ENCYCLOPEDIA OF

THE ANCIENT WORLD

ENCYCLOPEDIA OF
THE ANCIENT WORLD

Volume 3
Phidias–Zurvanism
Indexes

Editor
Thomas J. Sienkewicz
Monmouth College, Illinois

—————— *Editorial Board* ——————

Lawrence Allan Conrad
North America
Western Illinois University

Geoffrey W. Conrad
South America
Indiana University

Christopher Ehret
Africa
University of California, Los Angeles

David A. Crain
Mesoamerica
South Dakota State University

Katherine Anne Harper
South and Southeast Asia
Loyola Marymount University

Robert D. Haak
Egypt, Mesopotamia, Near East
Augustana College

Chenyang Li
East Asia
Central Washington University

Thomas H. Watkins
Greece, Rome, Europe
Western Illinois University

Managing Editor, **Christina J. Moose**

SALEM PRESS, INC.
Pasadena, California   Hackensack, New Jersey

Editor in Chief: Dawn P. Dawson

Managing Editor: Christina J. Moose *Research Supervisor:* Jeffry Jensen

Project Editor: Rowena Wildin *Research Assistant:* Jeff Stephens

Acquisitions Editor: Mark Rehn *Production Editor:* Joyce I. Buchea

Assistant Editor: Andrea E. Miller *Graphics and Design:* James Hutson

Photograph Editor: Philip Bader *Layout:* William Zimmerman

Administrative Assistant: Dana Garey *Additional Layout:* Eddie Murillo

Maps by: Electronic Illustrators Group, Morgan Hill, Calif.
Cover Design: Moritz Design, Los Angeles, Calif.

Library of Congress Cataloging-in-Publication Data

Encyclopedia of the ancient world / editor, Thomas J. Sienkewicz.
   p. cm.
Includes bibliographical references and index.
   ISBN 0-89356-038-3 (set) — ISBN 0-89356-039-1 (v. 1) — ISBN 0-89356-040-5 (v. 2) — ISBN 0-89356-041-3 (v. 3)
   1. Civilization, Ancient—Encyclopedias. I. Sienkewicz, Thomas J.

CB311 .E54 2001
930′.03—dc21

2001049896

First Printing

CONTENTS

KEY TO PRONUNCIATION

Many of the topics covered in the encyclopedia may be unfamiliar to students and general readers. For most of the more unfamiliar topics covered in these volumes, the editors have attempted to provide some guidelines to pronunciation upon first mention of the topic in text. These guidelines do not purport to achieve the subtleties of the languages in question but will offer readers a rough equivalent of how English speakers may approximate the proper pronunciation.

Symbols	Pronounced As In	Spelled Phonetically As
a	answer, laugh, sample, that	AN-sihr, laf, SAM-pul, that
ah	father, hospital	FAH-thur, HAHS-pih-tul
aw	awful, caught	AW-ful, kawt
ay	blaze, fade, waiter, weigh	blayz, fayd, WAYT-ur, way
ch	beach, chimp	beech, chihmp
eh	bed, head, said	behd, hehd, sehd
ee	believe, cedar, leader, liter	bee-LEEV, SEE-dur, LEED-ur, LEE-tur
ew	boot, lose	bewt, lews
g	beg, disguise, get	behg, dihs-GIZ, geht
i	buy, height, lie, surprise	bi, hit, li, sur-PRIZ
ih	bitter, pill	BIH-tur, pihl
j	digit, edge, jet	DIH-jiht, ehj, jeht
k	cat, kitten, hex	kat, KIH-tehn, hehks
o	cotton, hot	CO-tuhn, hot
oh	below, coat, note, wholesome	bee-LOH, coht, noht, HOHL-suhm
oo	good, look	good, look
ow	couch, how	kowch, how
oy	boy, coin	boy, koyn
s	cellar, save, scent	SEL-ur, sayv, sehnt
sh	champagne, issue, shop	sham-PAYN, IH-shew, shop
uh	about, butter, enough, other	uh-BOWT, BUH-tur, ee-NUHF, UH-thur
ur	birth, disturb, earth, letter	burth, dihs-TURB, urth, LEH-tur
y	useful, young	YEWS-ful, yuhng
z	business, zest	BIHZ-ness, zest
zh	vision	VIH-zhuhn

MAPS

COMPLETE LIST OF CONTENTS

Volume 1

OVERVIEWS

ENCYCLOPEDIA

Volume 2

Volume 3

ENCYCLOPEDIA OF

THE ANCIENT WORLD

PHIDIAS

ALSO KNOWN AS: Pheidias
BORN: c. 490 B.C.E.; Athens, Greece
DIED: c. 430 B.C.E.; Elis, Greece
RELATED CIVILIZATIONS: Classical Greece, Athens
MAJOR ROLE/POSITION: Sculptor

Life. Ancient writers regarded the Athenian artist Phidias (FIHD-ee-uhs) as the greatest sculptor of Greece. They applauded his colossal seated statue of Zeus at Olympia, one of the Seven Wonders of the World, which was fashioned of gold and ivory over a wooden core. When Pericles—the leading Athenian politician of the fifth century B.C.E.—initiated an ambitious building project on the Acropolis, Phidias was chosen to design most of the sculptural ornamentation for the Parthenon. The interior of the temple housed his universally acclaimed gold and ivory statue of Athena Parthenos, the virgin, standing some 40 feet (12 meters) high and portrayed as a warrior deity in the full panoply of battle. A novel feature of the Parthenon was its 525-foot-long (160-meter-long) continuous frieze adorning the top of the exterior wall. Carved in low relief, the superb frieze portrayed the Panathenaic procession honoring Athena, when the people wound their way up from the city to the Acropolis to bring the goddess a great embroidered robe.

Influence. The frieze gives a clear impression of the influential Phidian style of sculpture, which idealized human figures and successfully created the illusion of space and rounded form. Most of the sculptures of the frieze and pediments of the temple remain, controversially, in the British Museum in London, where they are popularly known as the Elgin Marbles.

ADDITIONAL RESOURCES

Brommer, Frank. *The Sculpture of the Parthenon.* Translated by Mary Whittall. London: Thames and Hudson, 1979.

Cook, B. F. *The Elgin Marbles.* London: British Museum Press, 1984.

Jenkins, Ian. *The Parthenon Frieze.* London: British Museum Press, 1994.

Palagia, Olga. *The Pediments of the Parthenon.* Boston: Brill, 1998.

SEE ALSO: Art and architecture; Greece, Classical; Parthenon; Pericles.

—*William E. Dunstan*

PHILIP II

BORN: 382 B.C.E.; Macedonia
DIED: 336 B.C.E.; Aegae, Macedonia
RELATED CIVILIZATIONS: Classical Greece, Macedonia, Thrace
MAJOR ROLE/POSITION: King of Macedonia

Life. Philip II began his reign by suppressing several pretenders to the throne and protecting Macedonia from foreign intruders, including the Athenians. To meet these threats, Philip created a new, mobile, formidable army, which in 357 B.C.E. he used to conquer the Greek city of Amphipolis. This victory gave him rich gold and silver mining regions, which freed him from financial worries. In 356 B.C.E., he sired Alexander (later the Great). By 354 B.C.E., he had won control of the entire Macedonian coast and much of Thrace. Philip used this opportunity to create new cities and encourage an urban life that survives today.

In 354 B.C.E., Thessaly invited Philip to lead them in the Third Sacred War (356-346 B.C.E.) to liberate Delphi from Phocian temple robbers. He first freed Thessaly from tyrants and, in return, became its legal ruler; he then defeated Phocis. Alarmed by Philip's success, Athens unsuccessfully challenged him in Thrace. In 349 B.C.E., he conquered and razed Olynthus, and in 346 B.C.E., he forced Athens to conclude with him the Peace of Philocrates.

After the peace, Philip campaigned in the north from 344 to 340 B.C.E., extending his power into modern Albania, Serbia, and Bulgaria. Turning again to Thrace, he attacked Perinthus and Byzantium, provoking Athens to declare war against him. In 339 B.C.E., he marched against Athens and found Thebes also arrayed against him. In 338 B.C.E., he defeated them at Chaeronea and, in 337 B.C.E., created the League of Corinth to establish peace in Greece. Conspira-

Philip II. (Library of Congress)

tors at the Macedonian court assassinated him in 336 B.C.E.

Influence. He made Macedonia the leading power in Greece, a position it held until the Roman conquest. Philip also laid the foundations for Alexander's achievements.

ADDITIONAL RESOURCES

Borza, Eugene N. *Before Alexander: Constructing Early Macedonia.* Claremont, Calif.: Regina Books, 1999.

Buckler, J. *Philip II and the Sacred War.* Leiden, Netherlands: E. J. Brill, 1989.

Cawkwell, G. *Philip of Macedon.* Boston: Faber and Faber, 1978.

SEE ALSO: Alexander the Great; Athens; Greece, Classical; Macedonia; Sacred Wars.

—*John Buckler*

PHILIP V

BORN: 238 B.C.E.; place unknown
DIED: 179 B.C.E.; Amphipolis, Macedonia
RELATED CIVILIZATIONS: Macedonia, Hellenistic Greece
MAJOR ROLE/POSITION: King of Macedonia

Life. Philip V, son of Demetrius II and Phthia (Chryseis) succeeded Antigonus III Doson to the throne of Macedonia in 221 B.C.E. In the Social War of 220-217 B.C.E., Philip successfully led the Achaean League against Aetolia and its allies, quickly extinguishing reports that he was only an insignificant youth.

In 217 B.C.E., Philip, noting Rome's preoccupation with the war against Hannibal of Carthage, began to move westward against Roman dependencies on the eastern coast of the Adriatic Sea. Rome's subsequent alliance with the Aetolians allowed it to largely stay out of the fighting in Greece while Philip brought the Aetolians to terms, concluding hostilities in 206 B.C.E.

Beginning in 203 B.C.E., Philip turned his sights on eastern territorial acquisition. The Romans declared war on Philip in 200 B.C.E., convinced by the Pergamenes and Rhodians that Philip threatened the freedom of the Greeks. After campaigns in 199 and 198 B.C.E., the Romans decisively defeated Philip at Cynosceph-

alae in Thessaly in 197 B.C.E. After defeat, Philip cooperated with the Romans and focused on Macedonian consolidation until the latter part of his life, when he made futile attempts to break with Rome.

Influence. Philip V stood in a long line of Hellenistic kings who sought to match the exploits and reconstitute the empire of Alexander the Great. Unfortunately, Philip and his Hellenistic contemporaries had to reckon not only with each other but also with the emerging might of Rome.

ADDITIONAL RESOURCES

Green, Peter. *Alexander to Actium: The Historical Evolution of the Hellenistic Age.* Reprint. Berkeley: University of California Press, 1993.

Gruen, Erich S. *The Hellenistic World and the Coming of Rome.* Berkeley: University of California Press, 1984.

Walbank, F. W. *Philip V of Macedon.* Cambridge, England: Cambridge University Press, 1940.

SEE ALSO: Achaean League; Alexander the Great; Carthage; Cynoscephalae, Battle of; Greece, Hellenistic and Roman; Hannibal; Macedonia; Rome, Republican.

—*Leah Johnson*

PHILIPPI, BATTLE OF

DATE: October, 42 B.C.E.
LOCALE: Philippi, a town overlooking plain and bay at Neapolis in Greece
RELATED CIVILIZATIONS: Republican and Imperial Rome
SIGNIFICANCE: The battle avenged the murder of Julius Caesar and marked the end of the Roman Republic.

Background. After the murder of Julius Caesar in 44 B.C.E., Brutus, one of the chief assassins, took possession of Macedonia, where he was joined by Cassius, another assassin, who commanded Syria. The two rivals for power, Caesar's friend Marc Antony and Caesar's heir Octavian (later the emperor Augustus), reconciled in 43 B.C.E. and formed (with Marcus Aemilius Lepidus) the Second Triumvirate. In the following year, Antony and Octavian (with twenty-eight legions) set out to recover the eastern provinces.

Action. The forces of Brutus and Cassius (with combined nineteen legions) were positioned along the Via Egnatia, west of Philippi (FIH-leh-pi); Brutus to the north was partly protected by a marsh. Brutus's forces successfully overran Octavian's camp, although Octavian avoided capture. Antony successfully attacked the camp of Cassius; Cassius, discouraged and not knowing of Brutus's success, committed suicide. The first battle was a stalemate. Three weeks later on October 23, Brutus began another battle. With his troops in flight, he also committed suicide.

Consequences. The battle marked the defeat of Brutus and Cassius, the leading assassins of Caesar, and left Rome in the power of the Triumvirate.

ADDITIONAL RESOURCE
Southern, P. *Augustus*. New York: Routledge, 1998.

SEE ALSO: Antony, Marc; Augustus; Brutus; Caesar, Julius; Cassius; Rome, Imperial; Rome, Republican; Triumvirate.

—*Thomas McGeary*

PHILISTINES

DATE: 1200-700 B.C.E.
LOCALE: Southeastern Mediterranean coast from the Yarkon River to the Egyptian border, the area controlled by the cities of Gaza, Ashkelon, Ekron, Ashdod, and Gath
SIGNIFICANCE: The Philistines, caught in the struggles between the Babylonians and Assyrians, both engaged in conflict and cooperated with the Israelites.

The collapse of civilizations in the eastern Mediterranean at the end of the Bronze Age set in motion the migration of the Sea Peoples. Their movements resulted in destruction of civilizations along the Mediterranean coast as far south as Egypt. The invasion of Egypt is documented in the reliefs of Rameses III at Medinet Habu (c. 1175 B.C.E.). The attack was thwarted and the invaders settled in the coastal plain north of Egypt. The various groups that established themselves on the coast are generally designated as "Philistines" (FIH-leh-steenz) from one of the major groups, the *prst* (Hebrew). This name came to designate the entire region during the time of the Roman emperor Hadrian, who named the area Provincia Palaestina.

The tradition of the Hebrew Bible indicates that these peoples were in conflict with the emerging Israelites. The archaeological record indicates that there were also periods of cooperation. Like the other small nations in the area, the Philistines were caught up in the conflicts between the superpowers of the day, suffering defeat and occupation by the Assyrian and Babylonian empires and a continual influence from the neighboring Egyptian rulers. By the end of the seventh century B.C.E., Philistia had ceased to exist as a distinct political entity.

No inscriptions of sufficient length have been discovered to identify a Philistine language. By the seventh century B.C.E., the language used was probably related closely to Phoenician and Hebrew. The Hebrew Bible indicates that the gods Dagan and Baal were worshiped in Philistia. The inscriptional materials indicate that a goddess (sometimes identified with Asherat) was gradually supplanted by local male deities.

ADDITIONAL RESOURCES

Dothan, Trude, and Moshe Dothan. *People of the Sea: The Search for the Philistines*. New York: Macmillan, 1992.

Ehrlich, Carl S. *The Philistines in Transition: A History from c. 1000-730* B.C.E. Vol. 10 in *Studies in the History and Culture of the Ancient Near East*. Leiden, Netherlands: E. J. Brill, 1996.

SEE ALSO: Bible: Jewish; Egypt, Pharaonic; Hadrian; Israel.

—*Robert D. Haak*

PHILO OF ALEXANDRIA

ALSO KNOWN AS: Philo Judaeus
BORN: c. 20 B.C.E.; Alexandria, Egypt
DIED: c. 45 C.E.; possibly outside Alexandria
RELATED CIVILIZATIONS: Imperial Rome, Egypt
MAJOR ROLE/POSITION: Theologian, philosopher

Life. The only firmly dated event known in Philo (FI-loh) of Alexandria's life is his participation in a delegation sent by Alexandrian Jews to the emperor Caligula in 39-40 C.E. He seems to have been prominent in the Alexandrian Jewish community, but that is all that can be said about him. He wrote commentaries on selected passages or topics in the Jewish scriptures and essays on standard philosophical topics such as the "eternity of the world." He read the Scriptures allegorically, enabling him to find connections between Jewish thought and Greek philosophy. In his eclectic system, God governs the world through his providence but is completely transcendent and communicates with creation only through intermediary beings, such as the Logos ("word"). It was this Logos, not God, who spoke to Moses in the burning bush. The goal of philosophy and theology, for Philo, was mystical union with God.

Influence. Little read in his own lifetime, Philo's work strongly influenced later Christian writers from Alexandria, especially Clement of Alexandria and Origen. They transmitted his ideas to other Greek and Latin theologians.

Philo of Alexandria. (Library of Congress)

ADDITIONAL RESOURCES

Goodenough, E. R. *An Introduction to Philo Judaeus*. 2d ed. Lanham, Md.: University Press of America, 1986.

Kamsler, H. M. "Philo Judaeus: Linking Biblical Judaism and Hellenistic Beliefs." *Jewish Biblical Quarterly* 26 (1998): 111-115.

Wolfson, H. A. *Philo: Foundations of Religious Philosophy in Judaism, Christianity, and Islam*. Cambridge, Mass.: Harvard University Press, 1948-1962.

SEE ALSO: Caligula; Clement of Alexandria; Greece, Hellenistic and Roman; Judaism; Moses; Origen; Rome, Imperial.

—*Albert A. Bell, Jr.*

PHILOCHORUS

BORN: c. 340 B.C.E.; Athens, Greece
DIED: c. 260 B.C.E.; Athens, Greece
RELATED CIVILIZATIONS: Classical and Hellenistic Greece
MAJOR ROLE/POSITION: Scholar, writer

Life. Few details are known about Philochorus's (feh-LAHK-uh-ruhs) life. He was a seer and prophet who interpreted omens for the Athenian state, but his historical significance derives from his work as a scholar. He was the author of twenty-seven works, most of them concerned with Athens and dealing with religious topics. However, he also wrote on chronology, Athenian inscriptions, and tragedy. His most famous work was his *Atthis* (n.d.; English translation of more than 170 fragments, 1949), a history of Athens from mythical times through the early third century B.C.E. Philochorus used earlier histories of Athens to write the *Atthis*, but he also conducted research into myths, poetry, and documents for further information.

Philochorus was put to death by Antigonus II Gonatas, king of Macedonia, some time in 260's, be- cause of his support of Ptolemy II Philadelphus, a king of Egypt who was then aiding Athens in its attempts to free itself from Macedonian control.

Influence. Although all of his works are now lost, Philochorus was extremely influential in antiquity. His *Atthis* became the standard history of Athens and was frequently cited by other ancient authors, and Christian writers often referred to Philochorus's religious works for his discussion of pagan beliefs and practices.

ADDITIONAL RESOURCES
Habicht, Christian. *Athens from Alexander to Antony.* Translated by Deborah Lucas Schneider. Cambridge, Mass.: Harvard University Press, 1997.
Harding, Phillip. *Androtion and the Atthis.* Oxford, England: Clarendon Press, 1994.

SEE ALSO: Athens; Greece, Classical; Language and literature.

—*James P. Sickinger*

PHILODEMUS

ALSO KNOWN AS: Philodemos
BORN: c. 110 B.C.E.; Gadara, Syria
DIED: c. 35 B.C.E.; Herculaneum, Campania
RELATED CIVILIZATION: Republican Rome
MAJOR ROLE/POSITION: Poet, philosopher

Life. Little is known of Philodemus's (fihl-eh-DEE-muhs) life and education. He was educated in Athens by Zeno the Epicurean and eventually came to Rome circa 75 B.C.E. under the patronage of the Piso family, in whose Italian villa at Herculaneum he probably remained until his death. He was famous as an erotic poet but known also as an Epicurean philosopher and teacher. He wrote on numerous subjects, including a history of philosophers, a book about anger, and a rare treatise on Epicurean theology, but he was especially devoted to the theory of art, going against popular sentiment by arguing that art was to be judged by its aesthetic value alone and not for its morals or logic.

Influence. As a poet and teacher, Philodemus had a direct impact on many Romans of his day, especially Vergil, Horace, Ovid, and Propertius, and though none of his prose was preserved by later scribes, he also played a crucial role in the late Republic, popularizing Greek philosophy for a Roman audience. The modern excavation of what may be his private library at Herculaneum has resulted in the recovery of numerous works of philosophy, both his own and those of Epicurus, which had been lost.

ADDITIONAL RESOURCES
Gigante, M. *Philodemus in Italy.* Ann Arbor: University of Michigan Press, 1995.
Glad, C. *Paul and Philodemus.* Boston: Brill, 1995.
Obbink, D. *Philodemus and Poetry.* New York: Oxford University Press, 1995.

SEE ALSO: Epicurus; Horace; Ovid; Propertius; Rome, Republican; Vergil.

—*Richard C. Carrier*

PHILOSTRATUS, FLAVIUS

BORN: c. 170 C.E.; island of Lemnos in the Aegean Sea
DIED: 245 C.E.; place unknown
RELATED CIVILIZATION: Imperial Rome
MAJOR ROLE/POSITION: Writer, philosopher

Life. Flavius Philostratus (FLAY-vee-uhs fuh-LAH-streht-uhs) was born into a wealthy family of Sophist philosophers. He studied philosophy and rhetoric, later becoming a teacher at the famous Academy in Athens. Philostratus traveled to Rome and was welcomed by Julia Domna, the wife of Emperor Lucius Septimius Severus (r. 193-211 C.E.). Philostratus wrote numerous works of philosophy and biography, including *Bio sophiston* (n.d.; *The Lives of the Sophists*, 1921), a collection of biographies of leading Pythagorean (pagan) philosophers, and the *Historia tou Apolloniou* (208-210 C.E.; *Life of Apollonius of Tyana*, 1912), the biography of a first century Pythagorean philosopher. This work dates from the period 208-210 C.E.

Although Philostratus does not specifically mention Christianity in his writings, he wrote against a backdrop of rising tensions between a pagan cultic sacrificial system that was badly in need of reform and Christianity, which considered itself morally and ethically superior to the idolatrous aspects of third century C.E.

paganism. Philostratus recounted the healing and miracle stories of the reformist philosopher Apollonius of Tyana (first century-104? C.E.), who denounced animal sacrifices, promoted a disciplined and ascetic lifestyle, and insisted that religious and/or cultic observances must be linked to ethical and moral behavior.

Influence. Philostratus's *Life of Apollonius of Tyana* presented Apollonius as a moral figure worthy of emulation. Anti-Christian writers of the third and fourth centuries used Philostratus's writings to counter the growing influence of the figure of Jesus as religious reformer and healer.

ADDITIONAL RESOURCES
Bunson, Matthew. *A Dictionary of the Roman Empire.* New York: Oxford University Press, 1995.
Frend, W. H. C. *The Rise of Christianity.* Philadelphia: Fortress Press, 1984.
Philostratus. *The Life of Apollonious of Tyana.* Cambridge, Mass.: Harvard University Press, 1912.

SEE ALSO: Apollonius of Tyana; Christianity; Julia Domna; Pythagoras; Rome, Imperial; Severus, Lucius Septimius.

—*Victoria Erhart*

PHINEAS

ALSO KNOWN AS: Phinehas; Pinhas ben Yaʾir; Phineas the Priest
FLOURISHED: second century C.E.; Palestine
RELATED CIVILIZATION: Imperial Rome
MAJOR ROLE/POSITION: Jewish poet and teacher of the tannaʾ, a Jewish religious tradition

Life. Phineas (FIHN-ee-uhs) was an ascetic who lived for a time in Lydda and was famous for his brilliance, piety, and ability to perform miracles. He was son-in-law of Rabbi Shimon ben Yohai and a contemporary of Rabbi Yehudah ha Nasi. He emphasized tithes to the point of fanaticism. His concern for cleanliness caused him never to accept an invitation to dine with another, including members of his family. In debate over Jewish religious law, he is reputed to have

been rigid, but his saintly character and pious living overshadowed that. Subsequent generations have ascribed authorship of Midrash Tadshe to him (known as the Baraitha of Phinehas ben Jair).

Influence. In his teaching, Phineas lamented the spiritual decline of the generations after the Babylonian destruction of the Jerusalem temple in 587 or 586 B.C.E. He therefore placed emphasis on right intention in religious behavior and drew up a well-known chain of virtues:

> Observance of the law leads to fastidiousness; fastidiousness to diligence; to cleanliness; abstinence, purity, fear of God, humility, holiness, modesty, piety, to the Holy Spirit, and to the resurrection of the dead which comes through Elijah.

ADDITIONAL RESOURCES

Kugel, James L. *The Bible as It Was*. Cambridge, Mass.: Harvard University Press, 1997.

Me'ir, Ofrah. "Hamurato shel R. Pinhas ben Ya'ir." In *Studies in Aggadah and Jewish Folklore*. Edited by Issachar Ben-Ami and Joseph Dan. Jerusalem: Magnes Press, Hebrew University, 1983.

SEE ALSO: Jerusalem, temple of; Judaism.

—*John M. Bullard*

PHOENICIA

DATE: 3000-500 B.C.E.

LOCALE: Lebanon, Israel, and Syria

SIGNIFICANCE: The Phoenician cities in North Africa, Sardinia, and Spain were islands of civic complexity in largely tribal areas, and they stimulated a dramatic increase in socioeconomic complexity among the indigenous peoples.

The term "Phoenicia" (fih-NEE-shee-uh) is derived from *phoinix*, the Greek word for "purple or crimson," probably an allusion to the purple dye that the Phoenicians extracted from the murex (a mollusk). Phoenicia referred to a territory encompassing the coastal plain of modern Lebanon, southern Syria, and northern Israel. The Phoenicians appear to have continued to call this region by its Semitic name, Canaan. From that homeland, the Phoenicians established colonies in Cyprus, North Africa, Sicily, Sardinia, and Spain. The most powerful of these colonies was Carthage.

History. Phoenicia represents a zone where Bronze Age (c. 3000-1200 B.C.E.) Canaanite city-state culture survived the onslaught of the Sea Peoples and the emergence of the nation-state Israelite, Moabite, Edomite, Ammonite, and Aramean kingdoms during the early

Solomon's fleet is shown arriving in Phoenicia, where trade flourished. (North Wind Picture Archives)

Iron Age (c. 1200-1000 B.C.E.). The major Phoenician city-states were Tyre, Sidon, Byblos, Arvad (Arwad), and Acre (ʿAkko). During the Bronze Age, Byblos was the most prominent of these cities. Phoenicia was an Egyptian vassal during much of its history. The main importance of Phoenicia during the Bronze Age was as a source of cedar for Egyptian temples and palaces. The Amarna tablets contain fourteenth century B.C.E. letters from Byblos indicating its vassalage to the pharaoh. Egyptian control had declined sufficiently by the late twelfth century B.C.E. so that the king of Byblos is recorded as asserting greater independence in the *Wen-Amon* or the *Journey of Wen-Amun* (possibly eleventh century B.C.E.; English translation in *Ancient Egyptian Literature*, 1976), the story of an Egyptian emissary of the Amun temple in Thebes who makes his way to Byblos to purchase cedar.

During the Iron Age (c. 1200-535 B.C.E.), Tyre and Sidon soon outstripped Byblos in political and economic importance. During the interlude between Egyptian and Assyrian domination, ranging from about 1200 to 850 B.C.E., local kingdoms and city-states flourished in the Levant. It was during this period that Hiram, king of Tyre, provided materials and personnel to Solomon, king of Israel, to aid in building the temple in Jerusalem, and Jezebel, daughter of Sidonian king Ethbaal, became wife of Ahab and queen over the northern Israelite kingdom.

Brief Assyrian activity in Phoenicia began with the campaign of Tiglath-pileser I (r. c. 1115-1077 B.C.E.). During the ninth and eighth centuries B.C.E., the Assyrian activity resumed, and the Phoenician city-states were forced to pay heavy tribute. When tribute failed to flow, punitive campaigns against Phoenician cities were launched under Sargon II (r. 721-705 B.C.E.), Sennacherib (r. 705-681 B.C.E.), and Esarhaddon (r. 680-669 B.C.E.). Tyre was besieged by both Sennacherib and Esarhaddon, and Sidon was destroyed by Esarhaddon, who repopulated a new Sidon with peoples from other parts of the Assyrian Empire. The tribute burden and Assyrian campaigns promoted the establishment and growth of Phoenician colonies in Cyprus and the western Mediterranean.

When Assyrian power was eclipsed by Babylon during the late seventh century B.C.E., Phoenicia passed into Babylonian control. After the capture of Babylon by the Persian Cyrus the Great in 535 B.C.E., Phoenicia became integrated into the vast Persian Empire. Phoenician cities provided ships and sailors for the Persian wars against the Greeks. However, the political and economic importance of the Phoenicians had shifted from their Levantine homeland to their colonies, especially Carthage in North Africa.

Architecture and city planning. Phoenician town planning and architecture are best known from the western Mediterranean colonies. However, excavations at Sarepta in Lebanon during the early 1970's revealed the first significant insight into Phoenician architecture in the homeland. The main type of construction method for domestic and industrial structures was the pier and rubble technique, in which piers, or columns of cut stone, were built at intervals of approximately 3 to 5 feet (0.9 to 1.5 meters) with fieldstones set in clay mortar to fill the interstices. House walls were flush against the street.

A temple to the goddess Tanit-Ashtart was uncovered at Sarepta, dating from the eighth to fourth centuries B.C.E. This temple, approximately 8.4 feet (2.6 meters) in width by 21 feet (6.4 meters) in length, was built of cut sandstone blocks laid in a header-and-stretcher pattern. The shrine exhibited many of the characteristics typical of Phoenician temples known in the western Mediterranean, including low benches along interior walls, an offering table at one end of the shrine, and a place for a sacred standing stone (*massebah*) or wooden pillar (*asherah*) in front the offering table.

Government. The government of Phoenician cities during the period from 3000 to 500 B.C.E. was a hereditary monarchy. In the Phoenician monarchies, close connections existed between royal and priestly power. One king of Tyre was a high priest, and at Sidon, the king also was priest of Ashtart. The ruling class below the royal house consisted of wealthy merchants.

Economics. The economy of Phoenicia was based on agriculture and maritime trade. The major Phoenician cities along the coast relied on agricultural hinterland areas to provide produce for urban consumption. Fishing also provided an important source of food. Phoenician commodities that were highly valued in the ancient world included cedar, purple-dyed cloth, and glass. These items were traded widely, with glass ingots recovered from a fourteenth century B.C.E. wreck off the Turkish coast, cedar supplied to Egypt and Israel, and purple-dyed cloth used for royal finery throughout the Near East and Eastern Mediterranean. Phoenician ivories and metal bowls have been found in wide distribution, from Assyria to Italy.

Navigation and transportation. The Phoenicians were renowned in the ancient world for their seafaring skill. Phoenician warships were a valuable asset to the

Persian Empire. Phoenician merchant vessels ventured throughout the Mediterranean and into the Atlantic, establishing trading stations as far away as Spain and Morocco. Phoenician traders also may have reached the British Isles. Under patronage of the Egyptian pharaoh Necho (609-593 B.C.E.), Phoenician ships reportedly circumnavigated the African continent, a feat not accomplished again until the sixteenth century by the Portuguese.

Religion and ritual. Little is known of religious life in Phoenicia during the Bronze Age, and only slightly more is known from the Iron Age. Much has been extrapolated from the Ugaritic texts and from the Bible. However, Ugarit was north of Phoenicia and never was considered part of Canaan, and the Bible is largely a hostile source. As a result, both should be used only as a supplement to primary Phoenician sources. These sources include votive inscriptions, treaties, archaeological excavations, and Philo Byblius, a Roman-era author who has been shown to draw on older source material written by a Phoenician priest, Sakkunyaton. The main Phoenician gods appear to have varied from city to city. At Tyre, the main deities were Bethel, apparently a local manifestation of El; Anat-Bethel, apparently his consort; and Melkart, a youthful god that appears to be connected with the "dying and rising" of natural forces. At Sidon, the main deities were Baal Shamim (the Lord of Heaven), Ashtart (a goddess of love and war), and Eshmun (a healing god). At Byblos, the main deities were Baal Shamim and Baalat, the Lady of Byblos. Other deities include Baal Hammon and Tanit, who become the chief deities of Carthage, Resheph (a god of plague), Gad (a god of luck), and Sid.

The foci of worship mainly were aniconic, consisting of standing stones (*masseboth*) or poles (*asheroth*). Sacred prostitution has been attributed to Phoenician temples by classical and biblical sources. Temple ritual centered on sacrifice. Types of sacrifice included an atonement offering, a peace offering, a whole burnt offering, and a meal offering. Evidence for child sacrifice has been cited in the Phoenician colonies, but it is scant in the homeland.

Death and burial. Phoenician burial customs included both inhumation and cremation. Burial normally occurred outside settlement areas. Inhumation was the more common practice. Grave types included shaft tombs, consisting of a shaft leading to rectangular chambers cut into rocky hillsides, and large subterranean halls with multiple rooms cut into the rock. The body of the deceased often was interred in a sarcopha-

gus. The elaborate sarcophagi of wealthy individuals frequently bore sculpted lids. Evidence of embalming has been noted, especially in royal tombs. Cremations occurred sporadically in time and space, with the exception of cremated child and infant remains that are found with votive stelae in religious precincts and that may be associated with human sacrifice. The earliest cremations occur at Phoenician sites during the twelfth and eleventh centuries B.C.E. The practice also occurred in the Phoenician colonies, especially during the eighth to seventh centuries B.C.E.

Language and literature. The Phoenician language belongs to the Canaanite group of Northwest Semitic languages. It is very close to biblical Hebrew. Little Phoenician literature has survived. Philo Byblius, writing in the second century C.E., draws on a lost theogony of the Phoenician priest Sakkunyaton. Phoenicians from Carthage also authored books that are cited and preserved in later fragments, including Hanno's *Periplus* (n.d.; *The Voyage of Hanno*, 1797; also known as *Periplus of Hanno*), an account of a voyage to West Africa, and a treatise on agriculture by Mago, quoted by the Roman writer Cato the Censor. Most preserved Phoenician texts are religious dedications or funerary epitaphs.

Writing systems. The Phoenicians used a twenty-two-letter alphabet that was nearly identical in script to the one used for biblical Hebrew. The Phoenicians were credited by the Greeks with inventing the alphabet. However, the first purely alphabetic writing system actually appears to have been created by peoples living in Canaan during the late Middle Bronze Age (c. 1700-1500 B.C.E.). The Phoenician alphabet is a direct descendant of that first linear alphabetic writing system. The Phoenicians probably did pass that alphabet to the Greeks during the early first millennium B.C.E., and they certainly introduced alphabetic writing into North Africa. During the Late Bronze Age (c. 1500-1200 B.C.E.) a variant alphabet, consisting of twenty-two cuneiform letters and based on the cuneiform Ugaritic alphabet, also was in use in Phoenicia, but this system disappeared shortly after the end of the Bronze Age.

Calendar and chronology. The Phoenician calendar appears to have been similar that of the early Israelites, a lunar calendar that was kept linked to the seasons by periodic insertion of extra months or days. Some preserved Phoenician month names (Ethanim, Bul, and Ziv) correspond to pre-Exilic month names in the Bible. Phoenician chronology appears to have been based on regnal years of particular rulers. This system naturally varied from city to city.

Visual arts. Three-dimensional sculpture was rare among the Phoenicians. However, Phoenician artisans excelled in the creation of reliefs, ceramic masks and figurines, ivory work, the production of metal vessels and figurines, and jewelry design. Phoenician visual arts were profoundly influenced by Egyptian styles of representation. Greek influence also can be seen in works after about 600 B.C.E. Reliefs often depicted gods approached by a human devotee. Although cult images generally were aniconic, the relief works show anthropomorphic deities, typically of three types: an enthroned bearded, mature god; a standing youthful god with right arm raised in smiting posture, holding a mace or lightning bolt; and a standing nude goddess, often accompanied by vegetation or animals. The human devotee is portrayed with raised right hand and a full-length beltless robe. Masks occur in smiling and grimacing forms. Figurines typically take the form of standing youthful male deities in smiting posture, standing nude goddesses, or seated enrobed pregnant women. Ivory work consisted largely of decorative furniture inlays, with floral designs, animals, and Egyptianizing images. Phoenician metal bowls, often with animal or human representations, were exported widely and have been recovered in Greece and Italy. Typical Phoenician jewelry included glass pendants in the shape of male or female heads and gold scroll-case pendants that may have housed magical formulas to ward off evil.

Current views. Most current research has focused on Phoenician colonies rather than on Phoenicia itself. One debate centers on the interpretation of cremated child and infant remains accompanied by votive markers as evidence for human sacrifice. Although most scholars contend that these remains represent sacrificial victims, other hypotheses are possible. For example, the remains may reflect those of children vowed as temple servants who died before actually beginning their service. To fulfill the vow, the deceased child may then have been offered in the manner of vowed animals. Another controversy focuses on the date of transmission of the alphabet to the Greeks.

ADDITIONAL RESOURCES
Edey, M. A. *The Sea Traders*. Alexandria, Va.: Time-Life Books, 1974.
Moscati, S., ed. *The Phoenicians*. New York: Rizzoli, 1999.

SEE ALSO: Ahab; Assyria; Babylonia; Canaanites; Carthage; Cyrus the Great; Esarhaddon; Sargon II; Sennacherib; Solomon; Tiglath-pileser I.

—Michael B. Hornum

PHRYGIA

DATE: 1200-700 B.C.E.
LOCALE: West-central Anatolia or Asia Minor (later Turkey)
SIGNIFICANCE: The most powerful Anatolian state between the fall of the Hittites and the rise of the Lydians, Phrygia influenced Greek culture.

Evidence of the Phrygian culture surfaced in the nineteenth century when archaeologists discovered relics of its tombs, forts, and inscriptions in Ancyra (modern Ankara, Turkey). From various artifacts found then and during post-World War II excavations, the period of Phrygia's (FRIH-jee-uh) dominance in Anatolia has been fixed at the eighth through sixth centuries B.C.E. Various artifacts also testify to peaceful Phrygian intercourse with many other civilizations. For example, bronze clasps called fibulae show Assyrian influence, and multicolored geometrically patterned pots suggest contacts with the Luwians, an eastern neighbor. Furthermore, Phrygia either owed its alphabet directly to the Phoenicians or got it from them indirectly by borrowing an archaic Greek version of Phoenician letters.

According to Greek writers—valuable sources of knowledge about this culture—the early Phrygian were west Europeans, probably Thracians, who migrated to Asia Minor around the time of the Trojan War. Indeed, Homer's *Iliad* (c. 800 B.C.E.; English translation, 1616) mentions them as Troy's allies; however, they later traded and otherwise cooperated with their Greek neighbors. In their new home, in the course of four hundred years, the Phrygians evolved from a barbarous people into an empire ruled by horse-owning, cultured aristocrats. Historians believe that their political progress came partly from their resettling the 3,000- to 5,000-foot (900- to 1,500-meter) high, mountainous plateau formerly inhabited by the Hittites.

Eventually, the Phrygian kingdom comprised the regions around Ancyra and Gordium and the hilly rural land between present-day Eskişehir and Afyon—with the Hittite association slightly differentiating east Phrygian culture from the rest. The chief cities were the capital, Gordium, bordering the Sangarius (later Sakaraya) River, and the religious center, Midas City (modern Yazilikaya, Turkey), rich in forestland. Tradition linked Gordium's founding to the peasant Gordius, who became the first Phrygian king and tied the Gordian knot that challenged Alexander the Great in the fourth century B.C.E. The next king was Gordius's son, Midas, immortalized in Greek legend for his golden touch.

The great wealth at the heart of this myth, archaeologists found, had actually existed—thanks to the Phrygians' skills in producing a highly valued wool, selling timber, raising horses, and working in wood, ivory, bronze, and glass. Furthermore, they produced much-admired carpets and were credited with inventing embroidery. Their religion was centered on the earth goddess Cybele, whose priests castrated themselves in initiation ceremonies, and it influenced the mystery cults of the Greeks and Romans.

The Phrygian empire fell to the Cimmerians, who invaded from beyond the Caucasus during the reign of King Sennacherib (r. 705-681), burned Gordium, and paved the way for Lydian rule.

ADDITIONAL RESOURCES

Bittel, Kurt. *Hattusha: The Capital of the Hittites*. New York: Oxford University Press, 1970.

Mellink, M. J. "The Native Kingdoms of Anatolia." In *The Cambridge Ancient History*. Vol. 3, part 2. Cambridge, England: Cambridge University Press, 1991.

Perrot, Georges, and Charles Chipiez. *History of Art in Phrygia, Lydia, Caria, and Lycia*. New York: A. C. Armstrong and Son, 1892.

SEE ALSO: Hittites; Homer; Lydia; Luwians; Midas; Phoenicia; Sennacherib.

—Margaret Bozenna Goscilo

PICTS

DATE: 200-700 C.E.

LOCALE: Scotland

SIGNIFICANCE: The Picts lived in ancient Scotland, fought fiercely against the Romans, and are best known for the carved symbol stones they left behind.

The Picts (pihktz) left virtually no documentary evidence about their lives. What little scholars know about the Picts has been derived from symbol stones, artifacts including silver jewelry, archaeological digs, and documents written by other early sources.

The first reference to the Picts occurs in a Roman poem dated circa 297 C.E. about attacks on Hadrian's Wall by Picts and Scots. It is unknown if the Roman poet referred to them as Picts because they tattooed their skins or if this was the name the people called themselves.

The eighth century C.E. historian Bede suggested that the Picts spoke a language different from that of any other people in Britain and that they handed down their kingship through matrilineal lines.

Some sources suggest that the southern Picts were first Christianized by Saint Ninian in the fifth century C.E., while crediting the Irish Saint Columba with introducing Christianity in the north and west during the sixth century. By the seventh century, there seems to have been a united Pictland. However, in about 843 C.E., Kenneth MacAlpine, king of the Scots, also became king of the Picts, forming the united land "Alba."

ADDITIONAL RESOURCES

Cummins, W. A. *The Picts and Their Symbols*. Phoenix Mill, England: Sutton, 1999.

Foster, Sally M. *Picts, Gaels, and Scots: Early Historic Scotland*. London: B. T. Batsford, 1996.

Sutherland, Elizabeth. *In Search of the Picts: A Celtic Dark Age Nation*. London: Constable, 1994.

SEE ALSO: Christianity; Columba, Saint; Rome, Imperial.

—Diane Andrews Henningfeld

PINDAR

ALSO KNOWN AS: Pindaros (Greek); Pindarus (Latin)
BORN: c. 518 B.C.E.; Cynoscephalae, near Thebes, Boeotia, Greece
DIED: c. 438 B.C.E.; Argos, Greece
RELATED CIVILIZATION: Classical Greece
MAJOR ROLE/POSITION: Choral lyric poet

Life. Pindar (PIHN-dur) composed elaborate and complex odes sung to musical accompaniment of lyres and pipes (reed instruments) and danced by choruses. Of his seventeen books of poems collected in the Hellenistic period, only four books containing forty-five epinician (victory) odes have been preserved in manuscript. These books, however, have established Pindar's fame as the greatest Greek lyric poet. In these poems, Pindar praises athletic victors throughout Greece, from powerful rulers such as Hieron I of Syracuse, Theron of Acragas, and Arcesilas of Cyrene to boys just beginning their athletic careers.

Varying in length from nineteen to nearly three hundred verses, the odes contain aphoristic reflections on life, brief mythological narratives, advice, prayers to gods, and praise of hard-won achievement. The odes are composed of stanzas called strophes, antistrophes, and epodes. These three stanzas make up triads, each of which is metrically identical in its poem. Pindar's style is grand, with abundant use of metaphor; his language is extremely complex and notoriously difficult to translate.

Influence. The Roman authors Horace and Quintilian acknowledged Pindar's greatness. After the Renaissance, the "Pindaric" ode became synonymous with any grand-style, serious poem. Imitators include French poet Pierre de Ronsard, English playwright Ben Jonson, English poet and playwright Abraham Cowley, French poet Nicolas Boileau-Despréaux, and English poet Thomas Gray.

ADDITIONAL RESOURCES
Race, W. H. *Pindar.* 2 vols. Cambridge, Mass.: Harvard University Press, 1997.
Young, D. C. "Pindar." In *Ancient Writers I*, edited by J. T. Luce. New York: Charles Scribner's Sons, 1982.

SEE ALSO: Greece, Classical; Hieron I of Syracuse; Horace; Languages and literature; Quintilian; Theron of Acragas.

—*William H. Race*

Pindar recites his poetry before an audience. (Library of Congress)

PISISTRATUS

ALSO KNOWN AS: Peisistratus
BORN: c. 612 B.C.E.; near Athens, Greece
DIED: 527 B.C.E.; near Athens, Greece
RELATED CIVILIZATION: Archaic Greece
MAJOR ROLE/POSITION: General, statesman

Life. Son of Greek physician Hippocrates and friend and kinsman of Athenian lawgiver Solon, Pisistratus (pi-SIHS-treht-uhs) distinguished himself as a soldier in the war against the Megarians (c. 570-565 B.C.E.) and became a leader of the citizens of northern Attica in their fight for equality. In 560 B.C.E., he seized power, ruling as tyrant for eight years until driven into exile on the island of Euboea by the aristocrats he had displaced. By 541 B.C.E., with the help of Thebes and Argos, he was able to defeat his enemies and return to power. According to historian Herodotus, Pisistratus accomplished his return with the help of Megacles on condition that he marry Megacles' daughter. Pisistratus arrived with an unusually tall woman from the Paeanian district and tricked the Athenians into believing she was Athena herself bringing back her favorite to rule her city. He ruled undisturbed until his death in 527 B.C.E., passing on his supremacy over Athens to his son, Hippias of Athens.

Influence. Herodotus noted that Pisistratus ruled according to established norms and that "his arrangements were wise and salutary." Pisistratus also improved the lot of Athens' poorest inhabitants. Among his accomplishments, Pisistratus stopped debt slavery, set up a court of appeals for citizens, reduced taxes on the poor, redistributed land, erected public buildings, decreed that those wounded in war should be supported by the state, and patronized the arts and literature.

ADDITIONAL RESOURCES
Herodotus. *The Histories: Book One.* Translated by David Grene. Chicago: University of Chicago Press, 1987.
Plutarch. "Solon." In *The Rise and Fall of Athens: Nine Greek Lives by Plutarch.* Translated by Ian Scott-Kilvert. London: Penguin, 1960.
Sancisi-Weerdenburg, Heleen. *Peisistratos and the Tyranny: A Reappraisal of the Evidence.* Amsterdam: J. C. Gieben, 2000.

SEE ALSO: Athens; Greece, Archaic; Herodotus; Hippocrates; Solon.

—Michael C. Paul

PITTACUS OF MYTILENE

BORN: c. 650 B.C.E.; Mytilene, Lesbos, Greece
DIED: c. 570 B.C.E.; Mytilene, Lesbos, Greece
RELATED CIVILIZATION: Archaic Greece
MAJOR ROLE/POSITION: Ruler of Mytilene

Life. After playing a leading role in the factional struggles over the rule of Mytilene (MIH-teh-leen) in the late seventh century B.C.E., Pittacus (PIHT-eh-kuhs) of Mytilene (r. c. 590-580 B.C.E.) was revered as a lawgiver and sage. Although the details of these struggles are somewhat sketchy, Pittacus seems to have helped overthrow the tyrant Melanchros (r. c. 612-609 B.C.E.) and then to have formed an alliance with Myrsilus, his successor (thus alienating his former ally, the poet Alcaeus of Lesbos). During this period, Pittacus helped fight against Athens for control of Sigeum (a territory on the Troad, later Yenişehir), which was subsequently awarded to Athens by arbitration. When Myrsilus died (c. 590 B.C.E.), Pittacus was popularly elected *aisymnētēs*, or absolute ruler, to put an end to the continuing civil strife and to reform the laws of Mytilene. Pittacus voluntarily laid down his rule after ten years and lived another ten years in retirement.

Influence. According to philosopher Aristotle, Pittacus did not radically reform the constitution, but he did create new laws. One of his laws doubled the penalty for offenses committed while drunk. Considered one of the Seven Sages of ancient Greece, Pittacus is best remembered for his sayings, such as "The painted wood [the law] is the best form of rule" and "It is hard to be truly good."

ADDITIONAL RESOURCES

Andrewes, A. *The Greek Tyrants*. London: Hutchinson, 1974.

Page, D. *Sappho and Alcaeus*. London: Oxford University Press, 1955.

SEE ALSO: Alcaeus of Lesbos; Aristotle; Athens; Government and law; Greece, Archaic.

—*Susan O. Shapiro*

PIYE

ALSO KNOWN AS: Piankhy; Piankhi
BORN: c. 765 B.C.E.; place unknown
DIED: c. 716 B.C.E.; place unknown
RELATED CIVILIZATIONS: Kush (Napata), Egypt
MAJOR ROLE/POSITION: Monarch, military leader

Life. When Piye was born, the Kushite kings not only ruled Kush (Napata) but also controlled much of central Egypt, including Thebes, home to the chief shrine of the god Amun-Re, sacred to the Kushites. Unusually gifted, Piye, at 6.5 feet (2 meters) in height, towered over his fellow Kushites, who believed him to possess supernatural powers.

When Piye became king circa 742 B.C.E., Thebes and the Amun cult were threatened by a Libyan chieftain named Tefnakht. In response, circa 730 B.C.E., Piye organized one of the most extraordinary military campaigns in history. He took his navy and army on a 1,200-mile (1,931-kilometer) journey down the Nile River to besiege the ancient capital of Memphis, Tefnakht's stronghold. All the great Nile cities fell to the Kushites; Memphis was conquered from the river, and Tefnakht

surrendered. Piye sailed back to his capital, Napata, and set up a stele detailing his expedition. The Kushite rulers founded the Twenty-fifth Dynasty, which ruled a united Egypt until circa 663 B.C.E.

Influence. Having developed one of the most advanced black cvilizations in Africa, the Kushite rulers also succeeded in preserving and expanding much of the cvilization of ancient Egypt, which was then in disarray.

ADDITIONAL RESOURCES

Burstein, Stanley M., ed. *Ancient African Civilizations: Kush and Axum*. Princeton, N.J.: Markus Wiener, 1998.

Johnson, E. Harper. *Piankhy the Great*. New York: Thomas Nelson and Sons, 1962.

Kendall, Timothy. "Kingdom of Kush." *National Geographic,* November, 1990, 103-123.

SEE ALSO: Africa, East and South; Egypt, Pharaonic; Napata and Meroe; Nubia; Shabaka.

—*Nis Petersen*

PLAINS PEOPLES

DATE: 8000 B.C.E.-700 C.E.
LOCALE: North American Great Plains, present-day central United States and southern Canada
SIGNIFICANCE: The Plains people endured significant ecological change over an extended period of time as they developed into hunting-and-gathering societies. Bison hunting was an important component of Plains life.

The Great Plains stretch from present-day Texas into the southern provinces of Canada. The Rocky Mountains provide the western boundary, and the eastern limit is considered the ninety-fifth meridian. Given the

vast size of the region, the lives of the people who inhabited the Plains varied in many ways. Those who lived to the north had to deal with harsher winters and shorter gathering seasons, while those farther south enjoyed milder winters and a long growing season. Despite the many differences in the day-to-day lives that different groups of Plains peoples led, they had at least one feature in common. They were in large measure influenced by climatic and environmental change.

The date of the arrival of the first humans on the Plains, called Paleo-Indians, is uncertain. They may have arrived around 9500 B.C.E. or even earlier. Before 8000 B.C.E., the Plains climate was mild, and wooded areas, bogs, and lakes dotted the plains. Paleo-Indians traveled in small bands, perhaps of twenty to fifty people. They gathered plant foods and hunted. Among their prey was the mammoth and other large mammals found in North America at that time.

The climate changed around 8000 B.C.E., becoming warmer, with less rainfall. Wooded areas declined and grasses dominated the Plains. The large mammals that Paleo-Indians relied on died off. The human role in this mass extinction is a matter of considerable debate among archaeologists. Some contend that the climate change was the sole cause of the extinctions, while others argue that Paleo-Indian overhunting was a contributing factor.

Whatever the reason for the mass extinction, Plains people turned to hunting bison, deer, and small mammals. The pursuit of smaller game may have required more time than hunting large animals such as mammoths and may have caused a shift in the lifestyles of Plains peoples. Lacking the horse, which would not be introduced into the region until Europeans arrived, hunters usually had to work as a team to kill bison. They either drove the animals into log or stone compounds or stampeded them over cliffs. One such site, Head-Smashed-In Buffalo Jump in southern Canada, was in use for some five thousand years. Because food gathering societies are usually organized into small bands, bison hunting may have been the one activity that brought the bands on the Plains together to visit and socialize.

Butchering sites and campsites remain the primary sources of evidence that scholars have regarding the Plains people between 8000 B.C.E. and 5000 B.C.E. Because the people were very mobile, they did not erect permanent shelters. They may have dug small pits that they covered for sleeping. Although the Plains people probably returned to the same locations year after year, the temporary nature of the camps has left little in the way of archaeological evidence. The nature of Plains clothing is a matter of speculation, although given the severe winters, the people must have developed sophisticated means of dressing and protecting their feet.

Climate change after 5000 B.C.E. again altered life on the Plains. A period of extended drought, lasting perhaps twenty-five centuries, made life difficult. Game and water became harder to find. A scarcity of archaeological sites from this period indicates that many people may have abandoned the Plains in pursuit of food. Some people, however, did remain. They continued to hunt and gather, living as nomads in search of food. They probably spent much of their time in river valleys and along the front range of mountains, where water and animals were more plentiful. Studies of campsites indicate that at this time bison was not an important part of the Plains diet, which consisted largely of small mammals and deer.

Around 2500 B.C.E., rainfall increased and game became more plentiful. Populations grew in size, but the lifestyle of the Plains people did not differ much from what it was during the drought era. One interesting development that occurred in Plains life during this period was the construction of stone circles, now known as medicine wheels. The purpose of the circles in unclear. Although they probably had some religious meaning, they also may have served as regional maps or astronomical calendars.

Life on the Plains underwent a dramatic change around 1 C.E. The Plains people began using pottery and constructing burial mounds. Whether they borrowed these practices from Indian communities to the east or eastern Indians migrated to the Plains is not clear. Archaeologists refer to the culture that developed at this time as the Plains Woodland, because it shares traits with early Plains culture and with that of woodland communities found east of the Mississippi. There is evidence that farming took place on some parts of the Plains, with maize, beans, and squash being the primary crops.

The Plains Woodland culture lasted until 700 C.E. Increased rainfall at that time made farming a more reliable source of food, and the Plains population increased. Although gathering remained an important component of Plains behavior, agriculture allowed for an increasingly sedentary lifestyle.

ADDITIONAL RESOURCES

Carlson, Paul H. *The Plains Indians*. College Station: Texas A&M University Press, 1998.

Frison, George C. *Prehistoric Hunters of the High Plains*. New York: Academic Press, 1978.

Jennings, Jesse C. *Ancient North Americans*. San Francisco: W. H. Freeman, 1983.

Krech, Shepard, III. *The Ecological Indian: Myth and History*. New York: W. W. Norton, 1999.

West, Elliott. *The Contested Plains: Indians, Gold-seekers, and the Rush to Colorado*. Lawrence: University Press of Kansas, 1998.

SEE ALSO: Archaic North American culture; Middle Woodland tradition; Paleo-Indians in North America.

—*Thomas Clarkin*

PLATAEA, BATTLE OF

DATE: late summer, 479 B.C.E.

LOCALE: Plataea, in Boeotia southwest of Thebes

RELATED CIVILIZATIONS: Classical Greece, Persia

SIGNIFICANCE: The Greek victory over Persia at Plataea (pleh-TEE-uh) freed Greece from the threat of subjugation to Persia.

Background. In 480 B.C.E., the Persians invaded Greece, destroyed an advance Spartan force at Thermopylae, and sacked Athens. After the Greek fleet defeated the Persians at Salamis, the Persian king Xerxes I retreated, leaving a sizable Persian army in Greece under Mardonius.

Action. In 479 B.C.E., the Persians sacked Athens again and took up a position in Boeotia. The Greeks, commanded by the Spartan regent Pausanias, marched north from Corinth to meet them. The Spartans held the Greek right wing and the Athenians the left. An initial engagement was indecisive, and for several days, both sides remained idle. When the Persians cut Greek supply lines and polluted their drinking water, Pausanias ordered a nighttime retreat to safer ground.

The Greek withdrawal was not completed by dawn, and the Persians attacked. The Spartans bore the brunt of the Persian assault, but their superior weaponry and discipline overwhelmed the more lightly armed Persians. When Mardonius was killed, the Persians lost heart and fled.

Consequences. Although the war with Persia continued, the Persians never again threatened mainland Greece. In 478 B.C.E., Greek forces crossed the Aegean Sea to Asia Minor and under Athenian leadership fought to free the eastern Greeks from Persian control.

ADDITIONAL RESOURCES

Green, Peter. *The Greco-Persian Wars*. Berkeley: University of California Press, 1996.

Lazenby, J. F. *The Defence of Greece, 490-479* B.C. Warminster, England: Aris & Phillips, 1993.

SEE ALSO: Greco-Persian Wars; Greece, Classical; Pausanias of Sparta; Persia; Salamis, Battle of; Thermopylae, Battle of.

—*James P. Sickinger*

The Persians (left) begin to fall against the Greeks, who would ultimately be triumphant. (North Wind Picture Archives)

PLATEAU PEOPLES

DATE: 8000 B.C.E.-700 C.E.

LOCALE: Columbia and Fraser River drainages of interior British Columbia, Washington, Oregon, Idaho, and Montana

RELATED CIVILIZATIONS: Shuswap, Thompson, Lillooet, Northern and Southern Okanagan, Kalispel, Spokane, Coeur d'Alene, Sanpoil-Nespelem, Lakes, Flathead, Pend d'Oreille, Kutenai, Yakima, Klickitat, Kittitas, Palouse, Nez Perce, Wasco, Wishram, Molala, Klamath-Modoc, Athapaskan

SIGNIFICANCE: The Plateau peoples were nonagricultural villagers who relied heavily on salmon for their livelihood.

The Columbia-Fraser Plateau is one of the ten culture areas of native North America and is sometimes grouped with the Northwest Coast as the "salmon area" because of the heavy reliance on that genus for food. Along the Fraser River in British Columbia lived peoples speaking Interior Salish languages—the Shuswap, Thompson, Lillooet, and northern Okanagan. Along the northern part of the Columbia River and its tributaries in today's United States lived both Salish speakers—Southern Okanagan, Kalispel, Spokane, Coeur d'Alene, Sanpoil-Nespelem, Lakes, Flathead, and Pend d'Oreille—and the linguistically isolated Kutenai. On the middle and lower Columbia and its tributaries were Sahaptin and Chinookan speakers—Yakima, Klickitat, Kittitas, Palouse, Nez Perce, Wasco, Wishram, and Molala. The most southern group, the Klamath-Modoc, straddled the Oregon-California border and spoke a language related to Sahaptin. Sahaptin and Klamath-Modoc are related to the Penutian languages found in California. Several small, isolated bands of peoples speaking Athapaskan languages, whose main area of distribution is in the Yukon and Alaska, are also found in the plateau. Archaeological research has shown that except for the Athapaskans, the ancestors of these peoples have resided in the plateau area for thousands of years.

As in most of North America, the earliest inhabitants, dating to about 9300 B.C.E., were hunters recognizable by the particular types of stone spear points they used. Clovis hunters, who used fluted spear points, are the earliest known inhabitants. Both isolated finds of these distinctive artifacts and caches at the Simon site in Idaho and the East Wenatchee site in Washington have been found. Clovis bone foreshafts also occur. At

8000 B.C.E., hunters still occupied the plateau but were using a new style of stemmed, unfluted, spear point and a distinctive crescent-shaped stone knife. Remains from the Lind Coulee and Marines Rockshelter sites are significant. Barbed bone points and harpoons used in fishing and small bone hooks that are parts of spear-throwers are also found. Bison bones and remains of smaller mammals and fish, but no salmon, are found in sites occupied by these later hunters.

Between 6000 and 5000 B.C.E., subsistence changed dramatically, and salmon gradually became a major food staple, although hunting was still important. The annual salmon runs are as predictable a food resource as the crops grown by farmers in other parts of the world. Salmon is preservable by drying and smoking, and the surplus from the large runs could be stored for future use. By 2000 B.C.E., people were living in permanent seasonally occupied villages of circular pit houses and relying on stored salmon to see them through the winter and early spring. A decline in temperature about 2500 B.C.E. may have precipitated an increase in the supply of salmon, a cold-water loving species. Archaeological sites at Kettle Falls and Five Mile Rapids and the Cascade phase sites, all on the Columbia River system, are significant for this period.

Increasing use of salmon between 5000 and 2000 B.C.E. is indicated by carbon isotope analyses of human bones that give a lifelong ratio of terrestrial protein to marine protein in the diet. In these upriver regions, the marine protein reached as high as 50 percent and could have come only from anadromous (river-ascending) salmon. Evidence for the extensive use of camas, a lily root, has been found in earth ovens dating to 3500 B.C.E., and there is evidence of roasting other edible roots in younger periods. Little early evidence for luxury goods is present except in western Idaho, where beads, pipes, and finely flaked stone knives and spear points made from exotic materials are found associated with burials that date between 4000 and 2500 B.C.E.

Except for the Athapaskan speakers, cultural and ethnic continuity is evident from at least 4000 B.C.E. on, even though there were changes in the sizes of villages and houses and in weaponry in the late prehistoric period. The earliest pit houses are small and shallow, whereas later ones are larger and deeper. At the Keatley Creek site, an extensively excavated village site of more than one hundred houses on the Fraser River near Lillooet, the largest pit house measures 76 feet (20 meters) in diameter. Both large and small pit houses occur there, and this fact has been taken as an indication of the presence of a stratified society with the wealthy families in the large houses and the poor in the smaller ones. Considerable evidence for the hunting of bison is present between 500 B.C.E. AND 500 C.E. on the Columbia Plateau and may be related to the introduction of the bow and arrow and its gradual replacement of the spear-thrower as the principal weapon for hunting. At various times, landslides on both the Columbia and Fraser Rivers have been taken as evidence of disruption of the supply of salmon, causing dislocation of resident populations. A slide at Texas Creek about 900 C.E. is thought to have blocked the Fraser River and forced abandonment of the large upriver villages.

Many pit house village sites have been test excavated throughout the plateau and indicate some variations in culture, but the basic plateau cultural patterns of winter pit-house villages in the major river valleys, a seasonal round of food collecting, and intensive storage of salmon, ungulates (hoofed animals), and roots are found throughout the area.

ADDITIONAL RESOURCES

Carlson, Roy L., and Luke DallaBona, eds. *Early Human Occupation in British Columbia.* Vancouver: University of British Columbia Press, 1996.

Hayden, Brian, ed. *The Ancient Past of Keatley Creek: Taphonomy.* Burnaby, B.C.: Simon Fraser University Archaeology Press, 2000.

Johnston, H. J. M., ed. *The Pacific Province.* Vancouver, B.C.: Douglas & McIntyre, 1996.

Richards, Thomas H., and Michael K. Rousseau. *Late Prehistoric Cultural Horizons on the Canadian Plateau.* Burnaby, B.C.: Simon Fraser University Archaeology Press, 1987.

Walker, Deward E., ed. *Plateau.* Vol. 12 in *Handbook of North American Indians.* Washington, D.C.: Smithsonian Institution Press, 1998.

SEE ALSO: Archaic North American culture; Archaic tradition, northern; Clovis technological complex; Paleo-Indians in North America.

—*Roy L. Carlson*

PLATO

ALSO KNOWN AS: Platon; Son of Ariston; né Aristocles
BORN: c. 427 B.C.E.; Athens, Greece
DIED: 347 B.C.E.; Athens, Greece
RELATED CIVILIZATION: Classical Greece
MAJOR ROLE/POSITION: Philosopher

Life. One of the most profound thinkers of Western civilization, Plato (PLAYT-oh) is the only author from Greek antiquity whose writings survive whole and intact. Though very critical of writing, Plato perhaps exemplifies the greatest command of Greek prose from antiquity. A collection of thirty-five dialogues and thirteen letters has been handed down under his name, though the authorship of some has been contested. Follower of Cratylus and Socrates and teacher of Aristotle, Plato was the first writer to bring together the chief components of philosophy: metaphysics, epistemology, ethics, and political theory.

Plato's family was prominent and of ancient nobility. His ancestors included Solon and Pisistratus. Plato's stepfather Pyrilampes was an intimate of Pericles, and his relatives included Charmides and Critias, both of whom served in the regime of the Thirty Tyrants. As a young man, Plato was a wrestler and playwright. He considered pursuing a public life, but the Peloponnesian War (431-404 B.C.E.), which ended in Athens' defeat and the oligarchy of 404 B.C.E., followed by a civil war and then a radical democracy, compelled Plato to withdraw from political affairs. He shunned public life altogether after his mentor Socrates was put to death by Athens in 399 B.C.E. Plato subsequently founded the first European institute of higher learning: the Academy.

Plato's writing and instruction continued for fifty years. Pythagoras, Empedocles, Anaxagoras, Heraclitus, Parmenides, and especially Socrates were influential in Plato's development. The solutions Plato crafted for the problems uncovered by those earlier thinkers were unparalleled. Plato also strongly opposed the relativistic teachings of the Sophists, and he viewed philosophy as the intellectual successor to Homer and the poets. Though Plato himself never engaged in public affairs, he did travel to Sicily on three occasions and tutored the young ruler Dionysius I the Elder of Syracuse. Plato died attending a wedding celebration, leav-

Plato. (Library of Congress)

open to a variety of interpretations. Uncovering Plato's philosophy is an exceedingly difficult task because he does not present ideas in his own name, compelling readers to contemplate philosophical problems for themselves.

Influence. Plato's impact cannot be quantified. His writings affected the entire intellectual development of Western civilization. Though Plato did not leave a well-rounded, dogmatic philosophical system and controversies exist on how to present Plato's thought, he serves as the father for all forms of philosophical idealism and dualism. Plato also is considered the inspiration for Platonism: a series of specific philosophical views, which Plato's companions and followers at the Academy initiated from Plato's dialogues and oral discussions. The movement produced over time an ever-changing but seemingly continuous philosophic dogma well into Roman times, and it claimed Plato as the founder.

ADDITIONAL RESOURCES

Guthrie, W. K. C. *A History of Greek Philosophy.* 6 vols. New York: Cambridge University Press, 1978-1990.

Kraut, R., ed. *The Cambridge Companion to Plato.* Cambridge, England: Cambridge University Press, 1993.

Randall, John Herman. *Plato: Dramatist of the Life of Reason.* Ann Arbor: University of Michigan Press, 2000.

SEE ALSO: Dionysius I the Elder of Syracuse; Greece, Classical; Parmenides; Peloponnesian War; Philosophy; Pre-Socratic philosophers; Pythagoras; Socrates.

—*Christopher Sean Planeaux*

ing his largest work, the *Nomoi* (360-347 B.C.E.; *Laws,* 1804), unfinished.

Plato crafted dramas: dialogues that feature his mentor Socrates (in all of the dialogues save two) engaged in conversations with a large number of leading intellectuals and prominent historical figures from the previous generation. These dialogues differ widely and are

PLAUTUS

ALSO KNOWN AS: Titus Maccius Plautus
BORN: c. 254 B.C.E.; Sarsina, Umbria, Italy
DIED: 184 B.C.E.; place unknown
RELATED CIVILIZATION: Republican Rome
MAJOR ROLE/POSITION: Comic playwright

Life. Few details are known about Plautus's (PLAWT-uhs) life. Of the approximately 130 comedies that he wrote for the Roman stage, only 21 survive. These plays, including *Asinaria* (*The Comedy of Asses,* 1774) and *Miles gloriosus* (*The Braggart Warrior,* 1767), belong to a genre called New Comedy, which fo-

cuses primarily on family problems, most commonly (but not exclusively) the love of a young man for a prostitute and the unsuccessful attempt of his father or her pimp to block their union.

Although Plautus's comedies are based on Greek originals, he did not merely translate them into Latin. Instead, he adapted them by adding material from native Italian drama that would appeal to his Roman audience. The most conspicuous of these alterations is the development of stock characters such as the young lover, the pimp, the braggart soldier, and the tricky slave. Plautus also inserted songs with complex meters, which made his plays similar to modern musicals.

Influence. Plautus's comedies were extremely popular in Rome and were revived hundreds of years after his death. Both Molière (*L'Avare*, pr. 1668; *The Miser*, 1672) and William Shakespeare (*The Comedy of Errors*, pr. c. 1592-1594) adapted them. Modern musical comedies and situation comedies display many of the same characteristics as Plautine comedy.

ADDITIONAL RESOURCES

Duckworth, G. *The Nature of Roman Comedy: A Study in Popular Entertainment.* Norman: University of Oklahoma Press, 1994.

Konstan, D. *Roman Comedy.* Ithaca, N.Y.: Cornell University Press, 1983.

SEE ALSO: Rome, Republican.

—*Shawn O'Bryhim*

PLEBEIAN SECESSION

DATE: 494 B.C.E.
LOCALE: Republican Rome
SIGNIFICANCE: Important element in the creation of early Republican institutions.

This event is traditionally regarded as a seminal event in the creation of Roman institutions after the expulsion of the last king of Rome. The Roman people, tired by debt and repeated warfare, refused to cooperate with their leaders and withdrew from the city to the nearby Alban Mountain, which has a long but obscure history as a center for regional festivals. The outcome of the mass protest was that the populace elected ten officials called tribunes to represent their interests. After the aristocracy recognized the permanent authority of the tribunes in the new Roman state, the populace returned and resumed cooperation with the aristocracy.

Modern historians have seen this episode as a key moment in a conflict between two social divisions in Roman society: the patricians and the plebeians (plih-BEE-ehns). No one can say exactly what these names mean, but the patricians are generally assumed to be a privileged group of Romans who attempted to monopolize key positions of power and leadership in the Roman state. The plebeians were everyone else. This so-called "struggle of the orders" was theoretically resolved in 287 B.C.E. by the empowerment of the plebeians with full legislative authority. However, this interpretation is by no means universally accepted. Some scholars believe that this particular conflict is better explained as a conflict between soldiers and leaders and that later supposed concessions by the ruling aristocracy to the people were merely predictable reforms in an expanding state.

ADDITIONAL RESOURCES

Cornell, T. J. *The Beginnings of Rome.* London: Routledge, 1995.

Mitchell, R. E. *Patricians and Plebeians: The Origins of the Roman State.* Ithaca, N.Y.: Cornell University Press, 1990

SEE ALSO: Rome, Prerepublican; Rome, Republican.

—*Randall S. Howarth*

PLINY THE ELDER

ALSO KNOWN AS: Gaius Plinius Secundus
BORN: probably 23 C.E.; probably Novum Comum (later Como), Italy
DIED: August 25, 79 C.E.; Stabiae Mount Vesuvius
RELATED CIVILIZATION: Imperial Rome
MAJOR ROLE/POSITION: Bureaucrat, author

Life. Born into the municipal aristocracy of Comum, Pliny (PLIHN-ee) the Elder followed an equestrian career. He served as cavalry officer in Germany and governor (procurator) in Spain, and at the time of his death, he was admiral (prefect) of the Roman fleet in the Bay of Naples. He perished in an attempt to save people living near Mount Vesuvius when it erupted in late August of 79 C.E.

Pliny is best known as a writer. Author of a military treatise as well as works on grammar, rhetoric, biography, and history (none extant), he is best known for his

Pliny the Elder. (Library of Congress)

encyclopedia of natural history, *Naturalis historia* (77 C.E.; *Natural History*, 1938-1963), in thirty-seven books, dedicated to the emperor Titus. Although largely uncritical, loosely organized, and replete with fanciful minutiae, the work is an invaluable treasure trove of information on Roman arts and sciences as they existed in the early first century C.E. Among the subjects he covered are agriculture, astronomy, earth sciences, chemistry, medicine, zoology, botany, and art.

Influence. Pliny's encyclopedia dominated the study of science and technology well into the Middle Ages and is frequently consulted by modern scientists interested in the history of their fields.

ADDITIONAL RESOURCES

Healy, John F. *Pliny the Elder on Science and Technology.* Oxford, England: Oxford University Press, 1999.

Pliny. *Natural History.* 10 vols. Cambridge, Mass.: Harvard University Press, 1938-1980.

SEE ALSO: Pliny the Younger; Pompeii and Herculaneum; Rome, Imperial; Science; Titus.

—*Robert I. Curtis*

PLINY THE YOUNGER

ALSO KNOWN AS: Gaius Plinius Caecilius Secundus
BORN: c. 61 C.E.; Comum (later Como, Italy)
DIED: c. 113 C.E.; Bithynia, Asia Minor (later in Turkey)
RELATED CIVILIZATION: Imperial Rome
MAJOR ROLE/POSITION: Writer, government official

Life. Pliny (PLIHN-ee) the Younger came from Rome's equestrian class, which supplied businessmen and government bureaucrats for centuries. He was adopted by his uncle, Pliny the Elder, and prepared to practice law and hold government offices. He was a renowned orator, but only one of his speeches, *Panegyricus* (100 C.E.; *Pliny's Panegyric*, 1644), a panegyric in honor of the emperor Trajan, survives. After holding some minor offices, Pliny obtained a consulship in 100 C.E. In 112 C.E., Trajan appointed him governor of Bithynia, a province in northern Turkey. No event in his life can be dated after that year. Though married several times, he was childless.

Throughout his life Pliny exchanged letters, actually literary essays, with numerous friends; while in Bithynia, he wrote frequently to the emperor. His *Epistulae* (97-109 C.E., books 1-9; c. 113 C.E., book 10; *The Letters*, 1748) consists of 248 letters in ten books. Book 10, perhaps published posthumously by friends, consists of business correspondence; the other nine books contain letters on various subjects. Most noteworthy are two letters describing the eruption of Mount Vesuvius in 79 C.E., which Pliny witnessed, and one detailing his persecution of Bithynian Christians.

Influence. Pliny's letters served as literary models, even as late as the eighteenth century. Volcanologists prize his description of the eruption of Vesuvius, and church historians find his account of the early Christians invaluable.

ADDITIONAL RESOURCES

Champlin, Edward. "Pliny the Younger." Vol. 2 in *Ancient Writers: Greece and Rome*, edited by T. J.

Luce. New York: Charles Scribner's Sons, 1982.

Sherwin-White, A. N. *The Letters of Pliny: A Historical and Social Commentary.* Oxford: Clarendon Press, 1966.

SEE ALSO: Christianity; Pliny the Elder; Rome, Imperial; Trajan

—Albert A. Bell, Jr.

PLOTINUS

BORN: c. 205 C.E.; possibly Lycopolis, Upper Egypt
DIED: 270 C.E.; Campania (now in Italy)
RELATED CIVILIZATIONS: Roman Greece, Imperial Rome
MAJOR ROLE/POSITION: Philosopher

Life. Plotinus (ploh-TI-nuhs) was educated in Alexandria. His mentor was Ammonius Saccas until 242 C.E., when he joined the emperor Gordian III's Persian expedition to learn the wisdom of the Persians and Indians. By 244 C.E., he had returned to Rome, where he established a Neoplatonic school of philosophy. It was respected by high officials in the government. His attempt to found a city, Platonopolis in Campania, though initially supported by the emperor Gallienus, was never realized. He opened his home to orphans and was reported to possess keen powers of discerning the hearts of people.

Plotinus was one of the greatest original thinkers of late antiquity, whose erudite lectures on Neoplatonic themes drew a number of gifted philosophers to his school, among whom was the great polymath and anti-Christian propagandist Porphyry of Tyre. The latter systematically arranged Plotinus's lectures into six books, each containing nine chapters, titled *Enneads* (c. 256-270; *The Enneads*, 1918). His *Life of Plotinus* (n.d.; translation, 1917) gives invaluable data about the great thinker.

Plotinus was a mystic who claimed to have experienced ecstatic union with the Supreme Principle, the One, several times in his life. According to his metaphysical theory of a hierarchy of reality, all lower orders of existent things emanate or process from the One, including intellect, soul, and humans. The goal of his philosophy was to purify the soul so that it could escape material reality and successfully make its ascent to the One.

Influence. Plotinus's Neoplatonic mysticism and metaphysical system influenced both pagan (Porphyry, Iamblichus of Syria, Proclus) and Christian writers (Saint Augustine, the Cappadocian Fathers) of late antiquity.

ADDITIONAL RESOURCES

Hornblower, S., and A. Spawforth, eds. *The Oxford Classical Dictionary.* Oxford, England: Oxford University Press, 1996.

O'Meara, Dominic J. *Plotinus: An Introduction to the Enneads.* Oxford, England: Oxford University Press, 1995.

Rist, John M. *Plotinus: The Road to Reality.* Cambridge, England: Cambridge University Press, 1967.

SEE ALSO: Augustine, Saint; Christianity; Greece, Hellenistic and Roman; Iamblichus of Syria; Philosophy; Porphyry; Rome, Imperial.

—Michael Bland Simmons

PLUTARCH

BORN: c. 46 C.E.; Chaeronea, Boeotia
DIED: after 120 C.E.; Chaeronea, Boeotia
RELATED CIVILIZATIONS: Roman Greece, Imperial Rome
MAJOR ROLE/POSITION: Greek biographer, philosopher

Life. Born during the reign of the Roman emperor Claudius, Plutarch (PLEW-tahrk) was studying philosophy at Plato's Academy in Athens when the emperor Nero toured Greece in 67 C.E. After completing his studies in Athens, Plutarch returned to Chaeronea, where he founded a philosophical academy of his own and continued to reside until his death during the reign of the emperor Hadrian. He traveled widely, however, at least twice to Italy.

An extraordinarily prolific writer, Plutarch consistently adopted a moral perspective. His surviving essays, dialogues, declamations, and collections of information have traditionally been grouped under the title *Ethika* (after c. 100 C.E.; *Moralia*, 1603); of particular autobiographical interest are "The Dialogue on Love" (found in *Moralia*) and the consolation he wrote to his wife on the death of their two-year-old daughter. His most famous work, the *Bioi paralleloi* (c. 105-115 C.E.; *Parallel Lives*, 1579), is organized into pairs of biographies of statesmen and military leaders, each pair consisting of the life of a Greek and that of his Roman counterpart (for example, Alexander the Great and Julius Caesar).

Influence. Plutarch's writings exerted a substantial influence on Western letters from the Renaissance through the nineteenth century. The plots of English playwright William Shakespeare's Roman tragedies, for example, are derived from the *Parallel Lives*.

ADDITIONAL RESOURCES

Barrow, R. H. *Plutarch and His Times*. Bloomington: Indiana University Press, 1967.

Russell, D. A. *Plutarch*. New York: Charles Scribner's Sons, 1973.

_____, trans. *Plutarch: Selected Essays and Dialogues*. Oxford, England: Oxford University Press, 1993.

Plutarch. (Library of Congress)

SEE ALSO: Alexander the Great; Caesar, Julius; Claudius; Greece, Roman; Hadrian; Nero; Philosophy.
—*Hubert M. Martin, Jr.*

POLYBIUS

BORN: c. 200 B.C.E.; Megalopolis, Arcadia, Greece
DIED: c. 118 B.C.E.; Greece
RELATED CIVILIZATIONS: Hellenistic Greece, Republican Rome
MAJOR ROLE/POSITION: Historian, ambassador

Life. Polybius (puh-LIHB-ee-uhs) was born into a prominent Greek family. His father, Lycortas, was a leading statesman of a southern Greek confederation of city-states, the Achaean League. In the second century B.C.E., Rome was expanding its influence in Greece. In Rome's Third Macedonian War (172-167 B.C.E.), Polybius served as an ambassador to the Romans and was able to save the Achaeans money by delaying an offer of aid. The pro-Roman policy did not help the Achaeans

when the Romans pursued a harsher policy, including sending a number of prominent Greeks into exile in Italy. Polybius was fortunate, serving in the house of Lucius Aemilius Paullus, a prominent Roman leader, and tutoring his two young sons. In this position, Polybius became acquainted with the Roman state and was permitted to travel extensively.

Following his exile, Polybius was an adviser to the Romans and was able to moderate some of Rome's demands when the Achaean League was conquered in the 140's B.C.E. *The Histories* (n.d.; translation, 1889), Polybius's main and greatest work, examined how Rome came to dominate the Mediterranean world. His other works include a history of the Numantine War (134-132 B.C.E.) and a treatise on military tactics (both now lost.)

Influence. While Polybius was most proud of his service to his countrymen, his examination of Rome and its "mixed" constitution has greatly affected governmental organizations, including the U.S. government.

ADDITIONAL RESOURCES

Von Fritz, Kurt. *The Theory of the Mixed Constitution in Antiquity*. New York: Columbia University Press, 1954.

Walbank, F. W. *A Historical Commentary on Polybius*. 3 vols. Reprint. Oxford, England: Clarendon Press, 1999.

SEE ALSO: Achaean League; Aemilius Paullus, Lucius; Greece, Hellenistic and Roman; Rome, Republican.

—*Frederick C. Matusiak*

POLYCLITUS

ALSO KNOWN AS: Polykleitos; Polycleitus
FLOURISHED: c. 460-410 B.C.E.; Argos or Sicyon
RELATED CIVILIZATION: Classical Greece
MAJOR ROLE/POSITION: Sculptor, theoretician

Life. Little is preserved about the life of Polyclitus (pahl-ih-KLIT-uhs), the most important sculptor in bronze of the fifth century B.C.E. He was a native Peloponnesian and a student of Ageladas (Hageladas) of Argos. A prolific sculptor, Polyclitus was best known for his nude athletic statues, such as the *Doryphorus* (c. 450-440 B.C.E.; *Spear Bearer*) and the *Diadumenus* (c. 430 B.C.E.; youth tying a ribbon around his head), which survive only in Roman copies. Polyclitus also made a celebrated statue of an Amazon for the temple of Artemis at Ephesus that was judged best in a competition with Phidias and other sculptors. Polyclitus's most famous work, however, was the gold and ivory cult statue created for the temple of Hera at Argos. Polyclitus was also the first artist known to have written a theoretical treatise, the *Kanon* (also known as *Canon*, now lost), which explored the laws of rhythm and proportion that were embodied in the *Doryphorus*. Eventually, Poly-

clitus became the head of a workshop and a school that continued to flourish throughout the fourth century B.C.E.

Influence. As a theoretician and sculptor, Polyclitus tried to define and capture the ideal human proportions. His work was frequently studied and copied by later Greek, Roman, and Renaissance artists.

ADDITIONAL RESOURCES

Borbein, Adolf H. "Polykleitos." In *Personal Styles in Greek Sculpture*, edited by Olga Palagia and J. J. Pollitt. Cambridge, England: Cambridge University Press, 1996.

Linfert, A. "Polykleitos." In *The Dictionary of Art*. Vol. 25. New York: Macmillan, 1996.

Moon, Warren G., ed. *Polykleitos, the Doryphoros, and Tradition*. Madison: University of Wisconsin Press, 1995.

SEE ALSO: Art and architecture; Greece, Classical; Phidias.

—*Ann M. Nicgorski*

POLYCRATES OF SAMOS

BORN: date and place unknown
DIED: c. 522 B.C.E.; Magnesia, Thessaly, Greece
RELATED CIVILIZATION: Archaic Greece
MAJOR ROLE/POSITION: Tyrant

Life. Polycrates (puh-LIHK-ruh-teez), supported by Lygdamis the tyrant of Naxos, seized Samos with

his two brothers in about 540 B.C.E. but not long after became sole ruler. His was the most famous of all the Aegean tyrannies. Polycrates of Samos aimed to maintain an independent Samos and to establish a Samian thalassocracy. He pursued an aggressive foreign policy, annexing neighboring islands and making treaties with Egypt and Cyrene. He also made the Samian navy a formidable force and was responsible for large-scale harbor fortifications. In 522 B.C.E., Oroetes, satrap of Sardis, who seems to have seen Polycrates' power as a threat, tricked him into leaving Samos with promises of money and other support. When Polycrates arrived in Magnesia, he was crucified.

Polycrates' reign was also one of culture. At his court were craftsmen such as Theodorus and the poet Anacreon of Teos, whom Polycrates wished to teach his son music. There is some chronological doubt as to whether he was responsible for the two great public works on Samos: the temple of Hera and the construction of the water tunnel through Mount Ampelus, which brought water into the city and took ten years to build.

Influence. Polycrates may have been the first Greek ruler to adopt triremes as the battleship for his navy, therefore changing the face of Greek naval warfare.

ADDITIONAL RESOURCES

Barron, J. P. "The Sixth Century Tyranny at Samos." *Classical Quarterly* 14 (1964): 210-230.
Shipley, G. *A History of Samos, 800-188* B.C. Oxford, England: Oxford University Press, 1987.

SEE ALSO: Greece, Archaic; Navigation and transportation.

—Ian Worthington

POLYGNOTUS

BORN: c. 500 B.C.E.; Thasos, Thrace, Greece
DIED: c. 440 B.C.E.; Thasos or Athens, Greece
RELATED CIVILIZATION: Classical Greece
MAJOR ROLE/POSITION: Painter

Life. The son, brother, and uncle of painters, Polygnotus (pahl-ihg-NOHT-uhs) moved to Athens, where his artistic innovations earned him the reputation of being the greatest painter of his age. He won praise for murals in public buildings in Athens and Delphi depicting such mythological themes as the conquering of Troy and Odysseus in the underworld. Some of his paintings were 15 feet (5 meters) high by 55 feet (16 meters) long, had as many as seventy figures, and were painted on wooden panels fixed to the walls. None of Polygnotus's works survives, but scholars are able to reconstruct how they looked from extensive literary descriptions—especially those by second century C.E. guidebook author Pausanias the Traveler—and from vase paintings by artists influenced by Polygnotus.

Previous painters arranged their figures on a one-dimensional plane. Polygnotus provided an illusion of depth by placing characters across a rising landscape. He excelled at carefully detailing women's headdresses and transparent garments and in portraying emotional facial expressions and gestures. Aristotle, in his *De poetica* (c. 335-323 B.C.E.; *Poetics*, 1705), praised Polygnotus on both moral and aesthetic grounds for showing the "ethos," or inner character, of his subjects.

Influence. Considered the greatest painter of the early Classical period, Polygnotus's technical innovations in depicting space and his delineation of individual character opened the way for even more realistic painting by his successors.

ADDITIONAL RESOURCES

Bruno, Vincent J. *Form and Color in Greek Painting*. New York: W. W. Norton, 1977.
Robertson, Martin. *A History of Greek Art*. 2 vols. New York: Cambridge University Press, 1975.
Stansbury-O'Donnell, Mark D. "Polygnotos's Iliupersis: A New Reconstruction." *Journal of Anthropological Research* 93, no. 2 (April, 1989): 203.

SEE ALSO: Aristotle; Art and architecture; Athens; Greece, Classical; Pausanias the Traveler.

—Milton Berman

POLYNESIA

DATE: 8000 B.C.E.-700 C.E.
LOCALE: South Pacific area bordered by Hawaii in the north, Aotearoa (New Zealand) to the southwest, and Rapa Nui (Easter Island) to the southeast
SIGNIFICANCE: Polynesia was explored, mapped, and settled by seagoing, canoe-building Pacific Island peoples before the dawn of recorded history.

After the last Ice Age (before c. 8000 B.C.E. until around 1600 B.C.E.), sea levels rose more than 325 feet (99 meters). What had been land masses of the Austronesian archipelago in the Pacific Ocean south of the equator were inundated by a glacial maximum that resulted in remaining lands becoming isolated islands reachable only by long sea journeys in finely crafted voyaging canoes.

Area inhabitants adapted the smaller, more ancient canoes that had been developed in such diverse places as India, Bali, and the Moluccas to follow the coastlines, carried by seasonal monsoon winds, and created massive outrigger canoes that were capable of navigating across vast distances. They were guided by ritual specialists called "wayfinders," who were trained from childhood to read the movements of stars, ocean currents, wave echoes, prevailing winds, and the habits of sea life. These ancient navigators were said to be able to smell land before it could be seen and see the reflections of islands shining from the bottoms of distant clouds. Built to carry as many as one hundred people and weighing upward of ten tons, the canoes were used to bring various peoples and their goods to all corners of the Polynesian triangle by 800 C.E.

Some historians speculate that, around 2500-1500 B.C.E., nomadic southeast Asians, possibly from Taiwan, migrated into and across the South Pacific region. Over the subsequent three thousand years they crossed more than 15 million miles (24 million kilometers) of unknown, open ocean to colonize every habitable island they encountered. Other authorities think early cultures evolved on the north coast of Papua New Guinea and not in Southeast Asia. Further evidence from recent finds will help continue the process of clarification and classification of materials and help to resolve ongoing provocative issues.

Austronesian-speaking Neolithic peoples from either Southeast Asia or Papua New Guinea who colonized the area called Oceania, which included Polynesia (pah-luh-NEE-zheh), Micronesia, and Melanesia, beginning circa 1600-1500 B.C.E., were the likely ancestors of Melanesians who first set out to populate Polynesia. They were lighter skinned, had broad noses, and came via Indonesia or the Philippines. They produced the distinctive Lapita pottery, which archaeologists use to trace the migrations of the ancestors of the Polynesian peoples with some precision.

Recent deoxyribonucleic acid (DNA) sample comparisons confirm the projected migratory path as originating in Southeast Asia, crossing to Taiwan, then south and west to the Philippines, Indonesia, New Guinea, Fiji, Samoa, Tahiti, New Zealand, to the north and farther west, and eventually to Hawaii and Rapa Nui.

Languages. The Austronesian languages shared by Polynesian peoples can be traced from Madagascar to halfway around the world on Easter Island. Proto-Austronesian originated on Taiwan around six thousand years ago. Motifs seen in contemporary tattooing and tape arts are very similar to the designs on ancient Lapita pottery. Most of the plants carried across the seas of Polynesia originated in Southeast Asia. The endemic diseases, leprosy and filaria parasite (the source of elephantiasis), never made it to the Americas. However, recent evidence hints at the possibility that some peoples now thought of as indigenous to coastal North America may have come into the North Pacific from eastern Polynesia using the same boat-building and navigating techniques as those seen in similar double-halted seagoing canoes of the Northwest Coast culture area.

"Polynesia" is a term invented by Charles de Broess in 1756 and was applied originally to all Pacific islands by Western peoples. The name comes from the Greek words *poly* (many) and *nesos* (islands). In 1831, in a famous lecture sponsored by the Geographical Society in Paris, a more restricted use of the term was proposed by Dumont d'Urville. At that time, Oceania was divided into three great cultural areas, with Micronesian ("small islands") north of the equator and Melanesian ("black islands") and Polynesian ("many islands") mostly to the south. The term "Polynesia," and the people known as Polynesians, share a vast triangle of open seas in the South Pacific.

The period of colonization. The Lapita peoples reached the Bismarck archipelago by 1500 B.C.E., Tonga (via Fiji) by 1300 B.C.E., and Samoa by 1000 B.C.E. By 100 C.E., they had left their ancient and mythic homeland, known as Havaiki, and moved onward to the Society Islands and the Marquesas (300 C.E.), Mangareva and Hawaii (500 C.E.), and Rapa Nui (700 C.E.).

Eastern Polynesian cultures used stone food pounders, carved wooden figures of the gods, and tanged adzes not evident in Samoa and Tonga to the west, indicating these developed later and locally. They sailed great canoes steered by huge hardwood paddles and powered by pandanus sails, carrying their animals and plants with them. They sailed to and from every locale, even against prevailing winds and oppositional currents. They fished along the way, and once they had arrived in a new place, immediately set up coconut groves, taro terraces, and fish ponds and established their culture in pristine environments never before seen by human beings. These were deliberate voyages of colonization. Ritual surrounded every aspect of Polynesian life, and the making of a canoe and preparing for a voyage were major cultural events and social undertakings. Making the canoes was a highly specialized craft. The training of navigators, or "wayfinders," likewise involved ritual specialization and took a lifetime to master.

The island ecosystems that Polynesian voyagers encountered had evolved in isolation and were populated by endemic life-forms that were very fragile and subject to decline caused by destructive competition from introduced species. Volcanic islands have varied altitudes, microclimates, and windward and leeward sides. Coral atolls are usually low and narrow, with little environmental range. Soil and water are usually poor on both types of islands, but atolls are the less desirable (unless underground freshwater sources can be tapped) and have less vegetation and a greater vulnerability to storms.

Polynesians did not just adapt to or change the biologically isolated environments they entered into as they colonized the South Pacific. They drastically altered each new ecosystem to reshape it to more closely match their distant memories of home. These were maritime people who settled to become agriculturalists like their ancestors. They introduced roots, trees, and vines for food and ornamentation, but they also dispersed pests such as Polynesian rats, geckos, snails, and insects. They cleared forests for farms, cut down trees to build houses and canoes, and hunted and gathered the defenseless endemic plants and animals, especially species such as wingless birds, driving them to near extinction, while cultivating wild plants and domesticating animals, which involved building fishponds, enclosures, irrigation projects, and often impressive monumental architecture. All of these resulted in vastly modified landscapes and environments.

Dogs, chickens, and pigs were carried along on the voyages. Sago, breadfruit, and banana replaced the Asian rice, millet, and grain crops carried across Polynesia as the migratory peoples moved south and east. They had an intricate and highly developed fishing technology that included finely crafted lines, various shapes of hooks, spear tips, nets, and other tools. These ancient maritime agriculturalists, coming into and going across Polynesia, developed into the many unique, discrete seagoing peoples with oceanic navigation skills, ground stone and shell adzes and other advanced Neolithic tools, and tame pigs and dogs who were collectively known as the Polynesians. In the process of adapting to each new island locale, the Polynesians developed into the dozens of distinctive cultures of the area.

Religion. Polynesian peoples had many gods representing such natural aspects as the oceans (Tangaroa), war (Tu), agriculture (Rono)—and many demanded human sacrifice. Such deities as Maui and Hina brought islands up from the bottom of the sea or fled to the Moon to avoid an incestuous brother. The polytheism of eastern Polynesia appears to have emanated from the Society Islands, carried from place to place by the myth speakers, or Arioi. Their beliefs led them to become enthusiastic temple builders. Known by the Polynesian term *marae*, these massive temple structures had platforms, terraces, and courtyards, with lava rock walls and internal structures made of large wooden slabs. They were used by religious groups for entertaining the gods and carrying out ceremonies and sacrifices as needed. Social ranking was determined by one's ancestors, and genealogies and other oral records were religiously preserved to maintain the order of island life.

Settlements. A high degree of contact was maintained between related and unrelated populations. Cultures developed and spread as, throughout prehistoric Polynesia, islands were further developed into territorial divisions. Clans and families lived together in small settlements, mostly along the coastlines or in fertile valleys farther inland. Higher-altitude areas were usually reserved for ceremonial use or war. Polynesians practiced intercropping and pond agriculture. Large populations could be fed by rich networks of taro, fish, and other ponds from the back of the alluvial valleys to the rich offshore fisheries.

After initial settlement was completed more than one thousand years ago, Polynesia changed rapidly as human beings left their indelible imprint, transforming the ancient seas and their islands as they became the vibrant, diverse, and dynamic Polynesia of the historical period.

ADDITIONAL RESOURCES
Irwin, G. *The Prehistoric Exploration and Colonization of the Pacific.* Cambridge, England: Cambridge University Press, 1992.

Terrell, J. *Prehistory in the Pacific Islands.* Cambridge, England: Cambridge University Press, 1989.

SEE ALSO: Australia, Tasmania, New Zealand; Hawaii; Melanesia; Micronesia.

—*Michael W. Simpson*

POMPEII AND HERCULANEUM

DATE: c. sixth century B.C.E.-79 C.E.

LOCALE: Along the southeastern shore of the Bay of Naples, Campania, Italy

RELATED CIVILIZATIONS: Republican and Imperial Rome

SIGNIFICANCE: Most significant archaeological sites in Italy reveal the architecture, art, and details of Roman daily life during the first century C.E.

Both Pompeii (pahm-PAY) and Herculaneum (hehr-kyew-LAY-nee-uhm) share a common mythological origin. According to Greek historian Dionysius of Halicarnasus, Hercules was given a parade (a *pompa*) near Mount Vesuvius by a settlement later named Pompeii, or "parade city." Hercules then founded the city named Herculaneum.

The earliest structures of Pompeii (the Doric temple of Hercules and the city walls) date no earlier than the sixth century B.C.E. The first residents of Pompeii were Oscans who allied themselves with Greeks living in Naples. By the fifth century B.C.E., Samnites had taken over and enlarged the city.

Two victims at Pompeii were immortalized in plaster almost two thousand years after being covered by volcanic ash from the eruption of Vesuvius. (Library of Congress)

The earliest reference to Herculaneum (by the philosopher in 314 B.C.E.) uses the Greek name Heracleion. Geographer Strabo wrote that Herculaneum also was settled by Oscans, although its city plan shows that it was modeled on Naples. From the end of the sixth century B.C.E., Herculaneum was definitely under the control of the Greeks before coming under the control of Samnites by the end of the fifth century B.C.E.

Pompeii and Herculaneum were taken under Roman control by Lucius Cornelius Sulla in 89 B.C.E. Although excavations at both Pompeii and Herculaneum provide spectacular insights into the daily lives of first century C.E. Italy, neither city was famous in antiquity. Historian Tacitus mentions a riot that took place in Pompeii's amphitheater (the oldest in Italy) between the residents of Pompeii and those of Nuceria in 59 C.E. Philosopher and writer Seneca the Younger records that Pompeii was seriously damaged by an earthquake four years later, and an inscription discovered in Herculaneum states that the emperor Vespasian restored the temple of Mater Deum in Herculaneum, which had been damaged by the same earthquake.

Residents of neither city suspected Mount Vesuvius was a volcano until August 24, 79 C.E., when a volcanic cloud rose from its peak. Writer Pliny the Younger described the whole event in two letters he wrote to Tacitus.

Lapilli (lava fragments) fell on Pompeii for three days, burying the city beneath 19 to 23 feet (6 to 7 meters) of debris. Although many of the 20,000 residents were able to escape, some stayed behind to hide or to loot. Volcanic material would later encase the bodies of these victims and formed human molds.

At first, the wind blew the volcanic cloud away from Herculaneum. When, however, Vesuvius expelled a column of volcanic mud into the sky, there was no time to escape. The column collapsed and flooded Herculaneum so quickly that only a few were able to run down to the sea to hide in seaside alcoves.

Excavators had removed usable building materials or salable artifacts from both cities before scientific archaeological procedures began to be followed. Because Pompeii was buried by lapilli, its excavation, begun in 1748 C.E., has been fairly easy. The volcanic mud that buried Herculaneum, however, became as hard as concrete, and very little of this city has been excavated since 1709 C.E.

ADDITIONAL RESOURCES

Jashemski, Wilhelmina. *The Gardens of Pompeii*. New Rochelle, N.Y.: Caratas Bros., 1993.
Maiuri, Amedeo. *Herculaneum*. Rome: Libreria dello Stato, 1956.
_____. *Pompeii*. Rome: Libreria dello Stato, 1957.
Ward-Perkins, Claridge. *Pompeii* A.D. *79*. Boston: Museum of Fine Arts, 1978.

SEE ALSO: Greece, Classical; Pliny the Younger; Rome, Republican; Seneca the Younger; Strabo; Sulla, Lucius Cornelius; Tacitus; Theophrastus; Vespasian.

—Bernard F. Barcio

POMPEY THE GREAT

ALSO KNOWN AS: Gnaeus Pompeius Magnus
BORN: September 29, 106 B.C.E.; probably near Rome
DIED: September 28, 48 B.C.E.; Pelusium, Egypt
RELATED CIVILIZATIONS: Republican and Imperial Rome
MAJOR ROLE/POSITION: Military and political leader

Life. A member of the senatorial aristocracy, Pompey (PAHM-pee) the Great began his career by organizing an army for the general Lucius Cornelius Sulla, who awarded him the name Magnus (the Great) in 81 B.C.E. While continuing to serve as a military leader, Pompey gained political power with a consulship and then an imperium that allowed him to pursue military campaigns. He helped defeat the army of Spartacus and formally incorporated the Eastern lands under Roman rule. In 59 B.C.E., Pompey entered into a triumvirate with Marcus Licinius Crassus and Julius Caesar and married Caesar's daughter, Julia. After Julia's death, Pompey formed an alliance with Quintus Caecilius Metellus Pius Scipio by wedding his daughter Cornelia and entered into a power struggle with his former father-in-law, Caesar, for the control of Rome and its empire. Civil war broke out when Pompey took

Pompey the Great. (Library of Congress)

command of the Republican forces against the armies of Caesar. Pompey was eventually murdered in Egypt, where he fled in the wake of Caesar's victories. His head was offered as a gift to his victorious rival.

Influence. Pompey the Great was a gifted military commander who brought the Eastern provinces under the rule of Rome. His assumption of absolute power, however, contributed to the death of the Roman Republic.

ADDITIONAL RESOURCES
Le Glay, Marcel. *History of Rome.* London: Blackwell, 1998.
Ruebel, James S., ed. *Caesar and the Crisis of the Roman Aristocracy.* Tulsa: University of Oklahoma Press, 1994.

SEE ALSO: Caesar, Julius; Julia (daughter of Julius Caesar); Rome, Imperial; Rome, Republican; Sulla, Lucius Cornelius.

—*Margaret Boe Birns*

POPPAEA SABINA

ALSO KNOWN AS: Augusta
BORN: 31 C.E.; Pompeii
DIED: 65 C.E.; place unknown
RELATED CIVILIZATION: Imperial Rome
MAJOR ROLE/POSITION: Wife of the emperor Nero

Life. Poppaea Sabina (pah-PEE-uh sah-BI-nah), the daughter of Titus Ollius, but named after her maternal grandfather, Poppaeus Sabinus, married the emperor Nero in 62 C.E.

Poppaea's first marriage was to Rufrius Crispinus, prefect of the Praetorian Guard, to whom she bore a son. In 58 C.E., she divorced Crispinus and married Marcus Salvius Otho, who was emperor for a few months in 69 C.E. Otho's boasts to Nero about his beautiful wife caused him to lose her. Nero sent her husband to be governor in western Spain, and she became Nero's mistress. Nero's mother, Agrippina the Younger, blocked his attempts to divorce his very popular wife, Claudia Octavia, and marry Poppaea. Nero had his mother murdered in 59 C.E. and, three years later, divorced and executed Octavia and married Poppaea.

Influence. Although Poppaea was renowned for her beauty and, according to Juvenal, lent her name to a popular cosmetic preparation, she also wielded political power in the imperial court. Her influence secured colonial status for her birthplace, Pompeii. The historian Flavius Josephus credits her with Jewish sympathies, and she procured the governorship of Judaea for her friend's husband, Gessius Florus.

Poppaea died while pregnant in 65 C.E. when Nero kicked her during an argument. His deep remorse at this act caused him to have her embalmed instead of cremated and buried in the mausoleum of the Julian family.

ADDITIONAL RESOURCES
Baumann, Richard A. *Women and Politics in Ancient Rome.* London: Routledge, 1994.
Griffin, Marian T. *Nero: The End of a Dynasty.* New Haven, Conn.: Yale University Press, 1985.

SEE ALSO: Acte, Claudia; Agrippina the Younger; Josephus, Flavius; Judaism; Nero; Rome, Imperial.

—*Christina A. Salowey*

PORPHYRY

ALSO KNOWN AS: Porphyry of Tyre; Malchos;
    Malchus
BORN: c. 234 C.E.; Tyre, Phoenicia (later Lebanon)
DIED: c. 305 C.E.; probably Rome
RELATED CIVILIZATION: Imperial Rome
MAJOR ROLE/POSITION: Philosopher

Life. Poprhyry (PAWR-feh-ree) was reared in Tyre, and studied at Caesarea in Palestine, and in Athens under Longinus. In 263 C.E., he became a disciple of Plotinus in Rome. By 270 C.E., he had moved to Sicily, where he heard of his master's death the same year. He then returned to Rome to assume leadership of the Neoplatonic school founded by Plotinus. He died circa 305 C.E. after editing the lectures of Plotinus, the *Enneads* (third century C.E.; English translation, 1916)

Sometime before the Diocletianic persecution (303-305 C.E.), he published two anti-Christian works, the *Kata Christanōn* (c. 270 C.E.; *Against the Christians*, 1830), in fifteen books, and *On the Philosophy of Oracles* (third century C.E.; English translation, 1959), in three books, which attacked the doctrines and practices of Christianity. Diocletian's new imperial theology attempted to inspire a renewed interest in a declining paganism in the Roman Empire, and the dissemination of Porphyry's polemical works may have been supported by the emperor himself. The argument that the greatest expression of piety was to honor the gods according to ancestral customs was the centerpiece of his (and Dio-

cletian's) anti-Christian program. Arnobius, the first Christian author to write in response to Porphyry, provides evidence that his works against Christianity were circulating in the Western Roman Empire by the late third century C.E.

Porphyry was a polymath who wrote on many subjects, including literature, philosophy, and religion. He was the greatest critic of Christianity in antiquity, and many wrote treatises against him. Imperial edicts of 333 and 448 C.E. ordered the burning of *Against the Christians*, and only fragments survive in Christian writings.

Influence. His publication of the *Enneads* and his writings on philosophy influenced the later development of thought in the West. His anti-Christian writings have given him the title of first critic of the Bible.

ADDITIONAL RESOURCES
Hoffmann, R. Joseph. *Porphyry's "Against the Christians."* Amherst, N.Y.: Prometheus, 1994.
Simmons, Michael Bland. *Arnobius of Sicca.* New York: Clarendon Press, 1995.
Smith, A. *Porphyry's Place in the Neoplatonic Tradition.* The Hague, Netherlands: M. Nijhoff, 1974.

SEE ALSO: Christianity; Diocletian; Longinus; Plotinus; Rome, Imperial.

—Michael Bland Simmons

POSIDONIUS

BORN: c. 135 B.C.E.; Apamea of the Orontes, Syria
DIED: c. 51 B.C.E.; place unknown, possibly Rhodes
RELATED CIVILIZATIONS: Hellenistic Greece,
    Republican Rome
MAJOR ROLE/POSITION: Philosopher

Life. Posidonius (pohs-ih-DOH-nee-uhs), a Stoic philosopher, studied under Panaetius of Rhodes before the latter's death in 104 B.C.E. He then became a citizen of Rhodes. Probably in the 90's B.C.E., he toured the Mediterranean world to collect material for his studies. Returning to Rhodes, Posidonius was elected to the office of the *prytany* and was sent on an embassy to Rome

in 87/86 B.C.E. Eminent Romans, such as Pompey the Great and Cicero, came to hear him. He died shortly after a second embassy to Rome in 51 B.C.E.

Posidonius's writings show a wide range of interests. For example, in his analysis of natural phenomena, he was most well known for his explanation of the relation between tides and the Moon. In ethics, his most profound contribution was in the field of psychology and the examination of the emotions. His *Histories* (now lost) continued Polybius's work, extending it from 146 to 86 B.C.E. An obsession with etiology, the examination of causes, underlies his exploration of all these subjects.

Posidonius. (Library of Congress)

Influence. The writings of Posidonius survive only in citations in later writers' works. His investigation of natural phenomena and history drew most interest in antiquity. Unfortunately, the fragmentary remains of his work do not adequately indicate his interest in etiology, which links the various parts of his once vast corpus.

ADDITIONAL RESOURCE

Kidd, I. G. *Posidonius*. 3 vols. Cambridge, England: Cambridge University Press, 1972-1999.

SEE ALSO: Cicero; Greece, Hellenistic and Roman; Panaetius of Rhodes; Polybius; Pompey the Great; Rome, Imperial.

—*Albert T. Watanabe*

POVERTY POINT

DATE: c. 1730-1350 B.C.E.
LOCALE: Lower Mississippi Valley, United States
RELATED CIVILIZATIONS: Middle Woodland tradition, Eastern peoples
SIGNIFICANCE: Poverty Point is known for its integrated large-scale earthworks, long-distance exchange, and novel stone and ceramic technologies with Archaic domestic and political economy.

Poverty Point culture developed in the food-rich but stone-poor Lower Mississippi Valley by intensifying fishing and acquiring stone resources via local and interregional exchange from sources up to a thousand miles away. The culture reached its high-water mark at the Poverty Point site, where a nested set of earthen half rings three-quarters of a mile (nine-tenths of a kilometer) across as well as six mounds were constructed. Calibrated radiocarbon dates indicate that construction spanned all or part of four centuries between 1730 and 1350 B.C.E. Altogether, human-made earth totaled nearly 1 million cubic yards (more than 765,000 cubic meters), enough to fill a 150-mile-long (241-kilometer-long) string of dump trucks lined up bumper to bumper. Despite their colossal size, the earthworks could have been raised by only a hundred people working nonstop for twenty-three years—a stupendous feat but still within the capabilities of dedicated fishers and hunter-gatherers.

Exchange empowered Poverty Point culture by fostering social reciprocity and a fund of unrequited obligation. As a consensual and corporate enterprise, construction drew down that energy fund, leveling social inequalities and fostering community pride and spiritual protection for everyone.

ADDITIONAL RESOURCES

Gibson, J. L. *Poverty Point*. Gainesville: University Press of Florida, 2000.
Webb, C. H. *The Poverty Point Culture*. Baton Rouge: Louisiana State University Press, 1982.

SEE ALSO: Eastern peoples; Middle Woodland tradition.

—*Jon L. Gibson*

These clay artifacts were found at the Poverty Point site. (AP/Wide World Photos)

POYKAI

ALSO KNOWN AS: Poygai; Sārayogi; Kāsārayogi
FLOURISHED: sixth or seventh century C.E.
RELATED CIVILIZATION: South India
MAJOR ROLE/POSITION: Saint

Life. Poykai (POY-ka-hi)was one of the first of the twelve *āḻvārs* (literally, "those immersed in the experience of god"), or saints, dedicated to the Hindu god Vishnu (Viṣṇu). Tradition recounts that Poykai was born from a golden lotus blossom sprouting in the temple tank of the Yathoktakari Temple at Kanchipuram in south India. He was among the early believers to begin countering the influences of Buddhism and Jainism that had flourished in south India for several centuries; as such, Poykai spearheaded a movement that led to the reemergence of Vishnu as an important deity in the region.

Poykai composed "centuries" of linked verse (groups of one hundred) called *antāti* in which the final verse becomes the beginning of the next verse; such verses created what was regarded as a "garland" of devotional verse for honoring the deity. In his ecstatic songs, he describes the nature of god, the nature of the soul, and the means to reach a oneness with god that is natural to the soul and separation from that which is the cause of all suffering. He declares that Vishnu is the sole support not just of Earth but of the entire universe. Vishnu, he claims, is the primal cause of all, the one who is responsible for the dissolution and creation of the world and the support of all creation. In other words, he regards Vishnu as continuous creative activity.

Influence. Poykai's artistic devotional songs influenced later *āḻvār* saints and generations of believers. The cult of Vishnu continues to be a major religious force in south India.

ADDITIONAL RESOURCE
Varadachari, K. C. *Alvars of South India.* Bombay, India: Bharatiya Vidya Bhavan, 1970.

SEE ALSO: Hinduism; India; Peyar; Pūtān.
—*Katherine Anne Harper*

PRAXITELES

BORN: c. 370 B.C.E.; Athens, Greece
DIED: c. 330 B.C.E.; place unknown
RELATED CIVILIZATION: Hellenistic Greece
MAJOR ROLE/POSITION: Sculptor

Life. Little is known of Praxiteles' (prak-SIHT-uhl-eez) personal life. He was famous for his art and greatly in demand; the finish of his statues was likened to living flesh. He, along with Scopas of Paros and Lysippus of Sicyon, steered late Classical Greek sculpture in a new direction, portraying real emotions with realistic, longer, slimmer bodies and smaller heads. These characteristics are evident in the *Hermes* of Praxiteles, the only intact major original work of these three artists. The expression of the god dangling a bunch of grapes before the infant Dionysus on his arm is light, playful, and relaxed. His weight is shifted so as to thrust a hip outward to create a pleasing S curve. Rather than lean and muscular, the body is soft, almost feminine. Pursuit of the feminine added to Praxiteles' fame. He was the first to sculpt a nude woman, his famous *Aphrodite of Knidos*, of which only copies survive.

Influence. The new approach to sculpture with which Praxiteles is associated linked the late Classical age in Greece with the Hellenistic period when Greek art, influenced and modified by other cultures, spread through the classical world.

ADDITIONAL RESOURCES
Gardner, Ernest A. *Six Greek Sculptors*. New York: Ayer, 1977.
Havelock, C. M. *The Aphrodite of Knidos and Her Successors*. Ann Arbor: University of Michigan Press, 1995.

SEE ALSO: Art and architecture; Greece, Hellenistic and Roman; Lysippus; Scopas.

—*Nis Petersen*

PRE-SOCRATIC PHILOSOPHERS

DATE: c. 600-400 B.C.E.
LOCALE: Magna Graecia (present Greece), western Turkey (Iona), and southern Italy
SIGNIFICANCE: The Pre-Socratics, often called the first philosophers and scientists, explored the basic makeup of the universe.

Inspired by various visions of the origin and order of the universe, these dozen or so early Greek thinkers, called "investigators of nature" by Aristotle and "Pre-Socratic philosophers" by later scholars, shared a passion for discovering the root nature of things. Modern knowledge of their ideas is based on fragments of their writings, and scholars recognize that this understanding has been colored by such philosophers as Aristotle, who first analyzed their doctrines.

Through religious myths, ancient Greeks tried to answer such questions as how the universe began, what its composition was, and what caused its order. Repudiating supernatural explanations, the Pre-Socratics answered these questions through natural rationales. The earliest Pre-Socratics came from Miletus in Ionia.

These Milesian philosophers believed that the universe's unity was grounded in the material of which it was made: For Thales of Miletus, it was water; for Anaximander, the "indefinite"; for Anaximenes, air; and for Heraclitus, fire. Thales' theory that water is the origin of all things was most likely derived from myths. Anaximander, who was critical of Thales, felt that if water were the originative stuff, then such things as fire could not have come into existence. For Anaximander, the universe was made not of any definite element but of the indefinite. Anaximenes tried to convince his fellow Milesians that the basic stuff was air, which produced all other things through condensation and rarefaction, and he was unbothered by the objection that condensed air is still air. Heraclitus modified the Milesian approach by explaining the unity of things through their structure rather than their material. Although he is famous for saying that no one steps twice into the same river, thus symbolizing his view that all is in flux, he also stressed a basic (though concealed) unity in the world. The river is stable in its flowing, and the flame is constant in its flickering.

Pythagoras was an Ionian who migrated to southern Italy, where he founded a school through which he taught the transmigration of souls and the numerical basis of all reality. According to his followers, he discovered that harmonious musical intervals could be expressed by simple ratios of integers. If music is numerical, then somehow the whole world must be. The Pythagoreans viewed objects as composed of geometrical unit-points (hence, numbers), which constituted lines, planes, and volumes.

Parmenides, who also lived in Italy, continued the Pre-Socratics' investigation into the nature of the ultimate reality. In a poem, he claimed that the only meaningful statement people can make about anything is that "it is." To say "is not" is to speak nonsense, for not-being is inconceivable: From nothing, nothing comes. Parmenides thus rejected change, since any change caused its subject to be what it was not before.

Other Pre-Socratics thought Parmenides' denial of diversity went against common experience. Accepting the reality of natural heterogeneity, Empedocles, Anaxagoras, and the Atomists proposed a plurality of homogeneous substances to explain the world's makeup—the four elements of Empedocles (earth, air, fire, and water), the "seeds" of Anaxagoras, and the atoms of Democritus. For centuries, Empedocles' cosmic system was the most popular of these proposals. Anaxagoras and the atomists produced two different answers to the question of the ultimate composition of matter—the continuous and the discrete. Anaxagoras, like Empedocles, maintained that change is the aggregation and dissemination of matter, but unlike Empedocles, he believed that the ultimate constituents ("seeds") were so arranged that between any two there was always a third. Unlike atoms, these seeds have no lower size limit.

Atomism, the culmination of the Pre-Socratic movement, originated with Leucippus and was developed by Democritus. Unlike Parmenides, the Atomists held that not-being, which they called the void, does exist, and furthermore, this void contains an indefinite number of indivisible atoms, which differed only in position, size, and shape. Though ancient Atomism was not a progenitor of the modern scientific atomic theory, the questions that the atomists and other Pre-Socratics investigated continued to concern thinkers for the next twenty-five hundred years.

Among the Pre-Socratic philosophers was Heraclitus of Ephesus, who is known for saying that no one steps twice into the same river. (Library of Congress)

ADDITIONAL RESOURCES

Kirk, G. D., J. E. Raven, and M. Schofield. *The Presocratic Philosophers: A Critical History with a Selection of Texts.* Cambridge, England: Cambridge University Press, 1983.

McKirahan, R. D. *Philosophy Before Socrates.* Indianapolis, Ind.: Hackett, 1994.

Mourelatos, Alexander P. D., ed. *The Pre-Socratics: A Collection of Critical Essays.* Garden City, N.Y.: Doubleday, 1993.

SEE ALSO: Aristotle; Democritus; Magna Graecia; Parmenides; Pythagoras.

—*Robert J. Paradowski*

PRISCIAN

ALSO KNOWN AS: Priscianus Caesariensis
BORN: fifth century C.E.; Caesarea, Mauretania (modern Algeria)
DIED: sixth century C.E.; Constantinople, Byzantium (modern Istanbul)
RELATED CIVILIZATIONS: Byzantium, Imperial Rome
MAJOR ROLE/POSITION: Grammarian

Life. Born in North Africa, Priscian (PRIHSH-ee-uhn) made his career as a teacher of Latin grammar in Constantinople. After the sack of Rome by the Vandals in 455 C.E., Constantinople became the capital of the empire and native speakers of Greek found themselves learning Latin as the official language of government. Latin was favored by the emperor Anastasius (r. 491-518 C.E.), for whom Priscian wrote a poem of praise, and by Justinian I (r. 527-565 C.E.).

In Constantinople, Priscian wrote the single most celebrated grammar of Latin, the *Institutiones Grammaticae* (fifth or sixth century C.E.; foundations of grammar). It consists of eighteen books, the last two of which were sometimes published separately, and totals more than a thousand pages in the modern scholarly edition. It openly acknowledges a debt to the Greek grammar of Apollonius of Alexander, the *Techne Grammatike* (second century C.E.; science of grammar), written nearly four hundred years earlier, and it

may owe something to the shorter Greek textbook of Aelius Donatus, written approximately two hundred years earlier. Taken together, the grammars of Priscian and Donatus became the standard textbooks of the Middle Ages, from which most schoolmasters took their lessons. Hundreds of manuscripts of Priscian's grammar have survived into modern times.

Influence. Priscian's methodical approach to language proved highly influential in the later Middle Ages, especially on the "speculative grammarians" who tried to explain grammar philosophically. The "speculative" approach was ridiculed by Renaissance Humanists such as Rabelais, but the same authors treasured Priscian's work for the numerous examples of elegant Latin from works otherwise lost to later centuries.

ADDITIONAL RESOURCES
Coyne, Patricia, trans. *Priscian of Caesarea's "De Laude Anastasii Imperatoris."* Lewisburg, Pa.: Edwin Mellen, 1991.
Robins, R. H. *The Byzantine Grammarians: Their Place in History.* New York: Walter de Gruyter, 1993.

SEE ALSO: Byzantine Empire; Donatus, Aelius; Imperial Rome.

—*Thomas Willard*

PRISCILLIAN

ALSO KNOWN AS: Priscillianus
BORN: c. 340 C.E.; Spain
DIED: 385 C.E.; Trier (later in Germany)
RELATED CIVILIZATION: Imperial Rome
MAJOR ROLE/POSITION: Religious figure

Life. In the 370's C.E., Priscillian (pruh-SIHL-yuhn) emerged as the leader of an ascetic movement in Spain that inculcated abstinence from meat, wine, and sex. The movement also evinced a taste for occultism, apocryphal scriptures, *au naturel* prayer, and nocturnal Bible study in which women participated. Such idiosyncrasies disconcerted more traditional Christians, and Priscillianist practices were condemned by the Council of Saragossa in 380 C.E. Nonetheless, Priscil-

lian's sympathizers engineered his appointment shortly afterward as bishop of Avila. When Priscillian vainly sought the aid of Pope Damasus and Bishop Ambrose of Milan, the usurping emperor Magnus Maximus, who was anxious to secure the backing of Catholic bishops, summoned a fresh council at Bordeaux, which this time was directed against the heresiarch himself. Priscillian appealed to Maximus in Trier, where he was tried on a charge of sorcery and executed: The sentence caused widespread shock.

Influence. As the only heretic of late antiquity to be put to death by civil jurisdiction, Priscillian was at first revered as a martyr in his native Spain; allegiance proved especially strong in the northwest. However, Priscillianist tenets were condemned by the Councils of

Toledo in 400 C.E. and of Braga in 563 C.E., so that by the seventh century the movement had died out.

ADDITIONAL RESOURCES

Burrus, V. *The Making of a Heretic: Gender, Authority, and the Priscillianist Controversy.* Berkeley: University of California Press, 1995.

Chadwick, H. *Priscillian of Avila: The Occult and the Charismatic in the Early Church.* Oxford, England: Clarendon Press, 1976.

SEE ALSO: Ambrose; Christianity; Rome, Imperial; Spain.

—Neil Adkin

PROCOPIUS

BORN: c. 500 C.E.; Caesaria in Palestine
DIED: c. 560-570 C.E.; place unknown
RELATED CIVILIZATION: Byzantine Empire
MAJOR ROLE/POSITION: Historian

Life. Procopius (pruh-KOH-pee-uhs), the greatest of the early Byzantine historians, wrote the *Polemon* or *De bellis* (550-553 C.E.; *History of the Warres*, 1653, better known as *History of the Wars of Justinian*) in seven books, covering the Persian, African, and Gothic wars, and later added an eighth on the victory over the Ostrogoths (to 553 C.E.). In his panegyric *Peri Ktismaton* or *De aedificiis* (c. 554 C.E.; *Buildings*, 1914-1940), he lauds Justinian I's building program. Procopius also wrote an invective against Justinian and the empress Theodora, as well as Belisarius and Antonia, called the *Anecdota* or *Historia arcana* (c. 550 C.E.; *The Secret History*, 1674). In this work, discovered in the Vatican library in 1623, the emperor and empress are depicted as demoniac tyrants who persecute dissenters and overtax the upper classes. Despite the contrast between this scurrilous polemic and the laudatory wars (except for Books 7 and 8) and the *Buildings*, *The Secret History* is now accepted as genuine.

Procopius accompanied Belisarius on his campaigns in Persia, Africa, and Italy. Sometime after 540 C.E., he became disillusioned with Belisarius and Justinian; the optimism of his earlier accounts faded. As a member of the secular elite, he followed classical literary models such as that of the historians Thucydides and Herodotus. His narrative of Justinian's reconquest focuses narrowly on military history, with little reference to religion, ecclesiastical events, policy analysis, or socioeconomic developments. For Procopius, personality drives events, although the person of Justinian never emerges from his writings.

Influence. Procopius's works provide the chief sources for the reign of Justinian. They contain both the traditional and the modern, the classical and the Byzantine, the positive and negative, and the secular and the Christian sides of the reconquest. Therefore, his writing reflects the ambiguities and contradictions inherent in imperial policy and in Byzantine society at the time.

ADDITIONAL RESOURCES

Cameron, A. *Procopius and the Sixth Century.* New York: Routledge, 1996.

Moorhead, John. *Justinian.* New York: Longman, 1994.

Procopius. *The Secret History.* Translated by G. A. Williamson. New York: Viking Penguin, 1966.

SEE ALSO: Belisarius; Byzantine Empire; Justinian I; Rome, Imperial; Theodora.

—Thomas Renna

PROPERTIUS

ALSO KNOWN AS: Sextus Propertius
BORN: 54-47 B.C.E.; Asisium (later Assisi, Umbria, Italy)
DIED: 16 B.C.E. or later; Rome
RELATED CIVILIZATION: Imperial Rome
MAJOR ROLE/POSITION: Poet

Life. Propertius (proh-PEHR-shee-uhs) seems to have come to Rome from Asisium, but little more is known. His *Elegies* (after 16 B.C.E.; first printed version, 1472; English translation, 1854) were published in four books; they cover a variety of amatory, literary, and patriotic topics. The first book, the so-called

Monobiblos (wr. c. 30-29 B.C.E.), sets the tone for the remainder of the collection. This book largely explores the poet's relationship with his lover Cynthia, who plays the role in Propertius's poetry that Lesbia does in Catullus's or Corinna in Ovid's. During the course of the collection, many ups and downs take place in the relationship and the lives of the two lovers; by the end, Cynthia is dead, and the poet has somewhat callously moved on.

Propertius's poetry is both passionate and deeply learned. His description of emotions often touches on the darker, almost pathological aspects of erotic love. The poems are laden with numerous references to mythology and to the Greek poetic tradition.

Influence. Propertius's work is the best example of Roman love elegy, and his portrayal of Cynthia was particularly important to Ovid's elegiac works. Although his fame dimmed for a time, he became influential again in the Renaissance. His influence can be seen in the works of many later authors, including the German poet Johann Wolfgang von Goethe and the American poet Ezra Pound.

ADDITIONAL RESOURCES
Hubbard, M. *Propertius.* New York: Charles Scribner's Sons, 1975.
Lyne, R. O. A. M. *The Latin Love Poets from Catullus to Horace.* Oxford, England: Oxford University Press, 1980.
Propertius. *Elegies.* Cambridge, Mass.: Harvard University Press, 2000.

SEE ALSO: Catullus; Ovid; Rome, Imperial.

—*Christopher Nappa*

PROTAGORAS

BORN: c. 485 B.C.E.; Abdera, Thrace
DIED: c. 410 B.C.E.; place unknown
RELATED CIVILIZATION: Classical Greece
MAJOR ROLE/POSITION: Teacher of rhetoric, writer

Life. Protagoras (proh-TAG-uh-ruhs), one of the earliest Sophists (itinerant teachers of rhetoric), was reputed to have been the first to accept fees for teaching. He traveled throughout Greece and to Sicily and in Athens was associated with the political leader Pericles. In 444 B.C.E., he was appointed to write laws for Thurii, an Athenian colony, perhaps at Pericles' request. Of many written works attributed to him, only fragments remain; however, he seems to have covered a wide range of subjects including grammar, theology (he was agnostic), and philosophy (his aphorism "the human is the measure of all things" earned him a reputation as a relativist). In the dialogue *Prōtagoras* (399-390 B.C.E.; *Protagoras,* 1804) by Plato, a long speech on the origins of society may closely resemble one of Protagoras's actual works. He has been called "the father of debate" because he said that "there are two contrary accounts [*dissoi logoi*] about everything." Though Protagoras was clearly a controversial figure, Plato contradicts a story that he was tried at Athens and banished.

Influence. Protagoras's most important accomplishment was probably in making argument and debate functional within the early democracies of the city-states.

ADDITIONAL RESOURCES
O'Brien, Michael, trans. "Protagoras." In *The Older Sophists,* edited by Rosamond Kent Sprague. Columbia: University of South Carolina Press, 1990.
Plato. *Protagoras.* Translated by C. C. W. Taylor. New York: Oxford University Press, 1996.
Schiappa, Edward. *Protagoras and Logos: A Study in Greek Philosophy and Rhetoric.* Columbia: University of South Carolina Press, 1991.

SEE ALSO: Athens; Greece, Classical; Pericles; Philosophy; Plato.

—*Janet B. Davis*

PRUDENTIUS, AURELIUS CLEMENS

BORN: c. 348 C.E.; Caesaraugusta, Spain
DIED: after 405 C.E.; Rome
RELATED CIVILIZATION: Imperial Rome
MAJOR ROLE/POSITION: Religious figure

Life. Aurelius Clemens Prudentius (aw-REE-lee-uhs KLEHM-ehnz prew-DEHN-shee-uhs), a Christian layman, has been called the first great representative of real Christian literature. Almost all that is known about him comes from his own writings. He practiced law and was a civil administrator, eventually holding a position at the imperial court. At a certain point in his life, he resolved to devote himself to Christian poetry. He published most of his works in a collection when he was fifty-seven years old.

His most famous works are his *Cathemerinon* (late third to early fourth century C.E.; *The Twelve Hymns*, 1898) and *Peristephanon* (late third to early fourth century C.E.; *The Martyrs' Crowns*, 1926). His work *Contra Symachum* (late third to early fourth century C.E.; *Against Symmachus*, 1926) took the Christian side in the controversy that arose over the removal of the altar of victory from the Roman senate house. His writings show a deep knowledge of the great Roman writers Vergil, Juvenal, Horace, and Lucretius.

Influence. Many of his poems became hymns in later Christian worship. His poem *Psychomachia* (late third to early fourth century C.E.; *The Psychomachia*, 1929), an allegory of conflict between virtues and vices, was influential in medieval Latin poetry.

ADDITIONAL RESOURCES

Malamud, Martha A. *A Poetics of Transformation: Prudentius and Classical Mythology*. Ithaca, N.Y.: Cornell University Press, 1989.

Peebles, Bernard Mann. *The Poet Prudentius*. New York: McMullen Books, 1951.

Roberts, Michael John. *Poetry and the Cult of the Martyrs: The Liber Peristephanon of Prudentius*. Ann Arbor: University of Michigan Press, 1993.

SEE ALSO: Christianity; Horace; Juvenal; Lucretius; Rome, Imperial; Vergil.

—*Leland Edward Wilshire*

PTOLEMAIC DYNASTY

DATE: 323-30 B.C.E.
LOCALE: Egypt, Cyrenaica, Palestine
RELATED CIVILIZATIONS: Hellenistic Greece, Macedonia, Egypt
SIGNIFICANCE: Ptolemy I Soter and his descendants ruled Egypt for nearly three hundred years and established Alexandria as the major center of Greek culture.

Following Alexander the Great's death, his lieutenants divided his vast empire. Ptolemy, one of Alexander the Great's ablest generals, chose Egypt as his share, becoming satrap in 323 B.C.E. and taking the title of king in 305 B.C.E. Ptolemy's policies set precedents for his successors.

Ptolemy I Soter created a large army and navy to maintain and expand his possessions. He granted land to Greek and Macedonian settlers willing to serve in his army and hired many mercenaries. By 321 B.C.E., Ptolemy dominated Cyprus and had turned Cyrenaic (modern Libya) into a protectorate. The Ptolemies fought five wars with the Seleucid Dynasty over possession of Palestine and Phoenicia before finally losing the territories in the second century B.C.E.

Having limited interest in Egyptian people or culture, Ptolemy I treated the inhabitants as inferior to Greeks and Macedonians. He supported Egyptian religion and rebuilt native temples in return for being recognized as pharaoh and worshiped as a god. Ptolemy used a highly centralized bureaucracy to control all aspects of the country's economic life, extracting enormous wealth from Egypt. Until Cleopatra VII, Egypt's last monarch, no Ptolemaic (tah-leh-MAY-ihk) ruler bothered to learn the Egyptian language.

Ptolemy I esteemed Greek civilization and wanted his capital, Alexandria, to replace Athens as the dominant center of Hellenic culture. He established a great library and museum, assembling a huge collection of written works and attracting outstanding artists, poets, scholars, and scientists from the entire Greek world. During his reign, he began construction of the great Pharos lighthouse, one of the Seven Wonders of the World.

Ptolemy II Philadelphus (r. 285-246), an even more voracious collector than his father; sought to obtain copies of every known work, expanding his father's library to some half million papyrus rolls, many containing more than one book. By wedding his sister Arsinoë, he began the Ptolemaic practice of sister-brother marriage. Under Ptolemy III Euergetes (r. 246-221 B.C.E.), the Ptolemaic Empire expanded to its maximum size, dominating many Aegean islands and coastal areas of Asia Minor.

The decline of Ptolemaic power began under Ptolemy IV Philopator (r. 221-205 B.C.E.). To defeat the Seleucids at the Battle of Raphia (217 B.C.E.), he enlisted Egyptians into his army. The resulting surge in Egyptian nationalism set off thirty years of native rebellions. In 164 B.C.E., the Syrian king, Antiochus IV Epiphanes, defeated the Egyptian army and captured Ptolemy VI Philometor. Only the intervention of Rome forced Antiochus to withdraw; Rome then treated Egypt as a protectorate. After choosing to ally with

Ptolemy I Soter, founder of the dynasty. (Library of Congress)

what proved to be the losing side in the Roman civil wars, Cleopatra VII committed suicide in 30 B.C.E. Her death ended the Ptolemaic Dynasty and Egypt became a province of the Roman Empire.

ADDITIONAL RESOURCES

Bowman, A. K. *Egypt After the Pharaohs, 332* B.C.-A.D. *642: From Alexander to the Arab Conquest.* Berkeley: University of California Press, 1986.

Ellis, Walter M. *Ptolemy of Egypt.* New York: Routledge, 1994.

Foss, Michael. *The Search for Cleopatra.* New York: Arcade, 1997.

SEE ALSO: Actium, Battle of; Alexander the Great; Alexandrian library; Diadochi; Egypt, Ptolemaic and Roman; Greece, Hellenistic and Roman; Macedonia; Pharos of Alexandria; Rome, Republican; Seleucid Dynasty.

—Milton Berman

RULERS OF THE PTOLEMAIC DYNASTY, 323-30 B.C.E.

Ruler	Reign
Philip III Arrhidaeus	323-317 B.C.E.
Alexander IV	323-311
Ptolemy I Soter	305-285
Ptolemy II Philadelphus	285-246
Ptolemy III Euergetes I	246-221
Ptolemy IV Philopator	221-205
Ptolemy V Epiphanes	205-180
Ptolemy VI Philometor	180-145
Ptolemy VII Neos Philopator	145
Ptolemy VIII Euergetes II	170-116
Ptolemy IX Soter II	116-107
Ptolemy X Alexander I	107-88
Ptolemy IX Soter II (restored)	88-80
Ptolemy XI Alexander II	80
Ptolemy XII Neos Dionysos	80-51
Cleopatra VII	51-30
Ptolemy XIII	51-47
Ptolemy XIV	47-44
Ptolemy XV Caesarion	44-30

PTOLEMY

ALSO KNOWN AS: Claudius Ptolemaeus
BORN: c. 100 C.E.; possibly Ptolemaic Hermii, Egypt
DIED: c. 178 C.E.; place unknown, possibly Egypt
RELATED CIVILIZATIONS: Hellenistic and Roman Greece, Roman Egypt, Imperial Rome
MAJOR ROLE/POSITION: Mathematician, astronomer, geographer

Life. Not to be confused with the Egyptian kings of the same name, Ptolemy (TAHL-eh-mee) led a life about which little is known except that he was a Hellenistic Egyptian and that his astronomical observations place him in the middle of the second century C.E. His major work, a definitive exposition of mathematical astronomy titled *Mathēmatikē syntaxis* (c. 150 C.E.; *Almagest*, 1948), is best known by its Arabic title, *Almagest*. He devised a complete astronomical system of concentric spheres from the Earth to the outermost sphere of fixed stars, explaining in detail the apparent retrograde motion of the planets. After Aristotle and Eratosthenes of Cyrene, Greek scientists recognized the Earth as spherical and partitioned it by latitude and longitude. Ptolemy's geography improved this knowledge, and the many errors it contains are caused by inaccurate measurements by surveyors and travelers, not by his method. He also wrote on optics, music, astrology, geometry, philosophy, and trigonometry.

Influence. Ptolemaic geocentric astronomy dominated Islamic and European cosmological thought until Nicolaus Copernicus developed a coherent heliocentric theory early in the sixteenth century. Ptolemy's Theorem, which states that for any quadrilateral ABCD inscribed in a circle, the sum of the products of the two pairs of opposite sides equals the product of its two diagonals, or $(AB \cdot CD) + (BC \cdot DA) = (AC \cdot BD)$, remains important in geometry.

ADDITIONAL RESOURCES

Britton, John Phillips. *Models and Precision: The Quality of Ptolemy's Observations and Parameters.* New York: Garland, 1992.

Gingerich, Owen. *The Eye of Heaven: Ptolemy, Copernicus, Kepler.* New York: American Institute of Physics, 1993.

Jones, Alexander. *Ptolemy's First Commentator.* Philadelphia: American Philosophical Society, 1990.

Newton, Robert R. *The Crime of Claudius Ptolemy.* Baltimore: Johns Hopkins University Press, 1977.

Smith, A. Mark. *Ptolemy and the Foundations of Ancient Mathematical Optics.* Philadelphia: American Philosophical Society, 1999.

Taub, Liba Chaia. *Ptolemy's Universe: The Natural Philosophical and Ethical Foundations of Ptolemy's Astronomy.* Chicago: Open Court, 1993.

SEE ALSO: Aristotle; Egypt, Ptolemaic and Roman; Eratosthenes of Cyrene.

—*Eric v.d. Luft*

PUBLILIUS SYRUS

FLOURISHED: mid-first century B.C.E.
RELATED CIVILIZATION: Republican Rome
MAJOR ROLE/POSITION: Actor

Life. Publilius (puh-BLIHL-ee-uhs) Syrus was a slave from Syria, as his name suggests, apparently from Antioch. He came to Italy, where he was freed because of his quick wit. After being educated at the expense of his former master, now his patron, he composed and performed in mimes (a type of imitative dramatic performance with male and female performers) throughout the Italian countryside before he made his debut at Rome. None of Publilius's mimes has survived, but two titles are known, *Putatores* ("the pruners") and *Mumurco* (probably "the mumbler"), as opposed to some forty-four titles of Decimus Laberius, a discredited Roman knight and Publilius's main rival. In 46 B.C.E., at games celebrating Julius Caesar's victory in the Battle of Thapsus, Publilius challenged his rivals to a literary contest in which they would compose and perform in scenes on a set theme. Cicero suffered through the performance, but Caesar declared Publilius the winner over Laberius. A century later, Publilius was regarded as "the founder of the mimic stage."

Influence. Seneca the Elder thought Publilius expressed moral ideas better than serious dramatists, and the only extant work under Publilius's name is a collection of moral maxims, originally compiled in the early empire as a booklet for the classroom. Subsequently, the collection was contaminated and enlarged. There are 734 surviving lines, amounting to a compendium of sometimes contradictory folk wisdom on various ethical topics, from which it is difficult to separate out the later additions and sayings that have been altered in various ways. The collection already had been modified by the time it reached the young Saint Jerome.

ADDITIONAL RESOURCES
Duff, J. Wight, and A. M. Duff, eds. *Minor Latin Poets*. Cambridge, Mass.: Harvard University Press, 1934.
Lust, Annette. *From the Greek Mimes to Marcel Marceau and Beyond*. Lanham, Md.: Scarecrow Press, 2000.

SEE ALSO: Caesar, Julius; Cicero; Rome, Republican; Seneca the Elder; Thaspus, Battle of.

—*F. E. Romer*

PUNIC WARS

DATE: 264-146 B.C.E.
LOCALE: Sicily, Italy, Spain, North Africa
RELATED CIVILIZATIONS: Republican Rome, Carthage
SIGNIFICANCE: Rome defeated Carthage in three wars and replaced it as the dominant power in the western Mediterranean. The Punic Wars marked Rome's transition from a regional power to a Mediterranean empire.

Background. Originally on friendly terms, Rome and Carthage fought increasingly over their respective spheres of influence. The settlement of the first war planted the seeds for the second war, and the third war was largely the product of the second.

Action. The First Punic (PYEW-nihk) War lasted from 264 to 241 B.C.E. When the city of Messina (in northeast Sicily) appealed to Rome for help against the Carthaginians, the Romans entered Sicily to defend Messina. The Romans seem to have feared the prospect of Carthaginians controlling territory so near to Italy. For more than twenty years, Rome and Carthage fought to control Sicily by land and sea. In 241 B.C.E., the Romans forced the Carthaginians to evacuate Sicily and pay a large war indemnity. Adding insult to injury, Rome soon bullied Carthage into surrendering the islands of Sardinia and Corsica (238 B.C.E.).

The Second Punic War (218-201 B.C.E.) saw the conflict between Rome and Carthage expand to include

This embossed steel shield depicts Scipio Aemilianus receiving the keys of Carthage at the end of the Third Punic War. (Hulton Archive)

Spain, Italy, and North Africa. From 237 to 219 B.C.E., the Carthaginians had carved out an empire in Spain. When the Carthaginian general Hannibal laid siege to Saguntum, a Spanish town allied with Rome, the Romans declared war on Carthage. Rather than waiting in Spain to meet the Roman armies, however, Hannibal surprised the Romans by marching overland from Spain, through southern France and across the Alps into Italy. During the first three years of the war (218-216 B.C.E.), Hannibal defeated the Romans at the battles of the Trebia River, Lake Trasimene, and Cannae. The Romans weathered these disasters largely because of their great reserves of manpower and the steadfast loyalty of many of their central Italian allies. Eventually, the tides of the war turned. From 216 to 204 B.C.E., the Romans steadily won back the Italian territory Hannibal had seized. Meanwhile, Roman armies gained control of Spain and defended Sicily from Carthaginian forces. In 204 B.C.E., the Roman commander Scipio Africanus invaded Africa and defeated Hannibal and Carthage at the Battle of Zama (202 B.C.E.).

After the prolonged struggles of the first two wars, the Third Punic War was anticlimactic. When Carthage broke its treaty with Rome and began to rearm itself in 149 B.C.E., the Romans laid siege to the city. The Romans captured Carthage after three years, razing the city and sowing salt in the surrounding fields in order to obliterate Carthage completely.

Consequences. Rome acquired from Carthage its first overseas provinces: Sicily, Sardinia, Corsica, and Spain. Ultimately, the Romans utterly destroyed Carthage, occupied the territory around Carthage, and named it the province of Africa.

ADDITIONAL RESOURCES

Cornell, Tim, Boris Rankov, and Philip Sabin. *The Second Punic War: A Reappraisal*. London: University of London, 1996.

Lazenby, J. F. *The First Punic War*. Stanford, Calif.: Stanford University Press, 1996.

Livy. *The War with Hannibal*. Translated by Aubrey de Sélincourt. London: Penguin Books, 1965.

Polybius. *The Rise of the Roman Empire*. Translated by Ian Scott-Kilvert. London: Penguin Books, 1979.

SEE ALSO: Cannae, Battle of; Carthage; Hannibal; Rome, Republican; Scipio Africanus; Zama, Battle of.

—*Jeremiah B. McCall*

PURANĀNŪRU

AUTHORSHIP: Composite; more than 150 poets
DATE: composed between first and third centuries C.E.
LOCALE: South India
RELATED CIVILIZATIONS: Dravidian, India
SIGNIFICANCE: One of eight Caṅkam classics, *Puranānūru* is one of the earliest Tamil classics of India before Aryan influence penetrated the south.

Puranānūru (pew-RAH-na-NEW-rew; English translation in *Tamil Heroic Poems*, 1973) literally means "the four hundred [poems] about the exterior." The "exterior" refers to life outside the family, which encompasses the king, the wars he fights, his greatness and generosity, his ethics in life for kings and commoners, the evanescence of life, and death. This anthology of four hundred poems written by more than 150 poets, including at least 10 women poets, is seminal to the understanding of South Asia's history, culture, religion, and linguistics.

Puranānūru describes a Tamil society that revolves around the king, whose generosity and valor are the main subjects of the poems that also celebrate the power of *karpu*, or woman's purity, which is of great importance to Tamils, both ancient and modern. Reference is also made to a caste system called *kuti* (now known as *jati*) that is peculiar to the Tamils and has no connection with the *varṇa* (caste) system described by the Aryans in the Vedas. Distinguished *Puranānūru* poets such as Kapilar and Auvaiyar paid eloquent tribute in their poems to kings Pari and Atiyaman, respectively, for their generosity and valor. Each of the *Puranānūru* poems is also assigned a *tinai*, defined as a place, region, or site, and each *tinai* corresponds to a tract of land, a time of day, a situation, and a *raga* (melody) in which it was sung. In the *puram* (exterior) poems, the *tinai* is further subdivided into a *turai*, or subject. These complex and sophisticated poems celebrate heroism and loyalty among men and chastity and purity among women.

ADDITIONAL RESOURCES
Hart, George L., and Hank Heifetz, trans. *The Four Hundred Songs of War and Wisdom: An Anthology of Poems from Classical Tamil—"The Purananuru."* New York: Columbia University Press, 1999.
Ramanujam, A. K. *Poems of Love and War from the Eight Anthologies and the Ten Long Poems of Classical Tamil.* New York: Columbia University Press, 1985.

SEE ALSO: Caṅkam; India.

—*Kokila Ravi*

PURĀṆAS

AUTHORSHIP: Compilation attributed to the mythical sage Vyāsa
DATE: fourth-sixth centuries C.E.
LOCALE: India
RELATED CIVILIZATIONS: Gupta Empire, India
SIGNIFICANCE: The *Purāṇas* are sectarian anthologies that determine the primary theological beliefs and practices in Hinduism.

The *Purāṇas* (pew-RAW-nahs) belong to the Gupta period of Indian history, when divergent sects, rituals, and theories fused into one neo-Brahmanical religion called Hinduism. These anthologies unified India religiously with a firm pantheon and mythology accepted throughout Hindu India. Long before the common era, the term *purāṇa* referred to "ancient tales and legends" of religious instructions. When the *Purāṇas* first appeared is difficult to ascertain. They claim great antiquity, and Vedic literature, recognizing their sacred origin, considered them the fifth Veda. Authorship was attributed to ancient *sūtas*, or bards, and compilation to the legendary sage Vyāsa. Orthodoxy considers the *Purāṇas* divinely inspired, with their chief narrators receiving their information through Vyāsa from god himself. Although the original *Purāṇas* can be traced back to the sixth century B.C.E., scholars believe that the existing works date from the golden age of the Guptas, the fourth to sixth centuries C.E., the dividing line between ancient and existing works.

Tradition dubbed eighteen *purāṇas* as *Mahāpurāṇas*; these along with a series of secondary works called *Upapurāṇas* formed a canon by the ninth century C.E. The *Bhāgavata Purāṇas* are devoted to Vishnu (Viṣṇu) and are the most significant, while the *Vāyu*, *Linga*, and *Kūrma* extol the god Śiva.

Although the character and contents of the most ancient *Purāṇas* are a mystery, the chief *Mahapurāṇas* contain much of the old legendary material. They convey the fundamental ideas of Hinduism through the mythological tales that are also woven into the lives of the people in festivals, ceremonies, and temple artwork so visible throughout the Hindu world. As sectarian texts, they center on the lives and deeds of the triune gods Brahmā, Vishnu, and Śiva and their incarnations as developed in the two theistic sects of Vaiṣṇavism and Śaivism. They brought into the mainstream of Indian religious thought deities and concepts from non-Brahmanical traditions and elevated the local cults to the level of Vedic religion. During the Vedic period, the *Purāṇas* became the religious belief system and literature of the lower castes, which were forbidden religious participation. The cosmogonic myths of the *Purāṇas* treat the formation of the world, the deeds of the gods, heroic figures of the past, genealogies of royal families and sages, festivals of the gods, prayer and proper manner of worship, deities of caste, and sacred sites and sanctuaries. They present a great insight into astrology, astronomy, politics, warfare, superstitions, medicine, agriculture, grammar, lexicography, and the Hindu social system. Considered the real Vedas for the masses, the *Purāṇas* exerted a profound influence on all aspects of life in Hindu India for at least two thousand years.

ADDITIONAL RESOURCES
Dimmitt, Cornelia, and J. A. B. Van Buitenen, eds. and trans. *Classical Hindu Mythology: A Reader in the Sanskrit Puranas.* Philadelphia.: Temple University Press, 1978.
Hazra, R. C. *Studies in the Puranic Records on Hindu Rites and Customs.* Calcutta, India: University of Dacca, 1940.
Kulkami, S. D., ed. *The Puranas: The Encyclopedia of Indian History and Culture.* Bombay, India: Bhishma, 1993.

Zimmer, Heinrich. *Myths and Symbols of Indian Art and Civilization*. New York: Harper and Row, 1962.

SEE ALSO: Gupta emperors; Hinduism; India; Vedas; Vedism.

—*George J. Hoynacki*

PŪTĀN

ALSO KNOWN AS: Pūttattār; Puda; Pudam; Bhoodath; Bhutam
FLOURISHED: sixth or seventh century C.E.; Tamil Nādu, India
RELATED CIVILIZATION: South India
MAJOR ROLE/POSITION: Hindu mystic

Life. Pūtān (PEW-tawn) was one of the early *ālvārs* (literally, "these immersed in the experience of god"), or saints, and spent his life in devotion to the Hindu god Vishnu (Viṣṇu). He was born at Mahabalipuram in the Chingleput District of Tamil Nādu; tradition asserts that he was born from the *kurukkaṭṭi* flower. It seems likely that he was a contemporary and an associate of both Poykai and Peyar. Pūtān was the first *ālvār* to claim to know god and to see the divine in dreams and while awake. Such mystical visions he describes as a gift from god to those who have rightly discerned or intuited the highest being and through devotion have sought him. Although his visions usually were of Lord Krishna (Kṛṣṇa), Pūtān was conversant on all of the avatars of Vishnu.

Pūtān's visions and spiritual insights found ecstatic expression in his songs, in which he explores the theme of transcendental knowledge. He also asserts that all souls are equal in the sight of god, the supreme, and that all souls have a divine destiny with god.

Influence. Pūtān was a powerful voice in the reestablishment of Hinduism and particularly the authority of the god Vishnu, after centuries of Buddhist and Jaina popularity in the Tamil country.

ADDITIONAL RESOURCE
Varadachari, K. C. *Alvars of South India*. Bombay, India: Bharatiya Vidya Bhavan, 1970.

SEE ALSO: Hinduism; India; Peyar; Poykai.

—*Katherine Anne Harper*

PYRAMID OF THE MOON

DATE: 200-700 C.E.
LOCALE: Central Mexico
RELATED CIVILIZATIONS: Maya, Teotihuacán
SIGNIFICANCE: The Pyramid of the Moon and other structures in central Mexico symbolized the advanced and distinctive cultures present in Mesoamerica before the arrival of the Europeans.

The Pyramid of the Moon is located in Teotihuacán, an ancient Mesoamerican city about 30 miles (48 kilometers) north of present-day Mexico City. The people who once lived there predated the powerful Aztec civilization by several hundred years. Teotihuacán peaked around 500 C.E. and had about 200,000 inhabitants. No one knows why the citizens of this city left or disappeared. They left no writing system, only ruins. These ruins are as mysterious as the Teotihuacános themselves. The later Aztecs called two of the great structures in the city the Pyramid of the Sun and the Pyramid of the Moon. A road labeled the Avenue of the Dead connected them. The Pyramid of the Moon is located at the northern end of this avenue.

The Pyramid of the Moon is about 460 by 490 feet (140 by 150 meters) at its base and was 148 to 151 feet (45 to 46 meters) high in its prime. Its walls were symmetrically aligned with the walls of every other structure in Teotihuacán. The Pyramid of the Moon was built to add height to stone temples and to make sacrifices to their deities. It underwent at least six facelifts, as made evident by the different styles of stone blocks present in the ruin. Each new addition was larger, covering the previous structure. The entire pyramid was probably built on top of several buildings. Numerous artifacts have been found in and around this structure, including obsidian pieces, figurines, ceramics, and jade carvings. In spite of these finds, the Pyramid of the Moon is still one of the least understood and most mysterious of all the ruins in Teotihuacán.

ADDITIONAL RESOURCES
Adams, Richard E. W., and Murdo J. MacLeod, eds. *Mesoamerica*. New York: Cambridge University Press, 2000.

Mendelssohn, Kurt. *Riddle of the Pyramids*. New York: Praeger, 1974.
Tompkins, Peter. *Mysteries of the Mexican Pyramids*. New York: Harper and Row, 1976.

SEE ALSO: Maya; Teotihuacán.

—*David Treviño*

PYRAMIDS AND THE SPHINX

DATE: c. 2649-c. 2514 B.C.E.
LOCALE: Egypt
RELATED CIVILIZATIONS: Pharaonic Egypt, Libya, Nubia, Phoenicia, Syria-Palestine
SIGNIFICANCE: The most widely known stone monuments of antiquity, these structures reveal a sophisticated level of state organization and architectural skill in Old Kingdom Egypt.

Although they were not the first pyramids constructed in Egypt, the three Fourth Dynasty pyramids of Giza were the finest pyramids the Egyptians built. They were linked to the worship of the Sun god Re. The pyramid symbolized the rays of the Sun, and the sacred *ben-ben* stone located in the Temple of the Sun in On (called Heliopolis by the Greeks) represented the primordial mound from which Re created the world. The pharaoh, or king, could ascend to the heavens after his death by means of the pyramid. His ascent was linked to creation and the daily rebirth of the Sun.

The largest Giza pyramid is the Great Pyramid of Khufu, the second pharaoh of the Fourth Dynasty. It is 481 feet (147 meters) high, and its base measures 756 feet (230 meters). Inside are several passages and cham-

The pyramids at Giza. (Corbis)

bers, including the Queen's Chamber and the Grand Gallery leading up to the King's Chamber where Khufu's sarcophagus was found empty. Pyramids were accompanied by other components, including a mortuary and valley temple connected by an enclosed causeway, smaller queen's and satellite pyramids, and boat pits. One of Khufu's full-sized boats has been reassembled, and it was probably intended to carry him through the heavens. The pyramid complex was a combination of a burial ground and palace for the dead king. Associated tombs were located nearby for other royalty and courtiers.

Khafre's pyramid is almost as big as that of Khufu but has chambers and passageways near to the ground and just beneath it. His valley temple and causeway are well-preserved. The Great Sphinx dates to Khufu or Khafre's reign and has the face of the pharaoh wearing the royal cloth (*nemes*) headdress on the body of a lion. The Great Sphinx is 66 feet (22 meters) tall and served as the guardian of the necropolis. At its east is a solar temple.

Menkaure's pyramid is only 213 feet (65 meters) high but is notable for having lower casing stones of red granite. There are three queen's pyramids, two being stepped.

The camp and cemetery of the workers who built the pyramids is located about two-thirds of a mile (one kilometer) southeast. The cemetery contains tombs of overseers, master craftsmen, and common laborers. Nearby was a bakery for making bread and brewing beer and a fish processing area. A wall with a bridge separated the workmen's area from the necropolis.

ADDITIONAL RESOURCES

Edwards, I. E. S. *The Pyramids of Egypt*. London: Penguin Books, 1993.

The Great Sphinx. (Corbis)

Lehner, Mark. *The Complete Pyramids*. London: Thames and Hudson, 1997.

Siliotti, Albert. *Guide to the Pyramids of Egypt*. New York: Barnes & Noble, 1997.

SEE ALSO: Egypt, Pharaonic.

—Sandra L. Orellana

PYRRHON OF ELIS

ALSO KNOWN AS: Pyrrho
BORN: c. 360 B.C.E.; Elis, Greece
DIED: c. 272 B.C.E.; buried in village of Petra, near Elis
RELATED CIVILIZATIONS: Classical and Hellenistic Greece
MAJOR ROLE/POSITION: Philosopher

Life. Pyrrhon of Elis (PIHR-ahn of EE-lihs), like Socrates, wrote nothing, and so information on his life must be gleaned from later sources. The founder of Greek Skepticism, he may have been influenced by Indian ascetics he encountered during Alexander the Great's eastern campaigns. For Pyrrhon, the senses were unreliable and people's beliefs neither true nor false. He recommended the simple life, free of beliefs, with a goal of mental and emotional tranquillity (*ataraxia*). The Skeptic should remain neutral with respect to things that cannot be known for certain and should avoid fruitless discussion about them. Pyrrhon made his daily life a demonstration of his Skeptical detachment and is said, for instance, to have displayed a legendary sangfroid during a storm at sea. Much of the biographical information recorded about him by Diogenes Laertius is, however, of dubious veracity.

Influence. Pyrrhon's response to the problem of knowledge marks the beginning of Greek Skepticism. It was the object of attacks by early Christian writers such as Gregory of Nazianzus but then lay dormant until the publication of a Latin translation of Sextus Empiricus's *Pyrrōneiōn Hypotypōseōn* (c. second century C.E., also known as *Pyrrhoniarum hypotyposes*; *Outlines of Pyrrhonism*, 1591) in France in 1562. From that time, Skepticism has strongly influenced the Western philosophical and intellectual tradition.

ADDITIONAL RESOURCES

Diogenes Laertius. *Lives of Eminent Philosophers*. Translated by R. D. Hicks. Cambridge, Mass.: Harvard University Press, 1991.

Hankinson, R. J. *The Sceptics*. London: Routledge, 1995.

Popkin, R. H. *The History of Scepticism from Erasmus to Spinoza*. Berkeley: University of California Press, 1979.

Unger, P. *Ignorance: A Case for Scepticism*. Oxford, England: Oxford University Press, 1975.

SEE ALSO: Alexander the Great; Christianity; Greece, Classical; Greece, Hellenistic and Roman; Gregory of Nazianus; Philosophy.

—*David H. J. Larmour*

PYTHAGORAS

BORN: c. 580 B.C.E.; Samos, Ionia, Greece
DIED: c. 500 B.C.E.; either Metapontum or Croton (Crotone), Italy
RELATED CIVILIZATIONS: Archaic and Classical Greece
MAJOR ROLE/POSITION: Philosopher, mathematician

Life. Pythagoras (peh-THAG-eh-ruhs) was the son of a Samian merchant and traveled extensively, studying as a youth in Tyre with the Chaldeans and Syrians and later in Miletus (Ionia) with the scientist-philosophers Thales of Miletus (possibly) and Anaximander. Subsequently, he went to Egypt, where he studied geometry and immersed himself in the mystical rites of the Diospolis temple. Taken from Egypt as a Persian prisoner-of-war, he continued his studies with the Magoi in Babylon, both absorbing their religion and perfecting his knowledge of mathematics and music. He returned to Samos, where he established his first society of mystic mathematician-philosophers, the "semicircle of Pythagoras."

In response to political turmoil and resistance to his teachings, he moved to Croton, off the coast of Italy. There he founded a secret philosophical and religious school including both men and women. The inner circle (*mathematikoi*) were expected to exercise strict physical and mental discipline, live communally, eat no meat, and wear no animal skins. Pythagoreans studied mathematical relationships, mathematical abstrac-

tions, and the concept of number as well as more mystical and spiritual subjects such as the belief in perfection through the transmigration of souls (hence their rever-

Pythagoras. (Library of Congress)

ence for animals) and spiritual purification through intellect and discipline. He fled to Metapontum, again to escape political turmoil and attacks on his school. Some evidence exists that he may have returned to Croton before his death.

As a result of his studies of music, mathematics, and astronomy, Pythagoras believed that the entire cosmos could be reduced to scale and numbers; reality was mathematical in nature and everything could be expressed in mathematical terms. He believed that certain symbols had mystical significance and that numbers had personalities. He described the "music of the spheres" and taught that the earth was the center of the universe and that celestial bodies moved in circular orbits. He noted that Venus was both the morning and evening star and that the Moon inclined to the equator. He also believed the brain was the locus of the soul and contributed to the mathematical theory of music when he discovered that tones and harmonies were ratios of whole numbers. He (or his school) developed a number of mathematical theorems, but he is best remembered for the Pythagorean theorem, an ancient idea in Babylon but one that he was able to prove.

Influence. Pythagoras was the first pure mathematician and was extremely important in the development of mathematics and philosophy. Although Pythagoras left no written works, details of his life and elements of his teachings can be found in the works of many early writers, including Plato, Aristotle, and other early scientists and philosophers.

ADDITIONAL RESOURCES
Gorman, Peter. *Pythagoras: A Life*. London: Routledge and Kegan Paul, 1979.
Kingsley, Peter. *Ancient Philosophy, Mystery, and Magic: Empedocles and Pythagorean Tradition*. Oxford, England: Clarendon Press, 1995.
O'Meara, Dominic J. *Pythagoras Revived: Mathematics and Philosophy in Late Antiquity*. Oxford, England: Clarendon Press, 1989.
Strathern, Paul. *Pythagoras and His Theorem*. London: Arrow, 1997.

SEE ALSO: Greece, Archaic; Greece, Classical; Philosophy; Science.

—*Robert R. Jones*

PYTHEAS

ALSO KNOWN AS: Pytheas of Massalia
BORN: c. 350-325 B.C.E.; Massalia, Gaul
DIED: after 300 B.C.E.; perhaps Massalia, Gaul
RELATED CIVILIZATION: Hellenistic Greece
MAJOR ROLE/POSITION: Geographer, historian

Life. Pytheas (PIHTH-ee-uhs) of Massalia most likely came from the Greek colony on the site of modern Marseilles. He was probably born into a merchant family and may have sailed the trading routes along the Atlantic coast. He appears to have traveled at least as far north as Britain and the Shetland Islands during a voyage lasting two or more years. In his lost work "On the Ocean," he recorded many astronomical and geographical observations, and, therefore, he may be categorized as a physical scientist. He also dealt with food supplies, social organizations, local customs, and the location of products suitable for trade. Although there may have been an economic purpose to Pytheas's voyage, his treatise does not seem to have been intended as a practical guide for mariners.

Influence. Many later writers quoted from Pytheas's treatise, which may have become a standard work of reference. He immortalized Thule (perhaps Iceland) as the furthermost location known to ancient geographers.

ADDITIONAL RESOURCES
Cary, M., and E. Warmington. *The Ancient Explorers*. London: Methuen, 1929.
Casson, L. *Ships and Seamanship in the Ancient World*. Princeton, N.J.: Princeton University Press, 1971.
Hawkes, C. F. C. *Pytheas: Europe and the Greek Explorers*. Oxford, England: Blackwell, 1975.
Roseman, Christina H. *Pytheas of Massalia, On the Ocean*. Chicago: Ares, 1994.
Thompson, J. O. *History of Ancient Geography*. New York: Bilbo and Tannen, 1965.

SEE ALSO: Britain; Greece, Classical; Greece, Hellenistic; Navigation and transportation; Trade and commerce.

—*David H. J. Larmour*

PYU

DATE: first-ninth centuries C.E.
LOCALE: Central Myanmar
RELATED CIVILIZATION: Burma
SIGNIFICANCE: The Pyu people contributed certain cultural attributes that survived to help shape Burmese culture of later periods.

The Pyu (pyew) were Tibeto-Burman speakers who migrated south into Burma from the Tibetan plateau, probably in the first century C.E., and established a kingdom in the Irrawaddy River Basin and the adjacent Yin, Mu, Nawin, and Kyaukse valleys. The Pyu called themselves Tirchul but were referred to as the Piao in Chinese records. They founded three capital cities: Beikthano, probably the earliest (the archaeological evidence has been carbon dated to the first century C.E.), Hmawza, the largest and most elaborate of the Pyu cities (Hmawza may be the city of Sri Ksetra mentioned by the Chinese Buddhist pilgrim Xuanzang), and Halin.

All three cities were large and attest an advanced culture that was ruled from a fortress palace located in the center of each city. The culture was based on both agriculture and trade. The cities demonstrate elaborate irrigation architecture that included hydraulic works, moats, tanks, canals, and reservoirs, all of which are evidence of a highly organized workforce and the importance of water in supporting the communities.

Archaeological remains of the early pre-Buddhist phase of Pyu culture attest the practice of cremation and the importance of the drum as a symbol of life, fertility, and riches. Drums were placed in pairs in graves to ensure renewal, and thus the Pyu formed part of the arc of drum cultures that extended throughout Southeast Asia and southwest China. Early on, the Pyu were a complex society consisting of rulers, royal officials, monks and priests, a range of craftspeople and traders, and farmer-irrigators.

When the Pyu first became Buddhists is impossible to determine, but it is evident that a transmission of ideas and technologies from India occurred during an early period. Their funerary brick constructions of the first century C.E. clearly resemble brickwork at Pāṭaliputra in north India dating to the second century B.C.E. Despite early contact with India, the archaeological finds demonstrate that the Pyu continued practicing funerary rituals connected with their ancient religion. Also, it can be determined from a seal of Indian origin dating to the second century C.E. that the Pyu were familiar with Indian Brahmi script and Pāli language. Nonetheless, the evidence suggests that Buddhism became influential only at a later time. Early in the fourth century C.E., a major monastic construction at Beikthano was raised, probably as the result of royal patronage. It is the first datable Buddhist monument in Burma. The plans of Pyu Buddhist stupas and monasteries demonstrate connections with the Buddhist monuments at the south Indian sites at Amaravātī and Nagarjunakonda in Andhra Pradesh dated between the second and the fourth centuries C.E. After the establishment of Buddhism, both males and females received education in monasteries and convents as novices, a practice that continues. Despite Buddhist training, the Pyu did not abandon many aspects of their previous religion.

Chinese records are an important source of information about the Pyu; they state that the Pyu claimed sovereignty over eighteen kingdoms, many of them in the southern portions of Myanmar. There is also evidence of the humane nature of the Pyu government; criminals were punished with only a few strokes of the whip.

ADDITIONAL RESOURCES

Stargardt, Janice. *The Ancient Pyu of Burma.* Cambridge, England: PACSEA, Cambridge, in association with the Institute of Southeast Asian Studies, 1990.

Tha Mayat, U. *Pyu Reader.* Canberra, Australia: National Library of Australia, 1967.

SEE ALSO: Amaravātī school; Arakanese; Buddhism; China; India; Xuanzang.

—Katherine Anne Harper

— *Q* —

QIJIA CULTURE

ALSO KNOWN AS: *Wade-Giles* Ch'i-chia culture
DATE: 2000-1000 B.C.E.
LOCALE: Gansu Province of northwestern China
RELATED CIVILIZATIONS: China, Central Asia
SIGNIFICANCE: The first known Chinese metalworking industry developed in this culture.

This Neolithic culture of northwest China may have been influenced by contemporary cultures in Mongolia and other parts of Central Asia. Archaeological evidence for this culture was first discovered by the Swedish geologist Johan Gunnar Andersson in 1923 at the village of Qijiaping, after which this culture is named. Since then, approximately 350 sites have been discovered.

The Qijia (CHIH-chiha) people lived in villages built on terraces on the Yellow River (Huang He). They built rectangular homes covered with clay plaster with round or circular hearths and surrounded by storage pits. Cemeteries were located near the villages and contained mostly individual burials with grave goods such as pottery, tools, and animal bones. Sheep, pig, dog, horse, and cattle bones provide evidence for the domestication of these animals. This culture is noted for its ceramics, mostly yellow with comb and incised designs and amphora shapes. Millet was a major crop. Also significant is the culture's copper metalwork. About fifty metal pieces, including rings, pendants, mirrors, and various tools, have been found. Most of these are copper but some are mixed with lead or tin.

ADDITIONAL RESOURCES

Chang, Kwang-chih. *The Archaeology of Ancient China.* 4th ed. New Haven, Conn.: Yale University Press, 1986.
Debaine-Francfort, Corinne. *The Search for Ancient China.* Translated by Paul G. Bahn. London: Thames and Hudson, 1999.

SEE ALSO: China; Yangshao culture.

—*Thomas J. Sienkewicz*

QIN DYNASTY

ALSO KNOWN AS: *Wade-Giles* Ch'in Dynasty
DATE: 221-206 B.C.E.
LOCALE: Central China
RELATED CIVILIZATION: China
SIGNIFICANCE: This large Legalist and feudal state emerged from the ashes of thirty-five years of civil war.

During the Chinese civil wars, people engaged in many heartless and cruel acts in their individual quests for power. When the Qin (chihn) family finally took control, these treacherous acts were not forgotten but instead encouraged Legalism. Legalism, characterized by strict rules enforced by the government, is based on the premise that humans are naturally selfish. Therefore, a system of regulations and consequences is needed so that people do not give in to their natural tendencies and so that order is maintained in society. The Qin did not want to lose power to anarchists and through civil war, so they sought to impose their ways on the people. Fearing that other ideologies would undermine their control, all other philosophies were prohibited—maverick scholars were even buried alive—and censorship was practiced in the form of book burning.

The Qin Dynasty had a strong military focus, and the first Great Wall of China was built during this period. Many technological developments took place during the Qin period, including the compass, which was engineered around the third century B.C.E. using a lodestone balanced on a round bronze plate.

The harsh rule of the Qin Dynasty led to its demise, and Legalism was soon discredited under the subsequent rule of the Han Dynasty (206 B.C.E.-220 C.E.).

ADDITIONAL RESOURCES
Bonavia, David. *The Chinese.* New York: Penguin, 1983.
Ebrey, Patricia Buckley, ed. *Chinese Civilization and Society: A Sourcebook.* New York: Free Press, 1981.
Sima Qian. *Records of the Grand Historian: Qin Dynasty.* Translated by Burton Watson. New York: Columbia University Press, 1993.

SEE ALSO: China; Great Wall of China; Han Dynasty; Legalists; Qin tomb.

—*Noelle Heenan*

QIN TOMB

DATE: c. 210 B.C.E.
LOCALE: Xianyang, near Xi'an, China
SIGNIFICANCE: According to the historical records, the tomb of China's first emperor contains many treasures, but it has not yet been opened by archaeologists.

When Shi Huangdi (259-210 B.C.E.) founded the Qin (chihn) Dynasty in 221 B.C.E., he became the first of 210 men and one woman to occupy the position of emperor of China. Over the next eleven years, until his death in 210 B.C.E., he would create the face of China that would endure over two millennia. Of the many grand and lasting projects constructed during his lifetime, perhaps the most intriguing is his own tumulus.

It is not known exactly when construction on his tomb was started: Some sources state that plans were being made as early as 246 B.C.E., when Shi Huangdi ascended the throne as King Zheng of the state of Qin, while others state that the actual construction did not start until 212 B.C.E., the year of his unification of China. According to the historical records, many of the

These terra-cotta soldiers, a short distance from the tomb itself, were discovered in 1974. (Corbis)

workmen were buried with him so that the secrets of the tomb would not be revealed to grave robbers. In addition, the emperor's childless concubines were entombed with him.

The contents of the tomb are still unknown because it has not been excavated, but the main historical record, Sima Qian's *Shiji* (first century B.C.E.; *Records of the Grand Historian of China*, 1960, rev. ed. 1993), offers a colorful description of its layout. More than 700,000 workers toiled at the site. The bronze-lined tomb was filled with valuable objects from far-off places as well as models of Shi Huangdi's own palaces and government buildings. A map of the empire was reproduced on the floor with the main rivers represented by veins of flowing mercury. The ceiling of the vault was decorated with descriptions of the constellations. Crossbows were arranged to discharge automatically should anyone try to desecrate the tomb. Finally, trees and grass were planted to make the tomb look like a hill. The total circumference of the tomb is 8 miles (nearly 13 kilometers), and it is approximately 145 feet (44 meters) high, about half of its height as reported in the third century C.E. Reportedly, the tomb has been plundered twice: the first time by rebels searching for weapons in 207 B.C.E. and again around the fifth century C.E. The inner tomb has not yet been opened by Chinese archaeologists, who are in the process of excavating the outer areas.

A significant find located less than two miles (a little more than three kilometers) from the tomb is the buried army consisting of nearly 8,000 life-size figures discovered in 1974. These soldiers, along with Shi Huangdi's tomb, are a testament to his love of the elaborate even in the afterlife.

ADDITIONAL RESOURCES

Chang, Wen-ti. *The Qin Terracotta Army*. London: Scala Books, 1996.

Cotterell, Arthur. *The First Emperor of China*. New York: Holt, Rinehart and Winston, 1981.

Fu, Tianchou, ed. *Wonders from the Earth*. San Francisco: China Books and Periodicals, 1989.

Guisso, R. W. L., and Catherine Pagani. *The First Emperor of China*. New York: Birch Lane Press, 1989.

SEE ALSO: China; Qin Dynasty; Shi Huangdi.

—*Catherine Pagani*

QU YUAN

ALSO KNOWN AS: *Wade-Giles* Ch'u Yuan; Qu Ping (*Wade-Giles* Ch'ü P'ing)
BORN: 340 B.C.E.; Hubei, China
DIED: 278 B.C.E.; Hubei, China
RELATED CIVILIZATIONS: China, Warring States
MAJOR ROLE/POSITION: Poet, thinker

Life. Qu Yuan (chew yew-an) was born into an aristocrat family in the Chu kingdom in the late Warring States era. At the time, the kingdoms of Qin and Chu were the strongest; each had the strength to unite the other kingdoms into a single China. Qu Yuan was trusted by the Chu king and served as the vice prime minister. He suggested that the king appoint able and virtuous persons to serve him and that he should form an alliance with the Qi kingdom against Qin so that the Chu could dominate a unified China.

After being betrayed by corrupt aristocrats, Qu Yuan lost the trust of the king and was exiled. In his exile, he wrote poems, including "Li Sao" (to leave from worries) and "Tian Wen" (to question Heaven), which are included in the collection *Chuci* (first collected in first century B.C.E., material added second century C.E.; *Chu Tz'u: The Songs of the South*, 1959). In 277 B.C.E., the Qin army invaded Chu. Qu Yuan could not bear to face his country's defeat and committed suicide, drowning in the Miluo River on the fifth day of the fifth month of the lunar calendar in 278 B.C.E.

Influence. Qu Yuan was the earliest great Chinese poet. The imagination, true emotions, and honorable integrity that are hallmarks of his poetry had a major influence on Chinese literature in later dynasties. The Chinese continue to revere him as a great thinker and patriot.

ADDITIONAL RESOURCES

Hawkes, David, ed. *The Songs of the South: An Ancient Chinese Anthology of Poems by Qu Yuan and Other Poets*. New York: Penguin Books, 1995.

Kuo, Mo-jo. *Chu Yuan: A Play in Five Acts*. Peking: Foreign Languages Press, 1978.

SEE ALSO: China; Qin Dynasty; Zhou Dynasty.

—*Lihua Liu*

QUINCTILIUS VARUS, PUBLIUS

ALSO KNOWN AS: Varus
BORN: date and place unknown
DIED: 9 C.E.; Teutoburg Forest (later in Germany)
RELATED CIVILIZATION: Imperial Rome
MAJOR ROLE/POSITION: Provincial governor, army commander

Life. Publius Quinctilius Varus (PUHB-lee-uhs kwihnk-TIHL-ee-uhs VAR-uhs) was a patrician and closely connected to the imperial family. Two of his known wives were Vipsania and Claudia Pulchra, daughters of Augustus's nieces Marcella Major and Minor. Vipsania's father was Augustus's colleague Marcus Vipsanius Agrippa; her half sister Vipsania married Augustus's stepson and successor Tiberius, with whom Varus was consul in 13 B.C.E. Varus's fathers-in-law and four nephews were consuls. Remains of an extensive villa overlooking the Anio (later Aniene) Valley near Tivoli at Quintiliolo are traditionally attributed to him.

Varus was proconsul of Asia 7/6 B.C.E., and as legate of Syria in 6-4/3 B.C.E., he intervened decisively at the death of Herod and the division of Judaea among Herod's sons. Augustus appointed Varus legate of Germany in 6/7 C.E., charging him to regularize the financial administration of a province created in 12 B.C.E. Deceived by ostensibly friendly natives—some of them Roman veterans and citizens—Varus led his army into an ambush in the Teutoburg Forest in 9 C.E. His army was destroyed, and he committed suicide.

Influence. Roman writers depicted Varus as corrupt, naïve, and militarily incompetent—as proved by the crushing defeat at Teutoburg Forest. Augustus's fault was greater: Distracted by the Pannonian revolt of 6-9 C.E., he overestimated Roman control and popularity in Germany and may have made a poor selection, as Varus had never commanded a large-scale campaign.

ADDITIONAL RESOURCES

Oldfather, William Abbott, and H. V. Canter. *The Defeat of Varus and the German Frontier Policy of Augustus*. Reprint. New York: Johnson, 1967.
Syme, R. *The Augustan Aristocracy*. Oxford, England: Oxford University Press, 1986.

SEE ALSO: Agrippa, Marcus Vipsanius; Augustus; Rome, Imperial; Teutoburg Forest, Battle of; Tiberius.
—*Thomas H. Watkins*

QUINTILIAN

ALSO KNOWN AS: Marcus Fabius Quintilianus
BORN: c. 35 C.E.; Calagurris, Hispania Tarraconensis (later Calahorra, Spain)
DIED: after 96 C.E.; place unknown
RELATED CIVILIZATION: Imperial Rome
MAJOR ROLE/POSITION: Rhetorician

Life. Quintilian (kwihn-TIHL-yehn) came to Rome at a time when Spanish provincials had become prominent in Rome. He may have received his education in Rome and was active in the courts there until he returned to Spain around 60 C.E. He was brought back to Rome by Servius Sulpicus Galba when he became emperor (r. 68-69 C.E.). Quintilian continued to be favored by the subsequent emperors Vespasian and Domitian, earning the honor of being the first teacher of rhetoric to be paid from the public treasury. In about 88 C.E., Quintilian retired after twenty years of teaching, but the emperor Domitian recalled him to tutor his two grandnephews. For this, Quintilian was awarded honorary symbols of the consulship.

Quintilian's major writing is the *Institutio Oratoria* (c. 95 C.E.; English translation, 1921) in twelve books. The so-called Minor Declamations may also be by him, or notes of his lectures. His book *De causis corruptae eloquentiae* (on the corruption of eloquence) is lost. The *Institutio Oratoria* is a fairly comprehensive treatise for the training of the orator from childhood to graduation.

Influence. Quintilian's influence as a teacher was considerable in his own day. Students and those heavily influenced by him include Pliny the Younger, Tacitus, Juvenal, and Martial. His writings were unknown through most of the Middle Ages until a single copy of the *Institutio Oratoria* was found in 1416 by Poggio Bracciolini. The Humanists were attracted to his attitude toward and method of education.

ADDITIONAL RESOURCES

Kennedy, George. *Quintilian*. New York: Twayne, 1969.

Quintilian. "From Institutes of Oratory." In *The Rhetor-ical Tradition*, edited by Patricia Bizzell and Bruce Herzberg. Boston: St. Martin's Press, 1990.

SEE ALSO: Domitian; Juvenal; Martial; Pliny the Younger; Rome, Imperial; Tacitus; Vespasian.

—*Robert W. Cape, Jr.*

QUINTUS SMYRNAEUS

ALSO KNOWN AS: Quintus of Smyrna
FLOURISHED: c. 375 C.E.; Asia Minor
RELATED CIVILIZATIONS: Roman Greece, Imperial Rome
MAJOR ROLE/POSITION: Epic poet

Life. Quintus Smyrnaeus (KWIHN-tuhs smehr-NEE-uhs) is known as the author of a surviving fourteen-book epic poem that describes the events between Homer's *Iliad* (c. 800 B.C.E.; English translation, 1616) and *Odyssey* (c. 800 B.C.E.; English translation, 1616). This epic poem *Posthomerica* (n.d.; *The Fall of Troy*, 1913) mimics the Homeric hexameters and the *Iliad* in style and structure. His narrative does not create new adventures for the heroes after Hector's death and up to the fall of the city of Troy but rather reflects previously written tales from the Trojan War cycle that survive only in summary and descriptive form. Quintus's work reveals the contemporary romanticizing of Greco-Roman literature and a desire to return to the classical forms; both trends later grew in the Byzantine world. The most often cited section of this poem is the first book, in which the tale of Achilles, the greatest hero of the Greeks, and Penthesilea, the queen of the Amazons, is detailed from the arrival of the fighting women to the romantic and tragic discovery of their femininity. This, too, is nothing more than an extension of contemporary trends in Greco-Roman literature.

Influence. Coming at the end of late antiquity, Quintus's greatest audience would have been the Byzantine courts and then Renaissance readers, who took his romantic model and applied it to the Trojan legend in their own works.

ADDITIONAL RESOURCES

Campbell, Malcolm. *A Commentary on Quintus Smyrnaeus Posthomerica XII*. Boston: E. J. Brill, 1981.

James, Alan. *A Commentary on Quintus of Smyrna Posthomerica V*. Boston: E. J. Brill, 1981.

White, Heather. *Studies in Late Greek Epic Poetry*. Amsterdam: Gieben, 1987.

SEE ALSO: Byzantine Empire; Greece, Hellenistic and Roman; Homer; Rome, Imperial.

—*Tammy Jo Eckhart*

QUR'ĀN

ALSO KNOWN AS: Koran
AUTHORSHIP: Muḥammad (c. 570-632 C.E.), through divine inspiration
DATE: revealed in installments c. 610-632 C.E.
LOCALE: Mecca and Medina
RELATED CIVILIZATION: Arabia
SIGNIFICANCE: The Qur'ān, the holy book of Islam, has been directing the daily lives of almost all Muslims for centuries. It has also served as the basis of canonical law for the Muslims.

According to the Muslim belief, the Qur'ān (kuh-RAN), which consists of many verses grouped in 114 chapters, was revealed to the Prophet Muḥammad through the archangel Gabriel or directly from God in its actual verbal form, not just in its meaning and ideas. The Prophet stayed in Mecca more than twelve years, from the day the first verses were revealed to him to his departure in 622 C.E. for Medina, where he lived another thirteen years. The last verse was revealed to him on the day of Great Pilgrimage in the tenth year of the flight (*hijrah*), three months before his death in 632 C.E. The Prophet dictated the verses to the scribes and told them where each verse should go. The chief scribe was Zayd bin Thābit. Most of the verses were written on palm branches, animal shoulder bones, leather, and thin stones.

A number of the companions of the Prophet, particularly those who had memorized the Qur'ān (*kurra'*), lost their lives at the Battle of Al-Yamama (633 C.E.). There was a threat that more might die in future battles. The caliph Abū Bakr set up a council under the chairmanship of Zayd bin Thābit and entrusted him with the collection of the Qur'ān. All the written verses were brought together, and everyone was invited to come forward with two witnesses if they had memorized any verses. The verses were put together according to the order in which the Prophet had recited them. Then all the companions of the Prophet were assembled, and the collected verses were read aloud to them. After their approval, the verses were made into a book and handed over to Abū Bakr. Before his death, Abū Bakr passed this copy to 'Umar ibn al-Khaṭṭāb, who then handed it over to his daughter Ḥafṣah before he died.

Huzayfah bin al-Yaman observed the disputes over the reading of the Qur'ān and warned the caliph. Therefore, in 651 C.E., Caliph 'Uthmān ordered Zayd bin Thābit and three other companions of the Prophet to prepare a new version based on the copy held by Ḥafṣah. Several transcripts were made from this final recension copy of the Qur'ān and were sent to major cities, including Al-Kufa, Basra, Damascus, and perhaps Mecca. All other copies were burned, and Ḥafṣah's copy was returned to her. However, Ibn Mes'ūd's copy in Al-Kufa reportedly remained in existence until the tenth century. These recension copies were difficult to read because they were written in Kufi script, which lacked vowels and diacritical marks. Al-Ḥajjāj ibn Yūsuf al-Thaqafī, 'Abd al-Malik's governor in Iraq, had these vowels and diacritical forms added to overcome this difficulty.

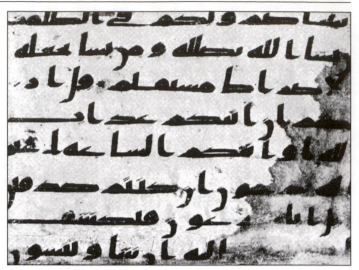

An excerpt from a ninth century C.E. version of the Qur'ān. (North Wind Picture Archives)

ADDITIONAL RESOURCES

Bell, Richard. *Introduction to the Qur'ān.* Edinburgh, Scotland: Edinburgh University Press, 1970.

Burton, J. *The Collection of the Qur'ān.* New York: Cambridge University Press, 1977.

Cragg, Kenneth. *The Event of the Qur'ān.* Rockport, Mass.: Oneworld, 1994.

The Encyclopaedia of Islam. Prepared by a number of leading orientalists; edited by an editorial committee consisting of H. A. R. Gibb et al. under the patronage of the International Union of Academies. New ed. Leiden, Netherlands: E. J. Brill, 1960- [2000].

Rippin, Andrew, ed. *The Qur'ān: Formative Interpretation.* Brookfield, Vt.: Ashgate, 1999.

SEE ALSO: Abū Bakr; Arabia; Islam; Muḥammad; 'Umar ibn al-Khaṭṭāb; 'Uthmān ibn 'Affān.

—*M. Mehdi Ilhan*

— R —

RADEGUNDA, SAINT

ALSO KNOWN AS: Radegund; Radegundis
BORN: c. 520/525 C.E.; Thuringia (later in Germany)
DIED: August 13, 587 C.E.; Poitiers (later in France)
RELATED CIVILIZATIONS: Merovingia, Rome
MAJOR ROLE/POSITION: Queen, nun

Life. Born into the Thuringian royal family, Radegunda (RAHD-uh-gihn-dah) was brought to France as a captive after the Franks conquered her homeland in 531 C.E. The Merovingian king Chlotar I (497-561 C.E.) married her in about 540 C.E., but they had no children, and when her brother was assassinated, Radegunda left court to adopt the religious life. For several years, she lived at her villa in Aquitaine, where she established a charitable institution for the indigent. In the late 550's C.E., with Chlotar's financial support, Radegunda founded a female monastery at Poitiers, where she lived until her death. Around 570 C.E., Radegunda sought and received a relic of the True Cross from Justin II, the Byzantine emperor. Subsequently, tense relations with Maroveus, the bishop of Poitiers, led to Radegunda's adoption of Caesarius's Rule for Nuns, which curtailed episcopal supervision of nunneries. Upon her death, Radegunda was immediately recognized as a saint, and her cult in Poitiers rivaled that of Saint Hilary.

Influence. Radegunda was the first female ruler to be recognized as a saint. Her career foreshadows that of other medieval queens who adopted a monastic life after they retired from court. However, Radegunda's life is extraordinary in that she retained significant political influence even after her retirement from court.

ADDITIONAL RESOURCES

McNamara, Jo Ann, et al. *Sainted Women of the Dark Ages*. Durham, N.C.: Duke University Press, 1992.
Van Dam, Raymond. *Saints and Their Miracles in Late Antique Gaul*. Princeton, N.J.: Princeton University Press, 1993.

SEE ALSO: Byzantine Empire; Chlotar I; Christianity; Merovingian Dynasty.

—*Martha G. Jenks*

RAIMONDI STONE

DATE: 400-200 B.C.
LOCALE: Chavín de Huántar, Callejon de Huaylas, Peru
RELATED CIVILIZATION: Chavín
SIGNIFICANCE: The most elaborately carved monument characteristic of the latest phase in the Chavín art style, the Raimondi stone depicts the "staff god," an anthropomorphic figure holding a staff in each hand, much copied throughout Peru.

The Raimondi (ri-MOHN-dee) stone defines the latest Chavín art style at its capital, Chavín de Huántar. The stone is attributed to the New Temple because of stylistic similarity to carved columns in the temple. Found by a nineteenth century naturalist, the Raimondi stone is the final and most elaborate representation of the Chavín supreme deity. It is carved in low-relief on a polished granite slab measuring 6.5 feet (1.98 meters) in height, 2.4 feet (0.74 meters) in width, and 0.6 feet (0.17 meters) in thickness. The staff god is shown in frontal view on the lower third of the stone; the rest of the stone is an elaborate headdress. Iconographically, there are repeated feline heads and snakes in the headdress and staffs, down-turned lips with fangs on the mouth, claws on the hands and feet, and a snake-feline costume. The image has bilateral symmetry, repetition of stylized elements, reversible organization, and generally a cluttered visual appearance. This powerful image was copied throughout the Andean region, in stone and textiles.

ADDITIONAL RESOURCES
Burger, Richard. *Chavín and the Origins of Andean Civilization*. New York: Thames and Hudson, 1992.
Moseley, Michael E. *The Incas and Their Ancestors: The Archaeology of Peru*. London: Thames and Hudson, 1992.

SEE ALSO: Andes, central; Chavín de Huántar.
—*Heather I. McKillop*

RĀMĀYAṆA

AUTHORSHIP: Composite; attributed to the legendary Vālmīki
DATE: c. 500 B.C.E., some material added later
LOCALE: India
RELATED CIVILIZATIONS: India, classical Southeast Asia
SIGNIFICANCE: This national epic has widely influenced literature and art in India and other cultures of South and Southeast Asia.

The *Rāmāyaṇa* (raw-MAW-yah-nah), or *Vālmīki-Rāmāyaṇa* (English translation, 1870-1889), is an epic poem of ancient India, consisting of about 24,000 stanzas divided into seven books and about 500 cantos and composed in a style of Sanskrit comparable in most ways to the style of India's other classical epic poem, the *Mahābhārata* (400 B.C.E.-400 C.E., present form by c. 400 C.E.; *The Mahabharata of Krishna-Dwaipayana Vyasa*, 1887-1896). Certain features—most prominently the use of formulaic repetitions with slight variations—suggest an origin in ancient oral tradition. Extant, however, are two main manuscript traditions, associated with north and south India. Of the epic's seven books, Books 2-6 are generally agreed to represent the older core of the poem. The first book ("Bāla–kāṇḍa," or "the book of the boy-prince") was seemingly added at a later time to explain the birth and youth of the hero of the epic, Rāma. The seventh book was added to tell the story of what happened to Rāma after the conclusion of his central adventure. Throughout the poem, however, are lines, passages, or entire groups of cantos that textual critics label as later interpolations.

The title *Rāmāyaṇa* is taken to mean "the adventures of Rāma." The epic's central narrative is a romance, recounting the birth of Rāmacandra, heir to the throne of the city-state Ayodhyā, his banishment through a palace intrigue, and his subsequent wanderings throughout India, accompanied by both his wife, Sītā, and brother Lakṣmaṇa. Sītā is abducted but is rescued, and Rāma is eventually restored to his rightful place as king in Ayodhyā. The poem's long sixth book describes in detail a battle between Rāma and his allies, the monkey army, against Rāvaṇa, the demon-king of Laṅkā who had abducted Sītā. A prominent character is the monkey Hanuman, Rāma's friend and helper. Hanuman was to become hugely popular in India, where he is understood as the paragon of religious devotion. In some parts of the epic, Hanuman is said to be the son of the wind-god, a status that grants him supernormal abilities. In general, later parts of the poem equate Rāma with Vishnu (Viṣṇu), the important central deity in later Hinduism. Sītā also has significant connections with early Vedic myth and may be divine in origin.

The Sanskrit *Rāmāyaṇa* has given rise to later versions in various languages, most prominently the *Rāmcaritmānas* in Avadhi from north India by Tulsīdās, often thought of as the "bible of (northern) India." Folk drama, sophisticated stage plays, and puppet shows have been based on the Rāma story. The Sanskrit text also has earned the name *ādi-kāvya*—"the first art poem."

ADDITIONAL RESOURCES
Brockington, John. *The Sanskrit Epics*. Leiden, Netherlands: E. J. Brill, 1998.
Goldman, Robert P., ed. *The Ramayana of Valmiki*. 5 vols. Princeton, N.J.: Princeton University Press, 1984-1996.
Richman, Paula, ed. *Many Ramayanas: The Diversity of Narrative Tradition in South Asia*. Berkeley: University of California Press, 1991.

SEE ALSO: Hinduism; India; *Mahābhārata*; Vālmīki.
—*Burt Thorp*

RAMESES II

ALSO KNOWN AS: Ramesses II; Usermare Ramses
BORN: c. 1300 B.C.E.; Egypt
DIED: 1213 B.C.E.; Egypt
RELATED CIVILIZATION: Pharaonic Egypt
MAJOR ROLE/POSITION: Pharaoh

Life. Rameses II (RAM-uh-seez), son of Seti I (second pharaoh of the Nineteenth Dynasty), was named regent by his father to ensure his succession and became pharaoh on his father's death in 1279 B.C.E. He inherited a kingdom that faced serious opposition from the Hittites of Anatolia in what is now Asian Turkey.

Rameses embarked on a military campaign to recapture northern territories lost in the fifteenth century B.C.E. In the fifth year of his reign, he prepared an attack on the Hittite stronghold of Kadesh in Syria but, misled by false intelligence, underestimated the size of the Hittite army. Only the arrival of another segment of Rameses' forces averted a potentially devastating defeat.

Rameses subsequently won many battles against states in Syria and Palestine, earning lasting renown as a military leader, but was never able completely to subdue the Hittites. Rameses finally settled for a peace treaty with his northern adversaries, even marrying a Hittite princess in 1245 B.C.E. Peace contributed to Egyptian prosperity and permitted Rameses to embark on a building campaign noted both for its large number of constructions and for the massive style of architecture that Rameses preferred.

The nickname "the Great" was bestowed on Rameses during the nineteenth century C.E. in response to the many monuments to his reign, most of them celebrating in words and pictures his martial triumphs. At Rameses' command, two colossi of him were constructed near the entrance to the Temple of Amun in Karnak (the northern half of ancient Thebes).

Rameses' most notable buildings included the Ramesseum, his mortuary temple at Thebes, and two temples at Abu Simbel in southern Egypt. The larger of these two temples included four statues of Rameses, each more than 65 feet (20 meters) high. The smaller temple was dedicated to his favorite wife, Nefertari. Both temples

Two statues of Rameses II at the temple at Abu Simbel. (PhotoDisc)

were cut into sections, moved, and reassembled in the 1960's to escape flooding from the new Aswan dam.

Rameses is usually identified as the pharaoh who contended unsuccessfully with Moses, leading to the Israelites' Exodus from Egypt. A fallen statue of Rameses inspired Percy Bysshe Shelley's sonnet "Ozymandias" (1818), on the transitory nature of earthly greatness.

Rameses' reign of sixty-six years was the second longest among Egypt's pharaohs. He was succeeded by Merneptah, one of the more than one hundred children that he fathered. Rameses' mummy was discovered in 1881 C.E., complete with skin, teeth, and hair, his visage reproduced in photographs so the world could see one of history's most powerful rulers.

Influence. Rameses led Egypt in its last great age of the pharaohs, achieving military success and altering the nature of Egyptian architecture with his massive constructions while delaying the disintegration of Egyptian power and influence that followed his death.

ADDITIONAL RESOURCES
Clayton, Peter A. *Chronicle of the Pharaohs*. New York: Thames and Hudson, 1994.
Menu, Bernadette. *Ramses II*. New York: Harry N. Abrams, 1999.
Schmidt, John D. *Ramesses II: A Chronological Structure for His Reign*. Baltimore: Johns Hopkins University Press, 1973.

SEE ALSO: Egypt, Pharaonic; Exodus; Hittites; Kadesh, Battle of; Merneptah; Moses; Rameses III; Seti I.
—*Edward J. Rielly*

RAMESES III

ALSO KNOWN AS: Ramsesses III
BORN: date and place unknown
DIED: 1156 B.C.E.; Thebes, Egypt
RELATED CIVILIZATION: Pharaonic Egypt
MAJOR ROLE/POSITION: Ruler or Pharaoh

Rameses III. (North Wind Picture Archives)

Life. Rameses III (RAM-uh-seez), who reigned from 1187 to 1156 B.C.E., was the second king of the Twentieth Dynasty, founded by his father, Setnakhte. A successful military leader, he repelled invasion attempts, first from Libya and later from the Sea Peoples, an alliance of Philistines, Sardinians, Cretans, and others. He continued the policies of his illustrious namesake of the preceding dynasty (Rameses II), who is thought to have been the biblical pharaoh who struggled with Moses. Rameses III also completed ambitious tree-planting and building projects, such as his famous mortuary temple, Medinet Habu. He was mortally wounded when one of his minor wives, Tiy, plotted unsuccessfully to usurp the throne for her son, in what is known as the Harem conspiracy. Rameses III died before the trial of the conspirators ended.

Influence. The reign of Ramses III marked a pivotal time in ancient Egyptian history because he is regarded as the last great pharaoh. After his rule, Egypt went into a period of decline, with economic, social, and internal political problems.

ADDITIONAL RESOURCES
Brugsch-Bey, Heinrich. *Egypt Under the Pharaohs*. London: Bracken Books, 1996.
Clayton, Peter A. *Chronicle of the Pharaohs: The Reign-by-Reign Record of the Rulers and Dynasties of Ancient Egypt*. New York: Thames and Hudson, 1998.
Forty, Jo. *Ancient Egyptian Pharaohs*. North Dighton, Mass.: JG Press, 1998.

Nelson, Harold Hayden. "Three Decrees of Ramses III from Karnak." *Journal of the American Oriental Society*, no. 2 (1935): 232-241.

SEE ALSO: Egypt, Pharaonic; Libyans; Philistines; Rameses II.

—*Alice Myers*

RECUAY

DATE: c. 200 B.C.E.-600 C.E.
LOCALE: Callejön de Huaylas Valley of the North Central Highlands, Peru
RELATED CIVILIZATION: Peru
SIGNIFICANCE: The Recuay produced monumental sculpture and elaborate pottery.

The Recuay were renowned for distinctive sociocultural traditions that emerged in Peru's northern highlands following the collapse of Chavín. The Recuay populated key highland regions for the purposes of agriculture, pastoralism, and exchange. Lower-altitude crops such as maize, fruits, and coca supplemented staples from higher zones such as potatoes and grains. Camelids served as pack animals (llamas) as well as primary sources of meat (mainly alpacas), supplemented by deer and guinea pigs.

Recuay centers include Huaraz, Tumshukayko (Caraz), Yayno (Pomabamba), Aija, and Pashash (Cabana). At these sites, defensive works, monumental architecture, corporate labor projects, and wealth distinctions are consistent with the existence of regional chiefdoms. A common social arrangement at other sites entailed largely egalitarian communities based around fortified hilltops serving to organize local households, production, ceremonial activities, and defense.

Highly sophisticated Recuay pottery, found mainly in funerary contexts, is characterized by thin wares often of white kaolinite clay, with polychrome and resist painting and sculptural decoration. Each pot is handmade; decorated shapes include bowls, jars, bottles, and effigies of humans and animals. Monolithic stone sculpture also distinguishes Recuay culture; artists rendered works in three dimensions (tenon-heads and statues) and in single-sided bas relief (vertical and horizontal slabs). Most sculptures were part of special secular and ceremonial constructions.

Recuay iconography is figurative and abstract—including geometric, zoomorphic (felines, serpents, birds, camelids, and mythical creatures), and anthropomorphic (warriors, leaders, women, and supernaturals) representations—emphasizing hierarchical status, fertility, ancestor worship, and warfare.

ADDITIONAL RESOURCES
Keatinge, Richard W. *Peruvian Prehistory.* New York: Cambridge University Press, 1988.
Stone-Miller, Rebecca. *Art of the Andes: From Chavín to Inca.* New York: Thames and Hudson, 1996.

SEE ALSO: Andes, central; Cajamarca pottery; Chavín de Huántar; Raimondi stone.

—*George F. Lau*

RES GESTAE DIVI AUGUSTI

ALSO KNOWN AS: *Monumentum Ancyranum*
AUTHORSHIP: Augustus
DATE: by 13 C.E., with slight posthumous editing in 14 C.E.
LOCALE: Rome
RELATED CIVILIZATION: Imperial Rome
SIGNIFICANCE: This work provides a rare glimpse of how an ancient political figure wished to depict himself, which, in the case of Augustus, is in quite traditional terms.

Literally "the deeds of the emperor Augustus," this list of his accomplishments was inscribed on bronze tablets outside his tomb at Rome. The original is long lost, but copies and translations inscribed elsewhere—most notably at the temple of Rome and Augustus in Ankara, Turkey—allow virtually the entire text to be reconstructed.

Like traditional epitaphs of other Roman aristocrats, *Res Gestae Divi Augusti* (*The Deeds of Augustus*, 1908) focuses on public accomplishments and honors: magistracies and priesthoods held, military victories, public buildings, and donations from his private purse. Also typical is its emphasis on instances in which Augustus can claim to have acted first, best, or most. Augustus also takes credit for victories won by his generals, buildings built by his family, and events (such as the arrival of ambassadors from India) that only coincidentally happened under his reign. His many domestic policy initiatives are treated only briefly and generally. Augustus puts a favorable spin on many items but never gives extensive narrative or justification.

ADDITIONAL RESOURCES
Brunt, Peter, and J. M. Moore. *Res Gestae Divi Augusti.* Oxford, England: Oxford University Press, 1967.
Galinsky, Karl. *Augustan Culture.* Princeton, N.J.: Princeton University Press, 1996.

SEE ALSO: Augustus; Languages and literature; Rome, Imperial.

—*Andrew M. Riggsby*

RIFT VALLEY SYSTEM

DATE: 3.5 million-c. 1 million years ago
LOCALE: Ethiopia, Uganda, Kenya, Tanzania, Mozambique
RELATED CIVILIZATION: East Africa
SIGNIFICANCE: The major site of early hominid excavations as well as a land form that influenced the migrations of early settlers, the Rift Valley system is often identified with the beginnings of human civilization.

The Rift Valley system is a system of earth rifts extending from Arabia to Mozambique at a length of 4,000 miles (6,400 kilometers) and a width of 18 to 60 miles (30-100 kilometers). Two major branches of the system are formed by the Eastern, or Great, Rift Valley and the Western Rift Valley. The Great Rift Valley extends from the Jordan River through the Dead Sea to the Gulf of Aqaba and continues to the south into the Ethiopian Denakil Plain to Lake Turkana, Naivasha, and Magadi in Kenya. The rift moves through Tanzania to the Mozambique Plain up to the Indian Ocean near Beira, Mozambique. The Western Rift Valley comes from the northern end of Lake Malawi along Lakes Rukwa, Tanganyika, Kivu, Edward, and Mobutu Sese Seko (Albert). These lakes are deep, and the bottom of Lake Tanganyika is below sea level. Some plateaus adjacent to the rift slope upward toward the valley with an average drop of from 2,000 to 3,000 feet (600-900 meters) to the valley floor. The Kikuyu and Mau escarpments, for example, drop more than 9,000 feet (2,700 meters). Margherita Peak of the Ruwenzori Range, along the border of Uganda and Congo, is the highest point within the Western Rift Valley.

The Great Rift Valley may be best known as the locale in which the earliest hominids (evolutionary precursors to *Homo sapiens*, or human beings) have been discovered. The most famous of these excavations have been conducted by the Leakeys (Louis, Mary, and Richard) at Olduvai Gorge in Kenya during the 1950's and 1960's and by Donald Johanson in the Afar Triangle. Johanson discovered Lucy, a 3-million-year-old skeleton of an early hominid, *Australopithecus afarensis*, in 1974 at a site called Hadar in the northern part of the valley. In 1978, in the southern part of the valley at Laetoli (Tanzania), Mary Leakey discovered hominid footprints dating to 3.5 million years ago. Other discoveries include the Taung child in 1924 (1.2 million years old), *Zinjanthropus boisei*, now called *Australopithecus boisei,* in 1959 (1.75 million years old), *Homo habilis* in 1972 (1.9 million years old), a boy *Homo erectus* in 1984 (1.6 million years old), and the "black skull" in 1985 (2.6 million years old). These and many other excavations of early hominids have led many paleontologists to conclude that human beings arose out of Africa.

ADDITIONAL RESOURCES
Gregory, John W. *The Great Rift Valley.* London: Frank Cass, 1968.
Johanson, Donald C., Leonora Johanson, and Blake Edgar. *Ancestors: In Search of Human Origins.* New York: Villard Books, 1994.
Johanson, Donald C., and James Shreeve. *Lucy's Child: The Discovery of a Human Ancestor.* New York: Morrow, 1989.
Oliver, Roland, and Michael Crowder, eds. *The Cambridge Encyclopedia of Africa.* Cambridge, England: Cambridge University Press, 1981.

SEE ALSO: Africa, East and South.

—*Alex L. Mwakikoti*

ROMAN ARCH

DATE: 1-500 C.E.
LOCALE: Roman Empire
RELATED CIVILIZATION: Imperial Rome

The Roman arch is a freestanding monument that commemorates a specific victory over a foreign foe by a Republican general or emperor, although later imperial arches also honor a particular member of the imperial family or even a city itself. Roman arches were built in Rome as well as in provincial cities throughout the empire, with fine examples surviving in modern France, Britain, Tunisia, and Turkey. Such arches served as a constant reminder of Roman power to both citizens and provincials.

The fornix, or honorific arch, is derived from the building technique which incorporates wedge-shaped bricks or stones placed in a semicircular format, with a keystone placed in the center to provide the necessary support against the pressure of the vault. The Romans used this technique to create freestanding arches that have architectural elements similar to that of a temple facade. Arches contain columns, usually engaged, resting on bases that support an entablature and frieze, which usually contains relief sculpture depicting a triumphal procession. The attic above the frieze contains a dedicatory inscription, which supports statues or trophies placed on top of the arch as further reminders of the commemorated victory. Many early imperial arches have only one arched, central passageway or bay. However, later arches, such as the arch of Lucius Septimius Severus (203 C.E.) and the arch of Constantine (312-315 C.E.) in Rome, contain three bays, one central bay flanked by two shorter and narrower bays.

The arch of Titus (c. 80 C.E.) is the most celebrated arch in Rome, commemorating Titus's defeat of the Jews and his capture of Jerusalem in 70 C.E. The arch spans the Via Sacra, the triumphal processional taken by victorious generals and emperors to display prisoners and booty to the Roman people. The bay contains two relief panels, each representations of Titus's triumphal procession. The "Spoils Relief" depicts Romans carrying religious items, including a menorah, plundered from the Temple in Jerusalem, and the "Triumph Relief" shows Titus in a chariot, crowned by Victory, who is accompanied by Genius Populi Romani, Genius Senatus, and Roma herself.

Roman imperial arches were also erected to commemorate events other than victory. Augustus erected an arch to his adopted sons, Gaius and Lucius, in the Roman Forum to identify them as legitimate heirs. The arch of Trajan in Beneventum honored Trajan's reconstruction of a highway, Via Traiana, from Beneventum (modern Benevento) to Brundusium (modern Brindisi).

In the later imperial age, the iconography shifted from celebrating victory over the enemies of Rome to triumph over rival emperors. The arch of Septimius Severus hailed victories over the Parthians, who acted as allies to Septimius Severus's rival Pescennius Niger (r. 193-194 C.E.). This theme was repeated in the provinces, as on the arch of Septimius Severus at Anazarbus (modern Turkey), which marked the spot of Niger's defeat. The Christian emperor Constantine the Great erected his arch to celebrate his defeat over his pagan rival, Maxentius, at the Milvian Bridge in 312 C.E.

ADDITIONAL RESOURCES

Anderson, J. C., Jr. *Roman Architecture and Society.* Baltimore: Johns Hopkins University Press, 1997.
Sear, Frank. *Roman Architecture.* Ithaca, N.Y.: Cornell University Press, 1982.

SEE ALSO: Art and architecture; Augustus; Constantine the Great; Milvian Bridge, Battle of; Roman Forum; Rome, Imperial; Severus, Lucius Septimius; Titus; Trajan.

—*Elizabeth A. Gardiner*

ROMAN FORUM

DATE: 1000 B.C.E.-700 C.E.
LOCALE: Rome, valley between the Capitoline, Palatine, Oppian, and Quirinal Hills
RELATED CIVILIZATIONS: Republican and Imperial Rome
SIGNIFICANCE: Civic center of Rome.

Before construction of the Cloaca Maxima (the main sewer) in sixth century B.C.E., the site of the Roman Forum was a marsh used for burials (ninth to sixth centuries B.C.E.). Once drained, the valley became a market that evolved into Rome's religious, economic, and governmental center. Under the kings and Roman Republic, the forum grew organically as individuals commissioned buildings for various functions. The Via Sacra was among the roads servicing the forum.

Sanctified sites appeared throughout the forum. The oldest, the Regia, Aedes Vestae, and Lacus Iuturnae, developed at the eastern end during the sixth and seventh centuries B.C.E. The fifth century B.C.E. temples of Saturnus and Castor lined the southern side, and the fourth century Aedes Concordiae occupied the west.

The central square, coupled with the surrounding shops (fourth century B.C.E.), provided space for business. The erection of the basilicas Aemilia (179 B.C.E.) and Sempronia (170 B.C.E.) behind the northern and southern storefronts offered more formal settings for economic or legal activities.

Governmental buildings occupied the northwestern corner of the forum, perhaps as early as the sixth century B.C.E. The Curia, or senate house, stood to the north of the comitium and rostra, sites of public assembly and debate. The Tabularium, or senate archive, was built along the eastern slope of the Capitoline in 80 B.C.E.

Julius Caesar and Augustus systematized the haphazard nature of the forum into something resembling an imperial forum, complete with approximate symmetry, closure, and focus. Caesar replaced the basilica Sempronia with the basilica Iulia (54 B.C.E.), restored the basilica Aemilia (54 B.C.E.), and rebuilt the Curia (44 B.C.E.) to align with his imperial forum and greatly reduce the size of comitum, thus symbolizing his political dominance. Augustus completed Caesar's interventions and added the Aedes Divi Iuli (29 B.C.E.) on the site of Caesar's funeral pyre. This temple, flanked by triumphal arches to Augustus and his heirs, became the focal point of the forum.

Subsequent generations maintained and modified the forum without significantly altering the organization of Caesar and Augustus. In fact, later interventions harmonized with their program, stressing allegiance. The Flavians added the temple of Vespasian (80 C.E.) facing the Aedes Divi Iuli, and the Antonines placed the temple of Faustina (141 C.E.) adjacent. The Severan arch (203 C.E.) stood near the Curia, opposite the arches of Augustus. Tetrarchic columns and anniversary monuments (all early fourth century C.E.) further ornamented the forum while announcing continuity. Maxentius's basilica and office of the urban prefect (both early fourth century C.E.) expanded the forum eastward.

Though paganism was outlawed in 346 C.E., Christianity did not come to the forum until the sixth century

This engraving depicts the north and east sides of the Roman Forum as it might have appeared when viewed from the north corner of the Rostra. (Hulton Archive)

conversions of the urban prefect's office into Santi Cosma e Damiano and the Palatine Palace's vestibule into Santa Maria Antiqua. The Curia became San Adriano in 630 C.E. Like pagan patronage in the forum, Christian intervention aimed at articulating political power.

ADDITIONAL RESOURCES

Claridge, Amanda. *Rome.* Oxford, England: Oxford University Press, 1998.

Favro, Diane. *The Urban Image of Augustan Rome.* Cambridge, England: Cambridge University Press, 1996.

Richardson, Lawrence, Jr. *A New Topographical Dictionary of Ancient Rome.* Baltimore: Johns Hopkins University Press, 1992.

SEE ALSO: Art and architecture; Augustus; Caesar, Julius; Christianity; Rome, Imperial; Rome, Republican; Maxentius; Vespasian.

—Diana H. Minsky

ROME, IMPERIAL

DATE: 31 B.C.E.-500 C.E.

LOCALE: Europe, west of the Rhine and south of the Danube; Northern Africa; Asia Minor; Palestine; Mesopotamia

SIGNIFICANCE: For at least two centuries, Imperial Rome exercised authority over one of the largest empires of all history, promoted trade, constructed roads and other infrastructure, and provided general prosperity and stability.

The impressive achievements of Imperial Rome were possible because of the foundations laid during the earlier age of the Republic. When the imperial monarchy was established under Augustus, the Romans had already gained control over colonies as far apart as Spain and Palestine. During the next two centuries, the Romans made additional conquests and effectively maintained hegemony over a large part of the civilized world. Beginning about 180 C.E., however, Rome began to experience destructive civil wars, economic crises, population decline, and barbarian invasions. During the fourth century, the weakened empire was divided between the East and the West, and the western portion of the empire was entirely taken over by Germanic tribes by the end of the 400's C.E.

History. In 31 B.C.E., Octavian, the adopted son of Julius Caesar, defeated the naval and land forces of Marc Antony and Cleopatra VII at the Battle of Actium, putting an end to the civil wars that had ravaged Rome for more than half a century. At first Octavian ruled as consul, but the senate in 27 B.C.E. gave him the honorific title of "Augustus," which became his formal name. Rather than declaring himself dictator, Augustus established a type of constitutional monarchy. In practice, nevertheless, he had the final word in deciding all gov-ernmental policies, and he was careful to maintain control over the army.

Augustus was often called *imperator*, or commander, and he is usually classified as the first of the Roman emperors. Claiming to restore republican institutions, Augustus preferred to be designated as *princeps*, or "first citizen," so that the period from Augustus until 180 C.E. is usually called the Principate. However, Augustus promoted the cult of emperor worship, which required people to pay homage to the emperor's *genius*, or guardian spirit. He expanded the empire as far as the Danube, and he reorganized provincial governments, with an emphasis on a more efficient means of collecting taxes. In addition, he rebuilt Rome and patronized the arts and letters. His rule initiated a period of peace that lasted about two hundred years, often called the Pax Romana, or "Roman peace."

For fifty years after Augustus's death in 14 C.E., the emperors came from the dynasty that Augustus founded, which was composed of the Julio-Claudian clans. Two emperors, Tiberius and Claudius, were considered to be wise and able administrators, but Caligula and Nero had reputations for being cruel and frivolous leaders. During these years, the emperor's special standing army, the Praetorian Guard, often intervened in politics; in 41 C.E., the Praetorians murdered Caligula and selected Claudius as emperor. Nero's inept rule led to rebellion and civil war, with four men claiming to be emperor after his death.

In 70 C.E., Vespasian restored order and founded the Flavian Dynasty, designating his sons Titus and Domitian as his successors. In effect, Vespasian transformed the Principate into a full-blown hereditary monarchy. The Flavians expanded the bureaucracy and expanded the boundaries of the empire. Although generally con-

THE ROMAN EMPERORS

Name	Reign	Name	Reign
Augustus	27 B.C.E.-14 C.E.	Carus	282-283
Tiberius	14-37	Numerian	283-284
Caligula	37-41	Carinus	283-285
Claudius	41-54	Diocletian (East)	284-305
Nero	54-68	Maximian (West)	293-305
Galba	68-69	Constantius (West)	305-306
Otho	69	Galerius (East)	305-315
Vitellius	69	Severus (West)	306-307
Vespasian	69-79	Maxentius (West)	306-312
Titus	79-81	Constantine the Great (East)	306-337
Domitian	81-96	Licinius (East)	308-324
Nerva	96-98	Constantine the Great (all)	324-337
Trajan	98-117	Constantine II (West)	337-340
Hadrian	117-138	Constans I (West)	337-350
Antoninus Pius	138-161	Constantius II (East)	337-361
Marcus Aurelius	161-180	Magnentius (West, usurper)	350-353
Lucius Verus	161-169	Julian (all)	361-363
Commodus	180-192	Jovian (all)	363-364
Pertinax	193	Valentinian I (West)	364-375
Didius Julianus	193	Valens (East)	364-378
Septimius Severus	193-211	Procopius (East)	365-366
Pescennius Niger	193-194	Gratian (West)	375-383
Caracalla	211-217	Valentinian II (West)	375-392
Geta	211-212	Theodosius I (all)	379-395
Macrinus	217-218	Maximus (West, usurper)	383-388
Elagabalus	218-222	Eugenius (West, usurper)	392-394
Severus Alexander	222-235	Honorius (West)	393-423
Maximin	235-238	Arcadius (East)	395-408
Gordian I	238	Theodosius II (East)	408-450
Gordian II	238	Constantius III (East)	421
Balbinus and Pupienus	238	Valentian III (West)	425-455
Gordian III	238-244	Marcian (East)	450-457
Philip the Arab	244-249	Petronius Maximus (West)	455
Decius	249-251	Avitus (West)	455-456
Gallus	251-253	Majoran (West)	457-461
Aemilian	253	Leo I (East)	457-474
Valerian	253-260	Libius Severus (West)	461-465
Gallienus	253-268	Anthemius (West)	467-472
Claudius II Gothicus	268-270	Olybrius (West)	472
Quintillus	270	Glycerius (West)	473-474
Aurelian	270-275	Leo II (East)	474
Tacitus	275-276	Julius Nepos (West)	474-475
Florian	276	Zeno (East)	474-491
Probus	276-282	Romulus Augustulus	475-476

sidered cruel, they did manage to maintain peace and to pave the way for the period of "five good emperors," a golden age lasting from 96 to 180 C.E.

These five rulers—Marcus Cocceius Nerva, Trajan, Hadrian, Antoninus Pius, and Marcus Aurelius—were effective commanders and competent administrators. Although not power-hungry despots, they were absolute monarchs determined to rule and preserve order on their own terms. Nerva reformed land law in favor of the poor, tolerated Christianity, and reformed taxation. His designated successor, Trajan, conquered much of the Parthian Empire, restored the Appian Way, and built a forum and a large aqueduct for Rome. Hadrian patronized artists, rebuilt the Pantheon, and constructed a protective wall in Britain. Marcus Aurelius was a Stoic philosopher who tried to help the poor and to decrease the violence of the gladiatorial shows. He also persecuted Christians as enemies of the empire.

In contrast to the other four good emperors, Marcus Aurelius designated his natural son, Lucius Aurelius Commodus, as his successor. The choice was unfortunate. Following Commodus's assassination, Lucius Septimius Severus founded a military dynasty that lasted from 193 to 235 C.E. The Severan Dynasty was followed by a period of constant civil wars and general anarchy, until the emperor Diocletian in 284 C.E. restored order and reorganized the empire into a tetrarchy (rule of four). The empire was divided into two parts, the East and the West, with each part having a military commander called an Augustus and an assistant called a Caesar. With the retirement of Diocletian in 305 C.E., civil wars recurred until Constantine the Great, the first emperor to endorse Christianity, again united the empire in 324 C.E.

Because of the weakened condition of Rome, Constantine moved his major capital to Byzantium, which was eventually renamed Constantinople. Later emperors were not able to reverse the decline of the West. In 410 C.E., Visigoth invaders under Alaric I sacked Rome. The last emperor of the West, Romulus Augustulus, was finally deposed in 476 C.E. The Western Empire was divided among a large number of seminomadic warrior societies, and the Eastern Empire, centered at Constantinople, would continue to survive for almost a thousand years.

Government and law. The emperor was the commander of the military, and he had almost unlimited power to issue legislative edicts and to execute their enforcement. The powers of the Roman senate, the courts, and army constantly changed, depending on circumstances and the force of individual personalities. The Romans never established good institutional means for the selection of the emperor, which meant that succession was often decided by warfare. The concepts of democracy and elected representation were generally missing from the political institutions of the empire.

During the imperial age, nevertheless, there was usually a strong commitment to the principle of rule by established law. Under the Principate, Augustus and his successors allowed eminent jurists such as Gaius and Ulpian to deliver opinions on the legal issues of trials, which produced the "classical age of Roman law." The Roman law included three major branches: the civil law, which was applicable to Roman citizens; the law of peoples, which was binding on all nationalities of the empire; and natural law, which assumed that humans could discern a rational order of nature. Although Roman jurists often endorsed the theory of equality before the law, slavery and other Roman institutions made it impossible to apply the theory in practice.

Military power. During the early years of the empire, the army was composed of Roman citizens who became professional soldiers by enlisting for twenty years of active duty. This army, famous for its training and discipline, conquered new territory and guarded the frontiers. The army also included engineers who designed bridges and roads. It was divided into legions, with each composed of about 6,000 infantry and 120 cavalry. Each legion was assisted by an auxiliary, a unit of the same size composed of noncitizens drafted for twenty years. At the height of the empire, the army probably included about 500,000 soldiers. Because of its great power, the army—especially the Praetorian Guard—sometimes intervened in political matters.

As the empire weakened, the army was increasingly dominated by Germans and mercenaries. By the fourth century C.E., the soldiers of the army had no real commitment to Roman power and traditions. As taxation became less efficient, the size and quality of the army declined, leaving the frontiers unprotected from barbarian invaders.

Economics. The prosperity of the Principate was based on a combination of manufacturing, agriculture, and the mutual benefits of trade. Manufacturers of the empire produced pottery, textiles, and numerous products of metal and glass. Romans traded with all parts of Eurasia, including India and China. The maintenance of the empire would not have been possible without efficient means of transporting soldiers and commercial goods. Each important region within the empire had a

IMPERIAL ROME, CIRCA 200 C.E.

busy port city to receive ships. Most merchant ships were sailing vessels dependent on the wind, and warships were usually galleys using slaves and prisoners to operate oars.

Even in good times, prosperity was unevenly distributed according to geography and social class. Italy usually had an unfavorable balance of trade, for it was never able to produce enough commodities to pay for the luxuries that were imported primarily from the East. By the fourth century C.E., Rome was increasingly drained of its money supply. As a consequence, the government lacked the means to pay for military protection or the maintenance of roads and other infrastructure.

Social structure. Roman society was divided into rigid social classes. The most basic distinction of the empire was between citizens and noncitizens. At first, only people from Rome could be citizens, but the privilege was later extended to other peoples throughout the empire. Citizens were divided into three categories: a small group of ruling aristocrats, a small number of

wealthy landowners and merchants, and the plebeians or lower-class majority. Noncitizens were divided into two groups: slaves and non-Roman nationalities who were allies of the Romans, called *socii*. Slaves had no legal rights. Most slaves were either prisoners of war or condemned criminals, although poor people sometimes were forced to sell their children into slavery.

Rural agricultural workers usually lived in conditions of extreme poverty. Although a small number of yeoman farmers possessed their own land, most rural workers were tenant workers, called *coloni*, concentrated in large estates, or villas. From the third century C.E., the majority of such workers were bound to the soil, forced into slavelike conditions. *Coloni* often escaped to the cities, and sometimes they joined bands of marauding robbers. Rural riots were increasingly a problem. During the empire's decline, many of the villas had already become self-sufficient units that resembled the manors during the Middle Ages.

Architecture and city planning. Roman architects pioneered in the construction of domes, amphitheaters, public baths, and race courses. The public buildings of the empire were massive and built to last. The Romans were the first to discover how to produce poured concrete. Although borrowing many ideas from the Etruscans, the Romans were also the first to make widespread uses of arches, barrel vaults, and domes. The largest domed structure was the Pantheon, which had a dome 142 feet (43 meters) in diameter. The Romans constructed several huge coliseums, including the one in Rome that accommodated 50,000 spectators.

The trade and urban centers of the empire would not have been possible without a vast network of stone roads, bridges, and aqueducts. Highways such as the Appian Way were constructed of layers of stone and gravel. At the time of Trajan, eleven aqueducts brought 300 million gallons (1.1 million liters) of water into Rome daily, providing running water and sewage for the homes of the wealthy. Numerous Roman structures, such as the Pont du Gard in France, remain standing in modern times.

Science. Although the Romans did not make especially great strides in theoretical science, they did put the findings of Hellenistic science to practical use in fields such as engineering and applied medicine. During the first century C.E., Pliny the Elder amassed a large encyclopedic work called *Naturalis historia* (77 C.E.; *Natural History*, 1938-1963). During the second century C.E., the Greek-speaking astronomer Ptolemy defended the geocentric view of the universe in his *Almagest* (also known as *Hē matheēmatikē syntaxix*, 146 or 147 C.E.; English translation, 1898). The physician Galen experimented with animal hearts and was probably the first to explain the process of respiration. Galen's medical encyclopedia, although containing many errors, remained the standard authority in the field until the sixteenth century.

Religion. Beliefs in animism, or spirits and mysterious forces, continued to be important during the empire. Until the advent of Christianity, Romans were tolerant polytheists who accepted a large number of gods and goddesses, with an emphasis on a pantheon of Greco-Roman deities such as Jupiter, Mars, Minerva, and Janus. Although Greek mythology and Greek philosophy were especially influential, syncretism with other traditions, such as those of Egypt and Persia, was also common. An official clergy conducted sacrifices and other rituals that were believed to promote peace and prosperity. Until the advent of Christianity, the civic religion mandated that everyone acknowledge the emperor's spirit as divine.

By the time of Augustus, many of the common people were attracted to mystery religions and cults from Egypt and Iran, with the worship of Isis, Mithra, and Cybele having especially great appeal. These new faiths centered around personal salvation and belief in a continued afterlife. Such practices helped to prepare the way for Christianity. Before the first Edict of Milan in 313 C.E., the government often persecuted Christians because of their stubborn refusal to participate in the civic religion. About 394 C.E., Theodosius the Great made orthodox Christianity the official religion of the empire, and the government attempted to suppress other religious traditions.

Recreation and entertainment. Under the empire, there were frequent holidays during which the government sponsored events of public entertainment. Chariot races, held in an arena called a *circus*, were especially popular. The poet Juvenal once wrote that the most important needs of the common people were "bread and circuses." Gladiator fights at the amphitheaters also attracted huge crowds. From the modern perspective, such fights were extremely cruel and violent. In addition to fighting wild animals, trained gladiators fought each other to the death. Condemned criminals and Christians were sometimes thrown to lions and other hungry beasts.

Romans also enjoyed less violent forms of recreation. They often went to the theater, where farcical comedies were especially appreciated. People frequently spent their leisure time at public baths, libraries, gymnasiums, and art galleries. Other amusements included dancing, magical shows, acrobatics, games similar to checkers, and hunting and fishing.

Literature. During periods of prosperity, Roman aristocrats were generous patrons of writers and artists. The Augustan age is often called the "golden age of Latin literature." The most famous poet of the age was Vergil, author of the *Aeneid* (c. 29-19 B.C.E.; English translation, 1553), an epic poem presenting an idealized view of a Trojan hero, considered an ancestor of aristocratic Romans. Another prominent poet, Horace, presented a detached analysis of human weaknesses in his *Satires* (35 B.C.E., 30 B.C.E.; English translation, 1567). The last great poet of the period, Ovid, preserved fifteen mythological tales in the *Metamorphoses* (c. 8 C.E.; English translation, 1567). The most prominent prose writer of the golden age was the historian Livy, whose mammoth *Ab urbe condita libre* (c. 26 B.C.E.-15 C.E.; *The History of Rome*, 1600) interpreted the past from a patriotic and moralistic perspective.

The century and a half after Augustus is commonly referred to as the Silver Age. Three philosophical writers—Seneca the Younger, Epictetus, and Marcus Aurelius—were eminent interpreters of Stoicism, teaching serenity and surrender to the benevolent order of the universe. Petronius Arbiter's *Satyricon* (c. 60 C.E.; *The Satyricon*, 1694) is considered one of first satirical novels in Western literature. The greatest historian of the period, Tacitus, wrote a narrative of the Roman past in *Ab excessu divi Augusti* (c. 116 C.E., also known as *Annales*; *Annals*, 1598) and *Historiae* (c. 109 C.E.; *Histories*, 1731), and his *De origine et situ Germanorum* (c. 98 C.E., also known as *Germania*; *The Description of Germanie*, 1598) favorably described the Germans as noble savages. Juvenal's five books of *Saturae* (100-127 C.E.; *Satires*, 1693) gave a biting critique of the vices and inequities of Roman society. During the later empire, the most important literary works were produced by Christian writers, including Saint Jerome, Saint Augustine, and the historian Eusebius of Caesarea.

Current views. In general, the Romans were not very interested in abstract thought, and they did not make many original contributions to philosophy or science. They excelled in the development of law, the administration of a large and diverse empire, and the construction of buildings and infrastructure. The Pax Romana produced peace and stimulated trade over a vast area, providing many advantages for the people who were a part of the empire. These benefits, however, were unequally distributed according to social position and location. The Romans did not build their political institutions on democratic principles and were unable to develop peaceful means for the transfer of political power. Roman leaders, therefore, had to rely primarily on fear and coercion to maintain their rule. The Roman Empire faced many challenges, and historians are easily able to identify multiple causes for its demise. The more difficult task is to explain how the empire survived as long as it did.

ADDITIONAL RESOURCES

Barton, Carlin. *The Sorrows of the Ancient Romans.* Princeton, N.J.: Princeton University Press, 1993.

Boren, Henry. *Roman Society: A Social, Economic, and Cultural History.* Boston: Houghton Mifflin, 1992.

Bradley, Keith. *Slavery and Society in Rome.* New York: Cambridge University Press, 1994.

Dupont, Florence. *Daily Life in Ancient Rome.* New York: Oxford University Press, 1992.

Potter, D. S., and D. J. Mattingly. *Life, Death, and Entertainment in the Roman Empire.* Ann Arbor: University of Michigan Press, 1997.

Veyne, Paul. *The Roman Empire.* Cambridge, Mass.: Harvard University Press, 1997.

SEE ALSO: Actium, Battle of; Alaric I; Antoninus Pius; Antony, Marc; Appian Way; Augustine, Saint; Augustus; Byzantine Empire; Caligula; Christianity; Claudius; Cleopatra VII; Constantine the Great; Constantinople; Diocletian; Domitian; Egypt, Ptolemaic and Roman; Epictetus; Eusebius of Caesarea; Four Emperors, year of the; Galen; Germany; Goths, Ostrogoths, Visigoths; Hadrian; Horace; Isis, cult of; Jerome, Saint; Juvenal; Livy; Marcus Aurelius; Milan, Edict of; Nero; Nerva, Marcus Cocceius; Ovid; Pantheon; Parthia; Petronius Arbiter; Pliny the Elder; Ptolemy; Romulus Augustulus; Seneca the Younger; Severus, Lucius Septimius; Tacitus; Theodosius the Great; Tiberius; Titus; Trajan; Vergil; Vespasian.

—*Thomas T. Lewis*

ROME, PREREPUBLICAN

DATE: 800-509 B.C.E.

LOCALE: Latium, central Italy

SIGNIFICANCE: Rome as a city and culture began as a monarchy whose kings successively added new territories and new customs to what became the Roman Republic.

From the founding of Rome in 753 B.C.E. (according to writer Marcus Terentius Varro) to the year 510 B.C.E., Rome was ruled by seven kings. The kings and the dates of their reigns given below are according to the traditional or "canonical" list; other traditions and archaeological evidence do not agree.

The first, Romulus (753-715 B.C.E.), established his supremacy by decreeing that the king would be preceded by twelve lictors and would have a special chair. He then established laws and created the senate as an advisory board. When neighboring peoples refused to intermarry with the Romans, Romulus developed a plan to hold a festival and invite the neighboring peoples to participate and see the new city. When a signal was given, the Romans seized the unmarried women and convinced them to become their wives. Later these very same women, known as the Sabine women, stopped the war between their fathers and husbands and joined the two peoples together, increasing Rome's population.

Romulus disappeared mysteriously one day. Because the people believed that the senators had murdered Romulus, a senator, Julius Proculus, announced that Romulus had appeared to him and said that he had been taken up by the gods. From then on, Romulus was worshiped as the god Quirinus. Because no method for succession had been established, the government passed into a period called an interregnum ("between reigns"). After a year of the interregnum, the people chose Numa Pompilius, a Sabine, as king.

Numa Pompilius (r. 715-673 B.C.E.) earned his reputation as a man of peace and religion. Numa's religious innovations included organizing of the cult of the Vestal Virgins, building the temple of Janus, and naming the first *pontifex maximus* (high priest). Numa also established the twelve-month lunar calendar. Because these months were only twenty-eight days long, Numa included an intercalary month—a varying period of days inserted when necessary to bring the lunar calendar back in line with the seasons.

After Numa's death, the people elected Tullus Hostilius (r. 672-641 B.C.E.) as king. Tullus had little interest in religion and immediately began expanding Rome's territory through conquest. Tullus conquered many towns, most notably bringing the population of Alba Longa to Rome. He ordered the construction of the Curia Hostilia, the senate house, and added the Caelian hill to the area of the city, which had previously consisted of the Palatine, Aventine, and Capitoline hills. When Rome was hit with a plague, Tullus turned to religion to save himself, but when he made a mistake in performing a ritual, his house was struck by lightning, and he was instantly killed.

Next, Ancus Marcius (r. 640-617 B.C.E.) was chosen as king. Ancus was the nephew of Numa, but unlike his uncle or his predecessor, he struck a balance between religion and warfare. Ancus established a special ritual for declaring war and ordered the *pontifex maximus* to make the procedures for all religious rituals public. Ancus added the Janiculum hill to Rome's control and ordered the construction of the first bridge across the Tiber River.

During Ancus's reign, an Etruscan couple came to Rome—Lucumo and Tanaquil. Lucumo changed his name to Lucius Tarquinius Priscus. Because they were wealthy and generous, the couple soon became well known. Lucius became an adviser to the king, and the couple was appointed as guardians for Ancus's young sons. When Ancus died, Lucius actively and successfully campaigned to become king.

Lucius Tarquinius Priscus (r. 616-579 B.C.E.) began a number of building projects in Rome: the Circus Maximus, the city wall, and the Temple of Jupiter Optimus Maximus. He also began the Roman games, doubled the number of Rome's mounted troops, and enlarged the senate.

Even though there was no concept of a father passing the kingship to a son, Ancus's sons felt that Lucius had usurped their right to rule. They therefore hired some herdsmen to assassinate Lucius. When Tanaquil heard the commotion caused by the attack, she had Lucius carried to their palace. She then summoned her son-in-law, Servius Tullius. Tanaquil issued the statement that Lucius was only injured and that Servius would rule until he recovered. Servius took the duties of the king, deciding some cases on his own, but pretending to refer others to Lucius. Soon, however, they revealed that Lucius was dead, but by that time, Servius had established his power.

Servius Tullius (r. 578-535 B.C.E.) established the first census, which counted approximately eighty thousand male citizens. Servius added the Quirinal, Viminal, and Esquiline hills to the city, and he made Rome the center of worship for the goddess Diana.

Although Servius had tried to make peace with Lucius's sons by marrying them to his daughters, one son (Lucius Tarquinius, better known as Superbus) and one of his own daughters (Tullia) plotted to take over. When Lucius believed he had enough support, he challenged Servius's right to rule because he had never been elected by the people. Even though the people voted overwhelmingly for Servius, Superbus could not accept defeat. One day he went to the senate house and summoned the senators. When Servius heard, he came to challenge Superbus, but Superbus seized the elderly king and hurled him down the steps of the senate house. Tradition has it that Tullia, riding in a cart, ran over her father's body.

In this way, Lucius Tarquinius Superbus (r. 534-509 B.C.E.) became the last king of Rome. He completed many of the building programs his father had begun, expanding the Temple of Jupiter, adding seats to the Circus Maximus, and building the Cloaca Maxima (the Great Sewer). Superbus, however, treated the Roman people harshly, killing those who were too wealthy or too powerful for his liking, but finally the Roman people expelled the Tarquins when the king's son, Sextus, raped Lucretia, a virtuous noblewoman. Thus ended the monarchy and began the republic.

Although this traditional version of Rome's past contains elements of folklore and legend, as archaeologists have uncovered more of the remains of early Rome, they have found that the archaeological record supports the essentials—the buildings, the influx of Etruscan culture, Etruscan rule and its later expulsion, and Rome's population growth through the addition of other peoples.

ADDITIONAL RESOURCES

Cornell, T. J. *The Beginnings of Rome: Italy and Rome from the Bronze Age to the Punic Wars (c. 1000-264 B.C.)*. New York: Routledge, 1995.

Gardner, Jane F. *Roman Myths*. Austin: University of Texas Press, 1993.

Scullard, H. H. *A History of the Roman World 753 to 146 B.C.* New York: Methuen, 1980.

SEE ALSO: Etruscans; Junius Brutus, Lucius; Lucretia.
—*T. Davina McClain*

ROME, REPUBLICAN

DATE: c. 500 B.C.E.-c. 31 B.C.E.
LOCALE: Italy and the Mediterranean World
SIGNIFICANCE: The city of Rome developed a distinctive republican government and conquered most of the Mediterranean world after gaining control over Italy. The resulting cultural synthesis was the foundation of subsequent Roman Imperial civilization and much of Western civilization in general.

Ancient accounts of the Roman Republic before the beginning of the Punic Wars in 264 B.C.E. are highly fictionalized and unreliable in detail, but modern archaeology and historical research confirm their general outline. Around 500 B.C.E., aristocratic leaders took advantage of dynastic struggles to overthrow the last kings of early Rome, who had become tyrants like those in contemporary Greek cities. They gradually developed a new system of government, later called the republic (*res publica*). It had four major parts: the magistracies, the senate, various popular assemblies, and the public priesthoods.

The magistracies were public offices filled by magistrates elected (usually annually) from the wealthiest landowning families (usually with aristocratic pedigrees). Eventually, there were two chief magistrates called consuls, who had the power of military command (*imperium*) outside Rome's sacred boundary (*pomerium*) and held the highest civil authority in the city. As needs increased, other, lower-ranking magistrates were created: praetors (eventually eight), curule aediles (two), and quaestors (eventually twenty). Praetors also had *imperium* and presided over the courts;

aediles supervised public buildings, festivals, and markets; and quaestors assisted other magistrates. All those magistrates and the consuls held the annual offices of the Republican course of offices (*cursus honorum*). The highest office of the *cursus* belonged to the two censors who were elected for eighteen months every five years to conduct a census of citizens, supervise public morals, and award public contracts. Each magistrate could veto another magistrate of equal or lower rank. In a crisis, a consul could appoint a dictator, who held sole power for up to six months. No one could veto a dictator. The dictatorship was not part of the *cursus*.

The senate was a council of experienced leaders who controlled the treasury and advised the current magistrates. Senators themselves also could be priests and magistrates. Their decrees were not laws but carried great moral authority. In the early Republic, some members probably were hereditary and the consuls probably appointed others for their year of office. Eventually, the censors appointed senators for life from the ranks of qualified former magistrates.

During the Republic, there were two major popular assemblies (*comitiae*) of all adult male citizens, who originally made up the army (*populus*). The centuriate assembly (*comitia centuriata*) was made up of groups of voters ranked according to wealth. Summoned by a magistrate with *imperium*, it elected the censors, consuls, and praetors; passed laws; and heard appeals from those convicted of capital crimes. The tribal assembly (*comitia tributa*) was made up of all adult male citizens grouped together by the urban and rural tribes (districts) in which they lived. It elected the aediles and quaestors and also could pass laws and hear appeals.

In the early Republic, the plebeian citizens established a separate council of the plebs organized by tribes (*concilium plebis*). It represented their interests through votes called plebiscites (resolutions of the plebs) and elected special plebeian officers called tribunes of the plebs (eventually ten). Within the city of Rome, the tribunes asserted the right to veto any arbitrary or abusive action taken by a magistrate—but not a dictator—against an individual plebeian or the plebs as a whole.

Many priesthoods were important elective or appointive public offices. Public priests came from the same wealthy families as the magistrates and often held magistracies at the same time. There were four major colleges (boards) of public priests: the pontiffs (including the Vestal Virgins and the priests of fifteen major deities under the leadership of the *pontifex maximus*, or supreme pontiff), augurs, fetials, and duovirs for making sacrifices. Their duties were to interpret the will of the gods and obtain divine favor for the community. Failure to perform the proper rituals or the discovery of unfavorable signs halted public business.

History. The early Republic and its neighbors fought for land to support growing populations. Leaders who defended Rome or expanded its territory won glory and popularity. Some of the earliest conflicts involved neighboring Etruscan and Latin cities. In 493 B.C.E., Rome and the cities of the Latin League decided to unite in the face of common attacks from nearby hill tribes like the Aequi, Volsci, and Hernici. During the fifth century B.C.E., Rome conquered the powerful Etruscan city of Veii, overcame the rugged hill tribes, and even came to dominate the Latin League.

About 390 or 386 B.C.E., a tribe of Gauls swept down from northern Italy and destroyed most of Rome before they left. Soon, old enemies and even many Latin allies who resented Rome's dominance attacked. The Romans defeated them and either absorbed them as Roman citizens, who had to serve in Roman armies, or forced them to accept defensive alliances. Rome's success led to wars with the powerful Samnite tribes of central Italy, the Greek cities in southern Italy, and the remaining independent Etruscan cities.

One of the most famous opponents was King Pyrrhus of Epirus. He invaded Italy with 28,000 men and seventy terrifying war elephants to help the Greek city of Tarentum (280 B.C.E.). His "Pyrrhic victories" were so costly that he finally had to withdraw when the Romans refused to surrender.

By 264 B.C.E., Rome had united all of peninsular Italy

by making former enemies full Roman citizens or loyal allies with rights of partial citizenship. Rome's inclusive attitude toward citizenship had constantly increased the manpower for further conquests in Italy. A central location in Italy, constant military innovations, and values that promoted discipline and self-sacrifice for the community had also aided conquest. Another major asset was the Romans' willingness to compromise to resolve internal conflicts in the face of external threats.

During the first two centuries of the Republic, compromises to end internal conflicts had created a fairer government and a more unified society. Some powerful families who had the hereditary right to supply important public priests tried to become an exclusive "patrician" aristocracy. Members of wealthy families who were identified as part of the plebs opposed patrician efforts to exclude them from the magistracies, the senate, and the public priesthoods. They often supported the demands of poorer members of the plebs for more land, relief from debt, and protection from abuse by magistrates. By 300 B.C.E., all wealthy citizens enjoyed the right to hold most public priesthoods and the magistracies that led to membership in the senate. Plebiscites were accepted as binding laws, and the tribunes of the plebs were recognized as legitimate "constitutional" officials. Eventually they even acquired the right to summon meetings of the senate and qualified as members. Plebeian agitation had also led to the creation of Rome's first written code of laws (the Twelve Tables, 451-450 B.C.E.), legal restrictions on the amount of public land that any one citizen could lease (367 B.C.E.), and the end of enslavement for debt.

Internal unity and control of Italy with its resources, manpower, and central location in the Mediterranean made the Roman Republic very powerful. The need to feed Rome's constantly growing city, the Romans' fear of strong neighbors, and their leaders' desire for wealth and glory led them to conquer most of the Mediterranean world except Egypt between 264 and 133 B.C.E. The three Punic Wars with Carthage (264-241, 218-201, and 149-146 B.C.E.) turned Sicily, Sardinia, Spain, and central North Africa into Roman provinces. Using Rome's great manpower and resources, leaders such as Fabius and the elder Scipio Africanus defeated the brilliant generalship of Hannibal in the Second Punic War. Between 225 and 133 B.C.E., the Romans took control of Cisalpine Gaul (northern Italy) and the Italian and French rivieras as far as Massilia (Marseilles).

King Philip V of Macedonia drew Rome into the conquest of the eastern Mediterranean by siding with

Hannibal in the Second Punic War. The four Macedonian Wars (215-205, 200-196, 172-167, and 149-148 B.C.E.) reduced Macedonia and Greece to Roman provinces. The Romans also attacked and defeated Antiochus the Great when he tried to expand the Seleucid Empire (191-188 B.C.E.). They gave Seleucid land to the kingdom of Pergamum and the maritime city of Rhodes but turned against them later. To avoid Roman conquest, Pergamum's last king willed his kingdom to Rome (133 B.C.E.).

Imperial conquests produced social, economic, political, and cultural changes that destroyed the Republic. Some leaders promised reforms to help those hurt by social and economic changes. Rivals and those fearing change, seeing no need to compromise, blocked many necessary reforms. Jealousy and frustration led to murder and civil wars. In 133 B.C.E., the tribune Tiberius Sempronius Gracchus was murdered when he campaigned for an unusual second consecutive term after he had obtained passage of a law to redistribute public land to the poor. Ten years later, his brother Gaius Sempronius Gracchus committed suicide after being attacked by enemies of his more extensive reforms.

By 90 B.C.E., Rome's treatment of its allies in Italy had become harsh as it demanded more and more troops for its wars and shared less of victory's fruits. When many allies demanded full Roman citizenship, the Romans selfishly refused. The bitter allies revolted in the Social War (91-87 B.C.E.), and the Romans finally granted citizenship to all of Italy south of the Po River. Later, Julius Caesar gave citizenship to Italy north of the Po.

Governing provinces and commanding wars against foreign enemies or rebellious slaves, provincials, and allies gave leaders great wealth and armies of loyal soldiers to bribe and intimidate voters or start civil wars. The first civil wars broke out between the rival leaders Gaius Marius and Lucius Cornelius Sulla and their respective supporters (88-86 and 83-82 B.C.E.). The victorious Sulla obtained an unlimited dictatorship to restore stability, but his reforms did not eliminate the causes of civil conflict.

Within ten years, other ambitious aristocrats had helped overturn Sulla's system and set off worse power struggles. In 63 B.C.E., Catiline conspired to seize power by stirring up a revolt of the poor and dispossessed. As consul, the orator Cicero foiled the plot, executed five of Catiline's accomplices, and drove him to die in a desperate battle.

Soon, three powerful senators, Pompey the Great,

Marcus Licinius Crassus, and Julius Caesar, formed the unofficial First Triumvirate (committee of three) to control Rome. Cicero opposed them and was briefly exiled (58-57 B.C.E.). After Crassus started a war against Parthia and was killed (c. 53 B.C.E.), personal rivalry between Pompey and Caesar escalated to civil war (49 B.C.E.). Traditionalists such as Cato the Younger, who feared that Caesar's ambitions would lead to monarchy, joined Pompey and fought on after Pompey's death until 45 B.C.E.

When Caesar had been made dictator for up to ten years in 46 B.C.E., the trend toward a monarchical government had become obvious to many. When he was made dictator for life in February of 44 B.C.E., some of his friends such as Brutus and Cassius conspired to assassinate him on March 15 (the Ides). That desperate act led to another round of civil wars and the official Second Triumvirate of Caesar's adopted heir, Octavian (the former Gaius Octavius and the future emperor Augustus), Marc Antony, and Marcus Aemilius Lepidus.

Later, Octavian forced Lepidus into retirement and challenged Marc Antony for supremacy. Queen Cleopatra VII of Egypt allied with Antony, but they lost the Battle of Actium to Octavian's forces (31 B.C.E.). They committed suicide when Octavian captured Egypt a year later. Soon, the senate hailed the triumphant Octavian as Augustus, the first Roman emperor (27 B.C.E.).

Government and law. The Republic was not a democracy. For most of Republican history, ballots were not secret. Complicated voting procedures and the necessity of going to Rome to vote severely limited voter participation. Public offices were unpaid, and wealth was a requirement for holding them. Therefore, a wealthy, landowning aristocracy always controlled the government. After 300 B.C.E., the government was made up of both patrician and plebeian families who dominated elections to the magistracies that led to membership in the senate. Among them was an even smaller elite, the consular nobility, families who had produced consuls.

Consuls and praetors or former magistrates appointed by the senate as proconsuls and propraetors governed the provinces with full civil and military power.

The Republic never had a public police force or public prosecutors. For most people, personal revenge and informal custom enforced by neighbors and the heads of families were enough. The most important public priests, the pontiffs, handed down the earliest laws of the state and controlled early legal procedure. After the publication of the Twelve Tables (451-450 B.C.E.), pontifical control over the law gradually yielded to magistrates such as the praetors and legal consultants (*iuris consulti, iuris prudentes*). Both the *praetor peregrinus* at Rome and provincial governors took into account relevant foreign laws to produce greater equity in cases involving Roman citizens and non-Romans. They built up a broadly applicable law of nations (*ius gentium*) parallel to Roman civil law.

Magistrates who granted a trial appointed a private judge (*iudex*) to try a case. Later, public standing courts (*quaestiones perpetuae*) presided over by praetors with juries of senators were established for serious crimes. In all cases, the plaintiffs had to act as prosecutors, and except in criminal cases in which the verdict involved capital punishment or payment of a fine to the state, the winner had to enforce judgment.

War and weapons. Men seventeen to forty-five owed active military service for up to sixteen years, six consecutively. From forty-six to sixty, they were liable for defending Rome's walls. They had to own at least two *iugera* of land (1.3 acres, or 0.5 hectare) to serve as light-armed infantry. The wealthiest men served as high officers and cavalry. Those of modest wealth made up the heavy infantry, the backbone of each Roman legion (3,000-6,000 men), originally armed and organized like the Greek phalanx.

The Romans organized the legion into increasingly flexible units during the Republic and adopted the javelin (*pilum*), short sword (*gladius*), and oblong shield (*scutum*) as the principal armament in addition to helmets, breastplates, and shin guards. Marius instituted rigorous training and made each soldier carry his own equipment in heavy packs to increase mobility and hasten the building of a fortified camp on the march each night.

Soldiers received shares of booty and supplemental pay. A law of Gaius Sempronius Gracchus provided free clothing and equipment. Marius eliminated the property requirement. Propertyless volunteers became long-term professionals more loyal to their generals than to the Republic. Except during the first two Punic Wars (264-241, 218-201 B.C.E.), the Republic relied mostly on Greek allies to supply naval forces.

Settlement and social structure. About 500 B.C.E., Rome was a city covering about 660 acres (267 hectares) and controlled a territory of about 300 square miles (about 780 square kilometers) with a total population of 25,000-40,000. Much of the population lived in small farming villages and towns. By the end of the Republic, Rome's urban core included about 4,200 acres (1,791

hectares), with about a million people drawn from Italy and the Mediterranean world. The total population of Italy was probably between six and seven million.

Hierarchical social structures with reciprocal duties and obligations characterized Roman life. Ancestors, the "greater ones" (*maiores*), and their customs (*mos maiorum*) received great respect. The head of the family hierarchy was the father of the family, the *paterfamilias*. His power (*patria potestas*) gave him absolute legal control over his family and its property, but he was morally obligated to protect the welfare of the family and consult with his wife and other closely related adults. Powerful men were patrons to weaker men called clients. Clients received their patrons' help and protection and performed whatever services they could in return.

At the bottom of the social ladder were numerous slaves. Racial prejudice was not a factor, but slaves from certain ethnic groups were prized for certain tasks. Loyal slaves who worked closely with their masters could expect eventual freedom, but slaves who worked in gangs on large estates or in dangerous operations such as mining were often badly treated. Freed slaves became Roman citizens but were like clients with legal obligations to their former masters.

Women. A woman was always legally subject to some male: father, husband, or guardian. Still, Roman women enjoyed a less restricted life than women in Classical Athens. Their role as mothers of legitimate children in marriage was extremely important. A married woman (*matrona*) managed the household, which was large and complex among the upper classes. She was not segregated from men inside the home, could go out in public unescorted, was well informed, was a trusted adviser to her husband, and could divorce him if she wished. Upper-class women were educated and had many opportunities to act independently in the late Republic. Unfortunately, lower-class women and female slaves suffered the hardships and exploitation that the poor and powerless often have experienced.

Agriculture and animal husbandry. The Roman economy was overwhelmingly agricultural. The Po Valley and the coastal plains of peninsular Italy provided flat, fertile ground for grains and field crops and winter pasturage for sheep, goats, and cattle. The hills and mountains of the interior provided summer pasturage for animals and slopes hospitable to grapes and olives. Grain, planted in the fall and harvested in early summer, could be sown among vines and olive trees, whose fruits were harvested in the fall. With these staple crops, a few chickens, sheep, goats, and pigs, possibly a mule or an

OX, a vegetable garden, access to public grazing land, and the sale or barter of small surpluses in the local market, a few *iugera* could support a farmer and his family.

Nevertheless, the margin of error for small farmers was always thin, and the division of property among heirs could quickly lead to a crisis of subsistence for many. Rome's overseas expansion rapidly undermined small farming in many parts of Italy. Cheap supplies of grain from Sicily and North Africa, large numbers of cheap slaves, and rapid urban growth greatly altered the agricultural economy. Supplying lucrative urban markets required the production of surpluses beyond the means of many poor farmers. Many sold out to creditors and wealthy neighbors and moved to cities such as Rome or looked for fresh starts in the Po Valley, Spain, or southern Gaul.

The wealthy amassed large villa estates, often called *latifundia* (broad lands). They used many slaves and the best equipment for the greatest output at the lowest cost. The villa system of production came to dominate Campania, Latium, and southern Etruria, which produced fruits, vegetables, olives, wine, wool, hides, meat, and cheese for urban markets. Those estates farther from Rome often specialized in high-value products that were profitable enough to move over long distances. Southern Italy specialized in cattle, sheep, and pigs, which could be herded to market. Really wealthy Romans would own several estates in different parts of Italy to spread out the risks from disasters and poor market conditions.

Trade, industry, and commerce. Rome's location on the Tiber at its lowest bridgehead made Rome a valuable trading center from the start. By the third century B.C.E., Rome had also become a major center of craft manufacturing. Fine bronze work and pottery were major exports. The local demand for furniture, terra-cotta sculptures, and carved stone grave monuments, altars, and sarcophagi was great. Greek and Carthaginian traders brought metals, ivory, gold jewelry, premium wines, and spices for sale in Rome and distribution to the rest of central Italy.

As the city grew, demands for construction materials, other goods, and personal services accelerated. Hundreds of small shops provided wine, hot food, meat, bread, metalwares, pottery, shoes, barbering, and laundering. Many people in the countryside produced bricks, roof tiles, timber, firewood, charcoal, stones, crates, and baskets.

Contracts for building public works, operating state-owned mines and forests, collecting taxes, and supplying Rome's armies attracted rich investors. They were

called *publicani* and formed legally recognized companies. The principal partners even sold shares to others. These companies submitted bids to the censors, who awarded contracts. Profits came from the difference between the amount bid and the revenue collected or expenses incurred. Although senators were legally forbidden to engage in these transactions and overseas commerce after 218 B.C.E., they often participated through friends and agents.

Rome became a great center of private money lending and banking. Partnerships financed cargoes for shipowners by profitable loans. Cities, provinces, and kingdoms borrowed huge sums to pay for taxes, tribute, and Roman military protection. Roman bankers kept deposits in their strongrooms and issued drafts on account or gave letters of credit, which could be cashed at branches in other cities or with other individuals.

Navigation and transport. Water provided the most efficient transport. Ships linked Rome directly or through the Campanian city of Puteoli with ports on the Atlantic coast of Spain, throughout the Mediterranean, and along the Black Sea. Riverboats and barges carried people and goods up navigable rivers such as the Tiber, the Rhone, and the Po to inland cities.

Starting with the Appian Way in 312 B.C.E., the Romans built a network of straight, well-drained, stone-paved highways. They linked Rome with the major cities and towns of Italy and the provinces and allowed Roman armies to march swiftly against any threat. They also aided the movement of people and light goods of high value.

Religion. At times, the Republican senate had tried to suppress foreign religions that seemed to threaten the state. Still, the large multiethnic population of late Republican Rome allowed many foreign cults and religions to flourish alongside traditional Roman religion. Many people found comfort in the mystery cults of universal deities such as Mithra, Cybele, and Isis from the eastern Mediterranean. Initiation rites created a sense of community and provided personal emotional connections with powerful protective deities in an impersonal and dangerous world.

Literature and thought. The language of the Romans was Latin, but close contact with Greek civilization from very early times is reflected in all aspects of Roman Republican literature. Formal Roman literature begins with a freed Greek slave named Lucius Livius Andronicus, who first translated Homer's *Odyssey* (c. 800 B.C.E.; English translation, 1616) into Latin and put on Latin versions of a Greek tragedy and comedy to celebrate the end of the First Punic War (241 B.C.E.). Later Republican poets such as Quintus Ennius, Plautus, Terence, Lucretius, and Catullus continued to write plays, epic poems, and lyric verse based on Greek models. Sometimes they adapted Greek subjects and themes for Roman audiences, and sometimes they wrote on personal or patriotic subjects and themes.

The earliest Roman historians were aristocrats who had fought in the first two Punic Wars and wrote on them in Greek to advertise Rome's greatness to the Greek world. The greatest early historian of Rome was the Greek hostage Polybius (c. 200-c. 118 B.C.E.). He wrote to convince fellow Greeks how pointless it was to resist Rome. The first important history of Rome in Latin was the *Origines* (168-149 B.C.E.; *Roman Politics*, 1951) of Cato the Censor (234-149 B.C.E.).

Despite his thundering against the bad moral influence of the Greeks, Cato studied Greek and used Greek models. His published speeches, treatise on rhetoric, and handbook on agriculture laid the groundwork for later orators and scholars such as Cicero, Julius Caesar, and Marcus Terentius Varro. Many of these writers also applied the thinking of great Greek philosophers such as Plato, Aristotle, the Stoics, and the Epicureans to the study of Roman social and political life.

Architecture and art. Around 264 B.C.E., the Romans began to remodel Rome in Classical Greek style. They often plundered works of art, monuments, and parts of buildings from Greek cities in southern Italy, Sicily, and Greece itself. The Romans' major contribution to Classical architecture was the extensive use of arches and vaults made of baked bricks or concrete. In the late second and early first centuries B.C.E., the Romans started building great symmetrical complexes that linked together a number of architectural elements and styles. Their combination of Greek columns framing Roman arches set a style that lasted for centuries.

Native bronze sculptures and terra-cotta reliefs were popular in the early Republic, but looted or copied Greek marble statues and reliefs became popular in the second century B.C.E. The Romans also decorated their floors and walls with mosaics and frescoes in the Hellenistic Greek style. Many were even versions of famous Greek paintings.

Legacy. Politically, the Roman Republic failed to withstand the pressures created by its imperial expansion. Culturally, however, it was a great success. Republican religion, literature, philosophy, architecture, and art blended Greek and native elements into a distinctive cultural synthesis that was the hallmark of the Roman Empire afterward.

ADDITIONAL RESOURCES

Crawford, M. H. *The Roman Republic*. 2d ed. Cambridge, Mass.: Harvard University Press, 1993.

Hornblower, S., and A. Spawforth, eds. *The Oxford Classical Dictionary*. Oxford, England: Oxford University Press, 1996.

Scarre, C. *The Penguin Historical Atlas of Ancient Rome*. Harmondsworth, England: Penguin Books, 1995.

Walbank, F. W., and A. E. Astin et al., eds. *The Cambridge Ancient History*. 2d ed. Cambridge, England: Cambridge University Press, 1989-1996.

Ward, A. M., F. M. Heichelheim, and C. Yeo. *A History of the Roman People*. 3d ed. Upper Saddle River, N.J.: Prentice Hall, 1999.

SEE ALSO: Antiochus the Great; Antony, Marc; Appian Way; Augustus; Brutus; Caesar, Julius; Carthage; Cassius; Catiline; Cato the Censor; Cato the Younger; Catullus; Cicero; Cleopatra VII; Crassus, Marcus Licinius; Ennius, Quintus; Etruscans; Fabius; Gauls; Gracchus, Tiberius Sempronius, and Gaius Sempronius Gracchus; Greece, Hellenistic and Roman; Hannibal; Homer; Isis, cult of; Latin League and War; Livius Andronicus, Lucius; Lucretius; Macedonia; Marius, Gaius; Parthia; Philip V; Plautus; Polybius; Pompey the Great; Punic Wars; Roman forum; Rome, Imperial; Rome, Prerepublican; Scipio Africanus; Seleucid Dynasty; Sulla, Lucius Cornelius; Terence; Triumvirate.

—*Allen M. Ward*

ROMULUS AND REMUS

FLOURISHED: traditionally eighth century B.C.E.; central Italy
RELATED CIVILIZATION: Prerepublican Rome
MAJOR ROLE/POSITION: Legendary founders of the city of Rome

Life. Roman legend held that the twin brothers Romulus and Remus founded the city of Rome in 753 B.C.E. According to the legend, Mars, the Roman god of war and the most important of the Roman deities in the early republic, had sired the twins. The twins were alleged to be the grandsons of Aeneas, a Greek warrior in Homer's *Iliad* (c. 800 B.C.E.; English translation, 1616), whom the Romans believed settled in Italy after the Trojan War. Aeneas linked the founding of Rome to the Greeks, whom the Romans greatly admired.

According to legend, the twins, orphaned at birth, were adopted and suckled by a female wolf. Images of the twins suckling beneath the female wolf became a common theme in Roman art. As adults, the twins founded the city of Rome. Romulus settled on the Palatine hill, and Remus settled on the Aventine. Remus became jealous of Romulus's settlement and showed his contempt by jumping over the unfinished walls. Romulus killed his brother in a rage and vowed, "So will die whoever else shall leap over my walls."

Influence. Romulus and Remus are remembered and honored as the legendary founders of Rome. Roman historians traced back to Romulus the seven kings who ruled until the founding of the Republic around 508 B.C.E. These kings, except for Romulus, are believed to have been actual historical figures.

Romulus, one of the legendary founders and the first king of Rome. (Hulton Archive)

ADDITIONAL RESOURCES

Grant, Michael. *History of Rome*. Englewood Cliffs, N.J.: Prentice Hall, 1978.

Hibbert, Fernand. *Romulus*. Port-au-Prince, Haiti: Editions H. Deschamps, 1988.

Wiseman, Timothy P. *Remus, a Roman Myth*. Cambridge, England: Cambridge University Press, 1995.

SEE ALSO: Rome, Prerepublican.

—*Barry M. Stentiford*

ROMULUS AUGUSTULUS

ALSO KNOWN AS: Flavius Momyllus Romulus Augustus
FLOURISHED: 475-476 C.E.; Italy
RELATED CIVILIZATION: Imperial Rome
MAJOR ROLE/POSITION: Child emperor

Life. Not much is known about Romulus Augustus's life and personality. His surname would have been Augustus, but it was changed to the diminutive form because of his young age. His father was Orestes, the Western Empire's master of soldiers. Following a civil war, Orestes forced the Western emperor Julius Nepos out of Italy. On October 31, 475 C.E., Orestes elevated his young son (who was probably between twelve and fourteen years of age) to the imperial throne. For about twelve months, Orestes ruled what was left of the Western Empire in his son's name.

Orestes infuriated the Germans under his command when he did not agree to their demands for additional lands. The warrior Odoacer led the Germans in a mutiny against the government. Odoacer's troops captured and executed Orestes at Placentia (later Piacenza, Italy) on August 28, 476 C.E. Rather than executing the young emperor, Odoacer exiled him to live with his relatives in southern Italy. Nothing is known about his subsequent life.

Influence. The exile of Romulus Augustulus is usually considered to have marked the end of the Roman Empire in the West.

ADDITIONAL RESOURCES
Nardo, Richard, ed. *The Fall of the Roman Empire*. San Diego, Calif.: Greenhaven Press, 1998.
Reece, Richard. *Later Roman Empire*. Charleston, S.C.: Tempus, 1999.

Scarre, Christopher. *Chronicle of the Roman Emperors*. London: Thames and Hudson, 1995.

SEE ALSO: Germany; Odoacer; Rome, Imperial.

—*Thomas T. Lewis*

ROSETTA STONE

AUTHORSHIP: Egyptian priests
DATE: March 27, 196 B.C.E.
LOCALE: Nile River delta
RELATED CIVILIZATION: Ptolemaic Egypt
SIGNIFICANCE: The discovery of this stone led to the decipherment of the ancient Egyptian demotic and hieroglyphic scripts.

The stela known as the Rosetta stone was found by French soldiers in August, 1799, near Rosetta (Rashīd),

The Rosetta stone provided the key to deciphering hieroglyphs. (Time and Life)

about thirty-five miles (fifty-six kilometers) northeast of Alexandria. It consists of an irregularly shaped stone of black basalt measuring approximately 3 feet, 9 inches (114 centimeters) by 2 feet, 4 inches (71 centimeters) by 11 inches (27 centimeters). Apparently broken in antiquity, it contains a commemorative inscription recording the beneficences of and honors due Ptolemy V Epiphanes. Three versions of the same decree (most likely passed by assembled priests at Memphis), in hieroglyphic symbols, demotic script, and Greek uncials, are found on the stela. It was recognized that this stone might be the key to unlocking the secrets of ancient Egyptian, knowledge of which had been lost (with the exception of Coptic) since late antiquity. If the subject matter of all three texts were the same, the Greek could be used to decipher the other two. This was the case, and after the stela came into the possession of the British and was transported to England, scholars such as Thomas Young and Jean-François Champollion soon turned their full attention to this valuable document. By the 1820's, substantial progress had been made on both scripts, forming the basis for much of modern knowledge of ancient Egyptian culture.

ADDITIONAL RESOURCES
Andrews, C. *The Rosetta Stone*. London: British Museum, 1981.
Budge, E. A. *The Rosetta Stone in the British Museum*. London: Religious Tract Society, 1929.
Parkinson, R. B., Whitfield Diffie, M. Fischer, and R. S. Simpson. *Cracking Codes: The Rosetta Stone and Decipherment*. Berkeley: University of California Press, 1999.
Sole, Robert, and Dominique Valbelle. *The Rosetta Stone: The Story of the Decoding of Hieroglyphics*. London: Profile, 2001.

SEE ALSO: Egypt, Ptolemaic and Roman; Languages and literature.

—*Robin G. Hanson*

RUTILIUS CLAUDIUS NAMATIANUS

FLOURISHED: c. 417 C.E.; Gaul and Rome
RELATED CIVILIZATIONS: Gaul, Imperial Rome
MAJOR ROLE/POSITION: Politician, poet

Life. Rutilius Claudius Namatianus (rew-TIHL-ee-uhs KLAWD-ee-uhs nuh-may-shee-AY-uhs) was born into an aristocratic Gallo-Roman family and pursued a political career in Rome, where he was master of offices in 412 C.E. and prefect of Rome in about 414 C.E. Namatianus is best known for his poem *De redito suo* (c. 417 C.E.; *On His Return*, 1907), in which he describes his journey home to Gaul in 417 C.E., only seven years after the sack of Rome by the Goths. Namatianus expresses profound loyalty toward Gaul but saves his highest praise for Rome, the mistress of the world. Although Namatianus refers to the destruction visited upon Italy and Gaul by the barbarian invasions, he expresses his belief in Rome's eternal destiny to rule the known world. Set in the context of more than one thousand years of Roman history, the Gothic sack of Rome appears to Namatianus to be a setback comparable to Hannibal's invasion of Italy.

Influence. *On His Return* provides surprising evidence of the optimism of at least some Romans about Rome's future, which suggests that modern scholars should exercise caution in viewing this period as one of unmitigated gloom. The poem also criticizes the asceticism of Christian monks and thereby provides a rare glimpse into the mind-set of an aristocratic pagan at a time when Christianity had become the dominant religion.

ADDITIONAL RESOURCES

Duff, J. Wight, and Arnold M. Duff. *Minor Latin Poets*. Cambridge, Mass.: Harvard University Press, 1982.
Matthews, John. *Western Aristocracies and Imperial Court* A.D. *364-425*. Oxford, England: Clarendon Press, 1990.

SEE ALSO: Christianity; Gauls; Goths, Ostrogoths, Visigoths; Rome, Imperial.

—*Martha G. Jenks*

— S —

SABINA, VIBIA

BORN: c. 86 C.E.; Spain
DIED: 136 C.E.; Italy
RELATED CIVILIZATION: Imperial Rome
MAJOR ROLE/POSITION: Wife of the emperor
  Hadrian

Life. Vibia Sabina (sah-BIHN-uh) was born in Spain, probably near Italica, the birthplace of her great-uncle Trajan and was the daughter of Matidia (Trajan's niece) and Lucius Vibius Sabinus. In 100 C.E., she married Publius Aelius Hadrianus (the future emperor Hadrian). Trajan's wife Plotina arranged the marriage between Sabina and Hadrian, who had lived with Trajan as his ward since the death of his father when Hadrian was a young boy. Sabina accompanied Hadrian on his travels throughout the empire, but there was little love lost between the two. Sabina was reported as saying that she made sure that she never conceived a child because any offspring of Hadrian would be a monster. Hadrian's affections were directed primarily toward a young Bithynian named Antinous.

Sabina was renowned for her striking beauty. In 130 C.E., Julia Balbilla carved a poem celebrating Sabina's beauty into the statue of Memnon in Egypt while Sabina and Hadrian were visiting the province. Sabina died in 136 C.E., reputedly from poisoning by Hadrian, who had once said that he would have divorced her if he had been a private citizen and not the emperor.

Influence. Sabina's marriage to Hadrian gave him the close familial ties and the legitimacy as Trajan's heir that he needed to become one of Rome's great emperors.

ADDITIONAL RESOURCES

Birley, A. R. *Hadrian: The Restless Emperor.* New York: Routledge Press, 1997.

Grant, M. *The Roman Emperors: A Biographical Guide to the Rulers of Imperial Rome, 31* B.C.-A.D. *476.* New York: Scribners, 1985.

SEE ALSO: Hadrian; Rome, Imperial; Trajan.

—T. Davina McClain

SACRED WARS

DATE: c. 600-300 B.C.E.
LOCALE: Delphi
RELATED CIVILIZATIONS: Classical Greece,
  Macedonia
SIGNIFICANCE: The First Sacred War was waged by
  the Amphictyonic League to justify the extension of
  its influence from Anthela (near Thermopylae) to
  Delphi. The Second Sacred War consisted of saber-
  rattling between Athens and Sparta preceding the
  Peloponnesian War. The Third and Fourth Sacred
  Wars provided religious justification for Philip II's
  entrance into central Greek politics and ultimate
  control over the Greek city-states.

The First Sacred War broke out when the city of Crisa's control over the temple of Apollo at Delphi either led to abuse of pilgrims or provoked jealousy among its neighbors. The Amphictyonic League, an organization of city-states that administered the temple of Demeter at Anthela, began a war against Crisa, with the help of allied reinforcements from Athens, Sicyon, and Thessaly. The details are obscure, but it seems that a long siege ended in 592/591 B.C.E., and Crisa was razed to the ground. By 582/581 B.C.E., the last resistance was overcome, and the Amphictyonic League consolidated its control over Delphi by founding the Pythian Games, which became part of the Panhellenic festival circuit.

The Second Sacred War is the only recorded military action during the Five-Year Truce between Athens and Sparta (concluded in 451 B.C.E.). Wishing to challenge Athens' imperialistic ambitions in central Greece, the Spartans seized control of the temple from the Phocians, allies of the Athenians, and gave it to the Delphians. The Athenians immediately marched out under Pericles and handed the temple back to the Phocians. Not long afterward, the Athenians lost their influence in central Greece after their defeat at the Battle of Coronea in 447 B.C.E.

The Third Sacred War began in 356 B.C.E., when the Amphictyonic League levied a heavy fine against the Phocians for the cultivation of sacred land. In desperation, the Phocians seized the sanctuary at Delphi and "borrowed" its treasures to pay armies of mercenaries. The conflict escalated when Philip II of Macedonia intervened in 354 B.C.E. He won the Battle of the Crocus Field in 353 B.C.E. but was prevented from capitalizing on his victory by a joint defense of the Phocians and Athenians at Thermopylae. The war then dragged on until 346 B.C.E., when Philip put a decisive end to the conflict and thereby extended his influence over central Greece.

The Fourth Sacred War broke out in 340/339 B.C.E., when the Athenian orator Aeschines denounced the Amphissans for the cultivation of the Crisaean Plain, which had been consecrated to Apollo at the end of the First Sacred War. After an unsuccessful expedition of the Amphictyonic League, Philip was invited to intervene in 339 B.C.E. Instead of heading for Amphissa, he seized Elatea (Elateia), a stronghold on the road to Thebes. This unexpected development resulted in the alliance of Athens and Thebes and finally in the Battle of Chaeronea in 338 B.C.E.

ADDITIONAL RESOURCES
Buckler, J. *Philip II and the Sacred War.* Leiden, Netherlands: E. J. Brill, 1989.
Ellis, J. R. *Philip II and Macedonian Imperialism.* London: Thames and Hudson, 1976.

SEE ALSO: Athens; Chaeronea, Battle of; Delphi; Greece, Classical; Macedonia; Pericles; Philip II.
—Frances Skoczylas Pownall

SAHARAN ROCK ART

DATE: c. 8000 B.C.E.-700 C.E.
LOCALE: Northern Africa
RELATED CIVILIZATION: North Africa
SIGNIFICANCE: The phases of Saharan rock art reflect the development of early North African cultures.

In 9000 B.C.E., the area now known as the Sahara was filled with vegetation and animal life. Previously nomadic groups established settlements there; their cultural development is chronicled in more than 30,000 paintings and engravings, half located near the southern Algerian area of Tassili.

These works are divided on the basis of subject matter into four periods: the Bubaline, Cattle, Horse, and Camel. The earliest period (c. 8000-5000 B.C.E.) the Bubaline, derives its name from large, naturalistic engravings of the now extinct buffalo *Bubalus antiquus*. Depictions also include other animals that inhabited the region at the time: elephants, giraffes, and rhinoceroses. Humans are depicted with throwing sticks and axes, reflecting their hunting lifestyle.

In the Cattle period (c. 5000-1500 B.C.E.), the *Bubalus antiquus* disappears. Domestic animals such as cattle become primary subjects, reflecting the change from hunting to herding. Other depictions include early examples of masked dancers and humans armed with bows.

From circa 1500 to 600 B.C.E., the Horse period, horses and chariots appear, reflecting innovations in travel and trade. In this period, humans are schematically presented with new weapons such as spears and shields.

The last phase of the rock art tradition, the Camel period (c. 600 B.C.E.), is marked by the introduction of the camel and carved inscriptions of the earliest Saharan writing. As the area became drier in the fifth to third millennia B.C.E., these cultures moved southward and eastward into the Nile River Valley.

ADDITIONAL RESOURCE
Perani, Judith, and Fred Smith. *The Visual Arts of Africa.* Upper Saddle River, N.J.: Prentice Hall, 1998.

SEE ALSO: Africa, North; African rock art, southern and eastern.
—Cassandra Lee Tellier

SAINT MUNGO PHASE

DATE: 2200-1200 B.C.E.
LOCALE: Lower Fraser River, British Columbia, Canada
RELATED CIVILIZATION: Northwest Coast cultures
SIGNIFICANCE: Saint Mungo represents the beginnings of significant Northwest Coast culture patterns that become more elaborate in later phases.

The Saint Mungo phase of the lower Fraser River, the Mayne phase of the Gulf Islands, and the Eayem phase of Fraser canyon are all contemporaneous expressions of the Charles culture of southwest British Columbia. The site at the Saint Mungo cannery is a shell midden. These phases all reveal a seasonal round of food gathering, and some sites yield evidence of fishing and mollusk collecting and others of elk hunting. Considerable data on subsistence, including presence of the earliest known Northwest Coast fish weir, come from the Glenrose cannery site, whereas most information on the developing art and ceremonial tradition was found at the Pender Canal site. Simple labrets (lip ornaments) were in use and may have been decorative rather than a mark of status differences, as they were in later phases. The presence of the fish weir, in which thousands of salmon could be captured at one time, is very important, as it indicates the presence of a storage economy, a necessity for the increasing sociocultural complexity evident in later cultural phases in this region.

ADDITIONAL RESOURCES

Carlson, Roy L., and Phillip M. Hobler. "The Pender Canal Excavations and the Development of Coast Salish Culture." *British Columbia Studies* 99 (1993).
Matson, R. G. *The Glenrose Cannery Site.* Archaeological Survey Papers 52. Ottawa, Ont.: National Museum of Man, 1976.

SEE ALSO: Archaic tradition, northern; Locarno Beach; Marpole phase.

—*Roy L. Carlson*

SAITE DYNASTY

DATE: 774-711 B.C.E. (Twenty-fourth Dynasty); Late Period, 664-525 B.C.E. (Twenty-sixth Dynasty)
LOCALE: Western delta on the Rosetta branch of the Nile, ancient Zau (modern Sa el-Hagar)
RELATED CIVILIZATION: Pharaonic Egypt
SIGNIFICANCE: This dynasty reunited Egypt, expanded trade, and revived the Old Kingdom art style.

The turbulent Twenty-fourth Dynasty of the Third Intermediate Period ended with a coalition against Nubian control of Thebes. The confederation of Tanis, Hermopolis, Heracleopolis, and Leotopolis rulers surrendered to Piye, founder of the Twenty-fifth Dynasty from Kush.

The later Saite monarchy (Twenty-sixth Dynasty) marks the last native independent rule before Persian conquest of Egypt. The Sais capital provided for political stability and a conduit for commerce between East and West. Around 615 B.C.E., Naukratis was established as a free port for Mediterranean trade. The 570 B.C.E. defeat of the Egyptian king Apries permitted Babylon to interfere with internal Egyptian affairs.

The Saite artistic renaissance actively revived Old Kingdom art styles and was intended to restore religious orthodoxy and pharaonic authority. Greek influences can be seen in the fluid outline of carved reliefs, with mannered and elegant reliefs replacing the rigid formality of Old Kingdom styles. Around 450 B.C.E., Herodotus described splendid Saite temples, but few traces remain at Sais because buildings were disman-

PHARAOHS OF THE SAITE DYNASTY, 664-525 B.C.E.

Pharaoh	Reign
Psamtik I	664-610 B.C.E.
Necho II	610-595
Psamtik II	595-589
Apries	589-570
Ahmose II	570-526
Psamtik III	526-525

tled for their materials, and sculptured objects were carried off.

ADDITIONAL RESOURCES
Baines, J., and J. Malek. *Atlas of Ancient Egypt*. Oxford, England: Oxford University Press, 1982.
Mysliwiec, Karol. *The Twilight of Ancient Egypt*.
Ithaca, N.Y.: Cornell University Press, 2000.
Smith, W. S. *The Art and Architecture of Ancient Egypt*. 1958. Rev. ed. Harmondsworth, England: Penguin Books,1981.

SEE ALSO: Egypt, Pharaonic; Herodotus; Piye.
—*Elizabeth L. Meyers*

SALAMIS, BATTLE OF

DATE: probably September 23, 480 B.C.E.
LOCALE: Saronic Gulf in Greece
RELATED CIVILIZATIONS: Classical Greece, Persia
SIGNIFICANCE: Victory over the Persians assured Greek independence and set the stage for a golden age.

Background. In 490 B.C.E., King Darius the Great of Persia (r. 522-486 B.C.E.) invaded Greece at Marathon. He wanted to punish Athens for its support of his Ionian Greek subjects and at the same time expand his empire into Europe. The Athenians defeated the Persians, forcing them to withdraw. Darius was succeeded by his son Xerxes I (r. 486-465 B.C.E.), who invaded Greece with a large army in 480 B.C.E. Athenian statesman Themistocles used the ten-year interval between the two invasions to make his city the leading power in Greece.

After an inconclusive battle at Artemesium and a Persian land victory at Thermopylae, the Allied Greek fleet fell back to the vicinity of the Saronic Gulf. Themistocles wanted the Greeks to engage the Persians in the narrow channel between Salamis (SA-luh-muhs) Island and the mainland. If they did, superior Persian numbers would be neutralized.

Greeks celebrate after their victory over the Persians at Salamis. (North Wind Picture Archives)

Action. As a ruse, Themistocles sent Xerxes a secret message that the Greek fleet was going to retreat. Xerxes took the bait. The Persian fleet, numbering about eight hundred triremes, was composed of subject peoples such as the Phoenicians. The Greek fleet had some three hundred triremes, the bulk coming from Athens. Superior Greek—especially Athenian—seamanship won the day. The Persian fleet was barely able to maneuver and was easy prey. A surprise flank attack by (Greek) Aeginetans and Megarans completed the victory.

Consequences. Xerxes retreated, abandoning the gains won to that point. The Persian king went home, leaving his army with Mardonius. Mardonius suffered a major defeat at Plataea, ending the Persian invasion.

ADDITIONAL RESOURCES

Meier, Christian. *Athens: A Portrait of the City in Its Golden Age*. Translated by Robert Kimber and Rita Kimber. New York: Metropolitan Books, 1998.

Warry, John. *Warfare in the Classical World*. London: Salamander Books, 1980.

SEE ALSO: Darius the Great; Greco-Persian Wars; Greece, Classical; Marathon, Battle of; Persia; Plataea, Battle of; Themistocles; Thermopylae, Battle of; Xerxes I.

—Eric Niderost

SALLUST

ALSO KNOWN AS: Gaius Sallustius Crispus
BORN: c. 86 B.C.E.; Amiternum, Sammium (later San Vittorino, Italy)
DIED: 35 B.C.E.; Rome
RELATED CIVILIZATION: Republican Rome
MAJOR ROLE/POSITION: Historian

Life. Sallust's (SAL-uhst) political career was not terribly distinguished, but he nonetheless became fabulously wealthy, largely as a result of his governorship of the wealthy province of Numidia. Much of his success was owed to the support of Julius Caesar, and when Caesar was assassinated, Sallust withdrew from public life. He chose to write history, which he felt was an especially suitable profession for a man who wished to avoid the corrupt world of politics but still serve his country by recording the events of the recent past. He wrote three major works, two of which survive in their entirety. The *Bellum Catilinae* (c. 42 B.C.E.; *The Conspiracy of Catiline*, 1608) is a vivid account of the conspiracy of Catiline in 63 B.C.E. The *Bellum Iugurthinum* (c. 40 B.C.E.; *The War of Jugurtha*, 1608) details the war against the Numidian king Jugurtha in the late second century B.C.E. The *Historiae* (begun c. 39 B.C.E.; English translation of fragments, *Histories*, 1789), of which only fragments survive, was his last work and covered the years 78 to 67 B.C.E.

Influence. A major theme in Sallust's surviving works is the moral decline and political corruption in the Roman Republic and how foreign luxuries and wanton political ambition had destroyed simple, old-fashioned Roman virtues. His diagnosis of Rome's ills is hardly unique, but his style is particularly lucid and his approach includes analysis of social and economic issues, rare among ancient historians, who usually concentrate on politics and personalities.

ADDITIONAL RESOURCES

Sallust. *Complete Works*. Translated by John C. Rolfe. Rev. ed. Cambridge, Mass.: Harvard University Press, 1985.

_____. *"The Jugurthine War"* and *"The Conspiracy of Catiline."* Translated by S. A. Handford. Harmondsworth, England: Penguin Classics, 1963.

_____. *Sallust, the Histories*. Translated by Patrick McGushin. Oxford, England: Clarendon Press, 1994.

Syme, Ronald. *Sallust*. Berkeley: University of California Press, 1964.

SEE ALSO: Caesar, Julius; Catiline; Jugurtha; Rome, Republican.

—Daniel J. Taravella

SALVIANUS

ALSO KNOWN AS: Salvian; Salvian of Marseille
BORN: c. 400 C.E.; northwestern Germany
DIED: c. 480 C.E.; place unknown
RELATED CIVILIZATIONS: Germany, Europe
MAJOR ROLE/POSITION: Priest, historian

Life. Little is known for certain about the life of Salvianus (sal-VEE-ay-nuhs). Born into what was probably a noble family in the area of Cologne or Trier, he lived through the destructive invasion of the Franks in 418 C.E. After their daughter's birth, he and his wife took up the ascetic life and gave away their wealth to the poor. Salvianus himself left his family to go to Lérins as a tutor and eventually ended up at Cassian's monastery in Marseilles, where he evidently spent the rest of his life.

Influence. Salvianus was a vigorous and highly rhetorical writer whose surviving works include his *Ad Ecclesiam* (fifth century C.E.; *Against Avarice*, 1618), written under the pseudonym of Timothy, attacking the vice of avarice in the Church in the most uncompromising of terms, as well as nine letters. His most famous work, *De gubernatione Dei* (fifth century C.E.; *On the Government of God*, 1700), is a spirited response to the barbarian invasions, in which he addresses the question of why God has not defended what is now a Christian empire. Salvianus defends the moral superiority of the barbarians and argues that faithless and pharisaical Christians have no right to complain about their well-deserved punishment at the hands of a God who excuses nobody on the basis of token affiliation with the Christian Church.

ADDITIONAL RESOURCES

Maas, M. "Ethnicity, Orthodoxy, and Community in Salvian of Marseilles." In *Fifth Century Gaul,* edited by J. F. Drinkwater. New York: Cambridge University Press, 1992.
Olsen, G. "Reform After the Pattern of the Primitive Church in the Thought of Salvian of Marseilles." *Catholic Historical Review* 68 (1982): 1-12.

SEE ALSO: Cassian; Christianity.

—*Carl P. E. Springer*

SAMARRAN CULTURE

DATE: 6300-5600 B.C.E.
LOCALE: Border of northern and southern Mesopotamia, present-day southern Iraq
SIGNIFICANCE: Samarran culture shows the first signs of irrigation agriculture and social differentiation in the prehistoric Mesopotamian world.

Archaeologists classify prehistoric cultures on the basis of material and cultural artifacts. On the basis of pottery styles and technology, archaeologists have traditionally divided Mesopotamian culture before the fourth millennium B.C.E. into two groups: northern and southern. However, Samarran (SAH-mahr-an) culture is on the border of the traditional dividing line and can best be described as a transitional, yet unique stage in the development of Mesopotamian civilization. Samarran pottery had a wide distribution for this period, overlapping with Hassan, Halaf, and Ubaid artifacts, suggesting that Samarran designs and style were popular and that they moved south with the advancement of agriculture.

Samarran potters developed a "tournette" technology that allowed the potter to turn the clay on a flat base in a circular pattern, resulting in finer-shaped ceramics. Samarran pottery shapes were simpler than the Halaf pottery, although both used the same initial production method. Samarran pottery was painted in matte colors only. Most archaeologists caution against assuming that any specialized group of potters developed at this period.

Sandwiched between the earlier Hassan and the slightly later Halaf cultures and contiguous for a brief time with Ubaid culture, Samarran culture differed in several ways. Samarran villages moved away from compound-style houses to individual homes perhaps for nuclear families, which would be common in the region for more than a millennium. However, these houses were different in size and style, suggesting that unlike other civilizations, the Samarrans had economically stratified villages, which in terms of population were the largest settlements in Mesopotamia until the Uruk period. Further evidence pointing to this development is the appearance of different graves, goods, and burial methods at Tell as-Sawwan by the end of the Samarran period. This same village also shows signs of early fortification in the remains of a moat and even what appear to be missile weapons; both of these finds suggest competition between villages.

At the village of Choga Mami, there is evidence of the earliest canal irrigation system in the world. Irrigation could explain the ability of the Samarrans to develop larger villages and of the population to stratify along economic lines because the largest houses are those closest to the canal. Other Samarran villages show evidence of flood irrigation in geographical and plant remains; irrigation was necessary because of the scant rainfall in the lower foothills and plains.

Most archaeologists and prehistorians speculate that Samarran technology and location made this culture the ideal transmitter of agriculture and material culture between the northern and southern regions of Mesopotamia.

Workers dig at a large Samarran burial site in Iraq. (AP/WideWorld Photos)

ADDITIONAL RESOURCES

Oates, D. *Studies in the Ancient History of Northern Iraq*. London: Oxford University Press, 1968.

Postgate, J. N. *Early Mesopotamia: Society and Economy at the Dawn of History*. New York: Routledge, 1994.

Roaf, Michael. *Cultural Atlas of Mesopotamia and the Ancient Near East*. Oxford, England: Equinox, 1990.

SEE ALSO: Halafian culture; Ubaid culture.

—Tammy Jo Eckhart

SAMMU-RAMAT

ALSO KNOWN AS: Semiramis (Greek)
FLOURISHED: c. 823-810 B.C.E.
RELATED CIVILIZATIONS: Assyria, Chaldean and Hellenistic Mesopotamia
MAJOR ROLE/POSITION: Queen of Assyria

Life. Sammu-ramat (SAHM-ew-rah-MAHT) was the wife of Shamshi-Adad V, king of Assyria, and the mother of his successor, Adad-nirari III. It is possible (although not certain) that she acted as regent for her son for several years after her husband's death. Her name appears in a memorial stela found at Ashur (Assur); this was an honor usually reserved for officials of the king and the king himself. She is also mentioned in a dedicatory inscription beside her husband's name, which indicates she was very significant. It appears that she played an important role in the reign of her son, and the governor of Calah (Nimrud) includes mention of her as "lady of the palace" in a separate inscription.

Sammu-ramat appears in the Greek sources (from historians Herodotus to Diodorus of Sicily) as Semiramis, one of two queens possessing superhuman qualities. Not only did she change the course of the Euphrates River, but she also was responsible for building the walls around Babylon and the watchtowers they contained. She is frequently mentioned along with Nitocris, "a woman of greater intelligence than Semiramis," who was also responsible for the construction of Babylon.

Influence. The traditions surrounding Sammuramat continued into the medieval period and beyond, and she is the subject of an opera composed by Italian Gioacchino Rossini.

ADDITIONAL RESOURCES
Sack, R. H. *Images of Nebuchadnezzar: The Emergence of a Legend.* London: Associated University Presses, 1991
Saggs, H. W. F. *The Might That Was Assyria.* London: Sidgwick & Jackson, 1984.

SEE ALSO: Assyria; Babylonia; Herodotus.
—*Ronald H. Sack*

SAMSON

FLOURISHED: c.1100 B.C.E.; Israel
LOCALE: Israel
RELATED CIVILIZATIONS: Israel, Philistines
MAJOR ROLE/POSITION: Warrior

Life. According to the biblical witness preserved in narratives spanning Judges 13-16, Samson was an accomplished military hero from the Israelite tribe of Dan. The triumphs of this physically overpowering rogue against neighboring Philistine men, however, were regularly offset by his failures with Philistine women, whose loyalties remained with their own people.

After being informed that her child would be remarkable, Manoah's wife bore a son. This son, Samson, obtained his parents' reluctant consent to marry a Philistine maiden. Their wedding feast turned sour when Philistine guests solved Samson's riddle by snatching the answer from his bride. In revenge, Samson tied blazing torches to three hundred foxes, releasing them in his enemies' grain fields. Credited with killing one thousand Philistines with the jawbone of an ass and carrying the city gates of Gaza uphill forty miles (sixty-four kilometers) to Hebron, Samson fell victim to the enchanting Delilah, who delivered him to her Philistine cohorts, who blinded him. Ultimately, Samson pulled down the pillars of the Philistine temple of Dagon, thereby killing three thousand worshipers and himself.

Influence. Whereas biblical legend presents Samson as a flawed Israelite Tarzan whose bawdy exploits elude historical verification, its testimony that Philistine-Israelite tensions rapidly escalated during those decades immediately predating the founding of the Israelite monarchy rings true. Samson's story has evoked two compelling artistic renderings—

Strongman Samson is depicted slaying a lion. (North Wind Picture Archives)

John Milton's dramatic poem *Samson Agonistes* (1671) and Camille Saint-Saëns' opera *Samson and Delilah* (1877).

ADDITIONAL RESOURCES

Crenshaw, James L. *Samson: A Secret Betrayed, a Vow Ignored*. Atlanta, Ga.: John Knox Press, 1978.

Gottwald, Norman K. *The Tribes of Yahweh*. Sheffield, England: Sheffield Academic Press, 1999.

SEE ALSO: Israel; Philistines.

—*J. Kenneth Kuntz*

SAMUEL

BORN: c. 1090 B.C.E.; Ramathaim-Zophim (or Ramah)
DIED: c. 1020 B.C.E.; Ramah
RELATED CIVILIZATION: Israel
MAJOR ROLE/POSITION: Religious figure

Life. According to the biblical books of Samuel, his mother, Hannah, who was childless, made a vow that if God gave her a son, he would be dedicated to the service of God at the sanctuary. She gave birth to a son and named him Samuel. When he was weaned, Hannah brought him to Shiloh, dedicated him to the service of God, and entrusted him to Eli, the priest. At the death of his mentor, Samuel assumed his priestly responsibilities. Samuel also was the last of the biblical judges. Each year, he went on a circuit from Bethel to Gilgal to Mizpah and back to Ramah, where his home was, adjudicating religious matters.

With the death of Eli and the realization that his sons were corrupt, the Israelites demanded that a monarchy be established. Samuel warned the Israelites that a monarchy meant conscription, taxation, and military service. Saul became Israel's first king, David its second. Samuel anointed both men. The emergence of monarchy in Israel was matched by the rise of prophetism. Samuel was the first of Israel's prophets.

Influence. A priest, a judge, a prophet—Samuel is described in the Bible as the greatest figure since Moses. At his death, all Israel mourned for him. The author of the biblical book of Hebrews includes Samuel among the great heroes of Israel's faith.

ADDITIONAL RESOURCES

Samuel. (North Wind Picture Archives)

Gordon, Robert P. *I and II Samuel: A Commentary*. Grand Rapids, Mich.: Zondervan, 1986.

_____. "Who Made the Kingmaker? Reflections on Samuel." In *Faith, Tradition, and History: Old Testament Historiography in Its Near Eastern Context*. Edited by A. R. Millard, James Karl Hoffmeier, and David W. Baker. Winona Lake, Ind.: Eisenbrauns, 1994.

Klein, Ralph W. *I Samuel*. Waco, Tex.: Word, 1983.

SEE ALSO: David; Israel; Judaism; Moses; Saul.

—*Mark J. Mangano*

SAPPHO

BORN: c. 630 B.C.E.; Eresus, Lesbos
DIED: c. 568 B.C.E.; Mytilene, Lesbos
RELATED CIVILIZATION: Archaic Greece
MAJOR ROLE/POSITION: Lyric poet

Life. Little is known of Sappho's (SAF-oh) life. The earliest historical documents—of doubtful authority—claim that she married a wealthy trader from Andros, and she speaks of a daughter in her poetry. Most of her life was spent at Mytilene, the principal city on the island of Lesbos. The popular tradition that she was not just a Lesbian (a person from Lesbos) but a lesbian (homosexual) appears to have developed much later; she was not linked with homoeroticism in the Hellenistic period. Sappho is one of the originators of the genre of monody, or solo song, short stanzaic poems sung by the poet to her own accompaniment on the lyre, apparently in her case to a small circle of women and girls, perhaps her students. Ancient authorities credit her with nine volumes of poetry, but only one complete poem and fragments of about a dozen others have survived. Her poems included several epithalamia, written to be performed at weddings, but most of her work appears to have been love poetry.

Influence. Sappho's importance in her own era was as one of the earliest and most accomplished performers of monody, and even the few lines that have survived establish her profound poetic skill beyond any doubt. In modern times, her name serves as the symbol of a specifically female literary tradition.

ADDITIONAL RESOURCES

Easterling, P. E., and B. M. W. Knox, eds. *Greek Literature.* Vol. 1 in *The Cambridge History of Classical Literature.* Cambridge, England: Cambridge University Press, 1985.
Williamson, Margaret. *Sappho's Immortal Daughters.* Cambridge, Mass.: Harvard University Press, 1995.

SEE ALSO: Greece, Archaic; Languages and literature.
                                              —*William Nelles*

SARACEN CONQUEST

ALSO KNOWN AS: Islamic conquest of Egypt;
    Muslim conquest of Egypt
DATE: 600-700 C.E.
LOCALE: Egypt
SIGNIFICANCE: The Arab conquest of Egypt in 641/642 C.E. began the Islamization of Egypt and ended Byzantine control of the country.

Background. The Muslim and Christian accounts of the conquest both imply that the Egyptians were at times partial to the Arabs because of continued conflict between the indigenous, monophysite Coptic Church and the orthodox Byzantine Church in Constantinople. Balādhurī and Ibn ʿAbd al-Ḥakam are the two main Islamic historians of the conquest of Egypt. Their accounts are supported in part by John of Nikiou, a Coptic bishop, who wrote a Christian chronicle that includes a short section presenting an Egyptian Christian perspective on the events.

Action. The conquest of Egypt was led by the general ʿAmr ibn al-ʿĀṣ, who led the battle for Egypt in the Delta region (639 C.E.) and negotiated for the surrender of Babylon (641/642 C.E.) and later for Alexandria (642 C.E.). Despite caliph ʿUmar ibn al-Khaṭṭāb's initial reluctance to support ʿAmr's invasion, the general convinced the caliph of the value of extending Muslim control into Africa and issued a decisive defeat against the Byzantine emperor, Heraclius.

Consequences. The conquest of Egypt provided a dependable food supply that could sustain the needs of an emerging Islamic empire. Egypt's proximity to Arabia proved useful for subsequent conquests into North Africa.

ADDITIONAL RESOURCES

Butler, Alfred J. *The Arab Conquest of Egypt.* Brooklyn, N.Y.: A & B Publishing Group, 1992.
Donner, Fred M. *The Early Islamic Conquests.* Princeton, N.J.: Princeton University Press, 1981.

SEE ALSO: ʿAbd Allāh ibn Saʿd ibn Abī Sarḥ; Arabia; Byzantine Empire; Christianity; Egypt, Ptolemaic and Roman; Islam.
                                    —*Darlene L. Brooks Hedstrom*

SARDURI I

BORN: date and place unknown
DIED: 830 B.C.E.; Urartu, Asia Minor
RELATED CIVILIZATION: Urartu
MAJOR ROLE/POSITION: King

Life. Sarduri I (sahr-DOOR-ee) ruled in Urartu from 840 to 830 B.C.E. and founded a dynasty that lasted for at least seven generations. Although there is some evidence of earlier rulers, they seem to have controlled more localized areas. The dynasty Sarduri I founded may have been formed in response to Assyrian incursions into the area. Under his rule, a unified state of Urartu was established and came into contact with the major powers of the day. A major conflict with the Assyrians took place in 834 B.C.E. during the reign of Shalmaneser III (r. 858-824 B.C.E.). The Assyrian army was led by Daian-Ashur.

Influence. The capital of Tushpa was established on Lake Van (in what later became eastern Turkey). Inscriptions of Sarduri I found there are written in Assyr-

ian, and the epithets mirror Assyrian royal inscriptions. Sarduri calls himself "the magnificent king, the mighty king, king of the universe, king of the land of Nairi, a king having none equal to him, a shepherd to be wondered at, fearing no battle, a king who humbled those who would not submit to his authority."

ADDITIONAL RESOURCES

Piotrovsky, Boris B. *The Ancient Civilization of Urartu.* Translated by James Hogarth. New York: Cowles, 1969.

Zimansky, Paul E. *Ecology and Empire: The Structure of the Urartian State.* Studies in Ancient Oriental Civilization 41. Chicago: The Oriental Institute, 1985.

_____. "The Kingdom of Urartu in Eastern Anatolia." In *Civilizations of the Ancient Near East,* edited by Jack M. Sasson. New York: Scribner, 1995.

SEE ALSO: Argishti I; Assyria; Sarduri II; Sarduri III; Urartu.

—Robert D. Haak

SARDURI II

BORN: date and place unknown
DIED: c. 735 B.C.E.; Urartu, Asia Minor
RELATED CIVILIZATION: Urartu
MAJOR ROLE/POSITION: King

Life. Sarduri II (sahr-DOOR-ee) ruled Urartu from circa 755 to 735 B.C.E. He continued the buildup of the Urartian empire that had begun under Argishti I. Urartu is believed to have reached its maximum size under Sarduri II. His military exploits include at least one campaign each year, and inscriptions commemorating his city building have survived.

In an alliance with Syrian powers, he confronted the Assyrian Tiglath-pileser III at Arpad in 743 B.C.E. He seems to have lost this battle but survived for several more years. In 735 B.C.E., Tiglath-pileser III besieged the capital of Tushpa. The capital itself held out, but the lower city was destroyed.

Influence. Urartu continued in its weakened state into the reign of his son, Rusas I (r. c. 735-713 B.C.E.).

ADDITIONAL RESOURCES

Piotrovsky, Boris B. *The Ancient Civilization of Urartu.* Translated by James Hogarth. New York: Cowles, 1969.

Zimansky, Paul E. *Ecology and Empire: The Structure of the Urartian State.* Studies in Ancient Oriental Civilization 41. Chicago: The Oriental Institute, 1985.

_____. "The Kingdom of Urartu in Eastern Anatolia." In *Civilizations of the Ancient Near East.* Edited by Jack M. Sasson. New York: Scribner, 1995.

SEE ALSO: Argishti I; Assyria; Sarduri I; Sarduri III; Tiglath-pileser III; Urartu.

—Robert D. Haak

SARDURI III

BORN: date and place unknown
DIED: 640/639 B.C.E.; Urartu, Asia Minor
RELATED CIVILIZATION: Urartu
MAJOR ROLE/POSITION: King

Life. Sarduri III (sahr-DOOR-ee), the son of Rusas II, ruled Urartu from circa 644 to 640/639 B.C.E. It is recorded that he sent gifts to the dominant Assyrian king, Ashurbanipal. There is also an Assyrian record of his visit to Assyria at or near the end of his reign. He seems also to have had contacts with the Umman-Manda, competitors of the Assyrians.

Influence. After the rule of Sarduri III, Urartian records indicate several further rulers but precise information is lacking. None of these rulers is mentioned in Assyrian records. Armenians invaded and took over Urartu in the late seventh century B.C.E.

ADDITIONAL RESOURCES

Piotrovsky, Boris B. *The Ancient Civilization of Urartu.* Translated by James Hogarth. New York: Cowles, 1969.

Zimansky, Paul E. *Ecology and Empire: The Structure of the Urartian State.* Studies in Ancient Oriental Civilization 41. Chicago: The Oriental Institute, 1985.

_____. "The Kingdom of Urartu in Eastern Anatolia." In *Civilizations of the Ancient Near East,* edited by Jack M. Sasson. New York: Scribner, 1995.

SEE ALSO: Argishti I; Ashurbanipal; Assyria; Sarduri I; Sarduri II; Urartu.

—*Robert D. Haak*

SARGON OF AKKAD

FLOURISHED: twenty-fourth to twenty-third century B.C.E.; Akkad, Mesopotamia
RELATED CIVILIZATIONS: Mesopotamia, Akkad, Sumer
MAJOR ROLE/POSITION: King

Life. Sargon (SAHR-gahn of A-kad) came from Akkad in Mesopotamia. Despite his humble, Semitic background, he was able to win a job with the Sumerian Ur-Zababa, king of Kish. When Ur-Zababa was overthrown, Sargon was able to seize the throne for himself. He would rule for fifty-five years, from c. 2334 to 2279 B.C.E.

Once in charge, Sargon immediately began a campaign of conquest. He first moved south and subjugated numerous city-states including Erech and Ur. He then moved east and conquered the Elamites. He then drove west to the Mediterranean Sea. Near the end of his reign, Sargon defeated a coalition of southern Sumerian city-states and established his dominance over all Mesopotamia. The state he had created was the world's first true empire.

Influence. Four rulers from Sargon's dynasty followed, but by 2100 B.C.E., his empire fell apart because of internal and external attacks. Sargon's example lived on in the region for centuries as numerous later kings attempted to emulate his achievements.

ADDITIONAL RESOURCES

Edwards, T. E. S., et al., eds. *The Cambridge Ancient History.* Vol. 1. Cambridge, England: Cambridge University Press, 1991.

Hallo, W. W., and W. K. Simpson. *The Ancient Near East: A History.* 2d ed. Fort Worth, Tex.: Harcourt Brace Jovanovich, 1998.

SEE ALSO: Akkadian Dynasty; Elamites; Sumerians.

—*Stefan G. Chrissanthos*

SARGON II

BORN: second half of the eighth century B.C.E.; Assyria
DIED: 705 B.C.E.; north of Assyrian Empire
RELATED CIVILIZATIONS: Assyria, Babylonia
MAJOR ROLE/POSITION: King of Assyria

Life. Sargon II became king of Assyria in 721 B.C.E. following a coup against his predecessor Shalmaneser V (r. 726-721 B.C.E.). Although he claimed to be a son of Tiglath-pileser III (r. 745-727 B.C.E.), Sargon probably usurped the throne with the assistance of the citizens of Ashur (Assur) and Harran.

Sargon's reign was characterized by numerous military campaigns. Early in his reign, Sargon faced opposition in Babylonia, where a Chaldean, Merodachbaladan, seized the throne. Merodachbaladan and his Elamite allies defeated the Assyrian army at Der. Meanwhile a coalition of Syrian states led by Hamath (Hamāh) rebelled against Assyria. Sargon defeated this coalition at Karkar (Qarqar) in 720 B.C.E. However, Sargon's most serious threat came from the kingdom of Urartu, located in the mountains north of the Assyrian heartland. In 714 B.C.E., Sargon invaded Urartu in a daring but brilliant operation that ended the Urartian threat. Sargon then turned his attention to Babylonia in a series of actions (710-707 B.C.E.), eventually dislodging Merodachbaladan and thus reclaiming Babylon for Assyria. Sargon died in battle in 705 B.C.E.

Influence. Building on the foundation laid by Tiglath-pileser III, Sargon maintained Assyrian control over areas crucial to Assyria in the face of significant threats from many directions. Sargon established a line of kings ("the Sargonids") who guided Assyria to greatness in the seventh century B.C.E. before the final collapse of the empire in 612 B.C.E. He also left an impressive architectural legacy. In addition to refurbishing temples and palaces at Ashur, Nineveh, and Calah (Nimrud), Sargon built a new capital city just northeast of Nineveh named Dur Sharrukin, today identified as Khorsabad.

ADDITIONAL RESOURCES

Boardman, John, et al., eds. *The Assyrian and Babylonian Empires and Other States of the Near East, from the Eighth to the Sixth Centuries* B.C. Vol. 3, part 2 in *Cambridge Ancient History.* 2d ed. Cambridge, England: Cambridge University Press, 1991.

Saggs, H. W. F. *The Might That Was Assyria.* London: Sidgwick & Jackson, 1984.

SEE ALSO: Assyria; Babylonia; Tiglath-pileser III; Urartu.

—*Thomas Vester Brisco*

SARMATIANS

DATE: 600 B.C.E.-900 C.E.

LOCALE: Ukraine

SIGNIFICANCE: From about 200 B.C.E. to 200 C.E., the Sarmatians ruled Ukraine and were thus one of the major precursors of Slavic Russia.

From the sixth to the fourth century B.C.E., the Sarmatians migrated from Asia into the Ural region, and from the fourth to the second century B.C.E. replaced the Scythians as rulers of the Ukraine. In the first century C.E., they threatened the Roman province of Moesia in the Danubian plain. General Tiberius Plautius Silvanus Aelianus defeated them in 63 C.E. In the second century C.E., they joined with several German tribes in an attack on the Roman Empire. Emperor Hadrian built a series of fortresses in Lower Moesia and Cappadocia to withstand the assaults.

In the third century C.E., the Goths replaced the Sarmatians as rulers of Ukraine, but many Sarmatians continued in positions of authority. However, the arrival of the Huns after 370 C.E. destroyed their nation.

By the sixth century C.E., they disappeared except for a small group that remained in Ossetia until the ninth century C.E.

Sarmatians spoke an Indo-European language related to Persian. They worshiped a fire god to whom they sacrificed horses. They were nomads but did engage in some agricultural pursuits. They made metal objects and pottery and cured hides. They traded in furs, fish, honey, metals, and grain with nearby Greek city-states and the eastern kingdoms on the borders of China.

ADDITIONAL RESOURCES

Davis-Kimball, Jeannine. *Kurgans on the Left Bank of the Ilek.* Berkeley, Calif.: Zinat Press, 1995.

Mielczarek, Mariusz. *The Sarmatians.* Oxford, England: Osprey, 2000.

SEE ALSO: Hadrian; Huns; Rome, Imperial; Scythia; Slavs.

—*Frederick B. Chary*

SĀSĀNIAN EMPIRE

ALSO KNOWN AS: Sāsānid Empire

DATE: 224-651 C.E.

LOCALE: Iran, Iraq, Armenia

SIGNIFICANCE: The Sāsānian Empire was the only power of the ancient world that was strong enough to stand up to the Roman Empire.

The Sāsānian (sa-SAY-nee-ehn) Dynasty was founded by Ardashīr I in 224 C.E. He defeated the last Parthian overlord of Persia. From the beginning, the Sāsānians depicted themselves as the true inheritors of ancient Persian power and greatness. They always tried to expand their empire's power and control of territory against the Eastern Roman Empire. As its height in the late fourth century C.E., the Sāsānian Empire controlled most of Syria, Mesopotamia, the Arabian Peninsula, Armenia, Iran, and Iraq. Zoroastrianism (ancient Persian fire worship) was established as the official religion of the Sāsānian Empire; Pahlavi/Middle Persian was its official language.

A number of groups in Sāsānian society all vied for dominance: interrelated aristocratic families, high-ranking members of the Zoroastrian clergy, military commanders, and other members of the ruling dynasty. Power gradually became centralized in the hands of the ruler but could be lost again under a weak ruler. The military played an important role in domestic Sāsānian politics, for the army could and did revolt against unpopular or ineffective leaders. However, the army also formed the defensive bulwark against the chronic threat of invasion by the Roman army. Over the four centuries of its existence, the Sāsānian Dynasty fought numerous battles against the Roman army. Overall, the Sāsānian military was successful at holding onto territory it cap-

SĀSĀNIAN EMPIRE, SIXTH CENTURY C.E.

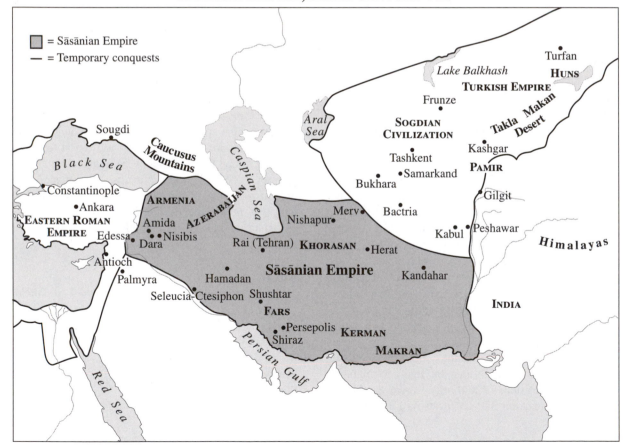

tured from the Romans, but the cost in money and troops weakened the Sāsānian Empire to the point that it could not survive its clash with the armies of Islam in the mid-seventh century. Although the Sāsānian Empire bested the Eastern Roman (Byzantine) Empire militarily, the Eastern Roman Empire survived it by more than eight hundred years.

Notable Sāsānian shahs include Shāpūr I (r. 240-272 C.E.), Shāpūr II (r. 309-379 C.E.), and Kavadh I (r. 488-531 C.E.), whose patronage of the Mazdakite religion brought the Sāsānian Empire to civil war but whose invasion of Roman Syria in 502-506 C.E. was successful. Khosrow I (r. 531-579 C.E.) reorganized most elements of Sāsānian civil society, including the systems of tax collection and land allocation. He also restructured the army to make it better equipped and more efficient. He curtailed the rising power of the aristocracy and reorganized the empire's civil administration into four administrative units. He invaded Roman Syria in 540 C.E. and looted the fabulously wealthy city of Antioch. This forced Emperor Justinian I to seek peace terms.

The last effective Sāsānian shah was Khosrow II (r. 590-628 C.E.). When the Eastern Roman Empire was weakened by internal strife in 602 C.E., Khosrow II invaded Syria and much of Asia Minor and eventually captured Jerusalem in 614 C.E. and Alexandria in Egypt in 619 C.E. Not until 627 C.E. were the Sāsānids driven out of the conquered territories. The expansionist policies of Khosrow II fatally weakened the Sāsānian Empire so that the Muslim army conquered the Sāsānian capital of Seleucia-Ctesiphon in 637 C.E. and annihilated the last significant remnants of the Sāsānian military at the Battle of Nahavānd in 642 C.E.

ADDITIONAL RESOURCES

Strauss, Barry. "Rome's Persian Mirage." *Military History Quarterly* 12, no. 1 (1999): 18-27.

Yarshater, Ehsan, ed. *The Seleucid, Parthian, and Sasanian Periods.* Vol. 3 in *The Cambridge History of Iran.* Cambridge, England: Cambridge University Press, 1983.

SEE ALSO: Ardashīr I; Byzantine Empire; Islam; Narses (Sāsānian emperor); Parthia; Persia; Rome, Imperial; Shāpūr I; Shāpūr II; Zoroaster; Zoroastrianism.

—*Victoria Erhart*

SĀTAVĀHANA DYNASTY

DATE: c. 200 B.C.E.-225 C.E.
LOCALE: Deccan region of south India
RELATED CIVILIZATION: India
SIGNIFICANCE: Earliest indigenous kingdom of the Deccan.

The Sātavāhana (SAH-tah-VAH-ha-nah) Dynasty, also called the Andhra Dynasty, rose to power in the Deccan after the demise of the Mauryan Dynasty in the region. The dynasty is known through coins, literary references, and some thirty-five inscriptions. According to the ancient lists of kings in various *purāṇas*, there were either nineteen kings who ruled for 350 years or twenty-nine rulers who reigned for 456 years. All accounts seem to agree that the founder of the line was King Simuka. The Sātavāhanas were Brahmans, and at least one king, Sātakarṇi I, performed the *aśvamedha* (Vedic horse sacrifice). They probably originated in the Godāvari region of modern Mahārāshtra. At the height of their power, they controlled the entire Deccan, embracing huge tracts of land stretching from sea to sea. Despite their Hindu allegiance, Buddhism flourished under Sātavāhana rule; it is recorded that the kings endowed land to Brahmans and Buddhists alike.

The Sātavāhana period was one of great industrial, commercial, and maritime activity in which the kingdom grew rich on trade with the Romans and various regions of South Asia. Liberal patrons of the arts and Buddhism, the Sātavāhanas' material prosperity was reflected in the art of the Andhradesha school, which created noble monuments throughout the Deccan. The Sātavāhanas had at least two different capitals, Pratishtana (Paithan in the Aurangabad District) and Dharanikota (Guntur District) near Amaravati. Sātavāhana rule ended in 225 C.E. when the Ikṣvāku Dynasty took over the region.

ADDITIONAL RESOURCE

Ajay Mitra Shastri, ed. *The Age of the Sātavāhanas.* New Delhi, India: Aryan Books, 1999.

SEE ALSO: Andhradesha school; Buddhism; Hinduism; Mauryan Dynasty; Rome, Imperial.

—*Katherine Anne Harper*

SAUL

FLOURISHED: eleventh century B.C.E.
RELATED CIVILIZATION: Israel
MAJOR ROLE/POSITION: Israel's first king

Saul, king of Israel (center), and Samuel. (North Wind Picture Archives)

Life. Saul was a charismatic military hero who summoned each Israelite tribe to rescue the men of Jabesh-Gilead, threatened by Ammonites who would spare them only if each man would gouge out his right eye. Saul's action saved the men and unified the tribes. This led to the creation of a monarchy to replace the loose tribal confederation, and Saul was chosen Israel's first king. His reign lacked monarchical organization, a capital city, court officials, taxation, conscript labor, and public works. His territory was limited to the hill country and portions of Gilead, and his reign was constantly bedevilled by the Philistines, who caused his death at the Battle of Mount Gilboa. His ambitious successor David, brought in as a youth to play music and sing to the depressed and self-doubting king, won over the hearts of the people. The prophet Samuel had anointed Saul king but later rejected him for usurpation of religious prerogatives.

Influence. The Bible presents Saul, perhaps unfairly, as a tragic hero, reflecting a southern, pro-David bias. That he exhibited some mental dementia is undenied, but his last hours reveal him as a truly regal figure.

ADDITIONAL RESOURCES
Fox, Everett. *Give Us a King! Samuel, Saul, and David.* New York: Schocken Books, 1999.
James, Fleming. *Personalities of the Old Testament.* New York : Scribners, 1938.

SEE ALSO: Bible: Jewish; David; Philistines; Samuel.

—*John M. Bullard*

SCAEVOLA, QUINTUS MUCIUS (AUGER)

ALSO KNOWN AS: Augur
BORN: mid-second century B.C.E.; place unknown
DIED: c. 88 B.C.E.; Rome
RELATED CIVILIZATION: Republican Rome
MAJOR ROLE/POSITION: Orator, statesman

Life. The details of Quintus Mucius Scaevola's (KWIHN-tuhs MYEW-shee-uhs SEE-vuh-luh) life and career remain mostly hidden. He advanced slowly but surely up the political ladder in Rome. He governed the Roman province of Asia while praetor circa 120 B.C.E. He was later tried for extortion but acquitted. He also held the consulship in 117 B.C.E.

Influence. Along with his cousin, Quintus Mucius Scaevola (also known as Pontifex), Scaevola the Augur dominated the Roman legal scene of his day. In the late Republic, Romans relied upon legal specialists to draw up contracts, advise trial lawyers, and provide opinions on points of law. Scaevola was a legal specialist known for his mastery of Roman law. He rarely served as a trial lawyer, instead preferring to offer his legal opinions to those seeking clarification of Roman laws. Many of the Roman elite sent their sons to observe Scaevola, a renowned legal expert, and learn legal science from him. He taught the renowned orator Lucius Licinius Crassus as well as the more famous orator and statesman, Cicero. Cicero remembered his mentor fondly and used him as a character in a number of his famous literary dialogues.

ADDITIONAL RESOURCES

Frier, Bruce W. *The Rise of the Roman Jurists: Studies in Cicero's "Pro Caecina."* Princeton, N.J.: Princeton University Press, 1985.

Robinson, O. F. *The Sources of Roman Laws: Problems and Methods for Ancient Historians.* London: Routledge, 1997.

Tellegen-Couperus, Olga. *A Short History of Roman Law.* London: Routledge, 1993.

SEE ALSO: Cicero; Rome, Republican; Scaevola, Quintus Mucius (Pontifex).

—*Jeremiah B. McCall*

SCAEVOLA, QUINTUS MUCIUS (PONTIFEX)

ALSO KNOWN AS: Pontifex
BORN: c. 130's B.C.E.; place unknown
DIED: c. 82 B.C.E.; Rome
RELATED CIVILIZATION: Republican Rome
MAJOR ROLE/POSITION: Jurist, statesman

Life. Quintus Mucius Scaevola (KWIHN-tuhs MYEW-shee-uhs SEE-vuh-luh) enjoyed a distinguished political career, holding Rome's highest political offices. As consul in 95 B.C.E., he coauthored a law expelling from Rome those Italians who had illegally enrolled as Roman citizens. Later, while governing the province of Asia, he rearranged the administration of the province and ended the Roman tax collectors' exploitation of the provincials. A supporter of Lucius Cornelius Sulla during the first civil war (88-82 B.C.E.), Scaevola was executed by the Roman authorities in 82 B.C.E.

Influence. Scaevola the Pontifex is best known for his contribution to the development of Roman civil law. He was a gifted orator as well as an expert on the intricacies of Roman law. Scaevola wrote an eighteen-book legal commentary, the first organized treatise on Roman civil law. This work set several precedents. First, it grouped similar Roman laws together in categories. Perhaps even more important, it contained hypothetical legal cases illustrating how various Roman laws should be applied. Both the categorization of law and the creation of hypothetical cases marked great innovations in Roman legal science, and Scaevola's work served as the foundation for later Roman legal commentaries.

ADDITIONAL RESOURCES

Frier, Bruce W. *The Rise of the Roman Jurists: Studies in Cicero's "Pro Caecina."* Princeton, N.J.: Princeton University Press, 1985.

Robinson, O. F. *The Sources of Roman Laws: Problems and Methods for Ancient Historians.* London: Routledge, 1997.

Tellegen-Couperus, Olga. *A Short History of Roman Law.* London: Routledge, 1993.

SEE ALSO: Rome, Republican; Scaevola, Quintus Mucius (Auger); Sulla, Lucius Cornelius.

—*Jeremiah B. McCall*

SCIPIO AEMILIANUS

ALSO KNOWN AS: Scipio the Younger; Publius Cornelius Scipio Aemilianus Africanus Numantinus
BORN: c. 185/184 B.C.E.; probably Rome
DIED: 129 B.C.E.; Rome
RELATED CIVILIZATIONS: Carthage, Republican Rome, Spain
MAJOR ROLE/POSITION: Statesman, military leader

Life. Scipio Aemilianus (SIHP-ee-oh ih-mihl-ee-AY-nuhs) inherited a proud aristocratic lineage and the familial connections that destined him for a career of service to the Roman state. His father was Lucius Aemilius Paullus, the conqueror of Macedonia at the Battle of Pydna (168 B.C.E.). While he was still a young man, he was adopted by Scipio Africanus, making him the eventual heir to the leadership of the prestigious and influential clan whose patriarch had defeated Carthage at the Battle of Zama (202 B.C.E.). Scipio Aemilianus was also related to the Gracchi brothers, Tiberius Sempronius Gracchus and Gaius Sempronius Gracchus, through marriage to their sister, Sempronia.

Although Scipio Aemilianus retained a lifelong interest in literature and the arts, he excelled in political and military affairs. During the mid-second century B.C.E., Rome faced two foreign challenges: the resurgent power of Carthage and perennial revolts in Spain. Scipio Aemilianus led the Roman armies that destroyed Carthage in the Third Punic War (149-146 B.C.E.). He ended Spanish unrest by seizing the city of Numantia in 133 B.C.E. After returning to Rome, he opposed the political and agrarian reforms of his brothers-in-law, the Gracchi. Scipio Aemilianus died unexpectedly shortly thereafter, leading to speculation that he had been murdered.

Influence. Scipio Aemilianus did little to address the growing socioeconomic distress prevailing in second century B.C.E. Italy. Although he defended property rights and the Roman constitution against the Gracchi, he also undermined Republican institutions through his circumventions of the senate's power and his bending of constitutional restraints in his own favor.

ADDITIONAL RESOURCES

Astin, A. E. *Scipio Aemilianus*. Oxford, England: Clarendon Press, 1967.

Richardson, J. S. *Hispaniae, Spain and the Development of Roman Imperialism, 218-82 B.C.* Cambridge, England: Cambridge University Press, 1986.

SEE ALSO: Carthage; Gracchus, Tiberius Sempronius, and Gaius Sempronius Gracchus; Punic Wars; Rome, Republican; Spain; Zama, Battle of.

—Michael S. Fitzgerald

SCIPIO AFRICANUS

ALSO KNOWN AS: Scipio the Elder; Publius Cornelius Scipio Africanus
BORN: 236 B.C.E.; Rome
DIED: 184/183 B.C.E.; Liternum, Campania (later Patria, Italy)
RELATED CIVILIZATIONS: Republican Rome, Carthage
MAJOR ROLE/POSITION: Military and political leader

Life. The son of an aristocratic Roman family, Scipio Africanus (SIHP-ee-oh af-rih-KAY-nuhs) enlisted in the Roman army and traveled to Spain with his father and uncle at the beginning of the Second Punic War in 218 B.C.E. He assumed command of the army at their deaths and proceeded to drive Carthaginian forces out of Spain. He commanded the Roman army which invaded Africa and defeated Hannibal at the Battle of Zama in 202 B.C.E., earning him the appellation "Africanus."

Though he was a successful and respected military leader and was elected to the highest Roman offices, Scipio Africanus's policies regarding the conflicts between Rome and the Greek states during the 190's B.C.E. were not accepted.

Scipio Africanus. (Library of Congress)

Scipio accompanied the army on the Roman campaign that led to victory over Antiochus the Great at Magnesia ad Sipylum in 190 B.C.E. He missed the battle because of illness, and his lenient terms were rejected by the senate. Upon his return to Rome, he and his brother were tried for financial mismanagement by Cato the Censor; Africanus was later accused of treason and died in disgrace.

Influence. Scipio Africanus's victory over Hannibal was possibly the most significant military success in Roman history. He was also important for his political influence. Rome would have been better served had it heeded his advice regarding the Greek states.

ADDITIONAL RESOURCES
Leckie, Ross. *Scipio Africanus*. Washington, D.C.: Regnery, 1998.
Scullard, Howard H. *Scipio Africanus in the Second Punic War*. Cambridge, England: The University Press, 1930.
_____. *Scipio Africanus: Soldier and Politician*. Reprint. Ithaca, N.Y.: Cornell University Press, 1970.

SEE ALSO: Antiochus the Great; Carthage; Cato the Censor; Hannibal; Magnesia ad Sipylum, Battle of; Punic Wars; Rome, Republican; Zama, Battle of.

—James O. Smith

SCOPAS

ALSO KNOWN AS: Skopas of Paros
BORN: possibly as early as 420 B.C.E.; Paros, Greece
DIED: late fourth century B.C.E.; place unknown
RELATED CIVILIZATION: Late Classical Greece
MAJOR ROLE/POSITION: Sculptor

Life. Most scholars agree that Scopas (SKOH-puhs) was part of a sculptural family that began with his grandfather Scopas and father, Aristandros, who was a renowned worker in bronze. None of Scopas's sculptural bases or signatures survives, although his works are described by Pliny the Elder, Pausanias the Traveler, Athenian politician Callistratus, and Strabo of Amasia.

Scopas's most notable achievements were accomplished at the mausoleum at Halicarnassus and the temple of Athena Alea at Tegea. Pausanias the Traveler reports that Scopas was the architect and sculptor of the cult statue at the latter site. He was most likely a sculptor trained to work in the famed Parian marble and has been credited with representations of Hecate, Asclepius and Hygieia, Artemis, Athena Pronaos, Heracles, Pothos, Eros, and Himeros.

Although the attribution of surviving sculptural pieces to Scopas is still a matter of debate among scholars, his style has been described as vivid with torsional action and full of emotional pathos.

Influence. Scopas was clearly one of the masters of fourth century B.C.E. sculpture, and his prominence is obvious from the outstanding number of sculptural pieces mentioned in ancient literature.

ADDITIONAL RESOURCES
Ridgway, Brunilde Sismondo. *Fourth-Century Styles in Greek Sculpture*. Madison: University of Wisconsin Press, 1997.
Stewart, Andrew F. *Skopas of Paros*. Park Ridge, N.J.: Noyes Press, 1977.

SEE ALSO: Art and architecture; Greece, Classical; Halicarnassus mausoleum; Mausolus; Pausanias the Traveler; Pliny the Elder.

—Christina A. Salowey

SCRIBONIA

BORN: c. 75 B.C.E.; Rome
DIED: 16 C.E.; place unknown
RELATED CIVILIZATION: Imperial Rome
MAJOR ROLE/POSITION: First wife of Caesar Augustus

Life. Scribonia (skrih-BOH-nee-uh) is best known as the wife of Octavian (the future Augustus) who bore the indignity of divorce on the very day she gave birth to his daughter Julia. Her marriage to him was rather short (40-39 B.C.E.) and had been arranged because of her ties with Pompey the Great.

Scribonia, from an important senatorial family, had previously married Scipio, who served as consul in Rome, and her brother Lucius Scribonius Libo was famous for his role throughout the Roman civil war. The marriage to Octavian was doomed to failure because of their age difference (she was much older) and because he was annoyed by her temper. A younger woman, the nineteen-year-old Livia Drusilla, stole the youthful Octavian away from her.

Although Livia would be married to Augustus for fifty-two years, Scribonia held the advantage of providing his only offspring, Julia. Therefore, Scribonia's influence continued behind the scenes while Julia married Marcus Claudius Marcellus, Marcus Vipsanius Agrippa, and Tiberius, all designated as possible successors to Augustus. However, Julia's adulterous affairs caused her to be exiled, and Scribonia followed her daughter into exile to Pandateria in 2 B.C.E. She outlived Julia and Augustus, who both died in 14 C.E.

Influence. Scribonia played an opposition role in Rome as she sought to discredit Livia and her son Tiberius.

ADDITIONAL RESOURCES

Ferrero, Guglielmo. *The Women of the Caesars*. New York: G. P. Putnam's Sons, 1925.

Suetonius. "Augustus." In *Lives of the Caesars*. Oxford, England: Oxford University Press, 2000.

SEE ALSO: Agrippa, Marcus Vipsanius; Augustus; Julia (daughter of Augustus); Livia Drusilla; Pompey the Great; Rome, Imperial; Tiberius.

—Fred Strickert

SCYLAX OF CARYANDA

FLOURISHED: sixth century B.C.E.
RELATED CIVILIZATION: Persia
MAJOR ROLE/POSITION: Navigator, geographer

Life. The Greek historian Herodotus reported that in about 515 B.C.E., Darius the Great sent Scylax of Caryanda (SI-laks of KAR-ee-an-duh), an island off Caria near Halicarnassus, and others whom he trusted on a journey. They traveled from northern India down the Indus River eastward to the sea and thence westward, in the thirtieth month, to the isthmus of Suez; after this circumnavigation, Darius conquered the Indians and made use of this sea.

Exactly where Scylax traveled is impossible to determine, but he appears to have based his *Periplus*, a geographical work, at least in part on his own experience. The Greek historian Herodotus knew Scylax in connection with India, the Indian Ocean, and geographical writings, and so did geographer and historian Hecataeus of Miletus in the sixth or fifth century B.C.E. and philosopher Aristotle in the fourth century B.C.E. There are numerous texts entitled *Periplus*, and Scylax's may have been the first; however, it survives only in fragments quoted by others. An extant fourth century B.C.E. *Periplus*, although often attributed to Scylax, was written too late to be his, although it probably borrowed on Scylax's authority for its descriptions of the coasts of Europe, Asia, and Libya. Strabo's *Geōgraphica* (c. 7 B.C.E.; *Geography*, 1917-1933) may have also used Scylax's work. The Latin poet Avienus cited Scylax as late as the fourth century C.E.

Influence. In writing what was probably the first Greek *periplus* at the end of the sixth century B.C.E., Scylax created a Greek literary genre that influenced not only merchants and seamen but also geographers and classical letters in general.

ADDITIONAL RESOURCES

Casson, Lionel. *The Ancient Mariners*. 2d ed. Princeton, N.J.: Princeton University Press, 1991.

Kaeppel, Carl. "The Periplus of Scylax." In *Off the Beaten Track in the Classics*. New York: Melbourne University Press, 1936.

SEE ALSO: Aristotle; Darius the Great; Hecataeus of Miletus; Herodotus; Persia; Strabo.

—O. Kimball Armayor

SCYTHIA

DATE: 1000-100 B.C.E.

LOCALE: Ukraine

SIGNIFICANCE: Scythia was a powerful state on the Black Sea during the Classical and Hellenistic ages of Greece and an ancient precursor of Russia and Ukraine.

In the ninth century B.C.E., the Chinese emperor Ji Jing (r. 872-781 B.C.E.) sent his army to face nomadic raiders near the Scythian (SIH-thee-uhn) homeland. This disruption, possibly along with a drought, forced the Scythians to move westward. The mobility and quickness with which they moved made them seem to appear out of nowhere in the land of the Cimmerians in southern Ukraine. Because the Cimmerians still fought on foot, the Scythians had no trouble in defeating them and taking over their state. In a thirty-year war beginning at the end of the eighth century B.C.E., the Scythians hunted the Cimmerians to extinction in the Volga River Valley, Armenia, the borders of Assyria, and Asia Minor. During the campaign, the Scythians made a temporary alliance with Assyria but abandoned it when the terms hindered their war against the Cimmerians. The Scythians remained in Asia and raided Syria and Palestine and even reached the border of Egypt. The Medes then drove the Scythians out of the region, forcing the main community back into the Ukraine. Smaller groups went into central Europe or eastward as far as India.

According to legend, the founder of the Scythians was Targitaos of the house of Phalatae. The first historical ruler was a chieftain named Colaxis. In 512 B.C.E., the Persian emperor Darius the Great hoped to extend his empire into the rich lands of the Danubian plain and therefore invaded Scythia. However, the fierce Scythian defense of their homeland under King Idanthyrus forced the emperor to abandon his European dream and retreat to Asia.

Idanthyrus's grandson Scyles introduced Greek fashions and styles into Scythia, sparking a revolt by his brother Ostomasades, who wanted to maintain traditional Scythian ways. Ostomasades murdered Scyles and took the throne. In 339 B.C.E., the ninety-year-old King Ateas was killed fighting Phillip II of Macedonia. Scythia began to decline with the arrival of the Sarmatians in the fourth century B.C.E. The Scythians held out until about 200 B.C.E., when the Sarmatians drove the last remnants into the Crimea. The last kings were Scylurus and his son Palakus around 100 B.C.E.

Social structure. The Scythians had a patriarchal society with an aristocratic class of great wealth, called by Greek historian Herodotus the "royal Scythians" in contrast to the general population of "Scythian ploughmen." When in transit, the Scythian men rode their horses, and the women and families rode in the ox carts bearing their tentlike homes with their possessions.

Government and economics. The Scythians divided their kingdom into four districts under governors who collected taxes and served as judges. They also collected tribute from the nearby Greek colonies. The aristocracy was nomadic, but the bulk of the commoners engaged in agriculture. Scythians also hunted and fished. They traded with the Greeks, exchanging forest and agricultural surplus for Greek luxuries. At the very end of their history, the Crimean Scythians minted coins.

Daily life and customs. Scythians counted their wealth in horses, and the upper classes owned many fine animals. Inferior horses served as food and draft labor. Scythians enjoyed inhaling the smoke of burning hemp seeds in groups. For this, they used cauldrons varying in size and shaped as truncated cones.

Death and burial. The Scythians had elaborate funerals lasting forty days. In addition to precious and ordinary objects, a Scythian's horses were buried with him. Companions who died around the same time built their graves near to one another. The tombs are chambers under huge mounds up to seven feet (a little more than two meters) in height and sometimes in excess of a thousand feet (about 300 meters) in diameter. Scythian graves reveal richly ornamented clothing, rugs of felt and wool, and wooden furniture. The Scythians decorated their bodies with tattooed religious symbols, including stars, designs, and imaginary animals. The tombs also contain richly decorated jewelry, tools, and utensils including the typical hemp seed cauldrons.

War and weapons. In time of war, the Scythians divided forces into three divisions. Troops were fed and dressed but not paid unless they brought back the heads of their foe; then they earned a share of their booty. Often they would gild or silver the victims' skulls and use them as drinking vessels for libations of blood and water. Scythians fought in bronze helmets and Greek-style chain mail with red felt linings. They carried round or rectangular shields of various materials and used a curved bow and arrows. They also used Persian swords and Chinese-style knives. Scythian weapons were made of bronze at first, but later they used iron.

They decorated their weapons in gold, iron, and precious stones, often in the shape of real or fantastic animals. Scythians were among the first masters of the horse, and they decorated their saddles and bridles with rich ornamentation in animal motifs. The Scythians also used the scorched-earth tactic in wars.

Religion and ritual. Scythians worshiped nature but had no temples or priests. Their chief goddess was Tabiti, protector of beasts and fire. They also worshiped deities of the sky, earth, water, and the Moon and adopted Greek gods as well, sometimes identifying them with their own. Although they had no priests, they did have a class of eunuchs who acted as soothsayers. These dressed as women and exhibited feminine characteristics in punishment, it is said, for a sacrilege against Tabiti.

Visual arts. Scythian art demonstrated their focus on animals. Sculptures, paintings, and reliefs all have the same theme, real and imaginary beasts decorated for magical and religious purposes. The Scythians worked in leather, wood, bone, felt, bronze, and later iron. They also used gold, silver, and gems. Golden stags, in particular, are an impressive legacy of their art. Although their art is mainly representational, it often approaches the abstract.

Current views. Although Herodotus divided the Scythians into two classes, the aristocracy and the "ploughmen," scholars today believe that only the aristocracy were true Scythians and the ploughmen were the remnants of the Cimmerians and earlier inhabitants.

ADDITIONAL RESOURCES

Cernenko, E. V. *The Scythians*. London: Osprey, 1983.

Jacobson, Esther. *The Art of the Scythians*. Leiden, Netherlands: E. J. Brill, 1995.

Rice, Tamara. *The Scythians*. New York: Praeger, 1961.

Rolle, Renate. *The World of the Scythians*. London: Batsford, 1989.

SEE ALSO: Assyria; Cimmerians; Darius the Great; Herodotus; Philip II.

—*Frederick B. Chary*

SEA PEOPLES

DATE: 8000 B.C.E.-700 C.E.

LOCALE: Oceania

RELATED CIVILIZATIONS: Melanesia, Micronesia, Polynesia

SIGNIFICANCE: The Sea Peoples, oceangoing voyagers, spread their culture throughout most of Oceania.

The Sea Peoples of Oceania were the original ocean voyagers, colonizing all of the region in less than three thousand years. Hunter-gatherers of southeast Asia who originated in Taiwan, they had expanded into the South Pacific from Australia and New Guinea by fifty thousand years ago. After 8000 B.C.E., and until around 1600 B.C.E., rising ocean levels inundated much of Oceania, preventing the spread of human populations. By 1500 B.C.E., the Lapita culture complex had spread from New Guinea in Melanesia as far east as Fiji, Samoa, and Tonga.

Around 200 B.C.E., early seafarers from Samoa and Tonga discovered and settled the Cook islands, Tahiti, the Tuamotus, and the Marquesas. By 300 C.E., colonizing voyages were sent from central or eastern Polynesia to Rapa Nui (Easter Island). By 700 C.E., Maori settlers from the Society Islands (or Cook Islands) had settled New Zealand.

As each island was settled, the culture of the original Sea Peoples of the South Pacific underwent gradual changes that led to the incredibly varied cultures of Oceania. Major groups include many identified with various islands such as Fiji, Samoa, Tonga, Tahiti, the Cooks, Tuamotus, Marquesas, Societies, Hive, Hawaii, and Aotearoa. The descendants of the Sea Peoples of Oceania speak many varieties of languages originating in Proto-Austronesian, vowel-rich, melodic, and closely related. Vocabulary and use of consonants varies widely from place to place, but the grammar and syntax are nearly universal throughout Oceania.

Until 700 C.E., the Sea Peoples were generally uniform culturally across the islands of Oceania, with local adaptations dependent on the distance of a colony from its original home, time in isolation, and environmental differences. They carried numerous plants and animals on their voyages, displacing many endemic species in the process of transforming every island they settled.

ADDITIONAL RESOURCES

Bellwood, P. S. *The Prehistory of Southeast Asia and Oceania*. Auckland, New Zealand: Collins, 1979.

Irwin, G. *The Prehistoric Exploration and Colonization of the Pacific*. Cambridge, England: Cambridge

University Press, 1992.

Terrell, J. *Prehistory in the Pacific Islands*. Cambridge, England: Cambridge University Press, 1989.

SEE ALSO: Australia, Tasmania, New Zealand; Melanesia; Micronesia; Polynesia.

—*Michael W. Simpson*

SECOND SOPHISTIC

DATE: c. 60-230 C.E.
LOCALE: Roman Europe and Mediterranean
RELATED CIVILIZATIONS: Roman Greece, Imperial Rome
SIGNIFICANCE: This movement of orators, who spoke on ancient and often fictional topics for popular entertainment, safely channeled rhetorical power away from politics in an era of tyranny and led to a renaissance of classical literature and history.

The Pax Romana, or "Roman peace," brought a general prosperity, including the proliferation of theaters and private schools and safety of travel, permitting the flourishing of itinerant philosophical orators. Artful and eloquent public speaking on philosophical topics and ancient themes became a popular form of entertainment, and its masters, who were also teachers, won high praise and the patronage of emperors and the elite. These men were compared by the historian Flavius Philostratus to the great sophists ("wise men" or "professors") of Classical Greece, who also traveled and taught philosophy and rhetoric, hence his coining of the phrase "Second Sophistic." The phenomenon traditionally begins with Nicetes of Smyrna under Nero and ends with Apsines under Marcus Aurelius Severus Alexander, but the most famous practitioners were Dio Chrysostom, Tiberius Claudius Atticus Herodes, Aristides, and Maximus of Tyre. Experts were expected to be able to give speeches extemporaneously and to defend either side of an argument. They also had to be widely read so that they could talk on antiquated subjects and spice their speeches with literary allusions and forms.

ADDITIONAL RESOURCES

Anderson, Graham. *The Second Sophistic*. New York: Routledge, 1993.

Sandy, Gerald. *The Greek World of Apuleius*. New York: Brill, 1997.

Swain, Simon. *Hellenism and Empire*. New York: Clarendon Press, 1996.

SEE ALSO: Aristides; Dio Chrysostom; Greece, Hellenistic and Roman; Philostratus, Flavius; Rome, Imperial.

—*Richard C. Carrier*

SELEUCID DYNASTY

DATE: 312 B.C.E.-64 B.C.E.
LOCALE: Mesopotamia, Coele-Syria (later Bekáa Valley), Anatolia, Persia
RELATED CIVILIZATIONS: Ptolemaic Dynasty, Hasmonean Dynasty, Hellenistic Greece, Republican Rome
SIGNIFICANCE: The Seleucid (suh-LEW-suhd) Dynasty maintained the preeminence of Greek culture over the indigenous peoples of the ancient Near East through a process of urbanization and economic centralization.

History. After the death of Alexander the Great in 323 B.C.E., there was a period of intense conflict among Alexander's generals, known as the Diadochi, for control of his empire. Though the idea of maintaining a single empire was their goal, no individual general was able to impose his will on the others, and the empire was divided among them. Seleucus I, one of the Diadochi, fought with Antigonus I Monophthalmos, who succeeded to the Macedonian throne, over control of Mesopotamia. Ptolemy I Soter, who ruled Egypt, helped Seleucus defeat Demetrius Poliorcetes, the son and coregent of Antigonus, at Gaza in 312 B.C.E. After this victory, Seleucus was able to take Babylon, which he made the seat of his government, declaring himself king and thereby establishing the Seleucid Dynasty as Seleucus I Nicator ("Victor"). After the Battle of Ipsus in 301 B.C.E., during which Antigonus died, there was a

THE HELLENISTIC WORLD, 185 B.C.E.

realignment of borders among the surviving Diadochi. Seleucus added the region from Syria to Babylon to his territories. Ptolemy I took Coele-Syria, Palestine, and the Phoenician cities, although Seleucus believed that these territories rightly belonged to him. Seleucus I was assassinated in 281 B.C.E. by Ptolemy Ceraunus, the son of Ptolemy I.

The next five Seleucid kings, Antiochus I Soter (r. 281-261 B.C.E.), Antiochus II (r. 261-246 B.C.E.), Seleucus II (r. 246-225 B.C.E.), Seleucus III (r. 225-223 B.C.E.), and Antiochus the Great (r. 223-187 B.C.E.), fought five wars (the Syrian Wars) with the Ptolemies over disputed territories until Antiochus the Great succeeded in taking Coele-Syria and Palestine from the Ptolemies in 198 B.C.E. by defeating the Egyptian general Scopas at the Battle of Paneas. Antiochus set about modernizing his kingdom by uniting military and civil administration. This modernization allowed the Seleucid kingdom to exercise enormous control over the politics, economy, and culture of the ancient Near East. When Antiochus the Great turned his attention to territories in Anatolia and Greece, he came into conflict with the Romans, who defeated him at the Battle of Magnesia ad Sipylum in 189 B.C.E. and ended Seleucid expansion in the west. In 187 B.C.E., Antiochus fell in battle and was succeeded by his son Seleucus IV Philopator (r. 187-175 B.C.E.). His uneventful reign ended with his assassination by his minister Helio-

dorus, whose unsuccessful *coup d'état* was put down by Seleucus's brother, who succeeded him as Antiochus IV Epiphanes (r. 175-164 B.C.E.).

Antiochus IV tried to manipulate factions within the Jewish community of Palestine in order to completely dominate the region. Not content with the results of his manipulation, he brutally proscribed the practice of Judaism and erected a statue of Zeus in the temple of Jerusalem. This was a departure from the Seleucid policy of religious tolerance. Antiochus's antireligious policies sparked the Maccabean revolution in 168 B.C.E. The conflict continued for twenty-five years. The fighting led to the end of Seleucid rule in Palestine and the establishment of an independent Jewish kingdom, the Hasmonean Dynasty (c. 143-37 B.C.E.), The Books of Daniel and 1 and 2 Maccabees speak of the Jewish resistance to Antiochus.

Following the death of Antiochus IV in 164 B.C.E., the reigns of the remaining Seleucid kings were marked by bitter and almost continuous civil wars. These made it impossible for the Seleucids to maintain control over their vast territories. These began slipping from their control until by 141 B.C.E., all lands east of the Euphrates River were gone. It was not long before the Seleucids were able to control little more than Syria and Cilicia. Pompey the Great ended the Seleucid Dynasty in 64 B.C.E., when he incorporated Syria into the Roman provincial system.

Settlements and economics. A high standard of urbanization marked the Seleucid territories. Seleucus I built several cities. The most important ones he named for himself: Seleucia. One of the three Seleucias was located on the northern coast of Syria four miles (six kilometers) north of the Orontes River. Its location on the sea made it an important communications and commercial center. His successors built another city, sixteen miles (twenty-six kilometers) inland at the intersection of major land routes connecting Syria with Mesopotamia and Anatolia. This city was named Antioch in honor of Seleucus's father, and it replaced Babylon as the center of east-west trade. Antioch had a population that eventually reached 500,000 and was the political, commercial, and cultural capital of the Seleucid Dynasty. Among the other important cities founded by the Seleucids were Antioch of Pisidia, Edessa, Beroea (later Veroia), and Dura-Europus (later Salahiyeh). These became important centers for the dissemination of Hellenistic culture, which became dominant in Seleucid territories.

The Seleucid economic system was marked by centralization that led to economic exploitation of the indigenous population of its territories and the development of state monopolies to institutionalize economic control. Trade, except for royal taxes, was free. The ruthless economic exploitation that characterized Seleucid rule was an important cause of the kingdom's fall. The Macedonian elite who controlled the economy had no long-range economic development in sight. Their principal concern was for immediate profit. Merchants cooperated with the ruling elite, who were supported by an army made up of mercenaries determined to maintain the political and economic status quo.

Government. The Seleucid kingdom was the most heterogenous of all the Hellenistic kingdoms. Its size was immense and its population diverse. Throughout its history, a Greek-speaking aristocratic class of Macedonian origin dominated the Seleucid state. In Anatolia and Mesopotamia, the Seleucids ruled the local population directly, but in the Persian territories, a local nobility administered the region for them. Although their political center was in Syria, the Seleucids wanted to extend their influence westward to the Aegean but were unable to do so because of the rise of Rome and the civil wars that destabilized the Seleucid state.

ADDITIONAL RESOURCES

Grant, Michael. *Hellenistic Greeks from Alexander to Cleopatra.* London: Weidenfeld & Nicolson, 1990.

Green, Peter. *Alexander to Actium: The Historical Evolution of the Hellenistic Age.* Reprint. Berkeley: University of California Press, 1993.

Sherwin-White, Susan M., and Amélie Kuhrt. *From Samarkhand to Sardis: A New Approach to the Seleucid Empire.* Berkeley: University of California Press, 1993.

SEE ALSO: Alexander the Great; Antiochus the Great; Diadochi; Egypt, Ptolemaic and Roman; Greece, Hellenistic and Roman; Judaism; Maccabees; Macedonia; Pompey the Great; Ptolemaic Dynasty; Rome, Republican; Seleucus I.

—*Leslie J. Hoppe*

SELEUCUS I

ALSO KNOWN AS: Seleucus I Nicator
BORN: c. 356 or 354 B.C.E.; Europus, Ancient Macedonia
DIED: c. 281 B.C.E.; Lysimacheia, Thrace
RELATED CIVILIZATIONS: Hellenistic Greece, Persia, Republican Rome
MAJOR ROLE/POSITION: Military and political leader

Life. Seleucus I (suh-LEW-kuhs) was the son of Antiochus I Soter, a general of Philip II of Macedonia, father of Alexander the Great . Although he accompanied Alexander on his campaigns of conquest, Seleucus was better known as an administrator than a general.

After Alexander's death in 323 B.C.E., Seleucus became one of the Diadochi, or "successors" to the conqueror hoping to fall heir to the intact empire but settling for a share. Seleucus's share, which he fought fiercely to acquire and hold, eventually included almost all of ancient Mesopotamia, including fabled Babylon where Alexander met his death, part of Persia and, for a time, parts of Asia Minor, including Syria. Seleucus hoped to gain Macedonia, the heartland of Alexander's empire. In 281 B.C.E., taking advantage of unsettled conditions in Macedonia, he invaded Europe—only to be assassinated in neighboring Thrace. After Seleucus's death, his empire began a slow decline.

Influence. The Seleucid Dynasty (312-64 B.C.E.)

became a major factor in the spread of the Hellenistic civilization. Antioch, Seleucus's capital, was not only one of the richest cities of the ancient world but also became an early center of the Christian faith.

ADDITIONAL RESOURCES
Grainger, John D. *Seleukos Nikator: Constructing a Hellenistic Kingdom.* New York: Routledge, 1990.

Kuhrt, Amélie, and Susan M. Sherwin-White, eds. *Hellenism in the East.* Berkeley: University of California Press, 1987.

SEE ALSO: Alexander the Great; Christianity; Greece, Hellenistic and Roman; Macedonia; Persia; Philip II; Rome, Republican; Seleucid Dynasty.

—Nis Petersen

SEMONIDES

ALSO KNOWN AS: Semonides of Amargos
BORN: c. 7th century B.C.E.; Samos, Greece
DIED: c. 7th century B.C.E.; Amargos, Greece
RELATED CIVILIZATION: Archaic Greece
MAJOR ROLE/POSITION: Colonial leader, poet

Life. Semonides (seh-MON-ih-deez) is a figure so historically obscure that he can only be identified with the small island he helped settle, around the year 680 B.C.E., as a colonist from the larger imperial island of Samos. Many sources depict him as a leader of the colonizing forces. What is not obscure is a large and almost complete poem about women *Te gene ton gynaikon* (seventh century B.C.E.; *Female of the Species*, 1975), which, at 118 lines, is the longest specimen of Greek iambic poetry to have survived and the longest piece of non-hexameter Greek verse that precedes the fifth century B.C.E.

Semonides views women as a plague created by Zeus to disturb the mental tranquillity of men. He caricatures women in terms of eight animal types, among which are the continually yapping bitch, the filthy and disorderly sow, the sly and manipulative vixen, the

overly proud mare, and the thieving hedonistic ferret. Only the busy and industrious bee is worthy of praise. Semonides also categorizes lazy and insensitive women made from the earth and temperamental women made from the sea.

Influence. Ignored by polite Victorian society and discussed only by a handful of German scholars as a work without charm or wit, Semonides' poem has come down to modern times as a means for understanding gender bias in ancient Greek society. The industrious bee and "the bitch" have also remained as stereotype caricatures misused in today's world.

ADDITIONAL RESOURCES
Lloyd-Jones, Hugh. *Females of the Species: Semonides on Women.* London: Duckworth, 1975.
West, M. L. *Greek Lyric Poetry.* Oxford, England: Clarendon Press, 1993.

SEE ALSO: Alcman; Greece, Archaic; Hesiod; Mimnermus; Stesichorus.

—Irwin Halfond

SEMPRONIA

FLOURISHED: first century B.C.E.
RELATED CIVILIZATION: Late Republican Rome
MAJOR ROLE/POSITION: Participant in Catiline's conspiracy

Life. Sempronia (sehm-PROH-nee-uh) was the wife of Decimus Junius Brutus, a consul in 77 B.C.E., and the mother of Decimus Junius Brutus Albinus, one of the men who took part in the conspiracy against Julius Caesar in 44 B.C.E. The primary source of information about her is the Roman historian Sallust. In 63 B.C.E.,

after twice failing to win a consulship, Catiline organized a conspiracy to take power in Rome by killing many senators and the newly elected consuls. In describing the range of Roman society that had been drawn into Catiline's plot, Sallust mentions Sempronia as one of Catiline's companions. Sallust describes her as having committed many crimes, including fraud, perjury, and murder. She danced and played music too well for a noble woman. In addition, Sallust credits Sempronia with a voracious sexual appetite, so much so that she sought men out more often than the other way around.

Influence. Sempronia is one of many women in the late republic who rejected traditional gender roles in favor of a more exciting life of intrigue and sexual freedom. Despite the negative characteristics, Sempronia displayed intelligence, wit, and charm. Yet she chose to participate in Catiline's conspiracy against the state.

ADDITIONAL RESOURCES
Gardner, Jane F. *Women in Roman Law and Society.* Bloomington: Indiana University Press, 1991.

Kleiner, Diana E., and Susan B. Matheson, eds. *I, Claudia: Women in Ancient Rome.* New Haven, Conn.: Yale University Art Gallery, 1996.
Sallust. *"The Jugurthine War"* and *"The Conspiracy of Catiline."* Translated by S. A. Handford. Harmondsworth, England: Penguin Classics, 1963.

SEE ALSO: Caesar, Julius; Catiline; Sallust.
—*T. Davina McClain*

SENECA THE ELDER

ALSO KNOWN AS: Lucius Annaeus Seneca
BORN: c. 55 B.C.E.; Corduba (later Córdoba, Spain)
DIED: c. 39 C.E.; possibly Corduba
RELATED CIVILIZATION: Imperial Rome
MAJOR ROLE/POSITION: Businessman, rhetorician

Life. Seneca (SEHN-ih-kuh) the Elder, though born in Corduba, lived much of his life in Rome. He was a successful businessman as well as an author of textbooks on rhetoric and oratory. Two of his books have survived, though in incomplete or abridged form. One, *Controversiae* (first century B.C.E. or first century C.E.; English translation, 1900), is a collection of exercises for use in classroom debates about legal issues; the other, *Suasoriae* (first century B.C.E. or first century C.E.; *Declamations*, 1974), provides topics for students who are practicing speeches intended to persuade listeners to support a proposed action.

Seneca the Elder had three sons, all of whom held positions in government. The eldest, Gallio, was proconsul of Achaea (Greece) in 52 C.E., where he heard the charges against Saint Paul mentioned in Acts 18:12. The middle son was Lucius Annaeus Seneca (known as Seneca the Younger), the statesman, philosopher, and playwright. The youngest, Mela, was an imperial procurator and the father of the epic poet Lucan. All three sons committed suicide in 65-66 C.E.

Influence. In his books, Seneca relates anecdotes about and quotations from many of the public speakers he had heard. He is an important source of information about oratory and rhetorical education in the early imperial period.

ADDITIONAL RESOURCES
Bonner, S. F. *Education in Ancient Rome.* Berkeley: University of California Press, 1977.
Sussman, L. A. *The Elder Seneca.* Leiden, Netherlands: Brill, 1978.

SEE ALSO: Rome, Imperial; Seneca the Younger.
—*Jo-Ann Shelton*

SENECA THE YOUNGER

ALSO KNOWN AS: Lucius Annaeus Seneca
BORN: c. 4 B.C.E.; Corduba (later Córdoba, Spain)
DIED: April, 65 C.E.; Rome
RELATED CIVILIZATION: Imperial Rome
MAJOR ROLE/POSITION: Statesman, philosopher, playwright

Life. Seneca (SEHN-ih-kuh) the Younger was born into a wealthy Roman family living in the province of Spain. His father, Seneca the Elder, sent him to Rome to be educated in the best rhetorical schools in preparation for a career in Roman politics. In addition to rhetoric, Seneca studied philosophy, particularly Stoicism. His public career was punctuated by reversals of fortune that would test the fortitude of even a Stoic saint. By 37 C.E., Seneca was a renowned public speaker and had won appointments to several political positions. However in 41 C.E., the emperor Claudius was persuaded by his wife, Messallina, to send Seneca into exile. In 49 C.E., after Valeria Messallina was executed for conspiring against Claudius, his new wife, Agrippina the Younger, convinced him to recall Seneca to Rome to be tutor for her twelve-year-old son, Domitius (later called Nero).

At Claudius's death in 54 C.E., the young Domitius (Nero) became emperor and retained Seneca as a close adviser. Despite the philosopher's influence, Nero became increasingly violent. In 59 C.E., for example, he ordered the bludgeoning death of his mother. In 62 C.E.,

Seneca the Younger. (Library of Congress)

Seneca asked Nero for permission to retire from the imperial court. In 65 C.E., he was accused, perhaps wrongly, of plotting to assassinate the emperor, and he committed suicide.

Despite the demands of his public life, Seneca was a prolific writer. He is the author of essays that elucidate Stoic teachings on such topics as mercy, anger, kindness, fate, happiness, and peace of mind. Also extant is a collection of 124 letters in which he discusses ethical issues. In addition, he composed a book about natural phenomena. Seneca is traditionally considered to be the author of nine tragedies on themes from Greek mythology, such as Medea, Oedipus, and Hercules. Also attributed to him is a satire about the death of the emperor Claudius, *Apocolcyntosis divi Claudii* (c. 54 C.E.; *The Deification of Claudius*, 1614).

Influence. Seneca's philosophic writings provide the best evidence for the nature of Stoicism in Rome during the early imperial period. The tragedies ascribed to him influenced many European playwrights, including Ben Jonson, Pierre Corneille, and, more recently, Ted Hughes.

ADDITIONAL RESOURCES
Campbell, R. *Letters from a Stoic.* Harmondsworth, England: Penguin, 1969.
Griffin, M. T. *Seneca: A Philosopher in Politics.* Oxford, England: Oxford University Press, 1976.
Motto, A. L., and J. R. Clark. *Senecan Tragedy.* Amsterdam: A. M. Hakkert, 1988.
Seneca, Lucius Annaeus. *Seneca in English.* Edited by Don Share. New York: Penguin, 1998.

SEE ALSO: Agrippina the Younger; Claudius; Epictetus; Lucan; Lucilius, Gaius (poet); Marcus Aurelius; Messallina, Valeria; Nero; Rome, Imperial.

—Jo-Ann Shelton

SENNACHERIB

ALSO KNOWN AS: Sinakhkheeriba
BORN: date and place unknown
DIED: 681 B.C.E.; Nineveh, Assyria
RELATED CIVILIZATIONS: Assyria, Babylonia
MAJOR ROLE/POSITION: King

Life. As the son and successor of Sargon II, Sennacherib (suh-NAK-uh-ruhb) began ruling over a well-knit Assyrian Empire in 705 B.C.E. Two years

later, he confronted an insurrection led by Merodachbaladan, who had reestablished himself as king of Babylon. Although the insurrection leader claimed Elam, Judah, and many Chaldean and Aramean tribes as allies, in three campaigns Sennacherib took Babylon and forced Merodachbaladan into Elamite exile.

Immediately, numerous western powers once subdued by Sargon II challenged Assyria's hegemony. Their open revolt triggered an Assyrian invasion in 701

B.C.E. that wrought widespread devastation. King Hezekiah of Judah suffered the obliteration of Lachish, his second largest city, and endured confinement in Jerusalem, his capital city, until Sennacherib unexpectedly and suddenly returned home. During the remainder of his reign, Sennacherib focused on palace construction in his newly chosen capital city of Nineveh and undertook further measures to ensure Assyria's supremacy over Babylonia.

Influence. Above all, Sennacherib astutely guided his nation's internal affairs and maintained a commanding position against rebellious enemy nations. Two artifacts have kept Sennacherib's memory alive— elaborate palace depictions of the Assyrian destruction of Lachish on display in London's British Museum, and George Gordon, Lord By-

Sennacherib. (North Wind Picture Archives)

ron's engaging poem "The Destruction of Sennacherib" (1815), ruminating on the king's near conquest of Jerusalem.

ADDITIONAL RESOURCES

Coogan, Michael D., ed. *The Oxford History of the Biblical World.* New York: Oxford University Press, 1998.

Kuhrt, Amelie. *The Ancient Near East, c. 3000-330* B.C. 2 vols. London: Routledge, 1995.

Von Soden, Wolfram. *The Ancient Orient: An Introduction to the Study of the Ancient Near East.* Translated by Donald G. Schley. Grand Rapids, Mich.: Wm. B. Eerdmans, 1994.

SEE ALSO: Assyria; Babylonia; Sargon II.

—*J. Kenneth Kuntz*

SEPTUAGINT

ALSO KNOWN AS: LXX
DATE: second century B.C.E.
LOCALE: Alexandria
RELATED CIVILIZATION: Hellenistic Greece
SIGNIFICANCE: The Septuagint allowed non-Hebrew speakers, both Jews and gentiles, to read the Bible and was instrumental in the spread of early Christianity.

The Septuagint (sehp-TEW-uh-juhnt; meaning "seventy" and abbreviated as LXX) is the Greek translation of the Old Testament. According to a work known as the *Letter of Aristeas* (between 200 B.C.E. and 33 C.E.;

English translation, 1917), the name arose because Egyptian Ptolemy II Philadephus (r. 285-246 B.C.E.), eager to have a copy of the Jewish law for his library in Alexandria but finding none available, commissioned seventy-two (more easily abbreviated as seventy) scholars to produce it. However, many modern scholars believe instead that the work was actually undertaken by the Jewish community in Alexandria for use by Jews who knew Greek better than Hebrew.

Although the LXX originally consisted of just the law of Moses, in time the rest of the books of the Bible were added along with other works known today as the Apocrypha. In the past, there was much discussion about the value of the LXX as a witness to the biblical text because it often differed from then known Hebrew manuscripts. However, the discovery of the Dead Sea Scrolls has since proved the antiquity of its text.

The LXX became the earliest Bible of Christianity. It was on the basis of its text that Christians tried to prove that Jesus Christ was the Messiah. Partly because of this, the LXX fell into disfavor among Jews. Disputes between Jews and Christians also led the learned theologian Origen (185-255 C.E.) to produce a schol-

arly edition of the LXX, known as the *Hexapla*, which unfortunately has not survived.

ADDITIONAL RESOURCE

Tov, E. *Textual Criticism of the Hebrew Bible*. Minneapolis, Minn.: Fortress Press, 1992.

SEE ALSO: Bible: Jewish; Bible: New Testament; Christianity; Judaism; Origen.

—*Erik W. Larson*

SESOSTRIS III

ALSO KNOWN AS: Senwosret; Senusert
BORN: date and place unknown
DIED: 1843 B.C.E.; place unknown
RELATED CIVILIZATION: Pharaonic Egypt
MAJOR ROLE/POSITION: King

Life. The reign of Sesostris III (suh-SAHS-truhs), an Egyptian king of the Twelfth Dynasty, marks the high point of the Middle Kingdom. During his reign there was a channel cut through the First Cataract of the Nile River at Aswan to allow ships to pass the barrier even when the river was at its lowest level. Sesostris's military campaigns in Nubia extended the Egyptian border south to Semna, at the southern end of the Second Cataract, where he set up a boundary stela at the end of a series of fortresses along the river in Nubia.

At home, Sesostris III was responsible for extensive changes in the government of Egypt, probably removing some of the political power from provincial governors. He ruled for at least nineteen years and perhaps as long as thirty-seven. He built himself two tombs. These include a pyramid at Dahshur, surrounded by the tombs

of women of the royal family, in whose burials some very beautiful jewelry was found. He himself may have been buried in a tomb complex at Abydos, where his funerary cult continued to honor him for two hundred years.

Influence. Sesostris III expanded Egypt's empire, and his political reforms consolidated power in the person of the king, subjugating the provincial governors to viziers that reported directly to the king himself.

ADDITIONAL RESOURCES

Clayton, Peter A. *Chronicle of the Pharaohs*. New York: Thames and Hudson, 1994.

Lehner, Mark. *The Complete Pyramids*. New York: Thames and Hudson, 1997.

Lichtheim, Miriam. *The Old and Middle Kingdoms*. Vol. 1 in *Literature of Ancient Egypt*. Berkeley: University of California Press, 1973.

SEE ALSO: Egypt, Pharaonic; Nubia; Pyramid and Sphinx.

—*Sara E. Orel*

SETI I

BORN: late fourteenth century B.C.E.; Egypt
DIED: 1279 B.C.E.; Egypt
RELATED CIVILIZATION: Pharaonic Egypt
MAJOR ROLE/POSITION: Pharaoh

Life. Seti I (SEHT-ee) was the son of Rameses I, founder of the Egyptian Nineteenth Dynasty. Following his father's short reign, Seti became pharaoh and set the pace for this important dynasty, militarily and culturally. He restored the New Kingdom's neglected em-

pire through numerous campaigns into Syria-Palestine. Two stelae describing Seti's campaigns were found at Beth Shean in Palestine. Other campaigns were made against the Libyans.

Seti's ambitious building projects (many finished by his son) include the famous Hypostyle Hall in the Temple of Amun at Karnak. This architectural marvel featured a forest of 134 huge columns and a 75-foot-high (23-meter-high) celestory for lighting. At Abydos, Seti built two elaborate temples with extensive historical

Mummy of Seti I. (Hulton Archive)

and religious decoration. The Hall of Records there depicts Seti and his young son Rameses II paying homage to a list of pharaohs from earliest times.

Seti constructed a royal residence near his ancestral home around Avaris in the northeastern Nile Delta. His son and successor, Rameses II, expanded this palace into his new capital Pi-Ramesse, apparently built by Hebrew slaves (Exodus 1:11). For this and other reasons, Seti is often regarded as the "pharaoh of the oppression," although his name does not appear in the Exodus account.

Influence. The thirteen-year rule (1290-1279 B.C.E.) of Seti I was one of rebirth for Egypt, politically and culturally. Seti's tomb, looted in antiquity, was one of the grandest in the Valley of the Kings. His mummy, found in a royal cache in secondary burial, is the finest of the royal mummies.

ADDITIONAL RESOURCES

Clayton, P. *Chronicle of the Pharaohs.* London: Thames and Hudson, 1994.

Redford, D. *Egypt, Israel, and Canaan in Ancient Times.* Princeton, N.J.: Princeton University Press, 1992.

SEE ALSO: Egypt, Pharaonic; Libyans; Pyramids and the Sphinx; Rameses II.

—*Daniel C. Browning, Jr.*

SEVERUS, LUCIUS SEPTIMIUS

BORN: April 11, 145 C.E.; Leptis Magna, Tripolitania (later in Libya)

DIED: February 4, 211 C.E.; Eboracum, Britain (later York, England)

RELATED CIVILIZATION: Imperial Rome

MAJOR ROLE/POSITION: Emperor

Life. Lucius Septimius Severus (LEW-shee-uhs sehp-TIHM-ee-uhs suh-VIHR-uhs) moved from Africa to Rome, where he formed close friendships with the sons of Rome's most important senators. His early exposure to Punic society in Tripolitania was later masked by his education in Greek and Latin language and culture. Severus became completely Italianized and would use his political connections to rise toward prominence.

Severus's rise to power was steady. In December, 169 C.E., he became a Roman senator. Six years later, he was named tribune of the plebs and later served in Syria, the Middle East, and Africa under the proconsul

Lucius Septimius Severus. (Hulton Archive)

and future emperor Pertinax. In the 180's C.E., Severus was the governor of the principal military province on the Danube and later the governor of Gaul. However, the civil wars of the 190's C.E., initiated by the killing of Emperor Pertinax, compelled Severus to secure his interests. In 193 C.E., he marched on Rome and seized political power. By 197 C.E., he had consolidated control of the empire. He spent the next fourteen years of his life expanding Rome's overseas territories. He fought against the Parthians, gaining Mesopotamia, and against desert tribes beyond Tripolitania and the British.

Influence. Severus, the African emperor, greatly expanded Rome's eastern territories and increased the role of the military in the governance of the empire.

ADDITIONAL RESOURCE
Birley, Anthony R. *Septimius Severus: The African Emperor.* New York: Routledge, 1999.

SEE ALSO: Africa, North; Caracalla; Christianity; Julia Domna; Rome, Imperial.

—*Michael J. Siler*

SEVERUS, SULPICIUS

BORN: c. 360 C.E.; Aquitania, Gaul
DIED: c. 420 C.E.; Aquitania, Gaul
RELATED CIVILIZATION: Late Roman Gaul
MAJOR ROLE/POSITION: Monk, writer, historian

Life. A noble educated in rhetoric, Sulpicius Severus (suhl-PIHSH-ee-uhs suh-VIHR-uhs) became a lawyer and married into a senatorial family. In 393/394 C.E., after the early death of his wife, he visited Bishop Martin of Tours, who had healed the eye of his lifelong friend Saint Paulinus of Nola.

Inspired by Saint Martin's monastery at Marmoutier, Severus and Paulinus gave away their wealth and built their own monasteries on the estate Primuliacum, west of Toulouse, and at Nola, Italy, respectively, between 394 and 396 C.E. Severus, in line with some Christian chronographers, envisaged the Second Coming of Christ five hundred years after his birth, the end of the sixth millennium after Creation. His *Vita S. Martini* (c. 397 C.E.; *Life of Martin*, 1866), which includes his *Three Letters*, and his *Dialogi* (404 C.E.; "Dialogues" in *The Western Fathers*, 1954), both about Saint Martin, portray "a man filled with God" in humankind's end-

phase. A similar finality pervades his *Chronica* (c. 402-404 C.E.; *Chronicle*, 1896-1899), a world history with emphasis on the Jewish people and the Christian Church to 400 C.E. Late in life, Severus befriended the Pelagians, active in Aquitania in the 420's C.E.

Influence. With Saint Martin and Paulinus, Severus pioneered Western ascetic monasticism. With Saint Athanasius of Alexander and Saint Jerome, he originated the genre of hagiography. In modern terms, he wrote a history survey with apocalyptic urgency.

ADDITIONAL RESOURCES
Stancliffe, Clare. *St. Martin and His Hagiographer: History and Miracle in Sulpicius Severus.* New York: Oxford University Press, 1983.
Van Andel, G. K. *The Christian Concept of History in the Chronicle of Sulpicius Severus.* Amsterdam: Hakkert, 1976.

SEE ALSO: Athanasius of Alexander, Saint; Christianity; Gauls; Jerome, Saint.

—*Reinhold Schumann*

SHABAKA

ALSO KNOWN AS: Sabacon; Shabaqo
BORN: date and place unknown.
DIED: 702 or 698 B.C.E.; place unknown
RELATED CIVILIZATIONS: Kush, Nubia
MAJOR ROLE/POSITION: Pharaoh

Life. Shabaka (SHAB-uh-kuh) and his older brother Piye were princes of African Kush who founded the Twenty-fifth Dynasty of Egypt. Their father, Kashta, the king of Kush, had governed Nubia, the southernmost part of the Nile Valley civilization, at a time when the

Egyptian state was fragmenting. Along with its internal struggles, Egypt was further preoccupied with the growing menace of Assyria and its military threats against Syria and Palestine. Taking advantage of Egypt's situation, Kashta started sending occasional military probes northward. After their father's death, Piye and Shabaka turned these expeditions into outright conquests. Defeating a coalition of petty rulers in a series of battles, Piye subjugated most of Upper Egypt. Proclaiming himself pharaoh, he revived and assumed all the traditional titles, including "He who unites the two lands." However, Piye left the delta region (Lower Egypt) independent and passed much of his reign (c. 742-c. 716 B.C.E.) in the city of Napata in Kush.

Shabaka, Piye's younger brother and virtual partner, ascended the throne circa 716 B.C.E. and immediately set out to be an even more vigorous ruler. He moved the capital north to the ancient Egyptian city of Thebes. His inauguration was deliberately structured after those of the ancient pharaohs, paying honor to the traditional gods and reviving old ceremonies. Shortly thereafter, through a combination of military force and diplomacy, Shabaka annexed the delta region, eastern Libya, and the Sinai. As a result, the Kushite regime held sway over more of the Nile Valley than any government since the Old Dynasty millennium.

Having reunited the Nile Valley, Shabaka sought to intensify his program of reviving traditional culture. He funded research in historical texts, seeking to authenticate his religious, ceremonial, and architectural reforms. Artistic forms drew inspiration from older Egyptian forms as well as Kushite models. An energetic builder, Shabaka enlarged religious complexes at Memphis, Thebes, Luxor, Abydos, and Karnak. Such policies all served to emphasize his conviction that Egypt and Kush were a single civilization and had been since the dawn of history.

Focused primarily on consolidating his power in the Nile, Shabaka's foreign policy concentrated on containing the rising power of an increasingly aggressive Assyria by supporting buffer states in Palestine. He apparently supported a Philistine revolt against Sargon II but then turned conciliatory when Assyrian forces captured the city of Ashdod.

However, around 704 B.C.E., when Hezekiah of Judah defied the Assyrian Sennacherib, he and his allies clearly expected Shabaka's intervention. In 701 B.C.E., Egyptian-Kushite forces checked the Assyrians at Eltekeh, thereby forestalling the Assyrian conquest of the Middle East for several decades.

Influence. Pharaoh Shabaka successfully reunified the Nile Valley civilization after years of separation and made his society a world power again.

ADDITIONAL RESOURCES

Grimal, Nicolas. *A History of Ancient Egypt.* Translated by Ian Shaw. New York: Barnes & Noble, 1997.

Redford, D. B. *Egypt, Canaan, and Israel in Ancient Times.* Princeton, N.J.: Princeton University Press, 1992.

Snowden, F. M., Jr. *Before Color Prejudice: The Ancient View of Blacks.* Cambridge, Mass.: Harvard University Press, 1983.

Welsby, D. A. *The Kingdom of Kush.* Princeton, N.J.: Markus Wiener, 1998.

SEE ALSO: Assyria; Egypt, Pharaonic; Hezekiah; Nubia; Sargon II; Sennacherib.

—Weston F. Cook, Jr.

SHANG DYNASTY

ALSO KNOWN AS: Yin Dynasty
DATE: c. 1600-1066 B.C.E.
LOCALE: Eastern and northeastern Henan Province, China
RELATED CIVILIZATION: China
SIGNIFICANCE: One of the earliest Chinese dynasties, Shang saw the development of a written language and the use of bronze metallurgy.

Archaeological evidence suggests that the Shang Dynasty, also known as the Yin Dynasty in its later stages, was formed in the eastern and northeastern region of Henan Province. It was a dynasty consisting of a series of towns united under the Shang king, a rebel leader who overthrew the last ruler of the Xia Dynasty (c. 2100-1600 B.C.E.).

The Shang civilization was based on agriculture, supplemented by hunting and animal husbandry. Two important events of the period were the development of a writing system and the use of bronze metallurgy. The earliest known examples of written Chinese are found on Shang period oracle bones, tortoise shells, and flat

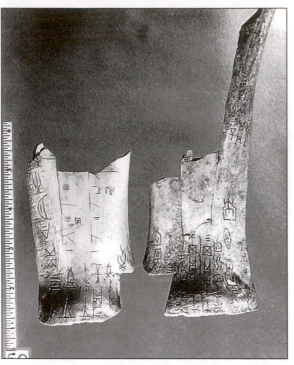

Oracle bones from the Shang Dynasty. (Time and Life)

cattle bones bearing inscriptions. During this period, bronze vessels displaying a fine workmanship and a high level of civilization were placed in royal tombs to accompany nobles in the afterlife. The Shang held their royal ancestors in high regard, honoring sacred ancestors with highly developed court rituals. Tablets bearing the ancestors' names were kept in the front of temples, and every royal event was announced aloud in the temples to inform the ancestors. These tablets were thought to contain the souls of the ancestors. A line of hereditary Shang kings ruled over much of northern China.

ADDITIONAL RESOURCES

Chang, Kwang-Chih. *Shang Civilization*. New Haven, Conn.: Yale University Press, 1980.

Keightley, David. *The Ancestral Landscape: Time, Space, and Community in Late Shang China, ca. 1200-1045* B.C. Berkeley, Calif.: Institute of Asian Studies, 2000.

SEE ALSO: China; Xia Dynasty.

—*Hong Xiao*

SHANG YANG

BORN: date and place unknown
DIED: c. 337 B.C.E.; China
RELATED CIVILIZATION: China
MAJOR ROLE/POSITION: Military leader, noble, writer

Life. Shang Yang of Wei led a Qin army to victory over Wei in 342 B.C.E. and was rewarded with the fief of Shang in 341 B.C.E., which gave him the title Lord Shang. Later legend has him executed, like Legalist Han Fei, by the ungrateful Qin. A body of Legalist writings, the *Shangjun shu* (also known as *Shangzi*; compiled 359-338 B.C.E.; *The Book of Lord Shang*, 1928) purporting to be Shang Yang's policies for strengthening Qin later circulated under his name. Scholar J. J. L. Duyvendak has noted their stylistic inconsistency. Later research has found within a military chapter of the work a possibly original core treatise on the civil basis of military success; other chapters are later. Chapter 13 is abridged in Chapter 53 of the *Han Feizi* (*The Complete Works of Han Fei Tzu: A Classic of Chinese Legalism*, 1939-1959, 2 vols.; commonly known as *Han*

Feizi), and the "Lord Shang" text probably took shape in what would become the Han Dynasty alongside the *Han Feizi*.

Influence. Shang Yang's position as a victim of Qin made him, like Han Fei, a viable name under which Han period Legalists, who could not openly recommend Qin policies, could shelter. Features of the Legalism that bore Shang Yang's name include an emphasis on agriculture and war, rewards and punishments, and weakening the people to strengthen the government.

ADDITIONAL RESOURCES

Duyvendak, J. J. L. *The Book of Lord Shang*. London: Probsthain, 1928.

Li, Yu-ning. *Shang Yang's Reforms and State Control in China*. White Plains, N.Y.: M. E. Sharpe, 1977.

Liu, Yongping. *Origins of Chinese Law*. New York: Oxford University Press, 1998.

SEE ALSO: China; Han Dynasty; *Han Feizi*; Legalism; Qin Dynasty.

—*E. Bruce Brooks*

SHĀPŪR I

ALSO KNOWN AS: Sapor I; Sābūr I
BORN: date and place unknown
DIED: 272 C.E.; place unknown
RELATED CIVILIZATIONS: Sāsānian Empire, Persia
MAJOR ROLE/POSITION: Political and military
   leader

Life. Shāpūr I (shah-PEWR), son of the founder of the Sāsānian Dynasty, ruled with his father Ardashīr I 240-242 C.E., then ruled in his own name 243-272 C.E. The early Sāsānian rulers sought to expand the territory under their control. Shāpūr I fought several campaigns against the Eastern Roman Empire in Syria, Mesopotamia, and Anatolia. Shāpūr I devastated the Roman cities of Dura Europus and Antioch in 256 C.E. and captured Roman emperor Valerian in 260 C.E., who died in Sāsānian captivity.

Shāpūr I deported captive Roman craftspeople to Sāsānian territory and used them to construct monumental cities in southern Persia. He thus began a long tradition of using foreigners to construct urban culture in the Sāsānian Empire. In 262 C.E., Shāpūr seized control of the independent kingdom of Armenia and appointed his own son as king. In addition to craftspeople, Shāpūr I imported scientific learning from the Roman Empire. Though Shāpūr remained attached to Zoroastrianism, he was tolerant of both Manichaeanism and Christianity.

Influence. Though not a conscious goal, Shāpūr I was responsible for the early spread of Christianity throughout the Sāsānian Empire because of his large-scale deportations of Roman craftspeople, many of whom were Christian.

ADDITIONAL RESOURCES

Strauss, Barry. "Rome's Persian Mirage." *Military History Quarterly* 12:1 (1999): 18-27.

Yarshater, Ehsan, ed. *The Seleucid, Parthian, and Sasanian Periods.* Vol. 3 in *The Cambridge History of Iran.* Cambridge, England: Cambridge University Press, 1983.

SEE ALSO: Ardashīr I; Armenia; Christianity; Manichaeanism; Narses (Sāsānian emperor); Persia; Rome, Imperial; Sāsānian Empire; Shāpūr II; Valerian; Zoroastrianism.

—*Victoria Erhart*

SHĀPŪR II

ALSO KNOWN AS: Sapor II
BORN: 309 C.E.; place unknown
DIED: 379 C.E.; place unknown
RELATED CIVILIZATIONS: Sāsānian Empire, Persia
MAJOR ROLE/POSITION: Political and military
   leader

Life. Shāpūr II (shah-PEWR) ruled 309-379 C.E., the longest reign of any Sāsānian ruler. He was named shah the day he was born. He greatly expanded Sāsānian power and territory. Shāpūr II gradually centralized power in the office of the ruler, forcing both the aristocratic and the priestly classes to give up some claims to authority. He expanded Sāsānian control into the Arabian peninsula, rebuilt the ancient Persian city of Susa, and founded the city of Nishapur, a city built using deported Roman craftspeople.

He expanded Sāsānian control against the Hunnic tribes on the eastern Persian frontier and fought numerous battles against the Romans to the west. Emperor Julian invaded Sāsānian territory in 363 C.E., but Shāpūr II defeated him. The Eastern Roman Empire was forced to give up vast stretches of territory east of the Tigris River. Shāpūr II also conquered large portions of Armenia. Wealth from conquered territories permitted Shāpūr II to construct extensive defensive fortifications along the Syrian and Mesopotamian frontiers.

Influence. Shāpūr II expanded Sāsānian power and territory and centralized power in the hands of the shah. He made Zoroastrianism the official religion of the Sāsānian Empire and was the first shah to initiate systematic and widespread persecutions of other religions in his territory.

ADDITIONAL RESOURCES

Strauss, Barry. "Rome's Persian Mirage." *Military History Quarterly* 12, no.1 (1999): 18-27.

Yarshater, Ehsan, ed. *The Seleucid, Parthian, and Sasanian Periods*. Vol. 3 in *The Cambridge History of Iran*. Cambridge, England: Cambridge University Press, 1983.

SEE ALSO: Arabia; Armenia; Huns; Persia; Rome, Imperial; Sāsānian Empire; Shāpūr I; Zoroastrianism.
—*Victoria Erhart*

SHEBA, QUEEN OF

ALSO KNOWN AS: Saba'; Bilqīs; Makeda
FLOURISHED: tenth century B.C.E.
LOCALE: Yemen and Eritrea
RELATED CIVILIZATIONS: Ethiopia (Abyssinia), Israel, Egypt, Assyria, Persia
SIGNIFICANCE: Celebrated for visiting King Solomon, the Queen of Sheba symbolizes ancient trading ties along the Red Sea and the deserts of Arabia before Islam.

The Queen of Sheba meets King Solomon. (North Wind Picture Archives)

Life. The tradition of the Queen of Sheba spans a long period of time. In both Jewish and Islamic history, the Queen of Sheba ruled the kingdom of Saba' in southwestern Arabia. In the Bible, Genesis, Psalms, Job, and the books of the prophets, Isaiah, Jeremiah, Ezekiel, and Joel, all mention the kingdom of Sheba, which was probably in Yemen, with its capital at Marib. In 1 Kings 10:1-13 and 2 Chronicles 9:1-12, the Queen of Sheba visits King Solomon to test his wisdom, arriving at the head of a camel caravan bearing gold, jewels, and spices—suggesting trade between ancient Israel and Arabia. She converts to Solomon's faith. In the New Testament, she is the Queen of the South (Matthew 12:42 and Luke 11:31). She is Bilqīs in the Islamic tradition, the subject of many legends. In the Qur'ān, she appears in two Suras: al Naml (the ant) 27 and Saba' (Sheba) 34. During Solomon's rule in Israel (c. 900 B.C.E.), his navy ensured southern trade through the Red Sea. The name Sheba is Hebrew for the Arabic name Saba'.

Across the narrow Red Sea in Africa, the Queen of Sheba appears in Ethiopia as Makeda. In this version, she leaves her capital at Axum to travel north to Jerusalem, where she conceives King Solomon's son, Menelik I, who founded the royal dynasty of Ethiopia. Born after Makeda's return to Africa, Menelik's descendants ruled Ethiopia as the Lions of Judah.

Whether she was from Yemen or Ethiopia, both countries were widely known as sources of frankincense, myrrh, and gold. In Yemen, high mountains shielded Marib, where a great dam irrigated crops, and merchants transported goods through the kingdom of Saba'. Carvings depicting trade expeditions of the Egyptian pharaoh Hatshepsut (r. c. 1502-1482 B.C.E.) to the south, Assyrian records (c. 700 B.C.E.), and later Babylonian and Persian records all attest extensive foreign trade with South Arabia and East Africa and to their rule by queens.

Later writers supplied detailed information about the southern Red Sea. The *Periplus Maris Erythraei* (also known as *Periplus*, first century C.E.; *Periplus of the Erythraean Sea*, 1980) was a guide for shipping by an anonymous Greek ship captain. Pliny the Elder wrote about the area in 60 C.E. King Ezana converted to Christianity in 350 C.E., linking Ethiopia with the Byzantine Empire against the Sāsānian Persians. After the prophet Muḥammad's death (632 C.E.), the Persian governor of Yemen converted to Islam, cutting off international trade and causing the region to be neglected by the rest of the world.

Influence. Archaeological and historical records clarify the interaction of people in the southern Red Sea as one of shared history and ideas. References to the Queen of Sheba are among these shared aspects of history; the names Bilqīs and Makeda indicate a type of ruler who appears frequently. The stories in the Old Testament and in the Qurʾān depicting the Queen of Sheba as a clever and rich woman probably indicate that more than one wise and wealthy queen ruled Yemen and Ethiopia.

ADDITIONAL RESOURCES
Clapp, Nicholas. *Sheba: The Quest for the Legendary Queen.* Boston: Houghton Mifflin, 2001.
Daum, Werner, ed. *Yemen: Three Thousand Years of Art and Civilization in Arabia Felix.* New Haven, Conn.: Yale University Press, 1988.
François, Jean François. *Arabia Felix from the Time of the Queen of Sheba: Eighth Century B.C. to First Century A.D.* Notre Dame, Ind.: University of Notre Dame Press, 2000.
Heldman, Marilyn, and Stuart Munro-Hay. *African Zion: The Sacred Art of Ethiopia.* New Haven, Conn.: Yale University Press, 1993.
Lassner, Jacob. *Demonizing the Queen of Sheba: Boundaries of Gender and Culture in Postbiblical Judaism and Medieval Islam.* Chicago: University of Chicago Press, 1993.

SEE ALSO: Africa, East and South; Arabia; Assyria; Bible: Jewish; Bible: New Testament; Egypt, Prepharaonic; Ethiopia; Ezana; Hatshepsut; Islam; Israel; Muḥammad; Persia; Pliny the Elder; Qurʾān; Solomon.

—*Lealan N. Swanson*

SHI HUANGDI

ALSO KNOWN AS: *Wade-Giles* Shih Huang-ti; Qin Shi Huangdi
BORN: 259 B.C.E.; Qin, northwestern China
DIED: 210 B.C.E.; China
RELATED CIVILIZATIONS: China, Qin Dynasty
MAJOR ROLE/POSITION: Emperor

Life. Shi Huangdi (SHEE HEWAHNG-dee), born Zheng (*Wade-Giles* Cheng), became king of the northwestern Chinese province of Qin in 247 B.C.E., when China was enduring a time of anarchy known as the Warring States period. However, beginning in 230 B.C.E., Zheng gradually brought most of the country under his rule, earning himself the nickname "the Tiger of Qin." By 221 B.C.E., for perhaps the first time ever, most of China was unified under one government. Zheng gave himself a new, more exalted title: Shi Huangdi ("first emperor"; all later Chinese rulers would bear the title "Huang"). While on the throne, Shi Huangdi established China's imperial bureaucracy, built the first Great Wall, and imposed a uniform system of writing.

At his death, he was buried with an army of seven thousand life-size terra-cotta figures.

Influence. Though the Qin Dynasty was short-lived, Shi Huangdi had a major impact on history through his establishment of a unified, imperial China, which would continue in various forms until 1911 C.E.

ADDITIONAL RESOURCES
Brooman, Josh. *Imperial China.* Harlow, England: Longman, 1991.
Cottrell, L. *The Tiger of Ch'in.* New York: Holt, Rinehart and Winston, 1962.
Twitchett, Denis, and Michael Loewe, eds. *The Ch'in and Han Empires.* Vol. 1 in *The Cambridge History of China.* Cambridge, England: Cambridge University Press, 1986.

SEE ALSO: China; Great Wall of China; Han Dynasty; Qin Dynasty; Qin tomb.

—*Stefan G. Chrissanthos*

SHINTŌ

DATE: c. 7500 B.C.E.-700 C.E.
LOCALE: The Japanese archipelago
RELATED CIVILIZATION: Japan
SIGNIFICANCE: Shintō was the original religion of the people of Japan.

Although Shintō (SHIHN-toh) is generally regarded as the original religion of the Japanese people, scholars do not agree as to when Shintō became part of the Japanese culture. Some scholars believe that Shintō, written with the Chinese characters "shen," which means spiritual power, and "tao," which means way, grew from the animistic religion of the Jōmon people who lived in Japan for thousands of years after 7500 B.C.E. Other scholars believe that elements of Shintō entered Japan when northern Mongoloid people, probably from Korea, invaded Japan after 1000 B.C.E. These scholars believe that the Shintō religion is a derivative of Korean shamanism.

Whatever its origin, the multitheistic Shintō religion was practiced by the ancient people of Japan. For them the gods, known as *kami*, were forces of nature. The spirits of the *kami* were found in rocks, mountains, lakes, and other natural things. *Kami* also controlled such processes as creativity, healing, and growth. The most important *kami* for the ancient people were the creation *kami*. Every Japanese clan had its personal *kami* and its own creation story. The creation story of one clan, the Yamato, eventually became the creation story for all of Japan.

Kami were very important to the ancient farmers. Agriculture was very difficult, and the farmers needed good growing conditions and good luck to succeed. They believed that their *kami* would help them, so there were frequent ceremonies and offerings to the *kami* who controlled wind and rain.

When the ancient people thought they had discovered the dwelling place of a god spirit, they would make a pile of stones and encircle it with a ring of stones. This area became a shrine to the god who lived there. Because the area was special, ordinary people were not allowed to enter it except during ceremonial times. Priests were responsible for mediating between the spirit world and the human world.

In the third and fourth centuries C.E., during the reign of the Yamato clan, the emperor of Japan was recognized as a living *kami*. His divinity was said to be greater than that of any other *kami*. Therefore, it was de-

termined that the emperor should have a permanent shrine, not just a pile of stones. The Shrine of Ise was built as a Shintō shrine to the emperor. At Ise, the Inner Shrine was devoted to the Sun goddess Amaterasu Ōmikami. In the Japanese creation story, Amaterasu was the mother of Prince Niniji, the grandfather of Jimmu, the first emperor of Japan.

At Ise, the ancient emperors of Japan conducted ceremonies to celebrate the *kami*. One of the most famous ceremonies was the Niiname Festival (first fruit festival) in which the emperor offered foods to the *kami* and shared a meal with them. At Ise Shrine, the doctrines of Shintō were systematized and disseminated. Certain objects sacred to the imperial family, such as the mirror (*yato no nagami*) that Amaterasu had passed on to her earthly children and a stone necklace (*yasaki no magatama*), symbol of the emperors, were stored there. Eventually the imperial code (*ritsuryō*) decreed that only the imperial family could worship at Ise. Ise became the center for imperial rites.

Ise Shrine was constructed very simply of wood so that it would be congruent with its natural setting. Every twenty years, it was totally reconstructed to correspond to the timetable of the natural cycle of renewal. The construction of the shrine at Ise affected the way that Shintō was practiced throughout Japan. Instead of using rock piles for shrines, the Japanese began to put up simple shrines made of raw cedar and cypress like the one at Ise. These shrines were also rebuilt every twenty years.

AMATERASU ŌMIKAMI

Amaterasu Ōmikami, the sun goddess, of the Shintō faith, was born from her father's left eye. When treated badly by her brother, the storm god Susanoo, she hid in a cave, bringing darkness to the world. The other gods determined to lure her out. They assembled many roosters and placed a mirror and jewels on a tree in front of the cave. Then, the goddess Amenouzume began to dance merrily to loud music, causing the other gods to laugh. Intrigued by the laughter and music, Amaterasu looked out. She was so taken by her bright reflection in the mirror that she left the cave. The other gods threw down a sacred rope made of rice straw to prevent her from returning to the cave, and light was restored to the world.

Around 552 C.E., Buddhism entered Japan from Korea. The followers of Shintō accepted Buddhism and embraced its gods as *kami*. Buddhist images appeared in shrines. As Shintō had no philosophy about an afterlife, the two religions could easily coexist.

After 700 C.E. In the late nineteenth century, the Shintō religion became associated with patriotism in Japan. The state Shintō religion emphasized the Japanese people's supremacy because of the divine origins of the Japanese emperor. After Japan's defeat in World War II, state Shintōism was abolished, and the emperor was no longer regarded as a god. The Shintō religion, however, continued to coexist alongside Buddhism.

ADDITIONAL RESOURCES

Bocking, Brian. *A Popular Dictionary of Shinto*. Chicago: NTC Publishing Group, 1997.

Ono, Sokyo. *Shinto: The Kami Way*. Osaka: Charles E. Tuttle, 1994.

Reader, Ian. *Simple Guide to Shinto: The Religion of Japan*. Kent, England: Folkestone, 1998.

SEE ALSO: Buddhism; Japan; Jimmu Tennō; Korea; Yamato court.

—*Annita Marie Ward*

SHŌTOKU TAISHI

ALSO KNOWN AS: Umayado no Miko (Prince Umayado)
BORN: 574 C.E.; Yamato, Japan
DIED: 622 C.E.; Yamato, Japan
RELATED CIVILIZATIONS: Japan, Korea, China
MAJOR ROLE/POSITION: Regent, crown prince

Life. In line for the throne at the death of Emperor Sushun in 592 C.E., Shōtoku Taishi (shoh-toh-kaw tah-EE-shee) deferred to his aunt, the wife of former ruler Bidatsu (572-585 C.E.), who became Empress Suiko. She appointed him regent and crown prince (593-622 C.E.).

Shōtoku Taishi was a devout Buddhist with a real understanding of Buddhist philosophy. Under his patronage, Buddhism was assured the favor of the Yamato nobility. Splendid temples were erected at government expense and richly endowed with lands. Impressive Buddhist ceremonies were woven into court ritual, and noble families were encouraged to direct their resources to the patronage of family temples. Buddhism as a religion and as a cultural force became an integral part of aristocratic life. It was a major carrier of Chinese civilization to Japan and opened the floodgates to further borrowings.

Shōtoku Taishi was well versed in the elements of Chinese civilization and was determined to transplant the Chinese political system to Japan as rapidly as the country could absorb it. He had tried to reestablish the Japanese position in Korea in 597 and 602 C.E. but failed. The new Chinese Sui Dynasty had also unsuccessfully tried to invade Korea and bring it to submission.

Shōtoku Taishi sent missions to China in 604, 606, and 614 C.E. to strengthen the Yamato position in Japan. Over the next two centuries, the policy of sending missions to China continued. Thirteen more official and innumerable private missions were sent to China between 630 and 838 C.E. to train young Japanese aristocrats on ways of governing and to develop their artistic skills and spiritual acumen.

The missions to China had an important impact on Japan. The Japanese applied the knowledge of political theory and practice acquired in China to the organization of a central government and a well-defined administrative system in their own country. Moreover, it was obvious to Shōtoku Taishi that the monks, scholars, artisans, and craftspeople, who were making their way to Japan from the Asian mainland in increasing numbers, represented a kind of civilization far in advance of anything hitherto known in Japan. They could teach principles of government that would be of great advantage to any statesman aspiring to sovereign power.

Shōtoku Taishi is credited with many other notable achievements, such as the issuance of the *Jūshichijō Kempō* (604 C.E.; *Prince Shotoku and His Seventeen-Article Constitution*, 1940), which synthesized Confucian and Buddhist concepts and also established Confucian ethical principles and Chinese centralized political institutions as the ideal in government. However, in the midst of studies on interests from abroad that would further affect Japan, Shōtoku Taishi died.

Influence. Shōtoku Taishi is viewed as the noble who established the ideal of Chinese centralized rule and laid the foundation for its achievement.

ADDITIONAL RESOURCES

Hall, John W. *Japan: From Prehistory to Modern Times.* Ann Arbor: University of Michigan Press, 1991.

Sansom, George B. *Japan: A Short Cultural History.* Stanford, Calif.: Stanford University Press, 1952.

SEE ALSO: Buddhism; China; Confucianism; Japan; Korea; Yamato court.

—*Edwin L. Neville, Jr.*

SHULGI

BORN: late twenty-second century B.C.E.; Iraq
DIED: 2047 B.C.E.; Iraq
RELATED CIVILIZATIONS: Iraq, Ur, Neo-Sumeria
MAJOR ROLE/POSITION: King

Life. Shulgi (SHOOL-gee; r. c. 2094-c. 2047 B.C.E.), the son of Ur-Namma, came to the throne of the Third Ur Dynasty rather young upon his father's death in battle. He focused on domestic politics in the first part of his reign, constructing and furnishing temples. In the middle of his reign, he installed one daughter as high priestess in Ur and arranged dynastic marriages for others. He also established a standing army and deified himself.

In the latter part of his reign, Shulgi campaigned repeatedly and expanded the state to its maximum, from Mesopotamia to western Iran. He built defensive walls and devised an intricate tax system that incorporated the newly acquired peripheral areas into the state economy. He instituted a statewide calendar and reformed systems of writing and measurement.

Shulgi supervised governors with generals selected mostly from royal families. The state chancellor, the king's right-hand man, helped to supervise vassal states.

Shulgi's dynasty flourished economically and culturally, and many Sumerian compositions originated in his reign. Hymns praised him as a divine king and multitalented sage who mastered the scribal arts.

Influence. Shulgi brought the Third Ur Dynasty to its apex and had a long-lasting influence on Mesopotamian literature and political ideology.

ADDITIONAL RESOURCES

Klein, Jacob. "Shulgi of Ur: King of Neo-Sumerian Empire." In vol. 3 of *Civilizations of the Ancient Near East,* edited by Jack M. Sasson et al. New York: Charles Scribner's Sons, 1995.

Kuhrt, Amélie. *The Ancient Near East, c. 3000-330* B.C. 2 vols. London: Routledge, 1995.

SEE ALSO: Sumerians; Ur-Namma.

—*Atsuko Hattori*

SIBYLLINE BOOKS

AUTHORSHIP: Compiled by Marcus Terentius Varro (116-27 B.C.E.)
DATE: composed c. 525 B.C.E.
LOCALE: Possibly Rome
RELATED CIVILIZATIONS: Republican and Imperial Rome
SIGNIFICANCE: Developed as a means of state divination, the Sibylline Books also served to effect senatorial policies via collective religious responses to critical situations.

The prophetesses known as the Sibyls originated in Asia Minor during the seventh century B.C.E. and spread throughout the Mediterranean world. Marcus Terentius Varro in *Antiquitates rerum humanarum et divinarum* (47 B.C.E., lost book; antiquities of human and divine things) names all sorts of Sibyls: Persian,

Libyan, Delphic, Cimmerian, Erythraean, Samian, Cumaean, Hellespontic, Phrygian, and Tiburtine. They could be consulted on a private or public basis, and collections of their responses were compiled and circulated. One of these collections reached Rome toward the end of the sixth century B.C.E., where it received official approval and came to be known as the *Libri Sibillini,* or Sibylline (SIH-buh-leen) Books.

Dionysius of Halicarnassus (30-8 B.C.E.) relays the legend of the books' advent: A foreign woman tried to sell the king Lucius Tarquinius Superbus nine books of Sibylline oracles. When he refused to buy them, she continually burned three books until only three remained. At his advisers' urging, Tarquinus purchased the remaining books, and they were kept in a stone chest beneath the temple of Jupiter on the Capitoline hill until the Social War of 91-87 B.C.E. They perished in the fire that destroyed the temple in 83 B.C.E. and were replaced with oracles gathered from other places. According to Dionysius, these oracles were the Romans' most guarded possession, sacred or profane, and the senate decreed that they could be consulted only during times of strife.

Unlike the Greeks, who allowed private persons as well as public officials to consult their oracles, the Romans restricted their use to state officials. Not even the priests in charge of the books could consult them without senate approval. As part of his religious reform, Augustus ordered a revision of the oracles and had them transferred to the temple of Apollo on the Palatine hill, but by then their days of influence had largely passed. Although interest in them revived under the emperors Lucius Domitius Aurelianus and Julian the Apostate, the Sibylline Books were reportedly burned during the reign of Honorius by order of his general Flavius Stilicho.

Scholars have traditionally credited the Sibylline Books with the progressive introduction into Rome of Greek and Eastern rites and deities, including Demeter (Roman Ceres), Dionysius (Liber), Kore (Libera), and Cybele, and the *lectisternium* (public offering of food to the gods), the *supplicatio* (thanksgiving in honor of the gods), and the *ver sacrum* ("sacred spring," a sacrifice of all fruits and animals produced in a particular spring). It is also possible that the Roman senate used the Sibylline Books to promote Greek cults and practices and thus to strengthen ties with Greek-speaking southern Italy and Sicily. Thus, the Sibylline Books were often a diplomatic tool rather than a vehicle to import foreign religious customs.

ADDITIONAL RESOURCES

Orlin, Eric M. *Temples, Religion, and Politics in the Roman Republic*. New York: E. J. Brill, 1997.

Parke, H. W. *Sibyls and Sibylline Prophecy in Classical Antiquity.* London: Oxford University Press, 1988.

Potter, D. S. *Prophets and Emperors: Human and Divine Authority from Augustus to Theodosius.* Cambridge, Mass.: Harvard University Press, 1994.

SEE ALSO: Augustus; Aurelianus, Lucius Domitius; Julian the Apostate; Religion and ritual; Rome, Imperial; Rome, Republican; Social War; Stilicho, Flavius; Varro, Marcus Terentius.

—Thomas J. Sienkewicz

SIDONIUS APOLLINARIS

ALSO KNOWN AS: Gaius Sollius Apollinaris Sidonius
BORN: 430 C.E.; Lugdunum (later Lyons, France)
DIED: c. 487 C.E.; Clermont
RELATED CIVILIZATIONS: Gaul, Imperial Rome
MAJOR ROLE/POSITION: Bishop, senatorial officeholder, man of letters

Life. A Christian and the son of a Gallic landowning family, Sidonius Apollinaris (si-DOH-nee-uhs uh-pahl-uh-NAR-uhs) enjoyed a classical Roman education in rhetoric and Roman tradition, preparing him for a public career. In 451 C.E., he married Papianilla, daughter of Eparchius Avitus. He entered imperial service in 455 C.E., when Avitus became the Western Augustus. His ability to use Latin panegyric to praise and publicize the Roman virtues of the emperor led to his reconciliation with Majorian in 458 C.E. and to the office of prefect of the city of Rome in 467 C.E. under Anthemius. Then in 469 C.E., the affairs of Gaul drew him home, and he was consecrated bishop of Clermont.

Romanized Clermont was caught up in the rivalries of the Burgundians and the expanding Ostrogoths. Sidonius worked for independence from both, and eventually he developed a working relationship with the Gothic court. He published nine books of his letters and twenty-four poems.

Influence. Sidonius's poetry and letters are not great literature. They are typical rhetorical creations lacking originality and filled with stilted language and obscure phrases. They provide insight on the lives of the Gallic aristocracy and show how Sidonius used the Church as the vehicle to preserve the virtues of Roman tradition.

ADDITIONAL RESOURCES

Drinkwater, J., and H. Elton, eds. *Fifth Century Gaul: A Crisis of Identity?* New York: Cambridge University Press, 1992.

Harries, J. *Sidonius Apollinaris and the Fall of Rome.* Oxford, England: Clarendon Press, 1994.

SEE ALSO: Avitus, Eparchius; Gauls; Goths, Ostrogoths, Visigoths; Rome, Imperial.

—Ronald J. Weber

SILK ROAD

DATE: traditionally opened in second century B.C.E., possibly in use as early as 2000 B.C.E.

LOCALE: From Ch'angan (later Xi'an, Shaanxi) in central China west to the Black Sea on the Northern route; west to Persia (later Iran), Mediterranean Sea, and Rome on the Central route; west to Afghanistan, Persia, and Northern India on the Southern route

RELATED CIVILIZATIONS: Han Dynasty, Tang Dynasty, Central Asia, Persia, Parthia, Syria, India, Imperial Rome

SIGNIFICANCE: This trade route reached from China into Central Asia, the Near East, and Europe. It facilitated the trade of numerous goods and an exchange of culture, including religion.

The Silk Road was the main caravan route from China to Europe, bringing horses, wools, silver, and gold to China in exchange for silk and other goods. Buddhism and Christianity also traveled over the road to China. The route, more than 7,000 miles (11,260 kilometers), had a number of branches, and people rarely traveled the whole distance. Trade was usually conducted by middlemen, including Northern Indians and Parthians.

In 138 B.C.E., Emperor Wudi of the Han Dynasty (206 B.C.E.-220 C.E.) sent General Zhang Qian and his one-hundred-man caravan from the capital city of Ch'angan to make contact with the Yuezhi and other desert tribes of Central Asia and to forge an alliance against the Xiongnu, who were raiding China. Although the Chinese general was captured by the Xiongnu and held for ten years, he continued through Kashi (Kashgar) and Fergana, eventually reaching the Yuezhi in Central Asia. He returned using what became the Southern route and was captured by a Tibetan group. He returned to Ch'angan thirteen years after he left. Intrigued by Zhang's reports of various kingdoms and powerful horses, Emperor Wudi sent additional missions to forge alliances, creating the Silk Road.

The Romans reportedly came into contact with silk in 53 B.C.E., when the Parthians waved banners of the shimmering material during a battle. The Parthians became middlemen in the trade of silk between the Romans and Chinese, venturing to Dunhuang and Loulan in the desert, and carrying the fabric to Persian, Syrian, and Greek traders. Other items included furs, ceramics, and cinnamon. In return, the Chinese received precious stones and metals such as jade, gold, and silver as well as ivory and coral. The oasis towns of the Taklamakan Desert through which the caravans passed became wealthy as a result of the trade.

The Silk Road was also a medium for the exchange of ideas, including Buddhism. A Han Dynasty emperor sent envoys to India to learn about the religion and bring it back to China. Along with the religion came paintings and sculpture. Monasteries and large Buddhist cave complexes were built in and near the desert oasis towns on the Silk Road. In c. 399 C.E., the first Chinese pilgrim, Faxian (337?-422? C.E.), traveled through Dunhuang and Khotan and crossed over the Himalayas to India, where he studied Buddhism. He visited as many as thirty countries, returning to China by sea fifteen years later.

China's most renowned religious pilgrim, Xuanzang (c. 602-664 C.E.), traveling at night on foot and by horseback, set out on the Silk Road in 629 C.E., studied in Indian monasteries for fourteen years, and returned to Ch'angan in 645 C.E. with more than five hundred sutras (Buddhist scriptures) and relics. He translated numerous Sanskrit sutras and other works into Chinese and wrote *Datang Xiyouji* (629 C.E.; *Buddhist Records of the Western World*, 1884), the story of his travels and a description of Buddhism. The Big Wild Goose pagoda, which still stands in Xi'an, housed his souvenirs, and the sixteenth century *Xiyou ji* (c. 1570-c. 1580, oldest surviving edition, 1592; *Journey to the West*, 1977-1983), a fictionalized account by Wu Cheng'en in which the Monkey King accompanies the pilgrim, has immortalized his journey. Manichaeanism and Nestorian Christianity also traveled the Silk Road, although they never reached the popularity of Buddhism.

The Silk Road flourished during the Tang Dynasty (618-907 C.E.), and Ch'angan became an international city. However, after the fall of Rome and the increase in Islamic power in the Levant, portions of the Silk Road became dangerous, and trade had declined by the end of the Tang Dynasty. At the end of the eighth century, the water supplies began drying up in many oasis towns. The spread of Islam also led to the destruction or abandonment of many Buddhist towns along the Silk Road. Trade revived somewhat during the Yuan Dynasty (1279-1368), when the Mongols controlled China. In the late thirteenth century, Marco Polo used the Silk Road to travel to China. His route took him over the Karakorams from Afghanistan into the Xinjiang Uighur region to the trading capital of Ürümqi, then from Kashi at the far west of China through high mountain passes to Samarkand in Central Asia.

ADDITIONAL RESOURCES
Arutyunyan, Soren. *The Silk Road*. Naples, Italy: Electa Napoli, 1994.
Bonavia, Judy. *The Silk Road: From Xi'an to Kashgar*. New York: Passport Books, 1993.
Elisseeff, Vadime, ed. *The Silk Roads: Highways of Culture and Commerce*. New York: Berghahn Books, 2000.
Foltz, Richard. *Religions of the Silk Road: Overland Trade and Cultural Exchange from Antiquity to the Fifteenth Century*. New York: St. Martin's Press, 1999.
Hopkirk, Peter. *Foreign Devils on the Silk Road*. London: Oxford University Press, 1986.
Whitfield, Susan. *Life Along the Silk Road*. Berkeley: University of California Press, 2000.
Yu, Ying-Shih. *Trade and Expansion in Han China: A Study in the Structure of Sino-Barbarian Economic Relations*. Berkeley: University of California Press, 1967.

SEE ALSO: Buddhism; Buddhist cave sculptures; China; Faxian; Han Dynasty; Tang Dynasty; Wudi; Xuanzang.
—*Ceferina Gayo Hess*

SIMA QIAN

ALSO KNOWN AS: *Wade-Giles* Ssu-ma Ch'ien
BORN: 145 B.C.E.; Longmen, China
DIED: 86 B.C.E.; China
RELATED CIVILIZATION: China
MAJOR ROLE/POSITION: Historian

Life. Sima Qian (soo-MAH chee-YEN) wrote the *Shiji* (first century B.C.E.; *Records of the Grand Historian of China*, 1960). He inherited the post of grand historiographer from his father, Sima Tan. The family had been astronomers before turning to history. The 130 chapters of the *Shiji* are divided into five subjects: annals, chronological tables, treatises on state matters, histories of states, and biographies. They carry China's history to about 100 B.C.E.

Sima Qian, out of filial piety and professionalism, wanted "to place on record the achievements of great men." He wrote good stories without much reference to supernatural causes. He used written sources and China's rich oral traditions.

Sima Qian recognized the jeopardy of knowledge and inquiry, highlighted by the Legalist first emperor Shi Huangdi's "burning of the books" in 213 B.C.E. He fell out of favor with emperor Wudi in 98 B.C.E. Given the choice of humiliating castration or honorable suicide, he chose life and finished writing his histories, which took twenty-seven years. His concern for truth and posterity may be compared with that of the Greek Socrates. Portions of his histories have been lost.

Influence. This influential, substantive, and methodological account has been the most famous of the Chinese histories for more than two thousand years. He has been compared to the Greek historians Herodotus and Thucydides.

ADDITIONAL RESOURCES
Ssu-ma Ch'ien. *Historical Records*. Translated by Raymond Dawson. New York: Oxford University Press, 1994.
Watson, Burton. *Ssu-ma Ch'ien: Grand Historian of China*. New York: Columbia University Press, 1958.

SEE ALSO: China; Shi Huangdi; Wudi.
—*Oliver B. Pollak*

SIMA XIANGRU

ALSO KNOWN AS: *Wade-Giles* Ssu-ma Hsiang-ju; Changqing
BORN: 179 B.C.E.; Chengdu, China
DIED: 117 B.C.E.; Maoling, Nan Yue, China
RELATED CIVILIZATION: China
MAJOR ROLE/POSITION: Poet

Life. Sima Xiangru (soo-MAH shee-AHNG-zhew) was a fencer, lute player, but primarily a *fu* poet of Western Han (206 B.C.E.-23 C.E.). His versatility won him a unique love, court positions, and a reputation as a great *fu* maker. *Fu*, a descriptive metered verse with rhyme interspersed with prose, became the preferred

court genre during the Han period. For Prince Xiao of Liang, Sima wrote his famous *Zixu Fu* (second century B.C.E.; *Sir Fantasy*, 1971), in which three speakers describe their pleasure at hunting. He later eloped with Zuo Wenjun, a widow and a lute player, to Chengdu, but poverty drove them back to Wenjun's home, where the couple ran a tavern for survival, winning historical fame as true lovers. Wenjun's wealthy father finally agreed to the marriage and gave the couple money.

Emperor Wudi called Sima to join the court, where he wrote *Shanglin Fu* (second century B.C.E.; "imperial park"), an ode to the emperor. He then pleaded illness and left the court. Provided for by his wife's fortune, Sima continued writing until his death. About thirty of his *fu* poems have survived, including the great *Nanshu Fulao* (second century B.C.E.; "refutation to the Sichuan elders"), which addresses taxation corruption and pop-

ular complaints. Most of his *fu* poems describe court prosperity but end with implicit satirical touches and remonstrations.

Influence. Sima's works helped establish the genre of *fu* poetry, which has been imitated by many subsequent Chinese poets.

ADDITIONAL RESOURCES
Perkins, Dorothy. *Encyclopedia of China: The Essential Reference to China, Its History and Culture.* New York: Roundtable, 1999.
Watson, Burton, trans. *Chinese Rhyme-Prose: Poems in the Fu Form from the Han and Six Dynasties Periods.* New York: Columbia University Press, 1971.

SEE ALSO: China; Han Dynasty; Six Dynasties; Wudi.
—*Charles Xingzhong Li*

SIMON MAGUS

ALSO KNOWN AS: Simon the Magician
FLOURISHED: first century C.E.
RELATED CIVILIZATION: Imperial Rome
MAJOR ROLE/POSITION: Magician

Life. The earliest account of Simon Magus (SI-muhn MAY-guhs) appears in the New Testament. According to Acts 8:4-24, Simon lived in Samaria and was well known for his practice of magic, which led to his being called "that power of God which is called great." Although the meaning of this phrase is debated, it indicates that either Simon claimed to be an exalted representative of God or he actually claimed to be God.

Simon was converted to Christianity by Philip, an evangelist from Jerusalem whose miracles of healing and exorcism impressed even Simon. However, the sincerity of his conversion came into question when the apostles Peter and John arrived. Seeing their ability to bestow the Holy Spirit, Simon offered them money if they would confer upon him the power to do the same. Instead, they soundly rebuked him and told him to repent. It is never mentioned in Acts whether Simon followed their advice or what became of him.

Subsequent Christian writers, however, state that Si-

mon Magus took up with a former prostitute named Helena and gathered many followers in Samaria. He was worshiped as "the first god" and Helena was considered "his first conception." Such terms indicate that Simon was promulgating an early form of Gnostic teaching. Later he traveled to Rome, where also he won great popularity and, according to some accounts, came into further conflict with Peter.

Influence. To combat the influence of teachers such as Simon, the Christian Church was compelled to formulate clearly its beliefs which, in turn, led to the development of Christian orthodoxy in the creeds of the fourth and fifth centuries C.E.

ADDITIONAL RESOURCES
Barrett, C. K. *A Critical and Exegetical Commentary on the Acts of the Apostles.* Edinburgh, Scotland: T & T Clark, 1994.
Bremmer, Jan N. *The Apocryphal Acts of Peter.* Leuven, Belgium: Peeters, 1998.

SEE ALSO: Christianity; Gnosticism; John the Evangelist, Saint; Peter, Saint.
—*Erik W. Larson*

SIMONIDES

BORN: c. 556 B.C.E.; Iulis, Island of Ceos (later Kéa), Greece
DIED: c. 467 B.C.E.; Syracuse, Sicily
RELATED CIVILIZATION: Classical Greece
MAJOR ROLE/POSITION: Lyric poet

Life. Nothing is known of Simonides' (si-MON-ih-deez) childhood or parentage other than that he was born near Iulis on the island of Ceos, fifteen miles (24 kilometers) from the southeast coast of Attica. He left Ceos after studying poetry and music and spent most of the remainder of his life in Athens. In addition to Pisistratus, the archon of Athens, his main patrons were the leaders of Syracuse and Thessaly. Simonides was chiefly known for his invention of the victory ode, a dithyramb offered to celebrate a prize won by a competitor at the religious or athletic festivals of ancient Greece. He was also famous as a maker of epigrams, the most famous of which is carved on a stone celebrating the successful defense of Thermopylae against the Persians: "Tell the Spartans, stranger passing by, that here we lie, obedient to their commands."

Influence. The choral forms that Simonides developed and popularized were widely used to celebrate the Greek victories over Persia and the ideals of Classical Greece after the war.

ADDITIONAL RESOURCES
Bowra, C. M. *Ancient Greek Literature*. New York: Oxford University Press, 1960.
Bowra, C. M., and T. F. Higham. *The Oxford Book of Greek Verse in Translation*. Oxford, England: Clarendon Press, 1948.
Carson, Anne. *Economy of the Unlost: Reading Simonides of Keos with Paul Celan*. Princeton, N.J.: Princeton University Press, 1999.
Lefkowitz, Mary. *The Lives of the Greek Poets*. Baltimore: Johns Hopkins University Press, 1981.
Podlecki, Anthony J. *The Early Greek Poets and Their Times*. Vancouver: University of British Columbia Press, 1984.

SEE ALSO: Athens; Bacchylides; Greece, Archaic; Greece, Classical; Pisistratus; Thermopylae, Battle of.
—*Robert Jacobs*

SIX DYNASTIES

DATE: 220-588 C.E.
LOCALE: China
RELATED CIVILIZATIONS: Han and Sui Dynasties, China
SIGNIFICANCE: Despite political turmoil, this period saw advances in technology and science and the flourishing of art, literature, philosophy, and religion.

In Chinese history, the Six Dynasties period began with the end of the Han Dynasty (220 C.E.) and ended with the reunification of China during the Sui Dynasty in 589 C.E. The name comes from six "legitimate" dynasties, each with its capital at Jiankang (modern Nanjing): the Wu (222-280 C.E.), the Eastern Jin (317-420 C.E.), the Southern Song (420-479 C.E.), the Southern Qi (479-502 C.E.), the Southern Liang (502-557 C.E.), and the Chen (557-588 C.E.). This period also included the Three Kingdoms (220-280 C.E.), the Western Jin (265-316 C.E.), and the Northern Dynasties (386-588 C.E.). It was a time of great political division and internal fighting; no centralized government existed, and much of the north as occupied by foreign nomads. The Confucian state religion was weakening, and Daoism and the imported Buddhist religion were becoming increasingly popular. In spite of the political chaos, great advances were made in science and technology, such as the invention of gunpowder, the wheelbarrow, and the kite. Literature, philosophy, and the arts also flourished.

The Six Dynasties period ended in 589 C.E. when a northern general named Yang Jian (better known as Wendi), who had established the Sui Dynasty (581-618 C.E.), overthrew the Chen Dynasty in the south and reunited China under one stable government.

ADDITIONAL RESOURCES
Hucker, Charles. *China's Imperial Past*. Stanford, Calif.: Stanford University Press, 1975.
Juliano, Annette. *Art of the Six Dynasties*. New York: China House Galleries, 1975.
Meskill, John, ed. *An Introduction to Chinese Civiliza-*

tion. Lexington, Mass.: D. C. Heath, 1973.

Tanigawa, Michio. *Studies in the History of the Six Dynasties*. Tokyo: Toho Gakkai, 1991.

SEE ALSO: Buddhism; China; Confucianism; Daoism; Han Dynasty; Sui Dynasty; Three Kingdoms.

—Alice Myers

SLAVS

DATE: 2000 B.C.E.-700 C.E.

LOCALE: Eastern and southeastern Europe

SIGNIFICANCE: The Slavs are the largest group of European peoples. After the ancient period, they formed the most nation-states in Eastern Europe.

Modern scholars define the Slavs as those whose native languages belong to the Slavic branch of the Indo-European family. Although definite historical references appear only in the first century C.E., linguistic and archaeological sources trace them back two or three millennia earlier.

History. The Slavic people coalesced in the area of central Europe around the Bug, Dnieper, and Vistula Rivers toward the end of the third millennium B.C.E. They were descendants of the Neolithic peoples who had earlier inhabited the region and groups of migrants who moved from all directions into the western part of the vast Eurasian plain. The latter included Indo-European speakers from the southeast who passed their tongue on to this proto-Slavic population. Around 2000 B.C.E., the Slavic language separated from the Baltic group; this can be designated as the historical starting point of the Slavs. Few records dealing with the ancient Slavs exist because they left no written documents. Their recorded history begins in the medieval period, when the various Slavic nations had already separated and adopted Christianity. There are a few scattered references in the ancient texts and a wealth of archaeological evidence through which, together with folklore and linguistic studies, researchers can piece together some of their history.

Some historians claim that a few of the peoples of the region mentioned by Herodotus—for example, the Budiani—were Slavs. More certainly the Venedi cited in the writings of the Romans were Slavs. Byzantine authors refer to the Sclavenes (from which their modern name comes) and the Anti. The former occupied the lands from the Danube to the Vistula, and the Anti lived in southern Ukraine.

Throughout the ancient period, the lands they inhabited were ruled by Cimmerians, Scythians, Sarmatians, Goths, and others. After the great migrations of the fourth and fifth centuries C.E. that upset the Roman Empire, the Slavs began to spread throughout central and eastern Europe and the Balkans. By that time, they had divided into three distinct groups: East, West, and South Slavs.

The Slavs occasionally invaded the Balkans during the reign of Justinian I (r. 527-565 C.E.), often along with other tribes. By the end of Justinian's reign, they had become allies (*foederati*) of the Byzantine Empire. However in 566 C.E., the Avars, a Turkish tribe, conquered the South Slavs and attacked the Byzantines south of the Danube. In the Avars' wake, the Slavs moved into the Balkans. They unsuccessfully besieged Thessalonica (modern Thessaloníki) but penetrated as far south as the Peloponnese while the Avars attacked Constantinople. By 640 C.E., they inhabited the whole peninsula except the coasts, western mountains, and Thrace. Heraclius (r. 610-641 C.E.) forced the Slavs to recognize his suzerainty, but the emperor's attention in the latter part of the seventh century C.E. turned to the Muslims, and in 681 C.E. (by tradition), the Turkic Bulgars, led by Asperuh, organized the Slavs north of Thrace on both sides of the Danube into the First Bulgarian Empire.

Law, social structure, and customs. The Slavs lived in blood-related clans, although marriage took place outside the clan. Their chiefs, whom they chose only as leaders in battle, did not have executive power. The Slavs believed that their ancient laws could not be changed, and the clan assemblies of all men old enough to bear arms decided what course corresponded to this law. Although members of the clan were more or less equal and even widows sometimes enjoyed the rights of their late husbands, they also kept slaves, usually prisoners of war, whom they often released after a period of time. Slavs also had a tradition of hospitality that obligated the clan to protect strangers who came into their midst as guests.

Settlements. Slavic houses were made from bushes and branches caked in mud, straw, reeds, and leaves. They usually lived along rivers and lakes. They stored their food in wooden containers that they buried in the ground with their other goods when under attack. Some of their villages had defensive walls.

Agriculture, animal husbandry, and trade. Slavs engaged in forest activities and rude agriculture. They hunted, fished, kept bees, and grew wheat, millet, flax, hemp, and other produce. They kept sheep, goats, swine, oxen, horses, and domestic fowl. They also were accomplished wood carvers and smelted iron and even gold. Trade with others was meager, although when the South Slavs moved into the Balkans, they maintained relations with the Byzantines.

Religion and ritual. Slavic religion was polytheistic without a hierarchy of deities. Slavic gods and goddesses represented different functions and natural spirits. The two common to all clans were Perun, the god of thunder and lightning, and Svarog. Other deities among the East Slavs according to the medieval *Povest Vremennykh Let* (c. 1112 C.E.; *The Russian Primary Chronicle, Laurentian Text*, 1953, also known as *Kievan Chronicle of Nestor, Russian Primary Chronicle, Chronicle of Nestor, Kiev Chronicle*) were Volos, Khors, Dazhbog, the father of Svarog, Stribogs, Simargl, and Mokosh. The *leshy*, or spirits of the forests, inhabited trees and entered into the temples and secular buildings made of the wood from those trees. Field spirits, or *polevoy*, were in charge of plants and were placated for harvests. Spirits of animals inhabited both wild beasts in hunts and domesticated animals on farms. The Slavs also believed in water demons.

The Slavs' wooden temples were divided into altars for the various gods. Slavic idols often exhibited supernumerary appendages, including multiple arms, legs, and heads. Slavs practiced animal sacrifice and distributed the burnt offerings to all clan members at communal feasts, a major rite in the religious celebrations of the Slavs. At these feasts, they honored and worshiped the founders of the clans and deceased ancestors by performing religious dances and plays. Wives attended their ancestral clans without their husbands, who belonged to other kinship groups. The Slavs practiced human sacrifice and various forms of mutilation, including decapitations, the tearing of limbs, and trepanation. Sometimes sacrificial victims were buried alive.

Slavic cosmology held that the earth was covered with water, and a god or spirit brought up sand from the depths to form the land. In various folk traditions, the spirit was either good or evil. The Slavs believed that both good and evil spirits who must be placated existed all around them. Especially they needed to heed the spirits of the dead. In particular, those who died young

or without fulfilling their destiny roamed the earth causing mischief. For example, they believed that if a maiden died before marriage, her spirit could kidnap children. Some Slavic myths also maintained the existence of two equal gods—good and evil.

Death and burial. Slavs engaged in the practice of second interment, disinterring bodies after a period of time and redressing them in new funerary wrapping. Slavs also worshiped the Moon. During eclipses, they engaged in rituals to kill the demons swallowing the Moon. The Sun's significance was relegated to a minor role as a nondivine bride of the Moon.

War and weapons. In war, the Slavs fought on foot in scattered arrays. A foot soldier's weapons included two small pikes, a heavy shield, a wooden bow, and arrows dipped in poison. For ease of movement, some Slavs went into battle barechested. They relied on surprise attacks and ambushes. Therefore, they preferred fighting in forests and inaccessible locales, avoiding open fields and fortresses. One tactic they used was to hide under water, breathing through reeds and then rising en masse to attack the foe.

Current views. In the past, scholars believed the Slavs were all descendants of the original Indo-European speakers. Currently the theories hold that they descended from a variety of earlier peoples, including the original Neolithic inhabitants. Some modern Slavs believe that the contemporary Slavic nations originated in ancient times, but most scholars maintain that the Slavs were originally one people and divided at the end of the ancient period into the three groups: East, West, and South Slavs.

ADDITIONAL RESOURCES

Conte, Francis. *The Slavs*. Boulder, Colo.: East European Monographs, 1995.

Dolukhanov, Pavel M. *The Early Slavs: Eastern Europe from the Initial Settlement to the Kievan Rus*. New York: Longman, 1996.

Godja, Martin. *The Ancient Slavs: Settlement and Society*. Edinburgh, Scotland: Edinburgh University, 1991.

Golab, Zbigniew. *The Origins of the Slavs: A Linguist's View*. Columbus, Ohio: Slavica, 1992.

Slupecki, Leszek P. *Slavonic Pagan Sanctuaries*. Warsaw: Polish Academy of Sciences, 1994.

SEE ALSO: Byzantine Empire; Justinian I; Rome, Imperial.

—*Frederick B. Chary*

SNEFRU

ALSO KNOWN AS: Sneferu
REIGNED: r. c. 2649-c. 2609 B.C.E.
RELATED CIVILIZATION: Pharaonic Egypt
MAJOR ROLE/POSITION: King

Life. Founder of the Fourth Dynasty of ancient Egypt, Snefru (SNEHF-rew) was the son (by a minor wife) of Huni, the last king of the Third Dynasty. He apparently consolidated his control of Egypt by marrying his half-sister Hetepheres, who was Huni's daughter by a senior queen.

Snefru is best known for his architectural activities. In addition to completing the funerary temple and pyramid of his father at Meidum, he built two pyramids of his own at Dahshur. The earlier of these two was the Bent Pyramid, so called because the slope of the walls changes from being very steep to much gentler for the upper courses. The reason for the change is unknown. He was apparently buried in the Red Pyramid, the first in a true pyramidal form. He also seems to have had a small provincial pyramid at Seila, near the Fayum. This makes Snefru the king with the most pyramids, with three of his own and credit for finishing a fourth in honor of his father. If all four are put together, the total volume of stone in these four monuments exceeds that in the pyramid construction of any other Egyptian king.

Influence. Patriarch of the Fourth Dynasty, Snefru consolidated power for his family, resulting in one of the most stable and architecturally productive periods of Egyptian history. During his reign, the funerary pyramid reached its final shape.

ADDITIONAL RESOURCES
Clayton, Peter A. *Chronicle of the Pharaohs*. New York: Thames and Hudson, 1994.
Lehner, Mark. *The Complete Pyramids*. New York: Thames and Hudson, 1997.

SEE ALSO: Egypt, Pharaonic; Pyramids and the Sphinx.
—*Sara E. Orel*

SOCIAL WAR

ALSO KNOWN AS: Italic War; Marsic War
DATE: 91-87 B.C.E.
LOCALE: Italy
RELATED CIVILIZATIONS: Republican Rome, Italy
SIGNIFICANCE: The rebellion of Rome's subject allies in Italy spurred Rome to extend full Roman citizenship throughout peninsular Italy.

Background. By the mid-third century B.C.E., Rome controlled nearly all peninsular Italy, with the majority of the Italian peoples having been made its subject military allies. As the allies' situation became gradually more oppressive, many of the allies felt it necessary to gain either full Roman citizenship or complete independence from Rome.

Action. After the murder of Marcus Livius Drusus, a tribune of 91 B.C.E. who had sought a diplomatic solution to the growing unrest of the allies, many of the allies rebelled. The major participants in the rebellion were the Marsi, Samnites, Hirpini, Frentani, Vestini, Marrucini, Paeligni, and Picentines, with disparate participation of the other peoples of Italy. The rebels chose Corfinium as their headquarters, renaming it Italia.

In the first year of the war, the insurgents met with considerable success in the fighting, which led Rome to make the political concession of offering Roman citizenship to those who had not rebelled or who put down their arms. This move greatly helped to turn the tide of the war in Rome's favor. By 87 B.C.E., only a few Samnites and Lucanians remained in arms, and they gradually surrendered.

Consequences. The extension of full Roman citizenship throughout Italy eventually led to an increased sense among urban and extra-urban Romans of common membership in one nation.

ADDITIONAL RESOURCES
Gabba, E. "Rome and Italy: The Social War." *Cambridge Ancient History*. Vol. 9. Cambridge, England: Cambridge University Press, 1994.
Keaveney, Arthur. *Rome and the Unification of Italy*. London: Croom Helm, 1987.

SEE ALSO: Rome, Republican.
—*Leah Johnson*

SOCRATES

BORN: c. 470 B.C.E.; Athens, Greece
DIED: 399 B.C.E.; Athens, Greece
RELATED CIVILIZATIONS: Athens, Classical Greece
MAJOR ROLE/POSITION: Philosopher

Life. Although Socrates (SOK-rah-teez) is one of the most influential philosophers of the Western world, little is known of his life or thoughts, because he left no written work. What is known about Socrates stems from the writings of those who knew him, with only the works of Aristophanes, Plato, and Xenophon surviving. In Aristophanes' play *Nephelai* (423 B.C.E.; *The Clouds*, 1708), Socrates is comedically depicted as adhering to a natural philosophy that has the effect of undermining human conventions such as the family. Alternatively, in Plato's corpus, Socrates' primary concern is not the natural world but the human world and human ideas such as justice. According to Plato, Socrates' quest for truth generally leaves the moral convictions of his interlocutors intact, if not improved. In all portrayals, Socrates questions accepted beliefs and pretensions to knowledge. The Socratic method of teaching was to let someone state a thesis and then draw out, through a series of questions, the underlying consequences and contradictions of that position, leading to a deeper analysis of the problem. In 400 B.C.E., Socrates was indicted for impiety and for corrupting young Athenians. He stood trial in 399 B.C.E. and was sentenced to death by drinking hemlock.

Influence. Socrates' influence led Plato, Antisthenes, Euclides, and Phaedon to become philosophers and start schools of their own. His method of teaching (as exhibited in many of Plato's dialogues), by posing a series of questions, the inevitable answers to which logically lead the answerer toward the truth, is still referred to as the "Socratic method." Socrates continues to exemplify the virtues of the examined life.

ADDITIONAL RESOURCES
Taylor, C. C. W. *Socrates*. Oxford, England: Oxford University Press, 1998.
West, Thomas G., and Grace Starry West. *Four Texts on Socrates*. Ithaca, N.Y.: Cornell University Press, 1984.

SEE ALSO: Aristophanes; Athens; Greece, Classical; Philosophy; Plato; Pre-Socratic philosophers; Xenophon.

—*Sara MacDonald*

Socrates. (Library of Congress)

SOLOMON

BORN: c. 991 B.C.E.; Jerusalem, Israel
DIED: c. 930 B.C.E.; Jerusalem, Israel
RELATED CIVILIZATIONS: Israel, Egypt, Phoenicia
MAJOR ROLE/POSITION: King, philosopher, poet

Life. Biblical literature (I *Kings* 1-11; I Chronicles 22-II Chronicles 9) relates that Solomon (SAHL-uh-

muhn) was a son of King David by Bathsheba. Solomon acceded to Israel's throne after David. Few biblical characters are as intriguing as Solomon, reputedly the richest king in history and wisest man in the world from biblical perspectives, receiving tribute from Egypt and Phoenicia and the testimony of the Queen of Sheba. Many implausible legends surround Solomon—such as being a great sorcerer and one who possessed a ring enabling him to understand animal languages—but he was politically canny, making trade alliances with nearby kings, including Hiram of Tyre, and marriage alliances with many others. He preferred peace to war, building the first temple in Jerusalem and embellishing it and his palace with Phoenician art and cedars and great luxury. He is perhaps best known to-day as the legendary wise ruler who solved the dispute between two women's claim to a child by offering to divide the child physically in half, thereby evoking the grief of the real mother and hence identifying which woman was telling the truth.

His reign marked the zenith of Israelite history, occurring in a power vacuum between weak Egyptian and Mesopotamian empires. He was reputed author of the biblical books Proverbs, Ecclesiastes, and Song of Songs (or Song of Solomon), although this last attribution is unlikely. His wisdom appears in observations of nature, especially plants, animals, and human behavior, in three thousand proverbs and more than one thousand songs. A man of legendary superlatives, he had seven hundred wives and three hundred concubines according to I Kings, but his excesses led to division of his kingdom into northern and southern realms at his death.

Influence. Solomonic legend continued through ancient history, even appearing in Pompeian wall painting, and into Judeo-Christian tradition in medieval as well as Islamic worlds as the most remarkable biblical potentate of the Near East.

ADDITIONAL RESOURCES

"Solomon." In *The Oxford Encyclopedia of Archaeology in the Near East*, edited by Eric Meyers. New York: Oxford University Press, 1997.

Thieberger, Frederic. *King Solomon.* 1978. Reprint. New York: Hebrew Publishing, 1998.

SEE ALSO: Bathsheba; David; Egypt, Pharaonic; Israel; Jerusalem, temple of; Phoenicia; Sheba, Queen of.

—*Patrick Norman Hunt*

King Solomon (kneeling). (Library of Congress)

SOLON

BORN: c. 630 B.C.E.; probably Athens, Greece
DIED: c. 560 B.C.E.; probably Athens, Greece
RELATED CIVILIZATION: Archaic Greece
MAJOR ROLE/POSITION: Politician, statesman, reformer, poet

Life. Solon (SOH-luhn) achieved prominence in Athens as a statesman, legislator, reformer, poet, and war veteran during an age of social crisis. Athens was experiencing dislocating economic conditions, and debt slavery was distorting what Athenians felt was their political culture. In his poetry, Solon reproached the rich for "avarice and arrogance." Solon was elected archon, or chief magistrate, for 594-593 B.C.E. and introduced sweeping, radical, but not revolutionary reforms.

He forbade the borrowing of money that took a security interest in the person and family of the borrower. He canceled all debts and current mortgages. This freed those who had been placed in servitude or enslaved for debt. In the name of family integrity, he produced a conservative reform that preserved private property and guided Greek democracy. Solon drew up a new law code, softening the laws created by Draco, whose severe punishments spawned the word "draconian," and adding laws in new areas. Attempts at repatriation of slaves sent to colonies were only partially successful. There was opposition to Solon's reforms, especially from the debt holders, and the founding charters of some Greek colonies contained provisions in which leaders pledged not to cancel debts.

Influence. Solon is the earliest Greek politician whose philosophy and deeds continue to resonate in the modern world.

ADDITIONAL RESOURCES
Ehrenberg, Victor. *From Solon to Socrates*. London: Methuen, 1968.
Plutarch. *The Lives of the Noble Grecians and Romans*. Translated by John Dryden, revised by Arthur Hugh Clough. New York: Modern Library, 1992.

SEE ALSO: Draco; Government and law; Greece, Archaic.

—Oliver B. Pollak

SONOTA CULTURE

DATE: 1-600 C.E.
LOCALE: Southern Manitoba, Canada; northern Dakotas; Minnesota
RELATED CIVILIZATIONS: Besant, Hopewell, Laurel
SIGNIFICANCE: This cultural phase is the earliest form of Woodland tradition in the northern plains.

The Sonota (soh-NOH-tuh) were migratory bison hunters, known primarily for their elaborate burial customs. They interred pipestone, obsidian, and bison offerings in mounds with the dead. Humans remains were placed in log chambers below the mounds. Their lithic tools were made primarily of Knife River flint, as were those of their neighbors to the west, the Besant culture. Sonota, Besant, and Hopewell cultures were all contemporary to one another.

The Sonota people followed the bison out onto the open grasslands to the north in spring and early summer, then south, to the edges of the eastern woodlands in the fall. They were experts at herding and cutting, capturing in jumps and pounds, and processing the large ungulates into forms that fulfilled most of their needs. The atlatl, a spear-thrower, was the primary hunting tool, although they may have adopted the use of the bow and arrow, and the corner or side-notched projectile points and expanded stemmed tips found at their occupation sites are unique to the Sonota culture.

They lived for several hundred years, in and around what are known as the Avery and Richard's Kill sites. They lived on the edges of the grasslands, near water, in sheltered valleys during that part of the year when they retreated from the open plains. Such areas provided ample fuel, bear, elk, deer, antelope, small game, rodents, fish, and many plant foods in the off season. Some evidence of plant domestication exists. Such sites were used mainly, however, as base camps, primarily for processing large kills—sometimes up to several hundred animals were trapped, killed, butchered, and dressed in fall and early winter.

Pottery associated with the Sonota culture is the earliest representation of Plains area ceramic wares. The pots are crude, undecorated, and were most probably used for cooking. Clay pottery was probably introduced from the Missouri River area of South Dakota.

The Sonota are known to have engaged extensively in trade networks spanning a vast area. Pottery styles from the Dakotas, shells from rivers to the south, the Gulf of Mexico, and the eastern seaboard, copper from the Upper Great Lakes, and flint from western North Dakota have all been found at Sonota sites.

ADDITIONAL RESOURCES
Bryan, Liz. *The Buffalo People*. Edmonton: University of Alberta Press, 1991.
Friesen, Gerald. *The Canadian Prairies: A History*. Toronto: University of Toronto Press, 1984.

Frison, George, C. *Prehistoric Hunters of the High Plains*. 2d ed. San Diego, Calif.: Academic Press, 1991.

SEE ALSO: Adena culture; Middle Woodland tradition; Plains peoples.

—*Michael W. Simpson*

SOPHOCLES

BORN: c. 496 B.C.E.; Colonus, near Athens, Greece
DIED: c. 406 B.C.E.; Athens, Greece
RELATED CIVILIZATION: Classical Greece
MAJOR ROLE/POSITION: Dramatist, military and civic leader, priest

Life. The handsome, gifted son of Sophilus, who was a wealthy manufacturer of armor, Sophocles (SAHF-uh-kleez) was given a good education, studying with the famous musician Lamprus and probably with the great tragic dramatist Aeschylus. At sixteen, Sophocles was chosen to lead the choral chant, or paean, celebrating the Athenian fleet's victory at Salamis.

However, Sophocles soon became best known as a dramatist. In 468 B.C.E., his tetralogy, or set of four plays, defeated that of Aeschylus to win the contest held at the Great Dionysia, Athens' most important religious festival. During his lifetime, Sophocles would win first prize about twenty times; he never placed lower than second. Of his 123 plays, only seven complete tragedies survive: *Aias* (early 440's B.C.E.; *Ajax*, 1729), *Antigonē* (441 B.C.E.; *Antigone*, 1729), *Trachinai* (435-429 B.C.E.; *The Women of Trachis*, 1729), *Oidipous Tyrannos* (c. 429 B.C.E.; *Oedipus Tyrannus*, 1715), *Ēlektra* (418-410 B.C.E.; *Electra*, 1649), *Philoktētēs* (409 B.C.E.; *Philoctetes*, 1729), and *Oidipous epi Kolōnōi* (401 B.C.E.; *Oedipus at Colonus*, 1729). About half of a satyr play, *Ichneutae* ("the trackers"), is also extant.

At least two of Sophocles' descendants also became tragic dramatists. One was Iophon, his son by his first wife, Nicostrate; the other was his grandson and namesake. Sophocles' second wife, Theoris of Sicyon, had borne him a son, Agathon, and it was Agathon's son, the younger Sophocles, who staged his grandfather's final play in 401 B.C.E.

Sophocles was also a prominent leader of his city-state. In 442 B.C.E., he was made a treasurer, collecting tribute from Athens' subject-allies. Two years later, he was one of ten generals who put down a revolt in Samos. It was said that this post was a reward for his play *Antigone*, but Sophocles' military ability is evident in that he was elected general at least once more. He also traveled on diplomatic missions, and in 413 B.C.E., when he was eighty-three, he served on a commission assigned to solve Athens' financial crisis.

After his death, Sophocles was honored as a hero for his part in bringing to Athens the worship of Asclepius, the god of healing, whose priest he became. However, the dramatist's final public act involved his art: Just months before his own death, he led a chorus of mourning for his younger rival Euripides.

Influence. Sophocles altered Greek drama by introducing scene painting, by increasing the size of the chorus, by writing each play in a trilogy as an independent unit, and by using three actors instead of just two, thus making it possible for plays to be more complex. Sophocles' magnificent poetry, his memorable characters, and his insights into the way human destiny is shaped by fate and frailty have continued to influence Western playwrights throughout the centuries.

Sophocles. (Library of Congress)

ADDITIONAL RESOURCES
Bowra, C. M. *Sophoclean Tragedy.* Oxford, England: Oxford University Press, 1944.
Dawe, R. D. *Sophocles: The Classical Heritage.* New York: Garland, 1996.
Nardo, Don, ed. *Readings on Sophocles.* San Diego, Calif.: Greenhaven Press, 1997.

Winnington-Ingram, R. P. *Sophocles: An Interpretation.* Cambridge, England: Cambridge University Press, 1980.

SEE ALSO: Aeschylus; Euripides; Greece, Classical; Performing arts; Salamis, Battle of.

—*Rosemary M. Canfield Reisman*

SOPHONISBA OF NUMIDIA

ALSO KNOWN AS: Saphanbaʿal
BORN: date and place unknown
DIED: c. 203 B.C.E.; place unknown
RELATED CIVILIZATIONS: Carthage, Republican Rome
MAJOR ROLE/POSITION: Queen and wife to Syphax, later wife of Masinissa

Life. As the highly charming, extremely intelligent, and very beautiful daughter of Hasdrubal, son of Gisgo, Sophonisba of Numidia (sahf-uh-NIHZ-buh of new-MIH-dee-uh) received an advanced education befitting a member of Carthage's ruling elite. Little is known of her royal upbringing, but she supported Carthage's conflict with Rome with a dedicated patriotism.

In spring, 204 B.C.E., Scipio Africanus's army of 25,000 men invaded Africa, signaling to Carthage its need for allies. Syphax, the Masaesylian king, was the central focus of both Punic and Roman diplomacy. Masinissa, a Numidian lieutenant of Hannibal in Spain and rival of Syphax, allied with Rome. In 205 B.C.E., Hasdrubal approved the marriage of Sophonisba to Syphax, cementing the Punic and Masaesylian alliance. However, in the Battle of the Great Plains, Hasdrubal and Syphax were defeated by the armies of Scipio and Masinissa, resulting in Syphax's death and Masinissa's capture of Sophonisba. She knew the victory's implications and quickly married Masinissa to turn him against Rome. Soon after, Scipio met with Masinissa and demanded Sophonisba as war booty. Instead, Masinissa sent Sophonisba poison, which she took with the same courage she had displayed throughout the conflict.

Influence. Sophonisba represented the strength, loyalty, and excellence of Punic womanhood, in line with the royal tradition established by Queen Dido, the founder of Carthage.

ADDITIONAL RESOURCE
Lancel, Serge. *Hannibal.* Oxford, England: Blackwell, 1998.

SEE ALSO: Carthage; Dido; Hannibal; Scipio Africanus.

—*Michael J. Siler*

SORANUS OF EPHESUS

ALSO KNOWN AS: Soranos Ephesios
FLOURISHED: second century C.E.; Ephesus and Rome
RELATED CIVILIZATIONS: Roman Greece, Imperial Rome
MAJOR ROLE/POSITION: Physician

Life. Soranus of Ephesus (sawr-AY-nuhs of EH-feh-suhs) was trained as a doctor in Ephesus and in Alexandria and practiced medicine in Rome. Nothing more is known with certainty of his life.

Soranus's approximately twenty books were renowned for clarity and scholarly detail. They included treatises on medical subjects such as hygiene, drugs, and terminology and a series of biographies of famous doctors. Everything is lost except for one complete book, *Gynaecology* (n.d.; *Soranus's Gynaecology*, 1956), and two chapters, covering broken bones and bandaging, from a work known as "On the Art of Surgery" (no English translation).

Influence. Soranus was the most influential teacher and theorist of the methodist school of medicine, which generally scorned anatomy and physiology. However, he merged these and other ideas into methodism with genius, emphasizing the importance of both theory and experience. His writings were quite influential in antiquity and the Middle Ages, eclipsed only by the works of the physician Galen. By preserving opinions and quotations from previous physicians in his works, Soranus has given modern scholars an excellent view of ancient medical debates and knowledge, and his discussion of contraception inspired scientific research in the mid-twentieth century on chemical birth control.

ADDITIONAL RESOURCES
Drabkin, I. "Soranus and His System of Medicine."
Bulletin of the History of Medicine 25 (1951).
Lloyd, G. E. R. *Science, Folklore, and Ideology.* Indianapolis: Hackett, 1999.
Riddle, J. *Contraception and Abortion, from the Ancient World to the Renaissance.* Cambridge, Mass.: Harvard University Press, 1992.
Temkin, O. *Soranus' "Gynaecology."* Baltimore: Johns Hopkins University Press, 1956.

SEE ALSO: Galen; Greece, Hellenistic and Roman; Medicine and health; Rome, Imperial.
—*Richard C. Carrier*

SOUTH AMERICA, SOUTHERN

DATE: 8000 B.C.E.-700 C.E.
LOCALE: Southern and southeastern Brazil, Paraguay, Uruguay, Argentina, and southern Chile
SIGNIFICANCE: Southern South American cultures became hunters and gatherers of a wide range of land and sea animals and plants and eventually farmers as they adapted to changes in the environment, including the loss of larger animals.

By 8000 B.C.E., or the end of the Paleo-Indian period, the orientation of subsistence in southern South America was changing from larger animals to more generalized hunting and gathering in an overall trend toward adaptation to environment and local species.

History. The first people in southern South America most likely migrated from North America through the Central American isthmus, moving down the Andes mountain chain in pursuit of large animals and settling into habitable areas. Numerous sites indicating previous human presence have been found in southern and southeastern South America. Besides Monte Verde, in southern Chile, which shows exceptional evidence of human occupation before 8000 B.C.E., other sites have been discovered as far south as southernmost Patagonia, on the Strait of Magellan. Excavations in Fell's cave and Palli Aike cave revealed remains dating to about 8000 B.C.E. and document continuing occupation in both Patagonia and Tierra del Fuego.

The Alice Boer site in São Paulo state, Brazil, which flourished during what is believed to have been a much colder and damper period than today, also points to the occupation of hunters and gatherers. Ancient cultures are clearly indicated in the human remains found in the Lagoa Santa cave and in the Santana de Riacho rock shelter in southeastern Brazil.

Around 6000 B.C.E., the population on the seashore began to increase. On the coasts of Brazil and Argentina, many shellfish gatherers appeared, having apparently abandoned the interior. A climatic shift to more hot and humid weather between 7000 and 4000 B.C.E. is thought to be related to this migration, which marked the beginning of the *sambaquis*, huge shell mounds that formerly lined the coast of Brazil.

Developments in southeastern South America had little apparent connection with the vast regional diversification or political grouping of the more expansionistic Andean states. Consequently, the juxtaposition between hunters and shoreline gatherers continued for centuries, and the shell mounds existed mainly as a response to population growth.

Agriculture. Potatoes appeared very early as a gathered crop at Monte Verde, but largely they grew wild throughout southeastern South America. Maize kernels have been discovered in early sites in Patagonia and also at the rock shelter at Santana de Riacho, essentially a nonagricultural area, beginning at about 3000 B.C.E. Manioc, a tuberous plant, proliferated widely from Brazil northward. The cultures of southeastern Brazil began slowly to become agricultural around 600-700 C.E.

Death and burial. Among early foraging groups, mourners painted their faces black, beat on the outside of the dead person's hut, fasted, and lamented. Much anger was directed toward the supreme deity, and fear of the dead and evil bush spirits was common. In southern Chile, the dead person and his effects were either buried or cremated. Patagonians left the corpse on a hilltop or in a cave along with some belongings. At the Santana de Riacho rock shelter, burials were commonly made inside the shelters. Bodies were wrapped in netting or in hammocks. A division of offerings was maintained as males were buried with stone tools, and females and juveniles were buried with wooden artifacts and vegetable offerings.

Burials in the *sambaquis* indicated a high degree of infant mortality. The deceased was often accompanied by personal adornments and a few grave goods. Burials seem to have been under houses, possibly multifamily residences.

Religion and ritual. Shellfish gatherers believed in a supreme being who was not a creator but a ruler—one who gave life to humans and who gave them animal and plant foods. They prayed to this being for success in fishing and hunting. Among some groups in Brazil, shamanism was highly developed for curing illness and working for the general welfare of the tribe. Also, much evidence in Argentina (as in most of South America) points to the widespread use of hallucinogens for curative purposes and religious rites.

Visual arts. Brazilian rock shelters are noted for their abundant petroglyphs, dating from the earliest occupation of Brazil. Rock art is difficult to date successfully because most of the shelters in which it occurs were occupied for centuries. Petroglyphs show humans in various activities, along with animals, especially deer, and geometric patterns.

Ceramics appeared much later in coastal Brazil than in Andean civilizations. The earliest *sambaquis* were preceramic, with the advent of pottery in Brazil about 500 C.E. or later. The major art form in South America, textiles, migrated to Rio de Janeiro about 550 C.E.

Women's life. In the earliest tribes of southernmost Chile, it was predominantly the women who gathered shellfish at low tide and dived from bark canoes with shell blades and baskets in their teeth.

Although little is known about textile production outside the Andean region, it is traditionally reported that in Rio de Janeiro, as elsewhere, women worked outside while men were weaving.

Current views. Besides finding that the subsistence basis of the earliest cultures was more diversified than had been supposed, recent study has determined the earliest reliable evidence for human presence in southern South America to be circa 10,000 B.C.E., although most sites date from 8000-6000 B.C.E. Some claims of great age have been made for several sites in Brazil, including the Pedra Furada rock shelter, which has been dated by recent research at 5000 B.C.E. and not 30,000 B.C.E. as some believed.

ADDITIONAL RESOURCES

Bird, Junius B. *Travels and Archaeology in South Chile.* Iowa City: University of Iowa Press, 1988.

Bruhns, Karen Olsen. *Ancient South America.* Cambridge, England: Cambridge University Press, 1994.

Fagan, Brian M. *People of the Earth: An Introduction to World Prehistory.* 9th ed. New York: Longmans, 1998.

McEwan, Colin, et al., eds. *Patagonia: Natural History, Prehistory, and Ethnography at the Uttermost End of the Earth.* Princeton, N.J.: Princeton University Press, 1998.

SEE ALSO: Andes, South; Archaic South American culture; Brazil, eastern; Paleo-Indians in South America.

—*Mary Hurd*

SOUTH AMERICAN INTERMEDIATE AREA

DATE: 8000 B.C.E.-700 C.E.

LOCALE: Colombia and Panama

RELATED CIVILIZATIONS: Monagrillo, Aristide, Tonosí, Tumaco/La Tolita, San Agustín/Tierradentro, Calima, Atlantic Coast cultures, Puerto Hormiga, Malambo, Momil

SIGNIFICANCE: The Intermediate Area lies between the two great civilization centers in the Americas, Mesoamerica and Peru. It is also the geographical link between Central and South America and shows cultural influences from both areas.

Paleo-Indians were present in the Intermediate Area from 8000 B.C.E. For the first five thousand years, people formed small, nomadic groups of hunters and foragers, using stone tools. The history of the Intermediate Area is defined along geographical contexts, the mountains versus the coastal lowlands. After 3000 B.C.E., lowland cultures continued to rely on fishing and hunting for food in contrast to the highland cultures, which began to rely more on agriculture. Population grew in the highland, agricultural communities, leading to the development of status differences. The political order that was required to organize the larger mountainous communities can be seen in the precise, repetitive, and orderly organization of visual images in the art.

Panama. The earliest definable ceramics culture in Panama is the Monagrillo culture (3000-1100 B.C.E.). In the latter half of this period, maize agriculture was adopted, leading to the use of slash-and-burn techniques and deforestation. The population grew significantly, and labor became more specialized. Ceramics were rudimentary in construction and lacked both necks and surface decoration. Around 900 B.C.E., black stylized designs of birds, serpents, and other animals were first painted on ceramics. The strong stylized figures that appear in this period came to define Panamanian ceramics throughout the pre-Columbian period.

The Aristide style (100 B.C.E.-300 C.E.) is associated with riverine villages in the central region of Panama that were characterized by a mixed economic pattern including hunting, fishing, and maize horticulture. Aristide ware can be identified by its use of black painting on a red background and geometric forms such as scrolls, cross-hatching, and chevrons. The painted area of the pot was enclosed within circumferential bands, a practice that was continued by later potters. From this period, shifts in ceramic style become important markers of cultural changes.

The Tonosí style (100 B.C.E.-500 C.E.) emerged somewhat later in essentially the same area under peoples with a similar lifestyle. However, the stylistic differences between the Aristide and Tonosí ceramics suggest that they were the products of distinct cultural groups. Tonosí ceramics were characterized by polychrome painting on buff-colored clay as well as black-on-red painting. The highly stylized figures included anthropomorphic, serpentine, and avian shapes painted with bold curving lines. By the late Tonosí period (500-600 C.E.), the design style evolved into the Conte style. The Conte painting style became denser, with images frequently crowded into the design space, anticipating a pattern characteristic of subsequent Panamanian styles.

Colombia. The evolution from the foraging lifestyle in Colombia to horticulture and chiefdomships led to a plethora of cultures. After the emergence of ceramics shortly before 3000 B.C.E., subsequent cultures included Tumaco/La Tolita, San Agustín/Tierradentro, Calima, and the Atlantic Coast groups.

In the Sinú region along the Atlantic coast, a number of cultures existed, including Puerto Hormiga (3200-

2000 B.C.E.), Malambo (800-600 B.C.E.), and Momil (600 B.C.E.-600 C.E.). These were lowland, coastal communities based on manioc horticulture until the later introduction of maize. Hunting and fishing were important supplemental activities. The ceramic art from this area is quite different from that found in southern Colombia in that it emphasizes female figures shown sitting or standing in power positions.

The Tumaco/La Tolita cultural complex (300 B.C.E.-350 C.E.) seems to have been important as a transmission zone for the metallurgical skills that were initially developed in Peru and later disseminated northward into Colombia along with the shaman/jaguar cult and the concept of the ritual urban center. The importance of the human figure in Tumaco ceramics and the gracefulness with which it was managed probably developed from the early Ecuadorian coastal cultures.

The Tumaco people lived in a dispersed settlement pattern with individual houses separated from one another. Their diet included shellfish, fish, birds, small mammals, corn, and beans, and they used cotton. During the Classic period (300 B.C.E.-90 C.E.), Tumaco emerged as a major ceremonial center with distinct social hierarchies. Earthen mounds were constructed, an urban concentration developed, and the production of ceramics increased. In the Postclassic period (90-350 C.E.), the area continued its rich figure-making tradition in ceramics.

Calima culture (1500 B.C.E.-700 C.E.) continued the ceramic figure tradition of Tumaco, but the figures were incorporated into small vessel shapes. The figures were usually full in volume and have carefully modeled facial features. Cross-hatching on the surface of the figure is frequently used for decoration.

San Agustín and Tierradentro (600 B.C.E.-700 C.E.) in the southern highlands were inhabited as early as 3300 B.C.E., but they did not become major ceremonial centers until 300 C.E. Both are necropolises characterized by elaborate funerary constructions. In San Agustín, the burials are in megalithic vaults with coffins carved of single pieces of stone, but in Tierradentro, the tombs are underground burial chambers with elaborately painted walls. The elaborate burials indicate the higher status people associated with chiefdomships. San Agustín is especially known for the stone sculptures associated with its sites. Sculptured guardians armed with clubs protect the entrances to the tombs, and other stone figures represent mythical beings in animal or human shapes.

ADDITIONAL RESOURCES

Helms, Mary W. *The Curassow's Crest: Myths and Symbols in the Ceramics of Ancient Panama.* Gainesville: University Press of Florida, 2000.

Labbé, Armand J. *Colombia Before Columbus: The People, Culture, and Ceramic Art of Prehispanic Colombia.* New York: Rizzoli, 1986.

_____. *Guardians of the Life Stream: Shamans, Art, and Power in Prehispanic Central Panamá.* Santa Ana, Calif.: Bowers Museum of Cultural Art, 1995.

SEE ALSO: Archaic South American culture; Paleo-Indians in South America.

—*Ronald J. Duncan*

SOUTHWEST PEOPLES

DATE: 9500 B.C.E.-700 C.E.

LOCALE: Southwestern United States

RELATED CIVILIZATIONS: Clovis technological complex, Folsom technological complex, Hohokam culture, Mogollon culture, Anasazi

SIGNIFICANCE: These peoples lived year-round in the arid Southwest, introducing agriculture and village life to the region, and are the ancestors to peoples such as the Pueblo and the Hopi.

For at least ten thousand years, maybe longer, people have struggled to make a homeland out of the arid Southwest. Apart from archaeology, little is known of the first peoples who came into the region more than ten thousand years ago, but the ancient remains contain evidence of ways of life that have persisted to modern times among the descendants of these peoples, including adobe and wattle-and-daub structure construction.

History. The American Southwest was wetter in ancient times and home to large animals such as the American mammoth and the American lion, now extinct. Peoples identified as Clovis, from the site in New Mexico where their spear points were first unearthed, moved into the region by about 9500 B.C.E. These people followed the migrating herds and slew them with arrow points especially designed to penetrate the rough hides of these animals. These points have small flutes in relation to the overall surface area. Recent discoveries elsewhere in the Western Hemisphere have challenged the notion that these Southwestern peoples invented the spear points that bear their name. The social organization and beliefs of these peoples cannot be determined from archaeological evidence.

As the climate changed around 8500 B.C.E., and the larger animals became extinct, peoples known as Folsom hunted smaller game and gathered native nuts and berries in the region. The Folsom point has a larger flute relative to its surface area and is better suited to slaying deer and elk. Like the Clovis people, Folsom hunters fixed the projectile point to a shaft and enhanced their ability to hurl this spear with an atlatl, a spear-thrower that lengthened the arc of the hunter's throw. The Folsom may have been descended from the Clovis people. Their numbers were relatively small, given the fragile resource base and paucity of rainfall in the region. Recent discoveries along the Continental Divide in Colorado indicate that these people ranged widely in search of food.

By 5500 B.C.E., food gathering had become more important to the Southwestern peoples, who began to trap small game such as rabbits with snares. These peoples, termed Archaic, migrated into the higher country in the summer, following the vegetation and animal herds, and remained in the lower elevations during the winter. Typically, fire pits are the most readily observed remains of early Archaic peoples. Relics found in caves, especially large concentrations of artifacts in given locations, seem to indicate that these people were less nomadic than their Clovis and Folsom ancestors. Among the artifacts found are woven bags, cradle boards for transporting infants, and sandals made from the yucca plant.

By about 1500 B.C.E., limited agriculture along watercourses characterized some of these Archaic groups. Corn and squash were grown first, and around 200 B.C.E., if not before, Archaic people cultivated beans. Agriculture laid the foundation for village life but also marked a turning point in social organization. People had to work harder to secure this food source, and most likely, social organization had to become more sophisticated. Furthermore, seeds and harvests were initially stored in natural shelters and later in specially designed storage pits. If artifacts and projectile points have been correctly interpreted, any given group of Archaic peoples ranged over less of the Southwest than did their Clovis and Folsom ancestors, and the style of manufacture varied from group to group.

Between 200 B.C.E. and 600 C.E., Southwest peoples increasingly moved toward agriculture and began to live in villages more or less full time. At first, they lived in pit houses but gradually built more elaborate structures out of stones and adobe. Early on, some of these structures seemed to have been devoted to civil or spiritual rituals that helped bind the village community together and mediate disputes among the peoples. The appearance of ceramic vessels by 200 C.E. serves as a watershed of the primacy of village life. These containers were too heavy and too fragile to be transported, but they did make it possible to cook food. In addition, late Archaic peoples developed specialized grinding tools, indicating that agriculture was their major source of food. At the same time, smaller archaic projectile points may be indicative of the introduction of the bow and arrow, which would have made small game hunting more efficient.

Increasingly, the architecture and ceramics indicate distinct cultural groups, such as the Hohokam in southern Arizona, the Mogollon in eastern Arizona, and the Anasazi in northern Arizona and New Mexico. Linguistic differences among peoples had appeared at or before the same time.

Current views. Scholars have traditionally viewed the peoples of the Ancient Southwest as benign, having had little impact on the environment and engaging in little conflict with one another. Indeed, inhabitants of the ancient Southwest were seen as the counterpoint to the modern, rapacious inhabitant of European descent. More recent research has raised the possibility of violent prehistoric warfare, especially as village sites in some places seem to have been built for the purposes of defense and the physical remains in mass graves seem to indicate the likelihood of death by combat. Even more controversial is that some inhabitants of the Southwest, either indigenous to the region or interlopers, may have practiced cannibalism as a means of controlling subject populations. All this remains speculative because the archaeological record, although large, is far from conclusive.

ADDITIONAL RESOURCES

LeBlanc, Stephen. *Prehistoric Warfare in the American Southwest*. Salt Lake City: University of Utah Press, 1999.

Plog, Stephen. *Ancient Peoples of the American Southwest*. London: Thames and Hudson, 1997.

Turner, Christy, and Jacqueline Turner. *Man Corn: Cannibalism and Violence in the Prehistoric American Southwest*. Salt Lake City: University of Utah Press, 1999.

SEE ALSO: Anasazi; Archaic North American culture; Archaic tradition, northern; California peoples; Clovis technological complex; Cochise culture; Folsom technological complex; Hohokam culture; Mogollon culture; Paleo-Indians in North America.

—Edward R. Crowther

SPAIN

DATE: 3000 B.C.E.-700 C.E.
LOCALE: The Iberian Peninsula, including the Balearic Islands
RELATED CIVILIZATIONS: Iberians, Celts, Celtiberians, Semites, Phoenicia, Carthage, Greece, Rome, Visigoths
SIGNIFICANCE: At the western edge of the Mediterranean Sea, Spain accommodated many different cultural and ethnic groups, which shared space until Rome's domination of the area.

Knowledge of ancient Spain is limited to archaeological evidence, epigraphs, and a sometimes conflicting literary record. As many of the ancient settlements are buried under existing cities, the history of this period will most likely remain incomplete.

Early history. By 3000 B.C.E., Spain was home to sedentary peoples who made pottery, erected megalithic tombs, worked copper, and inhabited fortified villages. Toward the beginning of the second millennium B.C.E., a wave of megalithic worshipers from the east initiated a period of agricultural prosperity in Andalusia, and in the north another megalithic people, the precursors of the Basques, settled in the Pyrenees. Bronze metallurgy was introduced between 1900 and 1600 B.C.E. and yielded more durable weapons. For better defense, many villages were relocated on heights.

Although it is often stated that the Iberians invaded Spain from North Africa (sometime between 4000 and 1600 B.C.E.) and spread northward, their origin is unknown. They are generally described as short, dark-skinned people, but the term Iberian does not indicate a specific race or ethnicity. Rather it is a generic label for the complex association of inhabitants of Spain's eastern and southern seaboard. The classicist Leonard Curchin would restrict the term Iberian to peoples of the east coast, because archaeological evidence in the south shows many orientalizing tendencies as a result of Semitic settlement along the Andalusian coast. He refers to the southern culture, centered on the Guadalquivir Valley, as Tartessian, home of the fabled Tartessus. The most interesting part of the Iberian culture that has been preserved are the stone sculptures, which are decorative (bulls, sphinxes, and other animals) or religious, such as the full-sized enthroned ladies called *damas*.

Between 900 and 600 B.C.E., successive waves of Celts crossed the Pyrenees and spread over the central Meseta and the western part of the peninsula. The Celts introduced into Spain iron metallurgy, the broad sword, and trousers. They were soon pressured by Iberians being forced southward by the Gauls. These Iberians moved into the central Meseta, fighting with and eventually dominating the Celts. With the establishment of peace, the two groups intermingled, forming the Celtiberians in the upper Ebro Valley and the eastern Meseta, although the Celts continued to occupy the west (Portugal and Galicia). Their economy depended on livestock raising and hunting as well as on cereal cultivation. The Celts and Celtiberians were divided into dozens of tribes (including the Vettones, Carpetani, and Arevaci) that controlled regions with settlements usually occupying hill forts. When threatened by a common enemy, the tribes formed coalitions under an elected war leader. They were renowned fighters using iron-tipped javelins and short, pointed double-edged swords, both of which were later adopted by the Romans.

The traders. Phoenician traders, attracted by Spain's mineral wealth, reached Spain's Atlantic coast about 1100 B.C.E. There they established Gadir (Cádiz). The Tartessian culture referred to above was likely a blend of Phoenician and local elements, in an area very close to Gadir. Evidence of Phoenician activity in southern Spain does not begin to accumulate until 800

B.C.E., when the Phoenicians came under the sway of the Assyrians and were expected to supply raw materials, especially silver and salt fish. Gadir became a prosperous colony and important commercial center, supporting the establishment of new colonies such as Onoba (Huelva), Malaca (Málaga), and Sexi (Almuñécar).

In the sixth century B.C.E., Assyria fell to the Babylonians, and Phoenicia's commerce with the far west was curtailed, permitting Carthage to gain supremacy over the Semitic colonies in the central and western Mediterranean. In Spain, Carthaginian (Punic) settlement was long restricted to the same coastal strip and offshore islands that had been settled by the Phoenicians. However, after Rome defeated Carthage in the First Punic War (264-241 B.C.E.), Carthage sent a force to conquer southern Spain as compensation for territorial losses in the central Mediterranean. Cartago Nova (Cartagena) was founded as the center of Carthage's Spanish operation. Hannibal led the Punic army deep into Spain, reaching Salamanca and perhaps the Ebro Valley. The east-coast city of Sagunto placed itself under Roman protection. Hannibal's siege of the city provoked the Second Punic War (218-201 B.C.E.). After losing to the Roman consul Scipio Africanus, the Carthaginians had to cede Spain and their remaining Mediterranean island possessions. Because Carthage started as a Phoenician colony, it is difficult to sort out the Carthaginian innovations from those of the Phoenicians. However, it is known that the Carthaginians introduced their knowledge of fish curing and use of esparto grass in making goods such as cordage and shoes.

Greek navigators first sailed along Spain's coasts in the seventh century B.C.E., attracted, like the Phoenicians, by Spain's reputed mineral wealth. Although many Greek pottery fragments have been found as far south as Huelva, no evidence—other than accounts in the writings of historians Herodotus, Strabo, and others—exists to demonstrate that Greeks had direct contact with southern Spain. In northern Spain, Greeks from Massilia (Marseilles) established daughter settlements of Emporion (Ampurias) and Rhode (Roses) around 575 B.C.E. Other places articulated with Emporion, once assumed to have been Greek colonies, either have been shown to be Phoenician (for example, Mainake, in the province of Málaga), or were simply landmarks for sailors (for example, Hemeroskopeion, near Ifach), or await intensive excavation (Saguntum). Nevertheless, Emporion ("a place of commerce") eventually succeeded Massilia as Greece's principal port of trade in the western Mediterranean. The Greeks certainly influenced Spain's trade, and they are credited with introducing the cultivated olive tree and grapevine into Spain.

The Romans. Roman subjugation of Spain was a long, often bloody process of about two hundred years. During and after the Second Punic War, the Romans tried to incorporate the Iberian Peninsula into their republic and, later, their empire. In 206 B.C.E., Scipio Africanus founded Itálica, near Seville, as a home for veteran soldiers. Hispania, as Romans called the peninsula, was soon divided into Hispania Citerior (Nearer Spain, the Ebro Basin and the Levantine coast) and Hispania Ulterior (Farther Spain); later, other divisions were recognized. Romanization proceeded slowly at first. There were frequent clashes with Spanish tribes until about 180 B.C.E. A period of relative peace prevailed until 155-133 B.C.E., when there was a final heroic effort on the part of the Spaniards to expel the conqueror. In 137 B.C.E., 20,000 Romans surrendered to a far smaller force of Numantians. In response, Rome sent 60,000 troops under Scipio Aemilianus to subdue Numantia (near Soria). Encircled by siege camps and circumvallation, many of the starving Numantians committed mass suicide rather than surrender dishonorably. After the fall of Numantia, all but northwestern Spain was conquered, but its pacification required another hundred years. Except for the northwest, the conflicts of the first century B.C.E. were more like civil wars involving Roman political factions.

Spain was profoundly influenced by the long Roman domination (218 B.C.E.-409 C.E.). Most of Spain's principal cities and towns were Roman and were eventually linked by about 12,000 miles (19,300 kilometers) of roads and stone bridges. Impressive architectural remains of the Roman period can still be seen throughout Spain: theaters, amphitheaters, aqueducts, bridges, triumphal arches, baths, and mosaics. Romans established numerous country estates (*villas*) with tenant farmers (*coloni*). Spain was one of the most productive parts of the Roman Empire, exporting wines, olive oil, olives, cereals, salt fish and fish sauce, gold, silver, lead, tin, copper, and iron.

Latin displaced other languages except for Basque. Spain's vernacular Latin, however, varied regionally, much as Spanish does. Roman gods and goddesses were added to those already worshiped in the peninsula, and Christianity took root in Spain even before its legalization under Constantine the Great in 313 C.E.

Native Spaniards, known as Hispano-Romans, made significant contributions to Latin culture as some developed into men of letters (including Seneca the Elder, Seneca the Younger, Lucan, and Martial) or even became Roman emperors (Trajan, Hadrian, and Theodosius the Great). In 380 C.E., Theodosius made Christianity the empire's official religion and denounced other faiths as heretical.

The Visigoths. In the fifth century C.E., the Visigoths, a Germanic people, operated in the south of France as an army of Roman auxiliaries. They were invited into Spain to oust Alani, Suebi, and Vandals, who had poured into Spain in 409 C.E. The Visigoths were to receive land in Aquitaine in compensation, but they stayed in Spain as the country's new governors. At first, the Visigoth kingdom centered on Toulouse, but as Franks pushed into southern France, the Visigoths established new capitals at Barcelona, Mérida, and, finally, Toledo.

There were about 200,000 Visigoths in Spain versus a Hispano-Roman population of about 6 million. Outnumbered and politically unstable, the Visigoths remained a kind of aristocratic-military elite that assimilated Hispano-Roman culture. They adopted Latin (adding several hundred of their own words to the vernacular), maintained Roman administration and law, and in 589 C.E., under King Reccared, converted from Arian Christianity to orthodox Christianity. Their main contributions to Spain were deurbanization and transmigratory flocks of sheep. A struggle for succession to the throne led to an African Berber army invading Spain in 710 C.E. and bringing Visigothic rule to an abrupt end the following year.

ADDITIONAL RESOURCES

Curchin, Leonard A. *Roman Spain: Conquest and Assimilation.* New York: Barnes & Noble, 1995.

Harrison, Richard J. *Spain at the Dawn of History.* London: Thames and Hudson, 1988.

Pierson, Peter. *The History of Spain.* Westport, Conn.: Greenwood Press, 1999.

SEE ALSO: Africa, North; Alani; Arian Christianity; Assyria; Carthage; Celts; Christianity; Franks; Greece, Classical; Hadrian; Hannibal; Lucan; Martial; Phoenicia; Punic Wars; Rome, Imperial; Rome, Republican; Scipio Aemilianus; Scipio Africanus; Seneca the Elder; Seneca the Younger; Theodosius the Great; Trajan; Vandals.

—*Steven L. Driever*

SPARTACUS

BORN: late second century B.C.E.; Thrace
DIED: 71 B.C.E.; southern Italy
RELATED CIVILIZATION: Republican Rome
MAJOR ROLE/POSITION: Gladiator, leader of a slave
revolt

Spartacus. (Library of Congress)

Life. The main sources for Spartacus (SPAHR-tah-kuhs) are Plutarch's *Life of Marcus Crassus* in *Bioi paralleloi* (c. 105-115 C.E.; *Parallel Lives*, 1579) and Appian's *The Civil Wars* in his *Roman History* (c. 130 C.E.; *Appian's Roman History*, 1899). Both accounts were written long after the revolt but most likely depend on the near-contemporary record of Sallust from his now lost work *Historiae* (begun c. 39 B.C.E.; English translation of fragments in *Histories*, 1789).

Originally an auxiliary soldier in the Roman army, Spartacus was enslaved and made a gladiator. While being trained at the gladiatorial school, Spartacus led a revolt that quickly acquired adherents from the local slave and free poor population in the environs of Capua in southern Italy. At its peak, Spartacus's following numbered between 70,000 and 120,000. In 73 and 72 B.C.E., Spartacus soundly defeated the Roman armies sent against him and succeeded in reaching Cisalpine Gaul. He had hoped his army would disband and return home, but they preferred to continue plundering Italy. Finally, in 71 B.C.E., Spartacus and his followers were crushed by armies under Marcus Licinius Crassus and Pompey the Great. Spartacus's body was never found, but thousands of his followers were crucified.

Influence. Modern historians have often seen Spartacus as an enemy of slavery as an institution, but the ancient evidence does not support this view. There is no question, however, that Spartacus was an intelligent, charismatic, and gifted leader ("more like a Greek than a Thracian," writes Plutarch) whose rebellion exposed deep social tensions in the Italian countryside and glaring incompetence among Rome's military elite.

ADDITIONAL RESOURCES

Appian. *The Civil Wars*. Translated by John Carter. Harmondsworth, England: Penguin Classics, 1996.

Bradley, Keith R. *Slavery and Rebellion in the Roman World*. Bloomington: Indiana University Press, 1989.

Plutarch. *The Fall of the Roman Republic*. Translated by Rex Warner. Baltimore: Penguin Books, 1980.

SEE ALSO: Appian; Crassus, Marcus Licinius; Plutarch; Pompey the Great; Rome, Republican; Sallust.
—*Daniel J. Taravella*

SPEUSIPPUS

BORN: c. 407 B.C.E.; place unknown
DIED: 339-338 B.C.E.; place unknown
RELATED CIVILIZATION: Classical Greece
MAJOR ROLE/POSITION: Philosopher

Life. Speusippus (spyew-SIHP-uhs), an Athenian, was the son of Eurymedon and Plato's sister Potone. He probably entered Plato's Academy when it was founded and is known to have traveled with Plato to Sicily in 361 B.C.E. After Plato's death, he became head of the Academy, a position he held until his own death. Little else is known about his life.

Influence. In the ancient world, Speusippus was known for having written a number of books on philosophy, of which only fragments remain. He disagreed with Plato on a number of points, such as the nature of pleasure (which he regarded as an evil), definition (which he regarded as impossible without knowledge of all that exists), and the forms (whose existence he denied). Although it is speculative, it seems likely that he criticized Plato using the notorious "Third Man" argu-ment (infinite regression). He in turn was criticized by Aristotle because he believed in a strict separation of different kinds of reality (such as sensible things and numbers). Aristotle likened this to a bad tragedy, saying that nature is not constructed from disconnected episodes.

ADDITIONAL RESOURCES

Dancy, R. M. "Ancient Non-Beings: Speusippus and Others." *Ancient Philosophy* 9 (1989): 207-243.

_____. *Two Studies in the Early Academy.* Albany, N.Y.: State University of New York Press, 1997.

Guthrie, W. K. C. *A History of Greek Philosophy.* 6 vols. New York: Cambridge University Press, 1978-1990.

Taran, Leonardo. *Speusippus of Athens: A Critical Study with a Collection of the Related Texts and Commentary.* Leiden, Netherlands: E. J. Brill, 1981.

SEE ALSO: Aristotle; Greece, Classical; Philosophy; Plato.

—John Pepple

SRI LANKA

DATE: 8000 B.C.E.-700 C.E.
LOCALE: Island on the Indian Ocean, to the south of the subcontinent of India
RELATED CIVILIZATIONS: India, Hellenistic and Roman Greece, Imperial Rome
SIGNIFICANCE: Many consider Sri Lanka to be the capital of Theravāda (Hīnāyāna) Buddhism for having preserved the complete texts of Buddhism.

Called Ceylon until 1972, pear-shaped Sri Lanka (sree-LAHN-kuh) has an area of 25,332 square miles (or 65,610 square kilometers). A shallow sea, Palk Strait, separates it from India and has permitted periodic contact. The island has a continuous record of settled and civilized life for more than two millennia, and for much of this time frame, Sri Lanka's historical profile bears many parallels to India. Overall, the culture and civilization of Sri Lanka are of the Indic pattern.

Prehistory. A datable sequence of strata for the early Stone Age in Sri Lanka has yet to be achieved. Thus far, the earliest stone implements of chert and quartz bear techniques similar to those found in India. Middle and Upper Paleolithic stages are not distinct or easy to correlate. Not only Indian paleolithic tools but also European ones are found on the island. The Mesolithic or Late Stone Age is marked by backed microlithic tools recovered in great abundance and bearing similarities not only to the Indian counterparts but also to those found in Java, Sulawesi, and Australia. This wide distribution suggests heightened activity or population increase. The microlithic industry probably began around 4000 B.C.E., if not earlier. The microliths were frequently found associated with bone implements (gouges, awls, fishhooks, and bipoints) and with specialized stone tools such as hammers, crushers, and pounders.

The transformation from food gathering to producing probably took place more than five thousand years ago. In comparison with the microliths, the Neolithic indicators are relatively sparse. Microliths continue to be found during this period, tending to be found with pebbles 4-5 inches (10-12 centimeters) long with abrasions and shallow drilled holes as well as larger, irregularly formed stone pieces marked with oval cavities and cup-shaped depressions on the sides. Probably these were used as anvils for drilling holes in beads. Pottery from simple dishes and pots also made its appearance; however, no metal was found in association. Burial finds at Bellan Bandi Palassa give clues as to burial practices and the phenotype of the island's early settlers. Personal adornment is evident in bone pendants, perforated shells, and hints of colored pigments. This Neolithic assemblage was named the Balangoda culture by an archaeologist. Between the Neolithic period and the onset of the Iron Age, estimated to have occurred at 600 B.C.E., is a temporal span that needs to be clarified and filled in.

Contemporaneous with the megalithic period, the Iron Age covers protohistorical Sri Lanka. As in Deccan and south India, this culture is characterized by burial sites. However, Sri Lankan burials did not achieve the elaborateness of the cist (stone-lined burial chamber) in Mysore or the sarcophagi of Madras. Perhaps Buddhism's entry into the island came too soon. The best-known burial site of this period is the Pomparippu cemetery. Its site yielded terra-cotta urns and pots of the black-and-red type. Some pots bear basket marking and incised lines; others had primitive Brahmi inscriptions (numerals). Also found at the site were evidence of cremation and inhumation, animal bones, bronze objects, and carnelian beads. Outline paintings, in monochrome and polychrome, and rock engravings are also associated with this period, although their precise status, prehistoric or protohistoric, is unresolved. Whether these art forms were produced by the aboriginal Veddas or not is moot.

Early settlers. Scholars have reconstructed the peopling of Sri Lanka as a series of migrations and subsequent admixtures of groups, a process that is reflected even in early islanders' origin myths. Various regions of India have been posited as the source of migrations; however, it is likely that the island's first human settlers were the Veddas, tribes of proto-Australoids resembling the pre-Dravidian hill tribes of India. The Veddas are characterized by slender build, small stature, dark complexion, and profuse wavy hair. Remnants of these migrants were eventually absorbed by the Indo-Aryans who emigrated from India around 500 B.C.E. and settled in various parts of the island. The most powerful of the clans and tribes were the Sinhalas, whose descendants were later called Sinhalese. Tamils probably came from Dravidian India in a long series of migrations stretching

from the second to the thirteenth centuries C.E.

The first historic colonists of Sri Lanka were Prince Vijaya and his seven hundred Sinhalese followers, who landed on the west coast of Puttalam in the sixth century B.C.E. Banished from India by his father, King Sinhabāhu, for misbehavior, Vijaya and company were put on a ship and driven away. The group landed on the island (Sri Lanka) described as inhabited by *yaksas* (demons). The demons were defeated and pursued into the interior. Vijaya subsequently married a *yaksa* princess (other interpretations claim a Tamil princess), who bore him two children. Later Vijaya sent her and the children to the Madurai court in India for a Pandu princess for him and for wives to his followers. He reigned as the first sovereign of Lanka, variously known in the chronicles as Sihaladipa (island of Sihalas) or Simhaladipa (island of the Lion), and formed a dynasty. He was succeeded by his brother's youngest son, Pāñduvāsudeva, who came with a thirty-two-person entourage. The capital, Tambapanni (sheet of copper), called Taprobane by Greeks and Roman authors, was transferred by the third ruler to Anuradhapura, where archaeology has revealed a long occupation. For more than a thousand years, it was to become the royal capital.

Conversion to Buddhism. According to the chronicles, the sixth king, Dēvānampiya Tissa (fl. c. 247-207 B.C.E.), was in power when Buddhism came to the island. The proselytizing zeal of King Aśoka of India and the missionary undertaking of one of his sons, Mahinda, brought Buddhism into the island. The Indian monk Mahinda was said to have memorized all the Buddhist teachings and tenets, which were written down in Pāli and thus preserved in full by local devotees. Reportedly, Mahinda converted Dēvānampiya Tissa in the year of the latter's coronation. In honor of his new faith, the Lanka king built a monastery in Anuradhapura called the Mahāvihāra and the first stupa, the Thuparama Dāgaba. Mahinda's sister, Saṅghamittā, a nun, followed him to the island and set up the first communities for women. She brought with her a slip from the Bodhi tree and planted it in the capital. After the death of Dēvānampiya Tissa, dynastic rivalries ensued.

At the end of the third century C.E., the throne was conquered by a Tamil (Hindu) king, Elara (204-161 B.C.E.), who was celebrated in the texts as a just leader. Soon Dutthagāmanī (r. 161-137 B.C.E.) recovered the throne for the Vijaya line through a single battle. Dutthagāmanī was the ruler of the princedom of Rohana in the southeast of the island. Dutthagāmanī has been hailed a hero and a symbol of Sinhalese nationalism. The cycle of peaceful dynastic rule and occasional struggle with an external peril became a common pattern for much of Sinhalese history. The Vijaya Dynasty ruled with occasional interruptions until 65 C.E.

At the beginning of the first century B.C.E., workers laid the foundation of the Abhayagiri monastery, the centerpiece of Vaṭṭagāmaṇi's reign (r. 89-77 B.C.E.). However, the founding of the monastery also marked the beginning of a religious schism that would last until 1200 C.E. Three other kings ruled before the end of the first Anuradhapura period: Mahāsena (r. 276-303 C.E.), Sirimeghavana (r. 303-331 C.E.), and Mahānama (d. 432 C.E.). Mahāsena built major irrigation systems and championed Buddhist sect heterodoxy. The dynasty ruled for four hundred years but was ended by a Pāṇḍyan invasion from south India.

Dhātusena (r. 459-477 C.E.) recovered the throne from the Pāṇḍyas and subsequently passed it on to his son, Kāśyapa I (r. 477-495 C.E.). Kāśyapa moved the capital from Anuradhapura to Sirigiya. However, on his dethronement, the capital was returned to Anuradhapura. The Anuradhapura period ended when Sri Lanka was annexed to the kingdom of the Cōḷas (993-1070 C.E.), and the capital was totally abandoned. More reigns and rulers followed as additional dynasties were formed and revived. All the kings were practicing Buddhists and patrons of Buddhist institutions. They built, maintained, and endowed monasteries and shrines, intervened to establish order, and prevented schisms in the Buddhist faith.

ADDITIONAL RESOURCES

Arasaratnam, S. *Ceylon.* Englewood Cliffs, N.J.: Prentice-Hall, 1964.
Boisselier, Jean. *Ceylon-Sri Lanka.* Geneva, Switzerland: Nagel, 1979.
Hammond, Norman, ed. *South Asian Archaeology.* Ridge Park, N.J.: Noyes Press, 1973.
Samarasinghe, S. W. R. *Historical Dictionary of Sri Lanka.* Lanham, Md.: Scarecrow Press, 1998.

SEE ALSO: Aśoka; Buddhism; Hinduism; India; Tissa, Dēvānaṃpiya; Vaṭṭagāmaṇi.

—*E. P. Flores-Meiser*

SRONG-BRTSAN-SGAM-PO

ALSO KNOWN AS: Song-tsen-gam-po
BORN: c. 608 C.E.; place unknown
DIED: 650 C.E.; place unknown
RELATED CIVILIZATIONS: Tang Dynasty, China, India, Nepal
MAJOR ROLE/POSITION: King, military and religious leader

Life. Known as the first Buddhist king of Tibet, Srong-brtsan-sgam-po (SRAWN-burt-SAHN-SKAHM-poh), while still a minor, attained the throne of what was to become the central Tibetan Empire about 627 C.E. Aided by powerful state ministers, he was responsible for the dramatic expansion and consolidation of the empire through military conquest and skillful diplomacy. In his lifetime, the empire controlled much of Central Asia, including what is today the Tibetan plateau, the Transhimalaya to the south, west, and north, western China, and the extremely important Silk Road. He moved the capital of his empire from the Yarlung valley to Lhasa, where it has been maintained through modern times.

Buddhism was established as a court religion during his reign, and, in time, it came to dominate religious practice on the plateau. He was buried in a massive mound in the Yarlung valley, which became the historic burial grounds of the Yarlung Dynasty.

Influence. Despite minor setbacks, Srong-brtsan-sgam-po created a stable empire in the central Tibetan region that was to last until the mid-ninth century C.E. Buddhism grew from a limited court religion to a powerful monastic and ecclesiastical force during this time, profoundly transforming the course of Tibetan civilization.

ADDITIONAL RESOURCES

Beckwith, S. *The Tibetan Empire in Central Asia.* Princeton, N.J.: Princeton University Press, 1987.
Sinor, Denis. *The Cambridge History of Early Inner Asia.* New York: Cambridge University Press, 1990.
Stein, R. A. *Tibetan Civilization.* Stanford, Calif.: Stanford University Press, 1972.

SEE ALSO: Buddhism; Silk Road; Tibet.

—*Mark Aldenderfer*

STATIUS, PUBLIUS PAPINIUS

BORN: c. 45 C.E.; Neapolis (later Naples, Italy)
DIED: 96 C.E.; Italy
RELATED CIVILIZATION: Imperial Rome
MAJOR ROLE/POSITION: Poet

Life. Born in the Greek city of Naples, Publius Papinius Statius (PUHB-lee-uhs puh-PIHN-ee-uhs STAY-shee-uhs) moved to Rome in about 65 C.E. By 83 C.E., he had became well established in Roman literary society, as shown by the public performance of his pantomime libretto *Agave* and the publication of an epic on Domitian's Germanic campaigns in or around this year; except for a fragment of the latter, these works and others that Statius composed for poetry competitions, in which he enjoyed varying degrees of success, have not survived.

The major work of his life, the *Thebaid* (c. 91 C.E.; English translation, 1928), a mythological epic consisting of twelve books, was begun in about 79 C.E. and published in about 91 C.E. This was followed by the publication of the first four books of occasional poems known as the *Silvae* (93-c. 96 C.E.; English translation, 1928) in about 93 and 95 C.E. Statius retired to Naples in 94 C.E. and died in 96 C.E., after which his *Achilleid* (c. 96 C.E.; English translation, 1928), an unfinished epic in two books, and the fifth book of the *Silvae* were published.

Influence. Statius fashioned a new type of poetry in the *Silvae* by combining features of Roman friendship poetry with elements of Greek encomiastic poetry. In the *Thebaid*, he created a mythic cosmos that provocatively reflects his contemporary Rome in political and cultural terms. Statius was much admired in the Middle Ages for his poetic achievements, and of all the Roman epic poets after Vergil, he is the most likely to appeal to modern readers.

ADDITIONAL RESOURCES

Dominik, William J. *The Mythic Voice of Statius: Power and Politics in the Thebaid*. Leiden, Netherlands: E. J. Brill, 1994.

Hardie, Alex. *Statius and the Silvae: Poets, Patrons, and Epideixis in the Greco-Roman World*. Liverpool, England: Francis Cairns, 1983.

SEE ALSO: Domitian; Languages and literature; Rome, Imperial; Vergil.

—William J. Dominik

STESICHORUS

BORN: 632/29 B.C.E.; Himera, Sicily, or Matauros, Italy
DIED: 556/53 B.C.E.; place unknown
RELATED CIVILIZATION: Archaic Greece
MAJOR ROLE/POSITION: Poet

Life. Practically nothing is known of Stesichorus's (stuh-SIHK-uh-ruhs) life. Ancient Greek tradition places him either in Himera or in Matauros. He composed lyric poetry for individual performance with lyre and perhaps for chorus. As a working poet of the era, he probably was patronized by aristocratic families and cities for which he composed works as part of civic celebrations. This relationship between poet and patron is better documented for Stesichorus's successors: Simonides, Pindar, and Bacchylides. The Greek historian Pausanias relates the fanciful story that Stesichorus was blinded for portraying Helen as an adulterer who followed Paris (Alexandros) to Troy. Stesichorus's retraction, which survives in fragments, gives an alternate version in which Helen's phantom image had gone to Troy, thus proving the real Helen's virtue. Pausanias says that as a result Stesichorus was given back his sight. The poet's works were collected in twenty-six books, of which quotations and fragmentary papyri survive. His poems achieve a heightened emotional effect from their combination of Homeric and other epic narratives with lyric meters.

Influence. Stesichorus's recastings of epic narratives of Troy (*Wooden Horse*, *Sack of Troy*, *Homecomings*, *Helen*, and *Oresteia*), stories of Thebes (*Eriphyle*, *Europia*, and a work on Oedipus's sons), Heracles' exploits (*Cycnus*, *Cerberus*, *Geryoneis*), and other mythological traditions (*Calydonian Boar Hunt*) became a valuable storehouse of material and storytelling patterns for the choral lyric poets Pindar and Bacchylides, for the Greek tragedians Aeschylus and Euripides, and even for Athenian vase painters.

ADDITIONAL RESOURCES
Campbell, David A. *Greek Lyric*. Cambridge, Mass.: Harvard University Press, 1993.
Mulroy, D. *Early Greek Lyric Poetry*. Ann Arbor: University of Michigan Press, 1992.
Segal, C. "Stesichorus." In vol. 1 of *The Cambridge History of Classical Literature*. Cambridge, England: Cambridge University Press, 1984.

SEE ALSO: Aeschylus; Bacchylides; Euripides; Greece, Archaic; Languages and literature; Pindar; Simonides; Troy.

—*Marc Mastrangelo*

STILICHO, FLAVIUS

BORN: c. 365 C.E.; place unknown
DIED: August 22, 408 C.E.; Ravenna, Italy
RELATED CIVILIZATION: Imperial Rome
MAJOR ROLE/POSITION: Military leader

Life. Born to a Vandal father and a Roman mother, Flavius Stilicho (FLAY-vee-uhs STIHL-ih-koh) pursued a career in the Roman army, becoming a trusted general to Emperor Theodosius the Great. When Theodosius died in 395 C.E., he entrusted the guardianship of his son Honorius to Stilicho. Despite considerable friction between Stilicho and the Eastern court in Constantinople, the West was well governed and defended under his care.

Stilicho, as master general of the West, defeated the Visigoths in Greece, the rebel Gildo in Africa, and Vandal raiders in Italy (395-401 C.E.). Large invasions of Italy by the barbarian kings Alaric I and Radagaisus were also repulsed (401-405 C.E.). These battles forced Stilicho to call many of the frontier armies away from their stations to the defense of Italy. As a result, a large barbarian invasion of Gaul went virtually unchecked (405-406 C.E.) and rebellion arose in Britain (406 C.E. onward).

Finally in 408 C.E., the young emperor Honorius, fearing that Stilicho was grooming his own son Eucherius to take the throne, had Stilicho and many of his key followers murdered.

Influence. Stilicho was a capable general who kept Italy safe from barbarians for many years. His murder was one of the colossal blunders in Roman history, as it caused thousands of his loyal soldiers to desert to the Goths and led directly to the Visigothic sack of Rome in 410 C.E.

ADDITIONAL RESOURCES
Bury, J. B. *History of the Later Roman Empire*. New York: Dover, 1978.
Gibbon, Edward. *Decline and Fall of the Roman Empire*. Reprint. New York: Modern Library, 1995.

SEE ALSO: Africa, North; Alaric I; Britain; Constantinople; Gauls; Goths, Ostrogoths, Visigoths; Rome, Imperial; Theodosius the Great; Vandals.

—*David Langdon Nelson*

STONEHENGE

DATE: 3100-1550 B.C.E.
LOCALE: Salisbury Plain, southern England
RELATED CIVILIZATIONS: Neolithic farming peoples, Britain
SIGNIFICANCE: This ancient structure reveals the engineering abilities of Stone Age peoples and raises questions about the sophistication of Neolithic astronomical observations.

Stonehenge is a circular megalithic stone structure, one of thirteen such structures of standing stones found in Britain. Scholars believe work began on Stonehenge about 3100 B.C.E., when a circle 320 feet (98 meters) in diameter was enclosed with a 6-foot (1.8-meter) bank. Flanked by two stones, Stonehenge's entrance is oriented to the northeast, the direction of the summer-solstice sunrise. This axis is marked by a 16-foot-high (5-meter-high), 35-ton (32-metric-ton) heel stone, located 96 feet (29 meters) past the entrance. Just inside the bank lies a circle 284 feet (87 meters) in diameter of fifty-six Aubrey holes. Named for antiquarian John Aubrey, these holes are evenly spaced some 16 feet (5 meters) apart, are between 2 and 4 feet (0.6-1.2 meters) deep, and were filled with chalk soon after being dug.

Stonehenge. (Corbis)

Excavations revealed that some holes contained human cremations from a later date. In this form, Stonehenge was used for several centuries and then abandoned.

Around 2700 B.C.E., communal long barrow graves were replaced with round barrows for individuals, containing copper daggers, gold earrings, fine pottery, and a distinctive type of drinking cup without handles. Once believed to have reflected an invasion of Beaker people, such artifacts now seem to reflect an emerging elite trading in flint, copper, tin, and prestige items while the people continued their Neolithic farming traditions. New henges began to appear, some near Stonehenge itself.

New work began at Stonehenge around 2100 B.C.E. By building two parallel chalk banks with exterior ditches more than one-third of a mile (roughly half a kilometer) long, the new builders created an avenue leading up to the northeast entrance. Eighty 6-foot (1.8-meter) bluestones, imported from the Preseli Mountains in Wales, were stood in two incomplete concentric circles. Researchers believe this may have been when four "station stones" were erected on the Aubrey Circle, imposing on it a rough rectangle. In 1978, a Beaker burial was discovered in the ditch, continuing the association of enclosures with death and ritual.

Between 2000 and 1550 B.C.E., the bluestones were removed, and large sarsen (foreign) sandstone blocks were brought from twenty miles to the north. Thirty blocks weighing 25 tons (23 metric tons) each were stood 3.5 feet (1 meter) apart to form a circle 100 feet

(30 meters) in diameter, then topped by lintels, creating a flat circular "sidewalk" elevated 16 feet (nearly 5 meters) above the ground. Inside was a horseshoe-shaped arrangement of five trilithons (each made of two upright blocks topped by a lintel), with the open end of the horseshoe oriented on the northeast axis. Sixty bluestones were added, forming circle 75 feet (23 meters) in diameter within the sarsen circle. Nineteen bluestones placed within the trilithons formed a bluestone horseshoe. The workmanship and innovative design of the sarsen circle occur in no other megalithic monument on earth.

Later alterations have been attributed to the Wessex culture of southern Britain's early Bronze Age, given that dozens of Wessex round barrows dot surrounding ridges. In 1965, Harvard astronomer Gerald Hawkins theorized that Stonehenge served as a giant astronomical observatory, noting that stone alignments marked key positions of the Sun and Moon. Archaeologists have questioned the alignments' precision, although Alexander Marshack has claimed that 25,000-year-old bones found in European sites have been engraved with precise day-to-day markings of the positions of the Moon. If Marshack is correct, ancient knowledge of astronomy could validate Hawkins's claims.

ADDITIONAL RESOURCES

Burl, Aubrey. *Great Stone Circles: Fables, Fictions, Facts.* New Haven, Conn.: Yale University Press, 1999.

Cunliffe, Barry, and Colin Renfrew. *Science and Stonehenge.* New York: Oxford University Press, 1997.

Hawkins, Gerald S., with John B. White. *Stonehenge Decoded.* Rev. ed. New York: Dorsett, 1987.

Marshack, Alexander. *The Roots of Civilization: The Cognitive Beginnings of Man's First Art, Symbol,* *and Notation.* Rev. ed. Mount Kisco, N.Y.: Moyer Bell, 1991.

Souden, David. *Stonehenge Revealed.* New York: Facts On File, 1997.

SEE ALSO: Britain; Celts.

—*Thomas J. Sienkewicz*

STRABO

BORN: 64/63 B.C.E.; Amasia, Pontus, Asia Minor
DIED: after 23 C.E.; probably Amasia or Rome
RELATED CIVILIZATIONS: Hellenistic and Roman Greece, Imperial Rome
MAJOR ROLE/POSITION: Geographer, historian

Life. Born to wealthy parents, Strabo (STRAY-boh) studied grammar, geography, and philosophy. For six years, he lived in Egypt and worked in the great library of Alexandria and traveled the Nile as far as Ethiopia. He also lived in Rome for six years but seems not to have traveled much beyond major roadways. He visited Crete and Corinth for short periods of time. His travel in Greece was very limited. At the time of his death, he was probably in Amasia or Rome. Almost nothing of his personal life is known.

Strabo wrote two major works, one of which survives. The lost work was a forty-seven-book history of Rome that he hoped would supplement Polybius's *The Histories.* His extant work is *Geōgraphica* (c. 7 B.C.E.; *Geography,* 1917-1933) in seventeen books. Books 1 and 2 are among the most important, being a critique of past works on the subject, almost all of which no longer exist. Indeed, much of what is known of Eratosthenes of Cyrene, Posidonius, and Eudoxus of Cnidus is found in Strabo's *Geography.* The remainder of the work presents his conceptions of Spain, Sicily, Italy, Greece, Egypt, India, and Persia as well as the Middle East. As he did not visit many of these places, he relied heavily on previous sources for his information. Occasionally, he failed to employ the most up-to-date sources available, for example, Julius Caesar's *Comentarii de bello Gallico* (52-51 B.C.E.; translated with *Comentarii de bello civili,* 45 B.C.E., as *Commentaries,* 1609), and he gave more credence to myth when dealing with Greece than was common by this time.

In part because his training in mathematics was limited, Strabo's geography was more cultural than physical, and he tended to undervalue the more scientific approach. He suggested (from Eratosthenes) that the inhabited world (*oikoumene*) was a single landmass surrounded by oceans and included Europe, Asia, and Africa with their associated islands. He hoped that his work would be read by the rulers of Rome so that they would understand the geography of the areas over which they ruled.

Influence. Strabo's work on geography provides a compendium of much of the knowledge of that subject in the first century of the common era. His commentaries and quotations from earlier writers are invaluable. Finally, his own style, never dull, provides insights into the thinking of educated Greco-Romans early in the Roman Empire.

Strabo. (Library of Congress)

ADDITIONAL RESOURCES
Dueck, Daniela. *Strabo of Amasia: A Greek Man of Letters in Augustan Rome.* New York: Routledge, 2000.
Strabo. *The Geography of Strabo.* Translated by Horace Leonard Jones. Reprint. Cambridge, Mass.: Harvard University Press, 1982.

Tozer, H. F. *A History of Ancient Geography.* New York: Biblio and Tannen, 1964.

SEE ALSO: Caesar, Julius; Eratosthenes of Cyrene; Eudoxus; Greece, Hellenistic and Roman; Posidonius; Rome, Imperial.

—*Terry R. Morris*

SUBARCTIC PEOPLES

DATE: 8000 B.C.E.-700 B.C.E.
LOCALE: Alaska, Northern Canada, Greenland.
RELATED CIVILIZATIONS: Eskimo-Aleut, Athapaskan, Algonquian, Northwest Coast
SIGNIFICANCE: The subarctic cultures and the closely related Arctic cultures represent the first human groups in the Americas and are most likely the ancestors of all subsequent groups now referred to as Indians or Native Americans.

The term "subarctic culture" is somewhat of a misnomer as at least three distinct groups of early people can be delineated in the vast area ranging from the Pacific to the Atlantic and from the Arctic to the Northwest Coast. Although these three groups appear to have migrated into North America independently of one another and no clear evidence has been found for any relationship among their languages, climatic and ecological conditions drove them to adapt very similar cultural traits.

History. The early history of the peoples of North America is sketchy at best. No tribes north of Mexico developed a written language, so the natives' own stories of their origins and development are entirely a matter of oral tradition and myth. Archaeological and genetic evidence gathered in modern times, however, suggests that at least two, and more likely three, migrations from Asia took place during the last Ice Age, roughly 20,000 to 12,000 years ago.

The earliest migration was probably that of the NaDene peoples, the ancestors of the Athapaskan and Algonquian cultures. These people almost certainly crossed from Siberia over the land bridge that existed between that area and Alaska until the melting of the glaciers, a land area referred to by modern archaeologists as Beringia. Their movement appears to have been very slow, as is attested by a huge variety of mutually indistinguishable languages. By the time of their first encounter with Europeans, the Vikings, about 1000 C.E., the Athapaskans ranged from Alaska to the Atlantic coast and from the Arctic circle to the Southwest.

The probable second migration was that of the Northwest Coast Indians, and even less evidence adheres to this group. They ranged from the Pacific coast of Alaska south to Washington and Oregon and spoke a group of languages apparently unrelated to any others.

The Eskimos and Aleuts are the most widespread group and apparently the last to enter North America. They are physically and genetically distinct from the other groups, generally short and stocky, with epicanthic folds that suggest a recent Asian origin. Their relatively recent entry onto the North American continent and their rapid spread are evidenced by the fact that their languages have changed very little over the millennia, and Eskimos from Alaska to Greenland can still understand one another.

Over a probable period of ten thousand years between the first entry of these peoples into North America and their first encounters with Europeans, little change took place in culture or beliefs. Life was literally a matter of survival. The large mammals they encountered in North America, which had never before encountered people, together with the extremely harsh climate, caused these people to be primarily concerned with the procurement of food.

The three groups must have encountered one another, but once again, evidence is scarce, and the three language groups do not appear to be related. The Athapaskans and Northwest Coast peoples appear genetically similar, but the Eskimo-Aleut groups are quite different. Linguistic evidence points to a connection with the peoples of Siberia, but the lack of written language makes this connection uncertain.

Social structure. Among all three groups, family structures were complex but very uncertain. Polygamy, both men marrying several women and vice versa, was common. Family relationships were emphasized down to several generations, but beyond this point, organization was loose.

The chief was generally agreed upon by mutual consent and selected based on real abilities, including hunting skills and judgment. Chiefs were never autocratic, and decisions were made by discussion among those considered most responsible.

The tribal groupings delineated by modern Americans and others are very generalized. A group of Athapaskans or Eskimos might be united in a loose sort of way by linguistic similarities and join together for hunts or religious ceremonies, but these groupings were always temporary. More permanent were bands of hunters, ranging from about fifty to two hundred.

Sexual differences were very highly emphasized. Boys were trained to be hunters, girls to be cooks and seamstresses. Chiefs and shamans were invariably male. Family structures were fluid; children were often adopted and considered no less a part of the family than those joined to it by birth.

Religion. The subarctic cultures never developed a pantheon of gods, as so many American and European cultures did. Their primary concern was with survival, which meant dealing with the spirits of the animals they hunted for a living. It was necessary to placate the spirits before they were killed for food. In many areas, animals were considered morally superior to their human hunters, and it was necessary to get their permission before killing them. Otherwise, the spirits of the dead animals could communicate with their living relatives and prevent the humans from further successful hunting. A great deal of emphasis was placed on song, accompanied by musical instruments, especially drums. Songs were developed for specific animals and also for specific weapons.

Hunting and fishing. In the subarctic area, where growing seasons could be limited to as little as sixty days of frost-free conditions, agriculture was virtually impossible and rarely developed. The subarctic cultures subsisted mainly on hunting large mammals, and when these were not available, on hunting smaller animals. Near coastal areas and large rivers, the practice of fishing, especially of salmon, was also important.

The lack of experience among the large mammals of North America with human beings may have led to their extinction. Fossil evidence suggests that the animals hunted by the early Americans included sabertooth tigers, wolves, and elk far larger than any found in modern times. These animals were apparently driven to extinction by the early hunters.

Current views. Changes in global environmental models of the last Ice Age have resulted in additional and alternate theories about how the first people came to North America. One theory is that about 9,000 years ago, when the Bering land bridge existed, in addition to those who crossed to North America by land, hunters in boats traveled the north Pacific Rim, settling along the coast of Alaska and Canada. In addition, deoxyribonucleic acid (DNA) evidence from studies of native Siberians and North Americans points to a possible interchange of people, of movement both to and from North America.

ADDITIONAL RESOURCES

Bone, Robert W. *Fielding's Guide to Alaska and the Yukon*. New York: Fielding Travel Books, 1990.

Crawford, Michael H. *The Origins of Native Americans: Evidence from Anthropological Genetics*. Cambridge, England: Cambridge University Press, 1998.

Pringle, Heather. *In Search of Ancient North America: An Archaeological Journey to Forgotten Cultures*. New York: John Wiley and Sons, 1996.

SEE ALSO: American Paleo-Arctic tradition; Archaic North American culture; Archaic tradition, northern; Ipiutak; Kachemak tradition; Maritime Archaic; Paleo-Indians in North America.

—*Marc Goldstein*

ŚŪDRAKA

ALSO KNOWN AS: possibly the same as Śaumila
FLOURISHED: c. 300-c. 600 C.E.
RELATED CIVILIZATION: North India
MAJOR ROLE/POSITION: Playwright

Life. A king called Śūdraka (shew-DRAW-kah) is known as the writer of the play *Mṛcchakaṭikā* (c. 300-c. 600 C.E.; *Mrchhakatika*, 1898, also known as *The Little*

Clay Cart). His identity, however, is surrounded in controversy. Although there is no reliable record of a ruler of that name in the list of Indian kings with whom the play can be associated, there are a few legendary references to a king of that name. Some believe that the author was actually a court poet named Śaumila who lived after the writer Bhāsa but slightly before the time of the poet Kālidāsa; however, the court in which Śaumila served is uncertain. Many experts believe the style of writing shares much with the work of Bhāsa and contend that Śūdraka and Bhāsa were the same person. Others insist that writer enlarged on Bhāsa's work *Cārudata* (second or third century C.E.; English translation, 1930-1931) by adding to it a subplot involving a lowborn revolutionary named Śūdraka who overthrew an unjust king. The preface to the play states that the writer committed suicide at the age of one hundred, but the statement works against the identification of Śūdraka in that he himself would have been dead at the time of writing the statement. *Mrchhakatika* is the only work credited to Śūdraka. Scholars doubt that such a brilliant writer, one who lived for a century, would have left behind only one work.

Despite the controversies about its origin, *Mricchakatika* is one of the best known and best loved of the surviving classical Sanskrit dramas. The plot revolves around the love affair of a beautiful courtesan named Vasanthasenā and a poor man of generous disposition named Cārudata. Of particular importance in this play is the information about the social conditions of the times, presumably the fourth century C.E.

Influence. The elegant classical Sanskrit writing was known to and inspired many later Indian writers. It also was the first Indian work to glorify a political revolution.

ADDITIONAL RESOURCES

Dandekar, R. N. *The Age of the Guptas and Other Essays*. Delhi, India: Ajanta Publications, 1982.

Devasarma, Visvanatha. *Shudraka*. New Delhi, India: Sahitya Akademi, 1999.

Oliver, Revilo Pendleton, trans. *The Little Clay Cart*. Urbana: University of Illinois, 1938.

SEE ALSO: Bhāsa; India; Kālidāsa.

—*Katherine Anne Harper*

SUEBI

ALSO KNOWN AS: Suevi
DATE: c. 150 B.C.E.-600 C.E.
LOCALE: Germany, Gaul, northwestern Spain and Portugal
RELATED CIVILIZATIONS: Republican and Imperial Rome
SIGNIFICANCE: The invasion of Gaul and Spain by these tribespeople added to the disruption that ended Roman rule in Western Europe.

The Germanic Suebi were constituted of a number of tribes including the Semnones, Marcomanni, Chatti, Hermunduri, Quadi, and perhaps Langobards. From the mid-second century B.C.E., these peoples were consolidating in and expanding from the region between the Elbe and Oder Rivers. In his *Comentarii de bello Gallico* (52-51 B.C.E.; *Commentaries on the Gallic War*, 1892), Julius Caesar describes battles with the Suebi as early as 58 B.C.E. Some Suebi migrated southward toward the Danube, and others remained in the northern homeland. From the Suebi who emerge as the Allemanni tribe in the fourth century comes the German territorial label Swabia (Schwaben).

The Huns' invasions of the later fourth century C.E. pushed many Suebic tribes into Roman Gaul. By 409 C.E., they had been defeated several times in battle but migrated south toward Spain, which they reached in 409 C.E. In 411 C.E., Rome recognized their settlements in Galicia and northern Portugal and employed them against the Vandals and Visigoths. Pagan and Catholic Suebi were converted to Arianism by the Visigothic contact, but during the reign of King Rechiarius (r. 445-456 C.E.), Bishop Martin of Braga (the capital) converted many to Catholicism. Extinction of the royal line, squabbling among minor chieftains, and Visigothic military victories reduced the Suebic kingdom to a Visigothic province (c. 585 C.E.).

ADDITIONAL RESOURCES

Collins, Roger. *Early Medieval Spain*. London: Macmillan, 1995.

Isidore of Seville. *Isidore of Seville's History of the Goths, Vandals, and Suevi*. Translated by G. Donini and G. B. Ford. Leiden, Netherlands: E. J. Brill, 1970.

Wolf, Keneth B., ed. *Conquerors and Chroniclers of Early Medieval Spain*. Liverpool, England: Liverpool University Press, 1990.

SEE ALSO: Allemanni; Arianism; Caesar, Julius; Christianity; Gallic Wars; Gauls; Germany; Goths, Ostrogoths, Visigoths; Rome, Imperial; Rome, Republican; Spain; Vandals.

—*Joseph P. Byrne*

SUETONIUS

ALSO KNOWN AS: Gaius Suetonius Tranquillius
BORN: 70 C.E.; Hippo Regius, North Africa
DIED: after 122 C.E.; place unknown
RELATED CIVILIZATION: Imperial Rome
MAJOR ROLE/POSITION: Biographer

Life. Little is known about Suetonius's (swee-TOH-nee-uhs) life. The few details are learned mostly from Pliny the Younger's *Epistulae* (97-109 C.E., books 1-9; c. 113 C.E., book 10; *The Letters*, 1748). Suetonius practiced law in Rome but abandoned this occupation to write. He traveled to Bithynia with Pliny the Younger. The emperors Trajan and Hadrian appointed him to governmental posts. These offices within the palace gave him access to private documents of the Julio-Claudian emperors, which he employed in his biographies. Suetonius, among others, was dismissed from his position by Hadrian because of an offense to the empress Sabina Vibia (122 C.E.).

Suetonius's surviving works include biographies of the Caesars and of famous men, including poets. His *De vita Caesarum* (c.120 C.E.; *History of the Twelve Caesars*, 1606) contains biographies of Julius Caesar and eleven emperors from Augustus to Domitian. The organization of these biographies is thematic rather than chronological. Suetonius records each emperor's birth, early life, accomplishments, personal traits, and death. He often includes lengthy quotations from original sources. His inclusion of scandalous detail made him popular. Suetonius also wrote the *De viris illustribus urbis Romeo* (106-113 C.E.; *The Lives of Illustrious Romans*, 1693), which included biographies of poets, philosophers, and historians. Only a few of these biographies have survived.

Influence. The authors of the *Historia Augusta* (c. 325 C.E.; *The Scriptores Historiae Augustae*, 1921-1932) followed Suetonius's biographical approach to history and recorded the lives of the emperors from Hadrian to Numerianus. Suetonius's style of biography continued to influence the writing of history for centuries.

ADDITIONAL RESOURCES

Launsbury, R. C. *The Arts of Suetonius*. New York: Peter Lang, 1987.
Suetonius. *Suetonius*. Cambridge, Mass.: Harvard University Press, 1998.
Wallace-Hadrill, A. *Suetonius: The Scholar and His Caesars*. New Haven, Conn.: Yale University Press, 1984.

SEE ALSO: Augustus; Domitian; Hadrian; Pliny the Younger; Rome, Imperial; Sabina, Vibia; Trajan.
—Emily E. Batinski

SUI DYNASTY

DATE: 581-618 C.E.
LOCALE: Luoyang, China
RELATED CIVILIZATION: China
SIGNIFICANCE: After four hundred disunited years since the collapse of the Han Dynasty, Emperor Wendi reunited China by founding the short-lived Sui Dynasty.

Wendi, a general to the last Northern Wei emperor, married his daughter to the emperor. When that emperor died, his infant grandson became emperor, but Wendi chose to displace his grandson and conquer the weak neighboring states, thereby founding the Sui (swee) Dynasty. Emperor Wendi began well with land distribution, peasant tax relief, currency stabilization, limited military service, standardized weights and measures, law softening and simplification, and reinstitution of civil service selection. His personal frugality led to such governmental saving that during his twenty-five-year reign, he gathered enough grain and cloth to protect against fifty years of crop failures. In the end, he became paranoid and executed many subordinates and their families before being assassinated (604 C.E.) by his son, Emperor Yang Di.

Before being named heir, Yang Di appeared to be obedient, kind, frugal, and diligent. Yang Di completed his father's building of the Grand Canal, created a more defensible capital at Luoyang, built thousands of ships to ply inland waterways, and rebuilt the deteriorated Great Wall. These expensive projects were compounded by his latter-day personal licentiousness and his many conquests of Vietnam, Mongolia, and Turkestan. His three disastrous Korean campaigns consumed much of the wealth his father had accumulated. Li Yuan, an aide, assassinated Yang Di (618 C.E.) and founded the three-hundred-year Tang Dynasty.

ADDITIONAL RESOURCES
Heinz, Carolyn Brown. *Asian Cultural Traditions*. Prospect Heights, Ill.: Waveland, 2000.
Murphey, Rhoads. *A History of Asia*. New York: Longman, 2000.

SEE ALSO: Han Dynasty; Tang Dynasty; Wendi; Yang Di.

—*Richard L. Wilson*

SULLA, LUCIUS CORNELIUS

ALSO KNOWN AS: Lucius Cornelius Sulla Felix
BORN: 138 B.C.E.; Rome
DIED: 78 B.C.E.; Puteoli
RELATED CIVILIZATION: Republican Rome
MAJOR ROLE/POSITION: Roman dictator

Life. Born to a patrician family, Lucius Cornelius Sulla (LEW-shee-uhs kawr-NEEL-yuhs SUHL-uh) pursued a military career. In North Africa, he served under Gaius Marius. Charged with defeating Jugurtha, the Numidian king, Sulla convinced Jugurtha's father-in-law, Bocchus, to betray Jugurtha. Although Sulla's efforts led to the defeat and capture of Jugurtha, Marius took the credit. This began a bitter feud between them that would have dire consequences for Rome.

Sulla continued to serve under Marius despite their differences. He distinguished himself in Gaul, Cilicia, and Cappadocia. Although a successful military officer, he received little acknowledgment for his service; most of the recognition went to his superior, Marius.

During the Social War, Rome's Italian allies rebelled in an attempt to create an independent state. Rome was victorious and Sulla became a hero, but his popularity became too much for Marius. A violent struggle ensued between the followers of Sulla and those of Marius. Murder followed murder, with each side seeking a complete purge of the other. In 86 B.C.E., Marius died of disease.

In 83 B.C.E., Sulla marched on Rome and massacred his enemies and Marius's remaining followers. Two years later, he became dictator. He abdicated in 79 B.C.E. and died a private citizen.

Influence. Sulla instituted numerous political reforms, including enlarging the senate and revising the

Lucius Cornelius Sulla. (Library of Congress)

law code. His march on Rome set a precedent that Julius Caesar followed in 49 B.C.E.

ADDITIONAL RESOURCES
Keaveney, Arthur. *Sulla: The Last Republican*. London: Croom Helm, 1982.
Plutarch. *The Fall of the Roman Republic*. Translated by Rex Warner. Baltimore: Penguin Books, 1980.

SEE ALSO: Africa, North; Caesar, Julius; Jugurtha; Marius, Gaius; Rome, Republican.

—*J. S. Costa*

SULPICIA

FLOURISHED: late first century B.C.E.
RELATED CIVILIZATION: Imperial Rome
MAJOR ROLE/POSITION: Poet

Life. Sulpicia (sewl-PIH-shee-ah) was the daughter of Servius Sulpicius Rufus and (probably) Valeria, the sister of her guardian, Marcus Valerius Messalla

Corvinus, the patron of the poet Albius Tibullus. Her six surviving elegiac poems are contained in the third book of the *Corpus Tibullianum* (n.d.; English translation, 1913), adjoined to the works of other writers of the circle of Messalla: the *Panegyricus Messallae*, six elegies by Lygdamus, and a collection of five poems on Sulpicia's love affair, probably by Tibullus.

Sulpicia's poems track the progress of her relationship with a young Roman nobleman she calls Cerinthus. Although her poems display a refreshing simplicity and naïveté (especially when compared with the labored and laborious Tibullus), there is a sense that the collection is too well organized. She traces too perfectly the course of the relationship—introduction, conflict, sickness—following the conventions established by Tibullus, Ovid, and Propertius. To her credit, however, the poems reflect genuine feelings and mercifully lack the extended mythological allusions that ulti-

mately mar the works of Rome's great elegists. Nothing is known of the eventual fate of Sulpicia or of the true identity of Cerinthus.

ADDITIONAL RESOURCES

Balmer, Josephine. *Classical Woman Poets*. Newcastle-upon-Tyne, England: Bloodaxe Books, 1996.

Keith, Allison. "Tandem Venit Amor: A Roman Woman Speaks of Love." In *Roman Sexualities*, edited by J. Hallett and M. B. Skinner. Princeton, N.J.: Princeton University Press, 1997.

Snyder, Jane McIntosh. *The Woman and the Lyre: Women Writers in Classical Greece and Rome*. Carbondale: Southern Illinois University Press, 1989.

SEE ALSO: Languages and literature; Rome, Imperial; Tibullus, Albius.

—Joseph P. Wilson

SUMERIANS

DATE: 3400-1800 B.C.E.
LOCALE: Mesopotamia, present-day Iraq
RELATED CIVILIZATIONS: Akkad, Babylonia
SIGNIFICANCE: The Sumerians created the first known civilization, ushering in an era of urbanization.

Sumer is the site of the world's first known civilization, located in southern Mesopotamia between the Tigris and Euphrates Rivers. The people living in this region learned to cultivate wheat and barley, domesticate sheep and goats, and predict the seasons using a lunar calendar. The invention of the bronze plow created a massive food surplus that allowed the Sumerians (sew-MEHR-ee-uhnz) to develop new skills that went beyond mere survival.

They began to keep economic records; this practice evolved into the first written language. The writing system known as cuneiform used wedge-shaped characters that were easily pressed into soft clay tablets. The Sumerians composed poetry and literature. Science, astronomy, medicine, and mathematics were taught in the first formal schools. Artisans became master potters, metalworkers, weavers, and scribes. Engineers created complex irrigation canals that brought water several miles inland, transforming the desert into fertile farmland. City planners designed palace and temple complexes, harbors, and roads within large residential districts. Ur, Kish, Uruk, and Lagash are a few of the large

walled cities that supported populations of 100,000 people. Epidemics were common in Sumerian cities because of the large populations and poor sanitary practices. They suffered from outbreaks of tuberculosis, bubonic plague, typhus, and smallpox.

Sumer was a confederation of independent city-states ruled by councils of wealthy landowners and elected kings. The elite ruling class supported itself through taxation of its citizens and tribute from surrounding groups. Collected wealth paid for armies, temples, roads, and public works. The Sumerian military was divided into ranks of infantry soldiers and charioteers. They wore leather armor and fought with bronze-tipped spears. Foreign war captives were forced into slavery, as were citizens who were in financial debt.

The role of priest or priestess was a powerful position held by members of the nobility. Sumerian gods were associated with the forces of nature. Their pantheon includes Utu the Sun god, Inanna the goddess of love and fertility, and Nanna the Moon god. Sacrifices were made and magnificent monuments called ziggurats were built to worship the gods.

The food surplus and centralization of the government made trade with other people possible. Sumerian trade routes spanned east to the Indus Valley and modern Afghanistan, where Sumerians obtained lapis lazuli and other precious stones. Syria supplied timber, Anatolia had tin and copper used for making bronze, and

SUMER AND AKKAD

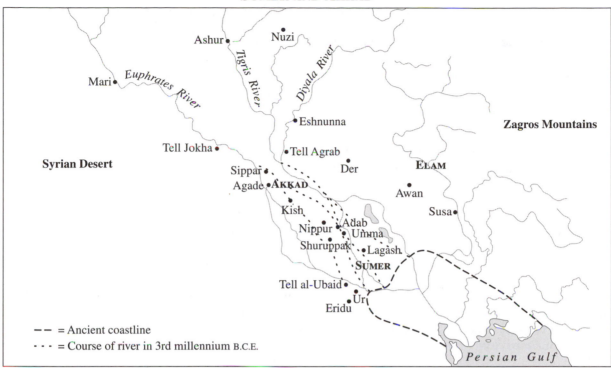

- - - = Ancient coastline
· · · = Course of river in 3rd millennium B.C.E.

luxury goods were imported from Egypt and Africa.

The city-states of Sumer were united about 2300 B.C.E. under the Akkadian leader Sargon. Shortly before 1800 B.C.E., the Sumerian civilization was assimilated by the Babylonians. It was not until the nineteenth century C.E., with the decipherment of the cuneiform language, that the Sumerians reentered the historical record. In 1922, C. Leonard Woolley's excavations at Ur uncovered magnificent royal tombs and the city's ziggurat, revealing the great accomplishments of the Sumerian people.

ADDITIONAL RESOURCES

Kramer, Noah. *The Sumerians: Their History, Culture, and Character.* Chicago: University of Chicago Press, 1963.

Kuhrt, Amélie. *The Ancient Near East, c. 3000-330 B.C.* 2 vols. London: Routledge, 1995.

Nemet-Nejat, Karen. *Daily Life in Ancient Mesopotamia.* Westport, Conn.: Greenwood Press, 1998.

SEE ALSO: Akkadian Dynasty; Babylonia; Sargon of Akkad.

—Kari Naso

ŚUṄGA DYNASTY

DATE: 185-151 B.C.E.
LOCALE: North India
RELATED CIVILIZATION: India
SIGNIFICANCE: Early Buddhist art flourished during the Śuṅga Dynasty.

Puṣyamitra Śuṅga (SHEWN-gah), a military officer who served the last Mauryan king, founded the Śuṅga Dynasty. Assassinating his predecessor, Puṣyamitra staged a palace revolt and seized the throne for himself and his descendants. A Brahman and an ardent advocate of Vedic religion, he had the Vedic horse sacrifice (*aśvamedha*) performed twice during his reign. The ritual established his suzerainty in his homeland, declared dominion over neighboring kingdoms, and reaffirmed Vedic authority after a long period in which Buddhism had been the preferred religion of the ruling class.

Under Puṣyamitra's successors, the northwestern sector of the kingdom was taken over by Greek invaders who eventually established diplomatic and trade relations with the Śuṅga court. Heliodorus, an ambassador of the Greco-Bactrian king Antialkidas, left an inscription (c. 120-100 B.C.E.) at Vidiśā declaring his devotion to the Hindu god Vāsudeva (Vishnu or Viṣṇu).

Although its rulers professed allegiance to Vedic religion, the Śuṅga period is noted particularly for the flowering of early Buddhist art. Great centers of Buddhism were established along the trade routes, funded primarily by merchants. The stupas (relic mounds) at Bharhut and Sanchi in the north and the *caitya* (hall of worship) complexes at Bhaja and Pitalkhora in the western Deccan are noted for the their artistry and important early iconography.

ADDITIONAL RESOURCE

Raychaudhuri, Hemachandra. *Political History of Ancient India: From the Accession of Parikshit to the Extinction of the Gupta Dynasty*. Delhi, India: Oxford University Press, 1996.

SEE ALSO: Buddhism; Buddhist cave temples; India; Vedism.

—*Katherine Anne Harper*

SUPPILULIUMAS I

ALSO KNOWN AS: Suppiluliuma; Shuppiluliumash; Subbiluliuma
BORN: fourteenth century B.C.E.; Hatti
DIED: c. 1322 B.C.E.; Syria
RELATED CIVILIZATIONS: Hittites, Egypt, Mitanni
MAJOR ROLE/POSITION: Military leader

Life. Suppiluliumas I (suh-pihl-ew-LEE-oo-mahs) first made a name for himself in the service of his father, Tudhaliyas II, campaigning against the neighboring Mitanni and rebellious elements within the kingdom of Hatti. Later, Suppiluliumas seized power after a prolonged civil war with his brother.

After coming to power, Suppiluliumas turned his attention to his Mitanni rivals. Of particular interest was the land of Isuwa, the gateway to the Mitanni kingdom. Before he could proceed, he had to isolate the Mitanni diplomatically. After assuring Akhenaton, the Egyptian pharaoh, that he would not encroach on Egyptian territories, Suppiluliumas married a princess of the Kassite ruling family to ensure the noninterference of the Babylonians.

Soon after, Suppiluliumas defeated the Mitanni militarily and overran their possessions. Egyptian-held Kadesh also fell victim to Hittite expansion. Later in life, he received a marriage alliance offer for one of his sons from the widow of Tutankhamen. Zannanza, the chosen prince, was murdered en route, increasing Egyptian-Hittite tensions. While preparing to attack Egyptian possessions, Suppiluliumas died of a plague carried by Egyptian prisoners.

Influence. The architect of the Hittite Empire, Suppiluliumas extended the reach of his land from Assyria to Egypt. His system of client-kings and viceroys served as an administrative body for the empire and a template for later empires.

ADDITIONAL RESOURCES

Bryce, Trevor. *The Kingdom of the Hittites*. New York: Oxford University Press, 1998.

Macqueen, J. G. *The Hittites and Their Contemporaries in Asia Minor*. 2d ed. London: Thames and Hudson, 1986.

SEE ALSO: Akhenaton; Babylonia; Kassites; Mitanni.

—*Abigail J. Gertner*

SŪTRAS

AUTHORSHIP: Various writers
DATE: second half of the first millennium B.C.E.
LOCALE: North India
RELATED CIVILIZATION: Vedic India
SIGNIFICANCE: This important body of work addresses both philosophical and practical realms of knowledge.

Written in Sanskrit, the *sūtras* (SEW-trahs) form the particular branch of late Vedic literature that is concerned with conveying expository information. The word *sūtra* means "a thread," and it is applied collectively to a broad group of treatises employing concise, aphoristic prose that attempts to distill as much meaning as possible into very few words, with rigid system-atization and a concern for a sacred language that, in order to be effective, must be completely correct. Thus, the *sutra* literature is concerned with the science of phonetics and, later, grammar, as was summed up by the grammarian Pāṇini. Included in this category of literature are the *Kalpa Sūtras*, or texts concerning rituals and works relating to the six Hindu *darśanas*, or orthodox schools of philosophy.

The *Kalpa Sūtras* deal with four main areas of knowledge: Vedic sacrifices as related in the *Śrauta Sūtras*, mathematical and geometric calculations necessary for construction of the ritual altars as found in the *Śulba Sūtras*, household ceremonies as set down in the *Gṛhya Sūtras*, and customary law as chronicled in the *Dharma Sūtras*. The texts presuppose knowledge of the Vedas and the *Brāhmaṇas* of their respective schools in that they often refer to them. The *Kalpa Sūtras* avoid doctrinal issues but focus rather on the details of the rituals and traditions current in each school. The *Śrauta Sūtras*, in particular, record the rules for extremely complex rituals involving three continuously burning sacred fires and the duties of as many as sixteen priests. Many of the more elaborate ceremonies endured for several days or even years. The works are not considered revelatory, and thus they bear the names of their respective authors.

The six philosophical schools of thought are known as the *darśanas*, or basic ways of looking at life. The *darśana sūtras* are the authoritative texts for the various philosophical systems. They include the *Nyāya Sūtra* by Gautama, the *Vaiśeṣika Sūtra* by Kaṇāda, the *Sāṃkhya Sūtra* by Kapila, the *Yoga Sūtra* by Patañjali, the *Mīmāṃsa Sūtra* by Jaimini, and the *Vedānta Sūtra* by Bādarāyana. Each philosopher saw different stages of the original source and explained his philosophy according to his vision. The Nyāya school was concerned with the rules of logic. The Vaiśeṣika school had an atomistic view of reality. Sāṃkhya philosophy articulated the distinction between pure consciousness and manifest reality. The philosophy of the Yoga school sought mystical perfection through spiritual practices. The Pūrva Mīmāṃsa (or Karma Mīmāṃsa) philosophy was concerned with ritual and argued that actions and the reactive fruits of those activities were the cause of cosmic manifestation. The Vedānta school distilled the wisdom of the *Upaniṣads*, emphasizing the individual soul and *brahman*. The concise language of these texts generally facilitated memorization and helped in the transmission of the knowledge. The writing of the *sutras* spans a long interval that extends between the composition of the Vedas and the rise of the epic literature. Buddhist and Jaina scriptures also employed the *sutra* style.

ADDITIONAL REFERENCES

Gopal, Ram. *India of the Vedic Kalpasutras*. Delhi, India: Motilal Banarsidass, 1983.

Muller, Max. *The Six Systems of Indian Philosophy*. London: Longmans and Green, 1919.

Paude, Govind Chandra. *The Dawn of Indian Civilization*. Delhi, India: Center for Studies in Civilization, 1999.

SEE ALSO: *Brāhmaṇas*; Hinduism; Pāṇini; *Upaniṣads*; Vedas.

—*Katherine Anne Harper*

SŪTTANIPĀTA

AUTHORSHIP: The Buddha (Siddhārtha Gautama) and his followers
DATE: sixth-fifth centuries B.C.E.
LOCALE: North India
RELATED CIVILIZATION: Early India
SIGNIFICANCE: An important anthology of early Buddhist teachings.

The *Suttanipāta* (SEW-tah-nee-PAW-tah; English translation in *Sacred Books of the Buddhists*, 1948) is part of a larger body of early Buddhist writings called the *Tipiṭaka* (collected c. 250 B.C.E.; English translation in *Buddhist Scriptures*, 1913), or "Three Baskets." Composed largely in verse, the *Suttanipāta* consists of dialogues, discourses, narratives, proverbs, and ballads based on the teachings of the historical Buddha, Siddhārtha Gautama. The various components presumably were collected and preserved by the immediate followers of the Buddha, and undoubtedly the canonical collection represents the earliest Buddhist writing. Written in Pāli, the work relates the doctrine of the Buddha and is believed to contain many discourses and speeches delivered by the enlightened master himself. The information is organized into five *nikāyas*, or subcollections: the Snake Chapter, the Lesser Chapter, the Greater Chapter, the Octet Chapter, and the Chapter on the Way to the Far Shore. The instructions are concerned with the hermit's or renouncer's way of life as opposed to monastic living, an indication that the materials predate the organization of Buddhist monastic orders. Throughout, the teachings stress the nature of sorrow, the shedding of unwholesome habits and states of mind, the conceits that come from holding onto practices or views, living the solitary contemplative life, the drawbacks of all attachments, abandonment of all attachments, directing loving and kindness toward all beings, and the method for reaching the highest level of spiritual attainment.

ADDITIONAL RESOURCES

Hare, E. M., trans. *Woven Cadences of Early Buddhists*. London: Oxford University Press, 1944.

Saddhatissa, H. *The Sutta Nipata*. London: Curzon Press, 1994.

SEE ALSO: Buddha; Buddhism; India; *Tipiṭaka*.

—*Katherine Anne Harper*

SUTTON HOO

DATE: c. 610-640 C.E.
LOCALE: Suffolk, England
RELATED CIVILIZATIONS: Anglo-Saxons, Celts, Scandinavia
SIGNIFICANCE: The richness of objects in the Mound I burial at Sutton Hoo provides extensive evidence for Anglo-Saxon art, culture, and society.

Sutton Hoo is an Anglo-Saxon cemetery with at least twenty mound burials and more than forty burials without mounds. Its fame rests on the Mound I burial excavated by Basil Brown in 1939. It was a ship burial, as shown by outlines of the wooden boards and the remaining iron rivets. No human remains were found, but the ship contained an extensive treasure, suggesting that it was a royal burial.

Many of the objects were metalwork such as clasps, a buckle, hanging bowls, and a helmet. Much of the metalwork was made by local craftspeople, but the designs and techniques demonstrate acquaintance with Germanic, Celtic, and Scandinavian art. Other pieces point to connections with the Continent and Byzantium, including a purse with Merovingian gold coins, a silver salver bearing stamps of Emperor Anastasius I (491-518 C.E.), and silver bowls and spoons that had some Greek inscriptions. The identity of the person that the burial commemorates is uncertain, but it is probably an East Anglian king of the first half of the seventh century C.E.

ADDITIONAL RESOURCES

Carver, Martin, ed. *The Age of Sutton Hoo*. Rochester, N.Y.: Boydell Press, 1992.

Evans, Angela C. *The Sutton Hoo Ship Burial*. London: British Museum, 1986.

Farrell, Robert T., and Carol Neuman de Vegvar, eds. *The Sutton Hoo Ship Burial: Fifty Years After*. Oxford, Ohio: American Early Medieval Studies, 1992.

SEE ALSO: Angles, Saxons, Jutes; Britain; Celts.

—*Karen K. Gould*

ŚYĀMILAKA

FLOURISHED: c. second half of fifth century C.E.
RELATED CIVILIZATION: North India
MAJOR ROLE/POSITION: Writer

Life. Śyāmilaka (SHYAW-mu-LAH-kah) was the writer of the *Pādātaḍitaka* (fifth century C.E.; *The Padataditaka of Syamilaka*, 1966), a classical Sanskrit one-act dramatic monologue. The text's colophon claims that Śyāmilaka was a native of north India and the son of Viśveśvaradatta. His writing seems to draw on Kashmiri tradition and, thus, may have had close links to the region. The highly polished classical Sanskrit and events mentioned in the play point to a date after 455 C.E. but before 510 C.E.

The fictitious city in which the drama takes place has been identified as Ujjain. The play centers on a type of character called the *viṭa*, a man about town and an erudite bon vivant with a talent for ridiculing society. The *viṭa* did not exist only in fiction but was a type of person connected to the *veśyā* (courtesan) culture. The *viṭa* of the *Pādātaḍitaka* once had means but squandered his wealth. He earned his living by acting as an intermediary between courtesans and potential patrons. Because of his erudition and familiarity with *veśyā* society, he was able to give interesting and humorous insights into and critiques of that world.

Influence. Because Śyāmilaka's style is so elegant, he was called a *mahākavi*, or great poet, a title that ranks him with such great poets as Kālidāsa. Śyāmilaka's brilliant prose and brisk repartee influenced later writers of comedy. Also, his depictions of daily life are so rich that his writing has been a reliable source of information on Indian history.

ADDITIONAL RESOURCE

Schokker, G. H. *The Padataditaka of Syamilaka*. Boston: R. Reidel, 1966.

SEE ALSO: India; Kālidāsa.

—*Katherine Anne Harper*

SYLVESTER I, SAINT

BORN: c. 265 C.E.; Rome
DIED: 335 C.E.; Rome
RELATED CIVILIZATION: Imperial Rome
MAJOR ROLE/POSITION: Bishop of Rome (pope)

Life. Sylvester was born at a time when the Roman world was beset by civil wars, barbarian invasions, and economic troubles. Like many people of his era, he looked to Christianity for solace and entered upon a spiritual life. He served in the lower grades of the clergy before becoming a priest early in the fourth century C.E. By then, the emperor Diocletian (r. 284-305) had restored order in the empire and begun the Great Persecution to force the Christians back to the Olympian cults. Sylvester resisted as a "confessor" and was sent into exile by the emperor Maximian (r. 293-305 C.E.) or his son Maxentius (r. 306-312 C.E.). However, with Constantine the Great's conversion in 312 C.E., Christianity became the favored religion in the Roman Empire, and the Church received imperial support.

Sylvester I was elected bishop of Rome in January of 314 C.E. and held that position until his death in December of 335 C.E.—his papal reign was thus contemporary with the imperial reign of the first Christian emperor, Constantine the Great (r. 306-337 C.E.). Constantine decided that because the Roman bishop was the successor of Peter, "prince of the apostles," he should have a palace for his official residence and a cathedral for public worship, so he granted the Laterani Palace at the east end of the capital to the bishop and erected a grand basilican church next to it—the old San Giovanni in Laterano (dedicated in 318 C.E.). Sylvester asked the zealous imperial convert to construct basilicas at the tombs of Rome's apostolic martyrs. The emperor consented and built the old San Pietro in Vaticano on the western side and the first San Paolo Fuori le Mura to the south of Rome (c. 319-329 C.E.). Constantine and his family patronized five more Christian basilicas around Rome and gave all eight of them to the papacy.

At the end of his reign, Sylvester built the parish church later known as San Martino ai Monti. This was the first of many parish churches that the popes built into the next century, completing the transformation of the ancient pagan capital into the medieval apostolic see. Sylvester was not able to attend the Council of Arles (314 C.E.) or the great Council of Nicaea (325 C.E.) but was represented at both by Roman delegates. The bishops at Arles followed Rome in condemning the Donatists, and those at Nicaea accepted the Western position that Christ shared the same substance with God the Father against the Arian heresy.

Influence. Sylvester was one of the earliest Roman bishops addressed as Papa (pope), and the imperial patronage and building programs in his reign helped elevate the status of the Roman see.

ADDITIONAL RESOURCES

McBrien, Richard P. *Lives of the Popes*. San Francisco: Harper, 1997.

Odahl, Charles. "The Christian Basilicas of Constantinian Rome." *The Ancient World* 26, no. 1 (1995): 3-28.

SEE ALSO: Arianism; Christianity; Constantine the Great; Diocletian; Donatus, Aelius; Nicaea, Council of; Rome, Imperial.

—*Charles M. Odahl*

SYMMACHUS, QUINTUS AURELIUS

BORN: c. 340 C.E.; place unknown
DIED: 402 C.E.; place unknown
RELATED CIVILIZATION: Imperial Rome
MAJOR ROLE/POSITION: Orator, government official

Life. Quintus Aurelius Symmachus (KWIHN-tuhs aw-REE-lee-uhs SIHM-uh-kuhs) was born to parents from politically prominent families; his paternal ancestors had served as senators since at least the early third century C.E. He won renown as a gifted orator, composing panegyrics of Valentinian I, Gratian, and Theodosius the Great. He served as quaestor, consul, proconsul (governor) of Africa, and prefect of the city of Rome (384-385 C.E.). In addition to his public orations, he wrote some nine hundred posthumously published letters. These include *Relationes* (n.d.; *The Relationes of Symmachus*, 1973), and forty-nine official dispatches to Valentinian II dealing with senatorial, legal, ceremonial, and other matters.

Symmachus is best known for his part in the fourth century C.E. struggle of religions. Like many senators of the day, he was a pagan who hoped that his faith might find accommodation within a world of Christian emperors and influential churchmen such as Saint Ambrose. The issues involved in the ongoing disconnection of state from pagan state-religion are crystallized in a famous dispatch (*Relatio* 3) to the emperor; eloquently advocating an ecumenical religious policy, Symmachus asks that an altar and statue of the goddess Victory be restored to the place they had occupied in the senate house since the time of Augustus. Ambrose interceded to quash the idea, and in 391 C.E., paganism was outlawed altogether.

Influence. Symmachus is a late example of the classic Roman ideal of the "good man, skilled in speaking." His unheeded plea for tolerance of others' religious beliefs has enduring relevance.

ADDITIONAL RESOURCES

Barrow, R. H. *Prefect and Emperor: The Relationes of Symmachus,* A.D. *384*. Oxford, England: Clarendon Press, 1973.

Cox, Claude E. *Aquila, Symmachus, and Theodotion in Armenia*. Atlanta, Ga.: Scholars Press, 1996.

SEE ALSO: Ambrose; Christianity; Gratian; Religion and ritual; Rome, Imperial; Theodosius the Great; Valentinian I.

—*James P. Holoka*

— T —

TA-SETI

DATE: 3500-3100 B.C.E.
LOCALE: Lower Nubia
RELATED CIVILIZATIONS: Sudanic civilization, Prepharaonic Egypt
SIGNIFICANCE: This Middle Nile kingdom grew powerful and wealthy, and at one time, it ruled Upper Egypt.

Ta-Seti (tah-EH-tee) was a fourth millennium B.C.E. kingdom that lay immediately south of Egypt proper, at the north end of the Nubian stretches of the Nile. Meaning "land of the bow," Ta-Seti was the Egyptian name for the kingdom and refers apparently to the archery skills of its fighting forces. What the inhabitants themselves called their country and state is no longer known.

In the second half of the fourth millennium B.C.E., Ta-Seti was one of what are suspected to have been a large number of small kingdoms stretching from possibly as far south as the confluence of the Blue and White Niles northward into Egypt. For a time between roughly 3400 and 3200 B.C.E., Ta-Seti became probably the most powerful of those kingdoms. The pictorial documents left by its kings reveal specifically that its armies conquered and ruled Upper Egypt.

The major sources of historical information about Ta-Seti come from the royal tombs at Qustul, where thirteen or more kings were buried. Excavations there show that the kingdom had strong cultural and economic connections both up and down the Nile. Imported items from as far away as the Syria-Palestine region turn up in the grave goods of the rulers. At the same time, it is clear from the overall archaeological record that Ta-Seti was the northern outlier of a much wider-spread Middle Nile culture area stretching as far south as the confluence of the Blue Nile, about 500 miles (800 kilometers) away. The peoples of this culture area belonged to what historians of Africa call the Sudanic civilization, and most or all of these peoples spoke languages of the Nilo-Saharan language family.

By the thirty-second century B.C.E., however, the power and wealth of Ta-Seti had entered into a steep decline. The balance of power shifted to the rulers of Upper Egypt, with its much more extensive areas suited to farming and its much greater concentrations of population. It is tempting to see the first moves toward Egyptian unification as, at least in part, a response to the earlier attacks from Ta-Seti, although other factors must have been involved as well. Sometime around 3100 B.C.E., the Upper Egyptian rulers brought all of Egypt under one rule. The final blow for Ta-Seti came when the First Dynasty king Aha sent his army southward to destroy the last remnants of the kingdom.

ADDITIONAL RESOURCES

Ehret, Christopher. "Sudanic Civilization." In *Agricultural and Pastoral Societies in Ancient and Classical History*, edited by Michael Adas. Philadelphia: Temple University Press, 2001.

Williams, Bruce. "The Lost Pharaohs of Nubia." *Archeology* 33, no. 5 (October, 1980).

SEE ALSO: Africa, North; Egypt, Pharaonic; Egypt, Prepharaonic.

—*Christopher Ehret*

TACITUS

ALSO KNOWN AS: Cornelius Tacitus
BORN: c. 56 C.E.; place unknown
DIED: c. 120 C.E.; probably Rome
RELATED CIVILIZATIONS: Imperial Rome, Germany
MAJOR ROLE/POSITION: Historian

Life. Little is known of the early life of Tacitus (TAS-uht-uhs), but he achieved success in Imperial Rome as senator, consul, and provincial governor of Western Anatolia. He is best known, however, for his historical studies.

Tacitus. (Library of Congress)

phy and ethnic composition of the island. *De origine et situ Germanorum* (c. 98 C.E., also known as *Germania*; *The Description of Germanie*, 1598) is the first ethnographic study of the Germanic tribes. *Historiae* (c. 109 C.E.; *Histories*, 1731) is a military, social, and political history of the Roman Empire from 68 to 90 C.E. His last great work, *Ab excessu divi Augusti* (c. 116 C.E., also known as *Annales*; *Annals*, 1598), is also a study of the empire but focuses on the era from 14 to 68 C.E.

Influence. As a politician and historian, Tacitus was in a unique position to witness and comment on the corruption, excesses, and immorality of first century C.E. Rome. His study of the Germans provides the first history of the people who came to dominate Europe after the Fall of Rome. He thus provides modern historians with a wealth of invaluable information on first century C.E. Europe.

ADDITIONAL RESOURCES

Benario, Herbert. *Introduction to Tacitus*. Athens: University of Georgia Press, 1975.
Mellor, Ronald. *Tacitus*. New York: Routledge, 1994.
Mendell, Clarence W. *Tacitus: The Man and His Work*. Hamden, Conn.: Archon Books, 1970.

SEE ALSO: Agricola, Gnaeus Julius; Germany; Rome, Imperial.

—Gregory S. Taylor

His first historical work, *De vita Julii Agricolae* (c. 98 C.E.; *The Life of Agricola*, 1591), is both a biography of his father-in-law Gnaeus Julius Agricola, who served as governor of Britain, and a study of the geogra-

TAHARQA

ALSO KNOWN AS: Tarku; Tirhakra; Tirhakah
FLOURISHED: seventh century B.C.E.
RELATED CIVILIZATIONS: Assyria, Kush
MAJOR ROLE/POSITION: King of Egypt's Twenty-fifth Dynasty

Life. Taharqa (tuh-HAHR-kuh) ascended the throne of Egypt from Napata in southern Kush (Nubia). Nephew of Shabaka, the founder of the Twenty-fifth Dynasty, Taharqa served as coregent with his cousin Shebitku (Shabitku) until his cousin's murder in 690 B.C.E., possibly at the hand of Taharqa.

Taharqa attempted to reunite Egypt with the Nubian state to establish an Egyptian military presence equal to Assyrian control of the northern delta. In 671 B.C.E.,

Taharqa formed an alliance with Baal, king of Tyre, and revolted against Assyrian occupation of Egypt. The alliance failed against Esarhaddon's army, and Taharqa was forced to flee to Napata. Treaty negotiations with Taharqa failed, and subsequent conspiracy plots among the delta rulers convinced Esarhaddon to invade Egypt. On his return to Egypt in 669 B.C.E., Esarhaddon died. Taharqa quickly reoccupied Thebes and then marched on to Memphis.

In 667 B.C.E., Ashurbanipal (son of Esarhaddon) led the Assyrian army against Egypt and defeated Taharqa in the eastern delta at Karbaniti. Again, Taharqa retreated south to Napata. Ashurbanipal pursued Taharqa and sailed south with the Assyrian army to Thebes. Within forty days, Ashurbanipal reaffirmed the pledge of Mentumehet and other Esarhaddon appointees in Thebes. Inscribed monuments in Thebes reveal Mentumehet's allegiance to Taharqa despite his submission to Ashurbanipal. Soon after Ashurbanipal's return to Nineveh, Taharqa returned to Thebes.

Delta governors left by Ashurbanipal plotted to divide rule of Egypt with Taharqa. Once the scheme was discovered, the Assyrians responded with severity. The sack of Thebes was depicted in relief at Nineveh and shows the bodies of conspirators impaled on city walls along with their flayed skins. To obtain Egyptian loyalty, Ashurbanipal's policy toward Egypt became conciliatory. Niku of Sais, sent in chains to Nineveh as a conspirator, was honored and returned to Memphis to rule. His son, Psamtik I, founder of the Twenty-sixth Dynasty, was made an Assyrian prince. Taharqa was left to spend the remainder of his rule isolated in Napata. At his death, Taharqa was succeeded by his brother-in-law Tanutamun, a son of Shabaka.

Influence. Taharqa's reign (r. 690-664 B.C.E.) left Egypt in disorder but served to change Assyrian military policy to a negotiated diplomacy. In the arts, Taharqa created numerous temples throughout Egypt, from Memphis to Philae. At Kawa, Taharqa reconstructed a vast temple to Amun abandoned by Amenhotep III during the New Kingdom (1550-1069 B.C.E.). The art of the dynasty is conservative and imitated earlier Old Kingdom models but includes traditional Kushite elements. Taharqa's tomb is located in Nun rather than the family cemetery at el-Kurru. Smaller temples by Taharqa are found at Buhen, Gebel Barkal, Qasr Ibrim, and Semna. At Karnak, a single papyriform column erected by Taharqa remains in the Temple of Amun.

ADDITIONAL RESOURCES

Baines, J., and J. Malek. *Atlas of Ancient Egypt.* Oxford, England: Oxford University Press, 1982.

Burstein, Stanley M., ed. *Ancient African Civilizations: Kush and Axum.* Princeton, N.J.: Markus Wiener, 1998.

Smith, W. S. *The Art and Architecture of Ancient Egypt.* Rev. ed. Harmondsworth, England: Penguin Books, 1981.

SEE ALSO: Ashurbanipal; Assyria; Egypt, Prepharaonic; Esarhaddon; Nubia; Shabaka.

—Elizabeth L. Meyers

TAI

DATE: beginning in the first century C.E.

LOCALE: Lowlands of south and southwest China and extreme northern Southeast Asia

SIGNIFICANCE: An ethnolinguistic group from whom emerged the peoples of modern-day Laos and Thailand.

Some two thousand years ago, the Tai people lived in the valleys and lowland areas of what is now southern China and extreme northern Southeast Asia, speaking similar tonal languages. They engaged in self-sufficient agriculture, with a diet consisting mostly of rice, fish, fowl, swine, and vegetables, while living in homes on stilts. Young people were allowed free choice of marriage partners, though there was wide sexual license. Women were accorded equal status with men. Adolescent boys engaged in tattooing as a rite of passage. *Müang*, or communities organized on a communitarian basis, were headed by *chao* (lords).

As imperial China expanded toward Vietnam, one group of Tais moved southwest into northern Laos and Vietnam. As the Chinese and Vietnamese asserted control up the Red River in the first few centuries C.E., they divided this group of Tais into two major groups. To the north of the Red River, the Chuang people of Kwangsi and the Tho and Nung of Vietnam developed in isolation from the rest of the Tai peoples. To the south of the Red River, the Tais settled in the region of Dien Bien Phu. The southern Tais are the ancestors of the present Lao, Shans, Thais, and the upland Tais, peoples that now live in Laos, Burma (Myanmar), northeastern India, southern Yunnan, and Thailand.

As the Chinese and Vietnamese encountered the *müang*, the *chao* were recognized as allies, enemies, or tributaries. In return for recognition of Chinese supremacy, the *chao* paid tribute but were left alone to preside over their *müang*. The Tais in turn exploited upland tribal peoples, using them as menial laborers and slaves, while the tribal chiefs were made vassals. Among the Tais, the *chao* enjoyed the support of the people for their skill in dealing with foreigners; the *chao* therefore developed political power and prestige and lived an increasingly refined lifestyle based on artistic, cultural, and technological advancements. The Tais, for example, are believed to have invented the outrigger canoe. Tais were also skilled in making artifacts and implements from copper, bronze, and iron.

Because of the high level of social and political organization of the Tais, they were able to migrate successfully into areas occupied by less sophisticated peoples. Because the areas immediately adjacent to the east of the southern Tais were mountainous, the Tais gradually migrated toward the Chaopraya River Basin, where they could reproduce their customary agricultural pursuits revolving around rice farming.

Many of the present Thais do not descend from the Tais but instead are of Chinese, Indian, Khmer, or Mon origins. However, most Tais intermarried with the indigenous peoples as they migrated southward along the Chaophraya River Basin after the eighth century.

ADDITIONAL RESOURCES

Gohain, B. K. *Origin of the Tai and Chao Lung Hsukapha*. New Delhi, India: Omsons Publications, 1999.

LeBar, Frank M., Gerald C. Hickey, and John K. Musgrave. *Ethnic Groups of Mainland Southeast Asia*. New Haven, Conn.: Yale University Press, 1964.

SEE ALSO: China; Laos; Mon-Khmer; Vietnam.

—*Michael Haas*

TAIZONG

ALSO KNOWN AS: *Wade-Giles* T'ai-tsung; Tang Taizong; Li Shimin (*Wade-Giles* Li Shih-min)
BORN: 599 C.E.; China
DIED: 649 C.E.; China
RELATED CIVILIZATIONS: Tang Dynasty, China
MAJOR ROLE/POSITION: Statesman

Life. Taizong (tid-ZOONG; his posthumous title) was the second Tang emperor, ascending the throne in 626 C.E. after murdering his brother and forcing his father, Gaozu (Li Yuan), to retire. The idealized paradigm of a Chinese emperor, he was educated in the Confucian classics and was a notable calligrapher and poet. Breaking little new ground, Taizong built on the accomplishments of his father and the previous Sui Dynasty. Like most great rulers, Taizong employed talented individuals. He reformed the central government as well as the administration of the provinces. He lessened the influence of the aristocracy and strengthened the examination system, thus increasing the position of the scholarly elite in the government.

Stressing Confucianism and its societal values, Taizong attempted to reduce the political influence of Buddhism by requiring that monks and nuns confine themselves to monasteries. Chinese imperial power was extended into Central Asia, and Chang'an, the capital, became the largest and most cosmopolitan city in the world. In the early years of his reign, Taizong was restrained, a learner open to advice and sensitive to criticism, but in the last decade, he acted more like an arrogant autocrat.

Influence. Less an originator than a consolidator, Taizong was a brilliant administrator and exemplary politician whose rule became the standard by which later reigns were measured.

ADDITIONAL RESOURCES

Paludan, Ann. *Chronicle of the Chinese Emperors*. New York: Thames and Hudson, 1998.

Perry, John C., and Bardwell L. Smith, eds. *Essays on T'ang Society*. Leiden, Netherlands: E. J. Brill, 1976.

SEE ALSO: Buddhism; China; Confucianism; Tang Dynasty.

—*Eugene Larson*

TALE OF THE TWO BROTHERS, THE

DATE: earliest manuscripts c. 1225 B.C.E.
LOCALE: Egypt
SIGNIFICANCE: This Egyptian tale parallels the biblical story of Joseph and Potiphar's wife.

The Tale of the Two Brothers strongly resembles the biblical story in which Potiphar's wife attempts to seduce her husband's slave Joseph and later accuses Joseph of rape. In the Egyptian tale, the older brother, Anubis, is married, and the younger one, Bata, like Joseph in the biblical story, is single and has a subordinate position, in this case working on his brother's farm. When Anubis is away, his wife tries to seduce Bata. Feeling that succumbing to her would be a betrayal of trust, he angrily spurns her. The biblical story adds a spiritual dimension to Joseph's refusal in that he declines to sleep with his master's wife because it would not only be a betrayal of trust but also a sin. Anubis's wife then falsely accuses Bata of trying to seduce her. At this point, the story becomes a fantasy. Anubis resolves to kill Bata, but the attempt is frustrated first by cows warning Bata that Anubis is coming and then by a stream full of crocodiles materializing between them. Bata demonstrates his innocence by swearing by the god Re-Harakhti and amputating his phallus. He then dies. Anubis, full of remorse, returns home and kills his treacherous wife. Bata returns to life and rises to prominence in the pharaonic court. In the biblical version, Joseph is accused of rape and imprisoned, although he is later released because of his ability to interpret dreams and rises to a position of importance in the Egyptian government.

ADDITIONAL RESOURCES

Hoffmeier, James K. *Israel in Egypt*. New York: Oxford University Press, 1996.

Hollis, Susan B. *The Ancient Egyptian "Tale of the Two Brothers": The Oldest Fairy Tale in the World*. Norman: University of Oklahoma Press, 1990.

SEE ALSO: Bible: Jewish; Egypt, Pharaonic; Israel.

—*Jonathon R. Ziskind*

TALIESIN

FLOURISHED: late sixth century to early seventh century C.E.
RELATED CIVILIZATIONS: Wales, Angles, Saxons, Celts
MAJOR ROLE/POSITION: Bard

Life. Taliesin (talh-YEHS-uhn) lived during the final age of Brythonic Celtic power that checked the final incursions of Saxons, Angles, and other groups (c. 570-590 C.E.). Although possibly from the Welsh area of Powys, Taliesin spent most of his professional life serving Urien in the Welsh kingdom of Rheged in northern Britain.

Little is known of Taliesin's life, except what can be gleaned from the surviving dozen poems he composed that describe the actions of the lords he served. Bards, highly esteemed and influential in Celtic cultures, praised a lord into favor or ridiculed him into disrepute. In such circumstances, Taliesin served briefly with a Powys lord and then moved north to serve Urien in Rheged. He composed poetry praising Urien's battle triumphs and generosity. As Urien aged, Taliesin also wrote poems about Urien's son Owain, who eventually died in battle (c. 604 C.E.), and another Welsh lord, Gwallawg of Elfin.

Influence. Taliesin's works represent the earliest examples of Welsh literature and language. His poems were later incorporated into a larger group, all attributed to him, *The Book of Taliesin* (c. 1300 C.E.), which inspired a medieval cult connected to the Arthurian tales. The mystical poems are markedly different in style and content from the original dozen poems, and scholars have agreed that the other poems were written later, probably by monks.

ADDITIONAL RESOURCES

Humphreys, Emyr. *The Taliesin Tradition*. Bridgend, England: Seren, 2000.

Pennar, Meirion. *Taliesin Poems*. Lampeter, Wales: Llanerch Press, 1988.

Williams, Sir Ifor. *The Beginnings of Welsh Poetry*. Cardiff: University of Wales Press, 1972.

SEE ALSO: Angles, Saxons, Jutes; Britain; Celts.

—*Kristin L. Gleeson*

TALMUD

AUTHORSHIP: First compiled by Rabbi Akiba (d. c. 135 C.E.)

DATE: 500 B.C.E.-700 C.E.

LOCALE: Galilee and Babylon

RELATED CIVILIZATIONS: Babylonia, Republican and Imperial Rome

SIGNIFICANCE: Developed by rabbis to preserve the record of previous generations, studying their own traditions for later generations, the Talmud, by the Middle Ages, became the center of Jewish life and the law of the community.

The earliest rabbis endlessly discussed and analyzed the Hebrew Bible, creating a rich tradition of oral literature that developed into laws regulating all Jewish life. Within a century of the destruction of the temple in Jerusalem in 70 C.E., rabbis were preparing the Oral Torah for permanent recording. The Mishnah, the core document of the Talmud (TAHL-mood), was complete by the beginning of the third century C.E.

The Mishnah is divided into six orders, each dealing with a broad area of Jewish life. These orders are divided into smaller topical sections called "webbings" or "tractates." The first order is "Seeds" and deals mostly with agricultural law, but the first tractate is titled "Blessings" and prescribes the life of prayer in Jerusalem in great detail. The Mishnah is the earliest teaching text, or curriculum of Jewish learning that still exists. After the creation of the Mishnah, a new body of oral Torah began to accumulate with the Mishnah at its core, as each new generation discussed both the Mishnah and the comments of the previous generation, especially the rabbis. This rapidly expanding mass eventually became an object of study in itself, called Talmud in Hebrew, which means "study." All modern forms of Jewish religion stand on this foundation.

There are two Talmuds. The earlier, or Jerusalem Talmud, dates from the first half of the fifth century C.E. It is a loose, elaborate commentary on certain tractates of the Mishnah and offers textual explanation, case precedents, stories, moral instruction, theological speculation, and legends about biblical characters and other, later people. However, it is only half the size of the Babylonian Talmud, which was completed about the first

An early version of the Talmud. (North Wind Picture Archives)

half of the sixth century C.E. The Babylonian Talmud, which is the one commonly used in modern times, is more clearly and elegantly written. The complete Babylonian Talmud was issued in English translation in the second half of the twentieth century and is now available in several forms.

The Talmud is printed in a style that reflects its character as discussion. In the middle of the page, in larger type, are the oldest stages of the conversation from the Mishnah. Where the Mishnah ends, often in the middle of the page, the Talmudic discussion begins, typically including many digressions. Surrounding the Talmudic text on the same page are the two most famous of the medieval commentaries. To the right is the commentary of Rashi (Rabbi Shlomo Itzhak, 1040-1105), the master of Jewish commentary. To the right of Rashi's commentary are the Tosafot, or supplements, which are amplifications of Rashi's commentary and references to other sections of the Talmud. Although the supplements attempt to unify all Talmudic literature into an integrated whole, they sometimes create obscurity.

ADDITIONAL RESOURCES
Heilman, Samuel. *The People of the Book*. Chicago: University of Chicago Press, 1983.
Mielzener, Moses. *Introduction to the Talmud*. New York: Bloch, 1968.

Neusner, Jacob. *Invitation to the Talmud*. Atlanta, Ga.: Scholars Press, 1998.

SEE ALSO: Bible: Jewish; Jerusalem, temple of; Judaism.

—*Sheila Golburgh Johnson*

TANG DYNASTY

ALSO KNOWN AS: *Wade-Giles* T'ang Dynasty
DATE: 618-907 C.E.
LOCALE: China
RELATED CIVILIZATIONS: Sui Dynasty, ʿAbbāsid Dynasty, Sung Dynasty
SIGNIFICANCE: The Tang Dynasty, in terms of power, prestige, and cultural achievement, represented one of the most brilliant periods of Chinese history.

In 618 C.E., Li Yuan, king of the Chinese province of Tang, established himself as Gaozu, or emperor of China (r. 618-626 C.E.). His son Li Shimin, who helped him to the throne, succeeded him as Taizong (r. 626-649 C.E.) and was most responsible for the brilliance of the Tang Dynasty. He extended Chinese power north into Mongolia and west along the Silk Road into Afghanistan in Central Asia. The power and prosperity of the Tang reached its zenith under Xuanzong (r. 712-756 C.E.). Unfortunately, it was also near the end of his reign that the long decline of the Tang Dynasty began. In 751 C.E., the Chinese were defeated at the Battle of Talas by a Muslim ʿAbbāsid army. This ended China's presence in Central Asia. Talas also sparked a rebellion against the Tang in 755 C.E. led by An Lushan, a provincial commander. This rebellion was ultimately crushed, but the Tang Dynasty never regained its former glory and power.

ADDITIONAL RESOURCES
Bingham, W. *The Founding of the Tang Dynasty*. New York: Octagon, 1970.
Pulleyblank, Edwin G. *Essays on Tang and Pre-Tang History*. Aldershot, England: Ashgate, 2001.
Twitchett, Denis, and John K. Fairbank, eds. *Sui and T'ang China*. Vol. 3 in *The Cambridge History of China*. Cambridge, England: Cambridge University Press, 1977.

SEE ALSO: China; Islam; Sui Dynasty; Taizong.
—*Stefan G. Chrissanthos*

Arts flourished during the Tang Dynasty. An earth spirit is captured in this artwork. (Hulton Archive)

TANTRAS

DATE: c. 400-1000 C.E.
LOCALE: India, Kashmir, Nepal, Tibet, China, Japan
RELATED CIVILIZATIONS: South and East Asia
SIGNIFICANCE: Esoteric texts associated with Hinduism and Buddhism.

Tantras (TAHN-trahs) refer to a group of Buddhist and Hindu texts that are specifically esoteric in their sect affiliations and teachings. The Sanskrit word *tan* means to weave, to stretch, or to expound; therefore, the tantras tend to expound on often obscure secret beliefs and rituals. Buddhism and Hindu Tantrism arose in contradistinction to the Vedic religion of the Brahmans. Considered heterodox in nature, Tantric practices and beliefs have their origins in an antiquity so remote that the earliest manifestations may never be known. Buddhist Tantrism is earlier than Hindu Tantrism by at least two centuries; the Buddhist *Guhyasmāja Tantra* may be as early as the third century C.E. Although it is difficult to date any of the surviving texts with accuracy, it is certain that Hindu Tantrism was widespread and a pan-Indian phenomenon by the fifth to sixth centuries C.E. The earliest Hindu text with specific Tantric content, though not called a tantra, is the *Devī Māhātmya* (c. 400-600 C.E.; English translation, 1885). Various sects in India produced tantras well through the medieval period.

Asserting the attainment of freedom from the Vedic belief in a never-ending cycle of reincarnation, the tantras offer spiritual liberation (*mukti* or *mokṣa*). Tantric practices promised emancipation from future lives, as well as earthly enjoyment and domination (*bhukti*). Accomplishing the dual goals is a difficult and lengthy process that takes place over a long period of time and under strictly controlled conditions.

The tantras generally emphasized in varying degrees the key practices: intricate and complex rituals, mantras (chanting incantations), spells and magic, secret sounds and syllables, magical diagrams called *yantras* (mandalas), special hand gestures, deliberately coded language, and restricted practices and initiations in which secret lore is passed from the guru to the student. Yogic exercises and meditation are essential components in Tantric rituals, particularly *kuṇḍalinī* yoga, in which creative energy is directed upward in the body along the nerve centers (*cakras*). Cultic rituals include formation of an elaborate macrocosmic/microcosmic cosmology located within the human body in which the deity is invoked in the heart. Both Buddhist and Hindu Tantric sects generally focus on a form of the Great Goddess as the primary deity and as the primary force of the universe. In addition, the sole and supreme creative force of the universe is called *śakti*. Often used as a name for the goddess herself, *śakti* is the ultimate principle of the universe, the source of all.

All tantras stress the absolute necessity of the guru to guide the uninitiated along the perilous road to emancipation. It is believed that the spells and incantations are so powerful that knowledge of them must be restricted only to those who are spiritually prepared. Thus, the tantras are written in selective and deliberately obscure, cryptic language. The revelatory secrets and connecting threads are the purview of the guru and the initiated alone.

ADDITIONAL RESOURCE
Gupta, Sanjukta, Dirk Jan Hoens, and Teun Goudraan. *Hindu Tantrism.* Leiden, Netherlands: E. J. Brill, 1979.

SEE ALSO: Buddhism; Hinduism; India; Tibet.
—*Katherine Anne Harper*

TAO HONGJING

ALSO KNOWN AS: *Wade-Giles* T'ao Hung-ching
BORN: 456 C.E.; Moling (later in Fujian), China
DIED: 536 C.E.; Huayang, China
RELATED CIVILIZATION: China
MAJOR ROLE/POSITION: Scholar

Life. Born into an aristocratic landowning family, Tao Hongjing (TAH-oh HONG-jihng) spent his early career in service to the Song and Qi courts. While tutoring the Qi emperor's sons, Tao began to study the major works of Six Dynasties Daoism, including those of the alchemist Ge Hong, the liturgical Lingbao (Spiritual Treasure) scriptures, and the Shangqing (Supreme Purity) scriptures revealed at Mao Shan from 367 to 370 C.E.

In 492 C.E., Tao retired to Mao Shan, where he spent the remainder of his life collecting, editing, and annotating the Supreme Purity scriptures. Tao was the first scholar to classify the Daoist deities hierarchically. He also composed a commentary on an ancient pharmacological text and created a guide for Daoist practice. Additionally, Tao devoted much of his life to the search for an alchemical elixir designed to secure "immortality" or transcendence (*xian*) from this world for its user. While focusing on the manipulation of medicinal herbs and minerals to create a consumable elixir, Tao greatly influenced the movement toward internal alchemy, through which a practitioner could become a transcendent by mental and physiological means.

Influence. Because of the influence of the Daoist community he established at Mao Shan, the Supreme Purity tradition subsequently became the dominant Daoist school during the Tang Dynasty, emphasizing meditation and internalized ritual practices. Tao is also regarded as the founder of critical pharmacology in China.

ADDITIONAL RESOURCES
Bokenkamp, Stephen. *Early Daoist Scriptures*. Berkeley: University of California Press, 1997.
Robinet, Isabelle. *Taoist Meditation: The Mao-shan Tradition of Great Purity*. New York: State University of New York Press, 1993.

SEE ALSO: Daoism; Ge Hong; Mao Shan revelations; Six Dynasties; Tang Dynasty.

—*Jeffrey Dippmann*

TAO QIAN

ALSO KNOWN AS: *Wade-Giles* T'ao Ch'ien; Tao Yuanming (*Wade-Giles* T'ao Yüan-ming)
BORN: 365 C.E.; Xinyang, China
DIED: 427 C.E.; Xinyang, China
RELATED CIVILIZATION: China
MAJOR ROLE/POSITION: Poet

Life. Born into a declining bureaucrat-scholar family when the Eastern Jin Dynasty (317-420 C.E.) was in its death throes, young Tao Qian (TAH-oh CHEE-ahn) aspired to stabilize the political turbulence. However, he grew disillusioned after serving as an adviser to two warlords for about ten years and experiencing their separatism and constant warfare. Assigned a magistracy, he served for only about eighty days, then resigned to live in seclusion as a poet and farmer. He never returned to office and died in poverty.

While living in seclusion, he took the pseudonym Tao Qian (Tao the Hermit) and wrote poetry, often about the joys of nature, human harmony with farming, and pleasant man-nature interactions. Modern critics judge him to be one of the greatest pastoral poets. His famous pieces *Guiqulai Ci* (fifth century C.E.; *Homeward Bound*, 1983) and *Gui Yuantian Ju* (fifth century C.E.; *Living on Native Land*, 1983) describe his immeasurable joy at shaking off the yoke of officialdom, his unsullied desire to live a simple, honest life, and his appreciation of lovely rural scenery. His masterpiece *Taohuayuan Ji* (fifth century C.E.; *Notes on the Land of Peach Blossoms*, 1983) depicts a lost utopia that contrasts with the political unrest of his day. His more than 130 poems and prose writings have all survived.

Influence. Tao Qian's creative writing, which explored multiple genres, including *fu* (verse with interspersed prose) and in particular lyric poetry, is held in high regard by modern scholars.

ADDITIONAL RESOURCES
Davis, A. R. *Tao Yuan-ming: His Works and Their Meaning*. 2 vols. Cambridge, England: Cambridge University Press, 1983.
Hightower, J. R. "The *Fu* of T'ao Ch'ien." *Harvard Journal of Asiatic Studies* 17 (1954): 169-230.
Kwong, Charles Yim-tze. *Tao Qian and the Chinese Poetic Tradition*. Ann Arbor: University of Michigan Press, 1994.

SEE ALSO: China; Sima Xiangru.

—*Charles Xingzhong Li*

TARQUINS

DATE: 616-510 B.C.E.
LOCALE: Rome
RELATED CIVILIZATIONS: Prerepublican Rome,
    Etruscans
MAJOR ROLE/POSITION: Kings

Lucius Tarquinius Priscus (traditionally, r. 616-579 B.C.E.) and Lucius Tarquinius Superbus (traditionally, r. 534-509 B.C.E.) were the fifth and seventh kings of Rome and were supposedly father and son. This relationship is questionable given the time separating their reigns. On the other hand, this century is so poorly documented that the dates of their reigns may actually be mistaken. Nevertheless, the Tarquins (TAHR-kwihnz) were important figures to the Romans because they were the last ruling family before the institution of the Republic.

The Tarquins were most likely Etruscan in origin and may have been partly responsible for the introduction of certain Etruscan customs such as the wearing of the toga, the triumph, and certain rituals of power. The Romans believed that Lucius Tarquinius Priscus actually conquered the Etruscans, but this seems unlikely. Rather, it is much more likely that Rome's geographic position at the southern edge of the Etruscan region put Rome in the position of absorbing influences from all the neighboring peoples, including the Latins, Sabines, and Greeks. All the kings of Rome seemed to have been outsiders; this is a probable reflection of strong lateral ties within the regional landed aristocracy and another indication that regional influences should be examined in any attempt to understand Rome's early cultural, economic, and political development. The archaeological record suggests that the period encompassed by the Tarquins' reigns was a prosperous one for Rome. Polybius, the Greek historian from the middle second century B.C.E., reports reading an inscribed treaty between Rome and Carthage that dates to the last year of the reign of Lucius Tarquinius Superbus. The terms of the treaty as reported by Polybius indicate that Carthage and Rome maintained cordial economic ties in this period.

Lucius Tarquinius Superbus was an especially important figure in Roman tradition as he was the quintessential tyrant. He was expelled from Rome in 509 B.C.E., after which the monarchy was abolished and the Republic instituted. The sources paint him and his wife as murderers of the sixth king of Rome, Servius Tullius, and their son Sextus as a rapist. It was this last outrage that supposedly precipitated the expulsion of the entire family from Rome and created the necessity for a new form of government. There are several surviving versions of the specific events, including the relationship of the expelled family and the leaders of the coup. These stories may be mostly hyperbole designed to gloss over what was in effect a revolution within an otherwise closely knit aristocracy. Little can therefore be reconstructed with any reliability. After Lucius Tarquinius Superbus was thrown out, Roman cooperation with the Etruscans gradually ceased.

The archaeological record suggests that the prosperity of the previous period faded over the next fifty years. During the same period, Rome moved toward closer cooperation with the Latin League, a group of cities to the south and west. Ironically, the Tarquins were most likely responsible for bringing Rome and the Latins closer together in the first place and, by extension, setting the stage for the eventual emergence of Rome as the dominant player in Italy.

ADDITIONAL RESOURCES
Cornell, T. J. *The Beginnings of Rome*. London: Routledge, 1995.
Smith, C. J. *Early Rome and Latium*. Oxford, England: Oxford University Press, 1996.

SEE ALSO: Etruscans; Junius Brutus, Lucius; Lucretia; Rome, Prerepublican.

—Randall S. Howarth

TELIPINUS

ALSO KNOWN AS: Telepinus
FLOURISHED: sixteenth century B.C.E.
RELATED CIVILIZATION: Hittite
MAJOR ROLE/POSITION: King

Life. Telipinus (tehl-ih-PI-nuhs; r. c. 1525-c. 1500 B.C.E.) is known as the last king of the Old Hittite Kingdom. Although he usurped the Hittite throne, he is arguably one of the most respected Hittite kings. Besides being a successful ruler in military and diplomatic respects, he was also a reformer. Telipinus consolidated his kingdom on its northern and southeastern borders. He untertook a military campaign against Hassuwa, an important city in in southeastern Anatolia, and put down a revolt in Lawazantiya in the Cilician region. Telipinus instituted some important legal reforms and, for the first time in Hittite history, entered into a treaty relationship with a neighboring country, the kingdom of Kizzuwatna in the Cilician region of Anatolia under the reign of a ruler named Isputahsus.

From Telipinus's reign several documents are preserved, including the above-mentioned treaty. However, the most important of them is the Edict of Telipinus, also known as the Proclamation of Telipinus. This document is primarily of an administrative-legal character; however, it also has a historical preamble that is the most important source for the history of the Old Hittite Kingdom.

In the preamble, Telipinus lists the reigns of his seven predecessors (from Labarnas I to Huzziyas I) and the events at the time of his own reign. He emphasizes the glories and mishaps the Hittite state had in the previous hundred years. His goal is clear: to demonstrate the fact that harmony in the royal family and in all sectors of the state will lead to the prosperity of the kingdom and that the assassinations of members of the royal family must be avoided. In this respect, he laudatorially describes the times of the first three Hittite rulers, Labarnas I, Hattusilis I, and Mursilis I. The last is known as the conqueror of Aleppo and Babylon.

According to the Edict of Telipinus, the unhappy phase of Hittite history begins with Hantilis I, who assassinated Mursilis I, his brother-in-law, and usurped the throne. After an ill-fated reign, he was illegitimately succeeded by his son-in-law Zidantas I, who systematically eliminated the other family members of Hantilis I. However, Zidantas I also was murdered by his own son Ammunas. Under the reign of Ammunas, the land of the Hittites was stricken by famine. The next king, Huzziyas I, ruled only for a short time and was removed by his brother-in-law Telipinus after a _coup d'état._

After the historical and didactic preamble, Telipinus enacts in his edict a concise law of succession, saying "Let a prince of the first rank become king. If there is no prince of the first rank, let one who is a son of the second rank become king. If, however, there is no prince, let them take a husband for a daughter of the first rank, and let him become king."

Istapariyas is known as the queen of Telipinus. She and his son, Ammunas, died under unknown circumstances before Telipinus. Telipinus was then succeded by Alluwamnas, who probably was his adoptive son.

Influence. Telipinus consolidated the kingdom and instituted legal reforms, including setting up a succession law for the kingship.

ADDITIONAL RESOURCES

Bryce, Trevor. _The Kingdom of the Hittites._ Oxford, England: Clarendon Press, 1998.

Gurney, Oliver R. _The Hittites._ 2d ed. London: Penguin Books, 1990.

SEE ALSO: Hattusilis I; Hittites; Labarnas I.

—_Oguz Soysal_

TEOTIHUACÁN

DATE: 1-750 C.E.

LOCALE: 25 miles (40 kilometers) northeast of Mexico City, Mexico

SIGNIFICANCE: Site of the Temple of the Sun and Temple of the Moon, Teotihuacán was the most organized and highly populated urban center in Mesoamerica during pre-Columbian times.

The construction of Teotihuacán (tay-oh-tee-wah-KAHN) continued for more than seven hundred years, and its expansive yet highly organized urban core reflects a master plan developed by its earliest inhabitants. The city is arranged on a grid with a major north-south street, currently known as the Avenue of the Dead, which intersects with another east-west street to divide the city into four quadrants. These quadrants contained barrios (neighborhoods) each with numerous apartment compounds and temples that housed thousands of people. The substantial buildings and walls of this ancient city were built from stone and plaster, and it is thought that 100,000 to 200,000 people lived at Teotihuacán during its height.

The most famous architectural features of Teotihuacán are the Pyramid of the Sun and the Pyramid of the Moon. The Pyramid of the Sun is the largest pre-Columbian pyramid in Mesoamerica and is thought to be dedicated to the goddess, the primary creator who is associated with creation and fertility. The Pyramid of the Moon is smaller and scholars believe it is dedicated to Tlaloc, the masculine deity of rain, lightning, and thunder.

Much of Teotihuacán history remains a mystery because there are no written records associated with the people of this culture. Although evidence indicates they had a system of writing and used astronomical calendars, they did not make any efforts to record historic dates, events, or even names of rulers. Furthermore, scholars do not know the language they spoke, and even the name Teotihuacán, (in Nahuatl, place of the gods) was a name given this city by the Aztecs, a culture that lived in the same region nearly six centuries later. The strict orientation and organization of the city plan, combined with the standardization of murals, ceramics, stone tools, symbols, and styles, indicate there was a strong central authority at Teotihuacán.

Teotihuacán was exceedingly influential on many levels throughout Mesoamerica. Its symbols of warfare and religion, such as the butterfly, Tlaloc eyes, and the atlatl (spear-thrower), have been found in many other Mesoamerican cultures, including the Maya, Mixtec, Toltec, and Aztec. During its most influential times, it is thought that Teotihuacán created long-distance political and economic ties with great Maya cities such as Tikal and Copán. Furthermore, the importance of Teotihuacán civilization, including the beliefs and ideas of its inhabitants, endured hundreds of years after 750 C.E. Evidence indicates the Aztec rulers and elite returned regularly to the abandoned city of Teotihuacán to conduct rituals and communicate with the ancients who came before them.

ADDITIONAL RESOURCES

Carrasco, David, Lindsay Jones, and Scott Sessions. *Mesoamerica's Classic Heritage: From Teotihuacán to the Aztecs*. Boulder: University Press of Colorado, 2000.

Stone carvings at Teotihuacán. (Corbis)

Coe, Michael. *Mexico*. New York: Thames and Hudson, 1994.

Pasztory, Esther. *Teotihuacán: An Experiment in Living*. Norman: University of Oklahoma Press, 1997.

SEE ALSO: Atlatl; Cholula; Copán; El Tajín; Mixtecs; Olmecs; Pyramid of the Moon.

—*Michelle R. Woodward*

TERENCE

ALSO KNOWN AS: Publius Terentius Afer
BORN: c. 190 B.C.E.; Carthage
DIED: 159 B.C.E.; en route to Greece
RELATED CIVILIZATIONS: Carthage, Republican Rome
MAJOR ROLE/POSITION: Playwright

Life. Born in Roman-occupied North Africa between 195 and 185 B.C.E. (and thus believed to be the first African writer of rank), Terence (TEHR-uhns) was brought to Rome as a boy slave and sold there to the senator Publius Terentius Lucanus, whose name he gratefully adopted. Lucanus provided for the young Terence's education and later set him free. An engaging person, Terence became a frequent guest in the literary circle around Scipio Aemilianus, whose admiration of Hellenistic culture and passion for the Latin language he shared. His first play, *Andria* (166 B.C.E.; English translation, 1598), attracted the attention of the prolific playwright Caecilius, who encouraged Terence's theatrical aspirations and ensured the plays' production by the troupe of Ambivius Turpio. In quick succession, Terence composed five more plays: *Hecyra* (165 B.C.E.; *The Mother-in-Law*, 1598), *Heautontimorumenos* (163 B.C.E.; *The Self-Tormentor*, 1598), *Eunouchus* (161 B.C.E.; *The Eunuch*, 1598), *Phormio* (161 B.C.E.; English translation, 1598), and *Adelphoe* (160 B.C.E.; *The Brothers*, 1598). The plays are all *fabulae palliatae*, domestic comedies mostly based on the Greek "New Comedy" of Menander. In contrast to the exuberance of his predecessor Plautus, Terence's plays are densely plotted (their characteristic feature is the intertwined "double plot") and elegantly written, a fact that contributed to their occasional failure in the public arena. Legend has it that Terence died on a voyage to Greece to procure new manuscripts by Menander.

Influence. Celebrated in antiquity as the only comic playwright to rival Plautus, Terence became a byword for pure Latin style during the Middle Ages. The influence of his domestic plays on the theater of the Italian Renaissance, William Shakespeare, and Molière, and

Terence. (Library of Congress)

through them on the modern theater, has been profound.

ADDITIONAL RESOURCES

Beacham, Richard. *The Roman Theatre and Its Audience*. Cambridge, Mass.: Harvard University Press, 1991.

Forehand, Walter. *Terence*. Boston: Twayne, 1985.

Konstan, David. *Roman Comedy*. Ithaca, N.Y.: Cornell University Press, 1983.

SEE ALSO: Carthage; Menander (playwright); Plautus; Rome, Republican; Scipio Aemilianus.

—*Ralf Erik Remshardt*

TERPANDER OF LESBOS

ALSO KNOWN AS: Terpandros
BORN: early seventh century B.C.E.; Antissa, Lesbos
DIED: late seventh century B.C.E.; perhaps Sparta
RELATED CIVILIZATION: Archaic Greece
MAJOR ROLE/POSITION: Musician, poet

Life. Modern scholars discount many of the more picturesque details that ancient authors present concerning Terpander of Lesbos (tur-PAN-dur of LEHZ-bohs), such as that he was forced to flee his homeland because of homicide and that he eventually died from choking on a fig. Fairly uncontroversial, though, is that he acquired fame as a musical performer in Lesbos and that he subsequently went to Sparta, where he won various musical competitions.

Terpander's career also had a literary dimension. In his time, music and poetry were closely associated, and various ancient sources refer to his performing both his own poems and those of Homer. Particularly suggestive in this regard is a passage in the *Iliad* (c. 800 B.C.E.; English translation, 1616) in which the warlike hero Achilles is presented as a kind of bard, celebrating the "fame of men." This combination of poetry and warfare sounds like an idealized picture of Sparta, where Terpander spent much of his career.

Influence. Terpander is generally credited with a dominant position in the establishment of Greek musical traditions; he possibly developed the seven-stringed lyre.

ADDITIONAL RESOURCES

Barker, Andrew. *The Musician and His Art*. Vol. 1 in *Greek Musical Writings*. Cambridge, England: Cambridge University Press, 1984.

Campbell, David A. *Greek Lyric*. Cambridge, Mass.: Harvard University Press, 1993.

SEE ALSO: Greece, Archaic; Homer; Performing arts.

—*Edwin D. Floyd*

TERTULLIAN

ALSO KNOWN AS: Quintus Septimius Florens Tertullianus
BORN: c. 155-160 C.E.; in or near Carthage (later in Tunisia)
DIED: after 217 C.E.; probably near Carthage
RELATED CIVILIZATION: Imperial Rome
MAJOR ROLE/POSITION: Religious figure

Life. Tertullian (tur-TUHL-yuhn) was born of pagan parents, enjoyed an extensive education, and led a life of unbridled immorality until at some time before 197 C.E., when he was converted to Christianity. By the end of the first decade of the ensuing century, disgruntlement at the laxity of Catholic morals had caused him to embrace the heresy of the apocalyptic and ascetically minded Montanists. He eventually found them wanting in puritanical rigor, and he appears to have responded by founding his own sect of Tertullianists. During the two decades that followed his adoption of Christianity, Tertullian produced numerous works, of which thirty-one survive and some dozen more have perished. This corpus is composed of apologetic tracts aimed at pagans, polemical refutations of heretics, and moral essays concerned with ecclesiastical discipline. All these works are written in a bizarre and contorted style that makes Tertullian one of the most difficult authors in the whole of Latin literature.

Influence. As one of the earliest writers of the Latin Church, Tertullian has exercised a vast influence on both its language and thought; of particular importance is his contribution to Christological and Trinitarian theology.

ADDITIONAL RESOURCES

Osborn, E. F. *Tertullian: First Theologian of the West*. New York: Cambridge University Press, 1997.

Rankin, D. *Tertullian and the Church*. New York: Cambridge University Press, 1995.

SEE ALSO: Christianity; Rome, Imperial.

—*Neil Adkin*

TEUTOBURG FOREST, BATTLE OF

DATE: 9 C.E.
LOCALE: Kalkriese, near Osnabrück, Germany
RELATED CIVILIZATION: Imperial Rome
SIGNIFICANCE: The Roman defeat at Teutoburg (TEW-tuh-burg) Forest ended its expansion efforts in the area.

Background. Expecting to continue three centuries of continuous expansion, most recently in Spain and the Alps, Augustus ordered the conquest of the lands east of the Rhine and the northern Balkan peninsula in 12 B.C.E. By 9 C.E., Rome was establishing a province between the Rhine and Weser Rivers (ultimate territorial goals are uncertain) and had crushed a revolt in Pannonia.

Action. Arminius (also known as Hermann) of the Germanic Cheruscan tribe set a trap between marshes and a limestone ridge (Kalkriese) and ambushed the Roman army returning to forts on the Rhine. Publius Quinctilius Varus's three legions plus auxiliaries, strung out in a long column, were almost entirely destroyed in a three-day engagement.

Consequences. Rome abandoned expansion across the Lower Rhine and redeployed legions along the west and south shores of the Rhine and Danube.

ADDITIONAL RESOURCES

Cornell, T. "The End of Roman Imperial Expansion." In *War and Society in the Roman World*, edited by J. Rich and G. Shipley. New York: Routledge, 1993.

King, A. *Roman Gaul and Germany*. Berkeley: University of California Press, 1990.

Maxfield, V. "The Germanies and Raetia." In *The Roman World*, edited by J. Wacher. New York: Routledge, 1987.

Schlüter, W. "The Battle of the Teutoburg Forest: Archaeological Research at Kalkriese near Osnabrück." In *Roman Germany: Studies in Cultural Interaction*, edited by J. D. Creighton and R. J. A. Wilson. Providence, R.I.: Journal of Roman Archaeology, 1999.

Wells, C. M. *The German Policy of Augustus*. Oxford, England: Clarendon Press, 1972.

SEE ALSO: Arminius; Augustus; Germany; Quinctilius Varus, Publius; Rome, Imperial.

—*Thomas H. Watkins*

THAPSUS, BATTLE OF

DATE: April 6, 46 B.C.E.
LOCALE: Thapsus, North Africa (Tunisia), southeast of Carthage
RELATED CIVILIZATION: Republican Rome
SIGNIFICANCE: Julius Caesar's victory over a republican army at Thapsus brought the African phase of Rome's civil war to a conclusion and moved Caesar decisively closer to complete mastery of the Republic.

Background. In January, 49 B.C.E., civil war erupted in the Roman Republic between Julius Caesar and senatorial forces led by Pompey the Great. As part of the ongoing struggle, Caesar besieged the North African coastal community of Thapsus (THAP-suhs) and its Pompeian garrison on April 4, 46 B.C.E. In response, a republican army led by Quintus Caecilius Metellus Pius Scipio and supported by King Juba I of Numidia moved to relieve the town.

Action. Scipio arrayed his army for battle on April 6, stationing legions in the center, supported by strong contingents of Numidian cavalry and elephants on both wings. In response, Caesar deployed his legions in the center in three lines, with elements of cavalry and light infantry positioned on the flanks. A spontaneous assault by Caesar's right, followed quickly by a charge of the entire army, shattered the resistance of Scipio's cavalry and elephants. A protracted infantry struggle then followed, which ended only when Caesar's veterans routed republican forces, thereby winning the battle.

Consequences. Thapsus proved the climactic battle of the African war and the turning point in Caesar's struggle with republican opposition in Rome. After defeating Scipio's army, Caesar returned temporarily to Italy before initiating a winter campaign in 45 B.C.E. against republican forces in southern Spain led by Gnaeus Pompeius Magnus, elder son of Pompey the Great.

ADDITIONAL RESOURCE
Dodge, Theodore A. *Caesar.* Mechanicsburg, Pa.: Stackpole, 1995.

SEE ALSO: Africa, North; Caesar, Julius; Pompey the Great; Rome, Republican.

—*Donathan Taylor*

THEMISTIUS

ALSO KNOWN AS: Themistios
BORN: c. 317 C.E.; Paphlagonia (later in Turkey)
DIED: c. 388 C.E.; Constantinople (later Istanbul, Turkey)
RELATED CIVILIZATIONS: Imperial Rome, Roman Greece
MAJOR ROLE/POSITION: Rhetorician, politician, philosopher

Life. Born into a rich rural family, Themistius (thuh-MIHS-chee-uhs) spent most of his life in Constantinople. He remained a pagan but was respected by the Christian authorities and held many high offices, including senator and, in 384 C.E., prefect of Constantinople. He admired Aristotle and used Aristotelian philosophy to mediate among classical pagan Platonism, Christian Neoplatonism, and fideistic Christianity. He ran his own school of philosophy and rhetoric, wrote interpretations and paraphrases of Aristotle, and served the emperor Theodosius the Great as tutor to his son, the crown prince Arcadius, later the first emperor of the Eastern Roman Empire. He was renowned in his lifetime for his political speeches, at least thirty-two of which survive.

Influence. Themistius's best-known work is his eulogy of his friend and former student, Julian the Apostate. Arabic scholars translated and carefully studied this eulogy and many of his other works either written about or addressed to Julian. In philosophy, his main importance was as a popularizer of Aristotle, not as an original thinker. Around 400 C.E., Vettius Agorius Praetextatus translated Themistius's paraphrase of Aristotle's *Analytica posterioria* (335-323 B.C.E.; *Posterior Analytics*, 1812) into Latin.

ADDITIONAL RESOURCES
Dihle, Albrecht. *Greek and Latin Literature of the Roman Empire from Augustus to Justinian.* London: Routledge, 1994.
Vanderspoel, John. *Themistius and the Imperial Court: Oratory, Civic Duty, and Paideia from Constantius to Theodosius.* Ann Arbor: University of Michigan Press, 1995.

SEE ALSO: Aristotle; Christianity; Constantinople; Greece, Hellenistic and Roman; Julian the Apostate; Rome, Imperial; Theodosius the Great.

—*Eric v.d. Luft*

THEMISTOCLES

BORN: c. 525 B.C.E.; Athens, Greece
DIED: c. 460 B.C.E.; Magnesia, Asia Minor
RELATED CIVILIZATIONS: Classical Greece, Persia
MAJOR ROLE/POSITION: Statesman, admiral, general

Life. The outstanding Athenian statesman of his generation, Themistocles (thuh-MIHS-tuh-kleez) was known for his vainglory as well as his foresight and resourcefulness. An archon in 493 B.C.E., he was chiefly responsible for Athens having a navy of two hundred triremes when Xerxes I invaded Greece in 480 B.C.E. Themistocles' strategy enabled the Greeks to trap and destroy the Persian armada in the straits between Attica and the island of Salamis (480 B.C.E.). He was instrumental in restoring and expanding the fortifications of Athens after the Persians retreated from Greece.

Themistocles was ostracized about 472 B.C.E. In exile, he began fomenting opposition to Sparta in the Peloponnese. With Spartan connivance, his political enemies at Athens then charged him with Medism (collaborating with Persia), and he was condemned to death in absentia. He escaped to the east, however, and Xerxes' successor granted him asylum and a fiefdom in Asia Minor, where he lived prosperously for the rest of his life.

Themistocles. (North Wind Picture Archives)

Influence. Themistocles' advocacy of a strong navy, a well-fortified city, and opposition to Sparta foreshadowed the policies of his successor, Pericles.

ADDITIONAL RESOURCES
Herodotus. *The Histories*. Translated by Robin Waterfield. New York: Oxford University Press, 1998.
Scott-Kilvert, I., trans. *The Rise and Fall of Athens: Nine Greek Lives by Plutarch*. New York: Penguin, 1960.
Strassler, Robert B., ed. *The Landmark Thucydides*. Vols. 1-2. New York: Free Press, 1996.

SEE ALSO: Greco-Persian Wars; Greece, Classical; Pericles; Salamis, Battle of; Xerxes I.

—Hubert M. Martin, Jr.

THEOCRITUS OF SYRACUSE

BORN: c. 300 B.C.E.; Syracuse, Sicily
DIED: c. 260 B.C.E.; place unknown
RELATED CIVILIZATION: Ptolemaic Egypt
MAJOR ROLE/POSITION: Poet

Life. Internal evidence dates Theocritus of Syracuse's (thee-AHK-ruht-uhs of SIHR-uh-kyews) poetry to the reign of Ptolemy II Philadelphus in Egypt. Probably originally from Syracuse but also linked through his poetry with Cos and Alexandria, Theocritus is famous for creating a bucolic world that provided inspiration for Vergil's *Eclogues* (43-37 B.C.E.; English translation, 1575, also known as *Bucolics*) and the later pastoral tradition. However, Theocritus's urban and mythological poems are equally artful and innovative, mixing genres and blurring distinctions between high and low culture. Therefore, the population of Theocritus's poetry includes—in addition to herdsmen and other rustics—housewives, soldiers, drinking companions, baby Heracles, and an adolescent Polyphemus in love. The urban mimes (short dramatic scenes) offer a special forum for exploring issues of contemporary importance, including gender relations, colonialism, and patronage. Theocritus's innovation is also evident in his artful reworking of motifs and techniques from epic, archaic lyric, New Comedy, and mime.

Influence. Although Theocritus seems to have avoided attaching himself officially to the Alexandrian museum and library, his poetry suggests lively relations with contemporary poets. Later, his poetry influenced such writers as the bucolic poets Moschus of Syracuse and Bion; the Roman poet Vergil; the Greek writer Longus; the English poets John Milton, Percy Bysshe Shelley, and Elizabeth Barrett Browning; and the modern Greek poet Constantine P. Cavafy.

ADDITIONAL RESOURCES
Burton, Joan B. *Theocritus's Urban Mimes: Mobility, Gender, and Patronage*. Berkeley: University of California Press, 1995.
Gutzwiller, Kathryn J. *Theocritus' Pastoral Analogies: The Formation of a Genre*. Madison: University of Wisconsin Press, 1991.
Hunter, Richard. *Theocritus and the Archaeology of Greek Poetry*. Cambridge, England: Cambridge University Press, 1996.

SEE ALSO: Egypt, Ptolemaic and Roman; Longus; Moschus of Syracuse; Vergil.

—Joan B. Burton

THEODERIC THE GREAT

ALSO KNOWN AS: Theodoricus; Theodoric
BORN: c. 454 C.E.; Pannonia
DIED: 526 C.E.; Ravenna
RELATED CIVILIZATIONS: Imperial Rome, Goths
MAJOR ROLE/POSITION: King

Life. Like his father, Theoderic (thee-AHD-uh-rihk) the Great became king of the Ostrogoths. Theoderic employed the Goths under his command alternately in support of and against the Byzantine emperor. In order to rid himself of his unreliable ally, the emperor Zeno dispatched Theoderic to expel the barbarian king Odoacer and his forces from Italy. Theoderic defeated Odoacer in 493 C.E., but instead of surrendering Italy to Byzantine control, he ruled as king of the Goths and of Italy.

As a youth, Theoderic had been a hostage at the imperial court in Constantinople, and his familiarity with Roman culture served him well in Italy, where he ruled as a Roman emperor in all but name. He retained the Roman administration, patronized classical culture, and bestowed high political office on Roman aristocrats who supported his rule. Despite his Arian faith, his relations with the papacy were good. The mildness of

Theoderic's rule was marred only by the execution of the philosopher Boethius and his father-in-law, Quintus Aurelius Memmius Symmachus. Their deaths can be attributed both to Theoderic's fear that they were plotting against him with the Byzantine emperor and to political strife over the succession.

Influence. Of the barbarian kings who succeeded to power after the fall of the Western Roman Empire, Theoderic was the most powerful. Even the historian Procopius praised Theoderic's rule, and subsequent barbarian kings emulated Theoderic's cultivation of Roman culture.

ADDITIONAL RESOURCES
Moorhead, John. *Theoderic in Italy*. Oxford, England: Clarendon Press, 1992.
Wolfram, Herwig. *History of the Goths*. 2d ed. Berkeley: University of California Press, 1988.

SEE ALSO: Arianism; Boethius; Byzantine Empire; Christianity; Goths; Odoacer; Procopius; Rome, Imperial.

—Martha G. Jenks

THEODORA

ALSO KNOWN AS: Empress Theodora
BORN: c. 497 C.E.; place unknown
DIED: 548 C.E.; Constantinople
RELATED CIVILIZATION: Byzantine Empire
MAJOR ROLE/POSITION: Byzantine empress

Life. Empress Theodora was an impressive leader of early Byzantine history. Her origins are unclear—she may have been the daughter of a Hippodrome bear keeper or perhaps a Mongol princess. She was an intelligent and beautiful actress who embraced Christianity, although she sympathized with the heretical sect. Theodora and Justinian I met while he was still a senator in Constantinople. Laws forbidding the union of a senator and an actress had to be bypassed before they could be married. Theodora became empress and unofficial co-ruler when Justinian ascended to the throne in 527 C.E. Her counsel assisted Justinian on more than one occasion. During the Nika Riots in 532 C.E., Procopius writes that Theodora rallied the fearful Justinian to action with these courageous words: "For an

Emperor to become a fugitive is a thing not to be endured ... purple makes a fine shroud." Theodora died of cancer in her forties. She is depicted in ceremonial regalia among the spectacular mosaics of San Vitale in Ravenna, Italy.

Influence. Theodora was involved in political and religious issues. She implemented laws improving the rights of women in divorce, rape, ownership of property, homelessness, and domestic violence.

ADDITIONAL RESOURCES
Browning, Robert. *Justinian and Theodora*. New York: Praeger, 1987.
Gies, Frances, and Joseph Gies. *Women in the Middle Ages*. New York: Harper Perennial, 1992.
Procopius. *The Secret History*. Translated by G. A. Williamson. New York: Viking Penguin, 1966.

SEE ALSO: Byzantine Empire; Christianity; Constantinople; Justinian I; Monophysitism; Procopius.

—Laura Rinaldi Dufresne

THEODORET OF CYRRHUS

ALSO KNOWN AS: Theodoretus; Theodoret of Cyrus
BORN: c. 393 C.E.; Antioch, Roman Syria
DIED: c. 458 C.E.; Cyrrhus
RELATED CIVILIZATIONS: Imperial Rome,
  Byzantine Empire
MAJOR ROLE/POSITION: Bishop, historian

Life. Theodoret of Cyrrhus (thee-AHD-uh-ruht) was born to an upper-class family in Antioch, Syria. When his parents died, he gave away all of his inherited property and joined a monastic community in Nicerte (c. 416 C.E.). In 423 C.E., he was consecrated bishop of Cyrrhus, where he served for about twenty-five years, ruling, writing, and building bridges, an aqueduct, and public baths.

In 431 C.E., he became embroiled in a theological conflict between his friend Nestorius and Cyril of Alexandria over the nature of Jesus Christ. Theodoret defended Nestorius by attacking Cyril's position. When Cyril died, Dioscorus, his successor as bishop of Alexandria, attacked Theodoret, first by gaining imperial decrees confining him to his see and then, in 449 C.E., by having him deposed by the Council of Ephesus (later known as the "Robber Council"). However, in July, 450 C.E., the emperor Theodosius II died and was succeeded by Marcian and his wife, Pulcheria, who were more fa-vorably disposed toward Theodoret. They invited him to attend the Council of Chalcedon in 451 C.E., where he was restored.

Influence. Theodoret became well known for his writings against Cyril (which were condemned in 553 C.E. at the Council of Constantinople). His *Historia ecclesiastica* (c. 430 C.E.; *The Ecclesiastical History*, 1612; better known as *Church History*) has also been important to modern historians because of the invaluable ancient documents that it preserves.

ADDITIONAL RESOURCES

Chestnut, Glenn F. *The First Christian Histories*. 2d ed. Macon, Ga.: Mercer University Press, 1986.
Theodoret. *Ecclesiastical History, Dialogues, and Letters*. Vol. 3 in *The Nicene and Post-Nicene Fathers*. 2d series. Translated by Blomfield Jackson. 1892. Reprint. Peabody, Mass.: Hendrickson, 1994.
Young, F. M. *From Nicaea to Chalcedon*. Philadelphia: Fortress Press, 1983.

SEE ALSO: Byzantine Empire; Chalcedon, Council of; Christianity; Cyril of Alexandria, Saint; Nestorius; Rome, Imperial; Theodosius II.

—*Stephen Felder*

THEODOSIUS OF ALEXANDRIA

BORN: beginning of sixth century C.E.; Egypt
DIED: 566 C.E.; Constantinople
RELATED CIVILIZATION: Byzantine Empire
MAJOR ROLE/POSITION: Church leader

Life. Little is known of Theodosius (thee-uh-DOH-shee-uhs) of Alexandria's early life. He became a priest and a disciple and friend of the theologian Severus of Antioch. Severus was leader of the moderate Monophysites. They held that Jesus Christ had a single nature, rather than the dual human and divine nature specified as orthodox truth by the Council of Chalcedon, in 451 C.E. Monophysitism was generally followed in Egypt.

Theodosius followed Severus and Patriarch Timothy III of Alexandria. When Timothy died in 535 C.E., Theodosius was elected patriarch, largely through Theodora, wife of the Eastern Roman Emperor, Justin-ian I. However, he only briefly occupied his office. In 537 C.E., he was deposed by Justinian for not accepting Chalcedon and summoned to Constantinople, where he remained in exile until his death.

After Severus's death, Theodosius became leader of the Monophysite cause and consecrated several bishops to the Arabs, who then set up a separate church. After Justinian's death, his successor, Justin II, tried to unite the church. Though Theodosius distanced himself from extreme forms of Monophysitism (that is, the Trinity being both three persons and three natures), he died before negotiations made further progress. He left a few writings in Syriac and Coptic.

Influence. His moderate Monophysitism ensured that although the church remained theologically divided, it was not split organizationally through Monophysitism being declared heretical.

ADDITIONAL RESOURCES
Bagnall, Roger. *Egypt in Late Antiquity.* Princeton, N.J.: Princeton University Press, 1993.
Frend, W. H. C. *The Rise of the Monophysite Movement.* Cambridge, England: Cambridge University Press, 1972.

SEE ALSO: Byzantine Empire; Chalcedon, Council of; Christianity; Justinian I; Monophysitism; Theodora.

—*David Barratt*

THEODOSIUS THE GREAT

ALSO KNOWN AS: Flavius Theodosius
BORN: January 11, 346 or 347 C.E.; Cauca, Gallaecia (later in Spain)
DIED: January 17, 395 C.E.; Mediolanum (later Milan, Italy)
RELATED CIVILIZATION: Imperial Rome
MAJOR ROLE/POSITION: Emperor

Life. In 368 C.E., Theodosius (thee-oh-DOH-shee-uhs) served in Britain on the military staff of his father, Theodosius the Elder, and later fought Germans on the Rhine frontier. In 373-374 C.E., as governor of Upper Moesia, he directed campaigns against the Sarmatians but retired to his family's Spanish estates after his father's execution for treason in 376 C.E.

After the Roman defeat at Adrianople in 378 C.E., the Western emperor Gratian named him commander of Roman forces on the Danube frontier, and in 379 C.E., he became coemperor in the east. From 379 to 382 C.E., he directed campaigns against the Visigoths that ultimately forced them back into Thrace, and he restored order to the Balkan provinces. In October of 382 C.E., he concluded a treaty with the Visigoths that represented a dramatic departure from earlier Roman policy toward barbarians. Unlike earlier barbarians, who had been permitted to settle in Roman territory as subjects of Rome, the Visigoths were allowed to live within the empire under their own leaders and laws as independent allies (*foederati*) of Rome.

In 380 C.E., Theodosius proclaimed Catholic Christianity as defined by the Council of Nicaea (325 C.E.) the official religion of the Eastern Empire. In doing so, he formally rejected Arianism. He subsequently accepted baptism and in 381 C.E. ordered that all Eastern churches be placed under the control of Catholic bishops. In 391-392 C.E., he issued edicts closing all pagan temples and banning pagan sacrifices and other rituals.

In 383 C.E., Roman troops in Britain proclaimed their commander Magnus Maximus emperor of the

Theodosius the Great. (Hulton Archive)

West. Maximus then invaded Gaul and executed Gratian, leaving Gratian's younger brother Valentinian II in control of Italy. In 387 C.E., Maximus invaded Italy; Theodosius consequently demonstrated his support for Valentinian through his marriage to Valentinian's sister Galla.

In the summer of 388 C.E., Theodosius defeated Maximus's forces at Siscia and Poetovio and subsequently executed Maximus. He remained in Italy from 388 to 391 C.E. in order to organize the government of the Western Empire. Valentinian II was named Western emperor but placed under the guidance of the Frankish general Arbogast. During this period, Theodosius began a close but sometimes turbulent relationship with Bishop Ambrose of Milan.

After Valentinian II was found dead in May of 392 C.E., Arbogast created a puppet Western emperor, Flavius Eugenius. On September 5-6, 394 C.E., Theodosius defeated the army of Arbogast and Eugenius at the Battle of the River Frigidus. This victory made Theodosius sole ruler of the empire; furthermore, because of Arbogast's and Eugenius's previous toleration of pagan religious practices, it was seen as a triumph for Christianity.

Influence. Because of his religious policies, Theodosius came to be known as "the Great." In addition, his treaty with the Visigoths established an important precedent and resulted in the settlement of more barbarian tribes as Roman allies. Their establishment of independent kingdoms within Roman territory contributed to the eventual collapse of central authority in the Western Empire during the fifth century C.E.

ADDITIONAL RESOURCES

Jones, A. H. M. *The Later Roman Empire, 284-602.* Norman: University of Oklahoma Press, 1964.

Williams, Stephen, and Gerard Friell. *Theodosius: The Empire at Bay.* New Haven, Conn.: Yale University Press, 1994.

SEE ALSO: Adrianople, Battle of; Ambrose; Britain; Christianity; Goths, Ostrogoths, Visigoths; Gratian; Nicaea, Council of; Rome, Imperial.

—Thomas I. Crimando

THEODOSIUS II

BORN: 401 C.E.; Constantinople
DIED: 450 C.E.; Constantinople
RELATED CIVILIZATIONS: Byzantine Empire, Imperial Rome, Persia, Huns
MAJOR ROLE/POSITION: Emperor

Life. Theodosius II's father, Arcadius, was tenth emperor of the Eastern Roman Empire. He died when Theodosius was only seven years old. Anthemius, Arcadius's last adviser, became regent for the infant emperor.

The Roman Empire, both Western and Eastern, was in a precarious state in the fifth century C.E.; in 410 C.E., Rome fell to the Huns, a barbarian tribe. The Eastern Empire was threatened by the Persian Empire to the east and the Huns to the north and west. Anthemius managed to keep these threats at bay and, in 413 C.E., began new fortifications for Constantinople, called the Theodosian Walls. He died circa 415 C.E.

The next influence over Theodosius was his older sister Pulcheria, an ardent Christian. She persuaded Theodosius to ban all pagans from public service in 416 C.E. In 421 C.E., he married Eudoxia the Younger. An attempt that year to alleviate the plight of Christians in Persia had to be abandoned to save Constantinople from a Hun attack. From this began a history of paying an annual tribute to the Huns. After each defeat (in 431, 441, and 447 C.E.), the tribute increased until it became a serious drain on the empire. Various attempts to help the Western Empire against barbarian tribes in Italy and North Africa were constantly hindered by these threats from the north and east.

Internally, Theodosius greatly expanded Constantinople as a seat of learning, adding thirteen Latin-speaking and fifteen Greek-speaking professors to the university faculty, especially with a view to increasing the efficiency of the civil service.

Theodosius became involved in several theological controversies that threatened the unity of the church. The main one concerned Nestorianism. Nestorius was patriarch of Constantinople and supported by Theodosius. However, a council in Rome in 430 C.E. condemned his teachings about the nature of Christ. Theodosius called an ecumenical council of all bishops at Ephesus in 431 C.E., but this agreed with the previous decision and Nestorius's teachings were declared heretical. The church was confused, but eventually most Nestorians moved to Persia.

In 440 C.E., Theodosius suspected his influential and often headstrong wife of adultery. She went to live in Jerusalem for sixteen years, starting many building projects there. When Theodosius died in mid-450 C.E. from a fall from his horse, he left no male heir. Pulcheria married Marcian, who was then proclaimed emperor.

Influence. Possibly Theodosius's main contribution to the empire was the compilation of the *Codex Theodosiusianus* (438 C.E.; *The Theodosian Code,* 1952), the first official attempt to codify Roman law. It included only laws made after 312 C.E., when the empire officially became Christian. It did make administering the law more uniform, and though still unwieldy, lasted until the *Codex Iustinianus* (529, 534 C.E.; English translation, 1915; better known as *Justinian's Codification*).

Though not a strong ruler, either militarily or intellectually, Theodosius managed to keep the Eastern Empire intact at a difficult period, to keep the church relatively united with Christianity as the dominant faith, and to build up Constantinople as a place of learning.

ADDITIONAL RESOURCES
Kaegi, W. E., Jr. *Byzantium and the Decline of Rome.*
Princeton, N.J.: Princeton University Press, 1968.
Treadgold, Warren. *A History of the Byzantine State and Society.* Stanford, Calif.: Stanford University Press, 1997.

SEE ALSO: Byzantine Empire; Christianity; Constantinople; Huns; Nestorius; Rome, Imperial; Persia.

—*David Barratt*

THEOGNIS

ALSO KNOWN AS: Theognis of Megara
BORN: c. 600 B.C.E.; place unknown
DIED: c. 500 B.C.E.; place unknown
RELATED CIVILIZATION: Archaic Greece
MAJOR ROLE/POSITION: Poet

Life. Virtually nothing is known about Theognis's (thee-AHG-nuhs) life. Ancient authorities debate his birthplace, referencing a Megara in Greece or Sicily. The former seems to be the better candidate, despite the fact that he wrote an elegy about Syracuse. Other fragments imply that he merely visited Sicily. What can be discerned through the fragments of his surviving works is that he belonged to aristocratic circles. Many of his poems are relevant to the symposium, such as drinking songs, political expositions, and pederastic love songs. His political views seemed to have put him at odds with the leaders of a democratic revolution. Betrayed by one of his friends, Theognis found himself bereft of his property and exiled. His travels took him to Euboea, Thebes, Sparta, and eventually Sicily. His poems, many addressed to his friend Cyrnus, are filled with invective against his enemies, the bemoaning of his state of poverty, and lampoons. Also, in some poems he attempted to give political and moral advice to his friend.

Influence. Despite the loss of much of his work and the doubtful authorship of some Theognic fragments, the ancient authors placed him on par with Hesiod and Solon. He appears to have been a prominent voice for aristocratic concerns during a century of political transition.

ADDITIONAL RESOURCES
Edwards, J. M. *Greek Elegy and Iambus*. Vol. 1. Cambridge, Mass.: Harvard University Press, 1982.
Mulroy, David. *Early Greek Lyric Poetry*. Ann Arbor: University of Michigan Press, 2000.
West, M. L. *Greek Lyric Poetry*. Oxford, England: Clarendon Press, 1994.

SEE ALSO: Greece, Archaic; Hesiod; Languages and literature; Solon.

—*Todd William Ewing*

THEOPHRASTUS

BORN: c. 372 B.C.E.; Eresus, Lesbos, Greece
DIED: c. 287 B.C.E.; Athens?, Greece
RELATED CIVILIZATIONS: Classical and Hellenistic Greece, Republican Rome
MAJOR ROLE/POSITION: Philosopher

Life. Theophrastus (thee-oh-FRAS-tuhs) was associated with the great Greek philosopher Aristotle during much of his active life. He appears to have met Aristotle sometime during the 340's B.C.E., perhaps in Asia Minor. He accompanied Aristotle when the latter moved to Macedonia (342-335 B.C.E.) and stayed with him when Aristotle returned to Athens. He succeeded Aristotle as the leader of the collection of scholars teaching philosophy in Athens in the late fourth and early third centuries B.C.E.

Influence. Although most of Theophrastus's writings have not survived, he carried on the philosophical

Theophrastus, known for his study of plants, as depicted on the frontispiece of a seventeenth century book on plants. (Library of Congress)

speculations of Aristotle, though not without some criticism of Aristotle's conclusions. Of the few works that have survived, the most significant are his study of fire (in which he expressed some disagreement with Aristotle's views) and his account of plants of the eastern Mediterranean, particularly its trees. He believed in close observation followed by rational evaluation of possible explanations of the observed phenomena. His study of plants laid the methodological foundations of modern botany, particularly through his descriptions of the methods of reproduction used by the different plants.

ADDITIONAL RESOURCES

Van Ophuijsen, Johannes M., and Marlein von Raalte. *Theophrastus: Reappraising the Sources.* New Brunswick, N.J.: Transaction, 1998.
Williams, Bernard. "Philosophy." In *The Legacy of Greece: A New Appraisal*, edited by M. I. Finley. Oxford, England: Oxford University Press, 1984.

SEE ALSO: Aristotle; Greece, Classical; Philosophy.
                                                —*Nancy M. Gordon*

THERA

DATE: 2000-1400 B.C.E.
LOCALE: Thera (modern Thíra), in the Cyclades
RELATED CIVILIZATIONS: Cyclades, Minoa
SIGNIFICANCE: Site of Bronze Age Akroteri, destroyed in a volcanic catastrophe, purported to have ended Minoan civilization and given rise to the Atlantis myth.

Thera (THIHR-uh), the largest island in the Santorini Archipelago, is about 62 miles (100 kilometers) north of Crete. Thera and the lesser island, Therasia (modern Thirasía), are remnants of a caldera (crater) rim formed by the collapse of an exploded volcano.

Thera's latest explosion, probably in 1623 B.C.E., was one of the largest volcanic explosions recorded in human history. In addition to blasting out a caldera, the volcano discharged an estimated 35,000-39,000 cubic yards (27 to 30 cubic kilometers) of volcanic debris, burying Bronze Age settlements on the archipel-

ago with thick ash and pumice. Airborne volcanic ash, mineralogically dated, occurs in archaeological excavations and natural exposures throughout the eastern Mediterranean, as far as the Nile Delta, Israel, and central Anatolia. This ash is about eight inches (twenty centimeters) thick off northern Crete. In addition, the eruption probably caused a tsunami, or tidal wave. Tsunami effects have been observed on the north coast of Crete, and some archaeologists credit a tsunami rather than an earthquake for tumbling large stone blocks in the ruins of Knossos. Also, geologists argue that glowing ash clouds from Thera could have crossed the sea to Crete to start the fires that accompanied Knossos's destruction. Finally, ash blown into the stratosphere by a large explosive eruption could cause temporary global cooling and crop failures. Indeed, volcanic traces in the Greenland ice cap and stunted growth recorded in tree-rings from California and Ireland indicate global cooling around 1623 B.C.E. and are widely ascribed to Thera's last explosive eruption.

Archaeological excavations. Before the great explosion, Thera and Therasia supported a thriving culture, named the Cycladic, but broadly included in the contemporaneous Minoan culture on Crete. Cycladic ruins and artifacts were first brought to light in 1866 in pumice quarries opened for the Suez Canal Company on Therasia. In 1869, extensive archaeologic excavation began when archaeologist and volcanologist Ferdinand Fouqué first found Akroteri at the south end of Thera. Between 1895 and 1903, German archaeologists excavated ruins near the town of Thera.

Akroteri, however, remains the most important Cycladic site and is a popular tourist destination. There, the Greek archaeologist Spyridon Marinatos began unearthing a rich, beautifully preserved city in 1967. After his death in 1974, Christos Doumas continued the project. The Akroteri excavation includes several large, well-constructed, multistory houses notable for very well-preserved frescos. These frescos completely cover the interior walls of entire rooms, illustrating ships, men, women, children, birds, plants, and monkeys in a naturalistic style. They closely resemble Minoan frescos on Crete but remain the finest uncovered Bronze Age artworks. The frescos, pottery, and other Theran artifacts clearly indicate strong affinity with the Cretan Minoan culture. In contrast to Pompeii and Herculaneum, also overwhelmed by volcanic debris, human remains are notably few on Thera. Either the inhabitants fled the island or they were trapped in an undiscovered refuge.

Thera as Atlantis. Archaeologists and other scholars speculate that Thera's explosion gave rise to the Atlantis myth. In his *Critias* (360-347 B.C.E.; English translation, 1793) and *Timaeus* (360-347 B.C.E.; *Timeaus*, 1793), Plato describes Atlantis as an island occupied by a highly civilized, powerful empire that, after being struck by violent earthquakes and floods, sinks into the sea during a single day and night. Thera and Knossos's destruction resembles this myth. Knossos and other Cretan cities and palaces were struck by an earthquake or possibly a tsunami and then destroyed by fire and abandoned at the height of the Minoan culture, about 1450 B.C.E. Akroteri also suffered an earthquake and was temporarily reoccupied before its volcanic destruction. No apparent cultural decline preceded either city's destruction, and both regions were subsequently occupied by people from mainland cultures. Therefore, although some explain the Cretan disaster as an overwhelming invasion, many archaeologists believe Thera's eruption caused the destruction on both Thera and Crete.

The sequence of pottery styles, however, indicates that Akroteri's destruction significantly predates Knossos's fall. The youngest pottery in Akroteri's ruins is considered of the same age as that of the Late Minoan IA age, an age defined by sequencing pottery decorative styles. These pots are somewhat older than the Late Minoan IB materials at ruined Knossos. These dates, however, are founded on correlating the Cycladic and Minoan decorative style sequences, and the calendar dates are based on Egyptian hieroglyphic records. None of this, however, is accepted by all archaeologists.

Radiocarbon dates do not support simultaneous destruction of Thera and Minoan Crete. The radiocarbon age of charcoal in the ruins of Akroteri ranges from 1740 to 1550 B.C.E., favoring a seventeenth century B.C.E. date for the eruption and for Minoan IA ceramics on Thera. Radiocarbon dates for Late Minoan IA or IB ceramics at Knossos are imprecise, but the subsequent Late Minoan II periods are placed at around 1510 to 1430 B.C.E. Again, however, many authorities consider the events synchronous.

In addition, Thera's eruption has been speculatively linked with the reddening of the Nile, pollution of water, and the three-day darkening of the sky reported in the book of Exodus. Pinkish-gray ash blown from Thera, identified in the Nile Delta, easily could have darkened the sky, colored the river, and polluted water supplies. Although the Exodus "plagues" are unrecorded in Egyptian hieroglyphics, historians believe they occurred sometime in the vicinity of Thera's eruption.

ADDITIONAL RESOURCES

Doumas, Christos G. *Thera, Pompeii of the Ancient Aegean*. London: Thames and Hudson, 1983.

Forsyth, Phyllis Young. "Thera in the Bronze Age." *American University Studies* 9, no. 187 (1997).

Fouqué, Ferdinand A. *Santorini and Its Eruptions*. Translated and with a new introduction by Alexander R. McBirney. Baltimore: Johns Hopkins University Press, 1998.

Hardy, D. A., ed. *Thera and the Aegean World III*. London: The Thera Foundation, 1990.

Sigurdsson, Haraldur. *Melting the Earth*. New York: Oxford University Press, 1999.

SEE ALSO: Art and architecture; Crete; Cyclades.

—*M. Casey Diana*

THERMOPYLAE, BATTLE OF

DATE: August, 480 B.C.E.
RELATED CIVILIZATIONS: Classical Greece, Persia
SIGNIFICANCE: A Greek defensive stand at Thermopylae (thuhr-MAH-puh-lee) paved the way for the subsequent defeat of Persian invaders.

Background. In 490 B.C.E., a Persian invasion force was routed by a much smaller Greek army on the plain of Marathon. A decade later, Persian ruler Xerxes I amassed an immense force (millions according to historian Herodotus) and invaded Greece, determined to avenge this humiliating defeat.

Action. The Greeks decided to delay the Persian advance down the eastern coast of Greece by deploying several thousand men at a narrow pass between the cliffs and the sea called Thermopylae ("hot gates"). Leading the Greeks was the Spartan king Leonidas and his 300-man royal guard. For two days, Leonidas and his elite troops repulsed Persian attacks, wreaking tremendous losses on their foes.

On the third day, a Greek traitor, Ephialtes, guided Persian forces through a mountain pass, outflanking Leonidas. Leonidas sent the majority of his troops to safety but remained at Thermoplyae with the 300 Spartans, some helots, and 1,100 Boeotians. They heroically fought to the death that day.

Consequences. Although the Persians won the battle, their losses were considerable, and the Greeks gained valuable time for the defense of their homeland. By the end of the next year, devastating defeats at Salamis and Plataea forced the Persians to withdraw from Greece, ending their hopes of imperial expansion.

ADDITIONAL RESOURCES
Green, Peter. *The Greco-Persian Wars*. Berkeley: University of California Press, 1996.

Pressfield, S. *Gates of Fire: An Epic Novel of the Battle of Thermopylae*. New York: Bantam Books, 1999.

SEE ALSO: Greco-Persian Wars; Greece, Classical; Leonidas; Marathon, Battle of; Persia; Plataea, Battle of; Salamis, Battle of; Xerxes I.

—*Paul John Chara, Jr.*

Persian and Greek warriors collide in a narrow pass at the Battle of Thermopylae. (North Wind Picture Archives)

THERON OF ACRAGAS

BORN: date and place unknown
DIED: c. 472 B.C.E.; probably Acragas (later Agrigento), Sicily
RELATED CIVILIZATION: Classical Greece
MAJOR ROLE/POSITION: Tyrant of Acragas

Life. Theron of Acragas (THEHR-ahn of AH-krah-gahz), son of Aenesidemus, ruled the city of Acragas on the island of Sicily from roughly 489 to 472 B.C.E., but the dates of his life cannot be determined precisely. Early in his reign, he allied with Gelon of Syracuse (who married Theron's daughter Damarete), the increasingly powerful ruler of Gela. They fought against the Phoenicians on the west side of the island before Gelon took over Syracuse in 485 B.C.E. In 483 B.C.E., Theron seized the city of Himera and expelled Terillus, ally of the Carthaginian general Hamilcar. This expulsion prompted a Carthaginian invasion of Sicily. In 480 B.C.E., however, Theron, in alliance with Gelon, subdued Hamilcar's forces at the Battle of Himera, reportedly at the same time that the Greeks overwhelmed the Persian attack at Salamis. Using spoils from the war, Theron repopulated Himera and enriched Acragas. After Gelon's death, tension arose between Theron and Hieron I, Gelon's brother and successor at Syracuse, but a marriage and alliance prevented hostilities.

Influence. Theron, although second in stature to Gelon, was renowned for bringing prosperity to Sicily. In Acragas, he was heralded as a hero after his death.

ADDITIONAL RESOURCES

Dunbabin, R. J. *The Western Greeks*. Oxford, England: Oxford University Press, 1999.
Finley, M. I. *A History of Sicily*. Vol. 1. London: Chatto & Windus, 1968.

SEE ALSO: Carthage; Gelon of Syracuse; Greece, Classical; Hieron I of Syracuse; Salamis, Battle of.

—*Wilfred E. Major*

THESPIS

BORN: before 535 B.C.E.; probably Icarios (Icaria) or Athens, Greece
DIED: after 501 B.C.E.; probably Athens, Greece
RELATED CIVILIZATION: Classical Greece
MAJOR ROLE/POSITION: Actor and playwright

Life. The name "Thespis" (THEHS-puhs) comes from a word that means "divinely speaking" or from a similar word that means "divinely singing." According to one tradition, Thespis's home was Icarios, or Icaria, in northern Attica, near Marathon. Yet an extant ancient source refers to him simply as "Athenian." He is credited with inventing the first actor, a character separate from the chorus performing at the festivals in honor of the god Dionysus. Perhaps his first dramatic efforts were rather crude representations of the doings of satyrs, lustful, mischievous goat-men. The etymology of the word "tragedy" can be traced to a word meaning "song of goats."

According to tradition, the first official prize for Athenian drama was presented in 534 B.C.E. to Thespis. Some scholars argue for a later date, 501 B.C.E. At least, Thespis can be said to have lived probably from before the earlier date until after the later. It is believed that Thespis combined in his own person the roles of writer, director, composer, choreographer, and lead actor. As the only one of his players to impersonate individual characters, Thespis would play one part after another in the same story, frequently changing his mask and disguise.

Influence. Thespis, through his creation of the first actor, changed the Dionysia festival from a pageant of song and dance into drama. Actors, "thespians," take his name to pay him homage.

ADDITIONAL RESOURCES

Flickinger, Roy C. *The Greek Theater and Its Drama.* 4th ed. Chicago: University of Chicago Press, 1961.
Green, J. R. *Theater in Ancient Greek Society.* New York: Routledge, 1996.
Thomson, George. *Aeschylus and Athens: A Study in the Social Origins of Drama.* London: Lawrence and Wishart, 1973.

SEE ALSO: Aeschylus; Aristophanes; Eupolis; Euripides; Greece, Classical; Sophocles.

—*Patrick Adcock*

THIRTY TYRANTS

DATE: 404-403 B.C.E.
LOCALE: Athens
RELATED CIVILIZATION: Classical Greece
SIGNIFICANCE: Democratic Athens comes under the rule of Spartan-supported tyrants for eight months.

Under the leadership of Critias of Athens, a pro-Spartan oligarchy (known as the Thirty Tyrants) ruled Athens for eight months. Intimidated by Lysander of Sparta, who arrived with the Peloponnesian fleet, the Athenians voted in favor of a proposal to install the Thirty shortly after Athens surrendered to Sparta in 404 B.C.E. In less than a year, the Thirty executed 1,500 people and confiscated the property of citizens and resident aliens. At the insistence of Theramenes, a fellow member of the Thirty, they created a list of 3,000 citizens permitted to participate in the oligarchy. Critias suspected Theramenes of disloyalty and had him convicted and executed.

In the winter of 403 B.C.E., Thrasybulus with a band of democratic exiles seized Phyle, a fortress on the Boeotian border. In May, 403 B.C.E., the democrats successfully captured the Piraeus, Athens' major port, and Critias fell in the fighting. The Thirty were then replaced by a board of ten rulers and withdrew to Eleusis. The Ten continued the war against the democratic exiles until Sparta, under pressure from its allies, restored the Athenian democracy. Several years later, the Athenians marched out against the remnant of the Thirty living in Eleusis and killed them.

ADDITIONAL RESOURCES

Krentz, Peter. *The Thirty at Athens*. Ithaca, N.Y.: Cornell University Press, 1982.
Tritle, Lawrence, ed. *The Greek World in the Fourth Century: From the Fall of the Athenian Empire to the Successors of Alexander*. New York: Routledge, 1997.

SEE ALSO: Athens; Critias of Athens; Greece, Classical; Lysander of Sparta.

—Andrew Wolpert

THOM'S CREEK

DATE: 1800 B.C.E.-800 B.C.E.
LOCALE: Georgia, South Carolina, coastal North Carolina
RELATED CIVILIZATION: Woodland tradition
SIGNIFICANCE: Associated with a distinctive and early sand-tempered pottery type, the Thom's Creek culture was an Early Woodland variant of the Late Archaic Stallings culture.

Centered in eastern Georgia and South Carolina (though known to have had a presence in coastal North Carolina), the Thom's Creek culture produced a distinctive pottery type between 1800 B.C.E. and 800 C.E. Thom's Creek pottery was sand-tempered (among the earliest of this type in the eastern United States), and the rims of vessels were often decorated with cord impressions. Although vessel shapes are not well documented, examples of bowls are known. The Stallings culture, a Late Archaic group that became entwined with the Thom's Creek culture, produced a fiber-tempered ware as early as 2550 B.C.E. Both ceramic types continued in use in the region until about 1050 B.C.E., when the Stallings ceramic type disappeared.

The Thom's Creek people were hunters and gatherers who ate deer, aquatic turtles, fish, and other wild creatures as well as nuts and other plant matter. Coastal sites are often associated with shell middens (mounds of discarded shells, indicating a diet of shellfish). The fact that inland sites generally lack these middens probably indicates a greater reliance in these areas on woodland food sources. Artifacts associated with the Thom's Creek culture include bone and antler awls, fishhooks, and projectile points as well as a variety of stone tools and the characteristic pottery.

Because of a paucity of archaeological evidence, not much is known about what sorts of dwellings the Thom's Creek people inhabited. Pits and hearths, accompanied by architectural traces, have been discovered, but these are more common at riverine and other inland sites that lack shell middens.

ADDITIONAL RESOURCES

Sassaman, K. E. *Early Pottery in the Southeast: Tradition and Innovation in Cooking Technology*. Tuscaloosa: University of Alabama Press, 1993.

Trinkley, M. B. "A Typology of Thom's Creek Pottery for the South Carolina Coast." *South Carolina Antiquities* 12 (1980): 1-35.

SEE ALSO: Eastern peoples; Middle Woodland tradition.

—*Jeremiah R. Taylor*

THREE KINGDOMS

DATE: 220-280 C.E.

LOCALE: China

RELATED CIVILIZATION: China

SIGNIFICANCE: The Three Kingdoms period marks the end of four centuries of unification in China and the beginning of the divisions that last until the seventh century C.E.

Following the demise of the Han Dynasty (206 B.C.E.-220 C.E.), clusters of political power based on geographical areas emerged. By the early third century C.E., the number of these entities was reduced to three. Control of the Han court and north China was achieved by Cao Cao (155-220 C.E.). In 208 C.E., he sought to eliminate southern warlords but was defeated at the Battle of Chibi on the middle Yangtze. This marked the beginning of the tripartite division of China that became the Three Kingdoms in 220 C.E.

Cao Cao dominated the north and his state became known as Wei; Sun Quan (182-252 C.E.), ruler of the Wu state, controlled the Yangtze valley and the coastal areas; and Liu Bei (161-223 C.E.), ruler of the Shu state, established power in the southwest and upper Yangtze. The equilibrium between these kingdoms was estab-lished through the acumen of the leaders of the two weakest states: Wu and Shu. After the death of their original leaders, these states became destabilized while the Wei state prospered. In 260 C.E., Wei annihilated Shu, thus isolating Wu. In 265 C.E., the Western Jin Dynasty ousted Wei and in 280 C.E. pacified Wu, unified China, and ended the Three Kingdoms period.

ADDITIONAL RESOURCES

Huang, Ray. *China: A Macro History*. Armonk, N.Y.: M. E. Sharpe, 1997.

Hucker, Charles O. *China's Imperial Past*. Stanford, Calif.: Stanford University Press, 1975.

Killigrew, John. "The Role of the Mou-shi in the Sanguo Zhi." *Journal of Asian History* 32, no. 1 (1998): 49-67.

Twitchett, Denis, and Michael Loewe, eds. *The Ch'in and Han Empires*. Vol. 1 in *The Cambridge History of China*. Cambridge, England: Cambridge University Press, 1986.

SEE ALSO: Cao Cao; Han Dynasty; Qin Dynasty.

—*John W. Killigrew*

THUCYDIDES

BORN: c. 459 B.C.E.; probably Athens, Greece

DIED: c. 402 B.C.E.; place unknown

RELATED CIVILIZATION: Classical Greece

MAJOR ROLE/POSITION: Historian

Life. Little is known about the early life of Thucydides (thew-SIHD-uh-deez). His father was named Olorus, and from him Thucydides inherited an estate and gold mine in Athens. He was a privileged youth and most likely traveled extensively. During his minority, he heard the historian Herodotus recite tales of distant lands and was animated with an interest in history. He was therefore aware of the historical opportunity provided when the Peloponnesian War (431-404 B.C.E.) erupted and began to collect information immediately. As a wealthy young man, he was expected to join the Athenian campaign, not just study it, but he contracted the plague sometime between 430 and 427 B.C.E. and initially was prevented from joining the war effort. Upon his recovery, he was appointed general and given command of a small squadron of ships. This command was short-lived, however, as his squadron failed to protect the Athenian colony Amphipolis from a Spartan invasion. For this failure, he was exiled in 424 B.C.E.

Thucydides. (Library of Congress)

1550). In eight sections, it tells the history of this conflict from its distant origins to 411 B.C.E. To do this, Thucydides relied on information gleaned from actual participants and observers, as well as his own knowledge and experience. The book begins with an analysis of the fear and mistrust between Athens and Sparta. A discussion on how these feelings led to war in 431 B.C.E. follows, and the remainder of the book details the participants and their battles in great depth. Although it breaks off seven years before the conclusion of the war and is laced throughout with admittedly fabricated speeches, Thucydides' work is a seminal study of the Peloponnesian War and has earned him recognition as one of the greatest historians.

Influence. Although not the first historian, Thucydides made major advances in the field. Rather than present all opinions regarding an event, he included only those he believed. He was the first to tell contemporary history and the first to tell any type of history without recourse to the influence of the gods. He thus made history a solely human forum and blamed the Peloponnesian War on human failings. Finally, his ability to tell military history and to recite the actions of politicians set the stage for future historians to focus their attention on the great personages and events of history.

He lived comfortably from the wealth of his mines and spent his time in exile researching the events and characters of the Peloponnesian War. With access, time, and money, Thucydides gathered an immense amount of information about the war and spent the rest of his life writing its history. With the end of the war, he returned to Athens to complete his work but died before so doing.

Although incomplete, the result of Thucydides' study was the *Historia tou Peloponnesiacou polemou* (431-404 B.C.E.; *History of the Peloponnesian War,*

ADDITIONAL RESOURCES

Conner, Walter R. *Thucydides*. Princeton, N.J.: Princeton University Press, 1984

Hornblower, Simon. *Thucydides*. Baltimore: Johns Hopkins University Press, 1987.

Owen, Clifford. *The Humanity of Thucydides*. Princeton, N.J.: Princeton University Press, 1994.

SEE ALSO: Greece, Classical; Herodotus; Languages and literature; Peloponnesian War.

—*Gregory S. Taylor*

THUTMOSE III

BORN: late sixteenth century B.C.E.; probably near Thebes, Egypt
DIED: 1450 B.C.E.; probably near Thebes, Egypt
RELATED CIVILIZATION: Pharaonic Egypt
MAJOR ROLE/POSITION: King

Life. Thutmose III (thewt-MOH-suh), the sixth king of the Eighteenth Dynasty, was the son of Thutmose II and an obscure woman of the harem named Isis.

Thutmose III succeeded his father in about 1504 B.C.E. Because he was a minor, real power fell to his stepmother and aunt, Hatshepsut, who eventually declared herself "king" and ruled for twenty years. Little is known of Thutmose during these years, although he must have matured as a military leader.

Upon Hatshepsut's death around 1482 B.C.E., Thutmose began a series of seventeen military campaigns that won for Egypt extensive territories in southern

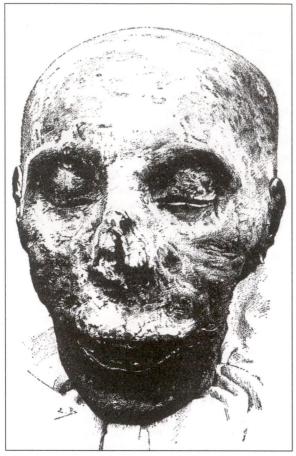

The mummified head of Thutmose III. (Library of Congress)

Syria and Palestine. He defeated a coalition of more than three hundred Canaanite and Syrian kings headed by the king of Kadesh at Megiddo in 1482 B.C.E. The real threat to Egyptian interest in western Asia, how-

ever, was the kingdom of Mitanni (Naharin), an Indo-Aryan/Hurrian state located east of the Euphrates River. Thutmose campaigned north against Tunip and Kadesh, rebellious states backed by Mitanni. In 1472 B.C.E., Thutmose crossed the Euphrates and attacked Mitannian forces. This campaign marked the farthest advance by Egypt into western Asia. In response, the kings of Assyria, Babylonia, and the Hittites sent gifts to Thutmose acknowledging the power of Egypt.

Thutmose also extended Egyptian control of Nubia southward to the Fourth Cataract, where he established a trading center at Napata. He added several structures to the temple of Amun-Re at Thebes to record his victories and honor the national god of Egypt. The last twelve years of his fifty-four-year reign were militarily uneventful. Upon his death, he was succeeded by his son Amenhotep II.

Influence. The campaigns of Thutmose III established an Egyptian empire that extended from Nubia in the south to Lebanon in the north. He is rightly regarded as one of the greatest Egyptian pharaohs.

ADDITIONAL RESOURCES

Edwards, I. E. S., et al., eds. *History of the Middle East and the Aegean Region c. 1800-1380* B.C. Vol. 2, part 1 in *The Cambridge Ancient History.* 3d ed. New York: Cambridge University Press, 1991.

Grimal, Nicolas. *A History of Ancient Egypt.* Translated by Ian Shaw. Oxford, England: Blackwell, 1992.

SEE ALSO: Assyria; Babylonia; Egypt, Pharaonic; Hatshepsut; Hittites; Mitanni.

—*Thomas Vester Brisco*

TIBERIUS

ALSO KNOWN AS: Tiberius Claudius Nero; Tiberius Caesar Augustus
BORN: November 16, 42 B.C.E.; Rome
DIED: March 16, 37 C.E.; Misenum
RELATED CIVILIZATION: Imperial Rome
MAJOR ROLE/POSITION: Emperor

Life. Tiberius served as emperor from the death of Augustus in 14 C.E. until his own death. The stepson

and adopted son of Augustus, he was forced to divorce his first wife in order to marry Augustus's daughter Julia. His advancement as the successor of Augustus was often interrupted as the emperor looked to younger members of the Julian family. Their deaths forced Augustus to turn again to Tiberius, and on Augustus's death, Tiberius held the proconsular *imperium* and tribunician power and thus was in a position to assume the imperial role. Tiberius, however, appears to have been ill-suited to imperial life in Rome—and the machinations of members of the Julian family and their supporters—and he removed himself from the city in 27 C.E., living mostly on Capri until his death.

Influence. Though Tiberius was the political and financial heir of Augustus, he never achieved the popular reverence accorded his predecessor. He was an able administrator and soldier, and as emperor, he adhered to many of the policies of Augustus. There is evidence that he would have liked to see the senate take a greater role in the administration of the state, but the imperial model was well entrenched.

ADDITIONAL RESOURCES

Levick, Barbara. *Tiberius the Politician*. London: Routledge, 1999.

Marsh, Frank Burr. *The Reign of Tiberius*. New York: Barnes and Noble, 1931.

Seager, Robin. *Tiberius*. Berkeley: University of California Press, 1972.

SEE ALSO: Augustus; Julia (daughter of Augustus); Rome, Imperial.

—*C. Wayne Tucker*

Tiberius. (Library of Congress)

TIBET

DATE: 200 B.C.E.-700 C.E.

LOCALE: Central Asia

RELATED CIVILIZATIONS: Burma, China, India, Nepal, Kashmir

SIGNIFICANCE: Tibetans adopted Buddhism, which they mixed with their native religion to create a Tibetan form of Buddhism that remains a vital religion.

Archaeological finds of prehistoric tools, villages, and megaliths in Tibet date back to the Old Stone Age. The artifacts support the view that Tibet has been a mingling area of diverse races and cultures by conquest and alliance for centuries. Although the Tibetans are an amalgam of many different peoples, the initial dominant groups were the sheep- and cattle-herding, nomadic, non-Chinese Chang tribes of eastern Central Asia centuries before the Christian era. They migrated from northeastern Tibet to the center, than west and south through the Himalayas into what is now northern and central Nepal. However, the nomads mixed far less than the later settled elements. In fact, nomadic culture was flourishing in this region by 3000 B.C.E.

What united these diverse groups as Tibetan was their language. The Tibetan and Burmese languages are related, although mutually unintelligible in their current forms. The Tibetan language has many regional and subregional dialects, but they are mutually understood, the dialect at Lhasa being the lingua franca. Except in a few localities, it was an oral language and did not take a written form until the advent of Buddhism in the sixth century C.E.

Long before the advent of Buddhism, nomadic groups from the northeast were clashing with and displacing some settled agriculturalists of southern and central Tibet. In the central region, people coalesced into tribes and petty kingdoms, some of which formed their own aristocracy (some aristocracies surviving to the late 1950's). This process of ongoing conflict between nomads and settled agriculturalists continued until the early seventh century B.C.E., after which infiltration from the north took the form of marriage alliances. In the valleys, rival chiefs had fortified strongholds, and chiefs had noble vassals who were served by bondsmen and subjects. Without strong leadership to counter hostile neighbors, the dominant level of existence was poverty. Around 500 B.C.E., small kingdoms had developed, but they remained hostile, relegating Tibetans largely to the mercy of their hostile neighbors. The result was that local chiefs combined to support an overlord chief who ruled in the Yarlung Valley. The confederacy under the Yarlung Valley rulers became the impetus for Tibetan power to go on the offensive.

The first person to become king of Tibet was gNiya'-khri (247 B.C.E., also known as Nyatri Tsenpo or Gnya'-khri brtsan-po), who subjugated the existing twelve warring kingdoms under him. His rule and those of the five generations that followed are known as the Six Thrones. Legend has it that battles during these times involved magic. Also according to legend, the lineage of the kings remained separate from that of the tribes, and kings took wives from the gods and nature spirits. Again according to mythology, there were no tombs because when the king's first son was old enough to ride a horse, the father would hand over the kingdom and disappear into the sky, leaving no corpse; thus, ancient Tibetan history or legend speaks of these kings as having the sky as their tomb. Estimates vary, but there were probably forty-two generations, spanning about 1,050 years, between the first Tibetan king and the last. Buddhism began making inroads in the third century C.E., when Buddhist scriptures were introduced, although they were not actively promulgated until the eighth century.

Although the Tibetans were strongly influenced by other cultures, one of their enduring qualities is that they noticeably modified outside traits to give them a Tibetan character. This is evident in the Tibetan version of Buddhism. Bon was the religion of Tibet just before Buddhism made its inroads, starting in the third century C.E. It was a form of shamanism, its worldview including a belief in gods, demons, and ancestral spirits who were responsive to priests or shamans. As Buddhism ascended, the two religions adopted characteristics from each other and resembled each other on many points. Although Chinese Buddhism was introduced in ancient times, the mainstream Tibetan Buddhist teachings stemmed from India, largely because of the influence of the Indian guru Padmasamsha.

Creditable Tibetan history begins late in the sixth century C.E., when three discontented vassals of a prince conspired to support a neighboring lord, Gnam-ri srong-brtsan (c. 570-c. 619 C.E.). Their new master was transformed from a prince of a small valley to a ruler of a vigorous military empire. It was his son, Srong-brtsan-sgam-po (c. 608-650 C.E.; also known as Song-tsen-gam-po), who forcibly brought Tibet to the Tang Dynasty of China. To pacify him, he was granted a princess as his bride. In addition, he married three women among important families and borderland people to form strong alliances with powerful clans. Srong-brtsan-sgam-po became known as the "religious king" and strongly influenced Tibet by supporting his wives in encouraging the spread of Buddhism. In fact, the spread of Buddhism was largely attributable to the skills of Wencheng, a Chinese princess married to Srong-brtsan-sgam-po. He had previously married Bhrileushi (or Bhrikuti) Devi, a Nepali princess and a Buddhist. From then on, the ruling families of Tibet adhered to a Tibetan form of Buddhism.

Srong-brtsan-sgam-po introduced writing, for which a script from India was borrowed. The script was used to translate Buddhist texts, many of which were already in Tibet. The introduction of writing also enabled genealogies, legends, stories, and history to be recorded. Laws and subsequently a constitution were codified and implemented. Srong-brtsan-sgam-po also extended Tibet's boundaries over Nepal, western Tibet, Tuyuhun, and other tribes on China's border, as well as invading India.

Peace was maintained between China and Tibet for twenty years after Srong-brtsan-sgam-po's death. Around 670 C.E., peace with China was broken, and Tibet, in conjunction with some western Turks, challenged China's control of the East-West trade routes through Central Asia.

ADDITIONAL RESOURCES
Coleman, Graham. *A Handbook of Tibetan Culture.* Boston: Shambhala, 1994.
Richardson, H. E. *A Short History of Tibet.* New York: E. P. Dutton, 1962.
Snellgrove, David, and Hugh Richardson. *A Cultural History of Tibet.* New York: Praeger, 1968.
Stein, R. A. *Tibetan Civilization.* Stanford, Calif.: Stanford University Press, 1972.
Thlku, Tarthang. *Ancient Tibet.* Berkeley, Calif.: Dharma, 1986.

SEE ALSO: Buddhism; China; India; Srong-brtsan-sgam-po.

—*Arthur W. Helweg*

TIBU

DATE: 3000 B.C.E.-700 C. E.
LOCALE: Central Sahara
RELATED CIVILIZATIONS: Libya, Sudanic civilization
SIGNIFICANCE: The Tibu created rock carvings and paintings that depicted the large animals that lived in the deserts of North Africa thousands of years ago.

The Tibu were descendants of a group of people who originally lived in the Sahara thousands of years ago. As the Sahara began to dry up, this group of people moved into the Tibesti and Ahaggar mountain ranges. The Tibu were originally a Neolithic hunting culture, but as animals began to disappear from their environment, they became subsistence farmers, living on the fringes of the mountain ranges until historical times. There is evidence that the culture, at least for part of its history, was matriarchal.

Members of the culture left behind paintings and carvings on the walls of the mountains in which they lived. These paintings and carvings show animals, such as giant buffalo, elephants, rhinoceroses, and hippopotamuses, which no longer exist in the area that the Tibu inhabited. Archaeological studies indicate that as the Sahara slowly dried up, images produced on the walls changed from wild jungle animals to domesticated cattle.

ADDITIONAL RESOURCES
Chippindale, Christopher, and Paul S. C. Tacon. *The Archaeology of Rock-Art.* New York: Cambridge University Press, 1998.
Coulson, David, and Alec Campbell. *African Rock Art.* New York: Abrams, 2000.

SEE ALSO: Africa, North; African rock art, southern and eastern; Saharan rock art.

—*Annita Marie Ward*

TIBULLUS, ALBIUS

ALSO KNOWN AS: Tibullus
BORN: c. 55 B.C.E.; place unknown
DIED: c. 19 B.C.E.; place unknown
RELATED CIVILIZATIONS: Republican and Imperial Rome
MAJOR ROLE/POSITION: Elegiac poet

Life. Little is known about the life of Albius Tibullus (AL-bee-uhs tuh-BUHL-uhs), except for what he says about it in his poetry and from comments in the verses of the Roman poet Horace. In Augustan Rome, under the patronage of Marcus Valerius Messalla Corvinus, Tibullus wrote two books of elegies, *Delia* (c. 26 B.C.E.) and *Nemesis* (c. 19 B.C.E.), both part of the *Corpus Tibullianum* (n.d.; English translation, 1913). The third and four books in this poetic corpus were very likely written by other poets in Messalla's literary circle, including the female poet Sulpicia. *Delia* deals primarily with Tibullus's love for a woman named Delia and a boy named Marathus and contains a celebration of Messalla's birthday and military triumph over the Aquitanian tribes, as well as a number of his other foreign and domestic exploits. *Nemesis* contains poems about Tibullus's love for another woman named Nemesis, a marvelous description of a country festival, and a celebration of the election of Messalla's son Messalinus to the sacred priesthood, charged with taking care of and reading the Sibylline Books. Throughout his elegies, Tibullus presents himself (or his persona) as living quietly in the country and worrying passionately about a love affair—a theme continuously interwoven with others in an artistic structure, with occasional tributes to literary predecessors such as Homer's *Odyssey* (c. 800 B.C.E.; English translation, 1616) and Vergil's *Aeneid* (c. 29-19 B.C.E.; English translation, 1553).

Influence. Tibullus was ranked among the four great Roman elegists (with Gallus, Propertius, and Ovid) and was eulogized by Ovid in *Amores* (c. 20 B.C.E.; English translation, 1597). Down through the centuries, poets have echoed or imitated him, especially the Italian poet Jacopo Sannazaro and the French poet André-Marie de Chénier.

ADDITIONAL RESOURCES
Ball, Robert J. *Tibullus the Elegist: A Critical Survey.* Göttingen, Germany: Vandenhoeck and Ruprecht, 1983.
Bright, David F. *Haec mihi fingebam: Tibullus in His World.* Leiden, Netherlands: E. J. Brill, 1978.
Cairns, Francis. *Tibullus: A Hellenistic Poet at Rome.* Cambridge, England: Cambridge University Press, 1979.
Lee-Stecum, Parshia. *Powerplay in Tibullus.* Cambridge, England: Cambridge University Press, 1998.

SEE ALSO: Homer; Horace; Ovid; Propertius; Rome, Imperial; Rome, Republican; Sibylline Books; Vergil.
—*Robert J. Ball*

TIGLATH-PILESER III

ALSO KNOWN AS: Pulu
BORN: early eighth century B.C.E.; place unknown
DIED: 727 B.C.E.; Babylonia
RELATED CIVILIZATIONS: Assyria, Babylonia
MAJOR ROLE/POSITION: King of Assyria

Life. Tiglath-pileser III (TIHG-lath-pi-lee-zur) came to the Assyrian throne by means of a coup in 745 B.C.E., ending decades of Assyrian weakness. Possibly of royal blood, the new king instituted a series of administrative and military reforms that gave him direct control over all the governmental machinery. He professionalized the army and used it not only to defeat Assyria's enemies but also to expand Assyrian territorial control.

Tiglath-pileser's extensive campaigns are virtually unmatched in Assyrian annals. In his first year, he campaigned to the south in Babylonia, where he consolidated Assyrian control by fending off Chaldean intrusions. Next, Tiglath-pileser smashed a coalition of Syrian states led by Arpad and backed by Urartu (743-740 B.C.E.). The Assyrian king annexed some territories west of the Euphrates and received tribute from others who submitted to Assyria. Tiglath-pileser used mass deportations to weaken national resolve among conquered peoples. From 739 B.C.E. onward, Tiglath-pileser campaigned in the north, eventually invading the kingdom of Urartu in the Lake Van region in 735 B.C.E. In the process, he also campaigned eastward into Median territory. From 734 to 732 B.C.E., Tiglath-pileser crushed an anti-Assyrian coalition in the Levant headed by Damascus and Israel. Finally Tiglath-pileser returned to Babylonia where he defeated a Chaldean usurper and formally assumed the title "king of Babylon" (728 B.C.E.). He died shortly thereafter in 727 B.C.E.

Influence. Tiglath-pileser III may be considered the true founder of the neo-Assyrian empire. His policies and campaigns laid the foundation for the rapid development of Assyrian power under Sargon II and his successors.

ADDITIONAL RESOURCES
Boardman, John, et al., eds. *The Assyrian and Babylonian Empires and Other States of the Near East, from the Eighth to the Sixth Centuries B.C.* Vol. 3, part 2 in *Cambridge Ancient History.* 2d ed. Cambridge, England: Cambridge University Press, 1991.
Roux, Georges. *Ancient Iraq.* 2d ed. London: Penguin Books, 1992.
Saggs, H. W. F. *The Might That Was Assyria.* London: Sidgwick & Jackson, 1984.

SEE ALSO: Assyria; Babylonia; Sargon II; Urartu.
—*Thomas Vester Brisco*

Tigranes the Great

ALSO KNOWN AS: Tigran or Dikran; Tigranes II
BORN: c. 140 B.C.E.; Armenia
DIED: c. 55 B.C.E.; Armenia
RELATED CIVILIZATIONS: Armenia, Parthia, Syria,
    Republican Rome
MAJOR ROLE/POSITION: King

Life. Either the son or brother of Artavasdes I, Tigranes (ti-GRAY-neez) was hostage to Mithradates II of Parthia before buying his freedom by yielding substantial land in Media (northwestern Iran). After forming an alliance with Mithradates VI Eupator of Pontus by marrying that ruler's daughter, Cleopatra, Tigranes began war against the Parthians when their empire

Tigranes the Great. (Library of Congress)

(southeast of the Caspian Sea) was temporarily weakened after the death of Mithradates II (c. 87 B.C.E.). He reconquered the seventy valleys he had offered for his freedom, then forced neighboring regents to become his vassals. He was offered the Syrian crown. He then reoccupied Cappadocia in eastern Asia Minor.

Grandly calling himself "King of Kings," he built Tigranocerta (modern Silvan), a huge royal city, on the borders of Armenia and Mesopotamia, to which he moved all his wealth, along with the inhabitants of twelve Greek towns.

Roman armies invaded Armenia in 72 B.C.E., and Tigranes suppressed a rebellion by his son. He surrendered to the Romans in 66 B.C.E. but was given back his kingdom and allowed to rule as client-king by Pompey the Great in exchange for Syria and other lands. After his death, he was succeeded by his son, Artavasdes II.

Influence. Tigranes turned Armenia into the strongest state in the Roman East by subduing neighboring regents and expanding his domain.

ADDITIONAL RESOURCES
Chahin, M. *The Kingdom of Armenia.* London: Croom Helm, 1987.
Hovannisian, Richard G., ed. *The Armenian People from Ancient to Modern Times.* New York: St. Martin's Press, 1997.
Khorenats'i, Moses. *History of the Armenians.* Translated by Robert W. Thomson. Cambridge, Mass.: Harvard University Press, 1978.

SEE ALSO: Armenia; Mithradates II; Mithradates VI Eupator; Parthia; Rome, Republican.

—*Keith Garebian*

Tikal

DATE: 200-900 C.E.
LOCALE: Northern Guatemala
RELATED CIVILIZATION: Maya
SIGNIFICANCE: Tikal was one of the earliest and most important centers in the central lowlands.

Tikal (tee-KAHL) is located in the central lowlands, an area known as the cradle of Maya civilization. It became one of the largest and most important cities in the area. By the first century B.C.E., large-scale construction was under way, and commerce extended east to the

Caribbean and south to the highlands.

By the beginning of the Classic period (250-600 C.E.), Tikal had become the capital of a state society and the center of a trade area that included trade with Teotihuacán, the great urban center of the Mexican highlands. During this period, the Maya developed hieroglyphic writing, extended their knowledge of astronomy and math, and created their calendars. The height of Maya civilization occurred between 600 and 800 C.E. Tikal became one of the most monumental sites ever constructed by the Maya. More than four thousand structures were built in an area of 6.3 square miles (16.3 square kilometers). Population estimates range between 60,000 and 90,000 in the sixth century C.E.

Invasions, ecological damage, overpopulation, and migration contributed to Tikal's dramatic decline between 800 and 900 C.E. By the tenth century C.E., Tikal had been abandoned.

ADDITIONAL RESOURCES
Henderson, John S. *The World of the Ancient Maya.* Ithaca, N.Y.: Cornell University Press, 1997.
Sabloff, Jeremy A., and John S. Henderson, eds. *Lowland Maya Civilization in the Eighth Century* A.D. Washington, D.C.: Dunbarton Oaks, 1993.
Schmidt, Peter, Mercedes de la Garza, and Enrique Nalda. *Maya.* New York: Rizzoli International, 1998.

SEE ALSO: Maya; Teotihuacán.

—Robert D. Talbott

TIMOLEON OF CORINTH

BORN: date and place unknown
DIED: after 337 B.C.E., Syracuse
RELATED CIVILIZATION: Classical Greece
MAJOR ROLE/POSITION: General

Life. In 344 B.C.E., the citizens of Syracuse appealed to Corinth, the mother city that had sent the first colonists to Syracuse, for aid in overthrowing Dionysius the Younger, who oppressed the city as tyrant. The Corinthian assembly provided a small army of mercenaries, appointing Timoleon (tih-MOH-lee-uhn) of Corinth as leader. Timoleon had earned a reputation as an opponent of tyranny by aiding the assassination of his older brother when he tried to become absolute ruler of Corinth.

Landing in Sicily that summer, Timoleon rapidly defeated two opposing armies, occupied Syracuse, and sent Dionysius the Younger into exile in Corinth. By 341 B.C.E., Timoleon had unseated the other Sicilian tyrants and successfully opposed a Carthaginian invasion. He wrote a constitution for Syracuse that protected the freedom of its citizens. By inviting new settlers from Greece, Timoleon repopulated Sicily, stimulating an economic revival.

In about 337 B.C.E., Timoleon retired from office, at that time an unheard-of act, and lived his remaining life near Syracuse. Although soon becoming blind, he continued to advise the Syracuse assembly.

Influence. Timoleon reestablished the rule of law and restored prosperity to Sicily. Plutarch, in his life of Timoleon, concludes that Timoleon had "done the greatest and noblest things of any Greek of his age."

ADDITIONAL RESOURCES
Talbert, R. J. A. *Timoleon and the Revival of Greek Sicily, 344-317* B.C. New York: Cambridge University Press, 1974.
Tritle, Lawrence A., ed. *The Greek World in the Fourth Century.* New York: Routledge, 1997.

SEE ALSO: Carthage; Dionysius the Younger; Government and law; Greece, Classical; Plutarch.

—Milton Berman

Tipiṭaka

AUTHORSHIP: Compilation, unknown
DATE: collected c. 250 B.C.E.
LOCALE: India
RELATED CIVILIZATIONS: Mauryan, Kushān, Gupta Dynasties, India
SIGNIFICANCE: The *Tipiṭaka* became the foundation of the Hīnāyāna, or Theravāda, school of Buddhism.

The *Tipiṭaka* (English translation in *Buddhist Scriptures*, 1913), the Buddhist canonical doctrine, existed only in the minds of Buddhist monks before the third century B.C.E. Its written form and codification grew gradually over several centuries as a result of four Buddhist councils convened primarily to collect and codify the dharma transmitted orally by the Buddha to serve as a guideline for monastic life. Hence, great care was taken to transmit the dharma as accurately as possible. The Pāli, Sanskrit, Chinese, and Tibetan versions are sectarian variants of a corpus that evolved during three centuries of oral transmission. The *Tipiṭaka*, or "Three Baskets" after the practice of filing prepared palm leaves of the dharma in baskets, covers the rules of discipline followed by monastic members, sermons of the Buddha on the dharma, and higher metaphysical subtleties of philosophy.

Shortly after Buddha's death, Kāśyapa, the great disciple of Buddha, proposed that a council be called to rehearse the dharma. Five hundred monks, who attended the First Buddhist Council at Rājagṛha under the auspices of King Ajātaśatru, addressed the ignorance and laxity that were prevalent in the Saṅgha. After seven months, they codified the rules into the *Vinaya Piṭaka* and the doctrine into the *Sūtra Piṭaka*. The *Sūtra Piṭaka*, the largest and most important "basket," was divided into five Nikāyas, or sections, which collectively represented the primary source of Buddha's message embodied in epigrams, dialogues, and tales from his life. Two sections, the *Jātakas*, with 547 birth stories of the Buddha exemplifying the dharma, and the *Dhammapada* (*Dharmapada*), with 423 epigrams of the Buddha, are some of the greatest pieces of Buddhist literature, popular throughout Buddhist Asia. The *Vinaya Piṭaka* covers 227 monastic rules addressing communal life, celibacy, charity, personal possessions, physical needs, interpersonal relations, and ecclesiastical offenses and punishments. Recitation in common every half month of the lunar calendar serves as means of self-purification.

One hundred years later, the Second Buddhist Council convened at Veśālī, sponsored by King Kālāsaka, to further reform the dharma. However, some believe that another "Second" Council met at Pāṭaliputra in 346 B.C.E. at the request of King Mahāpadma Nanda to tackle unresolved problems from the Veśālī council. Clarification of the dharma was critical because seventeen philosophical schools had emerged whose heresies had to be purged. In the process, a schism erupted over minor doctrinal points that resulted in a permanent split of the Saṅgha into the Theravāda (Hīnāyāna) and Mahāyāna schools.

The growing schism provoked the Mauryan king Aśoka to convene the Third Buddhist Council at Pāṭaliputra, at which heretics were expelled and the third piṭaka, the *Abhidharma*, was formulated, representing technical, psychological, metaphysical, and general philosophical doctrine for the Buddhist elite. The Fourth Buddhist Council, held by Kaniṣka in Kashmir in the first century C.E., resulted in a *Tipiṭaka* composed in Sanskrit, extant now only in fragments. The *Vinaya* and *Sūtra* pitakas were codified shortly after Buddha's death, and the *Abhidharma* appeared later, during the Third Council.

ADDITIONAL RESOURCES

Ch'en, Kenneth K. C. *Buddhism: The Light of Asia.* New York: Educational Series, 1968.
Conze, Edward. *A Short History of Buddhism.* London: George Allen and Unwin, 1980.
Dialogues of the Buddha. Translated by T. W. Rhys Davids. Delhi, India: Motilal Banarsidass, 2000.

SEE ALSO: Aśoka; Buddha; Buddhism; Dhammapada; *Jātakas*; Kaniṣka.

—*George J. Hoynacki*

TIRUTTAKKATEVAR

FLOURISHED: c. 900 C.E.; India
RELATED CIVILIZATIONS: Dravidian, India
MAJOR ROLE/POSITION: Poet

Life. Tiruttakkatevar (TEE-rew-TAH-kah-TEH-vahr) is the author of the celebrated Tamil epic *Cīvakacintāmaṇi* (c. 900 C.E.). A descendant of the Cōḷas, Tiruttakkatevar is said to have become a Jaina ascetic at a young age and lived in Madurai. The epic hero of *Cīvakacintāmaṇi*, Cīvakan, is depicted as the perfect man—a peerless lover, brave warrior, and master of all arts, who is gentle and considerate, full of sympathy and consideration for all living beings, and in total harmony with his surroundings. Tiruttakkatevar's ascetic status prompted non-Jaina poets to challenge his contribution to the *akam* (internal) genre, which consists of love poems. To counter this criticism, he composed an erotic epic poem titled *Mananul* (the book of marriage), the publication of which triggered doubts regarding his ascetic status. It is said that he held a red-hot iron rod in his bare hands to prove his celibacy.

Influence. In *Cīvakacintāmaṇi*, Tiruttakkatevar in-troduced a new poetical meter known as *viruttam*, which he re-created from the existing folk poetry. Later poets such as Kampar and Sekkizhar adopted *viruttam* meter in their poetry, finding it more suitable for expressing a variety of emotions. Unlike *akaval*, the prevalent meter, which is written in four-foot lines with a difference in rhyme, *viruttam* is a very flexible meter that allows any number of metric feet per line but mandates that the poem itself must have only four lines and that every line must have the same number of metric feet.

ADDITIONAL RESOURCES

Ramanujan, A. K. *Poems of Love and War from the Eight Anthologies and the Ten Long Poems of Classical Tamil*. New York: Columbia University Press, 1985.

Varadarajan, Mu. *A History of Tamil Literature*. Translated by E. A. Viswanathan. Delhi, India: Sahitya Akademi, 1988.

SEE ALSO: India; Jainism.

—*Kokila Ravi*

TIRUVALḶUVAR

ALSO KNOWN AS: Thiruvalluvar
FLOURISHED: third to fourth centuries C.E.; Maturai, India
RELATED CIVILIZATION: India (Tamil)
MAJOR ROLE/POSITION: Poet

Life. Tiruvaḷḷuvar (TEE-rew-VAH-lew-vahr) is the author of *Tirukuraḷ* (third or fourth century C.E.; English translation, 1987), the widely read Tamil classic. Very little is known about his life. Scholars have varied theories about his birth; some consider him to be of the weaver caste, and others deem that he is of mixed parentage, with a lower-caste mother and Brahman father. The general assumption is that he was born in Maturai and lived in Mylapore (modern Chennai). The *Tiru-kuraḷ*, composed in the *kural-venpa*, or the short verse meter, is written as three books, one each on *aram* (the way), *porul* (material), and *inbam* (joy). It has 133 chapters with ten couplets in each, making a total of 1,330 verses. These verses are words of wisdom that relate to love, ethics, economics, and politics.

Tiruvaḷḷuvar's ideas were probably influenced by Jain traditions and written in the years between the Caṅkam era and the *bhakti* era when the Tamil country was exposed to Jain and Buddhist influences. Tiruvaḷḷuvar is exalted as a Tamil sage. As an effective educator, Tiruvaḷḷuvar uses simple language that is clear, precise, and forceful. In addition, he uses wisdom and humor that make his verses the most quoted in the Tamil language.

ADDITIONAL RESOURCES

Diaz, S. M. *Aphorisms of Valluvar: Commentary and Comparative Study*. Madras, India: International Society for the Investigation of Ancient Civilizations, 1982.

Tiruvalluvar. *The Kural*. Translated by P. S. Sundaram. Madras, India: P. S. Sundaram, 1987.

_____. *Weaver's Wisdom*. Translated by Sivaya Sub-ramuniyaswami. Kapaa, Hawaii: Himalayan Academy, 1999.

SEE ALSO: Buddhism; India; Jainism.

—Salli Vargis

TISSA, DĒVĀNAMPIYA

FLOURISHED: c. 247-207 B.C.E.
RELATED CIVILIZATION: Ancient Sri Lanka
MAJOR ROLE/POSITION: King

Life. Dēvānampiya Tissa (deh-vaw-nahm-PEE-yah TEE-sah) was the first Buddhist king of Sri Lanka. According to tradition, he was converted to the new religion by Mahinda, the son of Aśoka, India's first emperor, who sent his son as a missionary to the southern island. The first meeting between Mahinda and Tissa reportedly occurred while the king was engaged on a hunting expedition at Missaka-pabbata (now called Mihintale), a mountain outside the capital at Anuradhapura. It was there that Mahinda converted the king and his entire entourage. The king, a particularly devout believer, was instrumental in the efforts to convert his family and subjects to Buddhism. He donated land for erecting the Mahāvihāra monastery, built in 207 B.C.E., the most famous of Buddhist monuments in Sri Lanka and a stronghold of Theravāda (Hīnāyāna) Buddhism. Other important monuments attributed to the patronage of the king include the Chettīya-pabbata, where the begging bowl of the historical Buddha Śākyamuni was enshrined; the Thuparama Dāgaba (stupa), which housed the Buddha's right collarbone and other bone relics; and the Hatthalhāka Vihāra, where a cutting from the Bodhi tree (the tree associated with the Buddha's enlightenment) was planted. Reception of the tree cutting was observed with a great ceremony in which Tissa waded neck-deep in the ocean, carrying the cutting on his head, then taking it to the shore, where he had a pavilion specially built for it. Eventually thirty-two saplings of the Bodhi tree were distributed throughout the island.

Influence. Tissa's influence was enormous in that he was instrumental in establishing Buddhism in Sri Lanka. The entire course of the island's history was altered by his conversion to and promotion of the new faith.

ADDITIONAL RESOURCES
Smith, Bardwell L. *Religion and Legitimation of Power in Sri Lanka*. Chambersburg, Pa.: ANIMA Books, 1978.
Trainor, Kevin. *Relics, Ritual, and Representation in Buddhism: Rematerializing the Sri Lankan Theravāda Tradition*. Cambridge, England: Cambridge University Press, 1997.

SEE ALSO: Aśoka; Buddha; Buddhism; Sri Lanka.

—Katherine Anne Harper

TITUS

ALSO KNOWN AS: Titus Flavius Vespasianus
BORN: December 30, 39 C.E.; place unknown
DIED: September 13, 81 C.E.; Aquae Cutilae (later Bagni di Paterno, Italy)
RELATED CIVILIZATION: Imperial Rome
MAJOR ROLE/POSITION: Statesman, military leader

Life. Born into an equestrian rather than a patrician family, Titus (TIT-uhs) commanded a legion in 67 C.E. under his father, Vespasian, during the First Jewish Revolt. Playing a conspicuous role in the events that brought Vespasian to the imperial throne in 69 C.E., Titus completed the conquest of Jerusalem, a feat commemorated by the arch of Titus, which still stands in Rome. He also developed a controversial attachment to Berenice, sister of King Agrippa of Judaea. Recognized by Vespasian as his heir, Titus conscientiously and ruthlessly served his father. There were rumors that he murdered Vespasian, but historians have rejected those allegations.

Titus's reign was brief and notable for events for which he bore little or no direct responsibility. In 79 C.E., Mount Vesuvius erupted, destroying Pompeii and Herculaneum. In 80 C.E., Rome was wracked by fire, followed by an outbreak of plague. It was during his reign that the Flavian Amphitheater, begun by his father and later known as the Colosseum, was completed. Titus died in 81 C.E. while at a spa; some said that the waters were too cold, others that he had been murdered by his brother and future emperor, Domitian.

Influence. Unlike his father, who had ended the civil wars following Nero's death, Titus was notable for hav-ing witnessed events such as the completion of the Colosseum and the eruption of Mount Vesuvius rather than for his personal accomplishments.

ADDITIONAL RESOURCES
Grant, Michael. *The Roman Emperors*. New York: Scribner's, 1985.
Suetonius. *The Twelve Caesars*. Translated by Robert Graves. London: Viking Press, 2000.

SEE ALSO: Domitian; Jewish diaspora; Pompeii and Herculaneum; Rome, Imperial; Vespasian.

—*Eugene Larson*

TIWANAKU

ALSO KNOWN AS: Tiahuanaco
DATE: earliest remains c. 200 B.C.E.
LOCALE: Titicaca Basin, northern Bolivia
RELATED CIVILIZATION: Wari (Huari)
SIGNIFICANCE: One of two sister states of the second round of empire in the Central Andes, whose religious iconography came to dominate the decorative arts.

The site of the prehistoric civilization of Tiwanaku is located at roughly 12,500 feet (3,800 meters) in the Titicaca Basin of the central Andes. Lake Titicaca is the largest lake in the world at this elevation. When the culture was first described 125 years ago, a number of specific similarities in design themes on the pottery, textiles, and other portable art objects were noted between this culture and several contemporary sites in Peru, resulting in the definition of a "Tiahuanacoid" empire including both Bolivia and Peru in sources before 1950. Since 1950, archaeologists have recognized two sister states: Wari (Huari) in Peru, and Tiwanaku in Bolivia. Before radiocarbon dating allowed precision in calibrating the age and duration of cultures, some fanciful notions about a great prehistoric metropolis perhaps as old as 10,000 years developed, contributing in part to Norwegian explorer Thor Heyerdahl's erroneous idea that the Tiwanaku folk colonized Easter Island.

History. Current evidence indicates that a series of small agro-pastoral polities began developing in the Titicaca Basin about 3,500-4,000 years ago, among the most important of which was Chiripa. Roughly 1,700 years ago, a series of political events resulted in the burgeoning growth of Tiwanaku into the paramount political center in the basin. Tiwanaku then began a series of expansive moves outside the basin but employed a variety of methods of economic and political control, which allowed the kingdom to establish a series of different relationships with separate areas and provided such a flexible system of interaction that Tiwanaku survived as the dominant political center for several centuries, not collapsing until about nine hundred years ago.

The Tiwanaku lords established a loose federation with the Cochabamba area to the east (later one of two "breadbaskets" of the Inca empire), so while there was extensive mimicking of Tiwanaku prestige goods, Cochabamba retained its independence. Tiwanaku also set up a small local "port of trade" presence with the semiprecious stone and mineral center of San Pedro de Atacama in central Chile. With the adjacent agricultural valleys in northern Chile, Tiwanaku sent intrusive settlers, who ended up in multiethnic local groupings. In the corn-growing areas of the Moquegua valley of southern Peru, Tiwanaku sent in colonists, completely replacing the local population and incorporating Moquegua into the highland state as a province. Relationships with the short-lived Wari conquest state in Peru (roughly 1,450-1,250 years ago) are more difficult to identify. Although pilgrimages by Wari people to the religious shrines in Tiwanaku apparently occurred, for the most part Wari seems to have been a much more totalitarian state, with its southern frontier with Tiwanaku defined by major fortifications such as Cerro Baul and Pikillacta.

Agriculture. The lake-shadow effect from Lake Titicaca produces an ameliorating impact on the local climate, which, together with its location near the equatorial zone, means that the area is free of snow most of the time and that more extensive agriculture is possible here than in areas of similar altitude. Although it was possible to grow some corn in the immediate area, the principal crops in prehistoric periods were various indigenous grains and seeds (from the chenopod, amaranth, and lupine families) and a wide variety of tubers (particularly several types of potatoes). The cold temperatures at night and the constant winds permitted "freeze-drying" of the tubers, yielding a desiccated product that could be stored for multiple years, thus allowing the people to develop considerable food surpluses. Domestic animals provided the other portion of an agro-pastoral economy, with llamas employed primarily as beasts of burden, moving goods in and out of the capital city, and alpacas the primary source of wool and meat. On the lake itself, small boats, propelled both by poling and by sails, made of cattail-like reeds, also provided a supplement of fish and waterfowl, and hunters in the altiplano tablelands brought in deer, guanaco, vicuna, and various small rodents and birds.

Religion and culture. The iconography of Tiwanaku is the most characteristic aspect of the culture. There was a principal godhead, with several different manifestations—in some situations depicted standing akimbo, holding staffs in outstretched hands, but in other situations, holding instead a *kero* (large drinking cup) for *chicha* (corn beer) in one hand and a shallow-incised tablet (for inhaling hallucinogenic snuffs) in the other. Attendants to this central figure include winged anthropomorphic and zoomorphic figures. These images occur on a wide variety of ceramic pots, on woolen and cotton textiles, and on stone, bone, and wooden artifacts. In the earliest manifestations, the figures are often in pairs and are known as *Pajano* (two-faced) in Aymara, the language of the original Tiwanaku people.

Dualism permeates the cultural fabric of the Aymara, so much so that at the time the Inca conquered the area, local polities or kingdoms were divided into halves, with cases of two "kings" being recorded, each one ascending to power in alternating years. This dualism is thoroughly integrated into the local clan system known as the *ayllu*, which in various local areas, because of the long temporal separation from its original roots as well as spatial separation, evolved into a variety of contrasting landowning and labor-managing kinds of local kin corporations.

ADDITIONAL RESOURCES

Albarracin-Jordan, Juan. *The Archaeology of Tiwanaku: The Myths, History, and Science of an Ancient Andean Civilization.* La Paz, Bolivia: Imprenta PAP, 1999.

Kolata, Alan L., et al. *Tiwanaku and Its Hinterland: Archaeology and Paleoecology of an Andean Civilization.* Washington, D.C.: Smithsonian Institution Press, 1996.

SEE ALSO: Andes, central; Andes, South.

—*David L. Browman*

TŌLĀMOLITTĒVAR

FLOURISHED: between 200 and 600 C.E., possibly as late as ninth or tenth century C.E.
RELATED CIVILIZATION: South India
MAJOR ROLE/POSITION: Writer

Life. Tōlāmolittēvar (toh-LAW-moh-lee-TEH-vahr) was the writer of a celebrated south Indian epic tale called *Cūḷamāni* (between 200 and 600 C.E., also known as *Śūlamāṇi*; the crest jewel). He is counted among the five minor *kāvyas* (poets) of Tamil literature. The work consists of 2,130 verses.

Tōlāmolittēvar was a Jain and, therefore, his writing includes a great deal of Jaina philosophy and strict enforcement of the principle of *ahiṁsā*, or nonviolence or noninjury to any living thing, including the prohibition against eating meat and taking alcoholic beverages. Throughout the epic, he explains that a good life stresses nonviolence and the seeking of salvation through self-sacrifice.

The story centers on a Jaina king who seeks to govern according to Jaina tenets. Included is the story of a prince who engages in various youthful escapades and numerous love affairs but who eventually renounces the world in typical Jaina fashion. It is through the character of the prince in particular that the writer explores erotic, heroic, and religious themes. In beautiful, mellifluous verse, Tōlāmoḷittēvar provides rich descriptions of his characters, city life, and rural scenes. He also explores and combines both the natural and supernatural worlds.

The dating of the *Cūḷamāni* and, therefore, the life of Tōlāmoḷittēvar is problematic. Many specialists argue for an early date between 200 and 600 C.E. Others believe that the work has characteristics common to later Tamil and place the work as late as the ninth to tenth centuries.

Influence. Tōlāmoḷittēvar provided a detailed and colorful tale about ancient Tamil culture. He is a rich resource for practical understanding of the everyday application of Jaina beliefs.

ADDITIONAL RESOURCE

Chakravarti, Appaswami. *Jaina Literature in Tamil.* New Delhi, India: Bharatiya Jnanapitha Publications, 1974.

SEE ALSO: India; Jainism.

        —Katherine Anne Harper

TOLKĀPPIYAM

AUTHORSHIP: Trinadhuma Agni, also known as Tolkāppiyanār
DATE: c. 250 B.C.E.
LOCALE: South India
RELATED CIVILIZATIONS: Dravidian, India
SIGNIFICANCE: This work codified an already existing large body of Tamil grammar and literature.

Tolkāppiyam (tuhl-KAW-pee-yahm; *Tol* meaning "hoary" and *kāppiyam* denoting literature), which codified the grammar and literature of Tamil language, provides evidence of numerous grammarians, a large body of literature, and a rich pool of artistic talent that existed in southern India several years before the work was created. *Tolkāppiyam* contains about 1,612 poems divided into three *adhikarams*, or categories: *Ezhuthadhikaram* (orthography), *Solladhikaram* (etymology), and *Poruladhikaram* (subject matter of poetry that applies to figures of speech, prosody, and idiom), each divided into nine chapters.

Ezhuthadhikaram, which analyzes Tamil phonology, sounds, and their production and classification, has 480 *sūtras*. *Solladhikaram* scrutinizes the origins of words and analyzes principles of word usage in literary, formal, and informal contexts. *Poruladhikaram* deals with the subject matter of poetry—the incidents of life. It consists of 660 *sūtras* and deals with the science of poetics pertaining to romantic love, affairs of the state, *rasa* (sentiment relating to poetry), figures of speech, meter, and traditional usage in poetry. *Porul* is classified as *Agamporul* and *Puraporul*—subjective and objective, home and abroad, and inside and outside. An interesting point to note is that land was then divided into five regions, each of which had its own music, deities, musical instruments, and other social customs.

ADDITIONAL RESOURCE

Rajam, V. S. *A Reference Grammar of Classical Tamil Poetry.* Philadelphia, Pa.: American Philosophical Society, 1992.

SEE ALSO: Caṅkam; India.

        —Kokila Ravi

TOTILA

ALSO KNOWN AS: Baduila
BORN: 515(?) C.E.; place unknown
DIED: 552 C.E.; place unknown
RELATED CIVILIZATIONS: Ostrogoths, Franks,
   Byzantine Empire
MAJOR ROLE/POSITION: Military leader

Life. Totila (TAHT-ihl-uh) was chosen as king of the Ostrogoths in Italy in 541 C.E. after his predecessor, Witigis, was captured by the Byzantine army and sent to Constantinople. Fighting in Italy against an army sent by Justinian I and led by Belisarius, Totila managed to capture Rome in 546 C.E. Belisarius beseeched Totila not to destroy the city, and it was saved. Later, however, when Totila chased the Byzantine army south, Belisarius retook Rome and rebuilt some of its fortifications. After Belisarius was recalled by Justinian I in 549 C.E., Totila recaptured the city.

In 551 C.E., Narses replaced Belisarius as commander in chief and entered Italy via the top of the Adriatic Sea and marched to Ravenna, which was still held by imperial troops. By the summer of 552 C.E., the Goths were engaged by Narses in the Apennines at Taginae near present-day Fabriano, where Totila was mortally wounded. In 555 C.E., Ostrogothic rule ended in Italy.

Influence. Although the Goths were ultimately defeated, Totila was able to challenge the force of the Byzantine Empire and conquer almost all Italy. He came to be regarded in the nineteenth century as a heroic and romantic figure.

ADDITIONAL RESOURCES

Dewing, H. B. *Procopius: History of the Wars.* Vol. 3. Cambridge, Mass.: Harvard University Press, 1992.
Fauber, Lawrence. *Narses: The Hammer of the Goths.* New York: St. Martin's Press, 1990.
Wolfram, Herwig. *History of the Goths.* Berkeley: University of California Press, 1988.

SEE ALSO: Belisarius; Byzantine Empire; Constantinople; Goths; Justinian I; Narses (Byzantine military leader); Rome, Imperial.

—*Brian Hancock*

TRAJAN

ALSO KNOWN AS: Marcus Ulpius Traianus
BORN: c. 53 C.E.; Italica, Baetica
DIED: c. August 8, 117 C.E.; Selinus, Cilicia
RELATED CIVILIZATION: Imperial Rome
MAJOR ROLE/POSITION: Emperor

Life. The Ulpii family were from Italica (Santiponce, Spain). Trajan's (TRAY-jehn) father was a prominent subordinate of Vespasian, whose son Domitian promoted Trajan to a consulship in 91 C.E. Trajan succeeded Marcus Cocceius Nerva without opposition and governed astutely and tactfully. He commemorated the conquest of Dacia (the Carpathian basin, 101-106 C.E.) in the magnificent forum complex (106-113 C.E.) adjoining those of his admired predecessors Julius Caesar, Augustus, and Vespasian, consolidated holdings in Britain and Africa, and annexed Arabia (Jordan). Baths, new port facilities, and an aqueduct improved the quality of life in Rome. Imperial judgments determined that Christians could be punished if they defied the government.

Although a Parthian war began well (114 C.E.), revolts in northern Mesopotamia compelled Trajan to retreat from Babylon in 117 C.E. He died of a stroke at Selinus (south Anatolian coast) in August. His ashes were placed at the base of the column in his forum.

Influence. The Roman senate proclaimed Trajan *optimus princeps,* or "optimal first citizen," meaning there could be no better emperor, for Trajan was tolerant, wise in selection of administrators, respectful of the senate, and popular with the armies. His successor was a cousin, Hadrian.

ADDITIONAL RESOURCES

Bennett, Julian. *Trajan, Optimus Princeps: A Life and Times.* Bloomington: Indiana University Press, 1997.
Campbell, B. *The Emperor and the Roman Army.* Oxford, England: Oxford University Press, 1984.
Millar, F. *The Emperor in the Roman World.* London: Duckworth, 1977.

Packer, J. E. *The Forum of Trajan at Rome*. Berkeley: University of California Press, 1996.

Sherwin-White, A. N. *The Letters of Pliny: A Historical and Social Commentary*. Oxford, England: Oxford University Press, 1985.

SEE ALSO: Africa, North; Arabia; Augustus; Britain; Christianity; Hadrian; Nerva, Marcus Cocceius; Parthia; Rome, Imperial; Trajan's column; Vespasian.

—*Thomas H. Watkins*

Trajan (seated). (Library of Congress)

TRAJAN'S COLUMN

DATE: 106-113 C.E.

LOCALE: Rome

RELATED CIVILIZATION: Imperial Rome

SIGNIFICANCE: One of greatest surviving examples of Roman relief sculpture, Trajan's column still stands today.

The large free-standing column of Trajan was the centerpiece of Trajan's forum in Rome and commemorated the emperor's two victorious military campaigns against the Dacians (101-102, 105-106 C.E.). Probably the creation of Apollodorus the Architect, the monument consists of a Luna marble pedestal, shaft, and capital that was originally topped by a gilded bronze statue of Trajan (replaced by one of Saint Peter in 1588). Although not intended to be a tomb, the remains of Trajan and his wife Plotina were housed in the pedestal after 117 C.E. The total height of the monument (125 feet, or

38 meters) records the amount of earth dug away from the Quirinal hill for the forum's construction. The column has an internal spiral staircase of 185 steps leading to an upper balcony. Light entered the interior through 40 slit windows that were added after the exterior decoration was finished. Reliefs of captured enemy armor cover the pedestal exterior, and the column shaft bears a helical band, 656 feet (200 meters) long and 2 to 4 feet (0.61-1.2 meters) high, carved with scenes from the actual campaigns. There are 155 individual scenes and more than 2,500 figures in the 23 superimposed spirals. Read from bottom up, the sculptural narrative records mainly generic Roman military events; only one-quarter is devoted to battle scenes. Decebalus, the Dacian leader, is depicted almost at the column's apex as a courageous man who preferred suicide to capture.

ADDITIONAL RESOURCES

Kleiner, Diana E., *Roman Sculpture*. New Haven, Conn.: Yale University Press, 1992.

Lepper, Frank, and Sheppard Frere. *Trajan's Column*. Gloucester, England: Alan Sutton, 1988.

Silverio, Francesco. *Trajan's Column*. Rome: Quasar, 1989.

SEE ALSO: Apollodorus the Architect; Art and architecture; Rome, Imperial; Trajan.

—*Lee Ann Turner*

TRIUMVIRATE

DATE: 60-53 and 43-32 B.C.E.
LOCALE: Rome
RELATED CIVILIZATION: Republican Rome

A triumvirate (tri-UHM-vuh-reht; Latin *triumviratus)* was a legally established board or commission composed of three members, a type of administrative organization common in the Roman Republic; its members were triumvirs (Latin *tresviri)*. Republican triumvirates oversaw the mint, public finances, prisons and capital punishment, and land distribution both at home and at colonial foundations. Modern historians use the term misleadingly. The so-called First Triumvirate, a misnomer, was simply a private power-sharing arrangement, beginning in 60 B.C.E., among Julius Caesar, Pompey the Great, and Marcus Licinius Crassus; it was never termed a triumvirate in its own day. Caesar benefited most from this private arrangement as he climbed to power.

The so-called Second Triumvirate, however, was constituted legally during the political crisis following Caesar's assassination. In 43 B.C.E., the senate appointed Octavian (later Augustus), Marc Antony, and Marcus Aemilius Lepidus to a five-year term as triumvirs to restore the government (*tresviri rei publicae constituendae)*. What appeared to be an instrument of reform provided a type of military dictatorship. When authorization ran out in 37 B.C.E. and the commissioners refused to step down, the senate reappointed them for a second five-year term, probably ending on January 1, 32 B.C.E., but the commission collapsed rapidly, with Lepidus being deposed in 36 B.C.E. and Antony eventually losing the naval battle at Actium in 31 B.C.E. After Actium, Octavian emerged as de facto head of the Roman Empire, even though he did not declare the political crisis over until 28 B.C.E. and had not yet entered into agreement with the senate (27 B.C.E.) or acquired the full legal power needed to be successful as emperor (23 B.C.E.).

ADDITIONAL RESOURCES

Oman, Charles William Chadwick. *Seven Roman Statesmen of the Later Republic*. London: E. Arnold, 1957.

Plutarch. *The Fall of the Roman Republic*. Translated by Rex Warner. Baltimore: Penguin Books, 1980.

SEE ALSO: Antony, Marc; Augustus; Caesar, Julius; Crassus, Marcus Licinius; Pompey the Great; Rome, Republican.

—*F. E. Romer*

TROY

DATE: c. 3000 B.C.E.-700 C.E.
LOCALE: Western coast of Turkey in the Hellespont, at the present-day city of Hisarlik
RELATED CIVILIZATIONS: Mycenaean, Archaic, Classical, Hellenistic, and Roman Greece
SIGNIFICANCE: Focal point of the earliest legends of Archaic Greek culture, Troy may have been destroyed by war, much the way the poet Homer describes, about 1250 B.C.E.

The site of Troy was inhabited as early as 3600 B.C.E. by Neolithic Asian peoples of the Dardanelles, but permanent structures do not appear until the third millennium. The name "Troy" refers to a number of different settlements at various times across four millennia. The first Troy, the Neolithic Asian settlement, took advantage of the strategic height of a plateau overlooking the Aegean Sea at the western mouth of the Dardanelles. The plateau is now nearly four miles (six kilometers) inland because of the silting of the rivers Scamander (Menderes) and Simoïs (Dümrek), but in the second millennium B.C.E., it was right on the bay at Cape Sigeum (Yenişehir). The natural defensive advantage of this promontory (known to archaeologists as Troy I) was strengthened sometime after 2500 B.C.E., making Troy II a royal fortress.

Somewhere around 2200 B.C.E., the royal fortress was sacked and burned, an event that Troy's first archaeologist, Heinrich Schliemann, mistook for the Trojan War recorded by Homer. The fire-scarred ruins of Troy II, however, were nearly one thousand years too early to be Agamemnon's Troy. Had he insisted on employing Greek mythology to guide archaeology, however, Schliemann could have justified his mistake by pointing to the tradition that Heracles sacked Troy a generation before the war over Helen. Three more successive "Troys" were constructed over the ruins of Troy II throughout the next four centuries. Then the Indo-European migration brought the ancestor of the Greek language (and perhaps a prototype of its mythology) into the region around 1800 B.C.E. This group introduced the art of domesticating and breeding horses, for which Troy was to become famous in Homeric tradition. Archaeological evidence of numerous Bronze Age horse bones corroborates the poetic claim: Troy was rich in horses.

Troy VI. The city of these Indo-European people, Troy VI, was the longest-lived settlement at Troy and may have been the city whose destruction sometime near 1250 B.C.E. was the nucleus of the Greek epic cycle. By 1500 B.C.E., Troy VI had documented contacts with a Mycenaean Greek empire. It may be possible, in fact, to consider Troy VI a part of that empire. It has been known since the early twentieth century that Troy and Mycenae shared architectural and pottery styles in the late Bronze Age. With the translation of the Linear B cuneiform in the 1950's, it was further learned that the two cities shared a common language as well, an ancestor of Homer's Greek.

The architectural features that Troy VI shared with Mycenae include the dome-vaulted tomb, the thick, upward-sloping sandstone walls, and high towers. The pottery style was dubbed "grey Minyan" by Schliemann, and archaeologists still use the term. The dome-shaped tomb, or *tholos*, was the telltale sign of Mycenaean architecture and provided rich finds to the archaeologist. The kings of Troy VI had their wealth buried with them much as the Egyptian pharaohs did. The walls were even more distinctively Mycenaean, matching walls of the same period excavated at Mycenae and Tiryns on the Greek mainland and at Knossos on the island of Crete. Greeks of the classical period called the style "cyclopean" because they could not imagine such massive sandstone rocks—square cut and more than three feet (a meter) thick—to be the work of human hands. Their peculiar pitch, a seventy-degree slope from the base, was noted by German archaeologist Friedrich Wilhelm Dörpfeld, who discovered the "cyclopean" walls of Troy VI in 1893. Poet Homer may have had this feature in mind when he related that Patroclus climbed the "angle" of the wall in the *Iliad* (c. 800 B.C.E.; English translation, 1616). Dörpfeld's assistants were able to scale the walls easily. Finally, the tower on the southern gate of Troy VI recalls similar structures in Mycenae and Tiryns.

Troy VII and beyond. The destruction of Troy VI about 1250 B.C.E. may well have been caused by war, though there is ample evidence of a major earthquake about that time. Troy lies on a major Anatolian fault, and archaeologist Carl Blegen had demonstrated earthquake damage in the previous three Troy settlements (III, IV, and V). Whatever the cause, the devastation of Troy VI led to a considerable drop in the standard of living in the subsequent settlement, Troy VII. Artifacts from Troy VII suggest a siege or refugee society, with rude shacks built over storage jars embedded in the

An archaeologist sketches as he looks over the southeastern gate of Troy. (North Wind Picture Archives)

ground. This "shantytown" Troy, built within the now-compromised walls of Troy VI, fell to invaders from the sea about 1180 B.C.E. Egyptian, Hittite, and other records corroborate the Trojan evidence of these marauders, though it is not clear where they came from.

Some time after the marauders left, new settlers arrived at the site. They brought with them a style of pottery that was a distinct step backward from the level of craftsmanship of Troy VII, the so-called knobbed-ware found at this time along the Danube or in Hungary. The style was also known much closer to Troy, in Thrace, and these new settlers may have been Thracians. By the end of the second millennium B.C.E., there was no trace of Troy VII. In fact, there is virtually no archaeological evidence of any human habitation of Troy from 1000 to 700 B.C.E.

Sometime before 700 B.C.E., colonists from the nearby island of Lesbos began a permanent settlement in Troy. The small market town (Troy VIII) was connected to Greek trade routes and became the focus of an odd custom in the Greek region of Locris on the Gulf of Corinth. The Locrians, beginning about 700 B.C.E. and continuing into the common era, selected a certain number of young girls each year to be sent to Troy as an expiation for the sin of Aias of Locris. According to Locrian tradition, Aias, a soldier in Agamemnon's expedition against Troy, defiled a temple of Athena at Troy. To make amends, the Locrians sent their daughters to serve in Athena's temple. Though many did just that, remaining in the temple of Athene into old age, many, during the nearly eight hundred years of this practice, were killed by the new Greek residents of "Ilion."

In the Hellenistic period, around 300 B.C.E., one of Alexander the Great's generals, Lysimachus, decided to rebuild the splendor that he thought must once have existed at Troy. He rebuilt the city walls in a glorious outer work that remained the outer walls for the Roman occupation of the city, New Ilium. Unfortunately, Schliemann's overzealous and now-outmoded digging methods (including dynamite) destroyed a great deal of this great wall.

Archaeologists consider both the Hellenistic and the Roman Troys to be a continuous settlement, Troy IX, the last structure that could be considered a city at Hisarlik. The city was sacked twice more: by the soldiers of Pontus, the Black Sea empire of King Mithradates VI Eupator, in 83-82 B.C.E., and by the Goths in 259 C.E. The Seljuk Turks took the city in 1070 C.E. and the Ottomans in 1306 C.E., though neither Turkish occupation could be called an invasion. There was by then not much to take, and the Troas had long been a melting pot.

In the Byzantine period, Troy might have become a major center of Constantine the Great's empire. In the late 320's C.E., having become the sole ruler of the Roman Empire, Constantine attempted to move the empire's capital to the site that was, according to poet Vergil's *Aeneid* (c. 29-19 B.C.E.; English translation, 1553), the homeland of the Roman people: Troy. The silting of the Scamander and Simoïs, however, made an inland capital at Hisarlik difficult to reach, and Constantine was forced to move his capital to his second choice, Byzantium, which he renamed Constantinople in 330 C.E. Nevertheless, Troy remained part of the Byzantine Empire, albeit as a remote backwater. It was a bishopric of the Byzantine church from the fourth to the eleventh century C.E., so it must have had some ecclesial importance, if only a continuation of the pagan importance Troy had as a "holy" city.

ADDITIONAL RESOURCES
Akurgal, Ekrem. *Ancient Civilizations and Ruins of Turkey.* Istanbul: Haset Kitabevi, 1983.
Blegen, Carl William. *Troy and the Trojans.* London: Thames and Hudson, 1963.
Boedeker, Deborah Dickman. *The World of Troy.* Pittsburgh, Pa.: Classical Association of the United States, 1998.
Fitten, J. Lesley. *The Discovery of the Greek Bronze Age.* Cambridge, Mass.: Harvard University Press, 1996.
Wood, Michael. *In Search of the Trojan War.* Berkeley: University of California Press, 1998.

SEE ALSO: Byzantine Empire; Constantine the Great; Greece, Archaic; Greece, Classical; Greece, Hellenistic and Roman; Greece, Mycenaean; Homer; Lysimachus.

—*John R. Holmes*

TULLIUS TIRO, MARCUS

BORN: 103 B.C.E.?; place unknown
DIED: 4 B.C.E.; Puteoli (later Pozzuoli, Italy)
RELATED CIVILIZATIONS: Imperial and Republican Rome
MAJOR ROLE/POSITION: Slave, scholar

Life. Marcus Tullius Tiro (MAHR-kuhs TUHL-ee-uhs TIH-roh) was a slave (and later freed) assistant to Cicero. His traditional date of birth is not directly attested but calculated from his purported lifespan of one hundred years. However, other, vaguer attestations have suggested to some that he may have been up to twenty years younger when he died. His name and national origin, as well as how he entered slavery and Cicero's household, are all unknown.

As Cicero's personal assistant, he worked on business and family matters but was especially important to his literary endeavors. Tiro did practical work (such as taking dictation) and served as a learned adviser. Cicero's letters also indicate a warm personal relationship, showing particular distress during Tiro's serious illness in 50 B.C.E. Tiro's manumission in 53 B.C.E. did not affect his position in the household.

Even after Cicero's death, Tiro was active in preserving and sometimes publishing his former master's works, including notes and letters not originally intended for the public. Works in his own right include a biography of Cicero, notes on grammatical topics, and "letters" on literary topics. Few fragments of any of these survive. His work appears to have been received critically in antiquity, perhaps because of his status as a freedman.

Influence. Tiro was crucial for preserving information about and boosting the reputation of his former master.

ADDITIONAL RESOURCES

Everitt, Anthony. *Cicero: A Turbulent Life*. London: John Murray, 2001.

McDermott, W. C. "M. Cicero and M. Tiro." *Historia* 21 (1972): 259-286.

Mitzschke, Paul Gottfried. *Biography of the Father of Stenography, Marcus Tullius Tiro*. Brooklyn, N.Y.: F. Hart, 1882.

SEE ALSO: Cicero; Rome, Imperial; Rome, Republican.
—*Andrew M. Riggsby*

TUTANKHAMEN

ALSO KNOWN AS: Tutankhaton
BORN: c. 1370 B.C.E.; probably Amarna, Egypt
DIED: c. 1352 B.C.E.; place unknown
RELATED CIVILIZATION: Pharaonic Egypt
MAJOR ROLE/POSITION: Pharaoh

Life. Tutankhamen (tew-tahn-KAHM-uhn) was either a brother or a son of the solar monotheist Akhenaton. Originally, his name was Tutankhaton, "living image of the Aton" (the Sun disk), but it was changed to honor Amun, the god of Thebes. During his nine-year reign, Aton's temples still functioned, but other gods' endowments were renewed. Meanwhile, campaigns were conducted to bolster Egyptian authority in Syria-Palestine and Nubia.

Early study of the mummy of Tutankhamen indicated that he died at eighteen. Though this estimate has been disputed, there can be no doubt that he became pharaoh when he was young and that he relied heavily on advisers. In this respect, the "god's father" Ay was particularly important. Under Akhenaton, Ay served as both a royal tutor and an army officer. Later, he oversaw Tutankhamen's funeral, married his widow, Ankhesenamen, and succeeded him as king.

Influence. Tutankhamen was of minor significance for Egyptian history. He presided over a transitional period—probably as a figurehead—and was omitted from king lists. He has been very important for Egyptology, however. His tomb, discovered by Howard Carter in 1922, contained a spectacular assemblage of burial goods. This treasure, which includes out-standing examples of the revolutionary Amarna style of art, has generated considerable excitement about Egypt.

Tutankhamen. (Library of Congress)

ADDITIONAL RESOURCES
Desroches-Noblecourt, Christiane. *Tutankhamen: Life and Death of a Pharaoh*. New York: Penguin, 1989.
Reeves, Nicholas. *The Complete Tutankhamun: The*

King, the Tomb, the Royal Treasure. London: Thames and Hudson, 1990.

SEE ALSO: Akhenaton; Ankhesenamen; Egypt, Pharaonic.

—*Steven M. Stannish*

TWELVE TABLES, THE

DATE: composed 451-450 B.C.E.
LOCALE: Rome
RELATED CIVILIZATION: Republican Rome
SIGNIFICANCE: The basis for a codified Roman law, the tables guided all future Roman law involving the family, civil disputes, and court procedure.

The Twelve Tables were written after Roman scholars visited Greece and studied the law of Solon. The Twelve Tables of law were a mix of Roman custom and Greek law. Though no copy of the laws exists today, many of the later Roman laws were based on the Twelve Tables. Initially, the Twelve Tables were accessible only to a small group of jurists known as pontiffs. They interpreted and applied the law until the public demanded that the law be published. This made the law accessible to most people and led to its growth and wider application.

The code regulated family relations, establishing the time-honored Roman tradition of *patria potestas*. Under this legal concept, the oldest male of the family was responsible for caring for the family's finances, food,

and shelter. This extended to all grown children. The Twelve Tables also regulated marriage, inheritance, and divorce. They related the procedures for trials and the punishments for those criminal acts covered under the law. They also required litigants to enforce their judgments.

ADDITIONAL RESOURCES
Justinian: The Digest of Roman Law. Translated by C. F. Kolbert. London: Penguin, 1979.
Mears, T. L. *The Institutes of Gaius and Justinian, the Twelve Tables, with Introduction and Translation*. Holmes Beach, Fla.: Gaunt, 1994.
Scullard, H. H. *A History of the Roman World*. London: Routledge, 1980.
Watson, Alan. *Rome of the Twelve Tables*. Princeton, N.J.: Princeton University Press, 1975.

SEE ALSO: Government and law; Justinian I; Rome, Republican; Solon.

—*Douglas Clouatre*

TYRTAEUS

FLOURISHED: mid-seventh century B.C.E.; Sparta
RELATED CIVILIZATION: Archaic Greece
MAJOR ROLE/POSITION: Hoplite general and martial poet

Life. Although Athenians claim Tyrtaeus (tur-TEE-uhs) was a schoolmaster called by an oracle to a Sparta in crisis, he was almost certainly a Spartan hoplite soldier who rose to emergency high command by using patriotic poetry and song to motivate. Five books of his poetry seem to have survived in Alexandria, of which

some 250 lines remain as *Eunomia* (seventh century B.C.E.; English translation in *Greek Literary Papyri*, 1942), a collection of fragments of war chants, quotations from patriotic, hortatory elegies, and part, at least, of one extraordinary constitutional poem.

The crisis that brought Tyrtaeus to Sparta was probably the Second Messenian War, a great Messenian revolt in the mid-seventh century B.C.E. that led to the final enslavement of the helots. He seems to have won the war, figuratively and perhaps even literally, by invoking the Spartans' Heraclid descent, their Delphic Apollonian kings, council, and demos, their law and order (*eunomia*), and their just and justified victories in the First Messenian War, all in stirring Ionian epic and lyric verse with echoes of the Greek Homer.

Influence. Tyrtaeus probably influenced the patriotic and political poetry of exhortation such as that produced by Solon and thereby Greek politics in general, but his Homeric lyrics may not have been influential in their own right.

ADDITIONAL RESOURCES

Forrest, W. G. *A History of Sparta*. London: Bristol Classics, 1995.

Huxley, G. L. *Early Sparta*. London: Faber and Faber, 1962.

SEE ALSO: Greece, Archaic; Homer; Messenian Wars; Solon.

—O. Kimball Armayor

— U —

UBAID CULTURE

DATE: 5200-3400 B.C.E.
LOCALE: Southern Mesopotamia, present-day Iraq
SIGNIFICANCE: The Ubaid culture flourished during the last great stage of prehistoric civilization in Mesopotamia.

In 1919, Harry R. Hall first excavated Tell al-Ubaid, a small mound located 3.7 miles (6 kilometers) west of Ur in southern Mesopotamia. C. Leonard Woolley, the famous excavator of Ur, also dug at Ubaid (EW-bayd) in 1923-1924. Woolley initiated the use of the name "Ubaid" to designate the long period of prehistory he associated with a distinctive painted pottery found first at Ubaid and then at Ur. Hall and Woolley found evidence of a great Sumerian temple dated to the third millennium B.C.E. and the remains of an extensive prehistoric civilization.

The prehistoric civilization employed a unique ceramic assemblage of painted pottery with geometric motifs in black on a background of greenish hue. Discovery of the same type of pottery at neighboring sites led to the conclusion that this Ubaid culture represented the last great stage of Neolithic society before the intensification of urbanization in Mesopotamia at the end of the fourth millennium B.C.E.

In addition to its distinctive pottery, the Ubaid culture is known for its use of curved nails, clay sickles, and molded bricks.

ADDITIONAL RESOURCES

Huot, Jean-Louis. "Ubaid." In *The Oxford Encyclopedia of Archaeology in the Near East*, edited by Eric M. Meyers. Oxford, England: Oxford University Press, 1997.

Lloyd, Seton. *The Archaeology of Mesopotamia: From the Old Stone Age to the Persian Conquest*. Rev. ed. New York: Thames and Hudson, 1984.

SEE ALSO: Samarran culture; Sumerians.

—*Stephen J. Andrews*

ULPIAN

ALSO KNOWN AS: Domitius Ulpianus
BORN: 172 C.E.?; Tyre
DIED: Summer, 223 C.E.; Rome
RELATED CIVILIZATION: Imperial Rome
MAJOR ROLE/POSITION: Lawyer

Life. Ulpian (UHL-pee-uhn) is one of the last of the canonical Roman jurists and perhaps the most prolific, with more than 280 works attributed to him. Yet despite the extent of his writings, little can be ascertained with certainty about his life. That he was born in the East, probably Tyre, of a family long since granted the Roman franchise is only a learned conjecture, and his putative birth date of 172 C.E. is a backdating from his association with Papinian as an assessor (along with his rival jurist, Paul) during the latter's praetorian prefecture. Ulpian at some point (possibly 202-209 C.E.) held the post *a libellis* (secretary for petitions) under Lucius Septimius Severus, and he accompanied Severus on his military expeditions to Parthia and Britain. After Severus's death, Ulpian appears to have held no major offices under his successor, Caracalla, but rather devoted himself to writing. The great bulk of his work dates from this period, including his famous commentaries on the praetor's edict, *Ad edictum praetoris* (third century C.E.; in *Rules of Ulpian*, 1880), in eighty-one books, as well as his *Ad Sabinum* (third century C.E.; in *Rules of Ulpian*, 1880), in fifty-one books. It has been theorized that much of this work was undertaken at the behest of the new emperor in order to clarify the Roman law for the new citizens enrolled by the *Constitutio Antoniana*, or Antonine constitution, which made Roman citizens of all free men and women in the empire of 212 C.E.

Ulpian was allegedly exiled, along with Paul, during the reign of Elegabalus, but this cannot be proved. He was clearly restored to power during the subsequent reign of Marcus Aurelius Severus Alexander, holding office as *praefectus annonae* (responsible for corn supply), then occupying some sort of extraordinary prefecture above the two praetorian prefects. For reasons unclear (possibly as a preemptive strike against men he believed were plotting against him), he executed the two praetorian prefects and became sole prefect, an office he maintained from late 222 C.E. until his own murder by the Praetorian Guards in mid-summer 223 C.E. The motives of the praetorians are not clear, although historian Dio Cassius claims that Ulpian was attempting to shore up the guard's notoriously lax discipline.

Influence. Ulpian's imprint can be seen in every area of Roman law. Most famously, citations from his work make up an estimated 40 percent of Justinian I's *Digesta*, also known as *Pandectae* (533 C.E.; *The Digest of Justinian*, 1920).

ADDITIONAL RESOURCES

Honore, Tony. *Ulpian*. Oxford, England: Clarendon Press, 1982.
Robinson, Olivia F. *The Sources of Roman Law: Problems and Methods for Ancient Historians*. New York: Routledge, 1997.
Wells, Colin. *The Roman Empire*. 2d ed. Cambridge, Mass.: Harvard University Press, 1992.

SEE ALSO: Britain; Caracalla; Dio Cassius; Justinian I; Parthia; Rome, Imperial; Severus, Lucius Septimus.

—Joseph P. Wilson

ʿUMAR IBN AL-KHAṬṬĀB

ALSO KNOWN AS: ʿUmar I; ʿUmar al-Farouq; al-Faruk
BORN: c. 586 C.E.; Mecca, Arabia
DIED: November 3, 644 C.E.; Medina, Arabia
RELATED CIVILIZATIONS: Islam, Arabia
MAJOR ROLE/POSITION: Caliph

Life. One of the early converts to Islam, ʿUmar ibn al-Khaṭṭāb (oh-MAHR ihbn ahl-kah-TAWB) was Muḥammad's father-in-law and, after Abū Bakr, the prophet's closest companion. Originally he was a member of a clan of the Meccan tribe of Quraysh and initially opposed Muḥammad. In or around 615 C.E., he converted to Islam, and by 622 C.E., he had accompanied Muḥammad and other Meccan Muslims to Medina. He took an active part in the Battles of Badr (624 C.E.) and Uhud (625 C.E.), protecting Muḥammad from the attacks of the Meccans. He and Abū Bakr were carrying dust while the prophet was digging at the Battle of Trench's (627 C.E.). He put his signature on the Treaty of Hudaybiyyah (628 C.E.). After Muḥammad's death in 632 C.E., he helped to bring about the Medinan Muslims' acceptance of the caliphate of Abū Bakr, a Meccan. Abū Bakr ruled for two years, and in 634 C.E., ʿUmar took over the caliphate.

During ʿUmar's rule, the Islamic state rose to worldwide influence. He defeated the Persians first at al-Qādisīyah (636 C.E.) and then at Nahāvand (642 C.E.), where he broke down the strength of Yazdegerd III and put an end to the Sāsānian Empire when Yazdegerd was finally killed in Khurasan (651 C.E.). The Byzantine presence in Greater Syria came to an end with a series of conquests that started with the Battle of Yarmuk (634 C.E.) and ended with the Patriarch Sophronius handing over the keys of Jerusalem to ʿUmar (637 C.E.). The fall of Alexandria (642 C.E.) meant the end of Byzantine rule in Egypt. He was stabbed to death by a Zoroastrian slave in 644 C.E.

Influence. ʿUmar is renowned for his administrative innovations and equal treatment of both Muslims and non-Muslims. The first Muslim ruler to use the title of Amir al-Muʾmineen (commander of the faithful), he is credited for persuading Abū Bakr to collect the writings of the Qurʾān, adopting the *Hijrah* calendar, introducing the *diwan* system, and imposing taxes. He was known for his asceticism, integrity, and justice, and more than five hundred Islamic traditions have been attributed to him.

ADDITIONAL RESOURCES

The Encyclopaedia of Islam. Prepared by a number of leading orientalists; edited by an editorial committee consisting of H. A. R. Gibb et al. under the patronage of the International Union of Academies.

New ed. Leiden, Netherlands: E. J. Brill, 1960-[2000].

Esposito, John, ed. *The Oxford History of Islam*. New York: Oxford University Press, 1999.

Holt, P., ed. *The Cambridge History of Islam*. Cambridge, England: Cambridge University Press, 1980.

Kennedy, Hugh. *The Prophet and the Age of the Caliphates*. London: Longman, 1986.

Walker, George Benjamin. *Foundations of Islam: The Making of a World Faith*. London: Peter Owen, 1998.

SEE ALSO: Abū Bakr; Arabia; Islam; Muḥammad; Qurʾān.

—*M. Mehdi Ilhan*

UMAYYAD DYNASTY

DATE: 661-751 C.E.
LOCALE: Arabia, the Middle East, Egypt, North Africa, Spain
RELATED CIVILIZATION: Arabia
SIGNIFICANCE: Umayyad caliphs created a unified empire out of the Arab conquests of the first three decades of Islam and doubled its size. They also presided over historic religious, cultural, and economic developments.

The Umayyad (oom-I-yuhd) family seized the Islamic caliphate after the murder of Caliph ʿAlī ibn Abī Ṭālib in 661 C.E., ending the 656-661 C.E. Muslim civil war. The Umayyads promptly moved the capital from Medina to Damascus. In 682 C.E., when Caliph Muʿāwiyah I sought to make Umayyad power dynastic, another civil war erupted. After 692 C.E., with the dynasty victorious, the Umayyads pursued territorial expansion and domestic consolidation. Arab armies swept westward over North Africa and into Spain and east into Afghanistan and Turkistan. Umayyad caliphs created a centralized bureaucracy, an official currency, and a tax code; made Arabic the language of government; and planted new garrison towns to supervise their Arab horsemen.

Ruling as champions of Islam, the Umayyads did not compel the conquered to become Muslims but forced non-Muslim subjects (*dhimmi*) to pay special taxes. Thousands of Persians, Berbers, and other non-Arabs embraced Islam, and these converts (*mawali*) came to outnumber the Arab Muslims. The regime's often heavy-handed rule stimulated Islamic religious and philosophical controversies. For example, Shīʿism rejected Umayyad claims to Islamic legitimacy and created its own distinctive vision as a spiritual and political alternative. In 749 C.E., a political and religious coalition led by the ʿAbbāsids unleashed a revolutionary movement (749-751 C.E.) that finally overthrew the Umayyads.

ADDITIONAL RESOURCES

Hawting, G. R. *The First Dynasty of Islam: The Umayyad Caliphate,* A.D. *661-750*. New York: Routledge, 2000.

Kennedy, Hugh. *The Prophet and the Age of the Caliphates*. New York: Longman, 1999.

SEE ALSO: ʿAlī ibn Abī Ṭālib; Arabia; Islam.

—*Weston F. Cook, Jr.*

UPANIṢADS

AUTHORSHIP: Compilation of various Indian sages
DATE: compiled c. 1000-c. 200 B.C.E.
LOCALE: Indian subcontinent
RELATED CIVILIZATIONS: India, Asia
SIGNIFICANCE: The *Upaniṣads* influenced Indian philosophy, religion, culture, and society for more than three thousand years and played a part in shaping Buddhist thought and the philosophies of West-

erners such as Arthur Schopenhauer and Ralph Waldo Emerson.

The *Upaniṣads* (ew-PAH-nih-shahdz)—from the Sanskrit *upa* (near), *ni* (down), and *sad* (to sit, collectively), meaning "sitting at the feet of the teacher"—make up the concluding portions of the Vedas and consist of the utterances and speculations of various sages concerning ultimate wisdom. The traditional number of *Upaniṣads* is 108, of which 10 are the most important. These "revealed" teachings make up the basis for the tradition of Vedantic philosophy and therefore influenced generations of subsequent Indian thinkers who used elements of the *Upaniṣads* to construct their own philosophical systems. The *Upaniṣads* elaborate on the tendency toward philosophical reflection and speculation to be found in the earlier *Rigveda* (also known as *Ṛgveda*, c. 1500-1000 B.C.E.; English translation, 1896-1897).

Although the *Upaniṣads* do not present a coherent system of thought, certain central philosophical doctrines do emerge. The ultimate ground of all reality is called *brahman*. This absolute reality of *brahman* makes up the objective universe as it manifests or projects itself into being. It is called *ātman* (or the finite soul) in its manifestation within the individual who knows it through introspection and intuition. Therefore, the individual soul is ultimately identical to the *brahman* and is infinite. This monistic wisdom is formulated in the often cited Vedantic doctrine: *tat tvam asi*, or "that you are." The experience of separation of self and universe, of the individual soul and the divine is in truth an illusion, or *māyā*. The pathway to the realization of this basic truth is through disciplined introspection—a journey into the intuitive self—and correct moral action. The goal is to realize fully the identity of the finite self with that of the infinite (to achieve deliverance, or *mokṣa*) and thus to be released from the sufferings of the finite being in its cycles of rebirth in time (known as *samsara*) and from the cosmic law of karma (actions and consequences).

Advaita Vedānta, which literally means "nondualism," is the best known and most influential school of Indian religious philosophy that is based on the *Upaniṣads*. It is also based on the Indian religious classic the *Bhagavadgītā* (c.200 B.C.E.-200 C.E.; *The Bhagavad Gita*, 1785). It teaches that *brahman* is the only absolute reality and that the individual self, the *ātman*, is illusory. In this respect, Advaita Vedānta has often been compared to Buddhism with its central teaching of *anatman*, or the idea that the self does not exist. Advaita Vedānta has become an international religious school through the work of teachers (or gurus) such as Swami Vivekananda and Paramahamsa Yogananda.

ADDITIONAL RESOURCES

Gupta, Bina. *The Disinterested Witness: A Fragment of Advaita Vedānta Phenomenology.* Evanston, Ill.: Northwestern University Press, 1998.

Olivelle, Patrick, trans. *Upaniṣads.* London: Oxford University Press, 1998.

Sharma, Arvind. *The Philosophy of Religion and Advaita Vedanta: A Comparative Study in Religion and Reason.* University Park: Pennsylvania State University Press, 1995.

Vraiaprana, Pravrajika. *Vedanta: A Simple Introduction.* Los Angeles: Vedanta Press, 1999.

SEE ALSO: *Advaita*; Buddhism; Hinduism; India; Vedas; Vedism.

—*Thomas F. Barry*

UR-NAMMA

ALSO KNOWN AS: Ur-Nammu; Ur-Engu
BORN: late twenty-second century B.C.E.; Iraq
DIED: 2095 B.C.E.; Iraq
RELATED CIVILIZATIONS: Iraq, Third Ur Dynasty, Neo-Sumeria
MAJOR ROLE/POSITION: King

Life. Ur-Namma (UR-NAHM-ah) was a governor of Ur and possibly a close relative of Utu-Hegal, the king of Uruk, who expelled the Gutians after the collapse of the Akkadian Dynasty. Historical inscriptions, year names, and literary compositions tell Ur-Namma's deeds. After Utu-Hegal's death, Ur-Namma established the Third Ur Dynasty in 2112 B.C.E. He eventually extended his state from Ur to southern Mesopotamia. He installed his children as high priestess and priest in Ur and Uruk, respectively. He built temples, including the famous ziggurat in Ur, as well as canals, because canal construction and maintenance were duties of Sumerian kings. He was the first ruler in Mesopotamia to issue a law code, although some scholars attribute it to his son Shulgi. Ur-Namma met death prematurely in a battle.

Influence. Ur-Namma reunited Mesopotamia and laid the foundation of the Sumerian renaissance during the Third Ur Dynasty. Sumerian civilization, refined in this period, became an important part of the Mesopotamian cultural tradition.

ADDITIONAL RESOURCES
Hallo, W. W., and W. K. Simpson. *The Ancient Near East: A History.* 2d ed. New York: Harcourt Brace Jovanovich, 1998.

Pritchard, James B., ed. *Ancient Near Eastern Texts Relating to the Old Testament.* 3d ed. Princeton, N. J.: Princeton University Press, 1969.

SEE ALSO: Shulgi; Sumerians.

—*Atsuko Hattori*

URARTU

DATE: c. 900-600 B.C.E.
LOCALE: Eastern Turkey
SIGNIFICANCE: Urartu was the leading opponent of the Assyrian Empire.

Urartu (oo-RAHR-tew; biblical Ararat) at its zenith embraced the lands stretching from Lake Urmia (Orūmīyeh) in northwestern Iran north to Lake Sevan and the middle Araxes (Araks) River, and then west to the Upper Euphrates. The heartland of Urartian civilization was the high plateau on the eastern shores of Lake Van. The southern border marched along the Tur Abdin and associated mountains that divide Transcaucasia from northern Mesopotamia. Urartu was ideal for raising livestock and rich in metals.

By consolidating the Nairi lands, Urartian kings posed a threat to the Assyrian Empire. Shalmaneser III (r. 858-824 B.C.E.) was the first Assyrian monarch to invade Urartu, attacking first King Sarduri I (r. 840-830 B.C.E.), who resided at Tushpa (Topprakale), the citadel of Van in what later became eastern Turkey. Urartian kings fielded disciplined heavy infantry, cavalry, and chariots. Given Urartu's remote location and difficult terrain, Urartian kings thwarted Assyrian armies by defending fortified citadels and driving off herds and flocks.

On the eastern shores of Lake Van, Urartian kings built their first fortress cities at Tushpa and Çavuştepe. Their westernmost fortress at Altintepe was founded astride the main route into eastern Anatolia. King Meinua (r. c. 810-781 B.C.E.) exploited a period of Assyrian weakness, extending his control southeast to Lake Urmia and westward to the Upper Euphrates. Meinua forged alliances with the neo-Hittite princes of Melid (Melitene) and Kummukh (Commagene), inveterate foes of the Assyrians. Neo-Hittite princes welcomed Urartian kings as allies against the Phrygians. Meinua's heirs Argishti I (r. c. 780-756 B.C.E.) and Sarduri II (r. c. 755-735 B.C.E.) imposed control northward to the middle Araxes and Lake Sevan. The revival of Assyrian power under Tiglath-pileser III (r. 745-727 B.C.E.) spelled the end of Urartian hegemony in neo-Hittite Syria and eastern Anatolia. In 714 B.C.E., Sargon II (r. 721-705 B.C.E.) broke the power of Rusa I (r. 734-714 B.C.E.), whose successors thereafter ruled as vassals of Assyria or Babylon, although arts enjoyed a brief renaissance under Rusa II (r. 685-645 B.C.E.).

Descended, in part, from Hurrian and Luwian immigrants of the late Bronze Age, the Urartians adapted the culture of the Hittite Empire. Urartian kings constructed vast irrigation systems, encouraged cultivation of new crops, and settled skilled immigrants and captives. They commemorated their building activities in monumental inscriptions in cuneiform, in both Akkadian and Urartian, the latter an Asiatic language related to Hurrian and so neither Indo-European nor Semitic in origin. A hieroglyphic syllabary of more than one hundred pictograms, still to be deciphered, was employed for administrative texts. Urartian craftspeople produced splendid ironwork, ceramics, and textiles that profoundly influenced the material culture of nascent Phrygian and Greek civilizations. Rituals and temples point to connections with the Hittite world. The principal Urartian god, Haldi, shared attributes with the Hurrio-Hittite weather god Teshub. The Urartians, although they spoke an Asiatic language, established the institutions and culture of later classical Armenia.

ADDITIONAL RESOURCES
Barnett, R. D. "Urartu." In *The Cambridge Ancient History.* 2d ed. Vol. 3. Cambridge, England: Cambridge University Press, 1994.

Burney, C., and D. M. Lang. *The Peoples of the Hills: Ancient Ararat and Caucasus*. New York: Praeger, 1972.

Zimansky, P. E. *Ecology and Empire: The Structure of the Urartian State*. Chicago: The Oriental Institute, 1985.

SEE ALSO: Argishti I; Armenia; Assyria; Babylonia; Hittites; Hurrians; Luwians; Phrygia; Sarduri I; Sarduri II; Sarduri III; Sargon II; Tiglath-pileser III.

—*Kenneth W. Harl*

ʿUTHMĀN IBN ʿAFFĀN

BORN: late sixth century C.E.; probably in Mecca
DIED: 656 C.E.; Medina, Arabian Peninsula
RELATED CIVILIZATION: Arabia
MAJOR ROLE/POSITION: Religious leader

Life. ʿUthmān ibn ʿAffān (ooth-MAHN-ihb-uhn-af-FAHN), a merchant, was a member of the important Umayyad clan in Mecca. The first important convert to Islam, he fled briefly to Abyssinia circa 615 C.E. to escape religious persecution. Although known as Dhu al-Nûûrayn ("Possessing Two Lights") because he married two daughters of the Prophet, he did not play a major role in Islam until he was elected successor to ʿUmar ibn al-Khaṭṭāb, the second caliph, in 644 C.E. His sudden political rise marks a resurgence in the power of the Umayyad clan.

His most significant act as caliph was the authorization of a single official version of the Qurʾān. He brought Iran, Ādharbāyjān, and portions of Armenia into the Islamic empire. He attempted to organize the Arabic tribes under a strong central power through the creation of landed fiefs and provincial governorships and drew power and wealth away from the army and into the hands of his own Umayyad clan.

ʿUthmān is often described as a pious but weak leader influenced by family members, especially his cousin and secretary, Marwān. Opposition to his authority, especially by ʿAlī ibn Abī Ṭālib and other members of the Prophet's companions, led to rebellions in Egypt and Iraq in 650 C.E. and to an Egyptian march against ʿUthmān in Medina in 655 C.E. ʿUthmān was attacked in his house and killed while reading the Qurʾān.

Influence. ʿUthmān's death led to a civil war that resulted in the eventual division of the Muslim world into three separate religious sects.

ADDITIONAL RESOURCES
Saunders, J. J. *History of Medieval Islam*. New York: Routledge, 1990.
Von Grunebaum, Gustave E. *Classical Islam: A History, 600-1258*. New York: Barnes & Noble, 1996.

SEE ALSO: ʿAlī ibn Abī Ṭālib; Arabia; Islam; Muḥammad; Qurʾān; ʿUmar ibn al-Khaṭṭāb; Umayyad Dynasty.

—*Thomas J. Sienkewicz*

UXMAL

DATE: flourished between c. 500-c. 900 C.E. and later
LOCALE: Yucatán Peninsula, Mexico
RELATED CIVILIZATION: Maya
SIGNIFICANCE: A major Classic period Maya site noted for its splendid architecture.

Uxmal (ewz-MAHL) is a beautiful but relatively small site found in the northwestern area of Mexico's Yucatán Peninsula. To the north lie the Puuc Hills, which give their name to the city's distinctive architectural style.

This site was occupied as early as pre-Classic times, and some ruins are Middle Classic in origin. The time of flourishing and major construction came during the Late Classic and Terminal Classic phases (600-900 C.E.).

Uxmal's main area is surrounded by a stone wall and contains magnificent edifices built mostly in the Puuc style. Building facades are decorated with elaborate representations of houses, rectangular shapes, and masks of Chac, the rain god. Carved loops, latticework,

The Pyramid of the Magician, Uxmal. (Corbis)

columns, and human and animal figures are also super-imposed. Some of the major buildings include the Pyramid of the Magician, built in five separate stages, and the Nunnery Quadrangle, a large compound whose four sides are multiroom buildings. The most striking and aesthetically pleasing building is the 328-foot-long (100-meter-long) Palace of the Governor, built over a staircase platform and divided into three sections. During the arid season, the Puuc-style buildings blend well with the background of distant hills and blue sky. Architects also varied the height of each structure to create a visually pleasing effect.

ADDITIONAL RESOURCES

Kelly, Joyce. *An Archaeological Guide to Mexico's Yucatan Peninsula.* Norman: Oklahoma University Press, 1993.

Kowalski, Jeff Karl. *The House of the Governor, a Maya Palace at Uxmal.* Norman: Oklahoma University Press, 1987.

SEE ALSO: Chichén Itzá; Maya; Palenque; Tikal.
                                                          —*David A. Crain*

— V —

VĀKĀṬAKA DYNASTY

DATE: third-fifth centuries C.E.
LOCALE: India
RELATED CIVILIZATIONS: India, Greece
SIGNIFICANCE: A prominent dynasty in central India.

The Vākāṭaka (vaw-KAW-tah-kah) Dynasty ruled in the northern Deccan Plateau of India (the present-day state of Maharashtra) between the third and fifth centuries C.E. The Vākāṭakas may have been a result of Greco-Indian liaisons, but they also had matrimonial alliances with the Nāgas, Āndhras, Guptas, and other indigenous groups.

Vindhyaśakti (c. 250-270 C.E.), the founder, is believed to have belonged to the Kilakilā ("leporous" or white) kings, who were Yavanas (Greeks or Kushāns). Initially a feudatory, he extended his influence over much of central India. His son, Pravarasena I (r. from c. 270 C.E.), reached the Narmada in the north by annexing the kingdom of Purika. The main line continued with Rudrasena I (c. 330), his son Pṛthvīṣeṇa I (c. 350), and Pṛthvīṣeṇa's son Rudrasena II (c. 400). Rudrasena II married Prabhāvatī, a daughter of Chandragupta II. She reigned after Rudrasena's early death until her sons became of age. Thus the Gupta influence was strong, and later rulers became Buddhist.

When the Guptas became involved in a war against the Hūṇas, or Huns, they expanded and, in the period of Pravarasena II's son Narendrasena (c. 450-470), spread but eventually came into conflict with the Nalas. During the reign of the last Vākāṭaka, Pṛthvīṣeṇa II (from c. 470 C.E.), Vākāṭaka power was temporarily revived.

The Vākāṭakas liberally patronized sculpture and graphic arts, and they generously endowed Hindu and Buddhist shrines, including Cave XVI at Ajantī. They were among the most glorious of the contemporary dynasties of the Deccan.

ADDITIONAL RESOURCES

Bakker, Hans. *The Vākāṭakas: An Essay in Hindu Iconology.* Groningen, Netherlands: E. Forsten, 1997.

Shastri, Ajay Mitra. *Vākāṭakas: Sources and History.* New Delhi, India: Aryan Books International, 1997.

Thaper, Romila. *A History of India.* Baltimore: Penguin Books, 1966.

Walker, Benjamin. *Hindu World: An Encyclopedic Survey of Hinduism.* London: Allen and Unwin, 1968.

SEE ALSO: Buddhism; Buddhist cave temples; Gupta emperors; Hinduism; Huns; India; Indian temple architecture.

—*Arthur W. Helweg*

VALENS

BORN: c. 328 C.E.; Cibalae, Pannonia
DIED: August 9, 378 C.E.; near Adrianople (later Edirne, Turkey)
RELATED CIVILIZATION: Imperial Rome
MAJOR ROLE/POSITION: Soldier, emperor

Life. An unknown career soldier, Valens (VAY-lehnz) was elevated to the position of Augustus of the Eastern Roman Empire by his brother, the Western Augustus Valentinian I, in March, 364 C.E. His only qualification was his absolute loyalty, and in short order, he had to put down the revolt of Procopius, another imperial candidate, and quiet the Visigoths. However, before he could settle the Visigoth problem, Valens was forced to turn his attention to the revolt of Theodorus in Antioch (winter of 371-372). From 372 to 378 C.E., he worked inconclusively against increasing Persian influence in the Middle East. Meanwhile, in 376 C.E., he granted the Visigoths asylum from the Huns in Roman territory south of the Danube River. Harsh treatment and poor administration caused the Goths to revolt in 378 C.E., and in a pitched battle near Adrianople, they destroyed nearly two-thirds of the Roman force and killed most of its officers, including Valens.

Influence. Valens never enjoyed the trust of the Roman elite, who regarded him as uneducated and boorish. In all, his mediocre career demonstrates the instability of the position of the Roman emperors and the mounting problems tearing down Roman rule.

ADDITIONAL RESOURCES

Cameron, Averil. *The Later Roman Empire:* A.D. *284-430*. Cambridge, Mass.: Harvard University Press, 1993.

Jones, A. H. M. *The Later Roman Empire, 284-602*. Norman: University of Oklahoma Press, 1964. Reprint. Baltimore: Johns Hopkins University Press, 1986.

SEE ALSO: Adrianople, Battle of; Rome, Imperial; Goths, Ostrogoths, Visigoths; Gratian; Huns; Procopius; Theodosius the Great; Valentinian I.

—*Ronald J. Weber*

VALENTINIAN I

ALSO KNOWN AS: Flavius Valentinianus
BORN: 321 C.E.; Cibalae, Pannonia
DIED: November 17, 375 C.E.; Brigetio, Pannonia
RELATED CIVILIZATION: Imperial Rome
MAJOR ROLE/POSITION: Emperor

Life. Valentinian I (val-uhn-TIHN-ee-uhn) served as an army officer under emperors Constantius II, Julian the Apostate, and Jovian. In 364 C.E., army commanders proclaimed him emperor; he assumed control of the Western Empire and named his brother Valens co-emperor in the East. Valentinian was quickly confronted with some major crises. From 366 to 369 C.E., he fought invading Germans on the Rhine frontier and directed military operations against invading Picts and Saxons in Britain. Valentinian also strengthened defenses on the Rhine and Danube frontiers while attempting to prevent further barbarian invasions by means of preemptive attacks on German tribes along both frontiers.

Although a Christian, Valentinian implemented a policy of religious toleration. He sought to improve the economic status of his soldiers by providing them with seeds and farm equipment, which enabled them to work as farmers in their spare time and thereby increase their income. He also attempted to check the power of the senators and great landowners while taking steps to help the empire's lower classes. In 375 C.E., Valentinian became enraged at the insolence of a German delegation, burst a blood vessel, and died.

Influence. Valentinian was an effective military leader and administrator who established a dynasty that ruled the empire until 455 C.E. He is generally considered one of the greatest rulers of the later Roman Empire.

ADDITIONAL RESOURCES

Burns, Thomas S. *Barbarians Within the Gates of Rome: A Study of Roman Military Policy and the Barbarians, c. 375-425* A.D. Bloomington: Indiana University Press, 1994.

Marcellinus, Ammianus. *The Later Roman Empire*. Translated by Walter Hamilton. New York: Penguin Classics, 1986.

SEE ALSO: Angles, Saxons, Jutes; Christianity; Constantius I-III; Germany; Picts; Valens.

—*Thomas I. Crimando*

VALENTINIAN III

ALSO KNOWN AS: Flavius Placidius Valentinianus
BORN: July 4, 419 C.E.; Ravenna, Italy
DIED: March 16, 455 C.E.; Rome
RELATED CIVILIZATIONS: Imperial Rome,
    Byzantine Empire
MAJOR ROLE/POSITION: Western Roman emperor

Life. Valentinian III (val-uhn-TIHN-ee-uhn) was the son of the patrician Constantius III and Galla Placida, daughter of the emperor Theodosius the Great. After a falling out between Galla Placida and her brother Honorius, the Western emperor, Valentinian III and his mother spent a period of exile at the court of the Eastern

Valentinian III. (Hulton Archive)

emperor, Theodosius II. Following Honorius's death, Theodosius II proclaimed Valentinian III as Caesar in 424 C.E. and as Augustus in 425 C.E. for the Western half of the empire. Until Valentinian III reached legal age, Galla Placida controlled the Western court except for Flavius Aetius, the *magister militum* (master of the soldiers). Concerned with Aetius's influence at court, Valentinian III had him murdered in 454 C.E. The following year, two of Valentinian's bodyguards and former supporters of Aetius murdered the emperor.

Influence. Although Valentinian III was a weak and ineffective emperor and the West continued to crumble slowly under his reign, he provided a sense of continuity with past emperors. With his death in 455 C.E., the disintegration of the West rapidly accelerated.

ADDITIONAL RESOURCES

Bury, J. B. *History of the Later Roman Empire: From the Death of Theodosius I to the Death of Justinian.* New York: Dover, 1978.

Jones, A. H. M. *The Later Roman Empire, 284-602.* Norman: University of Oklahoma Press, 1964. Reprint. Baltimore: Johns Hopkins University Press, 1986.

Liebeschuetz, J. H. W. G. *From Diocletian to the Arab Conquest.* Northhampton, England: Variorum, 1990.

SEE ALSO: Constantius I-III; Rome, Imperial; Theodosius the Great; Theodosius II.

—*R. Scott Moore*

VALERIAN

ALSO KNOWN AS: Publius Licinius Valerianus
BORN: date and place unknown
DIED: 260 C.E.; place unknown
RELATED CIVILIZATION: Imperial Rome
MAJOR ROLE/POSITION: Roman emperor

Life. Born to an old aristocratic family, Valerian (vah-LIHR-ee-ehn) was a prominent senator who was consul under Marcus Aurelius Severus Alexander (r. 222-235 C.E.). In 253 C.E., Valerian commanded an army in Raetia while serving the emperor Trebonianus Gallus. Upon Gallus's assassination and the death of Marcus Aemilius Aemilianus, Valerian was hailed by his troops as emperor and marched on Rome. Both Valerian and his adult son, Gallienus, received confirmation as co-emperors from the Roman senate. Valerian supervised the Roman East, while his son ruled the West. This arrangement helped Rome's two-front war against the Sāsānians in the East and the Western Germanic tribes.

In 254 C.E., Valerian successfully campaigned in Asia Minor and in the Black Sea region against incursions of Heruli and Goths. In an attempt to reaffirm traditional Roman religion, the emperor issued a series of edicts against Christianity in 257 and 258 C.E., which forced clergy to perform sacrifices to the state gods and forbade Christians from congregating. Disaster overtook Valerian in 260 C.E. when he was defeated by the Persian king Shāpūr I. During the negotiations, Valerian was taken prisoner and died in captivity.

Influence. Valerian was one of the last senatorial emperors, making way for a new breed of provincial soldier-emperors during the third century C.E. His shared rule with Gallienus paved the way toward further delegation of imperial authority under Diocletian's tetrarchy.

ADDITIONAL RESOURCE
Potter, D. *Prophecy and History in the Crisis of the Roman Empire*. Oxford, England: Oxford University Press, 1990.

SEE ALSO: Christianity; Gallienus; Germany; Goths, Ostrogoths, Visigoths; Persia; Rome, Imperial; Sāsānian Empire; Shāpūr I.

—Byron J. Nakamura

VALERIUS FLACCUS, GAIUS

FLOURISHED: first century C.E.
RELATED CIVILIZATION: Imperial Rome
MAJOR ROLE/POSITION: Poet

Life. Virtually nothing certain is known about Gaius Valerius Flaccus (GAY-uhs vuh-LIHR-ee-uhs FLAK-uhs) except that he was the author of the *Argonautica* (first century C.E.; English translation, 1863), an epic poem on the voyage of Jason and the Argonauts to Colchis in search of the Golden Fleece. It is not certain that he was a *quindecimvir* (member of a college of the Roman priesthood), a claim based mainly on a few lines in the proem to the *Argonautica*. Whether his *Argonautica* was composed during the reign of Domitian and one or two of the other Flavian emperors (Vespasian, Titus) is also difficult to say, but he may have commenced writing it around 80/81 C.E. Valerius is indebted most heavily in his treatment to the *Argonautica* of Apollonius Rhodius and in his style to Vergil. The narrative breaks off midway through the eighth book, in which Jason, who has fled from Colchis with Medea, is contemplating returning her. It is uncertain whether the incomplete state of the *Argonautica* is the result of the second half of this book being lost in transmission or is caused by Valerius's having died before he finished it, which is more likely the case.

Influence. Valerius not only reshaped the famous story of the Argonauts to make it relevant to the contemporary world of the Roman Empire but also explored issues relevant to human society at large, including heroic achievement and human emotions.

ADDITIONAL RESOURCES
Hershkowitz, Debra. *Valerius Flaccus' Argonautica: Abbreviated Voyages in Silver Latin Epic*. Oxford, England: Oxford University Press, 1998.
McGuire, Donald T. *Acts of Silence: Civil War, Tyranny, and Suicide in the Flavian Epics*. New York: Olms-Weidmann, 1997.

SEE ALSO: Apollonius Rhodius; Domitian; Rome, Imperial; Vergil.

—William J. Dominik

VALERIUS MAXIMUS

FLOURISHED: c. 20 C.E.; Rome
RELATED CIVILIZATION: Imperial Rome
MAJOR ROLE/POSITION: Author

Life. Little is known of Valerius Maximus's (vuh-LIHR-ee-uhs MAK-suh-muhs) personal life other than the few facts he mentions in the course of his work. He appears to have been well connected politically. He presents himself, for example, as a friend to the consul of 14 C.E., Sextus Pompeius Magnus. Valerius Maximus published *Fatorum et dictorum memorabilium libri ix* (c. 31 C.E.; *Memorable Deeds and Sayings*, 1888), a collection of some one thousand historical anecdotes in nine books. The anecdotes are arranged by categories of virtue and vice (including religion observed, religion neglected, bravery, and cruelty) and further subdivided within each chapter according to whether the story in question derives from Roman or foreign (usually Greek) history. Valerius dedicates his *Memorable Deeds and Sayings* to the emperor Tiberius, whom he treats throughout his work as a living god. The anecdotes themselves are highly rhetorical and endeavor to encourage personal morality and ethical conduct through the study of historical situations stripped of historical context.

Influence. As a moralist, Valerius was revered throughout the Middle Ages and Renaissance. With the advent of critical approaches to history, Valerius fell into disfavor and neglect, although the 1990's began to see renewed interest in Valerius's work as a helpful guide to ideological currents in Tiberian Rome.

ADDITIONAL RESOURCES

Bloomer, W. Martin. *Valerius Maximus and the Rhetoric of the New Nobility.* Chapel Hill: University of North Carolina Press, 1992.

Shackleton Bailey, D. R., ed. and trans. *Valerius Maximus: Memorable Deeds and Sayings.* 2 vols. Cambridge, Mass.: Harvard University Press, 2000.

Skidmore, Clive J. *Practical Ethics for Roman Gentlemen: The Work of Valerius Maximus.* Exeter, Devon, England: University of Exeter Press, 1996.

SEE ALSO: Rome, Imperial; Tiberius.

—Hans-Friedrich Mueller

VALERIUS PROBUS, MARCUS

BORN: c. 20 C.E.; Berytus (later Beirut, Lebanon)
DIED: c. 105 C.E.; place unknown
RELATED CIVILIZATION: Imperial Rome
MAJOR ROLE/POSITION: Author, grammarian

Life. Marcus Valerius Probus (MAHR-kuhs vuh-LIHR-ee-uhs PROH-buhs) spent his life studying old Latin authors and texts that were not popular in Rome, where he spent at least some of his adult life. Valerius Probus did not establish an official school to study grammar, paleography, and Latin literature, but his reputation as a careful textual scholar was so well known that he acquired a small group of scholars as his students. He was concerned primarily with preserving the accuracy of older Latin texts, particularly the works of Vergil, Horace, and Terence. Many copies of works by these authors had been made, and numerous scribal errors and notations, inaccurate emendations, and misreadings had crept into published versions of well-known texts. Valerius Probus produced more accurate versions of older Latin texts and included various marginal notations to indicate how a disputed phrase was to be read. He worked from the oldest and therefore theoretically most accurate manuscript of a text. He claimed to have produced a copy of the works of Vergil based on an ancient manuscript written by Vergil himself.

Influence. Valerius Probus is best known for his corrected versions of older Latin texts, which were shared with his followers. He also left a few short works on points of Latin grammar.

ADDITIONAL RESOURCES

Reynold, L. D., and N. G. Wilson. *Scribes and Scholars: A Guide to the Transmission of Greek and Latin Literature.* Oxford, England: Clarendon Press, 1984.

Suetonius. *De grammaticis et rhetoribus.* Edited and translated by Robert A. Kaster. New York: Oxford University Press, 1995.

SEE ALSO: Horace; Languages and literature; Rome, Imperial; Terence; Vergil.

—Victoria Erhart

VĀLMĪKI

FLOURISHED: c. 500 B.C.E.
RELATED CIVILIZATION: India
MAJOR ROLE/POSITION: Poet

Life. Vālmīki (vawl-MEE-kee) is a largely legendary figure credited with composing the *Rāmāyaṇa* (c. 500 B.C.E., some material added later; English translation, 1870-1889). He is said to have been a contemporary of its hero Rāma, who—while also a product of legend—may have been drawn from a historical personage who ruled the kingdom of Kośala in Northern India in the sixth century B.C.E. According to legend, Vālmīki was born the son of a forest sage but eventually turned to robbery to support his large family. After an encounter with the sage Narada, however, he abandoned his life of crime for one of meditation. In one fanciful story, he meditated in one position for so long that an anthill covered him; Narada dubbed him Vālmīki, playing on the Sanskrit word for anthill. Vālmīki is said to have become a poet after witnessing a hunter kill a bird with an arrow. He castigated the hunter by uttering a spontaneous *śloka,* or Sanskrit couplet, the form he later expanded in the *Rāmāyaṇa.*

Influence. As the *Rāmāyaṇa* is designated the *adikāvya,* or "first poem," in Hindu tradition, so Vālmīki has earned the title of *adikavi,* or first poet. He is credited with establishing both the metrical structure and narrative form of the classical Hindu epic.

ADDITIONAL RESOURCES
Goldman, Robert P. *The Ramayana of Valmiki: An Epic of Ancient India.* Princeton, N.J.: Princeton University Press, 1984.
Richman, Paula, ed. *Many Ramayanas: The Diversity of a Narrative Tradition in South Asia.* Berkeley: University of California Press, 1991.

SEE ALSO: Hinduism; India; *Rāmāyaṇa.*

—Luke A. Powers

VANDALS

DATE: c. 400-532 C.E.
LOCALE: Gaul, Spain, and North Africa
SIGNIFICANCE: The raids of the Vandals placed stress on the western half of the Roman Empire and contributed to its decline.

The Vandals were a Germanic people originally from the Scandinavian area. They crossed the Rhine River in 406 C.E. and migrated into Gaul. Traveling southward, ravaging the countryside as they went, they entered Spain three years later, in 409 C.E., and settled in the western and southern areas of the Iberian Peninsula with the intention of remaining there permanently. In 429 C.E., under the command of King Gaiseric, the Vandals crossed the Mediterranean into North Africa. Once there, they began to pillage and plunder the area. Other enemies of the Roman Empire, such as the Moors and Donatists, joined in the attacks on Roman-controlled areas in North Africa. The Vandals defeated the Roman forces in North Africa and captured the city of Hippo in 431 C.E. Their successes in North Africa forced the emperor Valentinian III to sign a treaty with the Vandals recognizing their control over Numidia and Mauretania in return for an annual tribute paid to the empire by the Vandals.

Four years later, in 439 C.E., Gaiseric broke the treaty by capturing the city of Carthage. This was a valuable conquest that offered many new resources to the Vandals, including a defensible harbor with naval vessels and a functional shipyard. Following the capture of Carthage, Gaiseric declared himself an independent ruler with no obligation or allegiance owed to Rome. Concerned over future Roman attempts to regain their lost holdings in North Africa, the Vandals created a buffer zone between North Africa and Italy by capturing the nearby islands, such as Sicily, Sardinia, Corsica, and the Balearic Islands. These locations were used as staging points for attacks on Italy and allowed the Vandals to make raids against the empire itself. In 455 C.E., a Vandal fleet was able to capture and loot the city of Rome. Byzantine attempts in 465 C.E. and 470 C.E. to recapture North Africa were unsuccessful, and a peace treaty was signed in 474 C.E. that acknowledged Vandal control over North Africa.

The Vandal kingdom lasted until the reign of the Byzantine emperor Justinian I, who initiated a "reconquest" of lost imperial holdings. During this successful recovery of lost lands conducted by the general Belisarius, Carthage was captured in 533 C.E., and the Vandal kingdom was destroyed. All Vandals taken as prisoners of war were organized into cavalry units and stationed in eastern provinces far from North Africa.

ADDITIONAL RESOURCES
Clover, Frank. *The Late Roman West and the Vandals.* Brookfield, Vt.: Variorum, 1993.
Randers-Pehrson, Justine Davis. *Barbarians and Romans: The Birth Struggle of Europe,* A.D. *400-700.* Norman: University of Oklahoma Press, 1983.
Wolfram, Herwig. *The Roman Empire and Its Germanic Peoples.* Translated by Thomas Dunlap. Berkeley: University of California Press, 1997.

SEE ALSO: Africa, North; Belisarius; Byzantine Empire; Carthage; Donatism; Gauls; Germany; Justinian I; Rome, Imperial; Spain; Valentinian III.

—R. Scott Moore

The Vandals in Italy under Gaiseric. (North Wind Picture Archives)

VARDHAMĀNA

ALSO KNOWN AS: Mahāvīra; Nigantha Nātaputra
BORN: c. 599 B.C.E.; Kṣatriyakuṇḍagrāma, India
DIED: c. 527 B.C.E.; Pārapuri, India
RELATED CIVILIZATION: Upaniṣadic India
MAJOR ROLE/POSITION: Jain ascetic monk

Vardhamāna (vahr-dah-MAW-nah) was born in Kuṇḍapura, Magadha Kingdom, during the reign of King Bimbusara. Together with the Buddha and Gośāla Maskarīputra, he was one of six unorthodox teachers at a time when life and society were in ferment in India. Named Jñātaputra Vardhamāna, he lived as a married householder for thirty years until the deaths of his parents, Siddhārtha and Trishalā. He then distributed his wealth among the poor, renounced the world, and for twelve years wandered about practicing rigorous austerities until he found full enlightenment at age forty-two. Initially, he was a sannyāsi of the ascetic Nirgarantha sect founded by Pārshvanatha, but he added regimens of chastity and nudity. During the next thirty years, he founded an order of Jain ascetics and became known as the Mahāvīra, or "Great Hero." He stressed *ahiṃsā*, or nonviolence, and constantly struggled against Brahman priests, caste, and materialism. At the age of seventy-two, he fasted to death at Pāvā near Patna. Jains consider him the twenty-fourth and final Tirthankara, or "builder of the ford." He stressed freedom from bondage to the material world through nonviolence, truthfulness, detachment, equality, chastity, and asceticism. His genius rested on systematization of Jain philosophy through rejuvenation of doctrines and beliefs to fit the changing times.

Influence. Jainism remained in India and became a driving force in its economic, social, and cultural life for more than twenty-five hundred years.

ADDITIONAL RESOURCES

Stevenson, Margaret. *The Heart of Jainism*. London: Oxford University Press, 1915.

Zimmer, Heinrich. *Philosophies of India*. Delhi, India: Motilal Banarsidass, 1990.

SEE ALSO: Buddha; Gośāla Maskarīputra; India; Jainism.

—*George J. Hoynacki*

VARRO, MARCUS TERENTIUS

ALSO KNOWN AS: Marcus Terentius Varro Reatinus
BORN: 116 B.C.E.; Reate, near Rome
DIED: 27 B.C.E.; Rome
RELATED CIVILIZATION: Republican Rome
MAJOR ROLE/POSITION: Politician and author

Life. Marcus Terentius Varro's (MAHR-kuhs tuh-REHN-shee-uhs VAR-oh) political career took him to the praetorship. He followed the cause of Pompey the Great in the civil war with Julius Caesar. Following the war, Caesar asked him to found the first public library in Rome, but subsequent events intervened to prevent its founding. Proscribed by Marc Antony in 42 B.C.E. but protected by Octavian (later Augustus), he devoted the rest of his life to scholarship.

Varro's literary output was extraordinary and covered a wide-ranging field of interests, including history, rhetoric, language, agriculture, music, philosophy, law, and religion, to name only a few. He was instrumental in developing Menippean satire. Most of his more than seventy compositions are no longer extant; the only complete the work is that on agriculture, *De re rustica*

(36 B.C.E.; *On Agriculture*, 1912). He wrote this work when he was eighty years old as a practical handbook for his wife. Rhetorician Quintilian considered him the "most intelligent man among Romans."

Influence. Varro's work on agriculture influenced all subsequent Roman writers on the subject, and Saint Augustine frequently consulted his work on "The Antiquity of Human and Divine Affairs." His date for the founding of Rome (April 21) became the official birth date, still observed.

ADDITIONAL RESOURCES

Cato and Varro. *On Agriculture*. Cambridge, Mass.: Harvard University Press, 1935.

Varro. *On the Latin Language*. 2 vols. Cambridge, Mass.: Harvard University Press, 1938.

SEE ALSO: Antony, Marc; Augustine, Saint; Augustus; Caesar, Julius; Pompey the Great; Quintilian; Rome, Republican.

—*Robert I. Curtis*

VASUBANDHU

FLOURISHED: fourth or fifth century C.E.
RELATED CIVILIZATIONS: Gupta Dynasty, India
MAJOR ROLE/POSITION: Buddhist philosopher

Life. Vasubandhu (vah-sew-BAHN-dew), Brahman by birth, was a great Buddhist scholar and native of Puruṣapura (Peshāwar), capital of Gandhāra in north-

west India. A leading authority on Sarvāstivāda, the realist school of Theravāda Buddhism, he was persuaded by his brother Asaṅga to espouse Yogācāra, the metaphysical idealist school of Mahāyāna. He served as minister to the Gupta monarch Samudragupta, whose patronage he enjoyed. He lived in various parts of India, most notably in Ayodhyā, where he died at age eighty.

According to his biographer, Paramārtha, Vasubandhu had a distinguished career as abbot of Nālandā with numerous disciples as his followers, the most notable being Diṅāga. He and Asaṅga were allotted the status of bodhisattvas, or potential buddhas, by Mahāyānists.

Vasubandhu's writings earned him great respect in both Buddhist schools. His greatest work, *Abhidharmakośa* (fourth or fifth century C.E.; *The Abhidharmakosa of Vasubandhu*, 1983), is a learned treatise on ethics, psychology, and metaphysics. As the quintessence of all Abhidharma texts and most important compendium of Sarvāstivāda tenets, it is treated as an authoritative work by all Buddhist sects. He also wrote *Paramārthasaptati*, a refutation of Sāṃkhya philosophy; *Vijñāptimatratasiddhi* (fourth or fifth century C.E.; *Vasubandhu's Vijñapti-matrata-siddhi*, 1980), the most important document of Yogāchāra; *Dashabhūmikashastra* (fourth or fifth century C.E.; English translation in *A Buddhist Doctrine of Experience*, 1982), a treatise on rebirth in Yogāchāra; and *Sukhāvativyuhopadesha*, a study of Pure Land philosophy.

Influence. Vasubandhu, the chief expounder of Mahāyāna after philosopher Nāgārjuna, strongly influenced Chinese and Japanese Buddhism. He is considered the twentieth patriarch of twenty-seven listed in Buddhist sources.

ADDITIONAL RESOURCES

Herman, A. L. *An Introduction to Buddhist Thought.* New York: University Press of America, 1983.

Thomas, Edward J. *The History of Buddhist Thought.* London: Routledge and Kegan Paul, 1951.

Vasubandhu. *Seven Works of Vasubandhu.* Translated by Stefan Anacker. Delhi, India: Motilal Banarsidass, 1998.

SEE ALSO: Asaṅga; Buddhism; Gupta emperors.
—*George J. Hoynacki*

VĀTSYĀYANA

ALSO KNOWN AS: Vātsyāyana Mallanāga
FLOURISHED: fifth century C.E.
RELATED CIVILIZATIONS: Gupta Dynasty, India
MAJOR ROLE/POSITION: Physician, logician, commentator

Life. Little is known about the life of Vātsyāyana (vaht-SAYH-yah-nah). He was a physician and commentator on Gautama's Nyāya school of orthodox philosophy. His *Nyāya-bhāṣya* (fifth century C.E.; English translation in *The Nyaya-sutras of Gautama: With the Bhasya of Vatsyayana*, 1912), is the oldest surviving commentary on philosophical Nyāya *sūtras*, which became a basic document of Nyāya interpretation. He is best known for his *Kāmasūtra* (fifth century C.E.; *The Kama Sutra of Vatsyayana*, 1883), a text on eroticism and social conduct in which sexual matters are exhaustively and elaborately explored. Once viewed in the West as a pornographic work, it is a classic example of analyzing and classifying every aspect of human experience in Hindu life. Dedicated to the god of love, Kāma, the work was compiled by Vātsyāyana while he was a religious student at Benares. Modeled on Kauṭilya's *Arthaśāstra* (dates vary, third century B.C.E.-third century C.E.; *Treatise on the Good*, 1961) in form and morals, it stresses sexual activity as a proper goal of life (dharma) for the householder in Indian society. It addresses marriage rites, parental duties in marriage, caste, intermarriage, duties of a devoted wife, images of conjugal love, polygamy, widowhood, remarriage, and forms of love making. It is a sophisticated, urbane, and pedantic classification of sex and love.

Influence. Vātsyāyana's commentaries established the foundation of Nyāya as a major philosophical school preoccupied with logical and epistemological issues. His *Kāmasūtra* shed much light on the sexual mores of ancient India, and nothing has dislodged it from the status it has maintained throughout the centuries.

ADDITIONAL RESOURCES

Gowan, Herbert H. *A History of Indian Literature.* New York: Greenwood Press, 1968.

Keith, Arthur Berriedale. *A History of Sanskrit Literature.* London: Oxford University Press, 1966.

Vatsyayana. *The Complete Kama Sutra: The First Unabridged Modern Translation of the Classic Indian Text by Vatsyayana.* Translated by Alain Daniélou. Rochester, Vt.: Park Street Press, 1994.

SEE ALSO: Hinduism; India; Kauṭilya.
—*George J. Hoynacki*

VAṬṬAGĀMAṆI

ALSO KNOWN AS: Vaṭṭagāmaṇi Abhaya; Valagam Ba
BORN: first century B.C.E.; place unknown
DIED: 77 B.C.E.; place unknown
RELATED CIVILIZATIONS: South Indian Dravidian kingdoms, India, Ceylon
MAJOR ROLE/POSITION: Monarch

Life. The first century B.C.E. was a tumultuous period in Ceylonese history. The reign of Vaṭṭagāmaṇi (vah-tah-GAW-mah-nee) in 103 B.C.E. was plagued by an invasion of south Indian Tamils who attacked Anuradhapura, forced him into exile to the mountains of Malaya in the central highlands, and ruled the country for almost fifteen years. In 89 B.C.E., Vaṭṭagāmaṇi returned, slew the last usurper, and restored Sinhalese rule, ending a chaotic period of banditry, famine, and attacks on Buddhist monasteries and clergy. He established the Abhayagiri Vihāra, made up of liberal monks from the orthodox Mahāvihāra monastery who were receptive to Mahāyāna doctrine. Doctrinal disputes erupted into a schism. Abhayagiri became an important Buddhist religious and political center of power that influenced Ceylonese secular history for twelve centuries until it reunited with Mahāvihāra.

During Vaṭṭagāmaṇi's reign, the Saṅgha (Buddhist community) was concerned that the codified oral tradition of the *Tipiṭaka* (collected c. 250 B.C.E.; English translation in *Buddhist Scriptures*, 1913) was in danger of disappearing. Five hundred monks gathered at the mountain retreat of Aluvihāra near Mātale north of Kandy and recorded the canon in Pāli on palm-leaf manuscript with commentaries in old Sinhalese. In 77 B.C.E., Vaṭṭagāmaṇi died, succeeded by his adopted son Mahaculi Mahatissa who ruled until 63 B.C.E.

Influence. Vaṭṭagāmaṇi's reign was directly responsible for supporting the preservation of the Pāli canon in writing, a landmark religious event in Buddhist history.

ADDITIONAL RESOURCES
The Mahāvamsa: The Great Chronicle of Sri Lanka. Fremont, Calif.: Asian Humanities Press, 1999.
Rahula, Walpola. *History of Buddhism in Ceylon.* Dehiwala, Sri Lanka: Buddhist Cultural Centre, 1993.

SEE ALSO: Buddhism; Sri Lanka.
　　　　　　　　　　　　　　　　—George J. Hoynacki

VEDAS

AUTHORSHIP: Compiled by several generations of Indo-Aryan priests/philosophers
DATE: 1500-1100 B.C.E.
LOCALE: Indian subcontinent
RELATED CIVILIZATION: Indo-Aryan
SIGNIFICANCE: Oldest Indo-European literary and philosophical documents; the *Rigveda* in particular was central to the development of later Indian religious and philosophical thought and practice.

There are four Vedas (VAY-duhs; the Sanskrit term *veda* signifies "wisdom") that deal with aspects of religious thought and customs: the *Rigveda* (also known as *Ṛgveda*, c. 1500-1000 B.C.E.; English translation, 1896-1897), the *Yajurveda* (c. 1500-1100 B.C.E.; *The Texts of the White Yajurveda*, 1899), the *Sāmaveda* (c. 1500-1100 B.C.E.; *Sama Veda of the Jaiminiyas*, 1938), and the *Atharvaveda* (c. 1500-1100 B.C.E.; *The Hymns of*

the Atharva-veda, 1895-1896). Each Veda contains four sections: *Saṃhitā* (hymns, prayers, benedictions), *Brāhmaṇas* (prose commentaries on the importance of the rites and ceremonies of sacrifice), *Āraṇyakas* (concerning forest-meditation retreats), and *Upaniṣads* (philosophical speculations concerning the ultimate questions of existence). The *Yajurveda* (sacrificial formulas) and *Sāmaveda* (melodies) are not important today; the *Atharvaveda* (magic formulas, spells, and incantations) would become important to the development of modern Indian (that is, non-Western, alternative) medical practices.

The *Rigveda* (hymns) remains the most significant document in that it contains the cosmologies (creation myths) of early Indo-European thought, some of the earliest manifestations of religious/philosophical consciousness in human civilization. It is made up of 1,017 hymns divided into ten books. The first and the tenth books contain most of the document's philosophical speculations. As in all primitive cosmologies, there are celebrations of numerous deities related to the occurrence of natural phenomena such as Sūrya (the Sun), Agni (fire), Dyaus (the sky or heaven), Vāyu/Vata (the wind), and Pṛthivī (Earth). Some deities are related to abstract human emotions, such as Śrāddha (faith) or Manyu (anger), and there are also numerous minor spirits and fairies associated with local forests, mountains, and fields.

Despite the polytheistic aspects of the *Rigveda*, the document also describes the monistic idea of *Ṛta*, or the unifying and absolute order (cosmic law/truth) of the universe, which seems to be ascribed to a single deity who has two names (or dimensions): Prajāpati (or the lord of all creation/creatures) and Viśvakarman (or the maker of the world). This idea evidences a tendency away from the primitive polytheism of the earlier village shaman and toward the philosophical monism of a later emerging scholarly priest class, who often voiced a sense of skepticism concerning the existence of a multitude of deities. Such a position presents a harmonized view of the universe that seeks to find a higher metaphysical unity amid the diversity of natural phenomena.

This monistic dimension of the *Rigveda* emerges in later Indian thought as the Vedantic notion of *brahman*, the ultimate nature and source of absolute reality, and the allied concept of *ātman*, or this divine reality as it is manifested in the individual soul.

ADDITIONAL RESOURCES

Frawley, David. *From the River of Heaven: Hindu and Vedic Knowledge for the Modern Age.* Salt Lake City, Utah: Morson, 1990.

King, Richard. *An Introduction to Hindu and Buddhist Thought.* Washington, D.C.: Georgetown University Press, 2000.

Knapp, Stephen. *The Secret Teachings of the Vedas: The Eastern Answers to the Mysteries of Life.* Bombay, India: Jaico Publishing House, 1993.

Ramamurty, A. *The Central Philosophy of the Rig-Veda.* Columbia, Mo.: South Asia Books, 1992.

Swami Prabhavananda. *Vedic Religion and Philosophy.* Los Angeles: Vedanta Press, 1983.

SEE ALSO: *Brāhmaṇas*; Hinduism; India; *Upaniṣads*; Vedism.

—Thomas F. Barry

VEDISM

DATE: c. 1500-c. 400 B.C.E.

LOCALE: India

RELATED CIVILIZATION: Indo-Aryan

SIGNIFICANCE: Vedism is the early manifestation of Hinduism. The basic structure of the religion was established with the emphasis on pilgrimages, a pantheon of gods, and religious literature.

Vedism (VAY-dih-zm), which means knowledge, is the complex of literature and religion that developed in India along with the Indo-European invasions. The basic structure of the later belief systems that evolved into Hinduism, Jainism, and Buddhism developed during this period, as did the organization of the caste system.

Classic Hindu works of literature, especially the Vedas, were first composed during this period. The four Vedas record early Indo-European thought, values, and legend beginning with the *Rigveda* (also known as *Ṛgveda*, c. 1500-1000 B.C.E.; English translation, 1896-1897), which contains poetic narratives of the epic stories of the Indo-European invasion of India. Each of the other Vedas covers a specific area of knowledge. The largely prose *Yajurveda* (c. 1500-1100 B.C.E.; *The Texts of the White Yajurveda*, 1899) is a prayer book that includes prayers and litanies to be used as devotional material. The *Sāmaveda* (c. 1500-1100 B.C.E.; *Sama Veda of the Jaiminiyas*, 1938) is a song book containing chants to be sung with sacrifices. The *Atharvaveda* (c. 1500-1100 B.C.E.; *The Hymns of the Atharva-veda*, 1895-1896) is a book of magical incantations, curses, and spells that may be used to help people deal with their basic daily fears, passions, hatreds or anger, and distress. Therefore, the Vedas include knowledge that ranges from the distant epic struggles in the beginning of time to ritual practices and songs for worship to something as banal as an incantation to protect one's property.

The *Rigveda* invokes the oldest Indo-European gods: Dyaus Pitar (the sky father god), Pṛthivī Matar (the Earth Mother goddess), and Mitra (the god of morality and faith). However, the more dramatic deities are the gods of the natural environment of India, one of whom was Indra (the god of storms), who wielded the mighty thunderbolt. Another nature god was Rudra (the mountain god), who could send destructive storms to the Himalayas, destroying settlements and lives.

Another god from the *Rigveda* who would survive into later Hinduism was Vishnu (Viṣṇu, the Sun or sky god). Agni was the god of fire, either on the earth or in the sky, but he was particularly present in the altar fire. As a cleanser and purifier, Agni removed evil and drove bad spirits away. Other gods included Varuṇa (a sky god), Yama (the god of the dead), and Soma (the god of drink). As the Indo-Europeans became more settled in India, adopting agriculture and living in permanent villages, religion evolved from their war and storm gods to Brahmanism.

The Brahmans were the priests, the religious elite. This next stage in the development of Vedism marks the institutionalization of Hinduism, when the priests rivaled the gods in importance. The Brahmā was the holy or godly power and presence that the priests could invoke and manipulate with their sacrificial rituals. Once they had settled in villages, the people built temples, and full-time priests were named. As priestly rituals became more sophisticated, people believed in the efficacy of the rituals, and the Brahmans became the center of religious life. The religious focus shifted from the other world to this world, and the utterance of prayers and the ritual services increased the importance of the priests.

The caste system was a part of the new Brahmanism, and the Brahmans were the ones who most benefited from it. They taught that the fundamental nature of society as formed by the gods was based on the divisions of the castes with the Brahmans at the top. Obeying the rules of caste behavior became a universal obligation within Hinduism, and people obeyed the rules in the hope that their position in life would be better in the next incarnation.

The literature that defines Brahmanism is called the *Brāhmaṇas*, which were compiled between the eighth and fifth centuries B.C.E. The *Brāhmaṇas* give detailed instruction on how to perform the various kinds of sacrifices in practice at the time, and they are thought to have been texts for teaching candidates for the priesthood. Along with the directions for the rituals are statements of worship and theology. The ultimate reality in the universe, which was greater than the individual gods, was the Brahmā (or *brahman*), the creator principle.

In the writings called the *Upaniṣads*, religious thinkers gradually became more abstract in their understanding of the ultimate spiritual reality. All being, whether it is material or spiritual, is a manifestation and part of the *brahman*. The heavens, earth (including nature), and even hell are of the *brahman*. The *brahman* includes all that is objective, or outside of one, and all that is subjective, including one's soul, innermost self, feelings, and self-consciousness. The soul or inner self is the *ātman*. The combination of the *brahman* (the objective all) and the *ātman* (the subjective or personal being) makes the ultimate reality, which is the *brahman-ātman*. True union with the *brahman* is the ultimate state of being for the person, the mystical experience of entering Nirvana.

Life is perceived as a cycle of reincarnation in which rebirth follows rebirth in what might seem like a continuous circle or wheel. The soul may have a higher or lower status in the next life, depending on the law of karma. "Karma" means deeds or works, and it is the ethical dimension of Hinduism. The law of karma says that the accumulation of one's deeds and thoughts affects the next rebirth. Good deeds gives an individual a higher place in the next life; bad deeds lower the position. *Mokṣa*, which is deliverance from the endless cycle of rebirths, can come through spiritual union with the *brahman* described earlier. As Vedism evolved into classic Hinduism, the gods changed significantly, but most of the religious concepts remained essentially the same.

ADDITIONAL RESOURCES

Embree, Ainslie T. *Sources of Indian Tradition*. 2d ed. New York: Columbia University Press, 1988.

Kinsley, David R. *Hinduism: A Cultural Perspective*. 2d ed. Englewood Cliffs, N.J.: Prentice Hall, 1993.

Noss, David S., and John B. Noss. *A History of the World's Religions*. 9th ed. New York: Macmillan College Publishing, 1994.

Smith, Huston. *The World's Religions: Our Great Wisdom Traditions*. San Francisco: HarperSanFrancisco, 1991.

SEE ALSO: *Brāhmaṇas*; Buddhism; Hinduism; India; Jainism; *Upaniṣads*; Vedas.

—*Ronald J. Duncan*

VEGETIUS RENATUS, FLAVIUS

FLOURISHED: fourth century C.E.
RELATED CIVILIZATION: Imperial Rome
MAJOR ROLE/POSITION: Government official, author

Life. Little is known of the life of Flavius Vegetius Renatus (FLAY-vee-uhs vuh-JEE-shee-uhs re-NAYT-uhs). His writings suggest he belonged to an upper-class Roman-Spanish family. He was certainly a Christian. Vegetius was not a military man but a high-ranking civilian official in the Late Roman Imperial government, perhaps the *comes sacrum largitionum* (finance minister) or *comes sacri stabuli* (count of the imperial stables). He authored two surviving works, *Mulomedicina* (n.d.; the treatment of mules), on veterinary medicine, and the better-known *De re militari* (between 383 and 450 C.E., also known as *Epitoma rei militaris*; *The Foure Bookes of Martiall Policye*, 1572, also translated as *Military Institutions of Vegetius*, 1767). The latter, a proposal for reforming the military through discipline and training—and replacing the barbarian troops the empire had come to rely on—was cloaked as a description of the "ancient" Roman army. It was dedicated to an anonymous emperor, probably Theodosius the Great.

Influence. *Military Institutions of Vegetius* was one of the most widely read books in the West from the early Middle Ages to the seventeenth century. Always a favorite with commanders (such as Richard the Lion-Hearted), Vegetius influenced the military theories of Niccolò Machiavelli (*Dell'arte della guerra*, 1521; *The Art of War*, 1560) and the development of the regiment by Maurice of Nassau (1567-1625).

ADDITIONAL RESOURCE
Milner, N. P. *Vegetius: Epitome of Military Science.* Liverpool, England: Liverpool University Press, 1993.

SEE ALSO: Rome, Imperial; Theodosius the Great.
—*Jonathan P. Roth*

VELLEIUS PATERCULUS, MARCUS

BORN: c. 19 B.C.E.; place unknown
DIED: after 30 C.E.; place unknown
RELATED CIVILIZATION: Imperial Rome
MAJOR ROLE/POSITION: Historian

Life. A soldier, magistrate, and senator, Marcus Velleius Paterculus (MAHR-kuhs vuh-LEE-yuhs puh-TUR-kyuh-luhs) began his career in the ranks of the army of Gaius Julius Caesar, son of Marcus Vipsanius Agrippa, at the turn of the millennium. He subsequently served for nine years in the army of Tiberius, and this association with Augustus's prospective successor proved to be the turning point in Velleius's career. Following Tiberius's ascension to the Roman throne, Velleius joined the ranks of the Roman senate and later began the composition of his *Annales* (c. 29 C.E.; *Compendium of Roman History*, 1924), an outline history of Rome in two books, from its beginnings to 29 C.E. Dedicated to Marcus Vinicius, the consul of 30 C.E., the work was intended for publication in the same year. Despite frequent references to a larger historical project, no other work survives under the name of Velleius Paterculus, who must have died soon after 30 C.E.

Influence. Velleius's summary treatment of Roman history is generally viewed by scholars as reaction to a tradition of voluminous historiography culminating in the 142 books of Livy's project (*Ab urbe condita libri*, c. 26 B.C.E.-15 C.E.; *The History of Rome*, 1600). Conclusions about the brevity of Velleius's work may be exaggerated by the fact that the first of the two volumes (mythological times to the fall of Carthage in 146 B.C.E.) is largely lost. Book 2 (146 B.C.E.-29 C.E.) is virtually complete, and more than two-thirds of the narrative is devoted to the eras of Julius Caesar, Augustus, and Tiberius. Despite accusations of partiality regarding his treatment of Tiberius, Velleius's account of the years between 14 and 29 C.E. should not be treated lightly, since it constitutes one of the very few eyewitness reports of a participant of contemporary events.

ADDITIONAL RESOURCES
Sumner, G. V. "The Truth About Velleius Paterculus: Prolegomena." *HSCP* 74 (1970): 257-297.

Woodman, A. J. "Questions of Date, Genre, and Style in Velleius: Some Literary Answers." *CQ* 25 (1975): 272-306.

_____. *Velleius Paterculus: The Caesarian and Augustan Narrative*. Cambridge, England: Cambridge University Press, 1983.

_____. *Velleius Paterculus: The Tiberian Narrative*. Cambridge, England: Cambridge University Press, 1977.

SEE ALSO: Augustus; Caesar, Julius; Livy; Rome, Imperial; Tiberius.

—*Sophia Papaioannou*

VENDAE

ALSO KNOWN AS: Wends
DATE: c. 400-800 C.E.
LOCALE: Modern northeast Germany, Poland, Czech Republic
RELATED CIVILIZATION: Germany
SIGNIFICANCE: These Slavonic peoples lived during the early Middle Ages in the area between the Elbe and Oder Rivers in what later became Germany.

The term Vendae (or "Wends") is somewhat confusing, having been used during the Middle Ages to refer to several groups, including a number of Germanic tribes, such as the similarly named Vandals. However, the term is properly used to refer to the Slavic groups that migrated west over the Oder River into what later became eastern Germany and parts of the Czech Republic and Poland.

The Vendae never developed the feudal system common to most of Europe at the time. They banded together in several loose confederations during the seventh century C.E. but never developed anything close to a unified state. They were thus easily overwhelmed by the more powerful and unified Germans, Czechs, Poles, and Danes nearby.

The individual Vendae tribes tended to remain independent, and they did not embrace Christianity until it was forced on them by invading Franks in the tenth century C.E. After this time, there were a number of short-lived attempts at rebellion, but they were never close to successful.

By the middle of the eighth century, the Vendae were politically controlled by the Carolingian Dynasty founded by Charlemagne.

ADDITIONAL RESOURCES
Grabois, Aryeh. *The Illustrated Encyclopedia of Medieval Civilization*. New York: Mayflower Books, 1980.
Gwatkin, H. M., et al. *Germany and the Western Empire*. Vol. 3 in *The Cambridge Medieval History*. Cambridge, England: Cambridge University Press, 1964.

SEE ALSO: Christianity; Franks; Germany.

—*Marc Goldstein*

VERCINGETORIX

BORN: c. 75 B.C.E.; central Gaul (later in France)
DIED: c. 46 B.C.E.; Rome
RELATED CIVILIZATIONS: Gaul, Republican Rome
MAJOR ROLE/POSITION: Military leader

Life. Born a prince, Vercingetorix (vur-sehn-JEHT-uh-rihks) was the son of Celtillus of the Arverni. In his youth, he had served in Julius Caesar's army as part of a Gallic goodwill contingent, derived from various regions of Gaul. Soon, however, the Druids, ancient priests of the Celts, called for a revolt. Dissension grew, and Vercingetorix was chosen to lead the rebellion. He organized the vast majority of the tribes of Gaul and Amorica. In 52 B.C.E., the revolt began. Vercingetorix would soon prove to be on par with Julius Caesar as a military strategist. Once, in an effort to cut Roman communication lines, he launched three simultaneous assaults on both pro-Roman Celtic tribes and Caesar's

Vercingetorix surrenders to Caesar. (North Wind Picture Archives)

troops. To weaken Roman resolve through starvation, he implemented a scorched-earth policy in Gaul that left nothing in its wake.

After countless skirmishes, the Romans eventually captured Vercingetorix. At Alesia, with the aid of mercenaries from Germania, Caesar forced Vercingetorix to surrender. He was taken back to Rome in chains, and in about 46 B.C.E., he was beheaded.

Influence. The failed revolt of Vercingetorix signaled the end of Celtic Europe. The Celts, who had prospered since the Iron Age, finally gave way to the combined onslaught of the Germanic tribes and the Romans.

ADDITIONAL RESOURCES

Eluere, Christine. *The Celts: Conquerors of Ancient Europe.* New York: Harry N. Abrams, 1993.

Green, Miranda. *The Celtic World.* New York: Routledge, 1996.

O'Hogain, Daithi. *Celtic Warriors: The Armies of One of the First Great Peoples in Europe.* New York: St. Martin's Press, 1999.

SEE ALSO: Caesar, Julius; Celts; Gauls; Germany; Rome, Republican.

—*Lloyd Michael Lohr*

VERGIL

ALSO KNOWN AS: Publius Vergilius Maro
BORN: October 15, 70 B.C.E.; Andes, Cisalpine Gaul
DIED: September 21, 19 B.C.E.; Brundisium (later Brindisi), Italy
RELATED CIVILIZATIONS: Republican and Imperial Rome, Celts, Greece
MAJOR ROLE/POSITION: Poet

Life. Vergil, the greatest of the Roman poets, sprang from peasant origins. The Roman historian Suetonius reports that his father was either a potter or a day-laborer who married his employer's daughter. Her name, Magia Pollia, contributed to the medieval practice of reading Vergil's works as poems of prophecy.

This peculiar form of bibliomancy, which came to be known as the *sortes Vergilianae*, also accounts for the corrupted form of the poet's name, "Virgil" (from *virga*, "wand"), which so frequently appears in modern texts.

Curiously, Vergil's birth in Cisalpine Gaul implies Celtic ethnicity. He would, therefore, have been considered a Gaul, at least in a legal sense, had Julius Caesar not extended Roman citizenship after Cisalpine Gaul became a province of Rome in 59 B.C.E. Vergil's early education, at Cremona and Mediolanum (Milan), followed the traditional Roman curriculum: rhetoric and literature with basic arithmetic. In his late teens, Vergil went to Rome and continued his studies, which in-

Vergil. (Library of Congress)

cluded philosophy and forensic rhetoric. This would indicate a future in law, though he seems to have spoken only once at court. He was by all indications constitutionally shy, a personality essentially unsuited to the speaking style of Roman lawyers.

Perhaps realizing that law was not a viable option, Vergil studied Alexandrine Greek under Epidius and philosophic Epicureanism under Siro, after which, in his early twenties, he returned to his family farm in Andes. In 41 B.C.E., land confiscations claimed his farm, among many others, for Marc Antony's veterans. Vergil's appeal to the young Octavian, later the emperor known as Augustus, saved his family's land. The poet's gratitude appears as the theme of the first of his ten *Eclogues* (43-47 B.C.E., also known as *Bucolics*; English translation, 1575), pastoral poems that parallel the Greek idylls of Theocritus of Syracuse.

The next phase of Vergil's life places him at Nola and Naples. It is possible that there was a second attempt at confiscation of his family's farm. It is certain, however, that for seven years he wrote his second masterwork the *Georgics* (c. 37-29 B.C.E.; English translation, 1589), four books of verse that chart the course of

the farmer's year in the style of the Greek *Erga kai Emerai* (c. 700 B.C.E.; *Works and Days*, 1618) of Hesiod. The *Eclogues* and *Georgics* brought Vergil into the literary circle of Gaius Maecenas, and this eventually brought him an imperial subvention from Octavian. It was, by general tradition, at the emperor's suggestion that Vergil began the best known of his poems, the twelve-book epic known as the *Aeneid* (c. 29-19 B.C.E.; English translation, 1553). The *Aeneid* parallels Homer's *Odyssey* (c. 800 B.C.E.; English translation, 1616) in its first six books and his *Iliad* (c. 800 B.C.E.; English translation, 1616) in its last six, though it concentrates on the aftermath of the Trojan War and seeks to establish the antiquity of the Roman "race."

Death, the result of a fever, overtook Vergil after a tour of the East, and he died at Brundusium. On his deathbed, Vergil asked that his unrevised *Aeneid* be destroyed; Augustus's intervention rescued the poem, and he commissioned two of Vergil's colleagues, Varius and Tucca, to edit it but to add nothing. It was in this way that Augustus saved one of the noblest epic poems ever written. It appeared in its final state sometime after 17 B.C.E., about two years after Vergil's death.

Influence. Vergil was buried at Naples, and his tomb became, especially in the Middle Ages, a place of superstitious reverence. His poetic works are widely known and read, and his *Aeneid* became one of the best-known epics in the Western world.

ADDITIONAL RESOURCES

Clausen, Wendell Vernon. *A Commentary on Virgil, Eclogues*. New York: Oxford University Press, 1994.

Johnson, William Roger. *Darkness Visible: A Study of Vergil's Aeneid*. Berkeley: University of California Press, 1976.

Martindale, Charles. *Cambridge Companions to Literature*. New York: Cambridge University Press, 1997.

Otis, Brooks. *Virgil: A Study in Civilized Poetry*. Oxford, England: Clarendon Press, 1964.

Williams, R. D. *The Aeneid*. Boston: Allen and Unwin, 1987.

SEE ALSO: Augustus; Rome, Imperial; Rome, Republican; Suetonius; Theocritus of Syracuse; Tibullus, Albius.

—*Robert J. Forman*

VERGINIA

BORN: date and place unknown
DIED: c. 449 B.C.E.; place unknown
RELATED CIVILIZATION: Republican Rome
MAJOR ROLE/POSITION: Legendary heroine, daughter of a Roman noble

Life. One of the best-known female heroines of ancient Rome, Verginia has gained immortality because of her tragic death, which traditionally occurred in 449 B.C.E., sixty years after the foundation of the Roman Republic. Two years earlier, the republican constitution had been suspended and ten commissioners (*decemviri*) had been appointed to codify the laws of Rome. These commissioners, however, refused to relinquish power when their tenure ended a year later. One of them, Appius Claudius Crassus Inregillensis Sabinus, lusted after Verginia, the maiden daughter of a noble officer, and subsequently directed one of his subordinates to claim that she was not freeborn but his own slave, so that he could have her for his own. The news reached Verginia's father, who hurried back to Rome and stabbed his daughter to death in order to save her honor and the honor of his family. The tragedy of Verginia brought to light Appius's machinations and led to a popular uprising and, eventually, to the expulsion of the *decemviri*.

Influence. The details of Verginia's tragedy follow closely the story of Lucretia, the Roman matron, who sixty years earlier had been raped by Sextus Tarquinius, the son of the last Roman king. Both women became the innocent victims of men who abused their political power to satisfy sexual lust, both died under tragic circumstances, and their deaths brought about the institution of a new government. The violation of powerless females became a trope, which interpreted political evolution in Rome in terms of a justified, imperative reaction against a regime no longer observant of the ideals of the community that it supposedly served.

ADDITIONAL RESOURCES

Fantham, E., and H. Foley et al. "Republican Rome I: From Marriage by Capture to Partnership in War—The Proud Women in Early Rome." In *Women in the Classical World*. Oxford, England: Oxford University Press, 1994.
Joshel, S. R. "The Body Female and the Body Politic: Livy's Lucretia and Verginia." In *Pornography and Representation in Greece and Rome*, edited by A. Richlin. Oxford, England: Oxford University Press, 1992.

SEE ALSO: Lucretia; Rome, Republican.

—*Sophia Papaioannou*

VESPASIAN

ALSO KNOWN AS: Titus Flavius Vespasianus
BORN: November 17, 9 C.E.; near Reate (later Rieti, Italy)
DIED: June 23, 79 C.E.; Aquae Cutilae (later Bagni di Paterno, Italy)
RELATED CIVILIZATION: Imperial Rome
MAJOR ROLE/POSITION: Roman emperor

Life. Vespasian's (veh-SPAY-zhee-uhn) family was of Sabine origins and equestrian standing. His older brother Flavius Sabinus was more prominent. After a praetorship, Vespasian commanded Legion II Augusta in the invasion of Britain, 43-47 C.E. He was consul in late 51 C.E. and proconsul of Africa in 62 C.E. Command against the Jewish rebels in 67 C.E. should have culminated his career.

Revolts against Nero (spring, 68 C.E.) led to the tumultuous Year of the Four Emperors. The governors of Egypt and Syria persuaded their armies to declare for Vespasian (July, 69 C.E.). The Danubian legions joined his cause and pushed toward Rome, where fighting in December occasioned the deaths of the city prefect Sabinus and the emperor Vitellius.

Vespasian reorganized several Anatolian provinces, trimmed expenditures, raised taxes, and initiated expansion in Britain and across the upper Rhine and Danube Rivers. Rewarding the region's extensive romanization, he granted Latin rights widely in Spain. In Rome, he built the Temple of Peace and Flavian Amphitheater. His sons Titus and Domitian followed him.

Influence. By posing as a civilian *princeps* and modeling himself on Claudius and Augustus, Ves-

Vespasian. (Library of Congress)

pasian restored the fundamentally civilian Principate. The Roman world enjoyed internal peace until 193 C.E.

ADDITIONAL RESOURCES
Levick, B. M. *Vespasian*. New York: Routledge, 1999.
Millar, F. *The Emperor in the Roman World*. London: Duckworth, 1977.
Nichols, J. "Vespasian and the Partes Vespasianae." *Historia Einzelschriften* 28 (1984).
Wellesley, K. *The Long Year:* A.D. *69*. 2d ed. Bristol, England: Bristol Classical Press, 1989.

SEE ALSO: Britain; Domitian; Four Emperors, Year of the; Nero; Rome, Imperial; Titus.

—*Thomas H. Watkins*

VIETNAM

DATE: beginning in second century B.C.E.
LOCALE: Northeastern part of mainland Southeast Asia, south of China.
SIGNIFICANCE: During the first few centuries of the common era, the Vietnamese came under Chinese cultural influences and reacted against Chinese political domination.

Most historians believe that the Vietnamese originated in the Yangtze Valley of southern China and moved into Vietnam's Red River Delta in prehistoric times. Until domination by the Chinese, the Vietnamese lived under ruling classes known as the Lac lords, who organized extensive irrigation systems.

In 207 B.C.E., as China's Qin Dynasty was collapsing, Chinese General Trieu Da created his own kingdom in the south. Known as Nan Yue (Southern Yue, after a province in China) or Nam Viet in the local language, this kingdom included the lands of the Lac lords and had its capital at Canton. In 111 B.C.E., Nam Viet became a part of the Chinese empire under the Han Dynasty.

With the beginning of the common era, the lands of Vietnam began to be influenced extensively by China. In 9 C.E., a Chinese political official named Wang Mang seized the throne of China. Although the Han Dynasty took power again in 23 C.E., the fourteen years of Wang Mang's rule saw extensive political disorder and opposition to the usurper. Refugees from the north, including many political and intellectual leaders, helped establish Chinese political traditions and Chinese writing in the south.

Despite the growing importance of Chinese civilization in Vietnam, the Lac lords retained a strong sense of their own independence. In 40 C.E., they rose against the Chinese. Led by the legendary Trung sisters, the Vietnamese rebels apparently opposed Chinese methods of tax collection. In 43 C.E., Chinese general Ma Yuan brutally suppressed the rebellion. The Lac ruling class was destroyed, and Vietnam came under direct Chinese rule.

Although they continued to stage periodic revolts against the Chinese, the Vietnamese adopted many northern customs, such as the mandarin, the bureaucracy based on tests in the Chinese literary classics. Confucianism and Daoism, the two religions that emerged in China, became part of Vietnamese civilization. Buddhism, which had spread to China from India, began to find adherents in Vietnam in the second and third centuries C.E. By the fifth century C.E., Chinese-style Māhāyana Buddhism had become one of Vietnam's predominant religions. The Chinese traveler Yijing (635-713 C.E.), who wrote in the seventh century C.E., described the city of Hanoi as a great center of Buddhist learning.

The Vietnamese rebel Ly Bon led a major but unsuccessful revolt against China from 544 to 547 C.E. When the Tang Dynasty came to power in China, in 618 C.E., the Chinese proceeded to crush resistance in Vietnam and to impose Chinese rule and Chinese customs even more forcefully. The Tang renamed the southern lands An Nam, or "the pacified south," and Vietnam was known to most of the world by this name until the twentieth century. Although the Vietnamese won independence from China in the tenth century C.E., Chinese civilization and the long struggle against Chinese domination had done much to shape their nation.

ADDITIONAL RESOURCES
Chapuis, Oscar M. *A History of Vietnam*. Westport, Conn.: Greenwood, 1995.
Taylor, Keith W. *The Birth of Vietnam*. Berkeley: University of California Press, 1991.

SEE ALSO: Buddhism; China; Confucianism; Daoism; Han Dynasty; Tang Dynasty.

—Carl L. Bankston III

VILLANOVAN CULTURE

DATE: 1000-600 B.C.E.
LOCALE: Northwestern Italian peninsula, Tuscany
RELATED CIVILIZATIONS: Prerepublican Rome, Etruscan
SIGNIFICANCE: This precursor to Etruscan and Roman civilization (named after a site called Villanova, in the Po Valley near Bologna) was the predominant culture of peoples inhabiting the northwestern Italian peninsula.

The origins of Villanovan culture are quite controversial, although it is associated with the third migration of Urnfield culture (the tradition of cremating the dead and placing the ashes in urns) into Northern Italy. The invasion theory proposes the movement of Early Iron Age Middle Europeans into the area before the first millennium B.C.E., and the migration theory suggests a movement of peoples from the southern Italian peninsula. The indigenous culture theory proposes the cultural development of native peoples during the Early Iron Age. Archaeological evidence suggests some similarities to Near Eastern and middle European cultures but also shows that some Villanovan sites coexisted in close proximity to other indigenous cultures without the overlap of artistic traditions.

Villanovan culture is characterized by two major artistic periods: Geometric and Orientalizing. The Geometric period (c. 1000-675 B.C.E.) begins the development of the basic native Italic styles, and the Orientalizing period (Early, c. 675-650 B.C.E., and Full, c. 650-600 B.C.E.) shows influences from Greece and the Near East and may have been the result of the migration of artisans (or imports) bringing Eastern artistic traditions to the region.

ADDITIONAL RESOURCES
Barker, Graeme, and Tom Rasmussen. *The Etruscans*. Oxford, England: Blackwell, 1998.
Bonfante, Larissa. *Etruscan Life and Afterlife*. Detroit, Mich.: Wayne State University Press, 1986.
Hencken, Hugh. *Tarquinia and Etruscan Origins*. New York: Frederick A. Praeger, 1968.

SEE ALSO: Etruscans; Neolithic Age Europe.

—David B. Pettinari

VINDOLANDA TABLETS

DATE: late first-early second century C.E.
LOCALE: Britain (Vindolanda)
RELATED CIVILIZATIONS: Britain, Imperial Rome
SIGNIFICANCE: Scarce ink-on-wood documents were found at Vindolanda and include personal and official correspondence from Roman Britain.

In 1973, the first of the documents known as the Vindolanda tablets were found in a third century C.E. fort. Two thin fragments, similar to woodshavings, were found. A closer examination revealed writing in ink on wood, but they deteriorated when exposed to air. In 1974, a few more documents were found, and the following year, more items were uncovered, bringing the total up to 202 (not all the finds contained writing).

Previous discoveries elsewhere in the Roman world were mostly of the stylus type, that is, hollowed-out wood filled with wax and then incised by a stylus. The Vindolanda tablets, like a collection of late fifth century C.E. North African documents (Tablettes Albertini), were written in ink-on-wood. In Switzerland, researchers have found more than four hundred similar documents at another military camp at Vindonissa.

The primary concerns expressed in the Vindolanda tablets are military: strength reports, assignments, manufacture of implements, and the like. There are some letters of military or administrative concern, and a few others detail everyday purchases such as clothing and give the prices for such items.

Influence. The finds demonstrate that strips of wood were used as a writing medium in the western half of the Roman Empire.

ADDITIONAL RESOURCES.
Birley, R. E. *Life and Letters on the Roman Frontier: Vindolanda and Its People.* London: British Museum Press, 1994.
_____. *Vindolanda: A Roman Frontier Post on Hadrian's Wall.* London: Thames and Hudson, 1977.
Bowman, A. K., and I. D. Thomas. *Vindolanda: The Latin Writing Tablets.* London: Society for the Promotion of Roman Studies, 1983.

SEE ALSO: Britain; Rome, Imperial; Writing systems.
—*Martin C. J. Miller*

VIŚĀKHADATTA

FLOURISHED: fourth century C.E. or later; India
RELATED CIVILIZATION: India
MAJOR ROLE/POSITION: Playwright

Life. Little is known of the life of Viśākhadatta (vee-SHAW-kah-dah-tah), nor is it certain when he lived. Possibly he was a contemporary of Chandragupta II (r. c. 380–415 C.E.) and therefore lived during the golden age of classical Sanskrit literature. He might have been attached to the king's court, as he says in the prologue of his surviving work that he was the grandson of a provincial governor. A lost play with Chandragupta II as its hero was apparently composed by Viśākhadatta. Various historians have, however, put his date either a generation earlier or even as late as 800 C.E.

Influence. Only one work by Viśākhadatta survives, the play titled *Mudrārākṣasa* (possibly fourth to eighth century C.E.; *Mudraraksasam*, 1900). As is typical for classic Indian drama, the text is composed in both prose and verse, and in several dialects, both classical Sanskrit

and the middle Indic dialects called Prākrit. Unique in classical Indian drama, *Mudrārākṣasa* centers on political intrigue and rapid action. The play portrays the possibly historical minister Kauṭilya as an effective and powerful, though deceitful, politician. Viśākhadatta's choice of subject and style, though highly attractive to modern readers, did not influence other dramatists in India.

ADDITIONAL RESOURCES
Dimock, Edward C., et al. *The Literatures of India: An Introduction.* Chicago: University of Chicago Press, 1974.
Seth, Chandi. *A Critical Study of the Dramam Mudrarakshasa of Visakhadatta.* Calcutta, India: Aparna Book Distributors, 1998.
Van Buitenen, J. A. B., trans. *Two Plays of Ancient India.* New York: Columbia University Press, 1968.

SEE ALSO: India; Kauṭilya.
—*Burt Thorp*

VITRUVIUS POLLIO, MARCUS

FLOURISHED: first century B.C.E.
RELATED CIVILIZATION: Imperial Rome
MAJOR ROLE/POSITION: Architect, engineer

Life. Marcus Vitruvius Pollio (MAHR-kuhs vuh-TREW-vee-uhs PAHL-ee-oh) was a skilled architect and military engineer who served under the emperor Augustus. Among the few buildings known to be by Vitruvius are the basilica at Fanum Fortunae. Vitruvius is best known for his treatise on architecture, *De architectura* (after 27 B.C.E.; *On Architecture*, 1914), which appears to be a compilation of earlier Greek treatises on architecture and engineering, combined with Vitruvius's own observations on the topics. The treatise is valuable in that it records important buildings from the early Imperial period and explains contemporary construction practices along with their strengths and weaknesses. Vitruvius often relates engineering and construction to philosophy and science, stating that one must be well versed in many areas to truly understand architecture. The encyclopedic text is divided into ten books covering subjects as diverse as town planning, the training of architects, building materials, temples and orders, civic and domestic buildings, pavement and plaster work, water supplies, measure and proportion, and military and civil engineering.

Influence. With a keen sense of history, Vitruvius recorded many aspects of ancient architecture, engineering, science, and philosophy that would otherwise be lost. His treatise served as the basis of much of Renaissance architecture and continues to be useful as a window into the ancient world.

ADDITIONAL RESOURCES

Kruft, Hanno-Walter. *A History of Architectural Theory: From Vitruvius to the Present.* New York: Princeton Architectural Press, 1994.

Vitruvius. *Vitruvius: Ten Books of Architecture.* Translated by Ingrid D. Rowland. Cambridge, England: Cambridge University Press, 1999.

SEE ALSO: Art and architecture; Rome, Imperial.

—Sonia Sorrell

— W —

WALLIA

ALSO KNOWN AS: Walya; Vallia
DATE: reigned 415-418 C.E.
RELATED CIVILIZATION: Visigoths
MAJOR ROLE/POSITION: King of the Visigoths

Life. Ataulphus, Wallia's predecessor, had married Galla Placidia, the daughter of the Roman emperor Theodosius. When Wallia was proclaimed king in 415 C.E., he attempted a crossing to Africa, but his transports were wrecked in a storm. In desperation, he concluded a treaty with the Roman general (later emperor) Constantius III for grain in exchange for Galla Placidia and military service to the empire. She was exchanged for 600,000 measures of corn, and Constantius eventually married her.

Wallia thus became an ally of the empire and determined to rid Spain of other barbarian tribes. The campaigns of the Visigoths from 416 and 418 C.E. almost completely destroyed the the Siling Vandals and Alani. In 417 C.E., Wallia sent two captive Vandal kings to the emperor Honorius. However, the Roman Empire was alarmed at the apparent ease with which Wallia des-patched his fellow barbarians and in 418 C.E. ordered him into Gaul, where the Visigoths were offered land in Aquitania. Wallia was pleased with this and marched with his people into their new homeland in 418 C.E. He died soon after.

Influence. Wallia destroyed the Siling Vandals and Alani in Spain and moved his people into Gaul, where the Visigothic capital was established at Toulouse.

ADDITIONAL RESOURCES

Blockley, R. C. *The Fragmentary Classicising Historians of the Later Roman Empire.* Liverpool, England: Francis Cairns, 1981.
Heather, P. J. *Goths and Romans, 332-489.* New York: Oxford University Press, 1991.
Wolfram, Herwig. *History of the Goths.* Berkeley: University of California Press, 1988.

SEE ALSO: Alani; Byzantine Empire; Constantius I-III; Goths; Theodosius the Great; Vandals.

—*Brian Hancock*

WANG BI

ALSO KNOWN AS: *Wade-Giles* Wang Pi
BORN: 226 C.E.; Jiaozuo, Henan, China
DIED: 249 C.E.; China
RELATED CIVILIZATION: Early China
MAJOR ROLE/POSITION: Philosopher

Life. Wang Bi (wahng BEE) was an eloquent child prodigy and a member of the state council of the kingdom of Wei (220-265 C.E.). He surpassed all his contemporaries in debates about Confucianism and Daoism. His era saw a tapering of the influence of classical Confucianism, which induced an uninhibited individuality that all writers endeavored to cultivate. Wang Bi, along with metaphysicians He Yan (d. 249 C.E.) and Xiao Houxun (209-254 C.E.), began to infuse Daoism into Confucianism to modify the latter. To Wang Bi, Confucianism focuses on all beings while Daoism focuses on an original creative nonbeing. In his *Laozi Zhu* (third century C.E.; English translation in *A Translation of Lao Tzu's Tao Te Ching and Wang Pi's Commentary*, 1977), a commentary on Laozi's *Dao De Jing*, Wang Bi remarks that all beings show patterns; these patterns may be reduced to one, which in turn comes from nonbeing. In this way, he colored the Dao with deism and argued in favor of the feudal ethical code of his age. He revised his early interpretation on Daoism in his *Zhouyi Zhu* (third century C.E.; partial translation in *The Classic of Changes: A New Translation of the I Ching as Interpreted by Wang Bi*, 1994), a commentary on the *Yijing* (eighth to third century B.C.E.; English translation, 1876; also known as *Book of Changes*, 1986), in which he adopted Daoist nomenclature and concepts and claimed that it was from that one pattern or principle that all things in the universe are derived. Wang Bi died in his early twenties.

Influence. Wang Bi's philosophy offset the influence of the long-established vogue of overelaborating Confucianism, emphasized philosophic reasoning, and initiated a tradition of intellectual discussion by the aristocracy on nonmundane matters.

ADDITIONAL RESOURCES

Perkins, Dorothy. *Encyclopedia of China: The Essential Reference to China, Its History and Culture.* New York: Roundtable, 1999.

Wagner, Rudolf G. *The Craft of a Chinese Commentator: Wang Bi on the Laozi.* Albany: State University of New York Press, 2000.

SEE ALSO: China; Confucianism; Daoism; *Han Feizi*; He Yan; Laozi; Three Kingdoms; *Wujing*.

—*Charles Xingzhong Li*

WANG CHONG

ALSO KNOWN AS: *Wade-Giles* Wang Ch'ung; Wang Zhongren (*Wade-Giles* Wang Chung-jen)
BORN: 27 C.E.; Shangyu, Kuaiji, China
DIED: 97 C.E.; Shangyu, Kuaiji, China
RELATED CIVILIZATION: Eastern Han Dynasty
MAJOR ROLE/POSITION: Philosopher

Life. Born into an impoverished noble family, Wang Chong (wahng CHUNG) was temperate and courteous. An outstanding student, he entered the Imperial College in the capital city of Luoyang. He lacked the money to buy books, so he often visited roadside bookstalls, where he would stand and read for long periods. Wang Chong held some petty official posts; however, none lasted long. He returned to his hometown to earn his livelihood by teaching. There, he finished his great philosophical work *Lun heng* (85 C.E.; *On Balance*, 1907-1911).

In his writings, Wang Chong demonstrated the monism of *qi* (air) and refuted philosopher Dong Zhongshu's theory that human acts cause natural events such as weather conditions. A Confucian, he attacked the contemporary version of Confucianism and rejected sages who claimed to be omniscient. A rationalist, he negated the prevailing beliefs about deities and ghosts using facts, which, along with experimental proof, he insisted must back any theory.

Influence. Wang Chong's philosophy was in opposition to contemporary thought. Unlike his contemporaries, who idealized the past, he held that the present was superior to the past. His philosophy never became extremely popular, although its value was affirmed after the spread of Marxism in China in the twentieth century.

ADDITIONAL RESOURCES

Chan, Wing-tsit, ed. and trans. *A Sourcebook in Chinese Philosophy.* Princeton, N.J.: Princeton University Press, 1963.

Fung, Yu-lan. *A Short History of Chinese Philosophy.* New York: Free Press, 1997.

SEE ALSO: China; Confucianism; Han Dynasty; Philosophy.

—*Lihua Liu*

WANG XIZHI

ALSO KNOWN AS: *Wade-Giles* Wang Hsi-chih; Yishao
BORN: c. 307 C.E.; Linxi, Shandong Province, China
DIED: c. 379 C.E.; near Shanyin, Zhejiang Province, China
RELATED CIVILIZATION: Early China
MAJOR ROLE/POSITION: Imperial officer, calligrapher

Life. Wang Xizhi (wahng SHEE-jee) was from a family of aristocrats and scholars. He was a court secretary of the Eastern Jin Dynasty (317-420 C.E.), general of Ningyuan prefecture, governor of Jingzhou, a general, and a civil administrator of Guiji in Zhejiang until he retired. He then maintained close contact with the literary scholars of his time.

Wang Xizhi learned calligraphy initially from Wei Shuo, a noted woman calligrapher, and further developed his skills by imitating the work of distinguished calligraphers of the past, such as Zhangzhi's (d. c. 192 C.E.) *caoshu* (cursive script) and Zhongyao's (151-230 C.E.) *kaishu* (standard characters). His calligraphy integrated styles of all schools into his own, showing a mighty, majestic appearance, limitless changes, and round and smooth motions. He was superb in all script styles, but especially so in *kaishu* and *xingshu* (running script). Most of his original works have not survived; only copies exist. These include his running script renderings of *Lanting Xu* (after 353 C.E.; preface to poems made at the Orchard Pavilion) and *Kong Shizhong* (n.d.; Kong the imperial attendant), and his cursive script rendering of *Shiqi Tie* (n.d.; seventeen models) and *Chuyue* (n.d.; the crescent Moon). His son, Wang Xianzhi (344-386 C.E.), was an equally accomplished calligrapher, and together they are known as the "two Wangs."

Influence. Wang Xizhi has been regarded as the sage of calligraphy and much admired in later dynasties and in modern China.

ADDITIONAL RESOURCES

Chang, L. L., et al. *Four Thousand Years of Chinese Calligraphy*. Chicago: University of Chicago Press, 1990.

Lai, T. C. *Chinese Calligraphy*. Seattle: University of Washington Press, 1973.

SEE ALSO: China.

—*Charles Xingzhong Li*

WAWAT

ALSO KNOWN AS: Lower Nubia
DATE: 2500–2300 B.C.E.
LOCALE: Nubian region of the Nile River, southern Egypt, northern Sudan
RELATED CIVILIZATION: Pharaonic Egypt
SIGNIFICANCE: Wawat was a center of population in the region south of Egypt.

An account from the tomb of Harkhuf (a Sixth Dynasty governor) mentions distinct regions of Lower Nubia, the land between the First and Second Cataracts of the Nile River. The most important of these regions were named Wawat (wah-WAHT), Irjet, and Satju. Wawat was a chiefdom north of Irjet in the area between Gerf Husein and Quarta. The Egyptians eventually gave the name of Wawat to all of Lower Nubia. Wawat, at first a trading partner with Egypt supplying cattle, minerals, copper, and gold, was later a source of exploitation.

Archaeological evidence reveals that the people of Lower Nubia (Wawat) and Upper Nubia (Kush), although related, were distinct. This evidence also suggests that the inhabitants of Wawat were generally peaceful while the people of Kush were warriors, often recruited into the armies of the Egyptian Empire. This combined group of herdsmen and soldiers resisted Egyptian domination until the reigns of Twelfth Dynasty Kings Senusret I and Senusret III. They were eventually assimilated into Egyptian culture, with all territory as far south as Semna annexed by Egypt.

ADDITIONAL RESOURCES

Emery, Walter B. *Lost Land Emerging*. New York: Charles Scribner's Sons, 1967.

O'Connor, David. *Ancient Nubia: Egypt's Rival in Africa*. Philadelphia: University Museum, University of Pennsylvania, 1993.

Taylor, John. *Egypt and Nubia*. London: British Museum Press, 1991.

Trigger, Bruce G. *History and Settlement in Lower Nubia*. New Haven, Conn.: Yale University Press, 1965.

SEE ALSO: Egypt, Pharaonic; Harkhuf; Nubia.

—*Craig E. Lloyd*

WEIYANG PALACE

DATE: c. 206-200 B.C.E.
LOCALE: Five miles northwest of Xi'an
RELATED CIVILIZATIONS: Western Han, China
SIGNIFICANCE: This structure exhibits the civil engineering abilities of the early Han Chinese and provides valuable evidence for studying the culture of that period.

Weiyang (way-YANG) palace, completed in 200 B.C.E., was a building complex situated in the southwest part of Chang'an, the capital of Western Han (206 B.C.E.-23 C.E.) and of nine subsequent dynasties: Xinmong, Western Jin, Early Zhao, Early Qin, Later Qin, Western Wei, Northern Zhou, Sui, and Tang. *Sanfu Huangtu* (c. 380-580 C.E.; maps of imperial palaces in mid-Shanxi) and archaeological discoveries during 1980-1983 and 1986-1987 show that the palace was built on the north slope of Mount Longshouyuan, surrounded by walls with four gates on each side with a circumference of 8.7 miles (14 kilometers). The palace had more than forty halls and pavilions, including the audience hall, where the emperor summoned his subordinates, halls for decree announcement, imperial ladies, weaving and dyeing, and water storage, and halls that functioned as an armory and a granary. The halls were connected to emergency passages. The audience hall, 38 feet (11.6 meters) high, 164 feet (50 meters) wide, and 547 feet (166.7 meters) long, was a terraced three-story building sitting on a mound, most likely with three flights and a central ramp leading to the top story. Its foundation, 656 feet (200 meters) long, 328 feet (100 meters) wide, and 38 feet (11.6 meters) high at its very north end, supported by sizable columns, remains in Majiazhai village. Excavated items include ancient building material, earthen ware, jade ware, bronze ware, iron ware, coins, and writing carved on pieces of bones, most of which are 2.8 inches (7.1 centimeters) long, 1.3 inches (3.3 centimeters) wide, and 0.18 inch (0.5 centimeter) thick.

ADDITIONAL RESOURCES

Ru Tighua and Peng Hualiang. *Ancient Chinese Architecture: Palace Architecture*. New York: Springer, 1998.

Scarpari, Maurizio. *Splendours of Ancient China*. London: Thames and Hudson, 2000.

SEE ALSO: China; Han Dynasty.

—*Charles Xingzhong Li*

WENDI

ALSO KNOWN AS: *Wade-Giles* Wen-ti; Yangjian (*Wade-Giles* Yang Chien)
BORN: 541 C.E.; China
DIED: 604 C.E.; China
RELATED CIVILIZATION: China
MAJOR ROLE/POSITION: Statesman

Life. Wendi (wehn-dee; his posthumous reign title) was descended from an aristocratic family that had long served the northern rulers during the period of division after the fall of the Han Dynasty in 220 C.E. His daughter married the heir of the Northern Zhou, and in 581 C.E., as Yangjian, the regent, he usurped the throne. He unified China for the first time in three centuries by defeating the southern state of Chen. Private armies were disbanded and the Great Wall was rebuilt. Chinese authority in Vietnam was increased, and the northern frontier tribes of the Tujue were neutralized, thereby creating an empire as great as that of the Han.

Claiming the mandate of heaven, the emperors' traditional justification to rule, Wendi established the Sui Dynasty. A Buddhist, he hoped to use Buddhism to unify the Chinese, but he also supported the traditional Confucian virtues. He built a new capital, linking it to the Yellow River by canal. Southerners were included in the bureaucracy, and the Han examination system for entry into government service was restored. Legal and tax reforms were also instituted. After his death in 604 C.E., it was rumored that he was murdered by his son and heir, Yang Di.

Influence. The Sui Dynasty ended shortly after Yang Di's death in 618 C.E., but Wendi's substantial accomplishments paved the way for the establishment of the more enduring Tang Dynasty.

ADDITIONAL RESOURCES
Paludan, Ann. *Chronicle of the Chinese Emperors.*
New York: Thames and Hudson, 1998.
Wright, Arthur F. *The Sui Dynasty.* New York: Knopf,
1978.

SEE ALSO: Buddhism; Confucianism; Han Dynasty;
Sui Dynasty; Tang Dynasty; Yang Di.

—*Eugene Larson*

WU HOU

ALSO KNOWN AS: née Wu Zhou (*Wade-Giles* Wu
Chao); Wu Zetian (*Wade-Giles* Wu Tse-t'ien)
BORN: 625 C.E.; place unknown
DIED: 705 C.E.; place unknown
RELATED CIVILIZATION: China
MAJOR ROLE/POSITION: Political leader

Life. Wu Hou (wew hoh), who was known for her
strong and able rule, governed China from about 660 to
705 C.E. She first entered the palace as a concubine of
Taizong of the Tang Dynasty. When the emperor died in
649 C.E., Wu entered a Buddhist convent. However, the
intelligent and beautiful woman did not wish to spend
the rest of her life there. In 650 C.E., she returned to the
palace and won the affection of Gaozong, becoming his
concubine and eventually his empress. After the death
of Gaozong in 683 C.E., Wu Hou installed two of her
sons as successive emperors. She ruthlessly used secret
police and informers to suppress conspiracies against
her. In 690 C.E., she claimed the throne for herself,
changed the name of the dynasty to Zhou, and introduced new titles for her officials.

Empress Wu restrained the great military aristocratic families and replaced them with professional bureaucrats. Under her rule, the civil service examination
system was fully organized as the basis for selection of
officials. In 705 C.E., in declining health, she was forced

to abdicate her power. She died a few months later. Her
monumental tomb, near modern Xian, testifies to the
extraordinary part that this empress played in Chinese
history.

Influence. Wu Hou was able to strengthen her authority through the support of Buddhist monks, some
scholars, and the common people. She understood the
art of government politics. Although she used her two
sons to retain power for herself, she did not seek to
place her family (Zhou) in the imperial line of succession. Over the years, many political leaders have imitated her.

ADDITIONAL REFERENCES
Brandaver, Frederick Paul, and Chün-chief Huang, eds.
*Imperial Rulership and Cultural Change in Tradi-
tional China.* Seattle: University of Washington
Press, 1994.
Fitzgerald, Charles P. *Empress Wu.* Melbourne: Austra-
lian National University, 1955.
Lin, Yutang. *Lady Wu: A True Story.* London: Heine-
mann. 1957.

SEE ALSO: China; Taizong; Tang Dynasty; Zhou Dynasty.

—*Carol C. Fan*

WUDI

ALSO KNOWN AS: *Wade-Giles* Wu-ti
BORN: 156 B.C.E.; place unknown
DIED: 87 B.C.E.; China
RELATED CIVILIZATIONS: Han Dynasty, China
MAJOR ROLE/POSITION: Emperor

Life. Wudi (wew-DEE), the fifth emperor of the Han
Dynasty (206 B.C.E.-220 C.E.), was the longest-ruling

emperor of China (r. 140-87 B.C.E.) until the eighteenth
century. Under him, Han China attained its apogee of
power and prestige.

Domestically, he expanded the central government's
authority. He curbed the power of the nobles by abolishing primogeniture among them and thus subdividing
their estates, impoverishing them through exactions of
lavish gifts, and abolishing their fiefdoms on many pre-

texts. He lessened merchant wealth and power by establishing state monopolies on essential items such as iron, salt, and liquor and curtailed the wealthy through reforms on lending laws, the establishment of state-controlled granaries, and other measures. He established Confucianism as the state ideology, founded a state university in the capital Chang'an (modern Xi'an), and began the concept of meritocracy in the recruitment of civil servants through a system of recommendations and confirmatory examinations. This later became the basis of a fully developed three-tier examination system based on Confucian texts.

Militarily, he launched several important campaigns that brought southern China (Fujian and Guangdong Provinces), the southwest (Yunnan and Guizhou Provinces), northern Vietnam, and north Korea into the Chinese empire. Although Korea and Vietnam would centuries later become separate states, they would retain their Chinese cultural heritage.

Most significant, he reversed the previous policy of appeasement of the nomadic Xiongnu along the northern and northwestern frontiers. In an eighteen-year-long campaign starting in 133 B.C.E., Han armies cleared them from the Ordos region (land along the northern bend of the Yellow River), Inner Mongolia, the Gansu corridor, and Chinese Turkestan. Han armies then crossed the Pamirs into present-day Russian Turkestan as far as Fergana, obtaining the fabled "blood-sweating horses" vital to the cavalry. His successors finally ended Xiongnu power by breaking up their tribal unity and securing the submission of the southern Xiongnu and expelling the northern Xiongnu westward into Europe.

Many small states in central Asia submitted to China, paying tribute; the rulers also sent their sons to the Han capital of Chang'an as hostages and to receive a Chinese education. The military-diplomatic arrangement, called the tributary system, became the basis of the Chinese world order. The Great Wall was extended westward; Chinese military colonists and Han protector-generals ensured peace. Han victories secured the Pax Sinica (Chinese peace) in eastern and Central Asia and opened the Silk Road, which extended to India, Persia, and the Roman Empire, ensuring extensive trade and cultural contacts.

Influence. Wudi's long reign was the high-water mark of cultural flowering. Sima Qian, the father of Chinese historical writing, Sima Xiangru, the noted Han poet, and Dong Zhongshu, the influential Han philosopher who interpreted Confucian ideology, all worked during Emperor Wudi's reign

ADDITIONAL RESOURCES

Ch'u, T'ung-tsu. *Han Social Structure*. Edited by Jack L. Dull. Seattle: University of Washington Press, 1972.

Dubs, Homer H., trans. *History of the Former Han Dynasty*. 3 vols. Baltimore: Waverly Press, 1938-1955.

Pirazzoli-t'Serstevens, Michele. *The Han Dynasty*. Translated by Janet Seligman. New York: Rizzoli, 1982.

Yu, Ying-Shih. *Trade and Expansion in Han China: A Study in the Structure of Sino-Barbarian Economic Relations*. Berkeley: University of California Press, 1967.

SEE ALSO: China; Confucianism; Dong Zhongshu; Han Dynasty; Sima Qian; Sima Xiangru; Xiongnu.

—Jiu-Hwa Lo Upshur

WUJING

ALSO KNOWN AS: Wade-Giles *Wu Ching*; Five Classics
DATE: 500-400 B.C.E.?
LOCALE: China
RELATED CIVILIZATIONS: Zhou and Han Dynasties, China
SIGNIFICANCE: Traditionally associated with Confucius, the *Wujing* form the basis of the classical Confucian texts and have had unequaled influence on Chinese life and education.

The five texts of the *Wujing* (WEW-jihng), the cornerstone of the Confucian classics, are so named because scholars after Confucius attributed to him a personal role in their editing, compilation, and transmission. Although this claim is dubious, the importance of the texts is undiminished. After the burning of the books by emperor Shi Huangdi in 213 B.C.E., Han scholars faced immense problems in their efforts to restore the classics. Confucius, who had come into power during the early Han Dynasty, is said to have reworked these texts, mak-

ing it impossible to discern the degree that some originals had been modified. Modern research can offer only
speculations about the original authors.

The *Wujing* are written in formal classic style characterized by such extreme brevity and exactness that
every character must be weighed to discern the meaning. Single characters are capable of giving a wide variety of connotations. They cannot be understood without the use of commentaries more lengthy than the texts
themselves, and they contain countless references and
allusions made clear only after years of tedious research.

The *Yijing* (eighth to third century B.C.E.; English
translation, 1876; also known as *Book of Changes*,
1986), possibly the oldest of the Five Classics, was first
used in divination. It referred to a theory of the universe
involving humans and nature in a system of the two cosmic forces, yin and yang. If properly understood and interpreted, the sixty-four hexagrams and eight trigrams
are believed to contain profound meanings applicable
to daily life.

Other classics include the *Shijing* (traditionally fifth
century B.C.E.; *The Book of Songs*, 1937), which contains 305 poems from antiquity that were used as a
model for later writers; the *Liji* (compiled first century
B.C.E.; *The Liki*, 1885; commonly known as *Classic of
Rituals*), a miscellany of texts that treat ceremonies and
rituals; the *Shujing* (compiled after first century B.C.E.;
English translation in *The Chinese Classics*, Vol. 5,
Parts 1 and 2, 1872; commonly known as *Classic of
History*), a collection of ancient records said to have
been selected and compiled by Confucius concerning
principles of statecraft and ethics; and the *Chunqiu*
(fifth century B.C.E.; *The Ch'un Ts'ew with the Tso
Chuen*, 1872; commonly known as *Spring and Autumn
Annals*), a record of events occurring in the state of Lu
during 722-464 B.C.E. and accompanied by traditional
commentaries.

In 136 B.C.E., the Han ruler Wudi declared Confucianism to be the state ideology of China and established doctoral chairs at the national university for the
teaching of the *Wujing*. Later on, the Confucian classics
became the core curriculum of Chinese education regarding moral standards, proper conduct, and instruction in government, law, literary composition, and religion. The *Wujing* has regulated Chinese life for two
thousand years.

ADDITIONAL RESOURCES

Confucius. *The Essential Confucius*. Translated by
Thomas Cleary. London: Book Sales Incorporated,
1998.

_____. *Shih-Ching: The Classic Anthology Defined
by Confucius*. Translated by Ezra Pound. Cambridge, Mass.: Harvard University Press, 1954.

Levy, Andre. *Chinese Literature: Ancient and Classical*. Translated by William H. Nienhauser. Bloomington: Indiana University Press, 2000.

Wu, Wei. *I Ching Wisdom: Guidance from the Book
of Changes*. Edited by Les Boston. Los Angeles:
Power Press, 1994.

SEE ALSO: *Chunqiu*; Confucianism; Confucius; Han
Dynasty; Shi Huangdi; Wudi.

—Mary Hurd

— X —

XENOPHANES

BORN: c. 570 B.C.E.; Colophon, Asia Minor
DIED: c. 478 B.C.E.; Magna Graecia, southern Italy
RELATED CIVILIZATION: Archaic Greece
MAJOR ROLE/POSITION: Poet, theologian, Natural philosopher

Life. Xenophanes (zih-NAHF-uh-neez), a son of Dexius (Orthomenus), lived an extraordinarily long life, reaching the age of ninety-two. He was driven to Sicily by the Persian invasion of Colophon in 545 B.C.E. and spent the rest of his life traveling around the Greek colonies of Zancle (Messina), Catana (Catania), Elea (Velia), and Syracuse. He condemned the luxury and degeneration of his contemporaries in the *silloi*, the first ancient Greek collection of satirical verses. Traditionally, he is said to have written epic poems dedicated to Colophon and Elea, and the poem "On Nature" (fragment, published in English in 1898), which presents his philosophical views on nature: All things come from earth and water, and water is the primary constituent of the Sun, clouds, winds, and rivers.

Influence. Rejecting the conventional beliefs of Homer and Hesiod that gods resemble men in body and character, Xenophanes proclaimed that there is one supreme divine being governing the universe with "the shaking of his thought." Distinguishing true knowledge from speculative opinion, he foreshadowed Parmenides' monism and the theory of knowledge of Plato, Aristotle, the Stoics, and the Skeptics.

ADDITIONAL RESOURCES

Guthrie, W. K. C. *A History of Greek Philosophy.* 6 vols. New York: Cambridge University Press, 1978-1990.

Kirk, G. S., J. E. Raven, and M. Schofield. *The Presocratic Philosophers.* 2d ed. Cambridge, England: Cambridge University Press, 1995.

Lesher, J. H. *Xenophanes of Colophon.* Toronto: University of Toronto Press, 1992.

Long, A. A. *The Cambridge Companion to Early Greek Philosophy.* Cambridge, England: Cambridge University Press, 1999.

SEE ALSO: Greece, Archaic; Hesiod; Homer; Languages and literature; Philosophy.

—*Svetla Slaveva-Griffin*

XENOPHON

BORN: c. 431 B.C.E.; near Athens
DIED: c. 354 B.C.E.; probably Corinth or Athens, Greece
RELATED CIVILIZATIONS: Classical Greece, Persia
MAJOR ROLE/POSITION: Historian

Life. Little is known about Xenophon's (ZEHN-uh-fuhn) early life, except that he was a member of Socrates' circle. In 401 B.C.E., he joined a revolt against the Persian king and led the Greek forces home afterward. He then served with the Spartan king Agesilaus II against the Persians in Asia Minor. Banished from Athens, Xenophon returned to Sparta with Agesilaus, who rewarded him for his service with a large estate at Scillus in the Peloponnese, where he remained until the Spartan defeat at Leuctra in 371 B.C.E. He spent the rest of his life at Corinth.

At Scillus, Xenophon began a productive literary career. His diverse output includes a number of Socratic works, technical treatises, and topics of political importance, including a history of Greece from 411 to 362 B.C.E., a favorable commentary on the Spartan constitution, a biography of Agesilaus, the gripping tale of his Persian adventure, and a fictional reconstruction of the life of Cyrus the Great. A common moral and didactic purpose unifies Xenophon's works.

Influence. Xenophon's *Ellēnika* (411-362 B.C.E.; *History of the Affairs of Greece*, also known as *Hel-*

Xenophon. (Library of Congress)

lenica, 1685) is the only surviving continuous narrative of Greek history from 411 to 362 B.C.E. His Socratic works provide a useful counterpart to Plato's portrait of Socrates.

ADDITIONAL RESOURCES

Dillery, John. *Xenophon and the History of His Times.* New York: Routledge, 1995.

Higgins, W. E. *Xenophon the Athenian.* Albany: State University of New York Press, 1977.

Hutchinson, Godfrey. *Xenophon and the Art of Command.* London: Greenhill Books, 2000.

SEE ALSO: Agesilaus II of Sparta; Cyrus the Great; Greece, Classical; Leuctra, Battle of; Persia; Socrates.

—*Frances Skoczylas Pownall*

XERXES I

ALSO KNOWN AS: Ahasuerus (biblical); Iksersa; Khsayarsan (Persian)
BORN: c. 519 B.C.E.; place unknown
DIED: 465 B.C.E.; Persepolis
RELATED CIVILIZATION: Persia
MAJOR ROLE/POSITION: Military leader, ruler

Life. The biblical story of Esther, while probably apocryphal, nevertheless presents an overview of Xerxes I's (zurk-seez) reign from the standpoint of intrigue within his court. The most comprehensive description of Xerxes' early years is found in the writings of Herodotus. Much of Xerxes' reign (r. 486-465 B.C.E.) was characterized by military struggles both within and around his empire. In the beginning of his reign, the Persian Empire stretched from the Indus River in the east to Libya in the west.

Following his suppression of revolts in Babylonia and Egypt, Xerxes assembled a large army for an invasion of Greece. After overcoming Greek resistance at the Battle of Thermopylae (480 B.C.E.), Xerxes captured and burned Athens. This marked the peak of his success. During the following decade, Greek armies defeated Xerxes at Salamis, Plataea, Mycale, and in southern Asia Minor. Probably as a result of the continual military disasters, Xerxes was assassinated in a palace coup.

Influence. Xerxes' goal was to surpass the military conquest of his father, Darius the Great. Instead, his military missions, primarily directed against Greece, resulted in a weakening of the Persian Empire.

ADDITIONAL RESOURCES

Gershevitch, I., ed. *The Cambridge History of Iran.* Cambridge, England: Cambridge University Press, 1985.

Yamauchi, E. *Persia and the Bible.* Grand Rapids, Mich.: Baker, 1990.

SEE ALSO: Athens; Darius the Great; Greece, Classical; Marathon, Battle of; Persia; Plataea, Battle of; Salamis, Battle of; Thermopylae, Battle of.

—*Richard Adler*

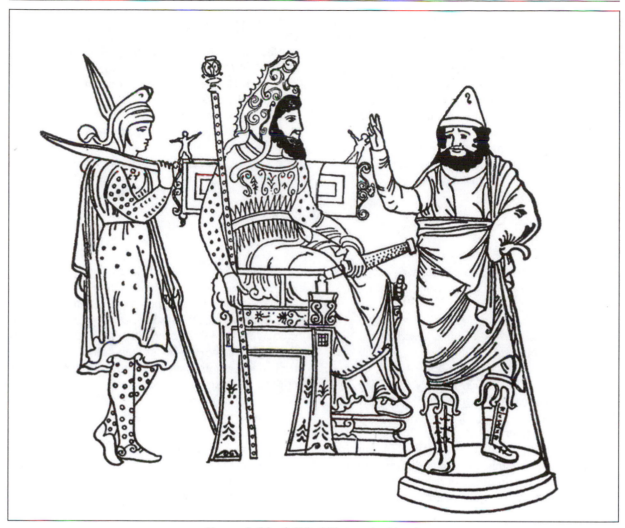

Xerxes I. (North Wind Picture Archives)

Xia Dynasty

Also known as: *Wade-Giles* Hsia Dynasty
Date: c. 2100-1600 b.c.e.
Locale: Erlitou, east of Luoyang in Henan, China
Significance: The Xia Dynasty, the first of the traditional twenty-four dynasties of China, was long thought mythical, but archaeological finds since 1957 have supported its existence.

Traditional Chinese histories referred to the existence of a dynasty predating the Shang Dynasty (1600-1066 b.c.e.), although no physical evidence existed until 1957. According to legend, the Xia (SHEE-AH) Dynasty was founded by Yu, who personified the ideal public servant. Yu was the last of five mythical pre-Xia "emperors." The five were credited with the development of fire, agriculture, animal domestication, writing, calendars, and flood control. The Xia Dynasty might simply be the late Longshan period, when various cultures merged.

The existence of the Xia Dynasty has never been firmly proven. Archaeological evidence uncovered near Zhengzhou in 1957, dubbed the Erlitou culture, dates from between 1900 to 1600 B.C.E. The site, surrounded by earthen walls 20 feet (6 meters) high and 1 mile (1.6 kilometers) square, might be the capital city of Yangcheng in traditional histories. One large complex, interpreted as a palace, was estimated to have taken 100,000 worker-days to build. Outside the walls were two foundries for casting bronze, indicating the existence of relatively advanced metallurgical skills. Regardless of whether this site was part of the Xia Dynasty, it does show the existence of centralized control in China before the Shang Dynasty.

ADDITIONAL RESOURCES

Chang, K. C. *The Archeology of Ancient China*. 4th ed. New Haven, Conn.: Yale University Press, 1987.
Gernet, J. *A History of Chinese Civilization*. Translated by J. R. Foster. Cambridge, England: Cambridge University Press, 1995
Keightler, D. *The Origins of Chinese Civilization*. Berkeley: University of California Press, 1983.

SEE ALSO: China; Longshan culture; Shang Dynasty.
—*Barry M. Stentiford*

XIAOWEN DI

ALSO KNOWN AS: *Wade-Giles* Hsiao-wen ti; Yuanhong (*Wade-Giles* Yüan Hung)
BORN: 467 C.E.; north China
DIED: 499 C.E.; China
RELATED CIVILIZATIONS: China, Xianbei
MAJOR ROLE/POSITION: Emperor

Life. Xiaowen Di (SHEE-AH-OH-when dee) was enthroned in 471 C.E. at the age of four; his grandmother, the Dowager Empress Feng (d. 490 C.E.), assisted him in governing the Northern Wei Dynasty (386-533 C.E.). Because Wei was a state with origins in the Toba branch of the Xianbei, who conquered all of north China, the two rulers recognized a dire need to regulate the claims of both the Xianbei and the Chinese aristocracy to high office, and they enforced sinicization. The state reallocated land under an equal land system and reorganized rural households under a three-headman system, grouping them into units of 5, 25, and 125, with the headmen responsible for tax collection and military recruitment.

In 493 C.E., Xiaowen Di relocated his capital from Datong to Luoyang and adopted a more drastic reform program. He outlawed the use of the Xianbei language at court, encouraged interethnic marriages, and insisted that Xianbei subjects adopt Chinese family names, follow Chinese customs, and wear Chinese clothing. He stressed agriculture (as opposed to nomadism), patronized Buddhism, and carved the Buddhist cave temples in Longmen. He also decreed that all Xianbei subjects in Luoyang regard the city as their home and not ask to be buried back in Datong. Xiaowen Di relentlessly crushed resisting Xianbei aristocrats, including Prince Xun, whom he put to death.

Influence. Xiaowen Di's reforms greatly unified north China, expedited the feudalization of the Xianbei, and promoted national harmony.

ADDITIONAL RESOURCES

Dien, Albert E. *State and Society in Early Medieval China*. Hong Kong: Hong Kong University Press, 1990.
Perkins, Dorothy. *Encyclopedia of China: The Essential Reference to China, Its History and Culture*. New York: Roundtable, 1999.

SEE ALSO: Buddhism; Buddhist cave temples; China; Northern Wei.
—*Charles Xingzhong Li*

XIE HE

ALSO KNOWN AS: *Wade-Giles* Hsieh Ho
BORN: mid-fifth century C.E.; place unknown
DIED: c. 533 C.E.; place unknown
RELATED CIVILIZATION: Southern Qi Dynasty, China
MAJOR ROLE/POSITION: Painter, art theorist

Life. Xie He (SHEE-EH heh) lived during the Southern Qi period (479-502 C.E.), when the capital was at Nanjing. He was known to be one of the most important painters and art critics around the fifth century C.E. He was a figure painter and known as an artist who excelled in detailed realism. Unfortunately, none of his works or even a copy of a copy of his works exists. However, his *Ku Hua Ping Lu* (late fifth century C.E.; record of the criticism of old paintings) remains the earliest extant statement of the essentials of Chinese painting.

The six laws of painting, which Xie He formulated in the first part of *Ku Hua Ping Lu*, represent a comprehensive attempt to create some theoretical basis for the evaluation of paintings. These six points on which paintings were to be evaluated are as follows: first, life and a spirit of vitality in the subject; second, mastery in the use of the brush; third, fidelity in portraying the subject; fourth, proper coloring; fifth, proper placement of elements (composition); and sixth, the transmission and perpetuation of the masterpieces by copying old masters.

Influence. Xie He's six laws have been quoted and discussed by scholars for fifteen centuries and have made his name one of the most renowned in the history of Chinese painting.

ADDITIONAL RESOURCES

Bush, Susan, and Hsiao-yen Shih. *Early Chinese Texts on Painting.* Cambridge, Mass.: Harvard University Press, 1985.

Siren, Osvald. *Chinese Painting: Leading Masters and Principles.* Reprint. New York: Hacker Art Books, 1973.

SEE ALSO: China; Gu Kaizhi; Yan Liben.

—*Juliana Y. Yuan*

XIE LINGYUN

ALSO KNOWN AS: *Wade-Giles* Hsich Ling-yün; Xie Kanglo (*Wade-Giles* Hsieh K'ang-lo)
BORN: 385 C.E.; Zhejiang Province, China
DIED: 433 C.E.; Canton, Nanhai, China
RELATED CIVILIZATIONS: China, Eastern Asia
MAJOR ROLE/POSITION: Poet

Life. Xie Lingyun (SHEE-EH LIHNG-yewn) was born into one of the most powerful aristocratic families of the Six Dynasties, one that was at the center of cultural and literary movements. The Xie family moved from Henan to Zhejiang province. His great wealth gave him all the leisure he needed. His book collection made him one of the most learned poets of his time, and he was famous as a calligrapher and painter. He was an eccentric and had a special love for nature. Xie spent much time wandering around the country looking at celebrated landscapes.

His poems were a blending of sentiment, reason, and beauty of nature with Daoism, Buddhism, and Confucian philosophy. Xie edited the southern version of the *Mahaparinirvana-sutra*, wrote a "discussion of essentials," and identified the combination of Nirvana and Samsara with the doctrine of Void. These were tasks well suited to a mind accustomed to the Daoist teachings of the *Dao De Jing* (possibly sixth century B.C.E.,

probably compiled late third century B.C.E.; *The Speculations on Metaphysics, Polity, and Morality of "the Old Philosopher, Lau-Tsze,"* 1868; better known as the *Dao De Jing*) and the *Zhuangzi* (traditionally c. 300 B.C.E., compiled c. 285-160 B.C.E.; *The Divine Classic of Nan-hua,* 1881; also known as *The Complete Works of Chuang Tzu,* 1968; commonly known as *Zhuangzi,* 1991).

Influence. Xie was regarded as the first of the nature poets and the founder of the school of mountains and waters poetry (*shanju fu*). His editions and commentary on Buddhism popularized this religion with educated Chinese scholars.

ADDITIONAL RESOURCES

Chang, Sun Kang-I. *Six Dynasties Poetry.* Princeton, N.J.: Princeton University Press, 1986.

Frodsham, J. D. *The Murmuring Stream: The Life and Works of the Chinese Nature Poet Hsieh Ling-yun (385-433), Duke of K'ang Lo.* Kuala Lumpur, Malaysia: University of Malaya Press, 1967.

SEE ALSO: Buddhism; China; Confucianism; Daoism; Six Dynasties; *Zhuangzi.*

—*Carol C. Fan*

XIN ZHUI'S TOMB

DATE: c. 150 B.C.E.
LOCALE: Mawangdui, near Changsha, China
RELATED CIVILIZATIONS: Han Dynasty, China
SIGNIFICANCE: This tomb is one of the most impressive and important ancient burial sites found in China.

Part of a family burial complex, this single-chamber crypt, also known as Han Tomb no. 1, was first excavated in 1972. The crypt was made of cypress planks buried in a thick layer of clay and charcoal. Its occupant, Xin Zhui (SHIN JEW-ay; *Wade-Giles* Hsin Chui), died circa 150 B.C.E. and was probably the wife of Li Cang, the marquis of Dai, who controlled the vicinity during the Han Dynasty (206 B.C.E.-220 C.E.) and was buried nearby. She is also known as Lady (duchess of) Dai. Her perfectly preserved body, now on display in a museum in Changsha, was entombed within four lacquer coffins and was surrounded by a variety of grave goods, including silks, lacquerware, tomb figures, food, and an elaborate funeral banner. These materials provide important evidence about the contemporary Chinese lacquer industry (centered in Changsha), artistic techniques, and religious beliefs. Especially noteworthy are the successful effort to inhibit decomposition of the corpse and the desire to provide the deceased with comfort in the afterlife. The paintings on the lacquer coffins depict landscape scenes, and those on the banner represent various stages in the funeral ceremony and the afterlife of the deceased. This burial reflects the traditions of the Chu culture of the Yellow River Basin and the central Yangtze Valley.

ADDITIONAL RESOURCES

Waley-Cohen, Joanna, trans. *The Lacquers of the Mawangdui Tomb.* Hong Kong: Oriental Ceramic Society, 1984.
Wang, Po-Yang. *Imperial Mausoleums and Tombs.* New York: Springer, 1998.

SEE ALSO: China; Han Dynasty.

—*Thomas J. Sienkewicz*

XIONGNU

ALSO KNOWN AS: *Wade-Giles* Hsiung-nu
DATE: 300 B.C.E.-500 C.E.
LOCALE: Northeastern to Central Asia
SIGNIFICANCE: China's nomadic enemies, the Xiongnu fought China and other groups for domination.

The horse-riding Xiongnu (SHYOHNG-new) first appeared on China's borders in the fourth century B.C.E., causing northern Chinese states to build defensive walls and develop cavalry forces. In 214 B.C.E., a newly unified China under the Qin Dynasty defeated the Xiongnu and connected the fragmentary walls to form the first Great Wall of China that stretched from present-day Pyongyang (north Korea) to Gansu in western China. The fall of the Qin in 206 B.C.E. threw China's northern defenses into chaos and allowed the Xiongnu to regroup.

Between 209 and 174 B.C.E., Maodun built the Xiongnu into a formidable power, defeating other nomadic tribes in northern Asia. In 200 B.C.E., his force of 300,000 cavalry defeated the equally large army, consisting mostly of infantrymen, of Liu Bang (posthumous name Gaozu), the founder of the Han Dynasty (206 B.C.E.-220 C.E.). Ten treaties were negotiated between the Han and Xiongnu between 198 and 135 B.C.E., in which several Chinese princesses were married to Xiongnu chiefs. The treaties also stipulated regular large gifts from China to the Xiongnu, despite which Xiongnu raids continued along China's border.

In a policy reversal, Emperor Wudi (r. 140-87 B.C.E.) launched a massive offensive against the Xiongnu beginning in 127 B.C.E. that culminated in the latter's defeat and expulsion to beyond the Gobi Desert to the shores of Lake Baikal in modern Russia. In 54 B.C.E. the Xiongnu split into two segments, the southern part submitting to the Han and the northern segment being expelled from China's borderlands, eventually moving into central Europe. There they were known as Huns and caused huge disruptions to local peoples and eventually toppled the Roman Empire in the west.

At the height of the Xiongnu's power, about a hundred tribes submitted to them. Along China's borders,

Xiongnu power was permanently broken during the mid-first century C.E. Remaining Xiongnu were absorbed into either the sedentary population or other newly powerful nomadic groups called the Xianbei and the Wuhuan. Reasons for the decline and fall of Xiongnu power were the primitive and unstable nature of their political structure, the corruption and softening of their warrior society by the tribute and gifts they exacted from their neighbors and victims, and the opposition of the Chinese and their other victims. Because they had no written language, sources of information about them come from their enemies and victims, mainly the Chinese, and from archaeological finds.

ADDITIONAL RESOURCES

Jagchid, Sechin, and Van Jay Symons. *Peace, War, and Trade Along the Great Wall.* Bloomington: Indiana University Press, 1989.

Sinor, Denis. *The Cambridge History of Early Inner Asia.* New York: Cambridge University Press, 1990.

Yu, Ying-Shih. *Trade and Expansion in Han China: A Study in the Structure of Sino-Barbarian Economic Relations.* Berkeley: University of California Press, 1967.

SEE ALSO: China; Han Dynasty; Huns; Wudi.

—*Jiu-Hwa Lo Upshur*

XUANZANG

ALSO KNOWN AS: *Wade-Giles* Hsüan-tsang; Xuanzhuang (*Wade-Giles* Hsüan-chuang)
BORN: c. 602 C.E.; Yanshi, Henan, China
DIED: 664 C.E.; Chang'an, China
RELATED CIVILIZATIONS: China, India
MAJOR ROLE/POSITION: Buddhist scholar

Life. Motivated by the diverse interpretations of the Buddhism that had been imported into China, Xuanzang (SHEWAHN-tsang) made a pilgrimage to India. He left Chang'an for that country in 629 C.E. and did not return until 645 C.E. While on his pilgrimage, he studied in Nalanda monastery, traveled widely in the region, and debated with local monks on Buddhism.

The story of his travels in Central Asia and India is related in several works, including the *Datang Xiyouji* (629 C.E.; *Buddhist Records of the Western World*, 1884). He is widely known for the voluminous translations of the Buddhist sutras he brought back from his travels. For their storage, Emperor Taizong built the still extant Big Wild Goose pagoda in 652 C.E. After his return, Xuanzang devoted his time to the study of the sutras, translated seventy-five of them, and initiated the school Weishi Zong (consciousness only), which did not last long because of its hair-splitting elaboration of the mind and the senses. He was buried in Xingjiao Temple, fourteen miles east of Xi'an. Xuanzang's experience became the source of the widely acclaimed novel *Xiyouji* (c. 1570-c. 1580, oldest surviving edition, 1592; *Journey to the West*, 1977-1983), by Wu Cheng'en (c. 1500-1582), in which a magical monkey king converts from the native Daoism to the imported Buddhism and assists Xuanzang on his pilgrimage.

Influence. Xuanzang has been considered the most accomplished Buddhist scholar and translator in China, and the account of his travels has been of tremendous value for historians.

ADDITIONAL RESOURCES

Perkins, Dorothy. *Encyclopedia of China: The Essential Reference to China, Its History and Culture.* New York: Roundtable, 1999.

Wriggins, Sally Hovey. *Xuanzang: A Buddhist Pilgrim on the Silk Road.* Boulder, Colo.: Westview Press, 1996.

SEE ALSO: Buddhism; China; Daoism; Silk Road; Tang Dynasty.

—*Charles Xingzhong Li*

XUNZI

ALSO KNOWN AS: *Wade-Giles* Hsün-tzu; Xun Qing
    (*Wade-Giles* Hsün Ch'ing); Xun Guang (*Wade-Giles* Hsün K'uang)
BORN: c. 307 B.C.E.; Zhou kingdom, China
DIED: c. 235 B.C.E.; Lanling, China
RELATED CIVILIZATION: China
MAJOR ROLE/POSITION: Philosopher

Life. Xunzi (SHEWN-tsih) was born in Zhao and may have studied in Lu. He visited Qin, became senior resident at the Jixia establishment in Qi in his fifties, and left in 254 B.C.E. to become director of territory, including former Lu, newly conquered by Chu. This position, combining administrative authority with a secure intellectual base, he held until 238 B.C.E., when the death of the Chu king destroyed his patron and ended his tenure. The writings gathered under his name, *Xunzi* (compiled c. 285-c. 255 B.C.E.; *The Works of Hsuntze*, 1928; commonly known as *Xunzi*), were produced over his long career by himself or close associates.

Unlike Mencius, Xunzi is a text-based rather than a tradition-based Confucian; he contributed to fixing the classical text canon. He attacked the Mencian view of human nature as tending inherently toward good and relied on education and ritual to overcome its evil tendencies. He rejected the Mencian rulership models drawn from remote and simple antiquity, preferring more relevant "later kings."

Influence. Xunzi is the bridge between early Confucianism and imperial Legalism. Li Si, the chief architect of Qin totalitarianism, was his student.

ADDITIONAL RESOURCES

Kline, T. C., and P. J. Ivanhoe, eds. *Virtue, Nature, and Moral Agency in the Xunzi*. Indianapolis, Ind.: Hackett, 2000.
Knoblock, John. *Xunzi*. Princeton, N.J.: Princeton University Press, 1990-1998.

SEE ALSO: Confucianism; Legalists; Mencius; Qin Dynasty; Zhou Dynasty.

—*E. Bruce Brooks*

XUSHEN

ALSO KNOWN AS: *Wade-Giles* Hsü Shen; Shuzhong
    (*Wade-Giles* Shu-chung)
BORN: c. 58 C.E.; Yancheng, Henan, China
DIED: c. 147 C.E.; China
RELATED CIVILIZATION: Early China
MAJOR ROLE/POSITION: Confucian commentator, lexicographer

Life. Xushen (SHEW-shehn) was an unrivaled Confucian commentator of the Eastern Han Dynasty (25-220 C.E.) and the first Chinese lexicographer in history. He was magistrate of Xiao county in Anhui and master of rituals under the supreme commander. During this period, commentaries were being written on the *Wujing*, the five Confucian classics. One of these classics, the *Liji* (compiled first century B.C.E.; *The Liki*, 1885; commonly known as *Classic of Rituals*), a miscellany of texts that treat ceremonies and rituals, directly concerned Xushen's position. As diverse interpretations emerged, Xushen was motivated to study the classical Chinese characters.

In addition to his book *Wujing Yiyi* (first or second century C.E.; alternative interpretations of the five Confucian classics), Xushen published the first Chinese dictionary, *Shuowen Jiezi* (c. 100 C.E.). It consisted of fifteen volumes containing 9,353 characters and 1,163 variants. It presented the meaning, structure, pronunciation, and etymology of each character up to his time. This dictionary introduced six categories for script structures, all but the last two of which are still accurate: *xiangxing* (pictograms), *zhishi* (simple ideograms), *huiyi* (compound ideograms), *singsheng* (phonograms), *jiajie* (phonetic loans), and *zhuanzhu* (derivatives). The entries are arranged under 540 radicals, a system that has since become the standard practice in most Chinese dictionaries, although alternatives have been developed. Extant is the edited copy by Xuxuan (916-991C.E.) of the Northern Song Dynasty (960-1127 C.E.).

Influence. Xushen's dictionary is one of the earliest

books of its kind and has been the most important work for research on classical Chinese.

ADDITIONAL RESOURCES
Hook, Brian, ed. *The Cambridge Encyclopedia of China*. 2d ed. New York: Cambridge University Press, 1991.

Watson, Burton. *Early Chinese Literature*. New York: Columbia University Press, 1962.

SEE ALSO: China; Confucianism; Confucius; Han Dynasty; *Wujing*.

—*Charles Xingzhong Li*

— Y —

YAM

DATE: 2500-2200 B.C.E.
LOCALE: Probably Upper Nubia, south of the Second Cataract
SIGNIFICANCE: Yam was a powerful Nubian kingdom that Harkhuf (a Sixth Dynasty governor) mentions in his accounts as a wealthy land engaged in trade with the later Egyptian Old Kingdom.

Yam was probably centered in the Kerma Basin, the most fertile region of Upper Nubia. The culture of Kerma was distinct from that of Lower Nubia and Egypt. Although material culture from Egypt has been found in excavated sites, these appear to have come in through trade and are not part of a shared culture. There are some continuities between Lower Nubian traditions and those of Kerma. For example, pottery styles reflect an underlying shared ceramic complex; however, there are clear innovations initiated by the people of Kerma. The pottery distinctively associated with Kerma is black-topped, and its lower part is a deep red. The upper and lower portions are separated by a whitish metallic band and a thinner black band. The interior of these vessels is glossy jet black. Of particular note is the thin wall of the containers and their sharp rims.

Burial practices at Kerma were similar to those in Lower Nubia. Additionally it has been observed from skeletal remains that the ancient people of Kerma resembled modern Nubians, and it is quite probable that the two populations share a common ancestry. The major variations that differentiate the Kerma societies from those of Lower Nubia may in fact be caused by the formidable wealth of the distinct kingdoms centered at Kerma. The royal tombs and monuments of Kerma excavated to date actually correspond to the Second Intermediate period (1650-1550 B.C.E.) of Egyptian history, which is after the decline of the Yam kingdom. More archaeological work may uncover an older tradition that corresponds to the Yam kingdom. The Yam kingdom, which ruled during the Egyptian Seventeenth Dynasty (c. 1580-1550 B.C.E.), was eclipsed by the kingdom of Kush, during the Egyptian New Kingdom under the Eighteenth Dynasty (1550-1295 B.C.E.).

According to Harkhuf's accounts, donkeys, ivory, incense, leopard skins, and ebony were some of the major notable items procured by Egypt in large quantities from the southern kingdom of Yam. This lucrative trade enhanced the wealth of the Yam rulers and placed luxury items in their coffers. The trade conducted with the south was carried out by overland caravans, not on flotillas, as was the case in the later Kush kingdom.

ADDITIONAL RESOURCES
Adams, William L. *Nubia: Corridor to Africa.* London: Penguin Books, 1977.
Burstein, Stanley M., ed. *Ancient African Civilizations: Kush and Axum.* Princeton, N.J.: Markus Wiener, 1998.
Shinnie, P. L. *Ancient Nubia.* New York: Kegan Paul International, 1996.

SEE ALSO: Egypt, Pharaonic; Harkhuf; Kerma; Nubia.
—*Catherine Cymone Fourshey*

YAMATO COURT

DATE: third-seventh centuries C.E.
LOCALE: Yamato plain in central Japan
RELATED CIVILIZATIONS: Japan, Korea, China
SIGNIFICANCE: The Yamato court was the precursor to the Yamato state (Japan).

From Jimmu Tennō's traditional ascension to the throne in 660 B.C.E. to that of Mommu in 697 C.E., the Yamato (YAH-mah-toh) court, as the predominant power in central Japan, extended its influence by securing the allegiance of surrounding families through marriage or military conquest and enlisting them in household organizations of increasing size and strength until it finally claimed sovereignty over Japan.

Continental influences, vital to Japan's development, produced an influx of Korean and Chinese professionals after 366 C.E., through the Korean kingdom of Paekche, which swelled the Japanese aristocratic class by one-third. However, the rise of Silla, which snuffed out Paekche, forced Japan to rethink its continental connections.

Official Japanese acceptance of Buddhism in 587 C.E. signaled the beginning of a wholehearted emulation of Chinese culture. Missions were sent directly to the Chinese capital starting in 604 C.E. to acquire Chinese expertise. Japan adapted the Chinese ideographs in order to write Japanese, accepted as much of the Chinese administrative system that fit the Japanese scene,

and produced formal histories based on the Chinese model.

With the construction of a permanent capital at Nara in the Yamato plain, the Japanese state had finally come into being.

ADDITIONAL RESOURCES

Hall, John W. *Japan: From Prehistory to Modern Times*. Ann Arbor: University of Michigan Press, 1991.
Sansom, George B. *Japan: A Short Cultural History*. Stanford, Calif.: Stanford University Press, 1952.

SEE ALSO: Buddhism; China; Japan; Jimmu Tennō; Korea; *Nihon shoki*.

—Edwin L. Neville, Jr.

YAN LIBEN

ALSO KNOWN AS: *Wade-Giles* Yen Li-pen
BORN: c. 600 C.E.; place unknown
DIED: 673 C.E.; place unknown
RELATED CIVILIZATIONS: Tang Dynasty, China
MAJOR ROLE/POSITION: Prime minister, court painter

Life. Yan Liben (YAHN LEE-behn) was born at the end of the sixth century C.E., during the reign of the first Sui Dynasty emperor. His father was already a painter of great renown in the capital. His elder brother Lide was also an official and a court painter. From an early age, Yan Liben was trained in the arts and became an official of the highest rank. In 668 C.E., he was appointed prime minister of the right.

Although he was considered one of the best early Tang painters and, despite his noble rank and high position, Yan Liben considered himself a mere servant of the emperors. At the requests of the Tang emperors Taizong and Gaozong, he portrayed scholar-officials, generals, foreign envoys, tribute bearers, and Buddhist and Daoist deities. Some of the later versions of his works that survive in various museums and collections are the *Emperor Scroll*, *The Tribute Bearers*, and

Scholars of the Northern Qi Dynasty Collating Classical Texts (all seventh century C.E.). He even designed the sculptures of Emperor Taizong's tomb, including the emperor's favorite horses, now in the Philadelphia Museum of Art. Upon his death, he was given the posthumous name of Wen Reng (true scholar).

Influence. Yan Liben recorded history through his paintings of important figures and the events of the court. He set the standard for all later figure painters.

ADDITIONAL RESOURCES

Loehr, Max. *The Great Painters of China*. Oxford, England: Phaidon Press, 1980.
Murck, Alfreda, and Wen Fong. *Words and Images: Chinese Poetry, Calligraphy, and Painting*. New York: Metropolitan Museum of Art, 1991.
Siren, Osvald. *Chinese Painting: Leading Masters and Principles*. Reprint. New York: Hacker Art Books, 1973.

SEE ALSO: Gu Kaizhi; Sui Dynasty; Taizong; Tang Dynasty; Xie He.

—Juliana Y. Yuan

YANG DI

ALSO KNOWN AS: *Wade-Giles* Yang Ti; Yang Guang (*Wade-Giles* Yang Kuang)
BORN: 569 C.E.; China
DIED: 618 C.E.; China
RELATED CIVILIZATIONS: Sui Dynasty, China
MAJOR ROLE/POSITION: Emperor

Life. Yang Di (YAHNG dee) was the second and last emperor of the Sui Dynasty (581-618 C.E.). He assisted his father-emperor in conquering the south and reunifying China, which had been divided for most of the three hundred years since the end of the Han Dynasty, and was viceroy of the south for ten years, with his headquarters at Yangzhou. In order to gain the crown, he framed (and possibly assassinated) his elder brother and took the throne in 604 C.E.

Yang Di was an active emperor who undertook massive national projects. To supplement his capital in Chang'an, he constructed an alternative capital in Luoyang, built huge granaries, rebuilt the Great Wall, paved roads connecting major cities and ports, and dredged countless rivers to link them with the Grand Canal. However, these projects were achieved through exorbitant corvée—unpaid labor extracted from one to two million laborers a year—and high taxes. He also fre-quently inspected parts of his empire with crowds of attendants (500,000 at one time) while sending military expeditions to all frontiers for territory expansion. Over time, his subjects found these excesses to be unbearable. Consequently, the response to Yang Di's three unsuccessful expeditions during 612-614 C.E. to conquer Koguryo was repeated revolts at home. He retreated to Yangzhou, but his garrison force mutinied and hanged him in 618 C.E.

Influence. Historians hold that Yang Di's tyranny and self-destruction taught the emperors of Tang (618-907 C.E.) to pay more attention to the interests of their subjects and that Yang Di's national building projects facilitated Tang's prosperity.

ADDITIONAL RESOURCES
Dillon, Michael, ed. *China: A Historical and Cultural Dictionary.* Surrey, England: Curzon, 1998.
Wright, Arthur E. *The Sui Dynasty.* New York: Knopf, 1979.

SEE ALSO: China; Great Wall of China; Koguryo; Sui Dynasty; Tang Dynasty.

—*Charles Xingzhong Li*

YANG XIONG

ALSO KNOWN AS: *Wade-Giles* Yang Hsiung; Yang Ziyun (*Wade-Giles* Yang Tzu-yün)
BORN: 53 B.C.E.; Sichuan, China
DIED: 18 C.E.; Luoyang, China
RELATED CIVILIZATION: Western Han Dynasty
MAJOR ROLE/POSITION: Poet, philosopher

Life. Yang Xiong (YAHNG shee-ong), whose father was a petty landlord, read extensively in his early youth. Though he lacked eloquence because of a stammer, he had a free and natural air that enabled him to get along with people. He became skilled in poetry and was appointed the close attendant of the emperor.

Later in life, Yang Xiong turned to the study of philosophy and dialect. He set forth the concept of *xuan*, "dark energy," or the absolute metaphysical reason for the formation and existence of all concrete things, in his *Tai Xuan Jing* (before 18 C.E.; *The Classic of the Great Dark*, 1983). He believed in the knowable nature of the universe and the importance of knowledge and stated that practicable knowledge was authentic knowledge. He also held that human nature was a mixture of good and evil. One became a good person by developing the good and an evil person by enhancing the evil.

Influence. Yang Xiong's poetry has continued to be appreciated and studied as an excellent model of Chinese literature, and his philosophy inspired later thinkers and enriched the treasure of Chinese thought.

ADDITIONAL RESOURCES
Knechtges, David R. *The Han Rhapsody: A Study of the Fu of Yang Hsiung.* Cambridge, England: Cambridge University Press, 1976.
Nylan, Michael, trans. *Yang Hsiung: The Canon of Supreme Mystery.* Albany: State University of New York Press, 1993.

SEE ALSO: China; Han Dynasty; Philosophy.
—*Lihua Liu*

YANGSHAO CULTURE

ALSO KNOWN AS: Painted Pottery culture
DATE: c. 5000-3000 B.C.E.
LOCALE: Center of the Yellow River region and beyond
RELATED CIVILIZATION: Neolithic China
SIGNIFICANCE: The Yangshao culture created some of the most magnificent Neolithic pottery known.

The Swedish archaeologist Johan Gunnar Andersson discovered the earliest Neolithic remains at Yangshao (YAHNG-shah-oh; *Wade-Giles* Yang-shao) village in western Henan Province early in the twentieth century. This culture was situated in the Yellow River Valley, which includes western Henan Province, central Shanxi Province, and southern Shaanxi Province. After Andersson's findings, more than a thousand archaeological sites were found, extending from western Shandong Province to as far west as Gansu and Xinjiang Provinces. A major site of the Yangshao culture is at Banpo, near Xi'an in Shaanxi Province, where a large village was excavated and divided into three sections: living area, cemetery, and firing kilns. Clearly, pottery was an important activity of this culture.

The Yangshao culture is distinguished by the full-bodied pottery of reddish clay, the majority of which has extraordinary geometric designs such as spirals and diamond and checkerboard patterns and painted black, brown, purple, and red pigments. A few have paintings of human faces, fish, birds, and frogs. Besides hunting and fishing, the Yangshao people cultivated millet and domesticated pigs and dogs. Their weapons and implements were made of stone, bone, or antler horn. Their dwellings were either at ground level or half sunken. The half-sunken houses were usually round and had cone-shaped thatched roofs.

ADDITIONAL RESOURCES
Loewe, Michael, and Edward L. Shaughnessy, eds. *The Cambridge History of Ancient China from the Origins of Civilization to 221 B.C.E.* Cambridge, England: Cambridge University Press, 1999.
Shangraw, Clarence F. *Origins of Chinese Ceramics.* New York: China Institute in America, 1978.

SEE ALSO: China; Liangzhu culture; Longshan culture.
—*Juliana Y. Yuan*

YANNAI

FLOURISHED: sixth century C.E.; Palestine
RELATED CIVILIZATION: Byzantium
MAJOR ROLE/POSITION: Religious poet

Life. Along with religious poet Eleazar ha-Kalir (Eleazar ben Kalir), Yannai was a famous author of sophisticated prayer-poems (*piyyutim*) intended for insertion at certain points in the Jewish synagogue liturgy. Little is known of his life other than that he lived in Palestine as a rabbi and wrote Jewish liturgical poetry. Yannai is the first synagogue poet, possibly following earlier Samaritan and Christian liturgical practice, to sign his compositions acrostically. He wrote a cycle of some 167 poetic insertions for the Amidah ("standing before God"), the main statutory prayer of the synagogue. Entitled *Maḥazor Yannai* (sixth century C.E.; English translation, 1919), these poems were designed to connect the most important prayer of the Sabbath service with the content of the weekly Torah reading and its Midrashic commentaries. This followed a triennial cyclical pattern used in the Byzantine period that lasted only until the Babylonian Torah-reading cycle replaced it, thus effectively eliminating these liturgical prayer-poems from common use and the need for creating them.

Influence. The *Maḥazor Yannai* and certain of Yannai's compositions for other occasions were highly prized and were copied for centuries for use in the synagogue liturgy. Many copies turned up in the Cairo Genizah. The literary heritage of Yannai constitutes a major source for knowledge of the literature, beliefs, and religious concepts of the sixth century synagogue.

ADDITIONAL RESOURCES

Kor, Avshalom. *Yannai's Piyyutim*. Tel Aviv, Israel: Universitat Tel-Aviv, 1988.

Spiegel, Shalom. *Fathers of Piyyut: Texts and Studies Toward a History of the Piyyut in Eretz Yisrael*. New York: Bet ha-midrash le-rabanum ba-Amerikah, 1996.

SEE ALSO: Bible: Jewish; Byzantine Empire; Judaism.
—*John M. Bullard*

YAYOI CULTURE

DATE: c. 300 B.C.E.-300 C.E.
LOCALE: Japan
SIGNIFICANCE: The Yayoi ushered in the wet-rice cultivation that shaped fundamental characteristics of the Japanese culture.

Yayoi (yah-YOH-i) pottery from around 300 B.C.E. recovered in Northern Kyūshū was expressly designed for the preparation and serving of rice. Rice growing was probably introduced to Japan by seafarers from the neighboring Asian continent as well as by refugees from war-torn China and the Korean peninsula. As a stable and nutritious food source, rice and its cultivation spread rapidly over most parts of Honshū by the end of the first century C.E. During this period, in addition to rice farming, the techniques of iron casting and weaving arose, resulting in the creation of related industries and trading of goods.

Labor-intensive, collective rice farming initiated social change. Loosely structured village communities were replaced by clans that yielded authority in their domains and produced the strict organization that ensured good rice harvests through collaborative effort. The Chinese chronicle *Weizhi* (compiled late third century C.E.) recorded that there were more than one hundred of these clans, constantly feuding until the legendary "Yamatai koku" clan under a female chieftain, Himiko, subjugated thirty of them, creating a powerful confederation in the early third century.

Japan's national traits of cooperative spirit and interpersonal harmony, observation of status relationships, and worship of Shintō gods for protection from natural elements were possibly derived from the agricul-

Yayoi pot with stand and lid. (© Sakamoto Photo Research Laboratory/Corbis)

tural practices of this era. The origins of the traditional Japanese obsession with ritual purification and the Japanese language may also find their roots in the behavior of the Yayoi population and their language of Wa.

SEE ALSO: Himiko; Japan; Jōmon, Yamato court.
—*Kumiko Takahara*

ADDITIONAL RESOURCES

Harris, David R. *The Origins and Spread of Agriculture and Pastoralism in Eurasia.* Washington, D.C.: Smithsonian Institution Press, 1996.

Mason, Penelope E. *History of Japanese Art.* New York: Abrams, 1993.

Tsunoda, Ryusaku. *Japan in the Chinese Dynastic Histories.* Translated by L. Carrington Goodrich. Kyoto, Japan: Perkins Oriental Books, 1968.

YOSE BEN YOSE

FLOURISHED: probably fourth or fifth century C.E.; Palestine
RELATED CIVILIZATION: Byzantium
MAJOR ROLE/POSITION: Jewish liturgical poet

Life. Practically nothing is known for certain about Yose ben Yose's (yoh-say behn YOH-say) life other than the presumption that he had been an orphan. Scholars hold varying opinions as to the dating of his life, ranging from early fourth century to as late as the seventh century. He is well known for his composition of prayer-poems (*piyyutim*) for use in the liturgy of the synagogue. These prayer-poems were inserted at certain points in the synagogue prayers as an embellishment, sometimes corresponding to appropriate readings from the Torah and Mishnah.

Influence. Some of the prayer-poems of Yose remain incorporated into the Orthodox rite for the Day of Atonement and into the Sephardic liturgy for both Yom Kippur and Rosh Hashanah. Yose's poetry is distinguished from that of his successors by clarity of expression, absence of rhyme, and, although rhythmic patterns are sometimes discernible, general absence of meter. There is occasional alliteration. Like those of his successors, Yose's prayer-poems overflow with references to the rabbinical literature known as Midrash.

ADDITIONAL RESOURCES

Elbogen, Ismar. *Jewish Liturgy: A Comprehensive History.* Translated by R. P. Scheindlin. Philadelphia: Jewish Publication Society, 1993.

Mirsky, Aharon. *Yosse ben Yosse: Poems.* Jerusalem: Mosad Byalik, 1991.

Spiegel, Shalom. *Fathers of Piyyut: Texts and Studies Toward a History of the Piyyut in Eretz Yisrael.* New York: Bet ha-midrash le-rabanum ba-Amerikah, 1996.

SEE ALSO: Bible: Jewish; Byzantine Empire; Judaism.
—*John M. Bullard*

YUE

ALSO KNOWN AS: *Wade-Giles* Yüeh
DATE: 500-300 B.C.E.
LOCALE: Zhejiang, China
RELATED CIVILIZATION: Zhou Dynasty
SIGNIFICANCE: Yue culture became a major component in the formation of Chinese civilization.

Yue (YEW-eh) culture covered most of the regional groups of southern China from Zhejiang to Hunan, Guangxi, and Guangdong. It was a peripheral ethnic group closely associated with Wu culture to the north. As early as the fifth century B.C.E., to be "Chinese" was a cultural rather than a racial distinction, and the central states of the Warring States period (475-221 B.C.E.) considered themselves "Chinese." The Yangtze states of Chu, Wu, and Yue, however, held an intermediary position with cultural groups considered Yi Ti, or "barbarian." Chinese culture was the only criterion of difference between being Chinese and being barbarian. Speculation classifies the Yue as speakers of

Austroasiatic languages related to those spoken in South and Southeast Asia. The Vietnamese are their descendants, "Viet" being their pronunciation of the term Yue.

The kingdom of Yue was located in Zhejiang of the Yangtze Delta. Its prehistory is obscure, but between 510 and 473 B.C.E., it emerged as a rival state in constant warfare with Wu, which it conquered. Yue then established supremacy over the lower Yangtze area. However, Yue was subsequently subjugated first by the Chu in 334 B.C.E. and then by the Qin in 223 B.C.E., which established the first empire of China.

ADDITIONAL RESOURCES

Creel, Herrlee Glessner. *The Birth of China*. New York: Frederick Ungar, 1967.

Fitzgerald, C. P. *China: A Short Cultural History*. London: Westview Press, 1985.

Loewe, Michael, and Edward L. Shaughnessy, eds. *The Cambridge History of Ancient China from the Origins of Civilization to 221* B.C.E. Cambridge, England: Cambridge University Press, 1999.

SEE ALSO: China; Qin Dynasty; Vietnam; Yue ware; Zhou Dynasty.

—*George J. Hoynacki*

YUE WARE

ALSO KNOWN AS: *Wade-Giles* Yüeh ware
DATE: 220-589 C.E.
LOCALE: Zhejiang Province, China
RELATED CIVILIZATION: China
SIGNIFICANCE: The greenish glazes on the Yue wares are the forebears of the celadon glaze.

Yue (YEW-eh) ware was a type of ceramics made in Yue kilns in Zhejiang Province, China, in the post-Han period of disunity (Three Kingdoms, Western and Eastern Jin Dynasties, Southern and Northern Dynasties). In general, ceramics can be divided into two basic categories: low-fired wares (earthenware or pottery), which are relatively soft and porous, suitable for funerary vessels and tomb sculptures, and high-fired wares (porcelain), which are relatively hard, durable, and impervious to water, suitable for everyday use. Most of Yue wares were low-fired wares. Yue ware is distinguished by its greenish glaze. The potters at the Yue kilns learned to apply greenish liquid glazes to their wares before firing. These early greenish glazes gradually developed into the green glazes on wares popularly known as celadon.

ADDITIONAL RESOURCES

Neave-Hill, W. B. R. *Chinese Ceramics*. Foreword by Sir Harry Garner. New York: St. Martin's Press, 1976.

Rawson, Jessica, ed. *The British Museum Book of Chinese Art*. New York: Thames and Hudson, 1993.

Valenstein, Suzanne. *A Handbook of Chinese Ceramics*. New York: Metropolitan Museum of Art, 1975.

SEE ALSO: China; Yue.

—*Yiwei Zheng*

Yue ware in the shape of a bear eating. (© Royal Ontario Museum/ Corbis)

YUEZHI CULTURE

DATE: c. 420 B.C.E.-c. 100 C.E.
LOCALE: East Turkestan, Turkestan, and Afghanistan
RELATED CIVILIZATIONS: Bactria, China, Kushān
SIGNIFICANCE: The first Indo-European empire in China, Yuezhi later served as a bridge to the Kushān Empire of India.

The Indo-European Yuezhi (YEW-eh jee; *Wade-Giles* Yüeh-chih) were probably Scythians who lived in Gansu Province (later Xingjiang) in the fifth century B.C.E. By about 250 B.C.E., they had established an empire that included most of Mongolia, the Altay region, the upper Yellow River, and the Tarim Basin. Primarily nomads, they produced jade while in Gansu. Their religion was a form of shamanism.

About 200 B.C.E., the Xiongnu, under Maodun (c. 209-174 B.C.E.), conquered all of Mongolia and in 176 B.C.E. drove the Yuezhi from Gansu to the Ili Valley. Twelve years later, Wulin, a vassal of the Xiongnu, forced them farther west. Some Yuezhi moved to the Tibetan mountains, but most occupied the territories between the Amu Dar'ya and Syr Dar'ya Rivers (Sogdia), driving Saka tribes into Bactria. Their new capital was Kienshih (Maracanda/Samarqand). In 138 B.C.E., Chinese emperor Wudi (r. 140-87 B.C.E.) unsuccessfully dispatched an ambassador to secure their assistance against the Xiongnu. Instead, following the Saka, the Yuezhi invaded Bactria and renamed the land Tokharistan. One of five branches of the Yuezhi, the Kushāns, extended their territories in Bactria and crossed the Indus River in 50 C.E. to establish the Kushān Empire in India. A Yuezhi state continued to exist for a while in Bactria under King Heraus.

ADDITIONAL RESOURCES

Frye, Richard N. *The Heritage of Central Asia: From Antiquity to the Turkish Expansion*. Princeton, N.J.: Markus Wiener, 1996.
Harmatta, János, B. N. Puri, and G. F. Etemadi, eds. *The Development of Sedentary and Nomadic Civilizations: 700 B.C. to A.D. 250*. Vol. 2 in *History of Civilizations of Central Asia*. Paris: UNESCO, 1994.

SEE ALSO: Bactria; China; Kushān Dynasty; Wudi; Xiongnu.

—*John D. Windhausen*

— Z —

ZAMA, BATTLE OF

DATE: October, 202 B.C.E.
LOCALE: Zama, in northern Africa west of Carthage
RELATED CIVILIZATIONS: Carthage, Republican Rome
SIGNIFICANCE: Rome's victory over Carthage in the Second Punic War (218-201 B.C.E.) made it the major power in the western Mediterranean.

Background. After Carthage lost its first war against Rome, its most successful general, Hamilcar, departed for Spain. His son Hannibal assumed command there in 222 B.C.E. and invaded Italy from the north over the Alps in 218 B.C.E.

Action. Hannibal defeated Roman armies at the Trebia River, Lake Trasimene, and Cannae. Capua, Syracuse, and Macedonia allied with him. Though Roman forces never defeated him in battle, they pushed Hannibal into southern Italy and defeated invasions by Hannibal's brothers Hasdrubal in 207 B.C.E. and Mago in 205.

In 203 B.C.E., Scipio Africanus invaded Africa. He defeated the Carthaginian defensive army, and Hannibal was called home. Hannibal marched west and met Scipio at Zama (ZAY-muh). Scipio turned back an ele-phant charge by blowing trumpets. The elephants stampeded and disrupted Hannibal's cavalry, which fled, pursued by the Romans. Scipio's legionnaires overwhelmed Hannibal's first and second lines and engaged his third line of Italian veterans. Soon after, Scipio's cavalry returned to envelop Hannibal's army.

Consequences. Scipio's victory ended the Second Punic War and eliminated Carthage as a major power. Rome was supreme in the western Mediterranean.

ADDITIONAL RESOURCES

Lazenby, J. F. *Hannibal's War: A Military History of the Second Punic War.* Warminster, England: Aris & Phillips, 1978.
Leckie, Ross. *Scipio Africanus.* Washington, D.C.: Regnery, 1998.
Seymour, William. *Decisive Factors in Twenty Great Battles of the World.* New York: St. Martin's Press, 1989.

SEE ALSO: Cannae, Battle of; Carthage; Hannibal; Punic Wars; Rome, Republican; Scipio Africanus.

—*James O. Smith*

ZAPOTECS

DATE: 200-700 C.E.
LOCALE: Oaxaca Valley, Mexico
SIGNIFICANCE: One of the first civilizations in Mexico, the Zapotecs developed advanced architecture and construction, urban social systems, and agricultural methods that influenced other Mesoamerican areas as far as Central America. They were the first Mesoamerican group to create a writing system and calendar.

Zapotec (zah-puh-TEHK) history can be divided into various periods, most of which correspond to Monte Albán, the most important Zapotec metropolis. The periods are Early (including Tierras Largas, San José, Guadalupe, and Rosario, 1400-500 B.C.E.), Monte Albán I (500-100 B.C.E.), Monte Albán II (100 B.C.E.-200 C.E.), Monte Albán III (200-700 C.E.), Monte Albán IV (700-950 C.E.), and Monte Albán V (950-1521 C.E.). The Classic Zapotec period, from about 200-700 C.E., corresponds to Monte Albán III. As scholars have learned more about the Classic stage, it has been broken down into two periods, IIIA and IIIB. Scholars have further identified transition times between certain periods to be particularly important and have labeled them Transition II-IIIA and Transition IIIA-IIIB.

Two funerary urns from (left) Zachila, Oaxaca, and (right) Huitzo, Oaxaca. (Courtesy Department Library Services, American Museum of Natural History)

By Transition II-IIIA, the Valley of Oaxaca was allied as a state and controlled by the Zapotecs. Monte Albán, an area of about 2.3 square miles (6 square kilometers), was the center of the civilization and consisted of various cities built on a series of flattened hilltops and containing ceremonial areas, temples, administrative buildings, plazas, ball courts, and living quarters. Monte Albán III was characterized by a highly complex political and social system, an ever-expanding population, and well-developed architecture. By IIIA, the Zapotecs, facing the threat of Mixtec incursions from the north and west, stopped their expansion into new lands and focused on maintaining control of valley areas already in their possession. They decolonized some of the outer regions of their land and moved inward. By IIIB, the Valley of Mexico's city of Teotihuacán had been destroyed, and the Classic Zapotec cultural and artistic traits reached their climax, relatively free of outside influences.

Monte Albán began declining during Period IV. Monte Albán city depopulated, and although cultural traditions remained in large part, there was a decided shift in the administrative and ruling functions of big cities. Smaller towns no longer served to support city centers.

Settlements and social structure. In Transition II-IIIA, the Valley of Oaxaca underwent a large population expansion and an increase in the use of fortified areas. The population reached its zenith of 115,000 during III. The most concentrated population was in Monte Albán city, home to about 16,500 people. The Tlacolula subvalley area grew greatly in density and included Jalieza, population 12,385. Four other towns with populations numbering in the thousands dotted the hills of the subvalley, and there were additional small villages in the flatlands. Roads connected cities.

Zapotec society was highly hierarchical, divided into nobles, commoners, and priests. Nobles were born into royalty; they ruled, fought wars, and supervised construction of temples and other buildings. They competed among themselves for access to more power and strategic marriages. In general, Zapotec rulers were first-born sons, but if a person was not deemed worthy, another son could gain the throne.

Priests had their own hierarchy: The most powerful priests, including the high priest, came from noble families. Less powerful priests were commoners trained for the priesthood. Commoners consisted of farmers, pottery makers, weavers, carpenters, shell workers, masons, and the like. They carried out the desires of the ruler, who communicated with them via various levels of nobles. Slaves, usually captives from battles, either worked or were sacrificed in rites.

Religion and ritual. Church and state were one and the same in Zapotec culture. Priests wielded much control. The ruling lord, though not a priest, was given much religious instruction. Both nobles and commoners were religious. Temples were generally made up of two rooms: Worshipers entered one room, and priests performed rites in the other. Rites included animal and human sacrifice, incense burning, self-sacrifice of blood, and use of hallucinogenic substances. Commoners' rituals may have also included use of hallucinogens, dancing, drinking, sacrifice, blood-letting, and fasting.

Ancestors of the royal family were venerated, and each town had its own group of ancestors. It was the duty of both commoners and nobles to please these ancestors.

The Zapotecs believed in a supreme being, infinite in time and space, beyond the realm of human contact. They also believed in other more palpable forces: Lightning was the strongest, accompanied by clouds, wind, rain, and hail. Sky and earth were the two halves that defined the cosmos. The entire world was divided into four quarters of black, red, white, and yellow, the center of which was blue-green.

The Zapotecs distinguished between animate and inanimate matter. All animate things contained *pee*, a life force ("wind/spirit"). *Pee* was responsible for movement and life, and all things with *pee* demanded respect. Animals were killed out of necessity, and hunters apologized to animals killed, offering the creatures' hearts to the gods.

Architecture and city planning. Zapotec cities were built on artificially flattened hilltops. Temples, palaces, plazas, and administrative buildings were located here. Architecture was planned and paid for by rulers, and commoner architects, masons, and laborers carried out the work. Construction was of stone, adobe, and wood. Classic period architecture increased in intricacy from IIIA to IIIB. Tombs, for example, were much larger, decorated with interior murals and elaborate carved decoration outside. Temples were built in flat-roof style, with two panels overhanging the build-

ings. Religious zeal was one reason for rulers to build temples, but attempts to impress commoners and other rulers were probably just as common. Temples were not destroyed, but new ones were built over the old.

Daily life, customs, and traditions. For the approximately 5 percent of all Zapotecs that were part of the ruling elite, daily life included living in a *quehui* (elaborate household). The *coqui* (hereditary lord) and his wife lived in a *yoho quehui* (royal palace) in the center of a Monte Albán city. Quehui were large squarish buildings divided into about ten to twelve rooms with an inner patio. Commoners outside of the ruling class lived in *yoho* (nonelaborate housing), about which less is known. These were located on the terraces of the flattened hilltops and in the valley. Those living on terraces may have been involved in the daily production of crafts such as pottery, while those who lived on good soils were more likely farmers. Commoners' daily lives were built around providing goods for the cities; this pattern was interrupted by various religious holidays in which all Zapotecs participated.

Death and burial. After death, nobles were placed in tombs below the palaces. They were buried with funerary urns, which were carved pieces depicting ancestors of the buried individuals, often in elaborate headdresses or masks. Tombs were large, often accessible from the ground-floor patio of the palace floor and featured murals and/or carvings. Royal burials sometimes included everyday pottery. Doors to the tomb were closed with a door stone, often carved. Tombs accommodated anywhere from one to a dozen bodies. The Zapotecs believed that after death, the noble dead rose above and became Cloud People, possessing powers of intercession with the gods.

War and weapons. Monte Albán I and II were periods of great expansion in which areas outside the Oaxaca Valley were conquered; by IIIA, expansion stopped, but more than two-thirds of all Zapotecs lived at sites with walls or other defensive structures.

Zapotec armies were created as needed, consisting of officers (nobles) and soldiers (commoners) recruited as necessary. Weapons included the obsidian-bladed sword, bow and arrow, atlatl (spear thrower), and sling. After marching into battle, Zapotec armies took the first prisoner captured and sacrificed him, saving the beating heart as an offering for the gods, and sometimes cooking and eating the body. War was waged to exact payment of a "tribute" from neighbors and to quell uprisings if they did not submit politically to the Zapotecs. More common than war, however, was the Zapotecs' skilled use of diplomacy, in which problems were solved with pacts or monetary offers. The peaceful relationship between Monte Albán and Teotihuacán is an example, recorded on a glyph, of such diplomatic relations between rulers.

Trade and commerce. Considerable evidence shows trade between the Zapotecs and Teotihuacanos; in fact, the Zapotecs had a small residential village on the outskirts of Teotihuacán, perhaps to facilitate trade. By the beginning of IIIA, Zapotec ambassadors had also traveled far southeast to Chiapa de Corzo, where Zapotec pottery has been found. Traded items were, however, visible only in palaces and other places of restricted access; trade most likely occurred as gift-giving between nobles.

Calendars and chronology. The Zapotecs had two calendars, ritual and solar. Both demonstrated their belief in a cyclical (nonlinear) time system. The ritual calendar contained twenty hieroglyphs ("day signs") and thirteen numbers, totaling 260 days. The four quarters of the calendar were calling "lightnings," each of which related to one of the world's four quarters. People were often named after the numbers and symbols corresponding to their birth dates. The ritual calendar was sacred and had *pee*. The solar calendar contained eighteen divisions of 20 days, plus 5 more days, totaling 365.

Language and literature. Zapotec belongs to the Otomanguean family of languages, of which there are five branches with many tongues. Whether more than one variant of Zapotec was spoken in the Classic period is unclear; currently the various Zapotec languages are different from each other. The Zapotec language was tonal; the meanings of words changed depending on the voice pitch employed. Scholars presume that nobles spoke a more elegant form of Zapotec than commoners.

Writing systems. The first writing to appear in Mesoamerica was at San José de Mogote, an Early period site in the Oaxaca Valley. Classic period Zapotec writing was on stone, in the form of carved symbols. These glyphs represented both ideas and sounds. Writing was developed by the nobles, first to record power struggles and sacrifices, then to express and promote themselves among other leaders and to share information with other nobles as well as commoners. Unlike other ancient Mexican writing systems such as that of the Maya, the Zapotec glyphs are still to a great extent undeciphered.

Visual arts. Zapotec art is visible in carvings and paintings on funerary urns, glyphs, figurines, tombs, and pottery. Visual arts were produced for nobles, by commoner artists. Subject matter includes representation of rulers (often in complex animal headdresses), ancestors, battles, diplomacy, and religious and social ritual. Materials included clay, jade, *tecalli*, and greenstone. In IIIA, the Oaxacan Valley style was further defined, and by IIIB, it was well established and quite ornate.

Agriculture and animal husbandry. Maize farming was a central part of Zapotec agriculture. Other crops included beans, avocados, chiles, cactus, agave, and tomatoes, all farmed by hand, as well as wild fruits and nuts. Turkeys and dogs were raised for food, while wild animals such as rabbits, deer, opossums, quail, and lizards were hunted.

Zapotec land presented various obstacles to farmers. High mountain soil was rocky and rugged, middle-range hilly soil was subject to washouts, and the rich valley soils had high rates of evaporation and low rates of rainfall, leading to drought. The Zapotecs designed systems of well and canal irrigation, terracing, and rainfall and floodwater farming to circumvent these problems.

Sports and entertainment. Ball courts built in Monte Albán II-III are standardized in size, suggesting a formal game. The game probably involved body contact (no hands) with a ball. One theory says that these I-shaped ball courts were the sites of games between communities, played to settle squabbles.

Current views. Scholarly research is attempting to determine exactly how and why the state developed in Oaxaca. Arguments include cultural/natural forces as well as emphasis on leaders forming the course of history.

ADDITIONAL RESOURCES

Blanton, Richard, et al. *Ancient Oaxaca*. Cambridge, England: Cambridge University Press, 1999.

Flannery, Kent, and Joyce Marcus. *Zapotec Civilization: How Urban Society Evolved in Mexico's Oaxaca Valley*. London: Thames and Hudson, 1996.

Paddock, John, ed. *Ancient Oaxaca: Discoveries in Mexican Archeology and History*. Stanford, Calif.: Stanford University Press, 1966.

SEE ALSO: Atlatl; Ball game, Mesoamerican; Monte Albán; Teotihuacán.

—*Michelle C. K. McKowen*

ZEALOTS

DATE: c. 100 B.C.E.-73 C.E.
LOCALE: Judaea
RELATED CIVILIZATION: Imperial Rome
SIGNIFICANCE: Believing only in the authority of God, the Zealots advocated resistance against Roman authority when Judaea was placed under Roman rule. They fought in defense of Jerusalem until its fall in 70 C.E.

Zealots started out as a religious faction maintaining strict observance of Mosaic law and emerged as a distinct political group during the reign of Herod the Great (r. 37-4 B.C.E.). They believed that Israel was a theocracy and God their only ruler. Their founder, Judah the Galilean, organized an uprising against Rome's direct rule and taxation in 6 C.E. Although the uprising was quickly extinguished, the group continued to advocate rebellion against the Romans. A violent fringe group of the Zealots, called Sicarii, carried hidden daggers and assassinated Romans and also prominent Jews who were suspected of collaboration.

The Zealots played another major role in inciting and sustaining the Jewish uprising against the Romans that began in 66 C.E. This led to the siege and capture of Jerusalem in 70 C.E. Another group of Zealots held the fortress of Masada, the spectacular thirteen-hundred-foot-high (roughly four-hundred-meter-high) rock on the edge of the Judaean desert, until 73 C.E. When it became apparent that the Romans would capture the fortress, which held nearly one thousand refugees, including women and children, the Zealots committed suicide rather than surrender.

ADDITIONAL RESOURCES
DeVaux, Roland. *The Early History of Israel*. Philadelphia: Westminster Press, 1978.
Johnson, Paul. *A History of the Jews*. 1987. Reprint. London: Phoenix, 2001.

SEE ALSO: Herodian Dynasty; Judaism; Masada, Battle of; Rome, Imperial.

—*Sheila Golburgh Johnson*

ZENGZI

ALSO KNOWN AS: *Wade-Giles* Tseng-tzu
BORN: c. 500 B.C.E.; place unknown
DIED: 436 B.C.E.; place unknown
LOCALE: Pre-Imperial state of Lu
RELATED CIVILIZATION: China
MAJOR ROLE/POSITION: Confucian religious leader

Life. Zengzi (TSENG-tsih) is traditionally regarded as one of the youngest disciples of Confucius; he was more likely a posthumous disciple. The eighth chapter of *Lunyu* (later sixth-early fifth centuries B.C.E.; *The Analects*, 1861) shows him as head of the Confucian school of Lu at his death in 436 B.C.E. The portrait of Confucius in the preceding chapter is probably his work; it presents Confucius not as an official mentor but as a sage teacher, counseling ceaseless effort at personal cultivation. This is the mystical strain in early Confucianism. When the school came under the leadership of Confucius's descendants, Zengzi was denied and derided, according to *The Analects*. In the early third

century B.C.E., he emerged as a paragon of filial piety.
Influence. A school of Zengzi evidently formed some time after his death and sponsored the new Zengzi image. *Da Xue* (possibly fifth century B.C.E.; *The Great Learning*, 1861), sometimes attributed to him, is a logical development of his interest in personal cultivation. His appearance in the classic of filial piety represents the transformed domestic Zengzi.

ADDITIONAL RESOURCES
Brooks, E. Bruce, and A. Taeko Brooks. *The Original Analects*. New York: Columbia University Press, 1998.
Legge, James. *Confucian Analects: The Great Learning, The Doctrine of the Mean*. Oxford, England: Oxford University Press, 1893. Reprint. Mineola, N.Y.: Dover, 1971.

SEE ALSO: China; Confucianism; Confucius.

—*E. Bruce Brooks*

ZENO OF CITIUM

ALSO KNOWN AS: Zeno the Stoic
BORN: c. 336-334 B.C.E.; Citium (modern Larnaca), Cyprus
DIED: c. 265-261 B.C.E.; Athens, Greece
RELATED CIVILIZATIONS: Phoenician, Hellenistic Greece
MAJOR ROLE/POSITION: Philosopher

Life. According to traditions recorded by historian Diogenes Laertius in the third century C.E., Zeno of Citium (ZEE-noh of SISH-ee-uhm) was the son of a Phoenician merchant. Shipwrecked near Athens about 312 B.C.E., he settled there and became the student of Crates the Cynic. At that time, the two major schools of Greek philosophy were the Cynics, who held to a strict morality, and the Cyrenaics, who sought the pleasure of the senses. Zeno admired Cynicism for its emphasis on virtue but opposed its distrust of reason and its pessimism. About 300 B.C.E., he began giving lectures on the Painted Porch (Stoa Poecile) in the Agora of Athens. He and his students became known as "Stoics," named after the porch. He taught there for the rest of his life and apparently wrote several books, but none of his writings survive.

Zeno taught that the universe is rationally ordered by a providential god. The duty of the people is to understood this order, which appears as fate, and to live in calm acceptance of it. To do so entails hard work. God obligates people to a threefold diligence: physics (the study of nature), logic (the study of reason), and ethics (the study of how to live properly), each equally important. Unlike the rival Epicurean school, which arose about the same time and recommended withdrawal from society for a life of quiet contemplation and refined pleasures, the Stoic school expected its adherents to be politically involved and useful in their communities, despite the pain and sacrifice. There is more pain than pleasure in life, but that fact should not bother Stoics. Accepting pain is just part of accepting fate.

Zeno of Citium, the founder of Stoicism, is not to be confused with Zeno of Elea, the discoverer of the four paradoxes of space, time, and motion.

Influence. Cleanthes succeeded Zeno as head of the Stoic school and was in turn succeeded by Chrysippus. These three thinkers are known collectively as the Early Stoics. The Middle Stoics were Panaetius and Posidonius, who taught on the Greek island of Rhodes in the second and first centuries B.C.E. Out of these two varieties of Greek Stoicism grew Roman Stoicism, eloquently stated by Cicero, Seneca the Younger, Epictetus, and Marcus Aurelius. Roman Stoicism influenced the early Christians, especially Saint Paul. The pagan Roman Stoics together with the earliest Christian Stoics are sometimes known as the Later Stoics.

ADDITIONAL RESOURCES

Colish, Marcia L. *The Stoic Tradition from Antiquity to the Early Middle Ages*. Leiden, Netherlands: E. J. Brill, 1985.
Diogenes Laertius. *Lives of Eminent Philosophers*. Translated by R. D. Hicks. Cambridge, Mass.: Harvard University Press, 1991.
Inwood, Brad. *Ethics and Human Action in Early Stoicism*. Oxford, England: Clarendon Press, 1985.

Zeno of Citium. (© Archivo Iconografico, S.A./Corbis)

Long, A. A. *Stoic Studies*. Cambridge, England: Cambridge University Press, 1996.

Reesor, Margaret E. *The Nature of Man in Early Stoic Philosophy*. New York: St. Martin's Press, 1989.

SEE ALSO: Athens; Christianity; Cicero; Epictetus; Epicurus; Greece, Hellenistic and Roman; Marcus Aurelius; Panaetius of Rhodes; Paul, Saint; Posidonius; Seneca the Younger.

—*Eric v.d. Luft*

ZENO OF ELEA

BORN: c. 490 B.C.E.; Elea, Italy
DIED: c. 440 B.C.E.; Elea, Italy
RELATED CIVILIZATION: Classical Greece
MAJOR ROLE/POSITION: Philosopher

Life. Zeno of Elea (ZEE-noh of EE-lee-uh) was a follower and defender of the "one and indivisible" philosophy of Parmenides, which directly opposed the atomists' idea of "being" composed of smaller and smaller parts. Zeno's book (now lost) used what has come to be called the *reductio ad absurdum* method of argument. Zeno began his defense by representing the atomists' idea as an extreme of multiplicity that led to contradictory conclusions and created a paradox that he believed proved the invalidity of "being" as multiple and many. His argument, however, was so confusing that it would take other philosophers in the Eleatic school to counter the atomist theory in the last half of the fifth century B.C.E.

Influence. Aristotle credited Zeno with the creation of the dialectic method of philosophical discussion, which Socrates used widely and which Aristotle disliked. Zeno and the Eleatic school's support for the "one and indivisible" theory never regained popularity after the end of the fifth century B.C.E. He is most famous for his "paradoxes," which are often studied out of their original context by philosophers, folklorists, historians, and mathematicians.

ADDITIONAL RESOURCES

Fans, J. A. *The Paradoxes of Zeno*. Brookfield, Vt.: Avebury, 1996.

Freeman, Kathleen. *Ancilla to the Pre-Socratic Philosophers*. Cambridge, Mass.: Harvard University Press, 1983.

Tejera, V. *Rewriting the History of Ancient Greek Philosophy*. Westport, Conn.: Greenwood Press, 1997.

SEE ALSO: Aristotle; Greece, Classical; Parmenides; Philosophy; Plato; Socrates.

—*Tammy Jo Eckhart*

ZENOBIA

ALSO KNOWN AS: Septima Zenobia; Bat Zabbai
BORN: c. 240 C.E.; Palmyra
DIED: after 274 C.E.; Italy
RELATED CIVILIZATIONS: Imperial Rome, Ptolemaic and Roman Egypt
MAJOR ROLE/POSITION: Queen, military leader

Life. When Zenobia's (zuh-NOH-bee-uh) husband, Odenathus, the client ruler of the Roman province of Palmyra, was assassinated in 267 C.E., Zenobia became regent on behalf of their young son. Declaring herself queen of Palmyra, she seized Egypt in 269 C.E. and conquered much of Asia Minor in 270 C.E. Although emperor Lucius Domitius Aurelianus "granted" her the titles and lands she had taken, she continued to flout Roman sovereignty by minting coins with Aurelianus's title of "Augustus" under her son's image and even with her own image on them rather than that of Aurelianus. Faced with increasingly open revolt from a woman who had already conquered about one-third of his empire, Aurelianus went to war and defeated her armies at Antioch and Emesa and besieged Palmyra in 272 C.E. Zenobia was captured and probably exhibited in Aurelianus's triumphal procession at Rome in 274 C.E. Zenobia apparently spent the rest of her life in retirement at a villa near Tivoli.

Influence. Zenobia was equally renowned for her power, beauty, and intellect and often characterized as the cultural heir to Cleopatra VII. A ruler and military leader as well as a scholar, who surrounded herself with philosophers and artists, she is an early example of a strong and independent woman.

ADDITIONAL RESOURCES
Sergeant, Philip Walsingham. *Dominant Women*. 1929. Reprint. Freeport, N.Y.: Books for Libraries Press, 1969.

Stoneman, Richard. *Palmyra and Its Empire: Zenobia's Revolt Against Rome*. Ann Arbor: University of Michigan Press, 1992.

SEE ALSO: Aurelianus, Lucius Domitius; Egypt, Ptolemaic and Roman; Rome, Imperial.

—William Nelles

ZEUS AT PERGAMUM, GREAT ALTAR OF

DATE: constructed c. 180-175 B.C.E.
LOCALE: Pergamum, in Asia Minor
RELATED CIVILIZATION: Hellenistic Greece
SIGNIFICANCE: The Great Altar is the most famous of all Hellenistic sculptural monuments.

The powerful city of Pergamum enjoyed a commanding position on the northwest coast of Asia Minor and served as the capital and showcase of the Attalid rulers, who gained royal status in the third century B.C.E. King Eumenes II (r. 197-159 B.C.E.) erected the colossal masterpiece known as the Great Altar on the Pergamene Acropolis to glorify the victories of his father Attalus I (r. 241-197 B.C.E.) against marauding Celtic-speaking Gauls (or Galatians), who had crossed from Europe to terrorize Asia Minor. The altar proper stood on a high base and was surrounded by an Ionic colonnade with projecting wings that flanked a broad staircase. The base below the surmounting colonnade carried a 400-foot (122-meter) encircling marble frieze called *Battle of Gods and Giants*, a battle in which the gods successfully fought for civilization against the violent forces unleashed by the monstrous giants. The sculptural ensemble suggests a parallel between the triumph of the gods and the victories of the Attalids, who saw themselves as preservers of Greek civilization against barbarism. Reflecting the dramatic compositions favored in Pergamene sculptors, the extravagant encircling frieze features larger-than-life figures, carved in high relief, who twist and turn with extraordinary vigor, the dramatic effect being further intensified by violent postures, anguished faces, and unruly hair.

ADDITIONAL RESOURCES
Pollitt, J. J. *Art in the Hellenistic Age*. Cambridge, England: Cambridge University Press, 1986.
Stewart, Andrew. *Greek Sculpture: An Exploration*. 2 vols. New Haven, Conn.: Yale University Press, 1990.

SEE ALSO: Attalid Dynasty; Art and architecture; Eumenes II; Gauls; Greece, Hellenistic and Roman.

—William E. Dunstan

ZEUXIS OF HERACLEA

FLOURISHED: late fifth century B.C.E.; Heraclea, Lucania, Italy
RELATED CIVILIZATION: Classical Greece
MAJOR ROLE/POSITION: Painter

Life. All that is known about the early life of Zeuxis (ZEWK-suhs) of Heraclea is that he was the pupil of either Damophilus of Himera or Neseus of Thasos, who were both active in Athens during the Peloponnesian War (431-404 B.C.E.). It was around this time that Zeuxis achieved wealth and fame as a painter.

He was a follower of Apollodorus of Athens, the inventor of shading, although Zeuxis pioneered a more painterly style and became known for remarkable illusionism and novel subject matter. Once, he competed with his rival Parrhasius, painting some grapes that fooled the birds; however, a curtain painted by Parrhasius fooled Zeuxis himself, and he was forced to admit defeat. Other well-known works by Zeuxis included a painting of Helen that reproduced the features of five beautiful virgins, and a painting of a female centaur nursing twins, one at her human breast and the other at her teat. No paintings by Zeuxis survive today.

Influence. Zeuxis was one of the most influential painters of ancient Greece. His innovative style was criticized by Plato and Aristotle and was discussed for generations afterward. The life and art of Zeuxis were a special inspiration for Renaissance and Neoclassical artists.

ADDITIONAL RESOURCES
Bruno, Vincent J. *Form and Color in Greek Painting.* New York: W. W. Norton, 1977.

Matheson, Susan B. "Zeuxis." *The Dictionary of Art.* Vol. 33. New York: Macmillan, 1996.
Pollitt, J. J. *The Art of Greece, 1400-31* B.C.: *Sources and Documents.* Rev. ed. New York: Cambridge University Press, 1990.

SEE ALSO: Apollodorus of Athens (artist); Aristotle; Art and architecture; Greece, Classical; Plato.
—*Ann M. Nicgorski*

ZHANGDI

ALSO KNOWN AS: *Wade-Giles* Chang-ti
BORN: 57 C.E.; China
DIED: April 9, 88 C.E.; China
RELATED CIVILIZATIONS: Han Dynasty, China
MAJOR ROLE/POSITION: Ruler

Life. Zhangdi (JAHNG-dee) was the fifth son of the emperor Mingdi (r. 58-75 C.E.) and his concubine Lady Jia, first cousin of Mingdi's childless empress Ma. The two women worked out a power-sharing arrangement whereby Zhangdi became heir apparent on April 8, 60 C.E., the same day that Ma was enthroned as empress. Ma had primary responsibility for the rearing of the future emperor.

Zhangdi became emperor on September 5, 75 C.E. In 77 C.E., he accepted as concubines two sisters from the Dou clan that rivaled the Ma. The elder Dou eventually became the emperor's consort, but no sons were born of this union. In 79 C.E., Zhangdi proclaimed as his heir Liu Qing, his third son, whose mother had been introduced into the emperor's harem by the Empress Ma. Later in the same year, however, Ma died, and the Empress Dou replaced Liu Qing as heir apparent with the emperor's fourth son, Hedi, whose mother was allied with the Dou. This marked the end of Ma political power. The Empress Dou raised Hedi, whose mother had died by 83 C.E.

Despite these dynastic intrigues, the reign of Zhangdi was marked by peace within China, significant improvement in land communication in the south, and successful military campaigns in Central Asia under general Ban Chao.

Influence. Following Zhangdi's death, the power of the dowager empress increased significantly at the Chinese court.

ADDITIONAL RESOURCES
Hucker, Charles O. *China's Imperial Past.* Stanford, Calif.: Stanford University Press, 1975.
Paludau, Ann. *Chronicle of the Chinese Emperors.* New York: Thames and Hudson, 1998.

SEE ALSO: Ban Chao; China; Han Dynasty.
—*Thomas J. Sienkewicz*

ZHIYI

ALSO KNOWN AS: *Wade-Giles* Chih-i
BORN: 538 C.E.; Hunan Province, China
DIED: 597 C.E.; Mount Tiantai, Zhejiang Province, China
RELATED CIVILIZATION: China
MAJOR ROLE/POSITION: Monk

Life. Zhiyi (JEE-yee) is considered to be the greatest of all Chinese Buddhist philosophers. He is especially renowned for his work in systematizing the diverse doctrinal and practical details that had come to plague Chinese Buddhism. After establishing a monastery on Mount Tiantai, Zhiyi spent his life creating the first truly Chinese school of Buddhism, effectively unifying the disparate aspects of sixth century C.E. Buddhism into a comprehensive system. Zhiyi's primary work involved the classification of the voluminous Buddhist scriptures so as to explain the often contradictory statements and doctrines preached by the Buddha. His system of "five periods and eight teachings" categorized the canon into various types of teachings introduced by the Buddha at different times in his career. Rather than contradicting one another, the scriptures were fully complementary and advanced a coherent body of religious truth. Particularly unique to Zhiyi's work was his unification of Buddhist practice with doctrine, what he referred to as analogous to the "two wings of a bird."

Influence. While technically considered the third patriarch of the Tiantai school, Zhiyi undoubtedly was the actual founder. His synthesis of practice and doctrine incorporated nearly everything that preceded it and undoubtedly inspired everything that followed. Zhiyi's practice of *zhiguan*, or concentration and insight, continues to be one of the most widespread meditation techniques in East Asian Buddhism.

ADDITIONAL RESOURCES

Hurvitz, Leon N. *Chih-i (538-597): An Introduction to the Life and Ideas of a Chinese Buddhist Monk.* Brussels: Institut Belge des Hautes Écoles Chinoises, 1962.
Swanson, Paul L. *Foundations of T'ien-t'ai Philosophy.* Berkeley: Asian Humanities Press, 1989.

SEE ALSO: Buddhism; China.

—Jeffrey Dippmann

ZHOU DYNASTY

ALSO KNOWN AS: *Wade-Giles* Chou Dynasty
DATE: c. 1066-256 B.C.E.
LOCALE: China
RELATED CIVILIZATION: Late Neolithic China
SIGNIFICANCE: The Zhou Dynasty shaped Chinese culture and marked the beginning of the collection of China's historical documents.

The Zhou (JOH) Dynasty is divided into two parts, the Western Zhou (1066-771 B.C.E.) and the Eastern Zhou (770-256 B.C.E.). The Western Zhou began when the last Shang ruler was overthrown by a chieftain of the Zhou tribe, a seminomadic clan from the Wei Valley in modern Shaanxi Province. The Zhou established a capital in Hao, near modern Xi'an. The Western Zhou shared the language and culture of the Shang, and their government was a feudal monarchy in which effective control depended primarily on familial ties. Through conquest and colonization, the early Zhou kings gradually united and ruled over much of the region north of the Yangtze River.

In 771 B.C.E. invading barbarians and rebel lords sacked the Zhou court and killed its king. Hao was ruined and no longer habitable. The new ruler moved the capital to Luoyi, near modern Luoyang, Henan Province, starting the Eastern Zhou period. Because of the fragmentation of the kingdom and the diminished power of the Zhou court, Chinese historians divide the Eastern Zhou into two periods: the Spring and Autumn (770-476 B.C.E.) and the Warring States (475-221 B.C.E.). It was during the Eastern Zhou period that China's recorded history took on its characteristic form, with the collections of documents and historical romances. It was also during this time that the decline of the ancient forms of religion and the transformation into Confucianism and Daoism took place.

Bronze food vessels and ladle from the Eastern Zhou Dynasty. (© Royal Ontario Museum/Corbis)

1166 · *Zhou style*

ENCYCLOPEDIA OF THE ANCIENT WORLD

Franke, Herbert, and Denis Twitchett. *Alien Regimes and Border States*. Vol. 6 in *The Cambridge History of China*. New York: Cambridge University Press, 1994.

A Journey into China's Antiquity: National Museum of Chinese History. Vol. 1. Beijing, China: Morning Glory, 1997.

Shaughnessy, Edward. *Sources of Western Zhou History: Inscribed Bronze Vessels*. Berkeley: University of California Press, 1991.

SEE ALSO: Confucianism; Daoism; Shang Dynasty; Zhou style.

—*Hong Xiao*

ZHOU STYLE

DATE: c. 771-256 B.C.E.
LOCALE: Shandong Province, through Henan, Hubei, and Hunan Provinces
RELATED CIVILIZATIONS: Zhou Dynasty, China
SIGNIFICANCE: Zhou style describes an artistic style that can be found in bronzes, jades, lacquerware, and all forms of art in the late Zhou Dynasty.

Although the late Zhou (JOH) Dynasty was marked by unrest and warfare, it also was a time when Confucianism and Daoism flourished. The arts flourished, performing new roles in society and becoming more refined. The bronzes of the Shang and early Zhou periods, mostly ceremonial wine and food vessels, were replaced by new shapes such as bells and mirrors that reflected different uses.

During the late Zhou period, a variety of new materials came to be used as Chinese craftspeople expanded their knowledge of techniques and raw materials. Bronzes were delicately inlaid with gold, silver, and semiprecious stones. Pictorial subjects, such as playful, intertwining snakes and dragons, decorated the backs

of bronze mirrors. The Zhou style could be found in almost every medium. Paintings from this period (few of which survive) depicted people and historic scenes. Lacquerware most likely developed in the south part of China during this period. The technique of layering fine cloth and lacquer mixed with color pigments to form objects that were light and waterproof is best demonstrated by wares from Changsha. Jade was used for funerary and ritual objects, and new shapes and finishes were added to the existing pottery tradition.

ADDITIONAL RESOURCES

Li, Xuebin. *Eastern Zhou and Qin Dynasties*. Translated by K. C. Chang. New Haven, Conn.: Yale University Press, 1985.

Watson, William. *The Arts of China to* A.D. *900*. New Haven, Conn.: Yale University Press, 1995.

SEE ALSO: China; Confucianism; Daoism; Zhou Dynasty.

—*Juliana Y. Yuan*

ZHUANGZI

ALSO KNOWN AS: *Wade-Giles Chuang-tzu*; *Chuang Chou*
AUTHORSHIP: Unknown; traditionally Zhuangzi (c. 369-286 B.C.E.)
DATE: traditionally c. 300 B.C.E.; probably compiled c. 285-160 B.C.E.
LOCALE: China
RELATED CIVILIZATION: China
SIGNIFICANCE: An appealing if miscellaneous literary embodiment of Daoist thought.

Zhuangzi (JEW-AHNG-tsih; *The Divine Classic of Nan-hua*, 1881; also known as *The Complete Works of Chuang Tzu*, 1968; commonly known as *Zhuangzi*, 1991) contains stories (some unfavorable) about the person Zhuangzi but does not claim him as its author. He figures in part as a philosophical opponent of Hui Shi, supposedly a late-fourth century minister in Wei. These stories may be merely emblematic, and there is no firm information on Zhuangzi from other sources.

The text is heterogeneous, and interpretations of it vary. Some parts advocate counterculture primitivism; others expound cosmology-based rulership. Some ideas (transmigration), motifs (the frog in the well), and literary devices (animal fables) are unique in China but have Indian parallels and may be echoes of Indian thought. Relations with Chinese texts generally imply a third century B.C.E. date; further additions were made during the Han Dynasty.

Themes appealing to modern readers include lyrical acceptance of death, transcending ordinary existence, and the inadequacy of logic to grasp ultimate reality.

Chapter 33 is not part of the text, but a Han survey of Warring States thought.

ADDITIONAL RESOURCES

Liu, Xiaogan. *Classifying the Zhuangzi Chapters*. Ann Arbor: University of Michigan Press, 1995.

Watson, Burton. *The Complete Works of Chuang Tzu*. New York: Columbia University Press, 1960.

SEE ALSO: China; Daoism; Laozi.

—*E. Bruce Brooks*

ZHUGE LIANG

ALSO KNOWN AS: *Wade-Giles* Chu-ko Liang
BORN: 181 C.E.; Yangdu, Shandong Province, China
DIED: 234 C.E.; China
RELATED CIVILIZATIONS: Eastern Han Dynasty, Three Kingdoms, China
MAJOR ROLE/POSITION: Political and military leader

Life. Born into a scholar-official family, Zhuge Liang (JEW-geh-LEE-AHNG) was orphaned during the Yellow Turban rebellion and raised by his uncle. He accompanied his uncle to the middle Yangtze region. As a precocious farmer-scholar, he became well known for his scholarship and insight into contemporary politics of the late Han Dynasty. In 206 C.E., he joined the staff of Liu Bei (r. 221-223 C.E.) and outlined for him a strategy for unifying China, ousting Cao Cao, and reviving the Han Dynasty. His plan called for an alliance with Sun Quan and the seizure of important geographic points to serve as a base for a two-pronged offensive to seize the north China plain and unify China. After 219 C.E., the political situation had changed and Zhuge Liang's plan was no longer viable.

After the death of Liu Bei in 223 C.E., Zhuge Liang served as prime minister of the Shu state (present-day Sichuan Province) and adviser to his son, who inherited the imperial title. Beginning in 228 C.E., he launched a series of campaigns north through the Qinling mountains. Failing to achieve any dramatic results, he died while campaigning in the Wei River valley. Over the centuries, controversy has arisen over whether these offensives were a variant of his earlier plan or a limited offensive to improve the strategic defensive position of Shu.

Influence. Zhuge Liang has been venerated in Chinese folklore as the epitome of the loyal but unsuccessful hero and acclaimed for his strategic acumen.

ADDITIONAL RESOURCES

Huang, Ray. *China: A Macro History*. Armonk, N.Y.: M. E. Sharpe, 1997.

Hucker, Charles O. *China's Imperial Past*. Stanford, Calif.: Stanford University Press, 1975.

Killigrew, John W. "Zhuge Liang and the Northern Campaign of 228-234." *Early Medieval China* 5 (1999): 55-91.

Twitchett, Denis, and Michael Loewe, eds. *The Ch'in and Han Empires*. Vol.1 in *The Cambridge History of China*. Cambridge, England: Cambridge University Press, 1986.

SEE ALSO: Cao Cao; China; Han Dynasty; Three Kingdoms.

—*John W. Killigrew*

Zi Si

ALSO KNOWN AS: *Wade-Giles* Tzu-ssu
BORN: c. 439 B.C.E.; place unknown
DIED: c. 378 B.C.E.; place unknown
LOCALE: Pre-Imperial state of Lu
RELATED CIVILIZATION: China
MAJOR ROLE/POSITION: Religious leader

Life. Tradition regards Zi Si (TZIH-see) as the grandson of Confucius, born before his death (479 B.C.E.) and providing a link between Confucius and later Confucianism, and as an adviser of Prince Mu of Lu (r. 410- 378 B.C.E.). These two claims are inconsistent: The latter is supported by early testimony, and the former must be abandoned. However, Zi Si was apparently the first of that family to serve as head of the Confucian school in Lu, following a period of disciple leadership in which the key figure was Zengzi.

For Zengzi's inner-cultivation approach, Zi Si substituted outer cultivation or ritual propriety (*li*) and official service. Chapter 11 (written by Zi Si's son) attacks Zengzi and other early disciples. An unknown text recovered from a third century tomb shows Zi Si defending ministers' right to criticize rulers; a logical development of his historical position. The Doctrine of the Mean, also associated with him, reflects a Mencian synthesis of this position and the self-cultivation of Zengzi.

Influence. With Zengzi, Zi Si was one of the two principal figures of Confucianism in the century after Confucius.

ADDITIONAL RESOURCES

Brooks, E. Bruce, and A. Taeko Brooks. *The Original Analects*. New York: Columbia University Press, 1998.
Legge, James. *Confucian Analects: The Great Learning, The Doctrine of the Mean*. Oxford, England: Oxford University Press, 1893. Reprint. Mineola, N.Y.: Dover, 1971.

SEE ALSO: China; Confucianism; Confucius; Zengzi.

—*E. Bruce Brooks*

Znaga

ALSO KNOWN AS: Zenaga
DATE: 2000 B.C.E.-700 C.E.
LOCALE: The Sahara and Sahel of southern Mauritania and northern Senegal between Medera and the Atlantic coast
RELATED CIVILIZATIONS: Bedouins, Berbers
SIGNIFICANCE: Bedouin people speaking the Znaga language, which descended from the proto-Berber language of the Afroasiatic language family, inhabit the Sahel, which links the Saharan and Niger Delta trade zones.

Znaga pastoralists were descendants of proto-Berbers who lived before 3000 B.C.E. in northern Africa. The ancestral Berbers migrated both westward toward the Atlantic and eastward on the frontiers of the Egyptian kingdoms. A major westward expansion of Berbers took place in the third millennium B.C.E. By the second millennium B.C.E., the ancestral Znaga communities took shape farther south, near the western Sahel at the edge of the Niger inland delta zone. Their position at the interface of the inland Niger Delta and Sahara afforded the ancestral Znaga an opportunity to be important participants in trade between the two zones. The ancestral Znaga raised sheep and goats, which they could exchange for delta products such as fish, rice, and copper. In the second millennium C.E., the Znaga became Arabized with the spread of Islam and Islamic culture across the Sahara.

ADDITIONAL RESOURCES

Applegate, Joseph R. "The Berber Languages." In Vol. 6 of *Current Trends in Linguistics*, edited by Thomas A. Sebeok. The Hague: Mouton, 1970.
Basset, René Marie Joseph. *Mission au Senegal*. Paris: Leroux, 1909.
McIntosh, Roderick. *Peoples of the Middle Niger: The Island of Gold*. Oxford, Mass.: Blackwell Publishers, 1998.

SEE ALSO: Africa, North; Berbers; Egypt, Pharaonic; Niger-Congo.

—*Catherine Cymone Fourshey*

ZOROASTER

ALSO KNOWN AS: Zarathustra
BORN: c. 628 B.C.E.; probably Rhages, northeastern Iran
DIED: c. 551 B.C.E.; probably northern Iran
RELATED CIVILIZATION: Persia
MAJOR ROLE/POSITION: Prophet

Life. The Zoroastrian tradition relates that Zoroaster (ZOHR-uh-was-tur) was from the Spitamid clan, which resided somewhere in eastern Persia or Central Asia in the first millennium B.C.E. Knowledge of him comes primarily from his utterances, which make up the most sacred part of the Zoroastrian scriptures, the *Gathas*. These hymns are a series of dialogues between him and the supreme deity, Ahura Mazda. These hymns indicate that he was unable to propagate his religion in his native land. Consequently, he left for eastern Persia, where he found the support of the local ruler, king Wishtasp. Wishtasp accepted Zoroaster's message and made it current in the territory under his rule. There were other Aryan religions and cults practiced by Karapans and Usijs, opponents of Zoroaster, who were competing with him.

Zoroaster was a reformer of the Aryan religion, which included many deities that were categorized as the Ahuras and Daivas. In his reform, he made Ahura Mazda ("wise lord") supreme and other Ahuras subordinate to him. The Ahuras are responsible for the creation of all that is good in this world. The Daivas, who kept their status as deities in India, became demons in Zoroaster's reform and were placed in constant opposition to the Ahuras. According to Zoroaster, Ahura Mazda created twin spirits, Angra Mainyu (Ahriman), a destructive force who chose deceit, darkness, and death, and Spenta Mainyu, a beneficent force who chose truth, light, and life. In this battle between the two forces, humans were given free will to choose which side to support. However, all people will be judged at the end of the world; those on the side of Ahura Mazda will remain in "the house of songs" (heaven), and those who have chosen otherwise will be sent to "the worst existence" (hell). Thus, Zoroaster's mission was to let people know of what was to come and whom to choose as their rightful god before the day of judgment. Later sources state that during his old age, Zoroaster was killed by an enemy to him and his religion.

Influence. Zoroaster replaced the polytheism, animal sacrifice, and magic that characterized Persian religion with an ethics-based, more spiritual monotheistic way of worship that would spread through the area and flourish for more than a thousand years.

ADDITIONAL RESOURCES
Bausani, Alessandro. *Religion in Iran: From Zoroaster to Baha'ullah.* New York: Bibliotheca Persica Press, 2000.
Boyce, Mary. *A History of Zoroastrianism: The Early Period.* Leiden, Netherlands: E. J. Brill, 1975.
Gnoli, Gherardo. *Zoroaster's Time and Homeland.* Naples, Italy: Instituto Universitario Orientale, 1980.

Zoroaster. (Hulton Archive)

Insler, Stanley. *The Gathas of Zarathustra*. Leiden, Netherlands: E. J. Brill, 1978.

Jackson, A. V. William. *Zoroaster: The Prophet of Ancient Iran*. 1898. Reprint. New York: Macmillan, 1965.

SEE ALSO: *Avesta*; Persia; Religion and ritual; Sāsānian Empire; Zoroastrianism.

—*Touraj Daryaees*

ZOROASTRIANISM

DATE: c. 700 B.C.E.-700 C.E.
LOCALE: Persia (modern Iran)
RELATED CIVILIZATION: Persia
SIGNIFICANCE: This influential religious movement in the ancient world had lasting influences on Judaism and Christianity.

The beginnings of Zoroastrianism (zohr-uh-AS-tree-uh-nih-zm) are obscure but linked to a historical figure, Zoroaster (also known as Zarathustra). There is scholarly debate as to when he lived, but his birth and death dates are generally given as circa 628 to circa 551 B.C.E. The religious tradition was firmly established by the reign of Persian emperor Darius the Great (r. 522-486 B.C.E.), who was a strong proponent of Zoroastrianism. Zoroastrianism has a body of scriptures, the *Avesta*, which includes a collection of poems, the *Gathas*, written in an old style and believed to have been composed by Zoroaster.

Zoroaster was the son of a priest of a pastoral group in what became northern Iran. Early in life, he exhibited an interest in religion. At age thirty, he had a religious experience in which he claimed to be transported by an angel to Ahura Mazda (the wise lord), who provided the first of a series of religious revelations. The most significant aspect of the revelation was that there was a single god, so Zoroaster began preaching against polytheism. He also emphasized the importance of ethical living. He met early opposition but eventually converted the Persian king, Hystaspes (Vishtaspa).

After Zoroaster's death, the religion continued to be influential in what was becoming the Persian Empire. With the Muslim conquest of the Persian Empire in 651 C.E., Zoroastrianism largely disappeared. A group known as the Parsees, who fled the Muslim invasion and settled in western India, still practice Zoroastrianism today.

Important beliefs of Zoroastrianism include the belief in monotheism and the expectation of a final judgment day. People will go to either heaven or hell depending on the moral quality of their lives. Also significant was the notion of a spiritual and moral dualism that exhibited itself in an ongoing battle of good against evil. According to Zoroaster, although there is only one god, there exists an evil force, Angra Mainyu (Ahriman), who is engaged in the struggle to capture human souls. The gods and spirits of polytheism were viewed as agents of evil. These beliefs—of a spiritual evil force at work in the world, of a final judgment day, and of the assignment to heaven or hell based on moral criteria—influenced Judaism and were eventually incorporated into Christianity.

ADDITIONAL RESOURCES

Clark, Peter. *Zoroastrianism: An Introduction to an Ancient Faith*. Sussex, England: Sussex Academic Press, 1999.

Hartz, Paula R. *Zoroastrianism*. New York: Facts on File, 1999.

Neusner, Jacob. *Judaism and Zoroastrianism at the Dusk of Late Antiquity: How Two Ancient Faiths Wrote Down Their Great Traditions*. Atlanta: Scholars Press, 1993.

Nigosian, Solomon A. *The Zoroastrian Faith: Tradition and Modern Research*. Toronto: McGill-Queens University Press, 1993.

Zaehner, R. C. *The Dawn and Twilight of Zoroastrianism*. New York: G. P. Putnam's Sons, 1961.

SEE ALSO: Avesta; Christianity; Darius the Great; Islam; Judaism; Persia; Religion and ritual; Zoroaster.

—*Charles L. Kammer III*

ZOSKALES

ALSO KNOWN AS: Za Hakala; Ze Haquile
FLOURISHED: mid-first century C.E.
RELATED CIVILIZATION: Axum
MAJOR ROLE/POSITION: King

Life. The *Periplus Maris Erythraei* (also known as *Periplus*, first century C.E.; *Periplus of the Erythraean Sea*, 1980), a Greek geographical text probably written by an Egyptian sea captain, contains a reference to an obscure local ruler named Zoskales (ZOHS-keh-leeze). In this work, he is described as administering a portion of the Red Sea coast of Africa centered on the port of Adulis (modern Zula, Eritrea). The anonymous writer states that despite Zoskales' reputed stinginess and acquisitiveness, he was a respectable sovereign and literate in Greek. The passage details goods imported to and exported from Adulis, illustrating its conomic connections with Europe and India. All other events or aspects of Zoskales' reign are unknown.

Most scholars believe that this literary description of Zoskales constitutes the earliest historical reference to the ancient Ethiopian kingdom of Axum and one of its rulers. Some scholars equate Zoskales with Za Hakala, a ruler named in a later Ethiopian list of kings. However, there is little positive evidence for this identification. Considerable debate also persists concerning the territorial extent of his realm and his power within it. Many Greek inscriptions are found at Axumite archaeological sites, suggesting that the royal use of that language as portrayed in *On the Periplus of the Erythraean Sea* may be correct.

Influence. The description of Zoskales in Greek literature provides the first historical indication of the Axumite kingdom and demonstrates significant economic and cultural interaction between the Hellenic world and Ethiopia.

ADDITIONAL RESOURCES

Burstein, Stanley M., ed. *Ancient African Civilizations: Kush and Axum*. Princeton, N.J.: Markus Wiener, 1998.

Casson, L. *The Periplus Maris Erythraei*. Princeton, N.J.: Princeton University Press, 1989.

Kobishchanov, Yuri M. *Axum*. Translated by L. Kapitanoff. University Park: Pennsylvania State University Press, 1979.

SEE ALSO: Axum; Ethiopia; Greece, Hellenistic and Roman.

—Ian Janssen

ZURVANISM

DATE: 300 B.C.E.-700 C.E.
LOCALE: Persia (modern Iran)
SIGNIFICANCE: Zurvanism was a heterodox development of Zoroastrianism.

Zurvan, also known as Zrvan in Avestan and Zurwan in Pahlavi, was the chief god of a late form of Zoroastrianism that developed in the late Achaemenian period and became important in the Parthian (245 B.C.E.-224 C.E.) and Sāsānian periods (224-651 C.E.) in Persia. Some have speculated that Zurvan may have been a pre-Zoroastrian god of the Medes.

From the third century C.E. onward, Zurvan ("time") was held to be the father of the twin spirits mentioned in a Zoroastrian text, the good Ormazd (Ahura Mazda) and the evil Ahriman (Angra Mainyu). Zurvanism was fatalistic in its outlook.

Because almost all the sources are late and non-Zoroastrian, there is considerable disagreement about the nature of this movement. The Denkard, a late, ninth century C.E. Pahlavi text, speaks of Zurvanism as a demon-inspired heresy.

Its very existence in the late Achaemenian and Parthian periods is more inferred than proven. Some scholars believe that Zurvanism was a dominant philosophical movement during the Sāsānian period. Others think that Zurvanism was the religion of the people as opposed to the Mazdaism (that is, Zoroastrianism) of the court. Some believe that Zurvanism was prevalent in southwestern Iran, while Mazdaism was popular among the Parthians.

ADDITIONAL RESOURCES

Boyce, Mary. *A History of Zoroastrianism: Under the Achaemenians*. Leiden, Netherlands: E. J. Brill, 1982.

————. *Zoroastrians: Their Religious Beliefs and Practices*. London: Routledge and Kegan Paul, 1986.

Clark, Peter. *Zoroastrianism: An Introduction to an Ancient Faith*. Sussex, England: Sussex Academic Press, 1999.

Zaehner, R. C. *The Dawn and Twilight of Zoroastrianism*. New York: G. P. Putnam's Sons, 1961.

————. *Zurvan: A Zoroastrian Dilemma*. Oxford, England: Oxford University Press, 1955.

SEE ALSO: Parthia; Persia; Sāsānian Empire; Zoroaster; Zoroastrianism.

—*Edwin Yamauchi*

Time Line

The following is *not* a listing of the articles in this encyclopedia; for a chronological listing of those articles, please see "Chronological List of Entries," at the end of this volume. Below are events and developments in the ancient world (to approximately 700 C.E. or somewhat later, depending on the region), selected by the editor as milestones in the early history of the nineteen regions covered: Africa, Anatolia, Arabia, Central Asia, China, Egypt, Europe, Greece, Japan, Korea, Mesoamerica, Mesopotamia, Middle/Near East, North America, Oceania, Rome, South America, South Asia, and Southeast Asia. Please note that dates, particularly those before the common era (or B.C.E.), are often approximate and may vary among sources.

—T.J.S.

AFRICA

To 8000 B.C.E.	Afrasan, Rub, Chifumbaze complex, Aquatic and Smithfield cultures are developing.
6000 B.C.E.	Settlements begin to appear along the Nile, Niger, and Congo Rivers.
6000 B.C.E.	East Sahelian culture begins in northern Africa.
3500 B.C.E.	Oldishi and Olmalenge traditions are developing.
3400-3200 B.C.E.	Ta-Seti culture flourishes in northeast Africa.
2700 B.C.E.	The culture of the Gash group develops near the border of modern Sudan and Ethiopia.
2500 B.C.E.	Wawats and Yam appear in Africa.
2400 B.C.E.	Kerma (Karmah) Empire builds a civilization on the Upper Nile.
2000 B.C.E.	Znaga culture develops in the Sahara.
1493 B.C.E.	The Kingdom of Kush begins to develop along the Upper Nile.
1000 B.C.E.	Bantu migration through southern Africa begins.
800 B.C.E.	Carthage is founded by Phoenicians from Tyre (legendarily under Queen Dido).
747 B.C.E.	Egypt is conquered by Kashta and his son Piye (Piankhi), kings of Nubia, initiating the Twenty-fifth, or Ethiopian, Dynasty.
716 B.C.E.	Shabaka, son of Kashta and Piye's younger brother, ascends the throne of Kush, relocating the capital to Thebes and effectively reuniting the Nile Valley civilizations.
700 B.C.E.	The languages of the Agaw, an ancient Cushitic-speaking people that lived in the northern and central Ethiopian plateau, begin to replace Omotic tongues in northern and central Ethiopia.
670 B.C.E.	The Kushites withdraw to the south and establish a new kingdom at Meroe.
600 B.C.E.	The Iron Age begins in Africa.
515 B.C.E.	The Greek explorer Scylax of Caryanda sails to the Indian Ocean.
500 B.C.E.	Early Ethiopian civilization develops in the highlands of the province of Tigray in the northeast part of Ethiopia.
500 B.C.E.	Nok culture flourishes in Central Nigeria.
264 B.C.E.	The First Punic War between Rome and Carthage begins. In this war, Rome gains control of Sicily.
218 B.C.E.	The Second Punic War between Rome and Carthage begins. The Carthaginian general Hannibal crosses the Alps to invade Italy.
202 B.C.E.	The Roman Scipio Africanus defeats the Carthaginian Hannibal in the Battle of Zama and ends the Second Punic War. Rome gains control of the entire western Mediterranean except the territory of Carthage in North Africa.
149 B.C.E.	The Third Punic War between Rome and Carthage begins. Carthage is destroyed in 146.
200 C.E.	Collapse of the Kushite civilization.
289 C.E.	After the nomadic Beja people conduct repeated raids on Egyptian border outposts, the Ptolemaic emperor Diocletian moves the Roman frontier back to Aswan.

300 C.E.	The kingdom of Axum (Aksum) develops in Ethiopia. Monophysite Christianity comes to Ethiopia during the reign of the emperor Ezana.
300 C.E.	Wagadu (Ghana) begins to develop.
410 C.E.	The Visigoths sack Rome and continue their pillage through Spain and North Africa.
430 C.E.	Augustine, bishop of Hippo and author of *Confessions* and *City of God*, dies in Numidia (modern Algeria).
460-497 C.E.	Arrival of the Nine Saints in Axum; they uphold the Monophysite Christian doctrine.
500-700 C.E.	The Nobatae civilization, successors to the kingdom of Meroe in Nubia, flourishes.
525 C.E.	King Kaleb of Axum defeats the Ḥimyarite kingdom of Yemen.
600 C.E.	Bantu migration reaches southernmost Africa.
639 C.E.	Islamic Arabs begin their African invasion with the conquest of Egypt.
652 C.E.	The king of Makouria and Egypt's Muslim rulers reach an agreement known as the Baqt, which institutionalizes economic relations and guarantees the sovereignty of Makouria, a non-Muslim kingdom—an event without precedent in early Islamic history. Nubia is left in peace and the Arabs enjoy a stable frontier until the fourteenth century C.E.
669 C.E.	The Muslim conquest reaches Morocco.

ANATOLIA

8000-7000 B.C.E.	People are living in painted brick houses at Hacilar, near Lake Burdur, which over the next millennium yields a sophisticated agricultural and pottery-making society.
6200 B.C.E.	The city of Çatalhüyük thrives on the plains of Anatolia.
3100 B.C.E.	Hurrian civilization begins in Anatolia.
1900-1700 B.C.E.	Written records refer to Assyrian kings such as Erishum, Sargon I, and Puzur-Ashur.
c. 1700 B.C.E.	The Old Hittite Kingdom begins under Hattusilis.
1500 B.C.E.	The Hittite king Telepinus proclaims his edict.
1400 B.C.E.	The New Hittite Kingdom begins.
1275 B.C.E.	A battle is fought at Kadesh between the Egyptian pharaoh Rameses II and Hittite king Muwatallis. Hittite victory halts Egyptian inroads into Syria.
1185 B.C.E.	The Hittite Empire falls to the Mediterranean Sea Peoples.
1180 B.C.E.	The New Hittite Kingdom ends.
1125 B.C.E.	The Trojan War is said to have ended with the fall of the city to the Greeks.
1100-1000 B.C.E.	Aegean Sea Peoples begin migrating to western Anatolia, and the Greeks settle in Ionia.
Mid-700's B.C.E.	The Kingdom of Urartu, the leading opponent of the Assyrian Empire, flourishes.
650 B.C.E.	Coinage is invented by the Lydians.
600 B.C.E.	Pre-Socratic philosophers begin philosophic inquiry in Ionia.
500's B.C.E.	Lydians conflict with Medians in eastern Anatolia. Persians begin infiltration.
546 B.C.E.	Cyrus the Great captures Sardis and ends the reign of Croesus, king of Lydia.
510 B.C.E.	The Greco-Persian Wars begin with the Ionian Revolt.
431-404 B.C.E.	The Greeks push back the Persians during the Peloponnesian Wars.
353 B.C.E.	Artemesia builds the Halicarnassus mausoleum for her dead brother Mausolus, tyrant of Caria in Anatolia.
333 B.C.E.	Alexander the Great destroys the Persians' Achaemenian Empire. Anatolia is divided between Egypt and the Seleucids thereafter, becoming the site of Celtic and Cappadocian incursions from the north and west.
133 B.C.E.	Rome has conquered western Anatolia and by the first century reorganizes all of Asia Minor politically into provinces of the Eastern Empire, centered on Constantinople.
6th cent. C.E.	Arab Muslims end Roman domination of Anatolia.

ARABIA

15th cent. B.C.E.	The Kingdom of Saba³ flourishes, associated with the Queen of Sheba, who visits King Solomon in Israel.
1st mill. B.C.E.	Ḥimyaritic kingdoms flourish from caravan trade.
65 B.C.E.	The Nabataean kingdom, which rules the region from the Gulf of Aqaba northward to the Dead Sea, makes first contact with Republican Rome.
25 B.C.E.	Nabataea is the base for the only Roman expedition to penetrate Arabia.
105 C.E.	Rome annexes Nabataea into Provincia Arabia.
272 C.E.	Rome attacks and defeats Palmyra in the Syro-Arabian Desert, a powerful kingdom at the starting point of the western trade route.
4th cent. C.E.	A century of domination by various Abyssinian Christian sects ends in economic disruption. Collapse of the Ma³rib Dam drives Ḥimyarites northward.
400's-500's C.E.	Feuding Bedouin tribes dominate the region. Mecca (governed by the Quraysh) and Medina served as trading posts along the extended caravan routes between South Arabia and the Fertile Crescent.
570 C.E.	The future prophet of Islam, Muḥammad, is born.
571 C.E.	Abyssinian Christians are driven out by Persians.
610 C.E.	Muḥammad has a religious experience that leads to the foundation of Islam.
630 C.E.	Muḥammad gains control of Mecca in Arabia.
637 C.E.	Arabs occupy Persia and begin the spread of Islam.
641 C.E.	The Arabs conquer Egypt.
651 C.E.	The Arab conquest of Iran ends the Sāsānian Dynasty.
661 C.E.	The Umayyad (Omayyad) Dynasty begins rule over the Empire of the Caliphates (Arab kingdom).
669 C.E.	The Muslim conquest reaches Morocco.

CENTRAL ASIA

5000-3000 B.C.E.	Kelteminar culture develops in Central Asia south of the Aral Sea.
3000 B.C.E.	Kitoi culture begins in Central Asia (present-day Russia)
2500 B.C.E.	Afanasievo culture begins in Siberia, Kazakhstan, Mongolia, and Xinjiang, representing the transition from the Neolithic to the Bronze Age in these areas.
2000 B.C.E.	The Mongols originate in the region around Lake Baikal, the natural boundary between Siberia and present-day Mongolia.
1750 B.C.E.	Andronovo culture, the bridge between the Neolithic and Bronze Age civilizations in Kazakhstan and Western Siberia, begins.
1250 B.C.E.	Karasuk culture begins to develop in southern Siberia, Mongolia, and Kazakhstan.
1000-690 B.C.E.	The Cimmerians, an Indo-European people related to the Thracians, live in the Ukraine.
8th cent. B.C.E.	The Scythians hunt the Cimmerians to extinction in the Volga River Valley, Armenia, the borders of Assyria, and Asia Minor.
c. 540 B.C.E.	Cyrus the Great conquers Bactria.
5th cent. B.C.E.	Bactria begins as a satrapy of the Achaemenian Dynasty of Persians between the Hisar and Hindu Kush Mountains (present-day Uzbekistan, Tajikistan, and Afghanistan).
4th cent. B.C.E.	The Xiongnu Huns begin to inhabit North and Central Asia.
330 B.C.E.	Alexander begins a campaign into Bactria.
245 B.C.E.	The Greco-Bactrian kingdom is established when Diodotus I, the Greek governor of Bactria, revolts against the Seleucid Dynasty.
200 B.C.E.-200 C.E.	The Sarmatians, one of the major precursors of Slavic Russia, rule Ukraine.
155-135 B.C.E.	The Greco-Bactrian ruler Menander rules in northwest India and Bactria.

130 B.C.E.	The Greco-Bactrian domains to the north of the Hindu Kush Mountains are overrun by nomads from Central Asia, the Sakas (Scythians).
100 B.C.E.	The Silk Road from China to Europe crosses the region.
95 B.C.E.	The Armenian Empire reaches its greatest size and influence under Tigranes II (the Great).
1st cent. B.C.E.	The Yuezhi conquer Bactria and found the Kushān Dynasty, which reaches its height in the second century C.E.
200-300 C.E.	The Antae confederation, representing an early attempt at unity among Slavic tribes, begins in the southern Ukraine.
300-600 C.E.	The Huns, migrating westward from Central Asia, drive German tribes across the borders of the Roman Empire, thereby altering the demographic composition of the west.
310 C.E.	Armenia is Christianized under Tiridates III.
350-555 C.E.	The Juan-Juan rule in Mongolia.
c. 400-700 C.E.	The golden age of Armenian culture.
451 C.E.	Attila the Hun is defeated at the Battle of Châlons by Roman and German forces.
mid-6th cent. C.E.	A federation of predominantly Turkish-speaking tribes from the Altay region expand the territories once controlled by the Juan-Juan.
620 C.E.	The Chinese invade Turkestan and Tibet.
670 C.E.	The fragile peace with China is broken as Tibet and western Turks challenge Chinese control of East-West trade routes.
744-840 C.E.	Uighur tribes evolve into the next major steppe power.

CHINA

6000 B.C.E.	Yangshao (Painted Pottery) culture begins.
3400 B.C.E.	Liangzhu culture emerges.
2800 B.C.E.	The Age of the Five Rulers begins.
2697 B.C.E.	Huangdi, the Yellow Emperor, is said to have begun his reign in this year.
2697 B.C.E.	Ling Lun, an official in the court of Huangdi, is said to have invented the first musical pipes in China.
2100 B.C.E.	The Xia (Hsia) Dynasty begins.
2000 B.C.E.	Qijia culture is starting.
2000-1000 B.C.E.	Longshan (Black Pottery) culture begins.
1600 B.C.E.	The Shang Dynasty, noted for its bronze vessels, begins.
1384 B.C.E.	Pan Geng founds the last capital city of the Shang Dynasty, Anyang; writing and art flourish.
1066 B.C.E.	Zhou (Chou Hsin) is conquered by Wuwang. The Western Zhou Dynasty, the first period in the Zhou Dynasty, begins.
771 B.C.E.	With death of King Yu, the Chinese capital is moved to Luoyang. The Western Zhou period ends and the second period in the Zhou Dynasty, the Eastern Zhou (Chunqiu), begins. The feudal system begins to deteriorate.
6th cent. B.C.E.	Laozi writes the *Dao De Jing*, initiating Daoism.
479 B.C.E.	Confucius, author of the *Analects* and founder of Confucianism, dies.
475 B.C.E.	The Warring States period in the Zhou Dynasty begins. This period is also known as the Hundred Schools of Thought.
400 B.C.E.	The Age of Philosophers ends.
400 B.C.E.	The Yuezhi form a kingdom in South China.
391 B.C.E.	Mozi, founder of Moism, dies.
350 B.C.E.	Shang Yang (Weiyang) rules China.
289 B.C.E.	Chinese Confucianist Mencius dies.
246 B.C.E.	The Chenkuo canal is completed.
235 B.C.E.	Xunzi, founder of Legalism, dies.

221 B.C.E.	Construction of the Great Wall of China begins.
221 B.C.E.	The Warring States period ends. The Zhou Dynasty is replaced by the Qin Dynasty.
206 B.C.E.	The Han Dynasty begins.
154 B.C.E.	Chinese rules of inheritance are changed by the Han emperor Jingdi.
141 B.C.E.	Wudi rules China and makes Confucianism the state religion.
124 B.C.E.	The Imperial University is founded in China.
108 B.C.E.	The Han emperors of China conquer Korea.
100 B.C.E.	The Silk Road develops from China to Europe.
9 C.E.	Wang Mang founds the Xin Dynasty in China.
78 C.E.	Kaniśka, emperor of India, convenes a Buddhist council in Kashmir and begins the spread of Buddhism to China.
105 C.E.	The Chinese court official Cai Lun invents paper.
142 C.E.	Daoism as an institutionalized religion begins when the incarnated god of the Dao, Taishang Laojun, appears to Zhang Daoling.
184 C.E.	The Daoist Rebellion of the Yellow Turbans against Later Han Dynasty in China takes place.
220 C.E.	The poet Cao Cao dies and leaves his son as the first Wei Emperor.
220 C.E.	The Han Dynasty ends and the period of the Three Kingdoms (Wei, Shu, Wu) begins.
265 C.E.	The Western Jin Dynasty begins.
280 C.E.	The Three Kingdoms period ends.
316 C.E.	The end of the Western Jin Dynasty begins two hundred years of unrest in China.
420 C.E.	The Southern and Northern Dynasties rule: the Huns in the north (the Northern, Eastern, and Western Wei, the Qi, and the Northern Zhou), and in the south the Song, Qi, Liang, and Chen.
581 C.E.	The Sui Dynasty begins.
588 C.E.	The Southern and Northern Dynasties end.
618 C.E.	The Sui Dynasty ends and the Tang Dynasty begins.
620 C.E.	The Chinese invade Turkestan and Tibet.
907 C.E.	The Tang Dynasty ends, to be followed by the "Five Dynasties" period.

EGYPT

6000 B.C.E.	Settlements begin to appear along the Nile, Niger, and Congo Rivers in Africa.
3100 B.C.E.	The earliest known hieroglyphic writing appears in Egypt while cuneiform is developing in Mesopotamia.
3050 B.C.E.	The Archaic period begins in Egypt (sometimes estimated as early as 3900 B.C.E.), consisting of the First and Second Dynasties.
2925 B.C.E.	Upper and Lower Egypt are united for the first time under one ruler, initiating the Early Dynastic period. The names of this period's rulers are preserved on the Palermo stone.
2800 B.C.E.	Egyptians begin the period of pyramid building in Egypt. Djoser's Step Pyramid Complex is built under the direction of the architect Imhotep.
2772 B.C.E.	A 365-day calendar is introduced in Egypt.
c. 2700 B.C.E.	The Old Kingdom begins, consisting of the Third, Fourth, Fifth, and Sixth Dynasties.
c. 2200 B.C.E.	The collapse of the Old Kingdom introduces the First Intermediate period, consisting of the Seventh, Eighth, Ninth, and Tenth Dynasties.
c. 2050 B.C.E.	The Middle Kingdom begins, consisting of the Eleventh and Twelfth Dynasties.
2000 B.C.E.	The cat is domesticated in Egypt.
1990 B.C.E.	Egypt's Twelfth Dynasty is considered the golden age of Pharaonic Egypt.
1790 B.C.E.	The Second Intermediate period begins, consisting of the Thirteenth to Seventeenth Dynasties. About this time, the Hyksos enter northern Egypt and introduce the horse and chariots.
1700 B.C.E.	Egyptians are practicing diagnostic medicine.

1640 B.C.E.	Egypt falls under Hyksos control. The end of the Middle Kingdom leads into the Second Intermediate period.
1570 B.C.E.	The New Kingdom begins in Egypt, consisting of the Eighteenth, Nineteenth, and Twentieth Dynasties. The temple at Karnak is constructed. The earliest examples of the Book of the Dead appear.
1493 B.C.E.	Thutmose I of Egypt destroys the Upper Nile kingdom of Kerma.
1380 B.C.E.	The Temple of Luxor is built by Amenhotep III.
1380 B.C.E.	Egypt is ruled by the monotheist pharaoh Akhenaton (Amenhotep IV).
1352 B.C.E.	The pharaoh Tutankhamen dies.
1275 B.C.E.	A battle is fought at Kadesh between the Egyptian pharaoh Rameses II and Hittite king Muwatallis. Hittite victory halts Egyptian inroads into Syria.
c. 1250 B.C.E.	*The Tale of the Two Brothers* is composed.
1182 B.C.E.	Rameses III defeats the Sea Peoples.
1085 B.C.E.	The disintegration of the New Kindgom introduces Egypt's Third Intermediate (post-empire) period, consisting of the Twenty-first through Thirty-first Dynasties.
747 B.C.E.	Egypt is conquered by Kashta and his son Piye (Piankhi), kings of Nubia, initiating the Twenty-fifth, or Ethiopian, Dynasty.
712 B.C.E.	The Late Kingdom begins.
671 B.C.E.	The Assyrian king Esarhaddon conquers Egypt.
664 B.C.E.	The Saite Dynasty begins.
529-525 B.C.E.	The Persian Cambyses II conquers Egypt and ends the Saite Dynasty.
332 B.C.E.	Alexander the Great's conquest in Egypt marks the beginning of Egypt's Ptolemaic period. The city of Alexandria is founded at the mouth of the Nile.
300 B.C.E.	The Greek Euclid publishes a treatise on geometry in Alexandria, Egypt.
285 B.C.E.	Ptolemy II begins his reign and orders the building of the library at Alexandria and a Greek translation of the Old Testament (Septuagint).
196 B.C.E.	The Rosetta stone is carved.
51-30 B.C.E.	Cleopatra VII, last of the Ptolemies, reigns.
31 B.C.E.	Octavian defeats Marc Antony and Cleopatra VII in the Battle of Actium. Octavian becomes Augustus, the first Roman emperor, and founds the Julio-Claudian dynasty. With the death of Cleopatra VII, he also becomes ruler of Egypt.
240's C.E.	The Egyptian Plotinus goes to Rome and founds Neoplatonism.
c. 300 C.E.	The Christian monastic movement begins.
641 C.E.	The Arabs conquer Egypt.
661 C.E.	The Umayyad (Omayyad) Dynasty begins rule over the Empire of the Caliphates (Arab kingdom).

EUROPE

4000 B.C.E.	The Beaker people begin to appear in Europe.
3200 B.C.E.	The Copper Age begins in Europe.
3100 B.C.E.	Construction of Stonehenge begins in Britain.
2600 B.C.E.	Minoan civilization begins to develop in Crete.
2300 B.C.E.	In Europe, the Copper Age ends and the Bronze Age begins.
2300 B.C.E.	The Beaker people reach Britain.
2000 B.C.E.	Slavs begin to coalesce in central Europe around the Bug, Dnieper, and Vistula Rivers, and a Slavic language begins to become distinct.
2000 B.C.E.	The Indo-Europeans reach Italy.
1100 B.C.E.	Hallstatt culture develops in present-day Austria.
1000 B.C.E.	Villanovan culture develops in northern Italy.

800 B.C.E.	The Celts begin their migration into the British Isles.
700 B.C.E.	The Iron Age begins in Europe.
600 B.C.E.	Etruscan civilization reaches its height in Italy with the invention of the arch, the invention of the vault, and the introduction of the alphabet.
450 B.C.E.	La Tène culture develops in present-day Switzerland.
400 B.C.E.	The Celts, having invented the spoked wheel with curved wooden rims, develop the shrink fitting of iron tires.
300 B.C.E.	The Greek navigator Pytheas of Massilia visits the British Isles.
100 B.C.E.	The Silk Road develops from China to Europe.
52 B.C.E.	Caesar defeats the Gauls under Vercingetorix at the Battle of Alesia and completes the Roman conquest of Gaul.
43 C.E.	Britain is conquered by the Roman emperor Claudius and becomes a Roman province.
60 C.E.	The British Queen Boudicca leads an unsuccessful revolt against Roman rule.
101 C.E.	The Roman emperor Trajan begins his conquest of Dacia (modern Romania).
275 C.E.	The emperor Aurelian (Lucius Domitius Aurelianus) withdraws Roman troops and administration from the province of Dacia (modern Romania).
289 C.E.	Germanic tribes known as the Allemani invade Italy.
300 C.E.	The Christian monastic movement begins.
378 C.E.	The Visigoths defeat the Romans in the Battle of Adrianople.
400 C.E.	The Angles and Saxons enter Britain.
410 C.E.	The Visigoths sack Rome and continue their pillage through Spain and North Africa.
451 C.E.	A Roman and Visigoth victory at the Battle of Châlons stops the advance of Attila the Hun into Europe.
476 C.E.	The German Odoacer becomes king of Rome. The Western Roman Empire ends.
481 C.E.	Clovis founds the Frankish state and establishes the power of the Merovingian Dynasty in Europe.
529 C.E.	Benedict of Nursia founds the monastery of Monte Cassino in Italy.
560 C.E.	Æthelbert becomes king of Kent, later the first British ruler converted to Christianity.
567 C.E.	Slavs advance into Dacia (modern Romania) and the Balkan peninsula.
568 C.E.	The Lombards gain control of major portions of Italy.
590 C.E.	Gregory the Great becomes pope and establishes the principles of the Roman papacy.
597 C.E.	Augustine of Hippo arrives in Kent to convert the population to Christianity.
600 C.E.	The medieval period (Middle Ages) begins.
616 C.E.	The law code of King Æthelbert, the oldest piece of writing in Old English, is completed.
624 C.E.	The Sutton Hoo burial takes place in Britain.
751 C.E.	The Frankish kingdoms are united under King Pepin (the Short), who deposes the last Merovingian king, Childeric III, and establishes the Carolingian Dynasty.

GREECE

2500 B.C.E.	Helladic civilization begins on mainland Greece.
2200 B.C.E.	The Indo-Europeans enter Greece.
2100 B.C.E.	The Middle Minoan civilization flourishes on Crete.
2000 B.C.E.	Middle Cycladic civilization begins in the Aegean.
1990 B.C.E.	Mycenaean civilization begins on mainland Greece.
1700 B.C.E.	An earthquake destroys palaces on Crete and a period of major rebuilding begins.
1700 B.C.E.	Linear A documents, such as the Phaistos disk, are written on Crete.
1600 B.C.E.	The earliest Linear B documents are written.
1500 B.C.E.	Late Cycladic civilization begins in the Aegean, Middle Minoan on Crete.
1500 B.C.E.	A volcanic eruption on Thera causes the destruction of most of the southern coast of Crete.

1400 B.C.E.	Mycenaeans rule at the Palace of Knossos in Crete.
1250 B.C.E.	The city of Troy falls, although this event is traditionally dated by the Greeks to 1184.
1100 B.C.E.	The Dorian invasion of Greece ends the Mycenaean period in Greece, the Cycladic civilization in the Aegean, and the Minoan civilization in Crete. The Greek Dark Ages begin.
1000 B.C.E.	In Greece, an alphabet develops from Semitic sources.
1000 B.C.E.	The Greeks settle in Ionia (western Anatolia).
800 B.C.E.	The *Iliad* and *Odyssey* are composed by Homer.
800 B.C.E.	City-states begin to develop in Greece as the Archaic period begins.
776 B.C.E.	The Olympic Games are established.
700 B.C.E.	Hesiod composes his *Theogony* and *Works and Days*.
700 B.C.E.	The Age of Lyric Poets begins.
700 B.C.E.	The Messenian Wars in the Greek Peloponnesus lead to Spartan military society.
627 B.C.E.	The Age of Tyrants begins when Periander gains control of Corinth.
621 B.C.E.	Draco codifies the laws of Athens.
600 B.C.E.	Pre-Socratic philosophers begin philosophic inquiry in Ionia.
594 B.C.E.	Solon becomes archon and introduces political and economic reforms in Athens.
530 B.C.E.	Pythagoras establishes a community in Croton, Italy, discovers the Pythagorean theorem, and founds the philosophy of Pythagoreanism.
525 B.C.E.	Greek drama begins to develop in Athens.
515 B.C.E.	The Greek explorer Scylax of Caryanda sails to the Indian Ocean.
510 B.C.E.	The Peisistratid tyrants are overthrown in Athens. The reforms of Cleisthenes lead to Athenian democracy.
500 B.C.E.	The Archaic period ends and the Classical Age begins in Greece.
500 B.C.E.	Greek black-figure pottery is replaced by red-figure pottery.
499 B.C.E.	The Greco-Persian Wars begin with the Ionian Revolt.
490 B.C.E.	A coalition of Greek city-states defeat the Persian king Darius in the Battle of Marathon.
480 B.C.E.	A coalition of Greek city-states defeat Persian king Xerxes in the Battle of Salamis.
478 B.C.E.	The Golden Age of Athens begins with the founding of the Delian League and the Athenian naval empire in the Aegean. During this period, the Athenians build the Parthenon. The Athenian Golden Age is marked by Athenian democracy, the great tragedies by Aeschylus, Sophocles, and Euripides, the histories of Herodotus and Thucydides, and the philosophy of Socrates.
431 B.C.E.	The Peloponnesian War between Athens and Sparta begins.
430 B.C.E.	The Greek sculptor Phidias (Pheidias) completes the statue of Zeus for the Temple of Zeus at Olympia.
404 B.C.E.	The Peloponnesian War ends with the destruction of Athens' Long Wall. Sparta assumes political dominance in Greece.
399 B.C.E.	Socrates is condemned to death in Athens.
370 B.C.E.	Hippocrates, father of Western medicine, dies in Thessaly.
353 B.C.E.	Artemisia II builds the Halicarnassus mausoleum for her dead brother Mausolus, tyrant of Caria in Anatolia.
350 B.C.E.	Cynicism is founded in Greece by Diogenes of Sinope.
338 B.C.E.	Philip II of Macedonia defeats the Greek alliance at Chaeronea and ends the independence of the Greek city-states.
333 B.C.E.	Alexander the Great defeats Darius III at the Battle of Issus and ends both the Achaemenian Dynasty and the Persian Empire.
332 B.C.E.	Alexander the Great's conquest in Egypt marks the beginning of Egypt's Ptolemaic period. The city of Alexandria is founded at the mouth of the Nile.
330 B.C.E.	Alexander begins a campaign into Bactria.

326 B.C.E.	Alexander the Great wins the Battle of Hydaspes and extends his conquests to the Indus Valley.
323 B.C.E.	Alexander the Great dies in Babylon.
323 B.C.E.	The Greek Classical Age ends and the Hellenistic Age begins.
300 B.C.E.	Zeno of Citium begins giving lectures on the Painted Porch (Stoa Poecile) in the Agora of Athens, founding the philosophy of Stoicism.
300 B.C.E.	The Greek navigator Pytheas of Massalia visits the British Isles.
300 B.C.E.	The Greek Euclid compiles a treatise on geometry, the *Elements*, in Alexandria, Egypt.
285 B.C.E.	Ptolemy II begins his reign in Egypt and orders the building of the library at Alexandria and a Greek translation of the Old Testament (Septuagint).
270 B.C.E.	Epicurus of Samos, founder of Epicureanism, dies in Greece.
146 B.C.E.	The Roman consul Mummius defeats the Achaean League and Greece becomes a Roman province.
60 C.E.	The Second Sophistic movement, a revival of Classical literary forms, begins.
162 C.E.	The Greek physician Galen begins his medical practice in Rome.
284 C.E.	The period of Late Antiquity begins in Roman Empire, when the emperor Diocletian restored order and reorganized the empire into a tetrarchy (rule of four).
305 C.E.	An organized Christian monastic movement begins under the direction of Saint Anthony of Egypt.
313 C.E.	The Emperor Constantine signs the Edict of Milan, legalizing Christianity in the Roman Empire.
320 C.E.	The Arian controversy begins among Christians in the Eastern Mediterranean.
325 C.E.	Constantine convenes the first ecumenical council of the Christian church at Nicaea.
330 C.E.	Constantine founds Constantinople as the new capital of Roman Empire.
361 C.E.	Julian the Apostate begins his reign as Roman emperor and attempts to suppress Christianity.
381 C.E.	The Christian Council of Constantinople outlaws Arianism as heresy and confirms the position stated in the Nicene Creed.
392 C.E.	The emperor Theodosius prohibits the worship of the pagan gods and closes their temples. Christianity becomes the sole religion of the Roman Empire. The last Olympic Games are held.
527 C.E.	Justinian starts his reign as emperor of the Eastern Roman Empire and begins his recodification of Roman law.
532 C.E.	Justinian begins construction of Haghia Sophia in Constantinople.
533 C.E.	Justinian conquers the Vandals in north Africa and begins the reunification of the Eastern and Western Roman Empires.
600 C.E.	The Late Antiquity period ends in the Roman Empire.
610 C.E.	The reign of the emperor Heraclius in Byzantium marks the beginning of the Byzantine period in the Eastern Roman Empire.
627 C.E.	Persia is conquered by the Byzantine Empire.

JAPAN

Before 8000 B.C.E.	Jōmon culture is developing in Japan.
c. 7500 B.C.E.	The indigenous Japanese religion Shintō grows from the animistic religion of the Jōmon people who lived in Japan for thousands of years after this time, though some scholars believe that elements of Shintō entered Japan when northern Mongoloid people, probably from Korea, invaded Japan after 1000 B.C.E.
7500 B.C.E.-700 C.E.	Ainu people inhabit the Japanese archipelago.
2500 B.C.E.	The Early Jōmon period ends and the Middle Jōmon period begins in Japan.
1500 B.C.E.	The Middle Jōmon period ends and the Late Jōmon period begins.

1000 B.C.E.	The Late Jōmon period ends and the Final Jōmon period begins.
607 B.C.E.	Jimmu Tennō founds the Japanese imperial dynasty.
300 B.C.E.	Yayoi people arrive and settle around Kyūshū, followed by the development of iron smelting and intensive irrigated wet-rice cultivation. Controversy surrounds their origins, whether indigenous or from mainland China.
After 232 B.C.E.	Himiko, female ruler of the Japanese federation known as the Yamatai, dies.
300-710 C.E.	During the Kofun period, massive keyhole-shaped burial mounds, tombs or tumuli (*kofun*), are build in the western Kinai region of Ōsaka, Kyōto, and Nara. The Japanese imperial system begins.
400's C.E.?	Ōjin Tennō, believed to be the first historical Japanese emperor (vs. the legendary Jimmu Tennō and other legendary sovereigns), reigns. The first Japanese state, the Yamato court, appears.
443 C.E.	The largest Kofun-period tomb, that of Emperor Nintoku, is completed.
552 C.E.	Buddhism arrives in Japan. It flourishes during the Yamato court, especially under crown prince Shōtoku Taishi.
587 C.E.	The empress Suiko, under the guidance of regent Prince Shōtoku, recognizes Buddhism, first imported from China and Korea in 552 C.E., as an official religion.
593-710 C.E.	The Asuka period marks the end of the Kofun period.
612 C.E.	The dancer Mimaji travels from the Korean kingdom of Paekche to Japan and introduces *gigaku*, a form of dance drama.
645-649 C.E.	The Yamato emperor Kōtoku issues the Taika ("great change") Reforms.
710-794 C.E.	The medieval Nara period sees the compilation of the government-sponsored histories of the Yamato state and the chronicles of events of the Kofun period and mythological past.
720 C.E.	Prince Toneri Shinnou compiles the massive *Nihon shoki*, the first of six official Japanese histories compiled by imperial order.

KOREA

3000 B.C.E.	Chulmun pottery, a brownish-gray pottery decorated with engraved oblique lines, appears near lakes and shorelines.
2333 B.C.E.	The Old Choson state is traditionally founded by Tangun, in the Taedong River basin. Other tribal states include Ma-Han, Jin-Han, and Pyun-Han.
1000-800 B.C.E.	The Korean Bronze Age begins; people are living on hillsides and in dugouts. Dolmens are used as tombs for elite leaders in southern Manchuria and the Korean peninsula.
4th cent. B.C.E.	The Iron Age begins in Korea with the use of iron plows, sickles, and weapons.
194 B.C.E.	Wiman (*Chinese* Wei Man) becomes the Choson ruler.
108 B.C.E.	The Han emperors of China overthrow the Choson state.
1st cent. B.C.E.	Korea's Three Kingdoms period (dominated by the Koguryo, Paekche, and Silla groups) begins.
Late 200's C.E.	The Paekche Dynasty is the dominant chiefdom in the Ma-Han confederacy and expands toward the confederation of tribes called the Koguryo Dynasty.
372 C.E.	Buddhism arrives in Korea.
391 C.E.	The Koguryo defeat the Paekche and Chinese Han dependencies, take Manchuria, and expand southward.
551 C.E.	Allied with the Silla, the Paekche recover some of the territory taken by the Koguryo, but two years later the Silla dominate.
668 C.E.	The Silla and Chinese Tang, having defeated the Paekche eight years earlier, override the weakened Koguryo, ending the Three Kingdoms period.
676 C.E.	The Silla drive out the Chinese and unify Korea, beginning the unified Silla period, which will last until 935 C.E.

MESOAMERICA

2000-1500 B.C.E.	The Early Formative period of Mesoamerican culture begins. The Maya begin living in villages and cultivating corn and squash.
1500 B.C.E.	Early Mixtec peoples are farming in western Oaxaca.
1200 B.C.E.	The rise of Olmec culture begins near the southern Gulf coast of Mexico.
1000 B.C.E.	The Early Formative period ends and the Middle Formative period begins in Mesoamerica. Early Mayan farmers settle in Belize.
850 B.C.E.	The Early Formative period ends and the Middle Formative period begins.
500 B.C.E.	The Zapotec capital at Monte Albán in the Oaxaca Valley begins development and will flourish past 700 C.E.
300 B.C.E.	The Middle Formative period of Mesoamerican culture ends and the Late Formative period begins.
100 C.E.	Teotihuacán, to become the most organized, highly populated, and sophisticated urban center in Mesoamerica during pre-Columbian times, begins development.
100 C.E.	Cobá, near the northeastern Yucatán coast, begins development and will flourish during the Classic period (600-900 C.E.) as one of the largest Mayan cities.
200-700 C.E.	The highly organized, hierarchical Zapotec civilization flourishes in the Oaxaca Valley.
c. 250 C.E.	The Mayan city of Tikal, in the central lowlands of northern Guatemala, becomes a trade hub and by the sixth century will have a population of up to 90,000.
300 C.E.	The Late Formative period of Mesoamerican culture ends, and the Classical period begins with sites such as Chichén Itzá. The Maya erect stelae, carved monuments with dates.
300-400 C.E.	El Tajín, the principal civic-ceremonial center of Veracruz civilization, begins development from an amalgamation of Mesoamerican cultures ultimately encompassing the Huastec, Totonac, and Otomi. The site depends on the obsidian trade between Teotihuacán, Puebla, and the Gulf coast and Maya regions.
400 C.E.	Maya civilization begins to influence Copán, the capital of the region surrounding western Honduras.
500's C.E.	The Itzá Maya begin building their center at Chichén Itzá in north-central Yucatán.
600 C.E.	Dzibilchaltún, a Mayan city in the northern part the Yucatán Peninsula occupied since around 800 B.C.E., functions as one of the region's largest cities with more than eight thousand structures and a population of about 25,000.
600-900 C.E.	During the height of the Mayan civilization, sometimes called the Late Classic, art, technology, and science are at their peak. High population densities in the cities increasingly tax the Mayan farmers who are providing labor to construct temples and grow food for city dwellers.
615 C.E.	King K'inich Janahb' Pakal assumes leadership of the Maya.
Late 600's C.E.	Palenque, near Chiapas, Mexico, flourishes as one of the most important Classic Mayan sites.
750 C.E.	Teotihuacán is destroyed.
900 C.E.	The Classical period of Mesoamerican culture ends, precipitated by overpopulation and overuse of the land.

MESOPOTAMIA

11,000-8300 B.C.E.	Natufian culture is growing in Mesopotamia.
6300 B.C.E.	The Samarran culture begins to develop in Mesopotamia.
5700 B.C.E.	The Halafian culture begins in Mesopotamia.
5200 B.C.E.	Ubaid culture begins in Mesopotamia.
5000 B.C.E.	The wheel is invented. By about 3000 B.C.E., the two-wheeled A-frame cart is in use.
3450 B.C.E.	Uruk and other cities appear in Mesopotamia.

3300 B.C.E.	Sumerian civilization begins in Mesopotamia, with city-states united about 2300 B.C.E. by Sargon I.
3100 B.C.E.	The earliest known hieroglyphic writing appears in Egypt while cuneiform is developing in Mesopotamia.
2600 B.C.E.	Elam is developing in Mesopotamia.
2334 B.C.E.	Akkadian civilization begins in Mesopotamia; Sargon I founds the capital city of Akkad.
2300 B.C.E.	Trade between the Indus Valley and Mesopotamia begins.
2100 B.C.E.	The Sumerian King List is written.
2000 B.C.E.	The Gilgamesh epic is written down.
2000 B.C.E.	The collapse of Sumer introduces the Old Babylonian period in Mesopotamia.
1990 B.C.E.	The Sumerian migration to Canaan and to Egypt under Abraham begins about this time.
1800 B.C.E.	Babylonians learn to use multiplication and division.
1763 B.C.E.	Hammurabi conquers Sumer and writes his law code.
1600-1100 B.C.E.	The Mitanni Empire flourishes in northern Mesopotamia.
1550 B.C.E.	The Kassites conquer Mesopotamia.
1225 B.C.E.	Assyrians under Tukulti-Ninurta capture Babylon.
810 B.C.E.	Queen Sammu-ramat (Semiramis) rules the Assyrian Empire.
755 B.C.E.	The Kingdom of Urartu in northern Mesopotamia reaches its height under Sarduri II.
722 B.C.E.	The Assyrians conquer Israel.
705 B.C.E.	Sennacherib rules the Assyrian Empire, founds the city of Nineveh, and establishes a library.
671 B.C.E.	The Assyrian king Esarhaddon conquers Egypt.
614 B.C.E.	The Babylonian defeat of the Assyrians and the destruction of the city of Nineveh mark the beginning of New Babylonian period.
605 B.C.E.	Nebuchadnezzar II reigns in Babylon and begins the Hanging Gardens of Babylon.
600 B.C.E.	Zoroaster (Zarathustra) founds Zoroastrianism in Persia.
587/586 B.C.E.	Jerusalem falls to Babylonian Nebuchadnezzar II. Solomon's temple is destroyed and the Babylonian Captivity of the Jews begins.
559 B.C.E.	The Achaemenian Dynasty is founded in Babylon.
546 B.C.E.	Cyrus the Great captures Sardis and ends the reign of Croesus, king of Lydia.
539 B.C.E.	Cyrus the Great captures Babylon, establishes the Persian Empire, and leads an expedition to the Indus River.
539 B.C.E.	The Jewish captivity in Babylon ends.
539 B.C.E.	The New Babylonian period ends.
529 B.C.E.	The Persian Cambyses II conquers Egypt and ends the Saite Dynasty.
521 B.C.E.	Darius I (the Great) rules Persia and establishes a road system and a postal service.
517 B.C.E.	Darius the Great begins the Persian conquest of the Indus Valley.
499 B.C.E.	The Ionian Revolt heralds the Greco-Persian Wars.
490 B.C.E.	A coalition of Greek city-states defeat the Persian king Darius in the Battle of Marathon.
480 B.C.E.	A coalition of Greek city-states defeat Persian king Xerxes in the Battle of Salamis.
333 B.C.E.	Alexander the Great defeats Darius III at the Battle of Issus, ending both the Achaemenian Dynasty and the Persian Empire.
323 B.C.E.	Alexander the Great dies in Babylon.
321 B.C.E.	Chandragupta Maurya pays one of Alexander's successors, Seleucus I, five hundred war elephants for control of the Indus region, establishing the Mauryan Dynasty.
245 B.C.E.	Arsaces I founds the Parthian Empire in Mesopotamia.
100 B.C.E.	The Silk Road develops from China to Europe.
224 C.E.	In the Battle of the Plain of Hormizdagān, Ardashīr I ends the Parthian Empire and begins the Sāsānian Empire.
Late 4th cent. C.E.	At its height, the Sāsānian Empire controls most of Syria, Mesopotamia, the Arabian Peninsula, Armenia, Iran, and Iraq.

488-531 C.E.	Kavadh I rules the Sāsānian Empire; his patronage of the Mazdakite religion brings the empire to civil war.
531-579 C.E.	Sāsānian king Khosrow I reorganizes Sāsānian society, including the systems of tax collection, land allocation, army organization, and civil administration.
540 C.E.	Khosrow I invades Roman Syria and loots Antioch, forcing Byzantine Roman emperor Justinian I to seek peace terms.
590 C.E.	Khosrow II comes to power.
602-619 C.E.	Sāsānian king Khosrow II invades Syria and Asia Minor, and captures Jerusalem and Alexandria.
627 C.E.	The Byzantine Empire conquers the Sāsānians.
637 C.E.	Weakened by Koshrow's expansionist policies, the Sāsānians are occupied by Arabs who begin the spread of Islam.
651 C.E.	The Islamic/Arab conquest of Iran ends the Sāsānian Empire. The Zoroastrian religion, which has dominated Persia for the past century, disappears.
661 C.E.	The Umayyad (Omayyad) Dynasty begins rule over the Empire of the Caliphates (Arab kingdom).

MIDDLE/NEAR EAST

8000-900 B.C.E.	The Canaanites inhabit the geographical area called the Levant, the eastern shores of the Mediterranean Sea, from western Greece to western Egypt.
1990 B.C.E.	The Sumerian migration to Canaan and to Egypt under Abraham begins about this time.
1600 B.C.E.	The alphabet is invented in Syria.
c. 1450-1430 B.C.E.	The Jewish people under Moses begin the Exodus from Egypt of Rameses III, and the Jewish settlement of Canaan begins.
c. 1400-1300 B.C.E.	The Aqhat epic is composed in Ugarit, near the Mediterranean coast in modern Syria.
1200-700 B.C.E.	The Philistines—who occupy the southeastern Mediterranean coast from the Yarkon River to the Egyptian border, the area controlled by the cities of Gaza, Ashkelon, Ekron, Ashdod, and Gath—are caught up in the conflicts between the superpowers of the day, suffering defeat and occupation by the Assyrian and Babylonian Empires and a continual influence from the neighboring Egyptian rulers.
1200 B.C.E.	The Age of Judges begins in Israel.
1100 B.C.E.	Arameans are settling in the Near East.
11th century B.C.E.	Saul rules as Israel's first king.
1050 B.C.E.	The Philistines invade Israel.
1000 B.C.E.	The Age of Judges ends and the Age of Kings begins in Israel as David founds a united kingdom with a capital at Jerusalem.
1000 B.C.E.	Semitic alphabet reaches Greece from the Near East.
c. 962 B.C.E.	Israel's King David dies in Jerusalem.
961 B.C.E.	Solomon succeeds David as king of Israel and begins the Jewish Temple in Jerusalem.
930 B.C.E.	With the death of Solomon, Israel is split into two kingdoms, Israel in the north and Judah in the south.
928 B.C.E.	The death of Solomon is followed by the division of Israel into two kingdoms, Israel and Judah.
c. 874-c. 853 B.C.E.	King Ahab reigns in Israel with his infidel queen Jezebel. The prophet Elijah functions as Ahab's nemesis, defending the faith of the Jews' god Yahweh.
750 B.C.E.	Hosea, Amos, and Micah are prominent in Israel's Age of Prophets.
722 B.C.E.	The Assyrians conquer Israel; the Jewish diaspora begins.
715 B.C.E.	Hezekiah becomes King of Judah and works to free his people from Assyrian dominance.
701-680 B.C.E.	The Old Testament prophet Isaiah dies in Judah.

627 B.C.E.	The prophet Jeremiah begins his career in Israel.
After 587 B.C.E.	The prophet Jeremiah dies in Egypt.
587/586 B.C.E.	Jerusalem falls to Babylonian king Nebuchadnezzar II. Solomon's temple is destroyed and the Babylonian Captivity of the Jews begins.
586 B.C.E.	The Book of Ezekiel is written.
539 B.C.E.	The Jewish captivity in Babylon ends.
520 B.C.E.	The rebuilding of the Temple in Jerusalem marks the beginning of the "Second Temple" period in Israel.
5th cent. B.C.E.	Early Judaism begins to emerge from the religion of ancient Israel.
4th-1st cent. B.C.E.	Essene monks living at Khirbat Qumran on the northwestern shore of the Dead Sea compose the Dead Sea Scrolls, containing all the books of the Old Testament except Esther.
c. 200 B.C.E.	The area now called Judaea passes under control of the Seleucid Dynasty.
168 B.C.E.	Antiochus IV Epiphanes, a Hellenistic Seleucid ruler, outlaws Judaism and the Maccabean revolt begins.
143 B.C.E.	The Maccabean revolt ends, and the Hasmonean Dynasty (c. 143-37 B.C.E.) begins.
63 B.C.E.	Roman occupation of Palestine begins.
37 B.C.E.-c. 70 C.E.	The Herodian Dynasty rules Judaea for Imperial Rome.
30 C.E.	Jesus of Nazareth is crucified in Jerusalem.
40 C.E.	Paul of Tarsus (later, Saint Paul) is converted to Christianity.
66 C.E.	In Israel, the Zealots spark the First Jewish Revolt against Rome.
73 C.E.	In the Battle of Masada, the unsuccessful Jewish revolt against Roman rule results in the fall of Jerusalem and the destruction of the Second Temple.
132 C.E.	The Second Jewish Revolt against Rome breaks out, led by Bar Kokhba.
135 C.E.	The Second Jewish Revolt ends, marking the beginning of two thousand years of Jewish exile. Akiba ben Joseph, the founder of rabbinic Judaism, and the Jewish revolutionary Bar Kokhba both die, respectively, in Caesarea and Bethar, Palestine.
Early 3d cent C.E.	The Mishnah, the core document of the Talmud, is complete.
311 C.E.	The Arrian Controversy begins among Christians in the Eastern Mediterranean.
661 C.E.	The Umayyad (Omayyad) Dynasty begins rule over the Empire of the Caliphates (Arab kingdom).

NORTH AMERICA

11,500 B.C.E.	Paleo-Indians begin to appear throughout North America.
Before 8000 B.C.E.	Early North American cultures appear: Archaic, Clovis, Folsom, and Dalton traditions.
8000 B.C.E.	In the Southwest, the Cochise culture begins. It is characterized by temporary camps along lakes and streams and people who most likely killed large game such as the mammoth for food, with later peoples relying on vegetation and small animals. The Cochise pass this knowledge of plants for food and medicinal uses to subsequent groups in the Southwest.
6000-1100 B.C.E.	This period is called Maritime Archaic in some parts of North America.
4000 B.C.E.	Old Copper culture, denoting the first peoples in North America to experiment with metal, begins near the western Great Lakes.
4000 B.C.E.	The Northwest Microblade tradition appears, though some scholars place this tradition as early as 9000 B.C.E.
4000 B.C.E.	The Casimoiroid Indians may have begun their migration to western Cuba from the Yucatán Peninsula as early as this time.
3500 B.C.E.	The Helton culture rises in the lower Illinois Valley and develops on the North American Plains.
3050-1750 B.C.E.	Bolyston Street Weir, a series of fishing traps near present-day Boston, is being built.
2500 B.C.E.	The Arctic Small Tool tradition is developing. Bolyston Street Weir is being built.

2200 B.C.E.	The Saint Mungo culture near the lower Fraser River, the Mayne phase of the Gulf Islands, and the Eayem phase of Fraser canyon appear, all expressions of the Charles culture of southwest British Columbia.
2000 B.C.E.	The Aleutian tradition begins.
2000 B.C.E.	The Ortoiroids may have come from South America to the West Indies as early as this time.
1800 B.C.E.	The Thom's Creek site is developing in North America.
1730-1350 B.C.E.	Poverty Point culture, characterized by large earthworks called mounds, flourishes in the Lower Mississippi Valley.
1500 B.C.E.	The Kachemak tradition in Alaska begins.
1500-400 B.C.E.	Locarno Beach culture flourishes on the Fraser River Delta and Gulf Islands of British Columbia, Canada, the Strait of Juan de Fuca, and Washington State.
1000 B.C.E.-100 C.E.	The Adena culture precedes maize cultivation and influences the development of the advanced Hopewell culture in the Ohio and Illinois Valleys.
700 B.C.E.	The Dorset phase begins, referring to the Eskimo/Inuit peoples who inhabited most of northern Canada for about fifteen hundred years.
500 B.C.E.	The first people to adapt to the modern coastal environment of the eastern United States, the Deptford people dominate the southeast during the Early Woodland period.
500 B.C.E.	The Marpole phase begins in the Pacific Northwest.
500 B.C.E.	The Norton tradition begins in Subarctic North America.
300 B.C.E.	The Caribbean peoples known as the Arawak may be migrating northward into the Caribbean and Florida from South America.
200 B.C.E.	During the Middle Woodland period, the Laurel culture begins on the Canadian Shield.
200 B.C.E.	The Saladoir people, ancestors of the Tainos (who greeted Christopher Columbus), are migrating toward the West Indies from South America. They are followed by the Island Carib.
100 B.C.E.-400 C.E.	During the Middle Woodland period in eastern North America (especially Ohio), Hopewell culture thrives, involving regionally distinct local cultures with a veneer of shared behaviors such as complex burial and effigy mound construction; long-distance acquisition, use, and ritual disposal of high-status trade goods; and an almost standardized iconography.
c. 1 C.E.	Hohokam culture begins in the Sonoran desert in the Southwest. The Hohokam peoples eventually construct an extensive network of irrigation canals.
c. 1 C.E.	The indigenous peoples of the Plains begin using pottery and building burial mounds, inaugurating the Plains Woodland culture.
c. 1 C.E.	Sonota peoples, migratory bison hunters known for their elaborate burial customs, appear in southern Manitoba, the northern Dakotas, and Minnesota.
100 C.E.	The Anasazi, renowned for their great pueblos and large, multistoried cliff structures, appear in the American Southwest.
200 C.E.	Mogollon culture begins in southeast Arizona, southwest New Mexico, and northern Sonora and Chihuahua.
400-500 C.E.	In the eastern Great Basin and western Colorado plateau, Fremont culture begins.

OCEANIA AND AUSTRALIA

38,000 B.C.E.	The first peoples to arrive in the largest islands in the South Pacific migrate from Eurasia and travel by sea south along the Australonesian archipelago, reaching Australia. The Djanggawul song cycle, one of the world's oldest continuously told myths of origin, is composed.
30,000-9000 B.C.E.	The Tabonian (stone flake) tradition appears in Southeast Asian islands.
By 8000 B.C.E.	Areas of Papua in Micronesia are inhabited.
5000 B.C.E.	The linguistic explosion and expansion of Austronesian speakers begins spreading from insular Southeast Asia.

3000 B.C.E.	Methods of irrigation are used in the New Guinea Highlands, where the pig has already been domesticated.
2000 B.C.E.	In Australia, flaked stone tools appear, coincidental with the arrival in Australia of a type of wild dog, the dingo.
2000 B.C.E.	South Asian peoples begin to settle on islands north of New Guinea, especially in the Bismarck Archipelago.
2000 B.C.E.	The Melanesian migration to central Polynesia begins.
1800-800 B.C.E.	The Marianas are characterized by a culture that makes red ware.
1500 B.C.E.	Polynesian islands are settled; Polynesians begin migrations into Fiji, as evidenced by Lapita culture, with distinctive shell decorations and pottery.
1300 B.C.E.	Polynesians have reached Tonga.
1300 B.C.E.	Nan Madol, in the Caroline islands, represents an early town or ceremonial center.
1000 B.C.E.	Polynesians reach Samoa.
1000-500 B.C.E.	Populations increase as new tools allow more efficient exploitation of marginal environments. Trade between isolated groups becomes more widespread.
800 B.C.E.	The Latte phase of the Marianas and western Micronesia begins to eclipse Marianas Red Ware culture. Latte construction consists of two parallel rows of upright coral or volcanic rocks slotted at the top and set on with generally hemispherical capstones.
500 B.C.E.	Melanesians begin to settle in Fiji.
300 C.E.	Polynesians settle the Marquesas Islands.
300 C.E.	Colonizing voyages from central or eastern Polynesia reach Rapa Nui (Easter Island).
450 C.E.	The Hawaiian Islands are settled by Polynesian peoples from the Marshall Islands and, later, from the Marquesas.
800 C.E.	Large canoes carrying as many as one hundred people are transporting people to all corners of the Polynesian triangle.
700 C.E.	Earliest possible Maori settlement of Aotearoa (New Zealand).

ROME

753 B.C.E.	Rome is founded by its first king, Romulus. The era of Prerepublican Rome begins.
c. 509 B.C.E.	The era of Republican Rome begins.
509 B.C.E.	The Roman monarchy is overthrown and is replaced by the Republic.
450 B.C.E.	The laws of the Twelve Tables are written in Rome.
390 B.C.E.	Rome is sacked by the Celts.
312 B.C.E.	Construction of the Appian Way begins.
265 B.C.E.	Rome completes its conquest of Italy.
264-241 B.C.E.	The First Punic War between Rome and Carthage results in Roman control of Sicily.
240 B.C.E.	Livius Andronicus, father of Roman literature, produces his first play and begins the golden age of Roman literature.
218-201 B.C.E.	The Second Punic War between Rome and Carthage results in Roman control of the entire western Mediterranean except the territory of Carthage in North Africa.
212 B.C.E.	The Greek scientist Archimedes dies during the Roman sack of Syracuse.
149-146 B.C.E.	The Third Punic War between Rome and Carthage results in the destruction of Carthage.
146 B.C.E.	The Roman consul Mummius defeats the Achaean League and Greece becomes a Roman province.
133 B.C.E.	The Gracchi brothers begin their reforms.
107 B.C.E.	Marius serves his first consulship in Rome.
91 B.C.E.	The Social War begins in Italy.
82 B.C.E.	Sulla becomes dictator in Rome.
73 B.C.E.	Spartacus begins the gladiatorial slave revolt in Italy.

63 B.C.E.	Roman occupation of Palestine begins.
63 B.C.E.	The consulship of Cicero is highlighted by the Catilinarian Conspiracy.
52 B.C.E.	Julius Caesar defeats the Gauls under Vercingetorix at the Battle of Alesia and completes the Roman conquest of Gaul.
49 B.C.E.	Julius Caesar crosses the Rubicon and begins a civil war in Rome with Pompey the Great.
44 B.C.E.	Julius Caesar is assassinated.
31 B.C.E.–500 C.E.	The era of Imperial Rome.
31 B.C.E.	Octavian defeats Marc Antony and Cleopatra VII in the Battle of Actium. Octavian becomes Augustus, the first Roman emperor, and founds the Julio-Claudian dynasty. With the death of Cleopatra VII, last of the Ptolemies, he also becomes ruler of Egypt.
19 B.C.E.	The Roman poet Vergil (P. Vergilius Maro) dies, leaving unfinished his epic masterpiece the *Aeneid*.
9 B.C.E.	The Ara Pacis (Altar of Peace) is dedicated by Augustus.
14 C.E.	The death of Caesar Augustus marks the end of the golden age of Roman literature and the beginning of the silver age.
43 C.E.	Britain is conquered by the Roman emperor Claudius and becomes a Roman province.
60 C.E.	The British Queen Boudicca leads an unsuccessful revolt against Roman rule.
69 C.E.	The Year of the Four Emperors ends with the accession of the emperor Vespasian, founder of the Flavian Dynasty.
70 C.E.	The unsuccessful Jewish revolt from Roman rule results in the fall of Jerusalem and the destruction of the Second Temple.
79 C.E.	The cities of Pompeii and Herculaneum are buried by the eruption of Mount Vesuvius.
80 C.E.	The Flavian Amphitheater (Colosseum) opens in Rome.
96 C.E.	The death of the emperor Domitian ends the Flavian Dynasty and introduces a period of Five Good Emperors (Nerva, Trajan, Hadrian, Antoninus Pius, and Marcus Aurelius).
106 C.E.	The Roman emperor Trajan conquers Dacia (modern Romania) and makes it a Roman province.
114 C.E.	Trajan's column is erected in Rome.
117 C.E.	The emperor Hadrian's reign begins, during which the Pantheon is built in Rome and Hadrian's Villa in Tivoli, Italy.
180 C.E.	The death of Marcus Aurelius ends the period of Five Good Emperors in Rome and marks the beginning of the decline of the Roman Empire.
263 C.E.	The Egyptian Plotinus goes to Rome and founds Neoplatonism.
275 C.E.	The emperor Aurelian (Lucius Domitius Aurelianus) withdraws Roman troops and administration from the province of Dacia (modern Romania).
284 C.E.	Diocletian begins the reorganization of the Roman Empire, inaugurating the period of Late Antiquity.
300 C.E.	The Christian monastic movement begins.
325 C.E.	Constantine convenes the first ecumenical council of the Christian church at Nicaea.
330 C.E.	Constantine founds Constantinople as the new capital of Roman Empire.
361 C.E.	Julian the Apostate begins his reign as Roman emperor and attempts to suppress Christianity.
378 C.E.	The Visigoths defeat the Romans in the Battle of Adrianople.
381 C.E.	The Christian Council of Constantinople outlaws Arianism as heresy and confirms the position stated in the Nicene Creed.
392 C.E.	The emperor Theodosius prohibits the worship of the pagan gods and closes their temples. Christianity becomes the sole religion of the Roman Empire. The last ancient Olympic Games are held.
395 C.E.	Rome is divided into two empires, the Western Roman Empire and the Eastern Roman Empire.

410 C.E.	The Visigoths sack Rome and continue their pillage through Spain and North Africa.
451 C.E.	A Roman and Visigoth victory at the Battle of Châlons (Catalaunian Fields) stops the advance of Attila the Hun into Europe.
476 C.E.	The German Odoacer becomes king of Rome. The Western Roman Empire ends.
600 C.E.	The Late Antiquity period ends.

SOUTH AMERICA

14,000 B.C.E.	Pre-Clovis peoples occupy South America's earliest widely accepted archaeological site, Monte Verde, in south-central Chile.
Before 8000 B.C.E.	The people living in Peru at this time had no pottery, so this period is called the Preceramic.
8000 B.C.E.	The earliest mummies are buried at Chinchorro.
8000 B.C.E.	Archaic culture begins in South America.
8000-500 B.C.E.	The Chinchorro people inhabit the Atacama Desert, four hundred miles of South American coastline stretching from Ilo in southern Peru to Antofagasta in northern Chile.
7500 B.C.E.	The oldest known pottery in the Americas is being made in eastern Brazil.
6000 B.C.E.	Coastal populations in Brazil and Argentina increase. Shellfish gatherers appear, having apparently abandoned the interior. A climatic shift to more hot and humid weather between 7000 and 4000 B.C.E. is thought to be related to this migration, which marks the beginning of the *sambaquis*, huge shell mounds that line the Brazilian coast.
5000 B.C.E.	Andean peoples have domesticated quinoa, corn, beans, and potatoes.
2500 B.C.E.	Andean peoples have tamed llamas, vicuñas, and alpacas.
1800 B.C.E.	The introduction of pottery ends the Preceramic period and begins the Initial (or Lower Formative) period.
1800-1600 B.C.E.	La Florida pyramid is built in the Andes near present-day Lima.
900 B.C.E.	The Middle Formative (Early Horizon) period begins in Peru and sees the rise of the Pukara and Chavín cultures.
850-460 B.C.E.	Chavín, a small agricultural village at a trade crossroads, becomes a major pilgrimage center, oracle, and religious shrine.
400-200 B.C.E.	The Raimondi stone, associated with the Chavín culture, is carved.
300 B.C.E.-90 C.E.	Tumaco in modern-day Colombia emerges as a major ceremonial center with distinct social hierarchies.
200 B.C.E.	The Chavín, or Middle Formative, period ends in Peru.
200 B.C.E.-200 C.E.	Akapana pyramid, the largest structure at the Tiwanaku site of pre-Incan ruins in Bolivia, southeast of Lake Titicaca, is built.
200 B.C.E.-600 C.E.	The Recuay occupy the Callejön de Huaylas Valley of the north-central highlands of Peru.
100-700 C.E.	During the Florescent, or Classic, period, the Nasca, Moche, and middle Tiwanaku cultures build their monuments and irrigation works. Huaca de la Luna and Huaca del Sol (temple of the Moon and Sun, respectively) are built.
300-400 C.E.	The city of Cajamarca, in Andean Peru, flourishes.
400 C.E.	In Amazonia, Marajóara culture begins to flourish.
500-1000 C.E.	The Middle Horizon period sees the rise of the Wari and late Tiwanaku cultures.

SOUTH ASIA

3500 B.C.E.	The Indus Valley civilization begins in South Asia, especially at Harappā and Mohenjo-Daro.
2300 B.C.E.	Trade between the Indus Valley and Mesopotamia begins.
2000 B.C.E.	South Asian peoples begin to settle on islands north of New Guinea, especially in the Bismarck Archipelago.

1600 B.C.E.	Aryans invade the Indus Valley during the Early Vedic period. Writing disappears in India.
1000 B.C.E.	The Late Vedic period begins, the *Rigveda* is written down, and the caste system develops in India.
1000 B.C.E.	Composition of Upaniṣads, Brāhmaṇas, and other Vedic texts begins in South Asia.
800 B.C.E.	A priestly caste of Brahmans appears.
600 B.C.E.	The Late Vedic period ends.
539 B.C.E.	Cyrus the Great captures Babylon, establishes the Persian Empire, and leads an expedition to the Indus River.
c. 527 B.C.E.	Vardhamāna Mahāvīra, founder of Jainism, dies.
517 B.C.E.	Darius the Great begins the Persian conquest of the Indus Valley.
515 B.C.E.	The Greek explorer Scylax of Caryanda sails to the Indian Ocean.
c. 500 B.C.E.	The legendary Vālmīki composes the *Rāmāyaṇa* in South Asia.
486 B.C.E.	Siddhārtha Gautama Buddha, founder of Buddhism, dies.
326 B.C.E.	Alexander the Great wins the Battle of Hydaspes and extends his conquests to the Indus Valley.
c. 321 B.C.E.	Chandragupta Maurya founds the Mauryan Dynasty.
256 B.C.E.	The edicts of Aśoka, Mauryan emperor of India and great Buddhist reformer, appear.
251 B.C.E.	The Hindus begin their conquest of Sri Lanka.
250 B.C.E.	A Buddhist council is held at Patna.
c. 200 B.C.E.	The Sātavāhana Dynasty, the earliest indigenous kingdom of the Deccan, begins in India.
185 B.C.E.	The Mauryan Dynasty ends in India.
40 C.E.	Thomas the Apostle brings Christianity to India.
78 C.E.	Kaniśka, emperor of India, convenes a Buddhist council in Kashmir and begins the spread of Buddhism to China.
100 C.E.	Tamil culture develops in South Asia.
200 C.E.	Composition of the *Bhaghavadgītā* is completed.
320 C.E.	The Gupta Dynasty begins in South Asia with a leader who, like the founder of the Mauryan Dynasty, bears the name Chandragupta.
400 C.E.	Composition of the *Mahābhārata* is finished in South Asia.
500 C.E.	The Pallava Dynasty begins in South Asia and introduces the Hindu golden age.
500 C.E.	The Gupta Dynasty is in decline; the period of the Successor States begins.
604 C.E.	Harṣa ascends the throne in north India, while Tamil kingdoms thrive in the south.

SOUTHEAST ASIA

13,000-4000 B.C.E.	The Hoabinhian tradition thrives in the Malayan region of Southeast Asia.
4000-1000 B.C.E.	Austronesian settlements expand from insular Southeast Asia eastward into the Philippines, Indonesia, Hawaii, and New Zealand, and westward into Madagascar.
3500 B.C.E.	The Nok Nok Tha site in Thailand shows earliest evidence of rice cultivation in Southeast Asia.
3000 B.C.E.	Evidence of metallurgy is found in Thailand, soon followed by evidence of pottery making and domesticated animals.
3000-900 B.C.E.	Ban Pao culture in Malaya displays use of barkcloth beaters, spindle whorls, and fishing equipment.
2666 B.C.E.	Arakanese civilization begins in Myanmar (Burma).
2500 B.C.E.	Austronesian-speaking (Malayo-Polynesian-speaking) seafaring people have invaded much of insular and parts of mainland Southeast Asia.
2000 B.C.E.	Mon-Khmer people are believed to have migrated into Southeast Asia from southwest China or from the Khasi Hills in northwest India. The subgroup that becomes known as the Khmer migrates farther east into what is now Cambodia.

1000 B.C.E.	Evidence of jar burials of cremated remains appears in the Philippines and Borneo.
6th cent. B.C.E.	Buddhist influence arrives in modern-day Thailand and Cambodia. The Dvaravati civilization begins.
500 B.C.E.	Pottery jar burials dating to this period at Sa Huynh in southern Vietnam constitute the earliest evidence of jar burials on mainland Southeast Asia.
c. 300 B.C.E.	Earliest dated evidence of the Dong Son culture, a mixed Bronze and Iron Age culture from the north credited with introducing rice cultivation in the Red River delta region of modern Vietnam.
100 B.C.E.-100 C.E.	Indian influence begins in Malaya.
1st cent. C.E.	The Pyu (also called the Tirchul or the Piao), Tibeto-Burman speakers, migrate south into Burma from the Tibetan plateau and establish a kingdom in the Irrawaddy River Basin and the adjacent Yin, Mu, Nawin, and Kyaukse Valleys. They found three cities: Beikthano, Hmawza, and Halin.
1st cent. C.E.	The Funan and Chenla kingdoms rise in present-day Cambodia.
1st cent. C.E.	The Tai people live in the valleys and lowland areas of what is now southern China and extreme northern Southeast Asia. They include the Chuang people of Kwangsi; the Tho and Nung of Vietnam; and southern Tais who become ancestors of today's Lao, Shans, Thais, and upland Tais (peoples who now live in Laos, Myanmar, northeastern India, southern Yunnan, and Thailand).
c. 550 C.E.	Chenla, led by King Bhavavarman, rebels against its status as vassal to Funan and assumes dominance in the region of modern-day Cambodia through constant warfare. Funan moves its capital south and seeks to subdue the rest of what is now known as Laos.
627 C.E.	King Isanavarman of Chenla annexes Funan.
790 C.E.	Jayavarman II, a prince of a small Khmer kingdom who claims descent from the kings of Funan, extends his power over a large part of Cambodia, laying the foundation for the influential Angkor civilization, named after the huge temple complex built by the successors of Jayavarman II.
802 C.E.	The kingdom of Angkor absorbs Chenla.
877 C.E.	Angkor's ruler chooses as his queen a member of the royal line of both the Funan and Chenla kingdoms. Accordingly, Angkor, the precursor to the present state of Cambodia, may be said to have superseded both Chenla and Funan.

—Thomas J. Sienkewicz

GLOSSARY

Although most of the unfamiliar and foreign words are explained within the text of this encyclopedia, this glossary serves to highlight some of the more important terms. This glossary consists of words that appear within the text of the encyclopedia and is not a comprehensive lexicon of the ancient world.

Advaita (Hinduism): literally, "without a second"; nondualism; the view that the only reality is *brahman*, the primary origin and essence of all things, and that the multiplicity of the universe as it is perceived is the result of illusion and ignorance

ahiṁsā (Hinduism/Jainism): principle of nonviolence, with the corollary practice of compassion for all living beings

Ahura Mazda (Persia): supreme god of Zoroastrianism; subordinate to him are all Ahuras (responsible for the creation of all that is good in this world) and the Daivas (demons)

akam (internal) genre (Tamil): genre in Caṅkam literature consisting of poems that describe inner and personal human experiences such as love and its emotional phases

Allah (Islam): deity (singular) worshiped by Muslims

āḻvārs (Hinduism): literally, "one immersed in the experience of god"; saints devoted to the cult of the Hindu god Vishnu

Amaterasu Ōmikami (Japan, Shintō): Sun goddess who, upset by her brother's actions, retreated into a cave and had to be coaxed out by the other gods

Amun (Egypt): also Amun-Re, sun god worshiped by Egyptians

anātman (Hinduism): the idea that there is no real self (personality or soul) that exists, that there is only the ultimate reality or "true suchness" of being

anekāntvādis (Jainism): limitations of human perception, illustrated by the blind men whose perceptions of the elephant are all different

anthropophagy: cannibalism

Apedemak (Africa): Nubian war god most often represented with the head of a lion and a human body, although sometimes with the body of a serpent

apirigraham (Jainism): the principle that greed and the desire for material possessions entangles and limits humans; the absence of such a desire frees humans not only in this world but also from the endless cycle of birth, suffering, and death

Apollo (Greece): god known for healing, purification, prophecy, care for the young, poetry, and music; portrayed as a young, handsome athletic man; many cults arose around him

archon (Greece, Athens): civilian head of state in sixth century B.C.E. Athens

Aristotle's Lyceum: Athenian school founded by the philosopher Aristotle

Artemis (Greece): goddess of the hunt and women's rites of passage (as from virginity into womanhood); many cults arose around her

asceticism: a simple way of life, usually involving self-denial, that is often followed by religious figures, who renounce materialism and sensualism to pursue a higher level of spirituality

Asclepius (Greece): god of healing, often depicted as a mature, bearded man with a staff with a snake coiled around it

Ashur (Assyria): god who ruled and controlled the land of Assyria and had supreme power over other deities, including Ishtar (goddess of love and war), Ninurta (warfare and hunting), Shamash (Sun), Adad (storm), and Sin (Moon)

Athena (Greece): goddess of war and crafts, known for patronage of crafts including carpentry and metalworking as well as for helping heroes

ātman (Hinduism): a person's spiritual component, or soul

Aton (Egypt): "solar disk"; Sun god, object of worship by Akhenaton

Attic orators: ten Athenian orators given classic status by the second century C.E.: Lysias, Isaeus, Hyperides, Isocrates, Dinarchus, Aeschines, Antiphon, Lycurgus, Andocides, and Demosthenes

Augusta (Rome): title used to describe the wife of the Roman emperor

Augustus (Rome): title given to Roman emperors; used to denote the higher position in the tetrarchy established by Diocletian

avatar (Hinduism): incarnation of a deity, often Vishnu

avidyā (Hinduism): ignorance

Ayurveda (India): the science of longevity, a kind of alternative medicine

bas-relief: sculptural relief; the raised part of the sculpture is shallow, without undercutting

bhakti (devotional) genre (Tamil): genre in Caṅkam literature consisting of devotional poems

biface: a stone tool having two faces

bishop of Rome: head of the Catholic Church; also pope

bodhi (Buddhism): wisdom

bodhisattva (Mahāyāna Buddhism): "enlightened being"; individual who has achieved enlightenment but delays passing over into Nirvana in order to help with the salvation of others

boustrophedon: a writing technique in which alternate lines are written in different directions

Brahmā (Hinduism): "the creator"; deity in Hinduism regarded as the supreme being, the source of all reality

brahman (Hinduism): the primary origin and essence of all things

Brahman: priestly caste, the most favored of the four main hereditary groupings of people within India's traditional caste system

Bronze Age: period between 4000 and 3000 B.C.E. and the start of the Iron Age in which human cultures used bronze for tools and other objects

Buddha (Buddhism): "enlightened one"; name for Indian prince Siddhārtha Gautama after he gained enlightenment

Caesar (Rome): title given to Roman emperors, used during the tetrarchy established by Diocletian to denote a position lower than that of Augustus

caliph (Islam): *khalīfah*; title to denote a temporal and spiritual head of Islam, successor to the Prophet Muḥammad

camelid (Andes): *Camelidae*, family of animals including alpacas, llamas, vicuñas, and guanaco, often used as pack animals

castes: hereditary groupings of people by social status and rank

celadon: greenish ceramic glaze, originated in China; also a name for pottery bearing this glaze

cenote: well or underground river exposed when the limestone covering it collapsed

censor (Rome): Republic official responsible for citizen and senate rolls

church: building in which worship (usually Christian) takes place

city-state (Greece): an independent state consisting of a city and its environs

concubine: mistress, woman included in household who performs many functions of a wife but has lower status than a spouse

cong (China): jade tube encased in rectangular blocks carved with reliefs of abstract masks representing animals, deities, or ancestors, found in burials beginning in the Neolithic Age

consul (Rome): the Republic's highest office; position was reduced in power after Rome became an empire

cremation: the burning of a body after death

cultigen: cultivated or domesticated version of an unknown wild plant

cuneiform: rigid and angular wedge-shaped characters or the script that was produced using them

Dao (Daoism): literally "road" or "way"; the source and principle of everything in the universe, which cannot be defined in a positive manner as it is not anything concrete, tangible, or fixed, although it is at work in everything

deme (Greece): local territorial district, unit of government in Attica

democracy: a government ruled by the people, usually through majority rule

despotism: rule by a despot, or autocrat, a rule with absolute power

dharma (Buddhism and Hinduism): divine law; the teachings of the Buddha, the truth, ultimate reality, the moral law or the right way, duty, and the true religion

dharma (Hinduism): law of the universe, to be followed by those wishing to fulfill their duties

Dionysus (Greece, Rome): Roman name Bacchus; god of wine and intoxication, also ritual madness, ecstasy, the mask (theater), realm of the dead; object of many cults

dithyramb (Greece, Athens): song sung by a chorus to honor Dionysus; performed in contests at festivals such as the City Dionysia

dolmen: monument consisting of two or more upright stones holding up a horizontal slab; thought to be tombs or burial sites

earthenware: pottery; low-fired wares, relatively soft and porous, suitable for funerary vessels and tomb sculptures

Eightfold Path (Buddhism): the path to Nirvana, consisting of right views, right resolve, right speech, right action, right work, right effort, right mindfulness, and right concentration

enlightenment (Buddhism): also Nirvana, *satori*, a state of freedom from desire and suffering

entablature (Greece): horizontal piece that rests on a

column in an architectural structure; its midsection consists of a frieze

epinician ode (Greece, Athens): *epinicia*; victory odes, choral songs usually performed after an athlete's victory, either at the festival or upon his return home

equites (Rome): equestrian class, positioned between the senate and citizens in the Republic, they filled bureaucratic posts in the empire

Eros (Greece): god of love; depicted as a young, beautiful man; numerous cults arose around him

eunuch: castrated man, often employed near women in a palace

foederati (Rome): allies of Rome whose relationship was established through treaty

Four Noble Truths (Buddhism): first truth is that life is suffering, which continues through an endless chain of rebirths; second that suffering is caused by desire; third that desire can be ended; fourth that right living according to Buddhist precepts (the Eightfold Path) is the way to end desire and enter Nirvana

frieze: a highly ornamented or sculpted band, usually on a structure or furnishings

fu (China): form of poetry that mixes prose with verse

geoglyphs (Andes, Nasca culture): large-scale line drawings of birds, monkeys, spiders, and plants, scratched into the surface of the earth and visible only from the sky

haniwa (Japan): unglazed terra-cotta cylinders and figurines placed on burial mounds during the Kofun period; their significance is unknown

harmost (Greece, Sparta): title of Spartan garrison commanders or military governors when abroad

helots (Greece, Sparta): *heilōtai*, state-owned serfs; believed to be between free men and slaves in status

henotheism: the worship of a single god while acknowledging the existence of other gods

heresy: religious teaching or belief deemed contrary to accepted dogma of the faith

hieroglyphs (Egypt): "sacred inscriptions"; Egyptian hieroglyphs contained three types of signs: pictograms, phonograms, and determinatives, clarifying symbols that indicated the category of ideas pictured; also used to describe scripts that use mostly pictorial characters

hijrah (Islam): Muḥammad's flight from Mecca to Medina in 622 C.E.

Hināyāna Buddhism (Buddhism): "the lesser vehicle," also known as Theravāda; a form of Buddhism in which each individual must achieve enlightenment and salvation by his or her own efforts

iconography: traditional symbols or pictures associated with a religious or legendary subject; also pictorial material illustrating a subject

ideograms: pictures or symbols used in a writing script to represent a concept or object but not the word used for that concept or object

imperator (Rome): originally an honor to a victorious general during the Roman Republic; title given to the head of the Roman Empire

inhumation: burial in the ground

Ionic column (Greece): column produced by ancient Greek architectural order in Ionia; was a fluted column with scroll-like ornamentation at its top

Iron Age: historical period beginning in about 1000 B.C.E. in western Asia and Egypt in which people smelted iron and used it in industry; followed Bronze Age

Isis (Egypt): goddess who was the exemplary wife and mother, the healer, the bestower of fertility and prosperity, the patroness of the dead, and the great magician; a large cult developed around her and spread to Greece and Rome

kachinas (American Southwest, Pueblo tribes): small religious statues

karma (Hinduism, Buddhism): the concept that all actions produce consequences and that the way a person leads his or her life determines the individual's chance for deliverance through reincarnation

kivas (American Southwest, Pueblo tribes): ceremonial structures, usually partly underground, containing rooms used for rituals

Kṣatriya: caste of nobles and warriors (administrators), the second-ranked caste in the four main hereditary groupings of people within India's traditional caste system

labrets (North America): lip ornaments, sometimes indicating social status

logogram: letters, signs, or symbols representing an entire word

Mahāyāna Buddhism (Buddhism): "the great vehicle"; a form of Buddhism in which individuals can reach enlightenment through the assistance of bodhisattvas, individuals who have achieved enlightenment but delay passing over into Nirvana in order to help with the salvation of others

mandate of heaven (China): authorization by heaven to rule, could be taken away if the emperor did not act properly

mastaba (Egypt): tomb structure that predated the pyramids, consisted of oblong structure with sloping sides and a flat roof

māyā (Hinduism): illusion

megaliths: large stones used in massive prehistoric structures

menhir: a single standing stone monolith

microlith: tiny blade tool, sometimes triangular, often set into a bone or wooden haft

Middle Way (Buddhism): spiritual journey, neither ascetic nor self-indulgent, to achieving Nirvana, a state of liberation, peace, and joy

mokṣa (Jainism): enlightenment, liberation from the cycle of rebirth, suffering, and death

monarchy: absolute rule by a single individual

monasticism: a way of life that involves seclusion or asceticism in a monastery

monoliths: single great stones often in the shape of columns or obelisks

monotheism: worship of a single god, admitting of no other gods

nagara: town or sacred city modeled after the legendary Mount Meru, having its highest point protruding from the center and a base consisting of a series of descending layers of terraces and palisades

necropolis: literally "city of the dead"; expansive and elaborate ancient cemetery

Neolithic Age: late Stone Age, historical period of time in which people used polished stone implements

New Comedy (Greece, Athens; Rome): comic plays or poems using situation comedy; many examine relationships, love, and family life

Nirvana (Buddhism): a state in which a person is freed from all desires and attachments, a state of release from existence

nomes (Egypt): administrative or geographical unit of area

Old Comedy (Greece, Athens): carnivalesque form of poetry/drama that made fun of topical people, institutions, and issues; its origins were in rituals of fertility and verbal abuse and its defining features were grotesque costumes, obscene language, and fantastic plots

oligarchy: rule by a small group, often for selfish or corrupt purposes

Panchamas (India): Untouchables, who were without inherited status or caste

papyrus: writing material made from the pith of the papyrus plant, a tall sedge

pater patriae (Rome): "father of the country"; prestigious title given to some emperors

patriarch (Christianity): bishops in the church who headed the most important sees or areas and therefore had special rights and powers

patricians (Rome): *Patricii*; noble class of Rome, highest strata in the Republic

Pax Romana (Rome): period of peace within the Roman Empire beginning after Augustus claimed victory at the Battle of Actium (31 C.E.)

pharaoh (Egypt): ruler of ancient Egypt

phonograms: characters used to represent phonetic elements, syllables, or words

pictograms: drawings or pictures used to represent words or parts of words

Pillars of the Faith, Five (Islam): Five Pillars of Islam (distinct from the Six Pillars of Faith); five fundamental tenets of Islam: First, the profession of faith; second, the five required prayers each day toward Mecca; third, yearly tithe to a religious official; fourth, observance of the month-long fast of Ramadan; fifth, the pilgrimage to Mecca

Plato's Academy: school of philosophy established by Plato and located in Athens

plebeians (Rome): plebs; general population of Rome, apart from the elites

polytheism: worship of more than one god

pontifex maximus (Rome): chief priest, head of Rome's state religion and all its establishments

pope: head of the Catholic Church; also bishop of Rome

porcelain: high-fired wares (pottery), which are relatively hard, durable, and impervious to water, suitable for everyday use

praetor (Rome): title used first for a consul, then a magistrate dealing with justice in Rome

Praetorian Guard (Rome): elite guard force of the Roman Empire created by Augustus

prefect of the Praetorian Guard (Rome): commander of the Praetorian Guard; the post gradually grew in power during the Roman Empire

princeps (Rome): "first man in the state"; unofficial honorary title given during the Republic

proconsul (Rome): governor of a province serving in

place of a consul during the Roman Republic; governor of a senatorial province during the Roman Empire

projectile points (Americas): arrowheads; stone points fastened to the end of projectiles (weapons)

puram (external) genre (Tamil): genre in Caṅkam literature consisting of poems that extol the virtues of heroism

quaestor (Rome): lowest-ranked magistrate, often associated with finances

reincarnation (Hinduism, Buddhism, Jainism): rebirth of a person into another life (body) after death; part of the cycle of death and rebirth

relic: object (sometimes a bone) venerated or held in high regard because of its association with a religious figure

saint (Christian): a holy person, living or dead

Saṅgha (Buddhism): community of monks, nuns, and lay people

satrap (Persia): provincial governor in ancient Persia

satya (Jainism): a renunciation of secular life

schism: a break between subgroups within a religious body

shaman: high priest or priestess, uses magic or rituals to heal people, predict the future, and control events (rain)

Shamash (Aramea, Babylonia, Sumer): also Samash; Sun god

shrine: place hallowed by its religious associations, often where a deity or religious figure is worshiped

Śiva (Hinduism): "the destroyer"; deity associated with cosmic change

sophists (Greece): itinerant teachers giving lectures throughout Greece

stela, stelae (plural): stone slab or pillar, usually with commemorative inscription

Stone Age: historical period preceding the Bronze Age; distinguished by peoples' use of tools and weapons made of stone

stratēgos (Greece): military commander or general; in fifth century C.E. Athens, they also had political importance

stupa (Buddhism): structure, usually in the shape of a dome, often containing a relic

Śūdras: caste of peasants, the fourth-ranked caste in the four main hereditary groupings of people within India's traditional caste system

śūnyatā (Buddhism): emptiness, which is without origin or decay and beyond all description and is pure consciousness and the essence of phenomena

swidden: agricultural field created by cutting and burning the vegetation covering the area

temple: building in which religious exercises (often Jewish or Buddhist) take place

tennō (Japan): emperor or empress

terra-cotta: glazed or unglazed fired clay

tetrarchy (Rome): system of collegiate government created by Diocletian in which two Augusti shared power with two junior Caesars

Three Jewels (Buddhism): The first was the Buddha; the second the dharma; the third the Saṅgha (community of monks)

Three Jewels (Jainism): *ratna traya*; three religious practices of right perception (*samyagdarśana*), right knowledge (*samyagjñāna*), and right conduct (*samyagcāritra*)

torii (Japan): sacred gateway to a shrine

totem: plant or animal that represents a clan or family

trepanation: the cutting or boring a hole into the skull for medical purposes

trireme: galley (ship) with three banks of oars

tumulus: burial mound

tyrannicides (Greece): killers of tyrants; often used to refer to those who killed Julius Caesar and Hipparchus of Athens

tyranny (Greece): monarchy set up by those who seized power (usually fringe members of the ruling aristocracy) in the city-states of seventh-sixth century B.C.E.

Vaiśya: caste of farmers and merchant, the third-ranked caste in the four main hereditary groupings of people within India's traditional caste system

vegeculture: the cultivation of multiple species within a single field

Vishnu (Hinduism): "the preserver"; deity who personifies eternal, unchanging qualities

viziers (Egypt): king's highest officials, acted as judges and collected taxes

wu-wei (Daoism): the principle of noncontention; to be waterlike, to follow the flow of nature and not to oppose it, to be flexible and yet to accomplish one's goals

yin and yang (Chinese): two forces, one passive and negative (yin), and the other active and positive (yang), that are to be balanced in life

yoga (Hinduism): mental and spiritual exercises designed to enable a person to reach spiritual enlightenment

Yogācara (Buddhism): a form of Buddhism that involves metaphysical idealism and meditation and stresses that only thought exists and that the external world is an illusion; the only reality is *śūnyatā*, or emptiness

Zen Buddhism (Buddhism): form of Buddhism in which meditation is used to reach spiritual enlightenment

Zeus (Greece): man god of the Greek pantheon; father of the gods who rules from Mount Olympus

ziggurat: Mesopotamian temple tower, built in pyramid form with a shrine at the top

GEOGRAPHICAL GUIDE TO THE ANCIENT WORLD

This guide categorizes the entries in the encyclopedia according to their main areas of coverage, placing them into one or more of twenty-two geographical areas. Each individual essay may be found in alphabetical order in the body of the encyclopedia.

AFRICA

Afrasans
Africa, East and South
Africa, North
Africa, West
African rock art, southern and
  eastern
Agaw
Alwa
Apedemak
Arkamani
Augustine, Saint
Axum
Bantu, Congo Basin
Bantu, Mashariki
BaTwa
Beja
Berbers
Capella, Martianus
Carthage
Chadic peoples
Chifumbaze culture
Copper Belt
Cushites
Cyprian of Carthage, Saint
Dido
Divinity
Eastern African Microlithic/
  Khoisan peoples
Ethiopia
Ezana
Frumentius, Saint
Garamantes
Gash civilization
Ghana
Hannibal
Henotheism
Juba I of Numidia
Juba II of Mauretania
Jugurtha
Kaleb
Kerma
Khoikhoi

Khoisans
Madagascar
Makouria
Mande
Napata and Meroe
Niger-Congo
Nilo-Saharans
Nilotes
Nine Saints
Nobatae
Nok culture
Nubia
Omotic peoples
Piye
Rift Valley system
Saharan rock art
Shabaka
Sheba, Queen of
Sophonisba of Numidia
Ta-Seti
Taharqa
Tibu
Wawat
Yam
Zama, Battle of
Znaga
Zoskales

ALEXANDRIA

Alexandrian library
Alexandrian patriarchs
Apollonius of Perga
Apollonius Rhodius
Aristarchus of Samos
Athanasius of Alexandria,
  Saint
Callimachus of Cyrene
Clement of Alexandria
Cyril of Alexandria, Saint
Hesychius of Alexandria
Menelaus of Alexandria
Monophysitism

Pharos of Alexandria
Philo of Alexandria
Septuagint

ARABIA AND MUSLIM
NEAR EAST

ʿAbd al-Malik
ʿAbd Allāh ibn al-ʿAbbās
ʿAbd Allāh ibn az-Zubayr
ʿAbd Allāh ibn Saʿd ibn Abī
  Sarḥ
Abraha
Abū Bakr
ʿĀʾishah bint Abī Bakr
ʿAlī ibn Abī Ṭālib
ʿAmr ibn al-ʿĀṣ Mosque
Arabia
Ḥusayn
Islam
Muʿallaqāt, Al-
Muḥammad
Qurʾān
Saracen conquest
ʿUmar ibn al-Khaṭṭāb
Umayyad Dynasty
ʿUthmān ibn ʿAffān

ARMENIA AND ANATOLIA

Anatolia
Argishti I
Armenia
Artavasdes II of Armenia
Attalid Dynasty
Croesus
Gyges
Hattusilis I
Hittites
Kaska
Labarnas I
Luwians
Lycia

Lydia
Midas
Montanism
Muwatallis
Phrygia
Sarduri I
Sarduri II
Sarduri III
Suppiluliumas I
Telipinus
Tigranes the Great
Urartu

BRITISH ISLES AND THE CELTS
Ælle
Æthelbert
Agricola, Gnaeus Julius
Aidan, Saint
Aneirin
Angles, Saxons, Jutes
Arthur
Augustine of Canterbury, Saint
Benedict Biscop, Saint
Boudicca
Britain
Caratacus
Cartimandua
Celts
Columba, Saint
Cunobelinus
Dallán Forgaill
Edwin
Hallstatt culture
Ireland
La Tène culture
Patrick, Saint
Picts
Stonehenge
Sutton Hoo
Taliesin
Vindolanda tablets

CENTRAL ASIA
Afanasievo culture
Andronovo culture
Antae
Attila

Bactria
Cimmerians
Huns
Karasuk culture
Kelteminar culture
Kitoi culture
Kushān Dynasty
Menander (Greco-Bactrian king)
Milinda-pañha
Mongolia
Sarmatians
Scythia

CHINA AND TIBET
Ban Gu
Banpocun culture
Black Pottery culture
Bodhidharma
Cai Lun
Cao Cao
Cao Zhi
China
Chunqiu
Confucianism
Confucius
Daoism
Dong Zhongshu
Faxian
Fu Hao's tomb
Ge Hong
Great Wall of China
Gu Kaizhi
Guang Wudi
Han Dynasty
Han Feizi
He Yan
Huainanzi
Huangdi
Hui Shi
Huiyuan
Laozi
Legalists
Liangzhu culture
Ling Lun
Liu Xie
Liu Yiqing
Longshan culture
Lü Buwei
Lu Ji

Mao Shan revelations
Mencius
Mozi
Mulanshi
Northern Wei Dynasty
Qijia culture
Qin Dynasty
Qin tomb
Qu Yuan
Shang Dynasty
Shang Yang
Shi Huangdi
Silk Road
Sima Qian
Sima Xiangru
Six Dynasties
Srong-brtsan-sgam-po
Sui Dynasty
Taizong
Tang Dynasty
Tao Hongjing
Tao Qian
Three Kingdoms
Tibet
Wang Bi
Wang Chong
Wang Xizhi
Weiyang palace
Wendi
Wu Hou
Wudi
Wujing
Xia Dynasty
Xiaowen Di
Xie He
Xie Lingyun
Xin Zhui's tomb
Xiongnu
Xuanzang
Xunzi
Xushen
Yan Liben
Yang Di
Yang Xiong
Yangshao culture
Yue
Yue ware
Yuezhi culture
Zengzi
Zhangdi

Zhiyi
Zhou Dynasty
Zhou style
Zhuangzi
Zhuge Liang
Zi Si

EGYPT
Akhenaton
Ankhesenamen
Anthony of Egypt, Saint
Book of the Dead
Cleopatra VII
Egypt, Pharaonic
Egypt, Prepharaonic
Egypt, Ptolemaic and Roman
Harkhuf
Hatshepsut
Herophilus
Hyksos
Hypatia
Imhotep
Isis, cult of
Merenptah
Montuhotep I
Nefertiti
Palermo stone
Ptolemaic Dynasty
Ptolemy
Pyramids and Sphinx
Rameses II
Rameses III
Rosetta stone
Saite Dynasty
Saracen conquest
Sesostris III
Seti I
Snefru
Tale of the Two Brothers, The
Thutmose III
Tutankhamen

EUROPE
Agapetus, Saint
Agathias
Alani
Alaric I
Alaric II

Alboin
Allemanni
Anastasius I
Anthemius of Tralles
Aristides of Miletus
Beaker people
Belisarius
Benedict of Nursia, Saint
Byzantine Empire
Cassiodorus
Cassivellaunus
Chlotar I
Clovis
Constantinople
Cyprus
Etruscans
Finnic peoples
France
Franks
Gauls
Germany
Goths
Haghia Sophia
Hallstatt culture
Jordanes
Justinian I
Justinian's codes
La Tène culture
Langobards
Malalas, John
Maroboduus
Merovingian Dynasty
Narses
Neolithic Age Europe
Paulinus, Saint
Procopius
Radegunda, Saint
Salvianus
Slavs
Spain
Suebi
Theoderic the Great
Theodora
Theodosius of Alexandria
Theodosius II
Totila
Vandals
Vendae
Vercingetorix
Wallia

GREECE
Achaean League
Achaean War
Achilles Painter
Aegospotami, Battle of
Aeschines
Aeschylus
Aesop
Aetolian League
Agariste
Agathon
Agesilaus II of Sparta
Alcaeus of Lesbos
Alcibiades of Athens
Alcman
Alexander the Great
Amasis Painter
Anacreon
Andocides
Antigonid Dynasty
Antiochus the Great
Antipater
Antiphon
Anyte of Tegea
Apollodorus of Athens (artist)
Apollodorus of Athens (scholar)
Apuleius, Lucius
Aratus
Archidamian War
Archidamus II of Sparta
Archidamus III of Sparta
Archilochus of Paros
Archimedes
Archytas of Tarentum
Argead Dynasty
Aristarchus of Samothrace
Aristides of Athens
Aristophanes
Aristotle
Artemis, temple of, at Ephesus
Aspasia of Miletus
Athens
Bacchylides
Brasidas of Sparta
Callicrates
Cassander
Chaeronea, Battle of
Cimon
Cleisthenes of Athens
Cleisthenes of Sicyon

Cleon of Athens
Colossus of Rhodes
Corinthian War
Crates of Athens
Cratinus
Crete
Critias of Athens
Cunaxa, Battle of
Cyclades
Cypselus of Corinth
Delphi
Demetrius Phalereus
Demetrius Poliorcetes
Democritus
Demosthenes
Diadochi
Diocles of Carystus
Diogenes of Sinope
Dionysius I the Elder of
    Syracuse
Dionysius the Younger
Draco
Eleusinian mysteries
Epaminondas
Ephialtes of Athens
Epicurus
Erasistratus
Eratosthenes of Cyrene
Erinna
Euclid
Eudoxus
Eumenes II
Eupalinus of Megara
Eupolis
Euripides
Four Hundred
Gaugamela, Battle of
Gelon of Syracuse
Gorgias
Gortyn, law code of
Granicus, Battle of
Greco-Persian Wars
Greece, Archaic
Greece, Classical
Greece, Hellenistic and Roman
Greece, Mycenaean
Halicarnassus mausoleum
Harmodius and Aristogiton
Hecataeus of Miletus
Heliodorus of Emesa

Herodas
Herodotus
Hesiod
Hieron I of Syracuse
Hieron II of Syracuse
Hipparchus
Hippias of Athens
Hippocrates
Histiaeus of Miletus
Homer
Hydaspes, Battle of
Iamblichus of Syria
Ibycus
Ictinus
Ion of Chios
Ionian Revolt
Isaeus
Isocrates
Issus, Battle of
King's Peace
Leonidas
Leucippus
Leuctra, Battle of
Linear B
Lucian
Lycurgus of Sparta
Lysander of Sparta
Lysias
Lysimachus
Lysippus
Macedonia
Magna Graecia
Mantinea, Battles of
Marathon, Battle of
Meleager of Gadara
Menander (playwright)
Menippus of Gadara
Messenian Wars
Miltiades the Younger
Mimnermus
Moschus of Syracuse
Mycenae, palace of
Myron
Nicander of Colophon
Nicias of Athens
Nicolaus of Damascus
Nicomachus of Gerasa
Olympias
Olympic Games
Oribasius

Orphism
Paeonius
Panaetius of Rhodes
Parmenides
Parthenon
Pausanias of Sparta
Pausanias the Traveler
Peloponnesian War
Periander of Corinth
Pericles
Phidias
Philip II
Philip V
Philochorus
Pindar
Pisistratus
Pittacus of Mytilene
Plataea, Battle of
Plato
Plotinus
Plutarch
Polybius
Polyclitus
Polycrates of Samos
Polygnotus
Posidonius
Praxiteles
Pre-Socratic philosophers
Protagoras
Pyrrhon of Elis
Pythagoras
Sacred Wars
Salamis, Battle of
Sappho
Scopas
Scylax of Caryanda
Semonides
Simonides
Socrates
Solon
Sophocles
Speusippus
Stesichorus
Strabo
Terpander of Lesbos
Themistocles
Theocritus of Syracuse
Theognis
Theophrastus
Thera

Thermopylae, Battle of
Theron of Acragas
Thespis
Thirty Tyrants
Thucydides
Timoleon of Corinth
Troy
Tyrtaeus
Xenophanes
Xenophon
Zeno of Citium
Zeno of Elea
Zeus at Pergamum, Great
    Altar of
Zeuxis of Heraclea

INDIA AND SOUTH ASIA

Advaita
Aiṅkururnūru
Ājīvikas
Akanāṉūṟu
Amaravātī school
Amaru
Ānanda
Andhradesha school
Appar
Āraṇyakas
Āryabhaṭa
Asaṅga
Ashvaghosa
Aśoka
Āśvalāyana
Bāṇa
Bhagavadgītā
Bharata Muni
Bhāravi
Bhartṛhari
Bhāsa
Bhavabhūti
Bodhidharma
Brāhmaṇas
Brahmanism
Buddha
Buddhism
Buddhist cave temples
Budhasvāmin
Campantar
Caṅkam
Cātaṉār

Chandragupta Maurya
Daṇḍin
Dhammapada
Gandhāra art
Gaudapāda
Gośāla Maskarīputra
Guṇāḍhya
Gupta emperors
Harivaṃśa
Harṣa
Hinduism
Hydaspes, Battle of
Iḷaṅkō Aṭikaḷ
India
Indian temple architecture
Indus Valley civilization
Jainism
Jātakas
Kālidāsa
Kalittokai
Kaniṣka
Karaikkal Ammaiyar
Kauṭilya
Kuruntokai
Kushān Dynasty
Mahābhārata
Mahābodhi temple
Mahendravarman I
Mauryan Dynasty
Menander (Greco-Bactrian
    king)
Milinda-pañha
Nārāyaṇa
Naṟṟiṇai
Nāṭya-śāstra
Pallava Dynasty
Pāṇini
Paripāṭal
Pārvatī Devī temple
Patiṉeṇkīḻkkaṇakku
Patirruppattu
Peruṅkatai
Peyar
Poykai
Puṟanāṉūṟu
Purāṇas
Pūtāṉ
Rāmāyaṇa
Sātavāhana Dynasty
Sri Lanka

Śūdraka
Śuṅga Dynasty
Sūtras
Suttanipāta
Śyāmilaka
Tantras
Tipiṭaka
Tiruttakkatevar
Tiruvaḷḷuvar
Tissa, Dēvānaṃpiya
Tōlāmoḷittēvar
Tolkāppiyam
Upaniṣads
Vākāṭaka Dynasty
Vālmīki
Vardhamāna
Vasubandhu
Vātsyāyana
Vaṭṭagāmaṇi
Vedas
Vedism
Viśākhadatta

JAPAN AND KOREA

Ainu
Gigaku
Haniwa
Himiko
Japan
Jimmu Tennō
Jingū
Jōmon
Kofun period
Koguryo style
Korea
Mimaji
Nihon shoki
Nintoku
Ōjin Tennō
Pak Hyokkose
Shintō
Shōtoku Taishi
Yamato court
Yayoi culture

MESOAMERICA

Altar de Sacrificios
Atlatl

Ball game, Mesoamerican
Chichén Itzá
Cholula
Cobá
Copán
Dzibilchaltún
El Tajín
Leyden plate
Maya
Mixtecs
Monte Albán
Olmecs
Palenque
Pyramid of the Moon
Teotihuacán
Tikal
Uxmal
Zapotecs

MESOPOTAMIA
Akkadians
Ashurbanipal
Assyria
Atrahasis epic
Babylonia
Esarhaddon
Fertile Crescent
Gilgamesh epic
Halafian culture
Hammurabi's code
Hurrians
Kassites
Manichaeanism
Mitanni
Natufian culture
Nebuchadnezzar II
Samarran culture
Sammu-ramat
Sargon of Akkad
Sargon II
Seleucid Dynasty
Seleucus I
Sennacherib
Shulgi
Sumerians
Tiglath-pileser III
Ubaid culture
Ur-Namma

MIDDLE EAST:
  ISRAEL AND SYRIA
Ahab
Akiba ben Joseph
Amos
Aqhat epic
Arameans
Bar Kokhba
Bathsheba
Ben-Hadad I
Bible: Jewish
Canaanites
Christianity
Damascus document
David
Dead Sea Scrolls
Elijah
Essenes
Exodus
Ezekiel
Ezra
Henotheism
Herodian Dynasty
Hezekiah
Hosea
Isaiah
Israel
James the Apostle
Jehu
Jeremiah
Jeroboam I
Jerusalem, temple of
Jesus Christ
Jewish diaspora
Johanan ben Zakkai
John the Baptist, Saint
John the Evangelist, Saint
Josiah
Judaism
Kadesh, Battle of
Maccabees
Mary
Masada, Battle of
Moabites
Moses
Paul, Saint
Peter, Saint
Philistines
Phineas
Phoenicia

Samson
Samuel
Saul
Solomon
Talmud
Yannai
Yose ben Yose
Zealots
Zenobia

NORTH AMERICA
Adena culture
Aleutian tradition
American Paleo-Arctic tradition
Anasazi
Archaic North American
    culture
Archaic tradition, northern
Arctic Small Tool tradition
Boylston Street weir
California peoples
Clovis technological complex
Cochise culture
Dalton tradition
Deptford culture
Dorset phase
Eastern peoples
Folsom technological complex
Fremont culture
Great Basin peoples
Helton phase
Hohokam culture
Ipiutak
Kachemak tradition
Laurel culture
Locarno Beach
Maritime Archaic
Marpole phase
Microblade tradition, Northwest
Middle Woodland tradition
Mogollon culture
Norton tradition
Old Copper complex
Paleo-Indians in North America
Paleo-Indians in South America
Plains peoples
Plateau peoples
Poverty Point
Saint Mungo phase

Sonota culture
Southwest peoples
Subarctic peoples
Thom's Creek

OCEANIA
Australia, Tasmania, New
   Zealand
Djanggawul cycle
Dreaming
Hawaii
Melanesia
Micronesia
Polynesia
Sea Peoples

PERSIA
Achaemenian Dynasty
Ardashīr I
Arsacid Dynasty
Artabanus I-V
Artemisia I
Artemisia II
Astyages
Atossa
Avesta
Cyaxares
Cyrus the Great
Darius the Great
Darius III
Greco-Persian Wars
Manichaeanism
Mausolus
Mithradates I
Mithradates II
Mithradates VI Eupator
Mithrism
Narses
Parthia
Persia
Sāsānian Empire
Scylax of Caryanda
Shāpūr I
Shāpūr II
Xerxes I
Zoroaster
Zoroastrianism
Zurvanism

ROME
Accius, Lucius
Achilles Tatius
Acte, Claudia
Actium, Battle of
Adrianople, Battle of
Aemilius Paullus, Lucius
Aeneas
Agrippa, Marcus Vipsanius
Agrippina the Elder
Agrippina the Younger
Alesia, Battle of
Alexander Polyhistor, Lucius
   Cornelius
Ambrose
Ammianus Marcellinus
Antipater of Idumaea
Antonia the Elder
Antonia the Younger
Antoninus Pius
Antony, Marc
Apollodorus the Architect
Apollonius of Tyana
Appian
Appian Way
Ara Pacis
Arausio, Battle of
Aretaeus of Cappadocia
Arianism
Aristides
Arminius
Arria the Elder
Arrian
Atticus, Titus Pomponius
Augustine, Saint
Augustus
Aurelianus, Lucius Domitius
Ausonius, Decimus Magnus
Avitus, Eparchius
Basil of Cappadocia, Saint
Bible: New Testament
Boethius
Brutus
Byzantine Empire
Caesar, Julius
Caligula
Calpurnius Siculus, Titus
Camillus, Marcus Furius
Cannae, Battle of
Capella, Martianus

Caracalla
Carrhae, Battle of
Cassian
Cassiodorus
Cassius
Catiline
Cato the Censor
Cato the Younger
Catullus
Celsus
Celsus, Aulus Cornelius
Chalcedon, Council of
Châlons, Battle of
Cicero
Cincinnatus, Lucius Quinctius
Claudian
Claudius
Claudius Caecus, Appius
Clement I
Clodia
Clodius Pulcher, Publius
Columella
Commius
Constans I
Constantine the Great
Constantius I-III
Corbulo, Gnaeus Domitius
Coriolanus, Gnaeus Marcius
Cornelia
Crassus, Marcus Licinius
Curtius Rufus, Quintus
Cynoscephalae, Battle of
Cyprian of Carthage, Saint
Denis, Saint
Dio Cassius
Dio Chrysostom
Diocletian
Domitian
Donatism
Donatus, Aelius
Ennius, Quintus
Epictetus
Eudocia
Eudoxia, Aelia
Eusebius of Caesarea
Eutropius
Fabius
Fabius Maximus, Quintus
Fabius Pictor, Quintus
Faustina I

Faustina II
Figulus, Publius Nigidius
Flamininus, Titus Quinctius
Flavian Amphitheater
Fortunatus, Venantius
Four Emperors, Year of the
Frontinus, Sextus Julius
Fronto, Marcus Cornelius
Fulgentius, Fabius Planciades
Fulvia
Galen
Galerius Valerius Maximianus,
    Gaius
Gallic Wars
Gallienus
Gellius, Aulus
Gnosticism
Gracchus, Gaius Sempronius
Gracchus, Tiberius Sempronius
Gratian
Gregory of Nazianzus
Gregory the Great
Hadrian
Hadrian's villa
Helena, Saint
Herodian
Heron
Hilary of Poitiers, Saint
Horace
Hortensia
Hyginus (land surveyor)
Hyginus, Gaius Julius
Ignatius of Antioch
Irenaeus, Saint
Isidore of Seville, Saint
Jerome, Saint
John Chrysostom, Saint
Josephus, Flavius
Julia (daughter of Augustus)
Julia (daughter of Julius Caesar)
Julia Domna
Julia Mamaea
Julian the Apostate
Junius Brutus, Lucius
Justin Martyr, Saint
Juvenal
Lactantius, Lucius Caelius
    Firmianus
Latin League and War
Leo I (emperor)

Leo I, Saint
Licinius, Valerius Licinianus
Licinius Lucullus, Lucius
Livia Drusilla
Livius Andronicus, Lucius
Livy
Longinus
Longus
Lucan
Lucilius, Gaius (poet)
Lucilius, Gaius (satirist)
Lucretia
Lucretius
Macrobius, Aurelius Theodosius
Maecenas, Gaius
Magnesia ad Sipylum, Battle of
Manilius, Marcus
Marcus Aurelius
Marcus Aurelius's column
Marius, Gaius
Martial
Maxentius
Maximian
Mela, Pomponius
Messallina, Valeria
Milan, Edict of
Milvian Bridge, Battle of
Minucius Felix, Marcus
Mummius, Lucius
Naevius, Gnaeus
Nemesianus
Neoplatonism
Nepos, Cornelius
Nero
Nerva, Marcus Cocceius
Nestorius
Nicaea, Council of
Nonnus of Panopolis
Octavia
Odoacer
Origen
Ovid
Pachomius, Saint
Pacuvius, Marcus
Palladius, Rutilius Taurus
    Aemilianus
Pantheon
Paulinus of Nola, Saint
Pelagianism
Persius Flaccus, Aulus

Petronius Arbiter
Phaedrus
Pharsalus, Battle of
Philippi, Battle of
Philodemus
Philostratus, Flavius
Plautus
Plebeian secession
Pliny the Elder
Pliny the Younger
Pompeii and Herculaneum
Pompey the Great
Poppaea Sabina
Porphyry
Priscian
Priscillian
Propertius
Prudentius, Aurelius Clemens
Publilius Syrus
Punic Wars
Pytheas
Quinctilius Varus, Publius
Quintilian
Quintus Smyrnaeus
Res Gestae Divi Augusti
Roman arch
Roman Forum
Rome, Imperial
Rome, Prerepublican
Rome, Republican
Romulus and Remus
Romulus Augustulus
Rutilius Claudius Namatianus
Sabina, Vibia
Sallust
Scaevola, Quintus Mucius
    (Auger)
Scaevola, Quintus Mucius
    (Pontifex)
Scipio Aemilianus
Scipio Africanus
Scribonia
Second Sophistic
Sempronia
Seneca the Elder
Seneca the Younger
Severus, Lucius Septimius
Severus, Sulpicius
Sibylline Books
Sidonius Apollinaris

Simon Magus
Social War
Soranus of Ephesus
Spartacus
Statius, Publius Papinius
Stilicho, Flavius
Suetonius
Sulla, Lucius Cornelius
Sulpicia
Sylvester I, Saint
Symmachus, Quintus Aurelius
Tacitus
Tarquins
Terence
Tertullian
Teutoburg Forest, Battle of
Thapsus, Battle of
Themistius
Theodoret of Cyrrhus
Theodosius the Great
Tiberius
Tibullus, Albius
Titus
Trajan
Trajan's column
Triumvirate
Tullius Tiro, Marcus
Twelve Tables, The
Ulpian
Valens
Valentinian I
Valentinian III
Valerian
Valerius Flaccus, Gaius
Valerius Maximus
Valerius Probus, Marcus
Varro, Marcus Terentius
Vegetius Renatus, Flavius
Velleius Paterculus, Marcus
Vergil

Verginia
Vespasian
Villanovan culture
Vitruvius Pollio, Marcus
Zama, Battle of

SOUTH AMERICA
Abipón
Akapana pyramid
Amazonia
Andes, central
Andes, south
Arawak
Archaic South American culture
Brazil, eastern
Cajamarca pottery
Caribbean
Chavín de Huántar
Chinchorro mummies
Huaca de la Luna
Huaca del Sol
La Florida pyramid
Lima culture
Moche culture
Nasca culture
Raimondi stone
Recuay
South America, southern
South American Intermediate
    Area
Tiwanaku

SOUTHEAST ASIA
Arakanese
Funan
Java
Laos
Malay

Mon-Khmer
Pyu
Tai
Vietnam

WORLDWIDE
Agriculture and animal
    husbandry
Art and architecture: The
    Americas
Art and architecture: East Asia
Art and architecture: Europe and
    the Mediterranean region
Art and architecture: India
Art and architecture: Southeast
    Asia
Art and architecture: West and
    South Africa
Calendars and chronology
Daily life and customs
Death and burial
Education and training
Government and law
Languages and literature
Medicine and health
Navigation and transportation
Performing arts
Philosophy
Religion and ritual
Science
Settlements and social
    structure
Sports and entertainment
Technology
Trade and commerce
War and weapons
Women's life
Writing systems

CHRONOLOGICAL LIST OF ENTRIES

The following list, in rough chronological order, identifies all entries in this publication with the exception of the general overview essays appearing at the beginning of volume 1 (which by their nature are surveys and therefore all fall into the temporal scope of this set, which ends at roughly 700 C.E.). Names of personages are ordered by their birth dates, where available, or otherwise by death or regnal dates. In many cases, the fact that dates are approximate or relegated generally to a century (especially for topics, events, or personages before the common era) results in a list that may not present the topics in strict chronological order. Rules of ordering entries were devised as follows: Those topics to which only general (e.g., century) chronological designations can be applied (e.g., centuries) fall first, followed by the more precise dates—those for which a specific year or, even more specifically, months and days, are known and generally accepted. Readers wishing to access the articles on these topics will find them in this and the preceding volumes alphabetically arranged by the first word appearing in the second column.

Date	Event	Date	Event
8000 B.C.E.-700 C.E.	Sea Peoples	3000 B.C.E.-700 C.E.	Cyclades
	South America, southern		Germany
	South American		Ireland
	Intermediate Area		Korea
	Sri Lanka		Spain
8000 B.C.E.-710 C.E.	Japan	c. 3000 B.C.E.-700 C.E.	Tibu
8000 B.C.E.-900 C.E.	Middle Woodland		Troy
	tradition	c. 3000-2200 B.C.E. to 700	Arakanese
8th millen. B.C.E.-	Cushites	C.E.	
early 1st millen. C.E.		Born 2704 B.C.E.	Huangdi
c. 7500 B.C.E.-700 C.E.	Ainu	c. 2700 B.C.E.-c. 2600	Ling Lun
	Shintō	B.C.E.	
7000-2400 B.C.E.	Archaic South American	2700-1400 B.C.E.	Gash civilization
	culture	fl. 27th cent. B.C.E.	Imhotep
6300-5600 B.C.E.	Samarran culture	Reigned c. 2649-c. 2609	Snefru
c. 6000-4000 B.C.E.	Banpocun culture	B.C.E.	
c. 6000-1100 B.C.E.	Maritime Archaic	c. 2649-c. 2514 B.C.E.	Pyramids and the Sphinx
6000 B.C.E.-700 C.E.	Abipón	2500–2300 B.C.E.	Wawat
	Cyprus	2500-2200 B.C.E.	Yam
Beginning c. 6000 B.C.E.	Omotic peoples	c. 2500-1900 B.C.E.	Arctic Small Tool
5700-5600 B.C.E.	Halafian culture		tradition
5200-3400 B.C.E.	Ubaid culture	2500-1100 B.C.E.	Afanasievo culture
5000-3000 B.C.E.	Kelteminar culture	2500 B.C.E.-700 C.E.	Agaw
c. 5000-3000 B.C.E.	Yangshao culture	c. 2494-2345 B.C.E.	Palermo stone
5000-1900 B.C.E.	Longshan culture	2400-1570 B.C.E.	Kerma
c. 5000 B.C.E.-700 C.E.	Chadic peoples	c. 2400 B.C.E.-551 C.E.	Isis, cult of
4000-1000 B.C.E.	Old Copper complex	fl. 24th-23d cent. B.C.E.	Sargon of Akkad
4000 B.C.E.-100 C.E.	Archaic tradition,	fl. c. 2300-2200 B.C.E.	Harkhuf
	northern	c. 2300-2100 B.C.E.	Akkadians
4000 B.C.E.-700 C.E.	Caribbean	c. 2300-1800 B.C.E.	Beaker people
c. 4000 B.C.E.-700 C.E.	Mande	c. 2300-1600 B.C.E.	Hurrians
Beginning c. 4000 B.C.E.	Nilotes	c. 2300-612 B.C.E.	Assyria
3500-3100 B.C.E.	Ta-Seti	2200-1200 B.C.E.	Saint Mungo phase
3500-2900 B.C.E.	Helton phase	c. 2100-1600 B.C.E.	Xia Dynasty
c. 3500-1700 B.C.E.	Indus Valley civilization	2100-1000 B.C.E.	Greece, Mycenaean
3400-2100 B.C.E.	Liangzhu culture	Late 22d cent. B.C.E.-	Ur-Namma
3400-1800 B.C.E.	Sumerians	2095 B.C.E.	
3100-1550 B.C.E.	Stonehenge	Late 22d cent. B.C.E.-	Shulgi
c. 3050–1750 B.C.E.	Boylston Street weir	2047 B.C.E.	
c. 3050-305 B.C.E.	Egypt, Pharaonic	Reigned 2061-2011 B.C.E.	Montuhotep I
c. 3000-2900 B.C.E.	Kitoi culture	2000 B.C.E.	Gilgamesh epic
3000-500 B.C.E.	Phoenicia	2000-1400 B.C.E.	Thera
3000 B.C.E.-700 C.E.	Athens	c. 2000-1100 B.C.E.	Hittites
	Bantu, Congo Basin		Black Pottery culture
	Beja	2000-1000 B.C.E.	Qijia culture
	Berbers	2000-700 B.C.E.	Mongolia
	Britain	c. 2000 B.C.E.-c. 500 C.E.	Mithrism
	Crete	c. 2000 B.C.E.-653 C.E.	Armenia

Date	Event	Date	Event
2000 B.C.E.-700 C.E.	Aleutian tradition	1250-700 B.C.E.	Karasuk culture
	Slavs	c. 1225 B.C.E.	*Tale of the Two Brothers, The*
	Znaga		
c. 2000 B.C.E.-800 C.E.	Mon-Khmer	c. 1200 B.C.E.	Fu Hao's tomb
c. 1900-1800 B.C.E.	Atrahasis epic	c. 1200-10th cent. B.C.E	Dido
1900-1500 B.C.E.	Babylonia	1200-700 B.C.E.	Philistines
Died 1843 B.C.E.	Sesostris III		Phrygia
Constructed 1800-1600 B.C.E.	La Florida pyramid	c. 1200-400 B.C.E.	Olmecs
		1200-300 B.C.E.	Atlatl
1800 B.C.E.-800 B.C.E.	Thom's Creek	c. 1200-c. 63 B.C.E.	Moabites
Compiled c. 1770 B.C.E.	Hammurabi's code	1200 B.C.E.-700 C.E.	Lycia
1750-800 B.C.E.	Andronovo culture	fl. c. 12th-10th cent. B.C.E.	Aeneas
c. 1730-1350 R.C.E.	Poverty Point	Died 1156 B.C.E.	Rameses III
fl. 17th cent. B.C.E.	Hattusilis I	c. 1100 B.C.E.	Samson
	Labarnas I	1100-700 B.C.E.	Arameans
c. 1664-c. 1555 B.C.E.	Hyksos	c. 1100-450 B.C.E.	Hallstatt culture
1600-1120 B.C.E.	Mycenae, palace of	fl. 11th cent. B.C.E.	Saul
1600-1100 B.C.E.	Kaska	c. 1090-c. 1020 B.C.E.	Samuel
c. 1600-1100 B.C.E.	Mitanni	c. 1066-256 B.C.E.	Zhou Dynasty
c. 1600-1066 B.C.E.	Shang Dynasty	c. 1032-c. 962 B.C.E.	David
16th cent. B.C.E.	*Book of the Dead*	Coined 1000 B.C.E. or earlier	Nārāyaṇa
fl. 16th cent. B.C.E.	Telipinus		
c. 1595-1160 B.C.E.	Kassites	1st millen. B.C.E.	Copper Belt
1530 B.C.E.-700 C.E.	Mixtecs	c. 1000-690 B.C.E.	Cimmerians
c. 1525-c. 1482 B.C.E.	Hatshepsut	1000-600 B.C.E.	*Avesta*
1500-1100 B.C.E.	Vedas		Villanovan culture
1500-400 B.C.E.	Locarno Beach	c. 1000-c. 200 B.C.E.	*Advaita*
c. 1500-c. 400 B.C.E.	Vedism	Compiled c. 1000-c. 200 B.C.E.	*Upaniṣads*
1500 B.C.E.-700 C.E.	Kachemak tradition		
c. 1450-c. 1430 B.C.E.	Exodus	1000-100 B.C.E.	Scythia
1400-1300 B.C.E.	Aqhat epic	1000 B.C.E.-100 C.E.	Adena culture
c. 1400-c. 1230 B.C.E.	Linear B	c. 1000 B.C.E.-c. 100 C.E.	Israel
c. 1400-700 B.C.E.	Luwians	1000 B.C.E.-700 C.E.	Bantu, Mashariki
c. 14th cent.-1322 B.C.E.	Suppiluliumas I		Celts
14th cent.-1294 B.C.E.	Muwatallis		Judaism
c. 14th cent. B.C.E.-390 C.E.	Delphi	c. 1000 B.C.E.-c. 700 C.E.	Laos
		1000 B.C.E.-700 C.E.	Persia
c. 1390-c. 1360 B.C.E.	Akhenaton		Roman Forum
c. 1371-c. 1351 B.C.E.	Ankhesenamen	1000 B.C.E.-900 C.E.	Maya
c. 1370-c. 1352 B.C.E.	Tutankhamen	fl. 10th cent. B.C.E.	Bathsheba
c. 1366.-c. 1336 B.C.E.	Nefertiti		Sheba, Queen of
Late 14th cent.-1279 B.C.E.	Seti I	c. 10th cent.-910 B.C.E.	Jeroboam I
		c. 991-c. 930 B.C.E.	Solomon
1300-1213 B.C.E.	Rameses II	c. 966 B.C.E.-70 C.E.	Jerusalem, temple of
c. 1300-c. 1200 B.C.E.	Moses	c. 900-c. 853 B.C.E.	Ahab
Early to mid-13th cent.-1204? B.C.E.	Merenptah	c. 900-600 B.C.E.	Urartu
		900-200 B.C.E.	Chavín de Huántar
c. 1275 B.C.E.	Kadesh, Battle of	fl. 9th cent. B.C.E.	Elijah

Date	Event
Early-late 9th cent. B.C.E.	Homer
c. 9th cent.-815 B.C.E.	Jehu
Probably fl. between 9th and 7th cent. B.C.E.	Lycurgus of Sparta
9th cent. B.C.E.- 4th cent. C.E.	Napata and Meroe
Died c. 841 B.C.E.	Ben-Hadad I
Died 830 B.C.E.	Sarduri I
fl. c. 823-810 B.C.E.	Sammu-ramat
800-509 B.C.E.	Rome, Prerepublican
800-500 B.C.E.	Greece, Archaic
800-400 B.C.E.	Etruscans
c. 800 B.C.E.-697 or 698 C.E.	Carthage
800 B.C.E.-700 C.E.	Dzibilchaltún
c. 8th cent. B.C.E.	Chifumbaze culture
fl. 8th cent. B.C.E.	Amos
	Hosea
Traditionally fl. 8th cent. B.C.E.	Romulus and Remus
Early 8th cent.-727 B.C.E.	Tiglath-pileser III
8th-5th cent. B.C.E.	*Āraṇyakas*
	Brāhmaṇas
776 B.C.E.-393 C.E.	Olympic Games
774-711 B.C.E.	Saite Dynasty
c. 771-256 B.C.E.	Zhou style
c. 765-c. 716 B.C.E.	Piye
c. 760-c. 701-680 B.C.E.	Isaiah
Died c. 756 B.C.E.	Argishti I
2d half of 8th cent.- 705 B.C.E.	Sargon II
c. 740-c. 687 B.C.E.	Hezekiah
738-696/695 B.C.E.	Midas
Died c. 735 B.C.E.	Sarduri II
Late 8th to mid-7th cent. B.C.E.	Messenian Wars
722 B.C.E.-700 C.E.	Jewish diaspora
c. 705-c. 645 B.C.E.	Gyges
705-330 B.C.E.	Achaemenian Dynasty
c. 704-669 B.C.E.	Esarhaddon
Died 702 or 698 B.C.E.	Shabaka
fl. c. 700 B.C.E.	Hesiod
700-600 B.C.E.	Gortyn, law code of
700-500 B.C.E.	Lydia
c. 700-c. 311 B.C.E.	Argead Dynasty
c. 700 B.C.E.-262 C.E.	Artemis, temple of, at Ephesus
700 B.C.E.-700 C.E.	Macedonia

Date	Event
700 B.C.E.-700 C.E.	Magna Graecia
c. 700 B.C.E.-700 C.E.	Zoroastrianism
c. 700 B.C.E.-900 C.E.	Dorset phase
Born 7th cent. B.C.E.	Archilochus of Paros
c. 7th cent B.C.E.	Semonides
fl. 7th cent. B.C.E.	Taharqa
Early 7th cent.-627 B.C.E.	Cypselus of Corinth
Early 7th cent.-late 7th cent. B.C.E.	Terpander of Lesbos
c. 7th cent.-600 B.C.E.	Draco
7th cent.-early 6th cent. B.C.E.	Alcman
7th cent.-585 B.C.E.	Cyaxares
c. 7th cent.-570 B.C.E.	Cleisthenes of Sicyon
7th cent. B.C.E.-395 C.E.	Eleusinian mysteries
c. 685-c. 627 B.C.E.	Ashurbanipal
Died 681 B.C.E.	Sennacherib
Born c. 670-640 B.C.E.	Mimnermus
c. 667-c. 587 B.C.E.	Periander of Corinth
fl. mid-7th cent. B.C.E.	Tyrtaeus
c. 650-c. 570 B.C.E.	Pittacus of Mytilene
c. 648-609 B.C.E.	Josiah
c. 645-after 587 B.C.E.	Jeremiah
Died 640/639 B.C.E.	Sarduri III
632-629 to 556-553 B.C.E.	Stesichorus
c. 630-c. 568 B.C.E.	Sappho
c. 630-562 B.C.E.	Nebuchadnezzar II
c. 630-c. 560 B.C.E.	Solon
c. 628-c. 551 B.C.E.	Zoroaster
c. 627-c. 570 B.C.E.	Ezekiel
c. 625-c. 575 B.C.E.	Alcaeus of Lesbos
616-510 B.C.E.	Tarquins
c. 612-527 B.C.E.	Pisistratus
604-6th cent. B.C.E.	Laozi
c. 601 to 590-c. 530 B.C.E.	Cyrus the Great
c. 600-c. 500 B.C.E.	Theognis
c. 600-400 B.C.E.	Pre-Socratic philosophers
c. 600-300 B.C.E.	Sacred Wars
600 B.C.E.-300 C.E.	Garamantes
600 B.C.E.-350 C.E.	Apedemak
600 B.C.E.-900 C.E.	Sarmatians
Beginning 6th cent. B.C.E.	Jainism
fl. 6th cent. B.C.E.	Astyages
	Atossa
	Scylax of Caryanda
c. 6th cent.-509 B.C.E.	Lucretia
c. 6th cent.-508 B.C.E.	Junius Brutus, Lucius

Date	*Event*	*Date*	*Event*
fl. 6th-5th cent. B.C.E.	Hecataeus of Miletus	c. 510-c. 451 B.C.E.	Cimon
6th-5th cent. B.C.E.	*Suttanipāta*	fl. c. 500 B.C.E.	Pāṇini
Beginning 6th or 5th cent. B.C.E.	Buddhism		Vālmīki
Probably early 6th cent. B.C.E.	Aesop	c. 500 B.C.E., some material added later	*Rāmāyaṇa*
c. 6th cent.-467 B.C.E.	Gośāla Maskarīputra	2d half of the 1st millen. B.C.E.	*Sūtras*
c. 6th cent. B.C.E.-79 C.E.	Pompeii and Herculaneum	c. 500-c. 440 B.C.E.	Polygnotus
		c. 500-436 B.C.E.	Zengzi
6th cent. B.C.E.-14th cent. C.E.	Ājīvikas	c. 500-400 B.C.E.	La Tène culture
		500-400 B.C.E.?	*Wujing*
c. 599-c. 527 B.C.E.	Vardhamāna	500-323 B.C.E.	Greece, Classical
c. 595-c. 546 B.C.E.	Croesus	500-300 B.C.E.	Yue
c. 590-c. 500 B.C.E.	Agariste	c. 500-50 B.C.E.	Gauls
c. 580-c. 500 B.C.E.	Pythagoras	c. 500-c. 31 B.C.E.	Rome, Republican
Born mid-6th cent. B.C.E.	Ibycus	500 B.C.E.-200 C.E.	Nok culture
Mid-6th cent.-493 B.C.E.	Histiaeus of Miletus	c. 500 B.C.E.-400 C.E.	Orphism
c. 575-c. 500 B.C.E.	Eupalinus of Megara	500 B.C.E.-500 C.E.	Deptford culture
c. 570-after 507 B.C.E.	Cleisthenes of Athens	c. 500 B.C.E.-700 C.E.	Ball game, Mesoamerican
c. 570-490 B.C.E.	Hippias of Athens		
c. 570-c. 485 B.C.E.	Anacreon	500 B.C.E.-700 C.E.	Khoikhoi
c. 570-c. 478 B.C.E.	Xenophanes		Madagascar
c. 566-c. 486 B.C.E.	Buddha		Marpole phase
c. 556-c. 467 B.C.E.	Simonides		Monte Albán
c. 555-c. 525 B.C.E.	Amasis Painter		Norton tradition
c. 554-489 B.C.E.	Miltiades the Younger		Talmud
551-479 B.C.E.	Confucius	5th cent. B.C.E.	*Chunqiu*
550-486 B.C.E.	Darius the Great	fl. 5th cent. B.C.E.	Apollodorus of Athens (artist)
c. 540-c. 478 B.C.E.	Gelon of Syracuse		
Before 535-after 501 B.C.E.	Thespis		Callicrates
			Coriolanus, Gnaeus Marcius
fl. late 6th cent. B.C.E.	Ānanda		
Late 6th cent.-1450 B.C.E.	Thutmose III		Ictinus
Born late 6th or early 5th cent. B.C.E.	Ezra		Leucippus
		fl. early 5th cent. B.C.E.	Artemisia I
c. late 6th cent.-470 B.C.E.	Pausanias of Sparta	c. early 5th cent.-after 451 B.C.E.	Cincinnatus, Lucius Quinctius
c. late 6th cent.-467 B.C.E.	Aristides of Athens		
Composed c. 525 B.C.E.	Sibylline Books	Early 5th cent.-427 B.C.E.	Archidamus II of Sparta
c. 525-c. 460 B.C.E.	Themistocles	5th-4th cent. B.C.E.	*Jātakas*
525/524-456/455 B.C.E.	Aeschylus	c. 5th cent.-120 B.C.E.	Bactria
Died c. 522 B.C.E.	Polycrates of Samos	5th cent.-1st cent. B.C.E.	Aetolian League
c. 520-c. 450 B.C.E.	Bacchylides	499-494 B.C.E.	Ionian Revolt
c. 519-465 B.C.E.	Xerxes I	499-449 B.C.E.	Greco-Persian Wars
c. 518-c. 438 B.C.E.	Pindar	c. 496-c. 406 B.C.E.	Sophocles
c. 515-after 436 B.C.E.	Parmenides	c. 495-429 B.C.E.	Pericles
Died 514 B.C.E.	Aristogiton	494 B.C.E.	Plebeian secession
	Harmodius	c. 493-340 B.C.E.	Latin League and War
c. 510-Aug. 20, 480 B.C.E.	Leonidas		

Date	Event	Date	Event
Sept., 490 B.C.E.	Marathon, Battle of	c. 430-367 B.C.E.	Dionysius I the Elder of Syracuse
c. 490-c. 440 B.C.E.	Zeno of Elea		
c. 490-c. 430 B.C.E.	Myron	c. 427-347 B.C.E.	Plato
	Phidias	Died 422 B.C.E.	Brasidas of Sparta
c. 485-c. 410 B.C.E.	Protagoras		Cleon of Athens
c. 485-406 B.C.E.	Euripides	Died c. 420 B.C.E.	Cratinus
c. 484-c. 425 B.C.E.	Herodotus	c. 420 to 350-340 B.C.E.	Isaeus
Aug., 480 B.C.E.	Thermopylae, Battle of	Possibly as early as	Scopas
Probably Sept. 23, 480 B.C.E.	Salamis, Battle of	420 B.C.E.-late 4th cent. B.C.E.	
c. 480-before 422 B.C.E.	Ion of Chios	c. 420-c. 100 C.E.	Yuezhi culture
c. 480-411 B.C.E.	Antiphon	418, 362, 207 B.C.E.	Mantinea, Battles of
c. 480-c. 370 B.C.E.	Gorgias	c. 412-403 to c. 324-321 B.C.E.	Diogenes of Sinope
479 B.C.E.	Confucianism		
Late summer, 479 B.C.E.	Plataea, Battle of	Spring-summer, 411 B.C.E.	Four Hundred
c. 475-after 428 B.C.E.	Aspasia of Miletus		
fl. late 5th cent. B.C.E	Zeuxis of Heraclea	c. 410-362 B.C.E.	Epaminondas
Late-5th cent.-395 B.C.E.	Lysander of Sparta	c. 407-339/338 B.C.E.	Speusippus
Died c. 472 B.C.E.	Theron of Acragas	Sept., 405 B.C.E.	Aegospotami, Battle of
c. 470-413 B.C.E.	Nicias of Athens	404-403 B.C.E.	Thirty Tyrants
c. 470-399 B.C.E.	Socrates	401 B.C.E.	Cunaxa, Battle of
c. 470-c. 391 B.C.E.	Mozi	fl. c. 400 B.C.E.	Āśvalāyana
Died 466 B.C.E.	Hieron I of Syracuse	fl. 400-350 B.C.E.	Archytas of Tarentum
Died 461 B.C.E.	Ephialtes of Athens	c. 400-338 B.C.E.	Archidamus III of Sparta
fl. c. 460-c. 430 B.C.E.	Achilles Painter	400-200 B.C.E.	Raimondi stone
fl. c. 460-410 B.C.E.	Polyclitus	c. 400 B.C.E.-200 C.E., present form by 400 C.E.	*Mahābhārata*
c. 460-403 B.C.E.	Critias of Athens		
c. 460-c. 370 B.C.E.	Democritus	400 B.C.E.-224 C.E.	Parthia
	Hippocrates	c. 4th cent.-323 B.C.E. and 280-146 B.C.E.	Achaean League
c. 459-c. 402 B.C.E.	Thucydides		
Composed 451-450 B.C.E.	Twelve Tables, The	4th cent. B.C.E.-1st cent. C.E.	Dead Sea Scrolls
c. 450-404 B.C.E.	Alcibiades of Athens		
c. 450-c. 400 B.C.E.	Paeonius	fl. early 4th cent.-late 3d B.C.E.	Claudius Caecus, Appius
c. 450-c. 385 B.C.E.	Aristophanes		
Died c. 449 B.C.E.	Verginia	397-319 B.C.E.	Antipater
fl. c. 449-c. 424 B.C.E.	Crates of Athens	c. 396-late 4th cent. B.C.E.	Dionysius the Younger
Constructed 447-432 B.C.E.	Parthenon	395-386 B.C.E.	Corinthian War
c. 445-c. 411 B.C.E.	Eupolis	c. 390-350 B.C.E.	Eudoxus
c. 445-c. 400 B.C.E.	Agathon	c. 390-315 B.C.E.	Aeschines
c. 445-c. 380 B.C.E.	Lysias	c. 390-c. 300 B.C.E.	Lysippus
c. 444-c. 360 B.C.E.	Agesilaus II of Sparta	386 B.C.E.	King's Peace
c. 440-c. 391 B.C.E.	Andocides	384-322 B.C.E.	Aristotle
c. 439-c. 378 B.C.E.	Zi Si	c. 384-322 B.C.E.	Demosthenes
436-338 B.C.E.	Isocrates	382-336 B.C.E.	Philip II
May, 431-Mar., 421 B.C.E.	Archidamian War	c. 380-330 B.C.E.	Darius III
May, 431-Sept., 404 B.C.E.	Peloponnesian War	c. 375-316 B.C.E.	Olympias
c. 431-c. 354 B.C.E.	Xenophon	c. 375-c. 295 B.C.E.	Diocles of Carystus

Date	*Event*	*Date*	*Event*
c. 372-c. 289 B.C.E.	Mencius	c. 310-c. 230 B.C.E.	Aristarchus of Samos
c. 372-c. 287 B.C.E.	Theophrastus	c. 307-c. 235 B.C.E.	Xunzi
Summer, 371 B.C.E.	Leuctra, Battle of	306-168 B.C.E.	Antigonid Dynasty
c. 370-c. 330 B.C.E.	Praxiteles	c. 305-c. 240 B.C.E.	Callimachus of Cyrene
c. 367-351 B.C.E.	Halicarnassus mausoleum	c. 305-c. 215 B.C.E.	Hieron II of Syracuse
		c. 304-c. 250 B.C.E.	Erasistratus
Died 365 B.C.E.	Camillus, Marcus Furius	c. 302-c. 238 B.C.E.	Aśoka
c. 361-281 B.C.E.	Lysimachus	Traditionally 300 B.C.E.	*Zhuangzi*
c. 360-c. 290 B.C.E.	Fabius Maximus, Quintus	Beginning in 300 B.C.E.	Daoism
		Constructed c. 300-285 B.C.E.	Pharos of Alexandria
c. 360-c. 272 B.C.E.	Pyrrhon of Elis	c. 300-c. 260 B.C.E.	Theocritus of Syracuse
c. 358-297 B.C.E.	Cassander	c. 300 B.C.E.-300 C.E.	Yayoi culture
356-June 10 or 13, 323 B.C.E.	Alexander the Great	300 B.C.E.-500 C.E.	Xiongnu
		300 B.C.E.- 600 C.E.	Mahābodhi temple
c. 356 or 354-c. 281 B.C.E.	Seleucus I	c. 300 B.C.E.-before 700 C.E.	Alexandrian library
Died 353/352 B.C.E.	Mausolus		
fl. mid-4th cent. B.C.E.	Erinna	300 B.C.E.-700 C.E.	Arawak
Died c. 350 B.C.E.	Artemisia II		Zurvanism
c. 350-325 to after 300 B.C.E.	Pytheas	fl. 3d cent. B.C.E.	Herodas
			Menippus of Gadara
c. 350-283 B.C.E.	Demetrius Phalereus	3d or 2d cent.-2d cent. B.C.E.	Moschus of Syracuse
c. 342-c. 292 B.C.E.	Menander		
341-270 B.C.E.	Epicurus	3d cent. B.C.E.-7th cent. C.E.	Indian temple architecture
340-278 B.C.E.	Qu Yuan		
c. 340-c. 260 B.C.E.	Philochorus	fl. early 3d cent. B.C.E.	Anyte of Tegea
Aug. 2, 338 B.C.E.	Chaeronea, Battle of	Between 295 and 260-Late 3d cent. B.C.E.	Apollonius Rhodius
Died after 337 B.C.E.	Timoleon of Corinth		
Died c. 337 B.C.E.	Shang Yang	Constructed 292-280 B.C.E.	Colossus of Rhodes
336-283 B.C.E.	Demetrius Poliorcetes		
c. 336-334 to c. 265-261 B.C.E.	Zeno of Citium	c. 287-212 B.C.E.	Archimedes
		Died c. 286 B.C.E.	Chandragupta Maurya
c. 335-c. 280 B.C.E.	Herophilus	c. 285-c. 205 B.C.E.	Eratosthenes of Cyrene
Spring, 334 B.C.E.	Granicus, Battle of	c. 284-c. 204 B.C.E.	Livius Andronicus, Lucius
Nov., 333 B.C.E.	Issus, Battle of		
Oct. 1, 331 B.C.E.	Gaugamela, Battle of	c. 282-133 B.C.E.	Attalid Dynasty
c. 330-c. 270 B.C.E.	Euclid	c. 275-c. 203 B.C.E.	Fabius
Spring, 326 B.C.E.	Hydaspes, Battle of	c. 270-c. 199 B.C.E.	Naevius, Gnaeus
Coined c. 323 B.C.E.	Diadochi	264-146 B.C.E.	Punic Wars
323-30 B.C.E.	Ptolemaic Dynasty	c. 262-c. 190 B.C.E.	Apollonius of Perga
323 B.C.E.-330 C.E.	Greece, Hellenistic and Roman	259-210 B.C.E.	Shi Huangdi
		255-216 B.C.E.	Aemilius Paullus, Lucius
323 B.C.E.-639 C.E.	Egypt, Ptolemaic and Roman	c. 254-184 B.C.E.	Plautus
		Collected c. 250 B.C.E.	*Tipiṭaka*
c. 321-185 B.C.E.	Mauryan Dynasty	c. 250 B.C.E.	*Tolkāppiyam*
fl. c. 315 B.C.E.?	Hui Shi	Reigned 248-220 B.C.E.	Arkamani
c. 315-c. 245 B.C.E.	Aratus	c. 247 B.C.E.-224 C.E.	Arsacid Dynasty
312-244 B.C.E.	Appian Way	fl. c. 247-207 B.C.E.	Tissa, Dīvānaṃpiya
312-64 B.C.E.	Seleucid Dynasty		

Date	Event	Date	Event
247-182 B.C.E.	Hannibal	2d cent. B.C.E.-3d cent. C.E.	*Patirruppattu*
c. 242-187 B.C.E.	Antiochus the Great		*Dhammapada*
c. 239-169 B.C.E.	Ennius, Quintus	c. 2d cent. B.C.E.-300 C.E.	Kushān Dynasty
238-179 B.C.E.	Philip V	Beginning 2d cent. B.C.E.	Vietnam
236-184/183 B.C.E.	Scipio Africanus	197 B.C.E.	Cynoscephalae, Battle of
Died 235 B.C.E.	Lü Buwei	Mar. 27, 196 B.C.E.	Rosetta stone
Probably compiled c. 235-c. 160 B.C.E.	*Han Feizi*	195-190 to before 100 B.C.E.	Cornelia
234-149 B.C.E.	Cato the Censor	190 B.C.E.	Magnesia ad Sipylum, Battle of
c. 229-174 B.C.E.	Flamininus, Titus Quinctius	c. 190-159 B.C.E.	Terence
c. 221 B.C.E.	Great Wall of China	190-after 127 B.C.E.	Hipparchus
221-206 B.C.E.	Qin Dynasty	185-151 B.C.E.	Śuṅga Dynasty
c. 220-130 B.C.E.	Pacuvius, Marcus	c. 185-109 B.C.E.	Panaetius of Rhodes
c. 217-c. 145 B.C.E.	Aristarchus of Samothrace	c. 185/184-129 B.C.E.	Scipio Aemilianus
Aug. 2, 216 B.C.E.	Cannae, Battle of	Constructed c. 180-175 B.C.E.	Zeus at Pergamum, Great Altar of
c. 211 B.C.E.-224 C.E.	Artabanus I-V	c. 180-after 120 B.C.E.	Apollodorus of Athens
c. 210 B.C.E.	Qin tomb	c. 180-c. 102 B.C.E.	Lucilius, Gaius
c. 210-135 B.C.E.	Menander (Greco-Bactrian king)	179-117 B.C.E.	Sima Xiangru
		c. 179-c. 104 B.C.E.	Dong Zhongshu
c. 206-200 B.C.E.	Weiyang palace	c. mid-2d cent.-88 B.C.E.	Scaevola, Quintus Mucius (Auger)
c. 206 B.C.E.-220 C.E.	Han Dynasty		
Died c. 203 B.C.E.	Sophonisba of Numidia	c. 170-86 B.C.E.	Accius, Lucius
Oct., 202 B.C.E.	Zama, Battle of	c. 168-c. 100 B.C.E.	Maccabees
fl. c. 200 B.C.E.	Fabius Pictor, Quintus	163-June, 133 B.C.E.	Gracchus, Tiberius Sempronius
c. 200 B.C.E.	Tiwanaku		
c. 200-138 B.C.E.	Mithradates I	Died 160-159 B.C.E.	Eumenes II
c. 200-c. 118 B.C.E.	Polybius	c. 160-104 B.C.E.	Jugurtha
c. 200 B.C.E.-200 C.E.	Akapana pyramid	157-Jan. 13, 86 B.C.E.	Marius, Gaius
c. 200 B.C.E.-c. 200 C.E.	*Bhagavadgītā*	156-87 B.C.E.	Wudi
c. 200 B.C.E.-225 C.E.	Sātavāhana Dynasty	153-121 B.C.E.	Gracchus, Gaius Sempronius
c. 200 B.C.E.-400 C.E.	Andhradesha school		
200 B.C.E.-600 C.E.	Lima culture	c. 150 B.C.E.	Xin Zhui's tomb
c. 200 B.C.E.-600 C.E.	Recuay	c. 150 B.C.E.-600 C.E.	Suebi
200-100 B.C.E. to 600 C.E.	Moche culture	146 B.C.E.	Achaean War
200 B.C.E.-700 C.E.	Huaca del Sol	145-87 B.C.E.	Mithradates II
	Laurel culture	145-86 B.C.E.	Sima Qian
	Mogollon culture	c. 140-c. 70 B.C.E.	Meleager of Gadara
	Tibet	c. 140-c. 55 B.C.E.	Tigranes the Great
Beginning c. 200 B.C.E.	Hinduism	138-78 B.C.E.	Sulla, Lucius Cornelius
2d cent. B.C.E.	*Huainanzi*	c. 135-c. 51 B.C.E.	Posidonius
fl. 2d cent. B.C.E.	Mummius, Lucius	c. 134-63 B.C.E.	Mithradates VI Eupator
2d cent. B.C.E.	Septuagint	c. 130's-c. 82 B.C.E.	Scaevola, Quintus Mucius (Pontifex)
	Nicander of Colophon		
Traditionally 2d cent. B.C.E., possibly 2000 B.C.E.	Silk Road	c. late 2d cent.-c. early 1st cent. B.C.E.	Aristides of Miletus
		Late 2d cent.-71 B.C.E.	Spartacus

Date	Event
c. late 2d cent.-225 C.E.	Amaravātī school
c. 117-c. 56 B.C.E.	Licinius Lucullus, Lucius
116-27 B.C.E.	Varro, Marcus Terentius
c. 115-53 B.C.E.	Crassus, Marcus Licinius
c. 110-c. 35 B.C.E.	Philodemus
109-32 B.C.E.	Atticus, Titus Pomponius
c. 108-62 B.C.E.	Catiline
Jan. 3, 106-Dec. 7, 43 B.C.E.	Cicero
Sept. 29, 106-Sept. 28, 48 B.C.E.	Pompey the Great
105 B.C.E.	Arausio, Battle of Oct. 6,
c. 105-c. 35 B.C.E.	Alexander Polyhistor, Lucius Cornelius
103?-4 B.C.E.	Tullius Tiro, Marcus
c. 100 B.C.E.	Damascus document
July 12/13, 100-Mar. 15, 44 B.C.E.	Caesar, Julius
c. 100-c. 25 B.C.E.	Nepos, Cornelius
c. 100 B.C.E.-73 C.E.	Zealots
c. 100 B.C.E.-c. 100 C.E.	Essenes
c. 100 B.C.E.-600 C.E.	Nasca culture
100 B.C.E.-700 C.E.	Gandhāra art
fl. 1st cent. B.C.E.	Cassivellaunus
	Commius
	Sempronia
	Vitruvius Pollio, Marcus
1st cent. B.C.E.	Hyginus, Gaius Julius
1st cent.-77 B.C.E.	Vaṭṭagāmaṇi
c. 1st cent.-32 B.C.E.	Artavasdes II of Armenia
c. 1st cent. B.C.E.-40 C.E.	Cunobelinus
c. 98-Oct. 15, 55 B.C.E.	Lucretius
Before 97-45 B.C.E.	Figulus, Publius Nigidius
95-46 B.C.E.	Cato the Younger
c. 95-after 45 B.C.E.	Clodia
c. 92-Jan., 52 B.C.E.	Clodius Pulcher, Publius
91-87 B.C.E.	Social War
c. 86-35 B.C.E.	Sallust
c. 85-Apr., 46 B.C.E.	Juba I of Numidia
c. 85-Oct. 23, 42 B.C.E.	Brutus
c. 85-80 to 40 B.C.E.	Fulvia
c. 84-c. 54 B.C.E.	Catullus

Date	Event
c. 82-Aug., 30 B.C.E.	Antony, Marc
79-54 B.C.E.	Julia (daughter of Julius Caesar)
fl. mid-1st cent. B.C.E.	Publilius Syrus
c. 75-c. 46 B.C.E.	Vercingetorix
c. 75 B.C.E.-16 C.E.	Scribonia
Oct. 15, 70-Sept. 21, 19 B.C.E.	Vergil
c. 70-8 B.C.E.	Maecenas, Gaius
69-Aug. 3, 30 B.C.E.	Cleopatra VII
69-11 B.C.E.	Octavia
Dec. 8, 65-Nov. 27, 8 B.C.E.	Horace
Born c. 64 B.C.E.	Nicolaus of Damascus
64/63-after 23 C.E.	Strabo
63-Mar., 12 B.C.E.	Agrippa, Marcus Vipsanius
Sept. 23, 63-Aug. 19, 14 C.E.	Augustus
60-53 and 43-32 B.C.E.	Triumvirate
59 B.C.E.-17 C.E.	Livy
58-50 B.C.E.	Gallic Wars
Jan. 30, 58 B.C.E.-29 C.E.	Livia Drusilla
c. 55-c. 19 B.C.E.	Tibullus, Albius
c. 55 B.C.E.-c. 39 C.E.	Seneca the Elder
54-47 to 16 B.C.E. or later	Propertius
June, 53 B.C.E.	Carrhae, Battle of
53 B.C.E.-18 C.E.	Yang Xiong
July-Oct., 52 B.C.E.	Alesia, Battle of
fl. last half of 1st cent. B.C.E.	Hortensia
c. 50 B.C.E.-c. 24 C.E.	Juba II of Mauretania
Aug. 9, 48 B.C.E.	Pharsalus, Battle of
Apr. 6, 46 B.C.E.	Thapsus, Battle of
Died 43 B.C.E.	Antipater of Idumaea
Mar. 20, 43 B.C.E.-17 C.E.	Ovid
Died 42 B.C.E.	Cassius
Oct., 42 B.C.E.	Philippi, Battle of
Nov. 16, 42 B.C.E.-Mar. 16, 37 C.E.	Tiberius
Born 39 B.C.E.	Antonia the Elder
39 B.C.E.-14 C.E.	Julia (daughter of Augustus)
c. 37 B.C.E.-70 C.E.	Herodian Dynasty
37 B.C.E.-668 C.E.	Koguryŏ style
Jan. 31, 36 B.C.E.-May 1, 37 C.E.	Antonia the Younger

Date	Event	Date	Event
Sept. 2, 31 B.C.E.	Actium, Battle of	Early 1st cent.-180 C.E.	Iamblichus of Syria
31 B.C.E.-500 C.E.	Rome, Imperial	Composed between 1st	*Puranānūru*
Constructed c. 27 B.C.E.-121 C.E.	Pantheon	and 3d cent. C.E.	
		Between 1st and 5th	*Kuruntokai*
fl. late 1st cent. B.C.E.	Sulpicia	cent. C.E.	
c. 25 B.C.E.-c. 50 C.E.	Celsus, Aulus Cornelius	0-750 C.E.	Teotihuacán
c. 20-48 C.E.	Messallina, Valeria	c. 1-42 C.E.	Arria the Elder
c. 19 B.C.E.-after 30 C.E.	Velleius Paterculus, Marcus	c. 1-c. 80 C.E.	Johanan ben Zakkai
		1-400 C.E.	Alani
c. 17 B.C.E.-19 C.E.	Arminius	c. 1-500 C.E.	Caṅkam
c. 15 B.C.E.-c. 55 C.E.	Phaedrus	1-500 C.E.	Roman arch
c. 14 B.C.E.-Oct. 18, 33 C.E.	Agrippina the Elder	1-600 C.E.	Sonota culture
		1-700 C.E.	Axum
Constructed 13-9 B.C.E.	Ara Pacis		Finnic peoples
Aug. 1, 10 B.C.E.-Oct. 13, 54 C.E.	Claudius		Hohokam culture
		c. 1-700 C.E.	Java
c. 7 B.C.E.-c. 27 C.E.	John the Baptist, Saint	6-67 C.E.	Corbulo, Gnaeus Domitius
c. 6 B.C.E.-c. 30 C.E.	Jesus Christ		
c. 5 B.C.E.-Mar. 29, 57 C.E.	Guang Wudi	Died 9 C.E.	Quinctilius Varus, Publius
c. 4 B.C.E.-Apr., 65 C.E.	Seneca the Younger		
fl. 1st cent. C.E.	Valerius Flaccus, Gaius	9 C.E.	Teutoburg Forest, Battle of
	Hyginus		
	Kauṭilya	Nov. 17, 9-June 23, 79 C.E.	Vespasian
	Longinus		
	Simon Magus	c. 10-c. 100 C.E.	John the Evangelist, Saint
	Manilius, Marcus		
	Mary	Aug. 31, 12-Jan., 41 C.E.	Caligula
	Calpurnius Siculus, Titus	By 13 C.E., posthumously edited 14 C.E.	*Res Gestae Divi Augusti*
	Lucilius, Gaius		
1st cent.-60 C.E.	Boudicca	Nov. 6, 15-Mar., 59 C.E.	Agrippina the Younger
c. 1st cent.-62 C.E.	James the Apostle	fl. c. 20 C.E.	Valerius Maximus
1st cent. C.E.-after 71 C.E.	Cartimandua	c. 20-48 C.E.	Messallina, Valeria
c. 1st cent.-end of 1st cent. C.E.	Acte, Claudia	c. 20-c. 105 C.E.	Valerius Probus, Marcus
		Probably 23-Aug. 25, 79 C.E.	Pliny the Elder
c. 1st cent.-102 C.E.	Kaniṣka		
1st cent.-104? C.E.	Apollonius of Tyana	fl. mid-1st cent. C.E.	Zoskales
Late nineties or early 2d cent. C.E.-2d cent.	Curtius Rufus, Quintus	27-97 C.E.	Wang Chong
		c. 30-Jan. 28, 98 C.E.	Nerva, Marcus Cocceius
1st-4th cent. C.E.	*Narriṇai*	c. 30-Dec. 20, 107 C.E.	Ignatius of Antioch
1st-6th cent. C.E.	Funan	31-65 C.E.	Poppaea Sabina
1st cent.-700 C.E.	Langobards	32-92 C.E.	Ban Gu
1st cent.-9th cent. C.E.	Pyu	34-62 C.E.	Persius Flaccus, Aulus
1st or 2d cent. C.E.	*Milinda-pañha*	c. 35-after 96 C.E.	Quintilian
Beginning 1st cent. C.E.	Christianity	c. 35-c. 103 C.E.	Frontinus, Sextus Julius
	Tai	Died c. 36/37 C.E.	Maroboduus
Early 1st cent.-after 51 C.E.	Caratacus	c. 37-c. 100 C.E.	Josephus, Flavius
		Dec. 15, 37-June 9, 68 C.E.	Nero
Early 1st cent.-c. 64 C.E.	Paul, Saint		

Date	Event	Date	Event
Mar. 1, c. 38-41 to 130 C.E.	Martial	fl. 2d cent. C.E.	Achilles Tatius
			Phineas
39-65 C.E.	Lucan		Soranus of Ephesus
Dec. 30, 39-Sept. 13, 81 C.E.	Titus	2d or 3d cent. C.E.	*Aiṅkururnūru*
			Akanāṇūṟu
c. 40-after 112 C.E.	Dio Chrysostom	fl. 2d or 3d cent. C.E.	Bhāsa
c. 40-c. 135 C.E.	Akiba ben Joseph		Longus
June 13, 40-Aug. 23, 93 C.E.	Agricola, Gnaeus Julius	2d cent.-235 C.E.	Julia Mamaea
		2d cent. C.E. (legendary date 711 B.C.E.)-3d cent. C.E.	Jimmu Tennō
fl. c. 44 C.E.	Mela, Pomponius		
c. 45-96 C.E.	Statius, Publius Papinius		
c. 46-after 120 C.E.	Plutarch	fl. early 2d cent. C.E.	Apollodorus the Architect
fl. c. 50 C.E.	Columella		
50 C.E.-121 C.E.	Cai Lun	Early 2d cent.-after 161 C.E.	Pausanias the Traveler
Composed c. 50-c. 150 C.E.	Bible: New Testament		
		c. late 2d cent.-250 C.E.	Minucius Felix, Marcus
c. 50-c. 730 C.E.	Goths	Probably born 2d cent. C.E.	Aretaeus of Cappadocia
Oct. 24, 51-Sept. 18, 96 C.E.	Domitian		
		2d-6th cent. C.E.	Allemanni
c. 53-c. Aug. 8, 117 C.E.	Trajan	fl. c. 100 C.E.	Nicomachus of Gerasa
c. 55-c. 135 C.E.	Epictetus	c. 100-c. 166 C.E.	Fronto, Marcus Cornelius
c. 56-c. 120 C.E.	Tacitus		
57-Apr. 9, 88 C.E.	Zhangdi	c. 100-c. 178 C.E.	Ptolemy
c. 58-c. 147 C.E.	Xushen	c. 100-200 C.E.	Gnosticism
c. 60-230 C.E.	2d Sophistic	100-700 C.E.	Alexandrian patriarchs
c. 61-c. 113 C.E.	Pliny the Younger		Anasazi
fl. c. 62 C.E.	Heron	c. 100-700 C.E.	Cobá
Died 64 C.E.	Peter, Saint		Huaca de la Luna
Died c. 66 C.E.	Petronius Arbiter	100-700 C.E.	Ipiutak
June, 68-July, 69 C.E.	Four Emperors, Year of the	c. 104-Oct. or Nov., 140 C.E.	Faustina I
70-after 122 C.E.	Suetonius	c. 105-c. 165 C.E.	Justin Martyr, Saint
c. 70-c. 130 C.E.	Menelaus of Alexandria	106-113 C.E.	Trajan's column
Constructed c. 72-96 C.E.	Flavian Amphitheater	c. 117-181 C.E.	Aristides
73 C.E.	Masada, Battle of	c. 120-c. 180 C.E.	Lucian
Jan. 24, 76-July 10, 138 C.E.	Hadrian	c. 120-140 to 202 C.E.	Irenaeus, Saint
		Apr. 26, 121-Mar. 17, 180 C.E.	Marcus Aurelius
c. 80-c. 150 C.E.	Ashvaghosa		
c. 86-136 C.E.	Sabina, Vibia	Born c. 125-128 C.E.	Gellius, Aulus
Sept. 19, 86-Mar. 7, 161 C.E.	Antoninus Pius	c. 125-138 C.E.	Hadrian's villa
		c. 125-after 170 C.E.	Apuleius, Lucius
c. 89-c. 155 C.E.	Arrian	c. 129-175 C.E.	Faustina II
c. 95 C.E.-c. 165	Appian	c. 129-199 C.E.	Galen
Died c. 99 C.E.	Clement I	Died 135 C.E.	Bar Kokhba
By end of the 1st cent. C.E.	Bible: Jewish	Apr. 11, 145-Feb. 4, 211 C.E.	Severus, Lucius Septimius
Late 1st-early 2d cent. C.E.	Vindolanda tablets	c. 150-c. 215 C.E.	Clement of Alexandria
		c. 150-c. 235 C.E.	Dio Cassius

Date	Event	Date	Event
c. 155-160 to after 217 C.E.	Tertullian	224-651 C.E.	Sāsānian Empire
		fl. mid-3d cent. C.E.	Ardashīr I
155-220 C.E.	Cao Cao	Mid-3d cent.-325 C.E.	Licinius, Valerius Licinianus
c. 156-300 C.E.	Montanism		
c. 167-217 C.E.	Julia Domna	226-249 C.E.	Wang Bi
c. 170-245 C.E.	Philostratus, Flavius	c. 230-800 C.E.	Manichaeanism
172?-summer, 223 C.E.	Ulpian	c. 234-c. 305 C.E.	Porphyry
fl. c. 178 C.E.	Celsus	c. 240-after 274 C.E.	Zenobia
c. 178-c. 250 C.E.	Herodian	c. 240-c. 320 C.E.	Lactantius, Lucius Caelius Firmianus
c. 180-192 C.E.	Marcus Aurelius's column		
		c. 245-Dec. 3, 316 C.E.	Diocletian
181-234 C.E.	Zhuge Liang	c. 248-c. 328 C.E.	Helena, Saint
c. 185-c. 254 C.E.	Origen	Died 249 C.E.	He Yan
Apr. 4, 188-Apr. 8, 217 C.E.	Caracalla	Died c. 250 C.E.	Denis, Saint
		c. 250-310 C.E.	Maximian
192-232 C.E.	Cao Zhi	c. 250-May, 311 C.E.	Galerius Valerius Maximianus, Gaius
fl. 3d cent. C.E.	Bharata Muni around		
fl. 3d cent. C.E.	Heliodorus of Emesa	c. 250-421 C.E.	Constantius I-III
3d cent.-after 238 C.E.	Himiko	c. 251-probably Jan. 17, 356 C.E.	Anthony of Egypt, Saint
fl. 3d or 4th cent. C.E.	Guṇāḍhya		
3d or 4th cent. C.E.	*Harivaṃśa*	c. 253-after 283 C.E.	Nemesianus
fl. 3d-4th cent. C.E.	Cātanār	Died 260 C.E.	Valerian
	Iḷaṅkō Aṭikaḷ	c. 260-May 30, 339 C.E.	Eusebius of Caesarea
	Tiruvaḷḷuvar	261-303 C.E.	Lu Ji
200-300 C.E.	Antae	c. 265-335 C.E.	Sylvester I, Saint
200 and 300 C.E.	*Nāṭya-śāstra*	Died 272 C.E.	Shāpūr I
c. 200-Sept. 14, 258 C.E.	Cyprian of Carthage, Saint	c. Feb. 17 or 27, 272-285 to May 22, 337 C.E.	Constantine the Great
3d-5th cent. C.E.	Vākāṭaka Dynasty	c. 283-Oct. 28, 312 C.E.	Maxentius
3d-6th cent. C.E.	Neoplatonism	c. 283-c. 343 C.E.	Ge Hong
3d-7th cent. C.E.	Yamato court	c. 292-346 C.E.	Pachomius, Saint
fl. 200-600 C.E.	Tōlāmoḷittēvar	c. 293-May 2, 373 C.E.	Athanasius of Alexandria, Saint
200-700 C.E.	Cholula		
	El Tajín	fl. 4th cent. C.E.	Vegetius Renatus, Flavius
	Picts		
	Pyramid of the Moon	4th cent. C.E.	*Kalittokai*
	Zapotecs		*Paripāṭal*
200-900 C.E.	Altar de Sacrificios		Asaṅga
	Copán		Ezana
	Tikal		Frumentius, Saint
c. 205-270 C.E.	Plotinus	fl. 4th cent. C.E. or later	Viśākhadatta
c. 206 B.C.E.-220 C.E.	Han Dynasty	fl. 4th or 5th cent. C.E.	Vasubandhu
c. 215-275 C.E.	Aurelianus, Lucius Domitius	fl. probably 4th or 5th cent. C.E.	Yose ben Yose
c. 218-268 C.E.	Gallienus	4th-6th cent. C.E.	*Purāṇas*
220-280 C.E.	Three Kingdoms	4th-7th cent. C.E.	*Haniwa*
220-588 C.E.	Six Dynasties	300-400 C.E.	Cajamarca pottery
220-589 C.E.	Yue ware	c. 300-500 C.E.	Gupta emperors

Date	Event
c. 300-600 C.E.	Huns
fl. c. 300-c. 600 C.E.	Śūdraka
300-700 C.E.	*Patiṉeṉkīḻkkaṇakku*
300-710 C.E.	Kofun period
c. 300-1200 C.E.	Ghana
Early 4th cent.?-late 4th cent. C.E.?	Jingū
Died c. 302 C.E.	Narses
c. 307-c. 379 C.E.	Wang Xizhi
309-379 C.E.	Shāpūr II
c. 309-c. 750 C.E.	Donatism
c. 310-c. 395 C.E.	Ausonius, Decimus Magnus
c. 310 C.E.-probably second half of 4th cent.	Donatus, Aelius
Oct. 28, 312 C.E.	Milvian Bridge, Battle of
313 C.E.	Milan, Edict of
c. 315-c. 367 C.E.	Hilary of Poitiers, Saint
c. 317-c. 388 C.E.	Themistius
320 C.E.	Leyden plate
c. 320-c. 400 C.E.	Arianism
321-Nov. 17, 375 C.E.	Valentinian I
c. 323-350 C.E.	Constans I
325 C.E.	Nicaea, Council of
c. 325-403 C.E.	Oribasius
c. 328-Aug. 9, 378 C.E.	Valens
c. 329-Jan. 1, 379 C.E.	Basil of Cappadocia, Saint
329/330-389/390 C.E.	Gregory of Nazianzus
c. 330-c. 395 C.E.	Ammianus Marcellinus
330-700 C.E.	Byzantine Empire
Apr. 2, 330-May 29, 1453 C.E.	Constantinople
331-June 26 or 27, 363 C.E.	Julian the Apostate
331-347 to probably 420 C.E.	Jerome, Saint
334-416 C.E.	Huiyuan
337?-422 C.E.?	Faxian
339-Apr. 4, 397 C.E.	Ambrose
c. 340-385 C.E.	Priscillian
c. 340-c. 400 C.E.	Kālidāsa
c. 340-402 C.E.	Symmachus, Quintus Aurelius
c. 345-c. 406 C.E.	Gu Kaizhi
Jan. 11, 346 or 347-Jan. 17, 395 C.E.	Theodosius the Great

Date	Event
c. 347-Sept. 14, 407 C.E.	John Chrysostom, Saint
c. 348-after 405 C.E.	Prudentius, Aurelius Clemens
c. 352 or 353-431 C.E.	Paulinus of Nola, Saint
Nov. 13, 354-Aug. 28, 430 C.E.	Augustine, Saint
359-Aug. 25, 383 C.E.	Gratian
c. 360-c. 420 C.E.	Severus, Sulpicius
360-435 C.E.	Cassian
c. 365-Aug. 22, 408 C.E.	Stilicho, Flavius
365-427 C.E.	Tao Qian
Received 367-370 C.E.	Mao Shan revelations
370's-Oct. 6, 404 C.E.	Eudoxia, Aelia
c. 370-c. 404 C.E.	Claudian
c. 370-410 C.E.	Alaric I
c. 370-Mar., 415 C.E.	Hypatia
fl. c. 375 C.E.	Quintus Smyrnaeus
375?-427 C.E.	Nintoku
c. 375-June 27, 444 C.E.	Cyril of Alexandria, Saint
Aug. 9, 378 C.E.	Adrianople, Battle of
c. 381-c. 451 C.E.	Nestorius
385 C.E.-433	Xie Lingyun
386-533 C.E.	Northern Wei Dynasty
c. 386-581 C.E.	*Mulanshi*
c. 393-c. 458 C.E.	Theodoret of Cyrrhus
Late 4th cent.-Nov. 10, 461 C.E.	Leo I, Saint
Late 4th cent.-early 5th cent. C.E.	Ōjin Tennō
c. 395-457 C.E.	Avitus, Eparchius
Died c. 399 C.E.	Eutropius
fl. 5th cent. C.E.	Capella, Martianus
Probably colonized 5th cent. C.E.	Hawaii
fl. 5th cent. C.E.	Hesychius of Alexandria
	Macrobius, Aurelius Theodosius
5th cent. C.E.	Nine Saints
fl. 5th cent. C.E.	Vātsyāyana
c. 400?-c. 460? C.E.	Palladius, Rutilius Taurus Aemilianus
c. 400-c. 470 C.E.	Nonnus of Panopolis
c. 400-474 C.E.	Leo I (emperor)
c. 400-c. 480 C.E.	Salvianus
5th cent.-6th cent. C.E.	Bodhidharma
	Priscian
Coined c. 400-c. 525 C.E.	Pelagianism

Date	Event	Date	Event
c. 400-532 C.E.	Vandals	fl. late 5th and early 6th cent. C.E.	Fulgentius, Fabius Planciades
5th cent.-Apr. 22, 536 C.E.	Agapetus, Saint	Late 5th-early 6th cent. C.E.	Pārvatī Devī temple
5th cent.-before 558 C.E.	Anthemius of Tralles		
5th-8th cent. C.E.	Makouria	c. late 5th cent.-535 C.E.	Kaleb
c. 400-700 C.E.	Alwa	c. 490-c. 578 C.E.	Malalas, John
	Angles, Saxons, Jutes	c. 490-c. 585 C.E.	Cassiodorus
	Buddhist cave temples	c. 497-548 C.E.	Theodora
	Franks	c. 497-561 C.E.	Chlotar I
	Fremont culture	fl. 6th cent. C.E.	Abraha
400-800 C.E.	Palenque		Arthur
c. 400-800 C.E.	Vendae		Jordanes
c. 400-1000 C.E.	Tantras		Karaikkal Ammaiyar
401-450 C.E.	Theodosius II		Yannai
c. 401-Oct. 20, 460 C.E.	Eudocia	Early 6th cent.-566 C.E.	Theodosius of Alexandria
403-444 C.E.	Liu Yiqing		
c. 406-453 C.E.	Attila	6th cent.-598 C.E.	Dallán Forgaill
Reigned 415 to 418 C.E.	Wallia	6th cent.-May 26, 604/ 605 C.E.	Augustine of Canterbury, Saint
fl. c. 417 C.E.	Rutilius Claudius Namatianus	6th cent.-616 C.E.	Æthelbert
c. 418-422 to Mar. 17, 493 C.E.	Patrick, Saint	6th cent.-Oct. 12, 632 C.E.	Edwin
		6th cent.-1000 C.E.	Chichén Itzá
July 4, 419-Mar. 16, 455 C.E.	Valentinian III	fl. 6th or 7th cent. C.E.	Peyar
			Poykai
c. mid-5th cent.-533 C.E.	Xie He		Pūtān
c. 430 C.E.-487	Sidonius Apollinaris	c. 500 to c. 560-570 C.E.	Procopius
c. 430-440 to 518 C.E.	Anastasius I	500-700 C.E.	Nobatae
c. 435-Mar. 15, 493 C.E.	Odoacer	c. 500-800 C.E.	Pallava Dynasty
fl. c. 2d half of 5th cent. C.E.	Śyāmilaka	c. between 500-c. 900 C.E. and later	Uxmal flourished
450-751 C.E.	Merovingian Dynasty	c. 505-565 C.E.	Belisarius
c. 450?-c. 491 C.E.?	Ælle	515(?)-552 C.E.	Totila
c. 450-c. 500 C.E.	Bhartṛhari	c. 520-525 to Aug. 13, 587 C.E.	Radegunda, Saint
451 C.E.	Châlons, Battle of		
	Chalcedon, Council of	c. 521-June 8/9, 597 C.E.	Columba, Saint
	Monophysitism	528-535 C.E.	Justinian's codes
c. 454-526 C.E.	Theoderic the Great	c. 530-540 to c. 600 C.E.	Fortunatus, Venantius
456-536 C.E.	Tao Hongjing	c. 532 C.E.	Agathias
c. 465-c. 532 C.E.	Liu Xie	537 C.E.	Haghia Sophia
c. 466-507 C.E.	Alaric II	538-597 C.E.	Zhiyi
c. 466-Nov. 29, 511 C.E.	Clovis	c. 540-604 C.E.	Gregory the Great
467-499 C.E.	Xiaowen Di	c. 541-c. 600 C.E.	Aneirin
fl. 475/476 C.E.	Romulus Augustulus	541-604 C.E.	Wendi
476-550 C.E.	Āryabhaṭa	c. 560-Apr. 4, 636 C.E.	Isidore of Seville, Saint
c. 480-c. 524 C.E.	Boethius	569-618 C.E.	Yang Di
c. 480-c. 547 C.E.	Benedict of Nursia, Saint	c. 570-June 8, 632 C.E.	Muḥammad
c. 480-574 C.E.	Narses	Died 572 C.E.	Alboin
483-565 C.E.	Justinian I	573-Aug. 23, 634 C.E.	Abū Bakr

Date	Event	Date	Event
574-622 C.E.	Shōtoku Taishi	c. 619-687/688 C.E.	ʿAbd Allāh ibn al-ʿAbbās
581-618 C.E.	Sui Dynasty	Beginning 622 C.E.	Islam
c. 584-644 C.E.	Paulinus, Saint	624-Oct. or Nov., 692 C.E.	ʿAbd Allāh ibn az-Zubayr
c. 586-Nov. 3, 644 C.E.	ʿUmar ibn al-Khaṭṭāb		
c. 590-c. 647 C.E.	Harṣa	625-705 C.E.	Wu Hou
599-649 C.E.	Taizong	626-680 C.E.	Ḥusayn
fl. late 6th-early 7th cent. C.E.	Daṇḍ	c. 628-Jan. 12, 689/690 C.E.	Benedict Biscop, Saint
	Taliesin	Died c. 630 C.E.	Mahendravarman I
fl. c. 7th cent. C.E.	Budhasvāmin	fl. c. 634 C.E.	Bhāravi
fl. 7th cent. C.E.	Bāṇa	642 C.E.	ʿAmr ibn al-ʿĀṣ Mosque
	Campantar	646-647 to Oct., 705 C.E.	ʿAbd al-Malik
fl. 7th or 8th cent. C.E.	Amaru	Died Aug. 31, 651 C.E.	Aidan, Saint
c. 7th cent.-655 C.E.	Appar	661-751 C.E.	Umayyad Dynasty
600-661 C.E.	ʾAlī ibn Abī Ṭālib	7th cent.-656 C.E.	ʿUthmān ibn ʿAffān
c. 600-673 C.E.	Yan Liben	7th cent.-656 or 658 C.E.	ʿAbd Allāh ibn Saʿd ibn Abī Sarḥ
600-700 C.E.	Saracen conquest		
c. 602-664 C.E.	Xuanzang	8th cent. C.E.	*Muʿallaqāt, Al-*
c. 608-650 C.E.	Srong-brtsan-sgam-po	fl. 700 C.E.	Bhavabhūti
c. 610-632 C.E.	Qurʾān	Compiled 720 C.E.	*Nihon shoki*
c. 610-640 C.E.	Sutton Hoo	Born c. 725 C.E.	Gaudapāda
fl. c. 612 C.E.	Mimaji	c. 900 C.E.	*Peruṅkatai*
612-800's C.E.	*Gigaku*	fl. c. 900 C.E.	Tiruttakkatevar
c. 614-678 C.E.	ʿĀʾishah bint Abī Bakr		
618-907 C.E.	Tang Dynasty		

WEB SITES

This list of Web sites dealing with the ancient world lists the name of the person or organization responsible for the site followed by the site's official title and its address (URL). The URLs for these sites were active as of June, 2001.

GENERAL

About.com
Ancient History
http://www.ancienthistory.about.com/homework/
ancienthistory/

About.com
Archaeology
http://archaeology.about.com/science/archaeology/

Archaeological Institute of America
Archaeology
http://www.archaeology.org/

Artifice, Inc.
The Great Buildings Collection: Architectural Types
http://www.greatbuildings.com/types.html

Ashmawy, Alaa K.
The Seven Wonders of the Ancient World
http://ce.eng.usf.edu/pharos/wonders/

Beavers, Anthony F.
Exploring Ancient World Cultures
http://eawc.evansville.edu/grpage.htm

Beavers, Anthony F., and Hiten Sonpal
Argos: limited area search of the ancient and
medieval Internet
http://argos.evansville.edu/

Beck, Sanderson
Ethics of Civilization. Vol. 1. To 30 B.C.
http://www.san.beck.org/EC-Contents.html

Beck, Sanderson
Ethics of Civilization. Vol. 2. 30 B.C. to 1453
http://www.san.beck.org/AB-Contents.html

Brown, Haines
Images from World History
http://www.hp.uab.edu/image_archive/

Crystal, Ellie
Ancient and Lost Civilizations
http://www.crystalinks.com/ancient.html

CyberSites, Inc.
The Ancient Vine
http://www.thevines.com/leaf/AA172989

Day, J. Charles
Enter the Mist: Comparative Mythology
http://www.geocities.com/cas111jd/

Discovery Communications
Ancient World History
http://www.discovery.com/guides/history/history.html

Dolan, Tom
Costumes of All Nations: From Earliest Times to the
Nineteenth Century
http://www.pconline.com/~tomdolan/costume/
costume1.htm

Donn, Don
Mr. Donn's Ancient History
http://members.aol.com/donnandlee/

Dowling, Mike
Mr. Dowling's Electronic Passport
http://www.mrdowling.com/

Emuseum of Minnesota State University at Mankato
Prehistory Exhibits
http://www.anthro.mankato.msus.edu/prehistory/

Gill, N. S.
Major Time Intervals
http://ancienthistory.about.com/homework/
ancienthistory/library/bl/bl_time_epoch_index.htm

Goetsch, Sallie, and C. W. Marshall
Didaskalia: Ancient Theater Today
http://didaskalia.berkeley.edu/

Halsall, Paul
Internet History Sourcebooks Project (IHSP)
http://www.fordham.edu/halsall/index.html

Hatch, Robert A.
Ancient Chronology
http://web.clas.ufl.edu/users/rhatch/
    HIS%2DSCI%2DSTUDY%2DGUIDE/
    0005%5FancientChronology.html

Hayden, Julia
Ancient World Web
http://www.julen.net/aw/

Joyce, David E.
History of Mathematics
http://aleph0.clarku.edu/~djoyce/mathhist/

Koeller, David W.
World History Chronology
http://campus.northpark.edu/history/WebChron/
    world/world.html

Lindemans, M. F.
The Encyclopedia Mythica
http://www.pantheon.org/mythica.html

National Geographic Society
National Geographic
http://www.nationalgeographic.com/

Nothiger, Andreas
World History Chart
http://www.hyperhistory.com/

Oriental Institute Museum
Virtual Museum–What's New?
http://www-oi.uchicago.edu/OI/MUS/QTVR96/
    QTVR96.html

Scaife, Ross
Diotima. Materials for the Study of Women and
    Gender in the Ancient World
http://www.stoa.org/diotima/

Smithsonian Institution
Smithsonian Magazine
http://www.smithsonianmag.si.edu/

Special Collections Library at Duke University
Duke Papyrus Archive
http://odyssey.lib.duke.edu/papyrus/

Stewart, Dave
Documents in Military History
http://www.hillsdale.edu/dept/History/Documents/
    War/

Thinkquest Team 16325
Empires Past
http://library.thinkquest.org/16325

University of Oregon
OSSHE Historical and Cultural Atlas Resource
http://darkwing.uoregon.edu/~atlas/

Witcombe, Chris
Images of Women in Ancient Art
http://www.arthistory.sbc.edu/imageswomen/

Zalta, Edward N., ed.
Stanford Encyclopedia of Philosophy
http://plato.stanford.edu/

AFRICA
Agatucci, Cora
African Timelines. Part I: Ancient Africa
http://www.cocc.edu/cagatucci/classes/hum211/
    timelines/htimeline.htm

Agatucci, Cora
African Timelines. Part II: African Empires
http://www.cocc.edu/cagatucci/classes/hum211/
    timelines/htimeline2.htm

Bayuk, Andrew
Guardian's Egypt
http://guardians.net/egypt/

Beavers, Anthony F.
Chronology: Egypt
http://eawc.evansville.edu/chronology/
    extract.cgi?place=eg

Hooker, Richard
Egyptian Timeline
http://www.wsu.edu:8000/~dee/EGYPT/
    TIMELINE.HTM

Information and Decision Support Center (IDSC),
    Arab Republic of Egypt,
Culture of Egypt
http://www.tourism.egnet.net/culture.htm

Ministry of Tourism, Egypt
Tour Egypt
http://touregypt.net/

Oriental Institute Museum
The Nubia Salvage Project
http://www-oi.uchicago.edu/OI/PROJ/NUB/
    Nubia.html

Oriental Institute Research Archives
Egypt and the Ancient Near East
http://www-oi.uchicago.edu/OI/DEPT/RA/ABZU/
    YOUTH_RESOURCES.HTML

Paris Guide
La gloire d'Alexandrie
http://www.smartweb.fr/alexandrie/index.html

Think Quest Team 6182
Ancient Egypt: Stayin' Alive
http://tqjunior.advanced.org/6182/index.html

Von Essen, John, Dan Damian, and Dwayne Benson
Ancient Nubia
http://library.advanced.org/22845/index.shtml

THE AMERICAS
Berger, Michael
The Maya Astronomy Page
http://www.michielb.nl/maya/

Boline, G.
GB On-Line's Mesoamerica
http://pages.prodigy.com/GBonline/mesowelc.html

Callahan, Kevin L.
Ancient Mesoamerican Civilizations
http://www.angelfire.com/ca/humanorigins/
    index.html

Canadian Museum of Civilization
Mystery of the Maya
http://www.civilization.ca/membrs/civiliz/maya/
    mminteng.html

Chance, Norman
Exploring the Past: An Archaeological Journey
http://borealis.lib.uconn.edu/ArcticCircle/
    HistoryCulture/journey.html

Hutchinson, Kit
Welcome to the Hutchinson Research Center and the
    Wonderful World of Anthropology
http://www.geocities.com/Athens/Forum/6558/
    index.html

Johnson, Troy
American Indian History and Related Issues
http://www.csulb.edu/projects/ais/

Louisiana Dept. of Culture, Recreation and Tourism
Poverty Point State Historic Site
http://www.crt.state.la.us/crt/parks/poverty/
    pvertypt.htm

National Park Service
Prehistory of Alaska
http://www.nps.gov/akso/akarc/index.htm

Qvision
Virtual Palenque: A Virtual Tour of Ancient Maya
    Ruins
http://www.virtualpalenque.com/

Thomas, N. L.
North American Indian Historical Sites:Mounds,
    Pyramids, Related National and State Parks
http://www.thepeoplespaths.net/special/mounds.htm

AUSTRALIA
Ciolek, T. Matthew
Aboriginal Studies WWW Virtual Library
http://www.ciolek.com/WWWVL-Aboriginal.html

EAST AND SOUTH ASIA
Brown, Stephen A.
Chinese Philosophy Page
http://main.chinesephilosophy.net/index.html

China.pages.com.cn
Chinese Culture
http://hzdf.zjpta.net.cn/chinese_culture/culture.html

Hong, Joseph
History of Korea
http://violet.berkeley.edu/~korea/history.html

Hong, Joseph
Welcome to Korean History at U.C. Berkeley
http://socrates.berkeley.edu/~korea/

Hooker, Richard
Ancient China
http://www.wsu.edu:8080/~dee/ANCCHINA/
    ANCCHINA.HTM

Hooker, Richard
Ancient Japan
http://www.wsu.edu:8001/~dee/ANCJAPAN/
    ANCJAPAN.HTM

Hudson, Mark
Sannai Maruyama: "A New View of Prehistoric
    Japan." *Asia-Pacific Magazine* 2 (1966): 47-48.
http://coombs.anu.edu.au/SpecialProj/APM/TXT/
    hudson_m_02_96.html

Khan, Omar, ed.
The Ancient Indus Valley
http://www.harappa.com/har/har0.html

Lal, Vinay
Ancient India
http://www.sscnet.ucla.edu/southasia/History/
    Ancient/ancient.html

Muller, Charles
Resource for the Study of East Asian Language and
    Thought
http://www.human.toyogakuen-u.ac.jp/~acmuller/

Pei, Ming L.
China the Beautiful
http://www.chinapage.com/china.html

Pei, Ming L.
Chinese Dynasties
http://www.chinapage.com/dyna1.html

Roth,Wolff-Michael, ed.
Information Package on China
http://www.educ.uvic.ca/faculty/mroth/438/CHINA/
    China.htm

EUROPE
Brigantia
Brigantia, the Iron Age Celtic Reenactment Society
http://www.ironage.demon.co.uk/brigantia/

Conley, Lawrence V.
The Celts and Saxon Homepage
http://www.primenet.com/~lconley/

Knox, E. L. Skip
Ancient Europe
http://history.idbsu.edu/westciv/ancient/

Mariboe, Knud
Encyclopedia of the Celts
http://celt.net/Celtic/celtopedia/indices/encycintro.html

Mìadhachàin, Seàn O, Godfrey Nolan, and John
    Wash
Who Were the Celts?
http://www.ibiblio.org/gaelic/celts.html

Monaghan, Nancy
Cead Míle Failte to Ancient Eire
http://www.geocities.com/Heartland/Park/6748/
    ancient.html

Pfrenger, Ken
Celtic Martial Arts Research Society (CMARS)
http://members.tripod.com/~maol/index-2.html

Riley, M. E.
Clothing of the Ancient Celts
http://www47.pair.com/lindo/Textiles_Page.htm

Riley, M. E.
Halstatt and La Téne Period
http://www47.pair.com/lindo/Classical.htm

GREECE AND ROME
Blank, David, et al.
The Philodemus Project
http://www.humnet.ucla.edu/humnet/classics/
    Philodemus/philhome.htm

Bonenkamp, Jan, Mathijs Horsthuis, and Marloes
    Mentink
Forum Romanum
http://library.thinkquest.org/11402/

Bowman, Laurel
Classical Myth: The Ancient Sources
http://web.uvic.ca/grs/bowman/myth/index.html

Burdett, Carolyn, Carol Maier, and Alaina White
Journey Back in Time to Ancient Rome
http://www.richmond.edu/~ed344/webquests/rome/
    frames.html

Burns, Janet
The Olympic Games: Facts from 776 B.C.
http://latin.about.com/homework/latin/library/weekly/
    aa090600a.htm

Crane, Gregory, ed.
The Perseus Digital Library
http://www.perseus.tufts.edu

Fisher, John
Ancient Greek (Hellenic) Sites on the World Wide
    Web
http://www.webcom.com/shownet/medea/
    grklink.html

Foss, Pedar W.
ROMARCH: Roman Art and Archaeology
http://acad.depauw.edu/romarch/

Getty Research Institute
19-Century Photography of Ancient Greece
http://www.getty.edu/gri/greece/

Meadows, David
The Atrium
http://web.idirect.com/~atrium/

Mitchell-Boyask, Robin
Images of the Trojan War Myth
http://www.temple.edu/classics/troyimages.html

O'Donnell, James J.
Cassiodorus
http://ccat.sas.upenn.edu/jod/texts/cassbook/
    toc.html

Talbert, Richard, et al., eds.
Atlas of the Greek and Roman World
http://www.unc.edu/depts/cl_atlas/

Thinkquest Team 26602
SPQR Online
http://library.thinkquest.org/26602/home.htm

Universal Artists, Inc.
Ancient Greece
http://www.ancientgreece.com

Webber, Christopher
Welcome to Ancient Thrace and Thracology
http://www.geocities.com/Athens/Aegean/9659/
    welcome.htm

Zeeman, E. Christopher
Gears from the Ancient Greeks
http://www.math.utsa.edu/ecz/ak.html

MESOPOTAMIA, ANATOLIA, AND THE MIDDLE EAST

Association Hatti
Hatti. Homeland of the Hittites
http://hatti.multimania.com/

Cahill, Nick
Early Mesopotamia
http://www.wisc.edu/arth/ah201/
    01.mesopotamia.1.html

Collins, Billie Jean
Hittite Home Page
http://www.asor.org/HITTITE/HittiteHP.html

Collins, Billie Jean
The Line of Hittite Kings
http://www.asor.org/HITTITE/Kings.html

Hooker, Richard
The Hebrews: A Learning Module
http://www.wsu.edu:8000/~dee/HEBREWS/
    HEBREWS.HTM

Hopkins, C. D.
Parthia.com
http://www.parthia.com/

Oriental Institute, University of Chicago
The Chicago Hittite Dictionary Project
http://www-oi.uchicago.edu/OI/PROJ/HIT/
    Hittite.html

Research Archives of the Oriental Institute
Abzu: guide to resources for the study of the ancient
    Near East available on the Internet
http://www-oi.uchicago.edu/OI/DEPT/RA/ABZU/
    ABZU.HTML

Ritmeyer, Leon
The Temple Mount in Jerusalem
http://dspace.dial.pipex.com/ritmeyer/

Sagiv, Tuvia
The Temple Mount in Jerusalem
http://www.templemount.org/index.html

Siren, Christopher B.
Hittite/Hurrian Mythology
http://pubpages.unh.edu/~cbsiren/hittite-ref.html

RELIGION
Alharamain Islamic Foundation
The Last Prophet of God Muhammed
http://www.prophetmuhammed.org/

Barkati Foundation
History of Islam
http://www.barkati.net/english/

Buddha Mind
Buddha's Life Story
http://www.abm.ndirect.co.uk/leftside/arty/his-life/
    life-intro.htm

Buddha Mind
Buddhist Architecture
http://www.abm.ndirect.co.uk/leftside/arty/
    architect.htm

Brachter, Dennis
Historical and Cultural Context of Scripture
http://www.cresourcei.org/historyculture.html

Ciolek, T. Matthew, and Joe Bransford Wilson, eds.
Buddhist Studies WWW Virtual Library
http://www.ciolek.com/WWWVL-Buddhism.html

Islamic Affairs Department of the Royal Embassy of
    Saudi Arabia
Islam
http://www.saudiembassy.net/profile/islam/
    islam_rise.html

Islamicity
Islam and Islamic History in Arabia and the Middle
    East
http://www.islamicity.org/Mosque/ihame/hist.htm

Madin, Michael
Academic Info: Religion Gateway
http://www.academicinfo.net/religindex.html

BIBLIOGRAPHY

This bibliography of secondary sources is intended primarily for the general reader, advanced high school student, and college undergraduate. It includes no primary sources or source books unless they include significant introductory or supplementary material. All entries are in English, and most are book length. No articles from scholarly or professional journals are included; however, there are a few references to general interest periodicals such as *National Geographic* and *Discover*. The time range covered in this bibliography, beginning with the rise of agriculture in the eighth millennium B.C.E. and ending with the seventh century C.E., parallels that of the encyclopedia itself.

GENERAL

These works deal with more than one geographic and cultural boundary. Included here, for example, are books dealing with Greco-Roman civilization or both North and South America or surveys on warfare, philosophy, or other topics in antiquity.

Ankarloo, Bengt, and Stuart Clark, ed. *Witchcraft and Magic in Europe: Ancient Greece and Rome*. Philadelphia: University of Pennsylvania, 1999.

Aveni, Anthony. *Stairways to the Stars: Skywatching in Three Great Ancient Cultures*. New York: John Wiley and Sons, 1997.

Barnard, Noel. *Early Chinese Art and Its Possible Influence in the Pacific Basin*. New York: Intercultural Arts, 1972.

Barnett, William K., and John W. Hoopes. *The Emergence of Pottery: Technology and Innovation in Ancient Societies*. Washington, D.C.: Smithsonian Institution Press, 1996.

Bellwood, Peter S. *The Prehistory of Southeast Asia and Oceania*. Auckland, New Zealand: Collins, 1979.

Bennett, Matthew, ed. *The Hutchinson Dictionary of Ancient and Medieval Warfare*. Chicago: Fitzroy Dearborn, 1998.

Boardman, John. *Oxford History of Classical Art*. Oxford, England: Oxford University Press, 1993.

Boardman, John, et al. *The Oxford History of the Classical World*. Oxford, England: Oxford University Press, 1986.

Bober, Phyllis Pray. *Art, Culture, and Cuisine: Ancient and Medieval Gastronomy*. Chicago: University of Chicago Press, 1999.

Bonnefoy, Yves. *Mythologies*. Translated by Wendy Doniger. Chicago: University of Chicago Press, 1991.

Boulnois, Luce. *The Silk Road*. Translated by Dennis Chamberlain. New York: Dutton, 1966.

Brown, Peter Robert Lamont. *Late Antiquity*. Cambridge, Mass.: Harvard University Press, 1998.

Burn, A. R. *Persia and the Greeks: The Defense of the West, 546-478 B.C.* Stanford, Calif.: Stanford University Press, 1984.

Burton, David M. *The History of Mathematics*. Boston: McGraw-Hill, 1999.

Butler, Alfred J. *The Arab Conquest of Egypt*. Brooklyn, N.Y.: A & B Publishing Group, 1992.

Cameron, Averil, and Amelie Kuhrt. *Images of Women in Antiquity*. Detroit: Wayne State University Press, 1983.

Campbell, Joseph. *The Masks of God: Oriental Mythology*. New York: Viking, 1962.

_____. *Transformations of Myth Through Time*. New York: Harper & Row, 1990.

Cantarella, Eva. *Pandora's Daughters*. Baltimore: Johns Hopkins University Press, 1987.

Casson, Lionel. *The Ancient Mariners*. 2d ed. Princeton, N.J.: Princeton University Press, 1991.

Claiborne, Robert. *The Birth of Writing*. New York: Time-Life Books, 1974.

Clayton, Peter A., and Martin J. Price, eds. *The Seven Wonders of the Ancient World*. New York: Routledge, 1998.

Commire, Anne. *Women in World History*. Waterford, Conn.: Yorkin, 1997.

Comrie, Bernard, ed. *The World's Major Languages*. New York: Oxford University Press, 1987.

Cook, Harry. *The Way of the Warrior*. Prudhoe, England: Warriors Dreams, 1999.

Copleston, Frederick. *Greece and Rome*. Vol. 1 in *A History of Philosophy*. New York: Doubleday, 1993.

Corliss, William R., ed. *Ancient Infrastructure: Remarkable Roads, Mines, Walls, Mounds, Stone Circles*. Glen Arm, Md.: The Sourcebook Project, 1999.

Coulter, Charles Russell, and Patricia Turner. *Encyclopedia of Ancient Deities*. Jefferson, N.C.: McFarland, 2000.

Cowan, C. Wesley, and Patty Jo Watson, eds. *The Origins of Agriculture: An International Perspective*. Washington, D.C.: Smithsonian Institution Press, 1992.

Creasy, E. S. *Fifteen Decisive Battles of the World*. New York: Dorset Press, 1987.

Daniels, Peter T., and William Bright. *The World's Writing Systems*. New York: Oxford University Press, 1996.

Davies, Glyn. *A History of Money: From Ancient Times to the Present Day*. Cardiff, Wales: University of Wales, 1994.

Davis, Paul K. *Encyclopedia of Invasions and Conquests: From Ancient Times to the Present*. Santa Barbara, Calif.: ABC-Clio, 1996.

Dawson, Doyne. *The Origins of Western Warfare: Militarism and Morality in the Ancient World*. Boulder, Colo.: Westview, 1996.

Diamond, Jared. *Guns, Germs, and Steel: The Fates of Human Societies*. New York: W. W. Norton, 1997.

Diringer, David. *The Alphabet: A Key to the History of Mankind*. 3d ed. New York: Funk & Wagnalls, 1968.

Diringer, David. *Writing*. New York: Praeger, 1962.

Dudley, D. R. *A History of Cynicism: From Diogenes to Sixth Century* A.D. London: Methuen, 1937. Reprint. London: Bristol Classical Press, 1998.

Duncan, David Ewing. *Calendar: Humanity's Epic Struggle to Determine a True and Accurate Year*. New York: Avon Books, 1998.

Durant, Will, and Ariel Durant. *The Story of Civilization*. 11 vols. New York: Simon and Schuster, 1935-1975.

Dyer, J. E. *History of the Planetary Systems from Thales to Kepler*. New York: Dover, 1953.

Edey, M. A. *The Sea Traders*. Alexandria, Va.: Time-Life Books, 1974.

Evans, James. *The History and Practice of Ancient Astronomy*. New York: Oxford University Press, 1998.

Fagan, Brian M. *Oxford Companion to Archaeology*. New York: Oxford University Press, 1996.

_____. *People of the Earth: An Introduction to World Prehistory*. 9th ed. New York: Longman, 1998.

Fantham, Elaine, H. Foley, et al. *Women in the Classical World*. Oxford, England: Oxford University Press, 1994.

Finger, Stanley. *Minds Behind the Brain: A History of the Pioneers and Their Discoveries*. New York: Oxford University Press, 2000.

Finley, M. I. *A History of Sicily*. London: Chatto & Windus, 1968.

Foley, Helene P. *Reflections of Women in Antiquity*. New York: Gordon and Breach Science, 1984.

Freeman, Charles. *Egypt, Greece and Rome: Civilizations of the Ancient Mediterranean*. Oxford, England: Oxford University Press, 1996.

Friis Johansen, Karsten. *A History of Ancient Philosophy: From the Beginnings to Augustine*. New York: Routledge, 1999.

Gabriel, Richard A., and Karen S. Metz. *A History of Military Medicine*. Vol. 1 in *From Ancient Times to the Middle Ages*. Westport, Conn.: Greenwood, 1992.

Georgano, G. N. *Transportation Through the Ages*. New York: McGraw-Hill, 1972.

Gillispie, C. C., ed. *Dictionary of Scientific Biography*. New York: Charles Scribner's Sons, 1976.

Glad, C. *Paul and Philodemus*. New York: E. J. Brill, 1995.

Golden, James L., Goodwin F. Berquist, and William E. Coleman. *The Rhetoric of Western Thought*. 5th ed. Dubuque, Iowa: Kendall/Hunt, 1993.

Goodrich, Norma Lorre. *Ancient Myths*. New York: New American Library, 1960.

Goody, Jack. *Death, Property, and the Ancestors*. Stanford, Calif.: Stanford University Press, 1962.

Gordon, Benjamin Lee. *Medicine Throughout Antiquity*. Philadelphia: Davis, 1949.

Grant, Michael. *Greek and Roman Historians*. New York: Routledge, 1995.

Grigg, D. B. *The Agricultural Systems of the World: An Evolutionary Approach*. New York: Cambridge University Press, 1974.

Grimal, Pierre, ed. *Larousse World Mythology*. Translated by Patricia Beardsworth. New York: G. P. Putnam's Sons, 1963.

Grimes, B. F. *Ethnologue: Languages of the World*. Dallas: Summer Institute of Linguistics, 1992.

Grmek, Mirko D., ed. *Western Medical Thought from Antiquity to the Middle Ages*. Translated by Antony Shugaar. Cambridge, Mass.: Harvard University Press, 1998.

Grube, G. M. A. *The Greek and Roman Critics*. London: Methuen, 1965.

Guirand, Felix, ed. *New Larousse Encyclopedia of Mythology*. Translated by Richard Aldington and Delano Ames. New York: Hamlyn, 1968.

Hackin, M. J., ed. *Asiatic Mythology*. Translated by F. M. Atkinson. New York: Thomas Y. Crowell, 1963.

Hägg, T. *The Novel in Antiquity*. Berkeley: University of California Press, 1983.

Harris, D. R., and G. Hillman, eds. *Foraging and Farming: The Evolution of Plant Domestication*. London: Unwin Hyman, 1989.

Harris, David R., ed. *The Origins and Spread of Agriculture and Pastoralism in Eurasia*. Washington, D.C.: Smithsonian Institution Press, 1996.

Harris, Stephen L., and Gloria Platzner. *Classical Mythology*. Mountain View, Calif.: Mayfield Publishing, 1995.

Hart, Michael. *The 100: A Ranking of the Most Influential Persons in History*. Secaucus, N.J.: Carol Publishing Group, 1992.

Hawley, Richard, and Barbara Levick. *Women in Antiquity: New Assessments*. New York: Routledge, 1995.

Haywood, John, Simon Hall, et al., eds. *The Complete Atlas of World History*. Vols. 1-3. Armonk, N.Y.: Sharpe Reference, 1997.

Heilbron, John L. *Geometry Civilized: History, Culture, and Technique*. Oxford, England: Clarendon Press, 1998.

Heinz, Carolyn Brown. *Asian Cultural Traditions*. Prospect Heights, Ill.: Waveland, 1999.

Hoerth, A. J., G. L. Mattingly, and E. M. Yamauchi, eds. *Peoples of the Old Testament World*. Grand Rapids, Mich.: Baker Books, 1994.

Hogben, Lancelot. *Mathematics for the Millions*. 4th ed. New York: W. W. Norton, 1983.

Holt, P. M., et al., eds. *Cambridge History of Islam*. 2d ed. New York: Cambridge University Press, 2000.

Hopwood, Keith, ed. *Ancient Greece and Rome: A Bibliographical Guide*. Manchester: Manchester University Press, 1995.

Hornblower, Simon, and Antony Spawforth. *The Oxford Classical Dictionary*. 3d ed. Oxford, England: Oxford University Press, 1996.

Howatson, M. C., ed. *The Oxford Companion to Classical Literature*. Oxford, England: Oxford University Press, 1989.

Hughes, J. Donald. *Pan's Travail: Environmental Problems of the Ancient Greeks and Romans*. Baltimore: The Johns Hopkins University Press, 1994.

Irwin, Keith Gordon. *The 365 Days*. New York: Thomas Y. Crowell, 1963.

Jackson, Donald. *The Story of Writing*. New York: Taplinger, 1981.

Jackson, Guida M. *Women Who Ruled: A Biographical Encyclopedia*. New York: Barnes & Noble, 1998.

Jean, Georges. *Writing: The Story of Alphabets and Scripts*. New York: Harry N. Abrams, 1992.

Jones, A. H. M. *The Cities of the Eastern Roman Provinces*. Oxford, England: Clarendon Press, 1937.

Jones, Barbara. *Design for Death*. Indianapolis: Bobbs-Merrill, 1967.

Jones, David E. *Women Warriors: A History*. Washington, D.C.: Brassey's, 1997.

Jones, W. T. *A History of Western Philosophy: The Classical Mind*. 2d ed. New York: Harcourt Brace Jovanovich, 1970.

Keegan, John. *A History of Warfare*. New York: Alfred A. Knopf, 1993.

_____. *The Mask of Command: A Study of Generalship*. New York: Little, Brown, 1982.

Kern, Paul Bentley. *Ancient Siege Warfare*. Bloomington: Indiana University Press, 1999.

Knox, Paul L., and Sallie A. Marston. *Places and Regions in Global Context: Human Geography*. Upper Saddle River, N.J.: Prentice-Hall, 1998.

Koestler, Arthur. *The Sleepwalkers: A History of Man's Changing Vision of the Universe*. New York: Grosset & Dunlap, 1963.

Kramer, Samuel N., ed. *Mythologies of the Ancient World*. New York: Anchor Books, 1961.

Kranz, Rachel. *Across Asia by Land*. New York: Facts on File, 1991.

Kruft, Hanno-Walter. *A History of Architectural Theory: From Vitruvius to the Present*. New York: Princeton Architectural Press, 1994.

Kuhrt, Amelie. *The Ancient Near East, c. 3000-330 B.C.* 2 vols. London: Routledge, 1996.

Landels, J. G. *Engineering in the Ancient World*. Berkeley: University of California Press, 1978.

Landels, John G. *Music in Ancient Greece and Rome*. New Brunswick, N.J.: Rutgers University Press, 1999.

Lawson, F. H. *A Common Lawyer Looks at the Civil Law*. Ann Arbor: University of Michigan Law School, 1953.

Lay, M. G. *Ways of the World*. New Brunswick, N.J.: Rutgers University Press, 1992.

Lefkowitz, Mary R., and Maureen B. Fant, eds. *Women's Life in Greece and Rome: A Source Book in Translation*. 2d ed. Baltimore: Johns Hopkins University Press, 1992.

Lightman, Marjorie, and Benjamin Lightman. *Biographical Dictionary of Ancient Greek and Roman*

Women. New York: Facts on File, 2000.

Ling, Roger. *Ancient Mosaics*. Princeton, N.J.: Princeton University Press, 1998.

Liu, Xinru. *Ancient India and Ancient China*. Oxford, England: Oxford University Press, 1999.

Lloyd, G. E. R. *Science, Folklore, and Ideology*. Indianapolis: Hackett, 1999.

Loew, Cornelius. *Myth, Sacred History and Philosophy*. New York: Harcourt, Brace & World, 1967.

Luce, T. James, ed. *Ancient Writers: Greece and Rome*. 2 vols. New York: Charles Scribner's Sons, 1982.

Lyons, A. S., and R. J. Petrucelli. *Medicine: An Illustrated History*. New York: Abrams, 1978.

Macey, Samuel L., ed. *Encyclopedia of Time*. New York: Garland, 1994.

Magill, Frank N., ed. *Great Lives from History: Ancient and Medieval Series*. Vol. 1. Pasadena, Calif.: Salem Press, 1988.

_____, et al., eds. *Dictionary of World Biography*. Vol. 1: *The Ancient World*. Pasadena, Calif.: Salem Press, 1998.

Majno, Guido. *The Healing Hand: Man and Wound in the Ancient World*. Cambridge, Mass.: Harvard University Press, 1982.

Mallory, J. P. *In Search of the Indo-Europeans*. Thames and Hudson: London, 1989.

Marcuse, Peter M. *Disease: In Search of Remedy*. Urbana: University of Illinois Press, 1996.

Maringer, J. *The Gods of Prehistoric Man*. New York: Alfred J. Knopf, 1960.

Marrou, H. I. *Education in Antiquity*. New York: Sheed and Ward, 1956.

Martindale, Charles. *Cambridge Companions to Literature*. New York: Cambridge University Press, 1997.

Meijer, Fik, and Onno van Nijf. *Trade, Transport and Society in the Ancient World: A Sourcebook*. London: Routledge, 1993.

Millar, Fergus. *The Roman Near East 31* B.C.E.-A.D. *337*. Cambridge, Mass.: Harvard University Press, 1993.

Montagu, John Drogo. *Battles of the Greek and Roman Worlds: A Chronological Compendium of 667 Battles to 31* B.C., *from the Historians of the Ancient World*. London: Greenhill Books/Stackpole Books, 2000.

Morford, Mark P. O., and Robert J. Lenardon. *Classical Mythology*. 5th ed. New York: Longman, 1995.

Morgan, Theresa. *Literate Education in the Hellenistic and Roman Worlds*. New York: Cambridge University Press, 1998.

Murphey, Rhoads. *A History of Asia*. New York: Longman, 2000.

Natkiel, Richard, and Anthony Preston. *Atlas of Maritime History*. New York: Facts on File, 1986.

Navia, Louis E. *Classical Cynicism: A Critical Study*. Westport, Conn.: Greenwood Press, 1996.

Neugebauer, Otto. *Astronomy and History*. New York: Springer, 1983.

_____. *A History of Ancient Mathematical Astronomy*. New York: Springer, 1975.

Newman, James. *The World of Mathematics*. Vol. 1. New York: Simon & Schuster, 1956.

Nichols, Deborah L., and Thomas H. Charlton, eds. *The Archaeology of City-States: Cross-cultural Approaches*. Washington, D.C.: Smithsonian Institution Press, 1997.

Obbink, D., ed. *Philodemus and Poetry: Poetic Theory and Practice in Lucretius, Philodemus, and Horace*. New York: Oxford University Press, 1995.

Oman, Charles W. *The Art of War in the Middle Ages,* A.D. *378-1515*. Rev. ed. Ithaca, N.Y.: Cornell University Press, 1953.

Osborne, Harold, ed. *The Oxford Companion to Art*. Oxford, England: Oxford University Press, 1970.

Osen, Lynn M. *Women in Mathematics*. Cambridge, Mass.: MIT Press, 1995.

Pantel, Pauline Schmitt, ed. *A History of Women in the West: From Ancient Goddesses to Christian Saints*. Translated by Arthur Goldhammer. Vol 1. Cambridge, Mass.: Harvard University Press, 1992.

Parkins, Helen, and Christopher Smith, eds. *Trade, Traders, and the Ancient City*. New York: Routledge, 1998.

Pfeiffer, R. *History of Classical Scholarship*. Oxford, England: Oxford University Press, 1968.

Pomeroy, Sarah B. *Goddesses, Whores, Wives, and Slaves*. New York: Schocken Books, 1975.

Porter, Roy. *The Greatest Benefit to Mankind: A Medical History of Humanity, from Antiquity to the Present*. New York: W. W. Norton, 1997.

_____, ed. *Medicine: A History of Healing: Ancient Traditions to Modern Practices*. New York: Marlowe & Company, 1997.

Powell, Barry B. *Classical Myth*. Englewood Cliffs, N.J.: Prentice Hall, 1995.

Puhvel, Jaan. *Comparative Mythology*. Baltimore: The Johns Hopkins University Press, 1987.

Raaflaub, Kurt, and Nathan Rosenstein, eds. *War and Society in the Ancient and Medieval Worlds: Asia, the Mediterranean, Europe, and Mesoamerica*.

Washington, D.C.: Harvard Center for Hellenic Studies, 1999.

Redford, D. B. *Egypt, Canaan, and Israel in Ancient Times*. Princeton, N.J.: Princeton University Press, 1992.

Reid, William. *Weapons Through the Ages*. New York: Crescent Books, 1976.

Reynold, L. D., and N. G. Wilson. *Scribes and Scholars: A Guide to the Transmission of Greek and Latin Literature*. Oxford, England: Clarendon Press, 1984.

Richard, C. *The Founders and the Classics*. Cambridge, Mass.: Harvard University Press, 1994.

Richards, E. G. *Mapping Time: The Calendar and Its History*. Oxford, England: Oxford University Press, 1998.

Richlin, A., ed. *Pornography and Representation in Greece and Rome*. Oxford, England: Oxford University Press, 1992.

Riddle, J. *Contraception and Abortion, from the Ancient World to the Renaissance*. Cambridge, Mass.: Harvard University Press, 1992.

Robinson, Victor. *Pathfinders in Medicine*. New York: Medical Life Press, 1929.

Rosenberg, Donna, ed. *World Mythology*. 2d ed. Lincolnwood, Ill.: NTC Publishing Group, 1994.

Roth, Leland. *Understanding Architecture*. New York: HarperCollins, 1993.

Ruck, Carl A. P., and Danny Staples. *The World of Classical Myths: Gods and Goddesses; Heroines and Heroes*. Durham, N.C.: Carolina Academic Press, 1994.

Ruhlen, Merritt. *The Origin of Language*. New York: Wiley & Sons, 1994.

Runciman, Steven. *The Medieval Manichee*. Cambridge, England: Cambridge University Press, 1955. Reprint. Cambridge, England: Cambridge University Press, 1982.

Sachs, Curt. *World History of the Dance*. New York: W. W. Norton, 1937.

Sammartino, Peter, and William Robert. *Sicily: An Informal History*. London: Associated University Press, 1992.

Schmeling, Gareth, ed. *The Novel in the Ancient World*. Leiden, Netherlands: E. J. Brill, 1996.

Schneer, Cecil. *The Evolution of Physical Science*. New York: Grove Press, 1960.

Sergeant, Philip Walsingham. *Dominant Women*. 1929. Reprint. Freeport, N.Y.: Books for Libraries Press, 1969.

Seymour, William. *Decisive Factors in Twenty Great Battles of the World*. New York: St. Martin's Press, 1989.

Sienkewicz, Thomas J. *World Mythology: An Annotated Guide to Collections and Anthologies*. Lanham, Md.: Scarecrow/Salem, 1996.

Sinnigen, William G., and Charles Alexander Robinson, Jr. *Ancient History from Prehistoric Times to the Death of Justinian*. 3d ed. New York: Macmillan, 1981.

Slatkin, Wendy. *Women Artists in History: From Antiquity to the 20th Century*. 3d ed. Englewood Cliffs, N.J.: Prentice Hall, 1997.

Smith, Wesley D. *The Hippocratic Tradition*. Ithaca, N.Y.: Cornell University Press, 1979.

Snowden, Frank M., Jr. *Before Color Prejudice: The Ancient View of Blacks*. Cambridge, Mass.: Harvard University Press, 1983.

_____. *Blacks in Antiquity*. Cambridge, Mass.: Harvard University Press, 1970.

Snyder, James D. *All God's Children: The Tumultuous Story of* A.D. *31-71: How the First Christians Challenged the Roman World and Shaped the Next Two Thousand Years*. Cape Town, South Africa: Pharos Books, 1999.

Snyder, Jane McIntosh. *The Woman and the Lyre: Women Writers in Classical Greece and Rome*. Carbondale: Southern Illinois University Press, 1989.

Sorenson, J. *Pre-Columbian Contact with the Americas Across the Oceans*. Provo, Utah: Research Press, 1990.

Southall, Aidan. *The City in Time and Space*. Cambridge, England: Cambridge University Press, 1998.

Spodek, Howard. *The World's History. Vol. I: To 1500*. Upper Saddle River, N.J.: Prentice Hall, 1998.

Starr, Chester G. *A History of the Ancient World*. 4th ed. New York: Oxford University Press, 1991.

Steel, Duncan. *Marking Time: The Epic Quest to Invent the Perfect Calendar*. New York: John Wiley & Sons, 2000.

Sutton, Dana F. *Ancient Comedy: The War of the Generations*. Boston: Twayne, 1993.

Takacs, Sarolta. *Isis and Sarapis in the Roman World*. Leiden, Netherlands: E. J. Brill, 1995.

Taton, Renee, ed. *Ancient and Medieval Science*. New York: Basic Books, 1963.

_____. *History of Science*. New York: Basic Books, 1963.

Taylor, John. *Egypt and Nubia*. London: British Museum Press, 1991.

Thomas, Julian. *Understanding the Neolithic*. 2d ed. New York: Routledge, 1999.

Tomlinson, Richard. *From Mycenae to Constantinople: The Evolution of the Ancient City*. London: Routledge, 1993.

Too, Yun Lee. *The Pedagogical Contracts: The Economics of Teaching and Learning in the Ancient World*. Ann Arbor: University of Michigan Press, 2000.

Tozer, H. F. *A History of Ancient Geography*. New York: Biblio and Tannen, 1964.

Vercoutter, Jean, et al., eds. *The Image of the Black in Western Art*. Vol. 1. Cambridge, Mass.: Harvard University Press, 1976.

Vervliet, Hendrik D. L., ed. *The Book Through Five Thousand Years*. New York: Phaidon, 1972.

Veyne, Paul, ed. *A History of Private Life: From Pagan Rome to Byzantium*. Cambridge, Mass.: The Belknap Press of Harvard University, 1987.

Vivante, Bella, ed. *Women's Roles in Ancient Civilizations: A Reference Guide*. Westport, Conn.: Greenwood Press, 1999.

Von Fritz, Kurt. *The Theory of the Mixed Constitution in Antiquity*. New York: Columbia University Press, 1954.

Votaw, John, and Thomas Greiss, eds. *Ancient and Medieval Warfare*. Wayne, N.J.: Avery Publishing Group, 1984.

Wahlbank, F. W., and A. E. Astin, et al., eds. *The Cambridge Ancient History*. 2d ed. Cambridge, England: Cambridge University Press, 1989-1996.

Walker, Christopher, ed. *Astronomy Before the Telescope*. New York: St. Martin's Press, 1997.

Warry, John. *Warfare in the Classical World*. London: Salamander Books, 1980.

Watson, Alan. *The Evolution of Law*. Baltimore: Johns Hopkins University Press, 1985.

Wenke, Robert J. *Patterns in Prehistory: Humankind's First Three Million Years*. 4th ed. New York: Oxford University Press, 1999.

West, M. L. *The East Face of Helicon: West Asiatic Elements in Greek Poetry and Myth*. Oxford, England: Clarendon Press, 1997.

Wetterau, Bruce. *World History: A Dictionary of Important People, Places, and Events, from Ancient Times to the Present*. New York: Henry Holt and Company, 1994.

Wickersham, John, ed. *Myths and Legends of the World*. New York: Macmillan, 2000.

Willis, Roy, ed. *World Mythology*. New York: Henry Holt and Company, 1993.

Yamauchi, E. *Foes from the Northern Frontier: Invading Hordes from the Russian Steppes*. Grand Rapids, Mich.: Baker Book House, 1982.

RELIGION

This category deals with Buddhism, Christianity, Islam, Judaism, and other religions that significantly cross the geographic and cultural boundaries of this bibliography. Religions that have had a narrower geographic focus appear in the appropriate geographic category; books on Hinduism, for example, are listed under South Asia, and Confucianism under China. Also included here are books that deal with more than one religion. Biographical material on religious figures, however, can be found under the appropriate geographic heading; for example, Jesus Christ under Israel and Muḥammad under Arabia.

Ackroyd, Peter, R., et al., eds. *Cambridge History of the Bible*. New York: Cambridge University Press, 1975.

Aune, D. E. *Prophecy in Early Christianity and the Ancient Mediterranean World*. Grand Rapids, Mich.: Wm. B. Eerdmans, 1983.

Beltz, Walter. *God and the Gods: Myths of the Bible*. New York: Penguin, 1983.

Berlin, Adele. *Poetics and Interpretation of Biblical Narrative*. Winona Lake, Minn.: Eisenbrauns, 1994.

Bondi, Roberta C. *Three Monophysite Christologies*. Oxford, England: Oxford University Press, 1976.

Bowe, B. *A Church in Crisis*. Minneapolis: Fortress Press, 1988.

Brown, Raymond E. *The Gospel According to John*. 2 vols. Garden City, N.Y.: Doubleday, 1970.

Buell, D. *Making Christians: Clement of Alexandria and the Rhetoric of Legitimacy*. Princeton, N.J.: Princeton University Press, 1999.

Burrus, V. *The Making of a Heretic: Gender, Authority, and the Priscillianist Controversy*. Berkeley: University of California Press, 1995.

Chadwick, Henry. *Early Christian Thought and the Classical Tradition: Studies in Justine, Clement, and Origen*. New York: Oxford University Press, 1984.

Chadwick, Owen. *A History of Christianity*. New York: St. Martin's Press, 1995.

Charanis, Peter. *Church and State in the Later Roman Empire: The Religious Policy of Anastasius the First, 491-518*. Madison: University of Wisconsin Press, 1939.

Ch'en, Kenneth K. C. *Buddhism: The Light of Asia*. Woodbury, N.Y.: Barron's Educational Series, 1968.

Conze, Edward. *A Short History of Buddhism*. London: Allen & Unwin, 1980.

Coogan, Michael D., ed. *The Oxford History of the Biblical World*. New York: Oxford University Press, 1998.

Coomaraswamy, Ananda K. *Buddha and the Gospel of Buddhism*. London: George G. Harrap & Company, 1928. Rev. ed. New York: Harper & Row, 1964.

_____. *Hinduism and Buddhism*. New York: The Wisdom Library, 1943. Reprint. Westport, Conn.: Greenwood, 1971.

Coomaraswamy, Ananda K., and Sister Nivedita. *Myths of the Hindus and Buddhists*. 1914. Reprint. New York: Dover, 1967.

Corless, Roger J. *The Vision of Buddhism*. New York: Paragon House, 1989.

Craigie, Peter C. *The Old Testament: Its Background, Growth, and Content*. Nashville: Abingdon Press, 1986.

Crowther, Duane S. *How to Understand the Book of Isaiah*. Bountiful, Utah: Horizon, 1998.

Davies, Philip R. *The Damascus Covenant: An Interpretation of the Damascus Document*. Sheffield, England: Sheffield Academic Press, 1983.

Davies, W. D., and Louis Finkelstein, eds. *The Cambridge History of Judaism*. 2 vols. Cambridge, England: Cambridge University Press, 1984.

Davis, Raymond. *The Book of Pontiffs*. Liverpool, England: Liverpool University Press, 1989.

De Lange, Nicholas. *Judaism*. New York: Oxford University Press, 1986.

Dumoulin, Heinrich. *Zen Enlightenment*. New York: Weatherhill, 1979.

Ehrman, Bart. *After the New Testament: A Reader in Early Christianity*. New York: Oxford University Press, 1998.

Elbogen, Ismar. *Jewish Liturgy: A Comprehensive History*. Translated by R. P. Scheindlin. Philadelphia: Jewish Publication Society, 1993.

Elliot, Charles. *Hinduism and Buddhism*. 3 vols. London: Routledge and Kegan Paul, 1954.

Esposito, John, ed. *Oxford History of Islam*. Oxford, England: Oxford University Press, 1999.

Feldman, Louis. *Josephus's Interpretation of the Bible*. Berkeley: University of California Press, 1998.

Ferguson, Everett. *Backgrounds to Early Christianity*. Grand Rapids, Mich.: Wm. B. Eerdmans, 1994.

Ferguson, John. *The Religions of the Roman Empire*. Ithaca, N.Y.: Cornell University Press, 1970.

Finegan, Jack. *The Archaeology of World Religions*. Princeton, N.J.: Princeton University Press, 1952.

Fisher, Mary, and Robert Luyster. *Living Religions*. Englewood Cliffs, N.J.: Prentice Hall, 1991.

Frend, W. H. C. *The Rise of Christianity*. Philadelphia: Fortress Press, 1985.

_____. *The Rise of the Monophysite Movement*. Cambridge, England: Cambridge University Press, 1979.

Fuellenbach, J. *Ecclesiastical Office and the Primacy of Rome*. Washington, D.C.: Catholic University of America Press, 1980.

Gibb, H.A.R., et al., eds. *The Encyclopedia of Islam*. 2d ed. 6 vols. Leiden, Netherlands: E. J. Brill, 1986.

Gonzalez, Justo L. *A History of Christian Thought*. Vol 1. Nashville: Abingdon Press, 1970.

Goodenough, E. *The Theology of Justin Martyr: An Investigation into the Conceptions of Early Christian Literature and Its Hellenistic and Judaic Influences*. Amsterdam, Netherlands: Philo Press, 1968.

Griggs, C. W. *Early Egyptian Christianity from Its Origins to 451* C.E. Leiden, Netherlands: E. J. Brill, 1990.

Hanson, R. P. C. *The Search for the Christian Doctrine of God: The Arian Controversy, 318-381*. Edinburgh, Scotland: T & T Clark, 1988.

Hawthorne, Gerald F., Ralph P. Martin, and Daniel G. Reid, eds. *Dictionary of Paul and His Letters*. Downers Grove, Ill.: InterVarsity, 1993.

Herman, A. L. *An Introduction to Buddhist Thought*. Boston: University Press of America, 1983.

Hinchcliff, P. *Cyprian of Carthage and the Unity of the Christian Church*. London: Chapman, 1974.

Jafri, J. H. M. *The Origins and Early Development of Shi'i Islam*. London: Longman, 1979.

Joshi, L. M. *Brahmanism, Buddhism, and Hinduism*. Seattle: Vipassana Research Publications, 1987.

Lieu, S. N. C. *Manichaeism in the Later Roman Empire and Medieval China*. Tübingen, Germany: J. C. B. Mohr, 1992.

Meeks, Wayne A., and Jouette M. Bassler. *The Harper Collins Study Bible: New Revised Standard Version.* New York: HarperCollins, 1993.

Murata, Sachiko, and William Chittick. *The Vision of Islam.* New York: Paragon House, 1994.

Neusner, Jacob. *Judaism and Zoroastrianism at the Dusk of Late Antiquity: How Two Ancient Faiths Wrote Down Their Great Traditions.* Atlanta: Scholars Press, 1993.

Noss, David S., and John B. Noss. *A History of the World's Religions.* 9th ed. New York: Macmillan, 1994.

Pearson, B. A., and J. E. Goehring, eds. *The Roots of Egyptian Christianity.* Philadelphia: Fortress Press, 1986.

Pelikan, Jaroslav. *Christianity and Classic Culture.* New Haven, Conn.: Yale University Press, 1993.

Reat, Noble R. *Buddhism: A History.* Fremont, Calif.: Asian Humanities Press, 1995.

Robinson, Richard H., and Willard L. Johnson. *The Buddhist Religion: A Historical Introduction.* Belmont, Calif.: Wadsworth, 1982.

Rudolph, Kurt. *Gnosis. The Nature and History of Gnosticism.* Translated by Robert McLachlan Wilson. San Francisco: Harper and Row, 1983.

Rutgers, L. V. *The Hidden Heritage of Diaspora Judaism.* Leuven, Netherlands: Uitgevrij Peeters, 1998.

Sarna, Nahum S. *Understanding Genesis.* New York: Schocken Books, 1966.

Schaff, P., and H. Wace, eds. *A Select Library of Nicene and Post-Nicene Fathers of the Christian Church.* New York: Charles Scribner's Sons, 1891. Reprint. Grand Rapids, Mich.: Wm. B. Eerdmans, 1980.

Skilton, Andrew. *A Concise History of Buddhism.* Trumbull, Conn.: Weatherhill, 1997.

Smith, Huston. *The World's Religions: Our Great Wisdom Traditions.* San Francisco: HarperSanFrancisco, 1991.

Tov, E. *Textual Criticism of the Hebrew Bible.* Minneapolis: Fortress Press, 1992.

Tsukamoto, Zenryu. *A History of Early Chinese Buddhism: From Its Introduction to the Death of Hui-yüan.* Translated by Leon Hurvitz. New York: Kodansha International, 1985.

Urban, Linwood. *A Short History of Christian Thought.* New York: Oxford University Press, 1995.

Vallee, Gerard. *The Shaping of Christianity: The History and Literature of Its Formative Centuries.* New York: Paulist Press, 1999.

Wolfson, H. A. *Philo: Foundations of Religious Philosophy in Judaism, Christianity, and Islam.* Cambridge, Mass.: Harvard University Press, 1948-1962.

Yamauchi, E. *Persia and the Bible.* Grand Rapids, Mich.: Baker, 1990.

AFRICA

The emphasis of this category is on North and sub-Saharan Africa. Books dealing specifically with Arabia and Egypt appear separately.

Adams, William L. *Africa in Antiquity: The Arts of Ancient Nubia and the Sudan.* Princeton, N.J.: Princeton University Press, 1977.

_____. *Nubia: Corridor to Africa.* London: Penguin Books, 1977.

Alimen, H. *The Prehistory of Africa.* Translated by Alan Houghton Brodrick. London: Hutchinson Scientific and Technical, 1957.

Ayoub, M. S. *The Rise of Germa.* Tripoli, Libya: Ministry of Tourism and Antiquities, 1968.

Bates, O. *The Eastern Libyans.* London: Macmillan, 1914.

Bendor, S. J. *The Niger-Congo Languages.* Lanham, Md.: University Press of America, 1989.

Bobb, F. Scott. *Historical Dictionary of Zaire.* Metuchen, N.J.: The Scarecrow Press, 1988.

Boonzaier, Emile, Penny Berens, Candy Malherbe, and

Andy Smith. *The Cape Herders: A History of the Khoikhoi of Southern Africa.* Athens: Ohio University Press, 1996.

Brett, Michael, and Elizabeth Fentress. *The Berbers.* Oxford, England: Blackwell, 1998.

Budge, Ernest A. Wallis. *The Queen of Sheba and Her Only Son Menyelik.* 2d ed. London: Oxford University Press, 1932.

Burstein, Stanley M., ed. *Ancient African Civilizations: Kush and Axum.* Princeton, N.J.: Markus Wiener, 1998.

Church, R. J. Harrison. *West Africa: A Study of the Environment and of Man's Use of It.* New York: Longman, 1980.

Clark, J. Desmond. *The Prehistory of Africa.* New York: Praeger, 1970.

Clark, J. Desmond, and Steven A. Brandt, eds. *From

Hunters to Farmers: The Causes and Consequences of Food Production in Africa. Berkeley: University of California Press, 1984.

Connah, Graham. *African Civilizations: Precolonial Cities and States in Tropical Africa, An Archeological Perspective.* Cambridge, England: Cambridge University Press, 1987.

_____. *Three Thousand Years in Africa.* New York: Cambridge University Press, 1981.

Daniels, Charles. *The Garamantes of Southern Libya.* Stoughton, Wis.: Oleander Press, 1970.

Davidson, Basil. *Africa: History of a Continent.* New York: Macmillan, 1972.

_____. *A History of West Africa to the Nineteenth Century.* Garden City, N.Y.: Doubleday, 1966.

Davies, W. V., ed. *Egypt and Africa: Nubia from Prehistory to Islam.* London: The British Museum Press, 1991.

De Beer, G. *Hannibal: Challenging Rome's Supremacy.* New York: Viking Press, 1969.

De Grunne, Bernard. *The Birth of Art in Black Africa: Nok Statuary of Nigeria.* Luxembourg: Banque Générale du Luxembourg, 1998.

Diop, Cheik Anta. *The African Origin of Civilization: Myth or Reality.* Westport, Conn.: Lawrence Hill, 1974.

Ehret, Christopher, and Merrick Posnansky, ed. *The Archaeological and Linguistic Reconstruction of African History.* Berkeley: University of California Press, 1982.

Emery, Walter B. *Lost Land Emerging.* New York: Charles Scribner's Sons, 1967.

Fagg, Bernard. *Nok Terracottas.* London: Ethnographica, 1977.

Forbath, Peter. *The River Congo: Discovery, Exploration, and Exploitation of the World's Most Dramatic River.* New York: Harper & Row, 1977.

Garlake, Peter. *The Hunter's Vision: The Prehistoric Art of Zimbabwe.* Seattle: University of Washington Press, 1995.

Gillon, Werner. *A Short History of African Art.* New York: Facts on File, 1984.

Gregory, John W. *The Great Rift Valley.* London: Frank Cass, 1968.

Grunne, Bernard de. *The Birth of Art in Africa: Nok Statuary in Nigeria.* Paris: A. Biro, 1999.

Hall, M. *Archaeology Africa.* London: James Currey, 1996.

Herbert, Eugenia W. *Red Gold of Africa: Copper in Precolonial History and Culture.* Madison: University of Wisconsin Press, 1984.

Hodges, Carleton, ed. *Papers on the Manding.* Bloomington: University of Indiana Press, 1971.

Hombert, Jean Marie, ed. *Bantu Historical Linguistics: Theoretical and Empirical Perspective.* Cambridge, England: Cambridge University Press, 1999.

Inskeep, R. R. *The Peopling of Southern Africa.* New York: Harper & Row, 1979.

Johnson, E. Harper. *Piankhy the Great.* New York: Thomas Nelson & Sons, 1962.

Kendall, Timothy. "Sudan's Kingdom of Kush." *National Geographic* 178, no. 5 (November, 1990): 103-123.

Knappert, Jan, ed. *Bantu Myths and Other Tales.* Leiden, Netherlands: E. J. Brill, 1977.

Kobishchanov, Yuri M. *Axum.* Translated by L. Kapitanoff. University Park: Pennsylvania State University Press, 1979.

Lancel, Serge. *Carthage: A History.* Translated by Antonia Nevill. Cambridge, Mass.: Blackwell, 1995.

_____. *Hannibal.* Oxford, England: Blackwell, 1998.

Leakey, Richard E. *Origins Reconsidered: In Search of What Makes Us Human.* New York: Anchor Books, 1992.

Lewis-Williams, J. D., and T. A. Dowson. *Rock Paintings of the Natal Drakensberg.* Pietermaritzburg, South Africa: University of Natal Press, 1992.

Martin, Phyllis M., and Patrick O'Meara. *Africa.* Bloomington: Indiana University Press, 1986.

Milburn, Mark. *Ancient Libya, Arabia, and the Sahara: Some Problems and Uncertainties.* Graz, Austria: Akademische Druck und Verlagsanstalt, 1977.

Monges, Miriam Ma'at-Ka-Re. *Kush, the Jewel of the Nile: Reconnecting the Root System of African Civilization.* Trenton, N.J.: Africa World Press, 1997.

Montaigne, Robert. *The Berbers: Their Social and Political Organisation.* Translated and with an introduction by David Seddon. London: Frank Cass, 1973.

Munro-Hay, Stuart. *Aksum: An African Civilization of Late Antiquity.* Edinburgh, Scotland: Edinburgh University Press, 1991.

Newman, James L. *The Peopling of Africa: A Geographic Interpretation.* New Haven, Conn.: Yale University Press, 1995.

Oliver, Roland, and Michael Crowder, eds. *The Cambridge Encyclopedia of Africa.* Cambridge, England: Cambridge University Press, 1981.

Perani, Judith, and Fred Smith. *The Visual Arts of Africa*. Upper Saddle River, N.J.: Prentice Hall, 1998.

Phillipson, David W. *African Archaeology*. 2d ed. Cambridge, England: Cambridge University Press, 1993.

————. *Ancient Ethiopia: Aksum, Its Antecedents and Successors*. London: British Museum Press, 1998.

Raven, Susan. *Rome in Africa*. 3d ed. New York: Routledge, 1993.

Reader, John. *Africa: A Biography of the Continent*. New York: Vintage Books, 1999.

Rogerson, Barnaby. *A Traveller's History of North Africa: Morocco, Tunisia, Libya, Algeria*. New York: Interlink Books, 1998.

Shaw, Thurstan. "The Nok Sculptures of Nigeria." *Scientific American* 22 (February, 1981): 154-166.

Shaw, Thurstan, et al., eds. *The Archaeology of Africa: Food, Metals, and Towns*. London: Routledge, 1993.

Shinnie, Peter L. *Ancient Nubia*. New York: Kegan Paul, 1996.

————. *Meroe: A Civilization of the Sudan*. New York: Frederick A. Praeger, 1967.

Simonis, Damien, David Willett, Ann Jousiffe, Geoff Crowther, and Hugh Finlay. *North Africa: A Lonely Planet Travel Survival Kit*. Victoria, Australia: Lonely Planet Publications, 1995.

Soren, David, Aicha Ben Abed Ben Khader, and Hedi Slim. *Carthage from the Legends of the Aeneid to the Glorious Age of Gold*. New York: Simon and Shuster, 1990.

Trigger, Bruce G. *History and Settlement in Lower Nubia*. New Haven, Conn.: Yale University Press, 1965.

Vansina, Jan. *Paths in the Rainforests: Toward a History of Political Tradition in Equatorial Africa*. Madison: University of Wisconsin Press, 1990.

Vogel, Joseph A., ed. *Encyclopedia of Precolonial Africa: Archaeology, History, Languages, Cultures, and Environments*. Walnut Creek, Calif.: Alta Mira Press, 1997.

Warmington, Brian Herbert. *Carthage*. New York: Praeger, 1960.

Welsby, D. A. *The Kingdom of Kush*. Princeton, N.J.: Marcus Weiner, 1998.

Zabkar, Louis V. *Apedemak Lion God of Meroe: A Study in Meroitic Syncretism*. Warminster, England: Aris & Phillips, 1975.

Zarroug, Mohi el-Din Abdalla. *The Kingdom of Alwa*. Calgary, Alta.: University of Calgary Press, 1991.

AMERICAS

Books on all the ancient cultures of the Americas, including the Arctic, North America, Mesoamerica, and South America.

Adams, Richard E.W. *Río Azul: An Ancient Maya City*. Norman: University of Oklahoma Press, 1999.

Aldenderfer, Mark. *Montane Foragers: Asana and the South-Central Andean Archaic*. Iowa City: University of Iowa Press, 1998.

Anderson, David G., and Kenneth E. Sasaman, eds. *The Paleoindian and Early Archaic Southeast*. Tuscaloosa: University of Alabama Press, 1996.

Arriaza, B. *Beyond Death: The Chinchorro Mummies of Ancient Chile*. Washington, D.C.: Smithsonian Institution Press, 1995.

Beck, Charlotte, ed. *Models for the Millennium: Great Basin Anthropology Today*. Salt Lake City: University of Utah Press, 1999.

Bense, J. A. *Hawkshaw: Prehistory and History in an Urban Neighborhood in Pensacola, Florida*. Pensacola: Archaeology Institute, University of West Florida, 1985.

Benson, Elizabeth P. *The Mochica: A Culture of Peru*. New York: Praeger, 1972.

Benson, Elizabeth P., and Beatriz de la Fuente, eds. *Olmec Art of Ancient Mexico*. Washington, D.C.: National Gallery of Art, 1996.

Bierhorst, John. *The Mythology of Mexico and Central America*. New York: William Morrow, 1990.

————. *The Mythology of North America*. New York: William Morrow, 1985.

————. *The Mythology of South America*. New York: William Morrow, 1988.

Bird, Junius B. *Travels and Archaeology in South Chile*. Iowa City: University of Iowa Press, 1988.

Blanton, Richard, et al. *Ancient Oaxaca*. Cambridge, England: Cambridge University Press, 1999.

Bone, Robert W. *Fielding's Guide to Alaska and the Yukon*. New York: Fielding Travel Books, 1990.

Brody, J. J. *The Anasazi Ancient Indian People of the American Southwest*. New York: Rizzoli, 1990.

Bruhns, Karen Olsen. *Ancient South America*. Cambridge, England: Cambridge University Press, 1994.

Bryan, Liz. *The Buffalo People*. Edmonton: University of Alberta Press, 1991.

Burger, Richard. *Chavín and the Origins of Andean Civilization*. New York: Thames and Hudson, 1992.

Burland, Cottie, Irene Nicholson, and Harold Osborne. *Mythology of the Americas*. New York: Hamlyn Publishing Group, 1970.

Byland, Bruch, and John Pohl. *The Archaeology of the Mixtec Codices: In the Realm of Eight Deer*. Norman: University of Oklahoma Press, 1994.

Carlson, Paul H. *The Plains Indians*. College Station: Texas A&M University Press, 1998.

Carlson, Roy L., and Luke DallaBona, eds. *Early Human Occupation in British Columbia*. Vancouver: University of British Columbia Press, 1996.

Carrasco, David, Lindsay Jones, and Scott Sessions. *Mesoamerica's Classic Heritage: From Teotihuacán to the Aztecs*. Boulder: University Press of Colorado, 2000.

Chapman, Jefferson. *Tellico Archaeology*. Knoxville: University of Tennessee Press, 1985.

Coe, Michael D. *America's First Civilization*. New York: American Heritage, 1968.

———. *The Maya*. 6th ed. London: Thames and Hudson, 1999.

———. *Mexico*. New York: Thames and Hudson, 1994.

Coles, Bryony, J. M. Coles, and Mogens Schou Jørgensen. *Bog Bodies, Sacred Sites, and Wetland Archaeology*. Exeter, England: Wetland Archaeology Research Project, 1999.

Cook, Thomas Genn. *Koster: An Artifact Analysis of Two Archaic Phases in West Central Illinois*. Evanston, Ill.: Northwestern University Archaeological Program, 1976.

Cordell, Linda. *Ancient Pueblo Peoples*. Montreal: St. Remy Press, 1994.

Cordell, Linda, and George Gumerman, eds. *Dynamics of Southwest Prehistory*. Washington, D.C.: Smithsonian Institution Press, 1989.

Crawford, Michael H. *The Origins of Native Americans: Evidence from Anthropological Genetics*. Cambridge, England: Cambridge University Press, 1998.

Croes, Dale. R. *The Hoko River Archaeological Site Complex*. Pullman: Washington State University Press, 1995.

Crown, Patricia L., and W. James Judge. *Chaco and Hohokam Prehistoric Regional Systems in the American Southwest*. Santa Fe, N.Mex.: School of American Research Press, 1991.

DeLaguna, Frederica. *The Archaeology of Cook Inlet, Alaska*. Philadelphia: University of Pennsylvania Press, 1934.

Dick, Herbert W. *Bat Cave*. Santa Fe, N.Mex.: School of American Research, 1965.

Dillehay, Tom D. *The Archaeological Context and Interpretation*. Vol. 2 in *Monte Verde: A Late Pleistocene Settlement in Chile*. Washington, D.C.: Smithsonian Institution Press, 1997.

———. *Paleoenvironment and Site Context*. Vol. 1 in *Monte Verde: A Late Pleistocene Settlement in Chile*. Washington, D.C.: Smithsonian Institution Press, 1989.

Dixon, E. James. *Bones, Boats, and Bison: Archeology and the First Colonization of Western North America*. Albuquerque: University of New Mexico Press, 1999.

———. *Quest for the Origins of the First Americans*. Albuquerque: University of New Mexico Press, 1994.

Donnan, Christopher B. *Ceramics of Ancient Peru*. Los Angeles: Fowler Museum of Cultural History, University of California, 1992.

———. *Moche Art and Iconography*. Los Angeles: University of California Press, 1976.

———. *Moche Occupation of the Santa Valley, Peru*. Berkeley: University of California Press, 1973.

Fagan, Brian M. *Ancient North America: The Archaeology of a Continent*. London: Thames and Hudson, 1995.

———. *The Great Journey: The Peopling of Ancient America*. New York: Thames and Hudson, 1987.

Farabee, William Curtis. *The Central Arawaks*. Oosterhout N.B., Netherlands: Anthropological, 1967.

Fash, William L. *Scribes, Warriors, and Kings: The City of Copan and the Ancient Maya*. New York: Thames and Hudson, 1991.

Fiedel, Stuart J. *Prehistory of the Americas*. Cambridge, England: Cambridge University Press, 1987.

Flannery, Kent, and Joyce Marcus. *Zapotec Civilization: How Urban Society Evolved in Mexico's Oaxaca Valley*. London: Thames and Hudson, 1996.

Friesen, Gerald. *The Canadian Prairies: A History*. Toronto: University of Toronto Press, 1984.

Frison, George C. *Prehistoric Hunters of the High Plains*. New York: Academic Press, 1978.

Gibson, John L. *The Ancient Mounds of Poverty Point: Place of Rings*. Gainesville: University Press of Florida, 2000.

_____. *Poverty Point: A Terminal Archaic Culture of the Lower Mississippi Basin*. Baton Rouge: Dept. of Culture, Recreation and Tourism, Louisiana Archaeological Survey and Antiquities Commission, 1996.

Giddings, James Louis. *The Archeology of Cape Denbigh*. Providence, R.I.: Brown University Press, 1964.

Grayson, Donald K. *The Desert's Past: A Natural Prehistory of the Great Basin*. Washington, D.C.: Smithsonian Institution Press, 1993.

Haas, Jonathan, T. Pozorski, and S. Pozorski, eds. *The Origins and Development of the Andean State*. Cambridge, England: Cambridge University Press, 1987.

Halsey, John R., ed. *Retrieving Michigan's Buried Past: The Archaeology of the Great Lakes State*. Bulletin 64. Bloomfield Hills, Mich.: Cranbrook Institute of Science, 1999.

Harris, Cole R., ed. *Historical Atlas of Canada*. Vol. 1. Toronto: University of Toronto Press, 1987.

Harrison, Peter. *The Lords of Tikal*. New York: Thames and Hudson, 1999.

Hayden, Brian, ed. *The Ancient Past of Keatley Creek: Taphonomy*. Vol. 1. Burnaby, B.C.: Simon Fraser University Archaeology Press, 2000.

Helms, Mary W. *The Curassow's Crest: Myths and Symbols in the Ceramics of Ancient Panama*. Gainesville: University Press of Florida, 2000.

Hemming, J. *Amazon Frontier: The Defeat of the Brazilian Indians*. Cambridge, Mass.: Harvard University Press, 1987.

Jennings, Francis. *The Founders of America: From the Earliest Migrations to the Present*. New York: W. W. Norton, 1993.

Jennings, Jesse D. *Ancient North Americans*. San Francisco: W. H. Freeman, 1983.

_____. *Prehistoric North America*. Mountain View, Calif.: Mayfield, 1989.

Johnson, Jolene K. *Hohokam Ecology: The Ancient Desert People and Their Environment*. Washington, D.C.: National Park Service, 1997.

Johnston, H. J. M., ed. *The Pacific Province*. Vancouver, B.C.: Douglas & McIntyre, 1996.

Jones, Dorothy M. *Aleuts in Transition*. Seattle: University of Washington Press, 1976.

Kelly, Joyce. *The Complete Visitor's Guide to Mesoamerican Ruins*. Norman: University of Oklahoma Press, 1982.

Kolata, Alan L. *The Tiwanaku*. Cambridge, Mass.: Blackwell, 1993.

_____. *Valley of the Spirits: A Journey into the Lost Realm of the Aymara*. New York: John Wiley and Sons, 1996.

Labbé, Armand J. *Colombia Before Columbus: The People, Culture, and Ceramic Art of Prehispanic Colombia*. New York: Rizzoli, 1986.

_____. *Guardians of the Life Stream: Shamans, Art, and Power in Prehispanic Central Panamá*. Santa Ana, Calif.: Bowers Museum of Cultural Art, 1995.

Laughlin, William S. *Aleuts: Survivors of the Bering Land Bridge*. New York: Holt, Rinehart and Winston, 1997.

LeBlanc, Stephen. *Prehistoric Warfare in the American Southwest*. Salt Lake City: University of Utah Press, 1999.

Luckert, Karl W. *Olmec Religion: A Key to Middle America and Beyond*. Norman: University of Oklahoma Press, 1976.

McAnany, Patricia A. *Living with the Ancestors: Kinship and Kingship in Ancient Maya Society*. Austin: University of Texas Press, 1995.

McAnany, Patricia A., and Barry Isaac, eds. *Prehistoric Maya Economies of Belize*. Research in Economic Anthropology, Supplement 4. Greenwich, Conn.: JAI Press, 1989.

McCartney, Allen P., Hiroaki Okada, Atsuko Okada, and William Workman, eds. *Arctic Anthropology: North Pacific and Bering Sea Maritime Societies, the Archaeology of Prehistoric and Early Historic Coastal Peoples*. Madison: University of Wisconsin Press, 1998.

McEwan, Colin, et al., eds. *Patagonia: Natural History, Prehistory and Ethnography at the Uttermost End of the Earth*. Princeton, N.J.: Princeton University Press, 1998.

Mackenzie, Donald Alexander. *Myths of Pre-Columbian America*. London: Gresham, 1923. Reprint. Boston: Longwood Press, 1978.

Martin, Susan R. *Wonderful Power: The Story of Ancient Copper Working in the Lake Superior Basin*. Detroit: Wayne State University Press, 1999.

Mason, Ronald J. *Great Lakes Archaeology*. New York: Academic Press, 1981.

Masuda, S., I. Shimada, and C. Morris, eds. *Andean Ecology and Civilization*. Tokyo: University of Tokyo Press, 1985.

Meltzer, David J. *Search for the First Americans*. Washington, D.C.: Smithsonian Institution Press, 1993.

Milanich, J. T. *Archaeology of Precolumbian Florida*.

Gainesville: University of Florida Press, 1994.

Miller, Arthur G. *At the Edge of the Sea: Mural Painting at Tancah-Tulum, Quintana Roo, Mexico*. Washington, D.C.: Dumbarton Oaks, 1982.

Miller, Mary, and Karl Taube. *The Gods and Symbols of Ancient Mexico and the Maya: An Illustrated Dictionary of Mesoamerican Religion*. London: Thames and Hudson, 1993.

Minority Rights Group, eds. *Polar Peoples: Self-Determination and Development*. London: Minority Rights Publications, 1994.

Moseley, Michael. *The Incas and Their Ancestors: The Archaeology of Peru*. London: Thames and Hudson, 1992.

————. *The Maritime Foundations of Andean Civilization*. Menlo Park, Calif.: Cummings, 1975.

Mountjoy, Joseph B. *Man and Land at Prehispanic Cholula*. Nashville: Vanderbilt University, 1973.

Murra, J., N. Wachtel, and J. Revel, eds. *Anthropological History of Andean Polities*. London: Cambridge University Press, 1989.

Niles, Judith. *Native American History: A Chronology of the Vast Achievements of a Culture and Their Links to World Events*. New York: Ballantine Books, 1996.

Olsen, Fred. *On the Trail of the Arawaks*. Norman: University of Oklahoma Press, 1974.

Paddock, John, ed. *Ancient Oaxaca: Discoveries in Mexican Archeology and History*. Stanford, Calif.: Stanford University Press, 1966.

Pasztory, Esther. *Teotihuacan: An Experiment in Living*. Norman: University of Oklahoma Press, 1997.

Phillips, James L., and James A. Brown, eds. *Archaic Hunters and Gatherers in the American Midwest*. New York: Academic Press, 1983.

Piña Chan, Román. *The Olmec: Mother Culture of Mesoamerica*. New York: Rizzoli, 1989.

Plog, Stephen. *Ancient Peoples of the American Southwest*. London: Thames and Hudson, 1997.

Pringle, Heather. *In Search of Ancient North America: An Archaeological Journey to Forgotten Cultures*. New York: John Wiley & Sons, 1996.

————. "The Sickness of Mummies." *Discover Magazine*, December 1, 1998, 75-83.

Richards, Thomas H., and Michael K. Rousseau. *Late Prehistoric Cultural Horizons on the Canadian Plateau*. Burnaby, B.C.: Simon Fraser University Archaeology Press, 1987.

Richardson, James B., III. *People of the Andes*. Washington, D.C.: Smithsonian Institution Books, 1994.

Rick, John. *Prehistoric Hunters of the High Andes*. New York: Academic Press, 1980.

Roberts, David. *In Search of the Old Ones: Exploring the Anasazi World of the Southwest*. New York: Touchstone, 1996.

Rogozinski, Jan. *A Brief History of the Caribbean: From the Arawak and the Carib to the Present*. New York: Facts on File, 1992.

Roosevelt, A. C., ed. *Amazonian Indians: From Prehistory to the Present, Anthropological Perspectives*. Tucson: University of Arizona Press, 1994.

————. *Moundbuilders of the Amazon: Geophysical Archeology on Marajó Island*. San Diego: Academic Press, 1991.

Sabloff, Jereny A., and John S. Henderson, eds. *Lowland Maya Civilization in the Eighth Century* A.D. Washington, D.C.: Dumbarton Oaks, 1993.

Sasaman, K. E. *Early Pottery in the Southeast: Tradition and Innovation in Cooking Technology*. Tuscaloosa: University of Alabama Press, 1993.

Sayles, E. R. *The Cochise Cultural Sequence in Southeastern Arizona*. Tucson: University of Arizona Press, 1983.

Scarborough, Vernon L., and David R. Wilcox, eds. *The Mesoamerican Ballgame*. Tucson: University of Arizona Press, 1991.

Schele, Linda, and David Freidel. *A Forest of Kings*. New York: William Morrow, 1990.

Schele, Linda, and Peter Mathews. *The Code of Kings: The Language of Seven Sacred Temples and Tombs*. New York: Charles Scribner's Sons, 1998.

Schmidt, Peter, Mercedes de la Garza, and Enrique Nalda, eds. *Maya*. New York: Rizzoli, 1998.

Scott, John F. *Latin American Art: Ancient to Modern*. Gainesville: University Press of Florida, 1999.

Sharer, Robert. *The Ancient Maya*. Stanford, Calif.: Stanford University Press, 1994.

Silverman, Helaine. *Cahuachi in the Ancient Nasca World*. Iowa City: University of Iowa Press, 1993.

Smith, Nigel J. H. *The Amazon River Forest: A Natural History of Plants, Animals, and People*. New York: Oxford University Press, 1999.

Snow, Dean. *The Archaeology of North America*. New York: Viking Press, 1976.

Soustelle, Jacques. *The Olmecs: The Oldest Civilization in Mexico*. Norman: University of Oklahoma Press, 1985.

Spores, Ronald. *The Mixtecs in Ancient and Colonial Times*. Norman: University of Oklahoma Press, 1984.

Stoltman, J. B. *The Laurel Culture in Minnesota*. Minnesota Prehistoric Archaeology Series. Saint Paul: Minnesota Historical Society, 1973.

Stone-Miller, Rebecca. *Art of the Andes from Chavín to Inca*. New York: Thames and Hudson, 1995.

Sturtevant, William C., ed. *Handbook of North American Indians*. 17 vols. Washington, D.C.: Smithsonian Institution Press, 1978-1996.

Swanson, Earl H., Warwick Bray, and Ian Farrington. *The Ancient Americas*. New York: Peter Bedrick Books, 1989.

Taube, Karl. *Aztec and Maya Myths*. Austin: University of Texas Press, 1993.

Terborgh, J. "A Dying World." *The New York Review* 47, no. 1 (January 20, 2000): 37-42.

Thomas, David Hurst. *Exploring Ancient Native America: An Archaeological Guide*. New York: Routledge, 1999.

Thompson, John Eric. *The Rise and Fall of Maya Civilization*. 2d ed. Norman: University of Oklahoma Press, 1966.

Tompkins, Peter. *Mysteries of the Mexican Pyramids*. New York: Harper & Row, 1976.

Townsend, Richard F., ed. *Ancient West Mexico: Art and Archaeology of the Unknown Past*. London: Thames and Hudson/Art Institute of Chicago, 1998.

Trigger, Bruce G., and Wilcomb E. Washburn, eds. *The Cambridge History of the Native Peoples of the Americas*. 3 vols. New York: Cambridge University Press, 1996.

Turner, Christy, and Jacqueline Turner. *Man Corn: Cannibalism and Violence in the Prehistoric American Southwest*. Salt Lake City: University of Utah Press, 1999.

Weaver, Muriel Porter. *The Aztecs, Maya, and Their Predecessors: Archeology of Mesoamerica*. 3d ed. San Diego: Academic Press, 1993.

Webb, C. H. *The Poverty Point Culture*. Baton Rouge: Louisiana State University, 1982.

Webb, William S., and R. S. Baby. *The Adena People, No. 2*. Columbus: Ohio Historical Society, 1957.

Webb, William S., and C. E. Snow. *The Adena People*. Knoxville: University of Tennessee Press, 1945.

West, Elliott. *The Contested Plains: Indians, Goldseekers, and the Rush to Colorado*. Lawrence: University Press of Kansas, 1998.

Winter, Marcus. *Oaxaca: The Archaeological Record*. Mexico, D.F.: Minutiae Mexicana, 1992.

Wright, James V. *The Laurel Tradition and the Middle Woodland Period*. Ottawa: National Museum of Canada, 1967.

_____. *Ontario Prehistory: An Eleven-Thousand-Year Archaeological Outline*. Ottawa: National Museums of Canada, 1972.

ANATOLIA

This geographic term refers to the west Asian peninsula most commonly associated today with Turkey. For works dealing with Anatolia under the Persian Empire, see Mesopotamia. For Ionian Greece or the Byzantine Empire, see Greece.

Akurgal, Ekrem. *Ancient Civilizations and Ruins of Turkey*. Istanbul: Haset Kitabevi, 1985.

Allen, R. E. *The Attalid Kingdom: A Constitutional History*. Oxford, England: Oxford University Press, 1983.

Bean, George. *Aegean Turkey*. New York: F. A. Praeger, 1966.

Bittel, Kurt. *Hattusha: The Capital of the Hittites*. New York: Oxford University Press, 1970.

Blegen, Carl William. *Troy and the Trojans*. London: Thames and Hudson, 1963.

Boedeker, Deborah Dickman. *The World of Troy*. Pittsburgh: Classical Association of the United States, 1998.

Brown, Dale. *Anatolia: Cauldron of Cultures*. New York: Time-Life, 1995.

Bryce, T. R. *The Lycians in Literary and Epigraphic Sources*. Copenhagen: Museum Tusculanum Press, 1986.

Bryce, Trevor. *The Kingdom of the Hittites*. New York: Oxford University Press, 1998.

Buccellati, G., and M. Kelly-Buccellati. *Urkesh and the Hurrians*. Malibu: Undena, 1998.

Burney, C., and D. M. Lang. *The Peoples of the Hills: Ancient Ararat and Caucasus*. New York: Praeger, 1972.

Fleming, William. *Arts and Ideas*. New York: Holt, Rinehart and Winston, 1997.

Freely, John. *The Aegean Coast of Turkey*. Istanbul: Redhouse Press, 1996.

Gurney, Oliver R. *The Hittites*. 2d ed. London: Folio Society, 1999.

_____. *Some Aspects of Hittite Religion*. Oxford, England: Oxford University Press, 1976.

Hanfmann, G. M. A. *Sardis from Prehistoric to Roman Times*. Cambridge, Mass.: Harvard University Press, 1983.

Hansen, Esther Violet. *The Attalids of Pergamon*. 2d ed. Ithaca, N.Y.: Cornell University Press, 1971.

Hansmann, George Maxim Anossov. *From Croesus to Constantine: The Cities of Western Asia Minor and Their Arts*. Ann Arbor: University of Michigan Press, 1975.

Hoffner, H. A., Jr. *Hittite Myths*. Atlanta: Scholars Press, 1990.

_____. *The Laws of the Hittites: A Critical Edition*. Leiden, Netherlands: E. J. Brill, 1997.

Keen, Antony G. *Dynastic Lycia*. Leiden, Netherlands: E. J. Brill, 1998.

Macqueen, J. G. *The Hittites and Their Contemporaries in Asia Minor*. 2d ed. London: Thames and Hudson, 1986.

Meredith, Anthony. *The Cappadocians*. Crestwood, N.Y.: St. Vladimir's Seminary Press, 1995.

Morganster, James, ed. *The Fort at Dereagzi and Other Material Remains in its Vicinity: From Antiquity to the Middle Ages*. Tübingen, Germany: Ernst Wasmuth, 1993.

Pedley, John Griffiths. *Sardis in the Age of Croesus*. Norman: University of Oklahoma Press, 1968.

Perrot, Georges, and Charles Chipiez. *History of Art in Phrygia, Lydia, Caria, and Lycia*. New York: A. C. Armstrong and Son, 1892.

Seton, Lloyd. *Ancient Turkey*. Berkeley: University of California Press, 1989.

Seval, Mehlika. *Let's Visit Ephesus*. Istanbul: Minyatur, 1998.

Wilhelm, G. *The Hurrians*. Warminster, England: Aris & Phillips, 1989.

Zimansky, P. E. *Ancient Ararat: A Handbook of Urartian Studies*. Delmar, N.Y.: Caravan Books, 1998.

_____. *Ecology and Empire: The Structure of the Urartian State*. Chicago: The Oriental Institute, 1985.

ARABIA

Included here are books on the history of the Arabian peninsula but especially on the rise of Islam through circa 700 C.E.

Al-Tabar. *The Sasanids, the Byzantines, the Lakhmids, and Yemen: The History of al-Tabari*. Translated and annotated by Clifford Edmund Bosworth. Albany: State University of New York Press, 1999.

Beshore, George. *Science in Early Islamic Cultures*. New York: F. Watts, 2000.

Chirri, M. J. *The Brother of the Prophet Muhammad (The Iman Ali)*. Qum, Iran: Ansanyan, 1996.

Donner, Fred M. *The Early Islamic Conquests*. Princeton, N.J.: Princeton University Press, 1981.

Hawting, G. R. *The First Dynasty of Islam: The Umayyad Caliphate,* A.D. *661-750*. Carbondale: Southern Illinois University Press, 1987.

Hitti, Philip K. *History of the Arabs*. London: Macmillan, 1940.

Hourani, Albert. *A History of the Arab Peoples*. Cambridge, Mass.: Farber, 1991.

Knappert, Jan. *Islamic Legends: Histories of the Heroes, Saints and Prophets of Islam*. 2 vols. Leiden: E. J. Brill, 1985.

Lewis, Bernard. *The Arabs in History*. Oxford, England: Oxford University Press, 1993.

Lings, Martin. *Muhammad*. New York: Inner Traditions, 1983.

Mansfield, Peter. *The New Arabians*. Chicago: J. G. Ferguson, 1981.

Shaban, M. A. *Islamic History,* C.E. *600-750: A New Interpretation*. Cambridge, England: Cambridge University Press, 1973.

CENTRAL ASIA

This category includes all of Asia except China, Japan, Korea, the Indian subcontinent, and the Indo-Chinese peninsula. Books on ancient Armenia, Bactria, Mongolia, and Scythia can be found here.

Bournoutian, George. *A History of the Armenian People*. Costa Mesa, Calif.: Mazda, 1993.

Cernenko, E. V. *The Scythians*. London: Ospre, 1983.

Chahin, M. *The Kingdom of Armenia*. London: Croom Helm, 1987.

Christian, David. *Inner Eurasia from Prehistory to the Mongol Empire*. Oxford, England: Blackwell, 1998.

Dani, A. H., and V. M. Masson, eds. *The Dawn of Civilization: Earliest Times to 700 B.C.* Vol. 1 in *The History of the Civilizations of Central Asia*. Paris: UNESCO, 1992.

Davis-Kimball, Jeannine. *Kurgans on the Left Bank of the Ilek*. Berkeley, Calif.: Zinat Press, 1995.

Davis-Kimball, Jeannine, Vladimir A. Bashilov, and Leonid T. Yablonsky. *Nomads of the Eurasian Steppes in the Early Iron Age*. Berkeley, Calif.: Zinat Press, 1995.

Derev'anko, Anatoliy P., ed. and comp. *The Paleolithic of Siberia: New Discoveries and Interpretations*. Edited by Demitri B. Shimkin and W. Roger Powers. Translated by Inna P. Laricheva. Urbana: University of Illinois Press, 1998.

Fairservis, Walter A., Jr. *Archeology of the Southern Gobi of Mongolia*. Durham, N.C.: Carolina Academic Press, 1993.

Fasken, William H. *Cimmerians and Scythians*. Haverhill, Mass.: Destiny, 1944.

Frye, Richard N. *The Heritage of Central Asia: From Antiquity to the Turkish Expansion*. Princeton, N.J.: Marcus Wiener, 1996.

Harmatta, János, B. N. Puri, and G. F. Etemadi, eds. *The Development of Sedentary and Nomadic Civilizations: 700 B.C. to A.D. 250*. Vol. 2 in *The History of the Civilizations of Central Asia*. Paris: UNESCO, 1994.

Hopkirk, Peter. *Foreign Devils on the Silk Road: The Search for the Lost Cities and Treasures of Chinese Central Asia*. London: Oxford University Press, 1986.

Jacobson, Esther. *The Art of the Scythians*. Leiden, Netherlands: E. J. Brill, 1995.

Khorenats'i, Moses. *History of the Armenians*. Translated by Robert W. Thomson. Cambridge, Mass.: Harvard University Press, 1978.

Kristensen, Anne K. G. *Who Were the Cimmerians, and Where Did They Come From?* Copenhagen: Den Kongelige Danske Videnskabernes Selskab, 1988.

Levine, Marsha, Yuri Rassamakin, Aleksandr Kislenko, and Nataliya Tatarintseva. *Late Prehistoric Exploitation of the Eurasian Steppe*. Cambridge, England: McDonald Institute for Archaeological Research, 1999.

Narain, A. K. *The Indo-Greeks*. Oxford, England: Oxford University Press, 1957.

Reeder, Ellen, ed. *Scythian Gold: Treasures from Ancient Ukraine*. New York: Abrams/Walters Art Gallery/San Antonio Museum of Art, 1999.

Rice, Tamara. *The Scythians*. New York: Praeger, 1961.

Rolle, Renate. *The World of the Scythians*. Berkeley: University of California Press, 1989.

Rosenfield, John M. *The Dynastic Arts of the Kushans*. Berkeley: University of California Press, 1967.

Sinor, Denis. *The Cambridge History of Early Inner Asia: From the Earliest Times to the Rise of the Mongols*. Cambridge, England: Cambridge University Press, 1990.

Stein, Aurel. *Serindia: Detailed Report of Exploration of Central Asia and Westernmost China, Carried On and Described Under the Orders of His Majesty's Indian Government*. 5 vols. Oxford, England: Clarendon Press, 1921.

EAST ASIA

Includes China, Japan, Korea, and Tibet.

Aikens, C. Melvin, and Takayasu Higuchi. *Prehistory of Japan*. San Diego: Academic Press, 1982.

Allan, Sarah. *The Heir and the Sage: Dynastic Legend in Early China*. San Francisco: Chinese Materials Center, 1981.

Ames, Roger T. *The Art of Rulership: A Study in Ancient Chinese Political Thought*. Albany: State University of New York Press, 1994.

Bagley, Robert W. *Ancient Sichuan: Treasures from a Lost Civilization*. Princeton, N.J.: Princeton University Press, 2001.

Bangs, Richard, and Christian Kallen. *Riding the*

Dragon's Back: The Race to Raft the Upper Yangtze. New York: Macmillan, 1989.

Barnes, Gina. *Protohistoric Yamato*. Ann Arbor: University of Michigan Center for Japanese Studies, 1988.

————. *The Rise of Civilization in East Asia: The Archaeology of China, Korea, and Japan*. New York: Thames and Hudson, 1998.

Beshore, George. *Science in Ancient China*. New York: F. Watts, 1998.

Bingham, W. *The Founding of the Tang Dynasty*. New York: Octagon, 1970.

Birch, Cyril. *Chinese Myths and Fantasies*. London: Oxford University Press, 1962.

Birrell, Anne M. *Chinese Mythology*. Baltimore: The Johns Hopkins University Press, 1993.

Bocking, Brian. *A Popular Dictionary of Shinto*. Chicago: NTC Publishing Group, 1997.

Bonavia, Judy. *The Silk Road: From Xi'an to Kashgar*. New York: Passport Books, 1993.

Bowring, Richard J., and Peter F. Kornicki. *The Cambridge Encyclopedia of Japan*. New York: Cambridge University Press, 1993.

Brooks, E. Bruce, and A. Taeko Brooks. *The Original Analects*. New York: Columbia University Press, 1998.

Brown, Delmer, ed. *Ancient Japan. The Cambridge History of Japan*. Cambridge, England: Cambridge University Press, 1988.

Brown, J. D. *Frommer's China: The Fifty Most Memorable Trips*. New York: Simon & Schuster, 1998.

Bush, Susan, and Hsiao-yen Shih. *Early Chinese Texts on Painting*. Cambridge, Mass.: Harvard University Press, 1985.

Cavendish, Richard. *Chinese Mythology*. 2d ed. New York: Peter Bedrick Books, 1985.

————. *The Local Cultures of South and East China*. Translated by Alide Eberhard. Leiden, Netherlands: E. J. Brill, 1968.

Chang, Kwang-Chih. *The Archeology of Ancient China*. 4th ed. New Haven, Conn.: Yale University Press, 1987.

————. *Shang Civilization*. New Haven, Conn.: Yale University Press, 1980.

————, ed. *Studies of Shang Archaeology*. New Haven, Conn.: Yale University Press, 1986.

Chen, Shou. *Empresses and Consorts: Selections from Chen Shou's Records of the Three States with Pei Songzhi's Commentary*. Translated by Robert Joe Cutter and William Gordon Crowell. Honolulu:

University of Hawaii Press, 1999.

Ch'u, T'ung-tsu. *Han Social Structure*. Edited by Jack L. Dull. Seattle: University of Washington Press, 1972.

Chung, Shih-tsu. *Ancient China's Scientists*. Hong Kong: Commercial Press, 1984.

Cleary, Thomas. *The Book of Leadership and Strategy: Lessons of the Chinese Masters*. New York: Random House, 1992.

Coleman, Graham. *A Handbook of Tibetan Culture*. Boston: Shambala, 1994.

Cotterell, Arthur. *The First Emperor of China*. New York: Holt, Rinehart and Winston, 1981.

Cottrell, L. *The Tiger of Ch'in: How China Became a Nation*. New York: Holt, Rinehart and Winston, 1962.

Creel, Herrlee Glessner. *The Birth of China*. New York: Frederick Ungar, 1967.

————. *Chinese Thought from Confucius to Mao Tsetung*. New York: New American Library, 1960.

Davis, F. Hadland, and Evelyn Paul. *Myths and Legends of Japan*. Mineola, N.Y.: Dover, 1992.

De Bary, Theodore, and Irene Bloom. *From Earliest Times to 1600*. Vol. 1 in *Sources of Chinese Tradition*. 2d ed. New York: Columbia University Press, 1999.

Dower, John W., and Timothy S. George. *Japanese History and Culture from Ancient to Modern Times: Seven Basic Bibliographies*. 2d ed. Princeton, N.J.: Markus Wiener, 1995.

Dubs, Homer H., trans. *History of the Former Han Dynasty*. 3 vols. Baltimore: Waverly Press, 1938-1955.

Dunn, Hugh. *Cao Zhi: The Life of a Princely Chinese Poet*. Beijing: New World Press, 1983.

Eberhard, Wolfram. *A History of China*. Berkeley: University of California Press, 1977.

Ebrey, Patricia Buckley. *The Cambridge Illustrated History of China*. Cambridge, England: Cambridge University Press, 1996.

Fairbank, John King. *China: A New History*. Cambridge, Mass.: Harvard University Press, 1992.

Fairbank, John King, and Edwin O. Reischauer. *China: Tradition and Transformation*. Boston: Houghton Mifflin, 1978.

Feng Yu-Lan. *A History of Chinese Philosophy*. 2 vols. Princeton, N.J.: Princeton University Press, 1952.

Feng, Yu-lan, and Derk Bodde. *A Short History of Chinese Philosophy*. New York: Free Press, 1997.

Fitzgerald, C. P. *China: A Short Cultural History*. London: Westview Press, 1985.

Fitzhugh, William W., and Chisato O. Dubrevil, eds. *Ainu: Spirit of a Northern People.* Olympia: University of Washington Press, 2000.

Franke, Herbert, and Denis Twitchett. *The Cambridge History of China.* Vol. 6. New York: Cambridge University Press, 1994.

Franz, Michael. *China Through the Ages.* Boulder, Colo.: Westview Press, 1986.

Fu, Tianchou, ed. *Wonders from the Earth.* San Francisco: China Books and Periodicals, 1989.

Gernet, Jacques. *A History of Chinese Civilization.* Translated by J. R. Foster and Charles Hartman. New York: Cambridge University Press, 1996.

Graham, A. C. *Disputers of the Tao: Philosophical Argument in Ancient China.* La Salle, Ill.: Open Court, 1989.

Guisso, R. W. L., and Catherine Pagani. *The First Emperor of China.* New York: Birch Lane Press, 1989.

Hall, John W. *Japan: From Prehistory to Modern Times.* Ann Arbor: University of Michigan Press, 1991.

Hane, Mikiso. *Premodern Japan: A Historical Survey.* Boulder, Colo.: Westview, 1991.

Hansen, Chad. *A Daoist Theory of Chinese Thought.* Oxford, England: Oxford University Press, 1992.

Harper, Donald. *Early Chinese Medical Literature: The Mawangdui Medical Manuscripts.* London: Kegan Paul, 1997.

Huang, Ray. *China: A Macro History.* Armonk, N.Y.: M. E. Sharpe, 1997.

Hucker, Charles O. *China's Imperial Past.* Stanford, Calif.: Stanford University Press, 1979.

Hulsewé, Anthony F. P. *China in Central Asia: The Early Stage, 125 B.C.-A.D. 23.* Leiden, Netherlands: E. J. Brill, 1979.

Johnson, D. W. *The Ainu of Northeast Asia.* East Windsor, N.J.: Idzat International, 1999.

Kang, In-Gu. *Ancient Korean History Based on the Archaeological Data.* Seoul: Hakyunmunwhasa, 1997.

Kayano, Shigeru, et al. *Our Land Was A Forest: An Ainu Memoir.* Boulder, Colo.: Westview Press, 1994.

Keightley, David N., ed. *The Origins of Chinese Civilization.* Berkeley: University of California Press, 1983.

Kennedy, M. *A Short History of Japan.* New York: New American Library, 1964.

Kidder, J. Edward. *Japan Before Buddhism.* New York: Praeger, 1966.

Kim, Young-Joo, et al. *Kyongiju: Old Capital of Shilla Dynasty Enlivened with 2000-Year History.* Seoul,

Korea: Yong-Soo Kim: Woojin, 1995.

Knechtges, David R. *The Han Rhapsody: A Study of the Fu of Yang Hsiung.* Cambridge, England: Cambridge University Press, 1976.

Kodansha. *An Illustrated Encyclopedia of Japan.* New York: Kodansha America, 1993.

_____. *Kodansha Encyclopedia of Japan.* New York: Kodansha International, 1983.

Lai, Whalen. *Tao-sheng's Theory of Sudden Enlightenment Re-examined: Interaction with Seng-chao, Hui-kuan, Kumarajiva, and Hui-yuan.* Honolulu: University of Hawaii Press, 1987.

Lau, D. C., and Roger T. Ames. *Yuan Dao: Tracing Dao to Its Source.* New York: Ballantine Books, 1998.

Legge, James. *Confucian Analects: The Great Learning, The Doctrine of the Mean.* Oxford, England: Oxford University Press, 1893. Reprint. Mineola, N.Y.: Dover, 1971.

Levy, Andre. *Chinese Literature: Ancient and Classical.* Translated by William H. Nienhauser. Bloomington: Indiana University Press, 2000.

Li, Xuebin. *Eastern Zhou and Qin Dynasties.* Translated by K. C. Chang. New Haven, Conn.: Yale University Press, 1985.

Li, Yu-ning. *Shang Yang's Reforms and State Control in China.* White Plains, N.Y.: M. E. Sharpe, 1977.

Loehr, Max. *The Great Painters of China.* Oxford, England: Phaidon Press, 1980.

Loewe, Michael. *Chinese Ideas of Life and Death.* London: Allen & Unwin, 1982.

Loewe, Michael, and Edward L. Shaughnessy, eds. *The Cambridge History of Ancient China from the Origins of Civilization to 221 B.C.E.* Cambridge, England: Cambridge University Press, 1999.

Lopez, Donald S., Jr., ed. *Religions of China in Practice.* Princeton, N.J.: Princeton University Press, 1996.

Lowe, Scott. *Mo Tzu's Religious Blueprint for a Chinese Utopia: The Will and the Way.* Lewiston, N.Y.: The Edwin Mellen Press, 1992.

Major, John S. *Heaven and Earth in Early Han Thought: Chapters Three, Four, and Five of the Huainanzi.* Albany: State University of New York Press, 1993.

Miki, Fumio. *Haniwa.* Translated by Gina Lee Barnes. Arts of Japan 8. New York: Weatherhill, 1974.

Mulhern, C. *Heroic with Grace: Legendary Women of Japan.* New York: M. E. Sharpe, 1991.

Munro, Neil Gordon. *Ainu Creed and Cult.* London: Routledge & Kegan Paul, 1962. Reprint. New York: Kegan Paul, 1996.

Neave-Hill, W. B. R. *Chinese Ceramics*. Foreword by Harry Garner. New York: St. Martin's Press, 1976.

Needham, Joseph. *Introductory Orientations*. Vol. 1 in *Science and Civilisation in China*. Cambridge, England: Cambridge University Press, 1954.

Nelson, Walter Henry. *Buddha: His Life and Teaching*. Los Angeles: J. P. Tarcher, 2000.

Ono, Sokyo. *Shinto: The Kami Way*. Osaka, Japan: Charles E. Tuttle, 1994.

Paludan, Ann. *Chronicle of the Chinese Emperors*. New York: Thames and Hudson, 1998.

Pearson, Richard. *Ancient Japan*. New York: G. Braziller/ Arthur M. Sackler Gallery, Smithsonian Institution, 1992.

————, ed. *Windows on the Japanese Past: Studies in Archaeology and Prehistory*. Ann Arbor: University of Michigan Center for Japanese Studies, 1986.

Peers, Chris. *Ancient Chinese Armies, 1500 B.C.-200 B.C.* London: Osprey, 1990.

————. *Imperial Chinese Armies: 200 B.C.-589 A.D.* London: Osprey, 1995.

Perry, John C., and Bardwell L. Smith, eds. *Essays on T'ang Society*. Leiden, Netherlands: E. J. Brill, 1976.

Piggott, Juliet. *Japanese Mythology*. 2d ed. New York: Peter Bedrick Books, 1983.

Pirazzoli-t'Serstevens, Michele. *The Han Dynasty*. Translated by Janet Seligman. New York: Rizzoli, 1982.

Pye, Lucian. *China: An Introduction*. Boston, Mass.: Little Brown, 1991.

Queen, Sarah Ann. *From Chronicle to Canon: The Hermeneutics of the Spring and Autumn, According to Tung Chung-shu*. New York: Cambridge University Press, 1996.

Rawson, Jessica. *Ancient China, Art and Archeology*. London: Duckworth, 1980.

————, ed. *The British Museum Book of Chinese Art*. New York: Thames and Hudson, 1993.

Reader, Ian. *Simple Guide to Shinto: The Religion of Japan*. Kent, England: Folkestone, 1998.

Richardson, H. E. *A Short History of Tibet*. New York: E. P. Dutton, 1962.

Robinet, Isabella. *Taoist Meditation: The Mao-Shan Tradition of Great Purity*. Albany: State University of New York Press, 1993.

Roth, Harold David. *The Textual History of the Huai-nan tzu*. Ann Arbor, Mich.: Association for Asian Studies, 1992.

Sage, Steven, F. *Ancient Sichuan and the Unification of China*. Albany: State University of New York Press, 1992.

Sailey, Jay. *The Master Who Embraces Simplicity: A Study of the Philosopher Ko Hung*. San Francisco: Chinese Materials Center, 1978.

Sanders, Tao Tao Liu. *Dragons, Gods and Spirits from Chinese Mythology*. New York: Schocken Books, 1980.

Sansom, George B. *Japan: A Short Cultural History*. Stanford, Calif.: Stanford University Press, 1952.

Shangraw, Clarence F. *Origins of Chinese Ceramics*. New York: China Institute in America, 1978.

Shaughnessy, Edward L. *Before Confucius: Studies on the Creation of the Chinese Classics*. Albany: State University of New York Press, 1997.

————. *Sources of Western Zhou History: Inscribed Bronze Vessels*. Berkeley: University of California Press, 1991.

Shun, Kwong-Loi. *Mencius and Early Chinese Thought*. Stanford, Calif.: Stanford University Press, 1997.

Siren, Osvald. *Chinese Painting: Leading Masters and Principles*. Reprint. New York: Hacker Art Books, 1973.

Soled, Debra E. *China: A Nation in Transition*. Washington, D.C.: Congressional Quarterly Press, 1995.

Stein, R. A. *Tibetan Civilization*. Stanford, Calif.: Stanford University Press, 1972.

Thlku, Tarthang. *Ancient Tibet*. Berkeley, Calif.: Dharma Publishing, 1986.

Trupp, Philip Z. *Ancient Wisdom I: The Spiritual Tale of the Scholar Chu Shui Hu*. Sterling, Va.: Capital Books, 2001.

Tsunoda, R., et al. *Sources of Japanese Tradition*. New York: Columbia University Press, 1958.

Twitchett, D., and John King Fairbank, eds. *The Cambridge History of China*. Vols. 1-3. Cambridge, England: Cambridge University Press, 1986.

Tyler, Rayall, and Robert Boynton. *Japanese Tales*. New York: Pantheon Books, 1989.

Valenstein, Suzanne. *A Handbook of Chinese Ceramics*. New York: Metropolitan Museum of Art, 1975.

Van der Sprenkel, Otto P. N. *Berkelbach: Pan Piao, Pan Ku, and the Han History*. Canberra: Australian National University, 1964.

Walls, Jan, and Yvonne Walls, eds. and trans. *Classical Chinese Myths*. Hong Kong: Joint Publishing, 1984.

Wang, Hsiao-po, and Leo S. Chang. *The Philosophical Foundations of Han Fei's Political Theory*. Honolulu: University of Hawaii Press, 1986.

Watson, William. *The Arts of China to* A.D. *900.* New Haven, Conn.: Yale University Press, 1995.

Wenqing, Wang. *Ten Major Museums of Shaanxi.* Hong Kong: Polyspring, 1994.

Whitfield, Roderick, and Anne Farrer. *Caves of the Thousand Buddhas: Chinese Art from the Silk Route.* New York: George Brazillier, 1990.

Wright, Arthur F. *The Sui Dynasty.* New York: Alfred A. Knopf, 1978.

Yi, Do-Hak. *Rewriting Paekche History.* Seoul: Purunyuksa, 1997.

Yi, Hyun-Hye. *Production and Trade of the Ancient Korea.* Seoul: Ilchogak, 1998.

Yim, Byung-Tae. *The Study of Korean Bronze Age Culture.* Seoul: Hakyunmunwhasa, 1996.

Yu, Ying-Shih. *Trade and Expansion in Han China: A Study in the Structure of Sino-Barbarian Economic Relations.* Berkeley: University of California Press, 1967.

Yu Jin. *The Great Wall.* Beijing: Cultural Relics Publishing House, 1980.

EGYPT

Books dealing with ancient Egypt from the Pharaonic period through the Arabic invasion. Users should also consult the material on Nubia in the Africa category for material dealing with Nubian rule of Late Kingdom Egypt.

Aldred, Cyril. *Akhenaten: King of Egypt.* London: Thames and Hudson, 1988.

———. *The Egyptians.* London: Thames and Hudson, 1998.

Allan, Tony, Michael Kerrigan, and Charles Phillips. *Realm of the Sun.* Alexandria, Va.: Time/Life Books, 1999.

Allen, Thomas G. *The Egyptian Book of the Dead.* Chicago: University of Chicago Press, 1974.

Ames, D., trans. *Egyptian Mythology.* New York: Tudor Publishing Company, 1965.

Andrews, C. *The Rosetta Stone.* London: British Museum, 1981.

Andrews, Carol, ed. *The Ancient Egyptian Book of the Dead.* Austin: University of Texas Press, 1990.

Arnold, Dorothea. *The Royal Women of Amarna: Images of Beauty from Ancient Egypt.* New York: Metropolitan Museum of Art, 1996.

Bagnall, R. S. *Egypt in Late Antiquity.* Princeton, N.J.: Princeton University Press, 1993.

Baines, J., and J. Malek. *Atlas of Ancient Egypt.* Oxford, England: Oxford University Press, 1982.

Bard, Kathryn A., and Stephen Blake Shubert, eds. *Encyclopedia of the Archaeology of Ancient Egypt.* London: Routledge, 1999.

Bowman, A. K. *Egypt After the Pharaohs, 332* B.C.-A.D. *642: From Alexander to the Arab Conquest.* Berkeley: University of California Press, 1986.

Breasted, James Henry. *Ancient Records of Egypt: Historical Documents from the Earliest Times to the Persian Conquest.* Chicago: University of Chicago Press, 1906-1907.

Brugsch-Bey, Heinrich. *Egypt Under the Pharaohs.* London: Bracken Books, 1996.

Budge, E. A. *The Rosetta Stone in the British Museum.* London: Religious Tract Society, 1929.

Capel, Anne K., and Glenn E. Markoe. *Mistress of the House, Mistress of Heaven: Women in Ancient Egypt.* Cincinnati: Hudson Hills/Cincinnati Art Museum, 1997.

Cerny, Jaroslav. *Ancient Egyptian Religion.* London: Hutchinson's University Library, 1952. Reprint. New York: Greenwood Press, 1979.

Clark, Robert T. *Myth and Symbol in Ancient Egypt.* New York: Grove Press, 1960.

Clayton, Peter A. *Chronicle of the Pharaohs: The Reign-by-Reign Record of the Rulers and Dynasties of Ancient Egypt.* New York: Thames and Hudson, 1998.

Daly, M.W., ed. *The Cambridge History of Egypt.* 2 vols. Cambridge, England: Cambridge University Press, 1998.

David, Rosalie. *The Experience of Ancient Egypt.* New York: Routledge, 2000.

David, Rosalie, and Antony E. David. *A Biographical Dictionary of Ancient Egypt.* London: Seaby Publications, 1993.

Desroches-Noblecourt, Christiane. *Tutankhamen: Life and Death of a Pharaoh.* New York: Penguin, 1989.

Edwards, I. E. S. *The Pyramids of Egypt.* London: Penguin Books, 1993.

El-Abbadi, Mostafa. *The Life and Fate of the Ancient Library of Alexandria.* Paris: UNESCO, 1990.

Ellis, Walter M. *Ptolemy of Egypt.* New York: Routledge, 1994.

Empereur, Jean-Yves. *Alexandria Rediscovered*. Translated by Margaret Maehler. London: British Museum Press, 1998.

Erman, Adolf. *The Literature of the Ancient Egyptians*. Translated by Aylward M. Blackman. London: Methuen, 1927. Reprint. New York: Arno, 1977.

Flamarian, Edith. *Cleopatra: The Life and Death of a Pharaoh*. New York: Harry N. Abrams, 1997.

Forty, Jo. *Ancient Egyptian Pharaohs*. North Dighton, Mass.: J G Press, 1998.

Foss, Michael. *The Search for Cleopatra*. New York: Arcade Publishing, 1997.

Frankfort, Henri. *Ancient Egyptian Religion*. New York: Harper & Row, 1961.

Frazer, Peter M. *Ptolemaic Alexandria*. Oxford, England: Clarendon Press, 1972.

Gardiner, Alan. *Egypt of the Pharaohs*. London: Oxford University Press, 1961.

_____. *The Kadesh Inscriptions of Ramesses II*. London: Oxford University Press, 1960.

Grimal, Nicolas. *A History of Ancient Egypt*. Translated by Ian Shaw. New York: Barnes & Noble, 1997.

Harris, J. R. *The Legacy of Egypt*. 2d ed. Oxford, England: The Clarendon Press, 1971.

Hart, George. *Egyptian Myths*. Austin: University of Texas Press, 1990.

Healy, Mark. *Armies of the Pharaohs*. London: Osprey, 2000.

Hoffman, Michael A. *Egypt Before the Pharaohs: The Prehistoric Foundations of Egyptian Civilization*. New York: Alfred A. Knopf, 1991.

Hornung, Erik. *The Ancient Egyptian Books of the Afterlife*. Ithaca, N.Y.: Cornell University Press, 1999.

Howe, Kathleen Stewart. *Excursions along the Nile: The Photographic Discovery of Ancient Egypt*. Albuquerque, N.Mex.: Santa Barbara Museum of Art, 1994.

Ions, Veronica. *Egyptian Mythology*. Rev. ed. New York: Peter Bedrick Books, 1982.

Johnson, Paul. *The Civilization of Ancient Egypt*. New York: HarperCollins, 1999.

Kemp, B. J. *Ancient Egypt: Anatomy of a Civilization*. New York: Alfred A. Knopf, 1989.

Lehner, Mark. *The Complete Pyramids*. London: Thames and Hudson, 1997.

Lesko, Barbara. *The Goddesses of Egypt*. Norman: University of Oklahoma Press, 1999.

Lewis, N. *Greeks in Ptolemaic Egypt: Case Studies in the Social History of the Hellenistic World*. Oxford, England: Clarendon Press, 1986.

_____. *Life in Egypt Under Roman Rule*. Oxford, England: Clarendon Press, 1983.

Lurker, Manfred. *Gods and Symbols of Ancient Egypt*. Translated by Barbara Cummings. London: Thames and Hudson, 1980.

Mendelssohn, Kurt. *Riddle of the Pyramids*. New York: Praeger, 1974.

Menu, Bernadette. *Ramesses II: Greatest of the Pharaohs*. New York: Harry N. Abrams, 1999.

Moran, W. L. *The Amarna Letters*. Baltimore: Johns Hopkins University Press, 1992.

Morenz, Siegfried. *Egyptian Religion*. Translated by Ann E. Keep. London: Methuen, 1973.

Pinch, Geraldine. *Magic in Ancient Egypt*. Austin: University of Texas Press, 1995.

Quirke, Stephen. *Ancient Egyptian Religion*. London: British University Press, 1992.

Redford, Donald B. *Akhenaten: The Heretic King*. Princeton, N.J.: Princeton University Press, 1984.

Reeves, Nicholas. *The Complete Tutankhamun: The King, the Tomb, the Royal Treasure*. London: Thames and Hudson, 1990.

Reeves, Nicholas, and Richard Wilkinson. *The Complete Valley of the Kings*. London: Thames and Hudson, 1996.

Rice, Michael. *Who's Who in Ancient Egypt*. London: Routledge, 1999.

Robins, Gay. *The Art of Ancient Egypt*. Cambridge, Mass.: Harvard University Press, 1997.

_____. *Proportion and Style in Ancient Egyptian Art*. Austin: University of Texas Press, 1994.

_____. *Women in Ancient Egypt*. Cambridge, Mass.: Harvard University Press, 1993.

Rousseau, P. *Pachomius: The Making of a Community in Fourth-Century Egypt*. Berkeley: University of California Press, 1985.

Rundle, Clark, R. J. *Myth and Symbol in Ancient Egypt*. London: Thames & Hudson, 1959.

Schmidt, John D. *Ramesses II: A Chronological Structure for His Reign*. Baltimore: Johns Hopkins University Press, 1973.

Shaw, Ian, and Paul Nicholson. *Dictionary of Ancient Egypt*. New York: Harry Abrams, 1995.

Siliotti, Alberto. *Egypt: Splendor of an Ancient Civilization*. New York: Thames and Hudson, 1994.

_____. *Guide to the Pyramids of Egypt*. New York: Barnes & Noble, 1997.

Silverman, David, ed. *Ancient Egypt*. New York: Oxford University Press, 1997.

Simpson, William Kelly, ed. *The Literature of Ancient Egypt*. New Haven, Conn.: Yale University Press, 1972.

Smith, W. S. *The Art and Architecture of Ancient Egypt*. Rev. ed. Harmondsworth, England: Penguin Books, 1981.

Stierlin, Henri. *The Pharaohs' Master Builders*. Paris: Editions Pierre Terrail, 1995.

Thompson, D. J. *Memphis Under the Ptolemies*. Princeton, N.J.: Princeton University Press, 1988.

Trigger, B. G., et al. *Ancient Egypt: A Social History.*

Cambridge, England: Cambridge University Press, 1983.

Tyldesley, Joyce. *Hatchepsut: The Female Pharaoh*. New York: Penguin Books, 1996.

Van Seters, J. *The Hyksos: A New Investigation*. New Haven, Conn.: Yale University Press, 1966.

Wells, Evelyn. *Hatshepsut*. Garden City, N.Y.: Doubleday, 1969.

Wilkinson, Richard H. *The Complete Temples of Ancient Egypt*. London: Thames & Hudson, 2000.

Wilson, John A. *The Culture of Ancient Egypt*. Chicago: University of Chicago Press, 1956.

EUROPE

The focus of this category is generally Europe except for Greece and Rome. Many entries deal with northern Europe, especially the Celts, and including Roman Britain.

Aini, Ranjanen. *Of Finnish Ways*. Minneapolis: Dillon Press, 1981.

Alcock, Leslie. *Arthur's Britain*. Baltimore: Penguin, 1982.

Astell, Ann W. *Job, Boethius, and Epic Truth*. Ithaca, N.Y.: Cornell University Press, 1994.

Birley, R. E. *Vindolanda: A Roman Frontier Post on Hadrian's Wall*. London: Thames and Hudson, 1977.

Blair, Peter. *An Introduction to Anglo-Saxon England*. 2d ed. Cambridge, England: Cambridge University Press, 1995.

———. *Roman Britain and Early England: 55 B.C.- A.D. 871*. New York: W. W. Norton, 1963.

Bowman, A. K., and I. D. Thomas. *Vindolanda: The Latin Writing Tablets*. London: Society for the Promotion of Roman Studies, 1983.

Bradley, Ian. *Columba, Pilgrim and Penitent*. Glasgow, Scotland: Wild Goose, 1996.

Braund, David. *Ruling Roman Britain*. New York: Routledge, 1996.

Brehaut, Ernest. *An Encyclopedist of the Dark Ages: Isidore of Seville*. 1912. Reprint. New York: B. Franklin Reprints, 1971.

Burns, Thomas S. *A History of the Ostrogoths*. Bloomington: Indiana University Press, 1991.

Campbell, James, ed. *The Anglo-Saxons*. New York: Penguin Books, 1982.

Carver, Martin, ed. *The Age of Sutton Hoo*. Rochester, N.Y.: Boydell Press, 1992.

Chadwick, Henry. *Priscillian of Avila: The Occult and the Charismatic in the Early Church*. Oxford, England: Clarendon Press, 1976.

Christie, Neil. *The Lombards*. Malden, Mass.: Blackwell, 1998.

Clancy, Thomas, and Gilbert Markus. *Iona: The Earliest Poetry of a Celtic Monastery*. Edinburgh, Scotland: Edinburgh University Press, 1995.

Collins, John. *The European Iron Age*. New York: Routledge, 1997.

Collins, Roger. *Early Medieval Spain*. London: Macmillan, 1995.

Conte, Francis. *The Slavs*. Boulder: East European Monographs, 1995.

Cummins, W. A. *The Picts and Their Symbols*. Phoenix Mill, England: Sutton Publishing, 1999.

Cunliffe, Barry. *The Ancient Celts*. Oxford, England: Oxford University Press, 1997.

Darvill, Timothy, and Julian Thomas, eds. *Neolithic Houses in Northwest Europe and Beyond*. Oxbow Monograph 57. Oxford, England: Oxbow Books, 1996.

Deansely, Margaret. *Augustine of Canterbury*. 2d ed. Southampton, England: Saint Austin Press, 1997.

De Blâacam, Aodh. *A First Book of Irish Literature*. Dublin: Educational Company of Ireland, 1934. Reprint. Port Washington, N.Y.: Kennikat Press, 1970.

Derry, T. K. *A History of Scandinavia*. Minneapolis: University of Minnesota Press, 1979.

Dillon, Myles. *Early Irish Literature*. Chicago: University of Chicago Press, 1948.

Dolukhanov, Pavel M. *The Early Slavs: Eastern Europe from the Initial Settlement to the Kievan Rus*. New York: Longman, 1996.

Drinkwater, J., and H. Elton, eds. *Fifth Century Gaul: A Crisis of Identity?* New York: Cambridge University Press, 1992.

Dyer, James. *Ancient Britain*. London: B. T. Batsford, 1990.

Ellis, Peter Beresford. *The Celtic Empire*. Durham, N.C.: Carolina Academic Press, 1990.

————. *Celtic Women*. Grand Rapids, Mich.: Wm. B. Eerdmans, 1995.

Eluere, Christine. *The Celts: Conquerors of Ancient Europe*. New York: Harry N. Abrams, 1993.

Evans, Angela C. *The Sutton Hoo Ship Burial*. London: British Museum Press, 1986.

Farmer, David Hugh, ed. *Butler's Lives of the Saints: May*. Rev. ed. Collegeville, Minn.: Liturgical Press, 1996.

Farrell, Robert T., and Carol Neuman de Vegvar, eds. *The Sutton Hoo Ship Burial: Fifty Years After*. Oxford, Ohio: American Early Medieval Studies, 1992.

Fauber, Lawrence. *Narses: The Hammer of the Goths*. New York: St. Martin's Press, 1990.

Fisher, Katherine Drew. *The Lombard Laws*. Philadelphia: University of Pennsylvania Press, 1973.

Flanagan, Laurence. *Ancient Ireland: Life Before the Celts*. New York: St. Martin's, 1998.

Foster, Sally M. *Picts, Gaels, and Scots: Early Historic Scotland*. London: B. T. Batsford, 1996.

Freeze, Gregory L., ed. *Russia: A History*. New York: Oxford University Press, 1997.

Frere, S. *Britannia: A History of Roman Britain*. New York: Routledge and Kegal Paul, 1987.

Fry, Peter, and Fiona Somerset Fry. *A History of Ireland*. New York: Barnes & Noble, 1993.

Gantz, Jeffrey, trans. *Early Irish Myths and Sagas*. New York: Dorset Press, 1981.

Gaski, Harald, ed. *Sami Culture in a New Era: The Norwegian Sami Experience*. Seattle: University of Washington Press, 1998.

Geary, Patrick J. *Before France and Germany: The Creation and Transformation of the Merovingian World*. New York: Oxford University Press, 1988.

Gies, Frances, and Joseph Gies. *Women in the Middle Ages*. New York: Harcourt, Brace, 1978.

Godja, Martin. *The Ancient Slavs: Settlement and Society*. Edinburgh, Scotland: Edinburgh University, 1991.

Goffart, Walter. *Narrators of Barbarian History*. Princeton, N.J.: Princeton University Press, 1988.

Golab, Zbigniew. *The Origins of the Slavs: A Linguist's View*. Columbus, Ohio: Slavica, 1992.

Goodrich, Norma Lorre. *King Arthur*. New York: Harper & Row, 1986.

Gordon, C. D. *The Age of Attila*. New York: Dorset Press, 1992.

Grabois, Aryeh. *The Illustrated Encyclopedia of Medieval Civilization*. New York: Mayflower Books, 1980.

Green, Miranda J. *Celtic Myths*. Austin: University of Texas Press, 1993.

————. *The Celtic World*. New York: Routledge, 1996.

————. *The Gods of the Celts*. Totowa, N.J.: Barnes and Noble Books, 1986.

Griffen, Toby D. *Names from the Dawn of British Legend: Taliesin, Anerin, Myrddinl, Merlin, Arthur*. Wales: Llanerch, 1994.

Grohskoph, Bernice. *The Treasure of Sutton Hoo*. New York: Athenaeum, 1970.

Gwatkin, H. M., et al. *Germany and the Western Empire*. Vol. 3 in *The Cambridge Medieval History*. Cambridge, England: Cambridge University Press, 1964.

Harrison, Richard J. *Spain at the Dawn of History*. London: Thames and Hudson, 1988.

Hayman, Richard. *Riddles in Stone: Myths, Archaeology and the Ancient Britons*. London: Hambledon Press, 1997.

Heather, P. J. *The Goths*. Malden, Mass.: Blackwell Publishing, 1997.

————. *Goths and Romans, 332-489*. New York: Oxford University Press, 1991.

Hill, David. *An Atlas of Anglo-Saxon England*. Toronto: University of Toronto Press, 1981.

Hitchcock, F. R. M. *Irenaeus of Lugdunum*. Cambridge, England: Cambridge University Press, 1914.

Hodder, Ian. *The Domestication of Europe: Structure and Contingency in Neolithic Societies*. Cambridge, Mass.: Basil Blackwell, 1990.

Holmes, Michael. *King Arthur: A Military History*. New York: Barnes & Noble, 1998.

Humphreys, Emyr. *The Taliesin Tradition: A Quest for the Welsh Identity*. London: Black Raven Press, 1983. 2d ed. Brigend, Wales: Seren, 2000.

Isidore of Seville. *Isidore of Seville's History of the Goths, Vandals, and Suevi*. Translated by G. Donini and G. B. Ford. Leiden, Netherlands: E. J. Brill, 1970.

James, E. *The Origins of France from Clovis to the Capetians*. New York: St. Martin's Press, 1982.

James, Edward. *The Franks*. Oxford, England: Blackwell, 1991.

James, Simon. *The World of the Celts*. New York: Thames and Hudson, 1993.

Jimenez, Ramon L. *Caesar Against the Celts*. Staplehurst, England: Spellmount, 1996.

Kaster, R. A. *Guardians of Language: The Grammarian and Society in Late Antiquity.* Reprint. Berkeley: University of California Press, 1997.

Kiszely, I. *The Anthropology of the Lombards.* British Archaeological Reports, International Series 61. 2 vols. Oxford, England: Oxford University Press, 1979.

Kivikoski, Ella. *Ancient Peoples and Places: Finland.* New York: Praeger, 1967.

Koch, John T. *The Gododdin of Aneirin: Text and Context from Dark Age North Britain.* Andover, Mass.: Celtic Studies, 1997.

Lacaze, Charlotte. *The Vie de St. Denis Manuscript.* New York: Garland, 1979.

Laing, Lloyd, and Jennifer Laing. *Anglo-Saxon England.* New York: Charles Scribner's Sons, 1979.

Lawrence, C. H. *Medieval Monasticism: Forms of Religious Life in Western Europe in the Middle Ages.* 2d ed. New York: Longman, 1989.

Lawrence, John. *A History of Russia.* 7th ed. New York: Meridian, 1993.

Lawson, J. *The Biblical Theology of St. Irenaeus.* London: Epworth, 1948.

Lienhard, J. *Paulinus of Nola and Early Western Monasticism.* Cologne, Germany: Peter Hanstein Verlag, 1977.

McBrien, Richard. *Lives of the Popes.* San Francisco: HarperCollins, 1997.

MacCana, Proinsias. *Celtic Mythology.* Rev. ed. New York: Peter Bedrick Books, 1985.

McNamara, Jo Ann, et al. *Sainted Women of the Dark Ages.* Durham, N.C.: Duke University Press, 1992.

Mänchen-Helfen, Otto. *The World of the Huns.* Berkeley: University of California Press, 1973.

Matthews, Caitlín, and John Matthews. *Guide to British and Irish Mythology.* Wellingborough: The Aquarian Press, 1988.

Matthews, John, ed. *An Arthurian Reader.* Wellingborough: The Aquarian Press, 1988.

Maxwell-Stuart, P. G. *Chronicle of the Popes.* New York: Thames and Hudson, 1997.

Moody, T. W., and F. X. Martin, eds. *The Course of Irish History.* Rev. and enlarged edition. Dublin, Ireland: Mercier Press, 1994.

Moorhead, John. *Theoderic in Italy.* Oxford, England: Clarendon Press, 1992.

Moscati, Sabatino. *The Celts.* New York: Rizzoli, 1991.

Murphy, Gerald. *Sage and Myth in Ancient Ireland.* Dublin: Colm O Lochlainn, 1955.

Musset, Lucien. *The Germanic Invasions: The Making of Europe* A.D. *400-600.* University Park: Pennsylvania State University Press, 1975.

Myres, J. N. L. *The English Settlements.* Oxford, England: Oxford University Press, 1986.

O'Faolain, Eileen. *Irish Sagas and Folk Tales.* Oxford, England: Oxford University Press, 1954.

O'Hogain, Daithi. *Celtic Warriors: The Armies of One of the First Great Peoples in Europe.* New York: St. Martin's Press, 1999.

O'Rahilly, Thomas F. *Early Irish History and Mythology.* Dublin: Dublin Institute for Advanced Studies, 1946.

Paul, the Deacon. *History of the Lombards.* Translated by W. D. Foulke. Philadelphia: University of Pennsylvania Press, 1974.

Pierson, Peter. *The History of Spain.* Westport, Conn.: Greenwood Press, 1999.

Piggott, Stuart. *Ancient Europe: From the Beginnings of Agriculture to Classical Antiquity.* Chicago: Aldine, 1968.

Potter, T. W. *Roman Britain.* Cambridge, Mass.: Harvard University Press, 1997.

Randers-Pehrson, Justine Davis. *Barbarians and Romans: The Birth Struggle of Europe,* A.D. *400-700.* Norman: University of Oklahoma Press, 1983.

Rankin, H. D. *Celts and the Classical World.* London: Routledge, 1995.

Richardson, J. S. *Hispaniae, Spain, and the Development of Roman Imperialism, 218-82* B.C. Cambridge, England: Cambridge University Press, 1986.

Rivet, A. L. F. *Gallia Narbonensis.* London: B. T. Batsford, 1988.

Rolleston, Thomas William. *Celtic Myths and Legends.* London: George G. Harrap, 1917. Reprint. New York: Avenel Books, 1985.

Ross, Anne. *Druids, Gods and Heroes from Celtic Mythology.* New York: Schocken Books, 1986.

Salway, Peter. *The Oxford Illustrated History of Roman Britain.* Oxford, England: Oxford University Press, 1993.

_____. *Roman Britain.* Oxford, England: Oxford University Press, 1981.

Scherman, Katherine. *The Flowering of Ireland: Saints, Scholars, and Kings.* Boston: Little, Brown and Company, 1981.

Sellner, Edward. *Wisdom of the Celtic Saints.* Notre Dame, Ind.: Ave Maria Press, 1993.

Shanzer, D. *A Philosophical and Literary Commentary on Martianus Capella's De Nuptiis Philologiae et Mercurii.* Berkeley: University of California Press, 1986.

Sherratt, Andrew. *Economy and Society in Prehistoric Europe: Changing Perspectives*. Princeton, N.J.: Princeton University Press, 1997.

Simpson, W. Douglas. *The Historical St. Columba*. Edinburgh, Scotland: Oliver and Boyd, 1963.

Sjoestedt, Marie-Louise. *Gods and Heroes of the Celts*. Translated by Myles Dillon. Berkeley: Turtle Island Foundation, 1982.

Slupecki, Leszek P. *Slavonic Pagan Sanctuaries*. Warsaw: Polish Academy of Sciences, 1994.

Stancliffe, Clare. *St. Martin and His Hagiographer: History and Miracle in Sulpicius Severus*. New York: Oxford University Press, 1983.

Stenton, F. M. *Anglo-Saxon England*. 3d ed. Oxford, England: Clarendon Press, 1971.

Stewart, Columbia. *Cassian the Monk*. Oxford, England: University Press, 1998.

Sutherland, Elizabeth. *In Search of the Picts: A Celtic Dark Age Nation*. London: Constable, 1994.

Tabacco, Giovanni. *The Struggle for Power in Medieval Italy*. Cambridge, England: Cambridge University Press, 1989.

Thompson, E. A. *The Huns*. Oxford, England: Blackwell, 1996.

Tilley, Christopher Y. *An Ethnography of the Neolithic: Early Prehistoric Societies in Southern Scandinavia*. New York: Cambridge University Press, 1996.

Todd, Malcom. *The Early Germans*. Oxford, England: Blackwell, 1992.

———. *The Northern Barbarians: 100* B.C.-A.D. *300*. Rev. ed. Oxford, England: Blackwells, 1987.

———. *Roman Britain*. 3d. ed. Oxford, England: Blackwell, 1999.

Trout, D. *Paulinus of Nola: Life, Letters, and Poems*. Berkeley: University of California Press, 1999.

Turner, P. F. J. *The Real King Arthur*. Alaska: SKS, 1993.

Van Dam, Raymond. *Saints and Their Miracles in Late Antique Gaul*. Princeton, N.J.: Princeton University Press, 1993.

Vitebsky, Piers. *The Saami of Lapland*. Austin, Tex.: Raintree Steck-Vaughn, 1994.

Webster, G. *Rome Against Caratacus: The Roman Campaigns in Britain,* A.D. *48-58*. London: B. T. Batsford, 1981.

Welch, Martin. *Discovering Anglo-Saxon England*. University Park: Pennsylvania State University Press, 1992.

Wells, Peter S. *Rural Economy in the Early Iron Age: Excavations at Hascherkeller, 1978-1981*. Cambridge, Mass.: Harvard University Press, 1983.

Wernick, Robert. *The Monument Builders*. New York: Time-Life, 1973.

Whitelock, Dorothy. *The Beginnings of English Society*. Baltimore: Penguin Books, 1966.

Whittle, Alasdair. *Europe in the Neolithic: The Creation of New Worlds*. New York: Cambridge University Press, 1996.

Wickham, Chris. *Early Medieval Italy*. Totowa, N.J.: Barnes & Noble, 1981.

Williams, Ann. *Kingship and Government in Pre-Conquest England, c. 500-1066*. London: Macmillan, 1999.

Williams, Ifor. *The Beginnings of Welsh Poetry*. Cardiff: University of Wales Press, 1972.

Wolf, Keneth B., ed. *Conquerors and Chroniclers of Early Medieval Spain*. Liverpool, England: Liverpool University Press, 1990.

Wolfram, Herwig. *History of the Goths*. Translated by Thomas J. Dunlap. Rev. ed. Berkeley: University of California Press, 1988.

Wood, Carol L. *An Overview of Welsh Poetry Before the Norman Conquest*. New York: Edward Mellen Press, 1996.

Wood, Ian. *The Merovingian Kingdoms, 450-751*. London: Longman, 1994.

GREECE

Includes not only the civilizations of mainland Greece but also the Minoan civilization, Ionian Greece, Magna Graecia (in southern Italy and Sicily), and the Byzantine Empire. For Hellenistic Egypt, however, see Egypt.

Alderink, L. J. *Creation and Salvation in Ancient Orphism*. Ann Arbor, Mich.: Scholars Press, 1981.

Allbutt, T. Clifford. *Greek Medicine in Rome*. London: Macmillan, 1921.

Altay, A. Selahaddin. *St. Sophia*. Istanbul: Basimevi Koll.Sti, 1978.

Anderson, Graham. *The Second Sophistic*. New York: Routledge, 1993.

Anderson, Warren D. *Music and Musicians in Ancient Greece*. Ithaca, N.Y.: Cornell University Press, 1995.

Andrewes, A. *The Greek Tyrants*. London: Hutchinson, 1956.

Artmann, Benno. *Euclid: The Creation of Mathematics.* New York: Springer, 1999.

Ashley, James. *The Macedonian Empire.* Jefferson, N.C.: McFarland, 1998.

Asmis, E. *Epicurus' Scientific Method.* Ithaca, N.Y.: Cornell University Press, 1983.

Bailey, Cyril. *The Greek Atomists and Epicuris.* New York: Russell and Russell, 1964.

Balmer, Josephine. *Classical Woman Poets.* Newcastle-upon-Tyne, England: Bloodaxe Books, 1996.

Barber, G. *Daphnis and Chloe: The Markets and Metamorphoses of an Unknown Bestseller.* London: British Library, 1989.

Barber, R. L. N. *The Cyclades in the Bronze Age.* Iowa City: University of Iowa Press, 1987.

Barker, Andrew. *The Musician and His Art.* Vol. 1 in *Greek Musical Writings.* Cambridge, England: Cambridge University Press, 1984.

Barnard, L. *Justin Martyr: His Life and Thought.* Cambridge, England: Cambridge University Press, 1967.

Barnes, Jonathan. *Aristotle and His Philosophy.* Chapel Hill: University of North Carolina Press, 1982.

_____. *Logic and the Imperial Stoa.* New York: E. J. Brill, 1997.

_____, ed. *The Cambridge Companion to Aristotle.* Cambridge, England: Cambridge University Press, 1995.

Barnes, T. D. *Athanasius and Constantius: Theology and Politics in the Constantinian Empire.* Cambridge, Mass.: Harvard University Press, 1993.

Barrow, R. H. *Plutarch and His Times.* Bloomington: Indiana University Press, 1967.

Bartsch, Shadi. *Decoding the Ancient Novel: The Reader and the Role of Description in Heliodorus and Achilles Tatius.* Princeton, N.J.: Princeton University Press, 1989.

Baynham, E. *Alexander the Great: The Unique History of Quintus Curtius.* Ann Arbor: University of Michigan Press, 1998.

Beazley, John Davidson. *Attic Red-Figure Vase-Painters.* Oxford, England: Clarendon Press, 1963.

_____. *Paralipomena.* Oxford, England: Clarendon Press, 1971.

Behr, C. A. *Aelius Aristides and the Sacred Tales.* Amsterdam, Netherlands: Hakkert, 1968.

Belcer, Jack Martin. *The Persian Conquest of the Greeks.* Konstanz, Germany: Universitatsverlag Konstanz, 1995.

Bell, Robert E. *Dictionary of Classical Mythology.* Santa Barbara, Calif.: ABC-Clio, 1982.

_____. *Women of Classical Mythology.* Santa Barbara, Calif.: ABC-Clio, 1991.

Beye, Charles Rowan. *Ancient Epic Poetry.* Ithaca, N.Y.: Cornell University Press, 1993.

_____. *Epic and Romance in the Argonautica of Apollonius.* Carbondale: Southern Illinois University Press, 1982.

Biers, William R. *The Archaeology of Greece: An Introduction.* 2d ed. Ithaca, N.Y.: Cornell University Press, 1996.

Billows, Richard A. *Antigonos the One-Eyed and the Creation of the Hellenistic State.* Berkeley: University of California Press, 1990.

Birchall, Ann, and P. E. Corbett. *Greek Gods and Heroes.* London: Trustees of the British Museum, 1974.

Blake Tyrrell, William, and Frieda S. Brown. *Athenian Myths and Institutions: Words in Action.* New York: Oxford University Press, 1991.

Boardman, John. *Athenian Black Figure Vases.* Reprint. New York: Thames and Hudson, 1991.

_____. *Athenian Red Figure Vases: The Classical Period.* New York: Thames and Hudson, 1989.

_____. *Early Greek Vase Painting: 11th-6th Centuries B.C.: A Handbook.* New York: Thames and Hudson, 1998.

_____. *Greek Art.* New York: Thames and Hudson, 1996.

_____, et al. *Greece and the Hellenistic World.* Oxford, England: Oxford University Press, 1988.

Bonhöffer, Adolf Friedrich. *The Ethics of the Stoic Epictetus.* New York: Peter Lang, 1996.

Borza, Eugene M. *In the Shadow of Olympus: The Emergence of Macedon.* Princeton, N.J.: Princeton University Press, 1990.

Bosworth, A. B. *Conquest and Empire: The Reign of Alexander the Great.* Cambridge, England: Cambridge University Press, 1988.

Bowersock, G. W. *Greek Sophists of the Second Century.* Oxford, England: Clarendon Press, 1969.

Bowra, C. M. *Ancient Greek Literature.* New York: Oxford University Press, 1960.

_____. *Sophoclean Tragedy.* Oxford, England: Oxford University Press, 1944.

Bowra, C. M., and T. F. Higham. *The Oxford Book of Greek Verse in Translation.* Oxford, England: Clarendon Press, 1948.

Brakke, D. *Athanasius and the Politics of Asceticism.* Oxford, England: Clarendon Press, 1995.

Branham, R. Bracht, and Marie-Odile Goulet-Caze,

eds. *The Cynics: The Cynic Movement in Antiquity and Its Legacy*. Berkeley: University of California Press, 1996.

Brommer, Frank. *The Sculpture of the Parthenon*. Translated by Mary Whittall. London: Thames and Hudson, 1979.

Brown, Norman O. *Hermes the Thief*. Madison: University of Wisconsin Press, 1947. 2d ed. New York: Random House, 1969.

Browning, Robert. *Justinian and Theodora*. New York: Praeger, 1987.

Bruno, Vincent J. *Form and Color in Greek Painting*. New York: W. W. Norton, 1977.

Bryant, Joseph M. *Moral Codes and Social Structure in Ancient Greece: A Sociology of Greek Ethics from Homer to the Epicureans and Stoics*. Albany: State University of New York Press, 1996.

Buckler, J. *Philip II and the Sacred War*. Leiden, Netherlands: E. J. Brill, 1989.

_____. *The Theban Hegemony, 371-362* B.C.E. Cambridge, Mass.: Harvard University Press, 1980.

Bulfinch, Thomas. *Myths of Greece and Rome*. Edited by Bryan Holme. New York: Penguin, 1979.

Burn, A. R. *The Lyric Age of Greece*. London: Edward Arnold, 1960.

Burn, Lucilla. *Greek Myths*. Austin: University of Texas Press, 1990.

Burnett, Anne Pippin. *The Art of Bacchylides*. Cambridge, Mass.: Harvard University Press, 1985.

Burton, Joan B. *Theocritus's Urban Mimes: Mobility, Gender, and Patronage*. Berkeley: University of California Press, 1995.

Bury, J. B. *The Ancient Greek Historians*. Reprint. New York: Dover, 1958.

Calame, Claude. *The Poetics of Eros in Ancient Greece*. Translated by Janet Lloyd. Princeton, N.J.: Princeton University Press, 1999.

Cameron, Alan. *Callimachus and His Critics*. Princeton, N.J.: Princeton University Press, 1995.

_____. *The Greek Anthology from Meleager to Planudes*. Oxford, England: Clarendon Press, 1993.

Cameron, Averil. *Agathias*. Oxford, England: Clarendon Press, 1970.

_____. *Changing Cultures in Early Byzantium*. Brookfield, Vt.: Variorum, 1996.

_____. *Procopius and the Sixth Century*. New York: Routledge, 1996.

Camp, John M. *The Athenian Agora: Excavations in the Heart of Classical Athens*. London: Thames and Hudson, 1986.

Carawan, Edwin. *Rhetoric and the Law of Draco*. Oxford, England: Oxford University Press, 1998.

Carpenter, Rhys. *The Architects of the Parthenon*. Harmondsworth, England: Penguin Books, 1970.

Cartledge, Paul. *Aristophanes and His Theatre of the Absurd*. London: Bristol Classical Press, 1999.

_____. *The Greeks: Crucible of Civilization*. New York: TV Books, 2000.

_____. *Sparta and Lakonia: A Regional History*. Boston: Routledge & Kegan Paul, 1979.

Caven, Brian. *Dionysius I: War-Lord of Sicily*. New Haven, Conn.: Yale University Press, 1990.

Cawkwell, G. *Philip of Macedon*. Boston: Faber and Faber, 1978.

Chadwick, John. *The Mycenaean World*. Cambridge, England: Cambridge University Press, 1976.

_____. *Reading the Past: Linear B and Related Scripts*. Berkeley: University of California Press, 1997.

Colish, Marcia L. *The Stoic Tradition from Antiquity to the Early Middle Ages*. Leiden, Netherlands: E. J. Brill, 1985.

Conacher, D. J. *Aeschylus: The Earlier Plays and Related Studies*. Toronto: University of Toronto Press, 1996.

Conner, Walter R. *Thucydides*. Princeton, N.J.: Princeton University Press, 1984.

Cook, B. F. *The Elgin Marbles*. London: British Museum Press, 1984.

Crouzel, Henri. *Origen*. Translated by A.S. Worrall. New York: Harper & Row, 1989.

Curd, P. K. *The Legacy of Parmenides: Eleatic Monism and Later Presocratic Thought*. Princeton, N.J.: Princeton University Press, 1998.

Davenport, Guy. *Archilochos, Sappho, Alkman: Three Lyric Poets of the Late Bronze Age*. Berkeley: University of California Press, 1980.

Dawe, R. D. *Sophocles: The Classical Heritage*. New York: Garland, 1996.

Diehl, Charles. *Byzantine Empresses*. New York: Knopf, 1963.

Dijksterhuis, E. J. *Archimedes*. 2d ed. Introduction by Wilbur Knorr. Princeton, N.J.: Princeton University Press, 1987.

Dillery, John. *Xenophon and the History of His Times*. New York: Routledge, 1995.

Dinsmoor, William Bell. *The Architecture of Ancient Greece*. New York: W. W. Norton, 1975.

Doumas, Christos G. *Thera, Pompeii of the Ancient Aegean*. London: Thames and Hudson, 1983.

Dover, K. J. *Aristophanic Comedy.* Berkeley: University of California Press, 1972.

Drees, Ludwig. *Olympia: Gods, Artists, and Athletes.* New York: Praeger, 1968.

Drews, Robert. *The Greek Accounts of Eastern History.* Cambridge, Mass.: Harvard University Press, 1973.

Dreyer, J. L. E. *A History of Astronomy from Thales to Kepler.* New York: Dover Press, 1953.

Drijvers, Jan Willem. *Helena Augusta: The Mother of Constantine the Great and the Legend of Her Finding of the True Cross.* New York: E. J. Brill, 1992.

Durando, Furio. *Ancient Greece: The Dawn of the Western World.* New York: Stewart, Tabori & Chang, 1997.

Easterling, P. E., and B. M. W. Knox, eds. *Greek Literature.* Vol. 1 in *The Cambridge History of Classical Literature.* Cambridge, England: Cambridge University Press, 1985.

Ellis, J. R. *Philip II and Macedonian Imperialism.* London: Thames and Hudson, 1976.

Ellis, Walter M. *Alcibiades.* New York: Routledge, 1989.

Errington, R. Malcolm. *A History of Macedonia.* Berkeley: University of California Press, 1990.

Evans, James A. S. *The Age of Justinian: The Circumstances of Imperial Power.* New York: Routledge, 1996.

————. *Herodotus.* Boston: Twayne, 1982.

Fans, J. A. *The Paradoxes of Zeno.* Brookfield, Vt.: Avebury, 1996.

Farnoux, Alexandre. *Knossos: Searching for the Legendary Palace of King Minos.* Translated by David J. Baker. New York: Harry N. Abrams, 1996.

Finley, M. I. *The Ancient Greeks.* London, England: Penguin Books, 1977.

————, ed. *The Legacy of Greece: A New Appraisal.* Oxford, England: Oxford University Press, 1984.

Fitten, J. Lesley. *The Discovery of the Greek Bronze Age.* Cambridge, Mass.: Harvard University Press, 1996.

Flickinger, Roy C. *The Greek Theater and Its Drama.* 4th ed. Chicago: University of Chicago Press, 1961.

Fontenrose, Joseph. *The Delphic Oracle.* Berkeley: University of California Press, 1978.

————. *Python: A Study of Delphic Myth and Its Origins.* Berkeley and Los Angeles: University of California Press, 1959.

Forde, S. *Ambition to Rule: Alcibiades and the Politics of Imperialism in Thucydides.* Ithaca, N.Y.: Cornell University Press, 1989.

Forrest, W. G. *A History of Sparta.* London: Hutchinson University Library, 1968.

Fouqué, Ferdinand A. *Santorini and Its Eruptions.* Translated and with a new introduction by Alexander R. McBirney. Baltimore: Johns Hopkins University Press, 1998.

Fowler, Barbara Hughes. *The Hellenistic Aesthetic.* Madison: University of Wisconsin Press, 1989.

Fox, Robin. *Alexander the Great.* New York: Penguin, 1994.

Frantz, Alison. *Late Antiquity,* A.D. *267-700.* Vol. 24 in *The Athenian Agora.* Princeton, N.J.: American School of Classical Studies at Athens, 1988.

Freely, John. *Istanbul: The Imperial City.* New York: Penguin Books, 1996.

Freeman, Kathleen. *Ancilla to the Pre-Socratic Philosophers.* Cambridge, Mass.: Harvard University Press, 1983.

Furley, William D. *Andocides and the Hermes: A Study of Crisis in Fifth Century Athenian Religion.* London: Institute of Classical Studies, 1996.

Gabbert, Janice J. *Antigonus II Gonatas: A Political Biography.* New York: Routledge, 1997.

Gagarin, Michael. *Drakon and Early Athenian Homicide Law.* New Haven, Conn.: Yale University Press, 1981.

————. *Early Greek Law.* Berkeley: University of California Press, 1986.

Gallop, D. *Parmenides of Elea.* Toronto: University of Toronto Press, 1984.

Gardner, Ernest A. *Six Greek Sculptors.* New York: Ayer, 1977.

Garland, Robert. *Daily Life of the Ancient Greeks.* Westport, Conn.: Greenwood Press, 1998.

Georgiadou, A., and D. H. J. Larmour. *Lucian's Science Fiction Novel: True Histories.* Leiden, Netherlands: E. J. Brill, 1998.

Gerber, Douglas E., ed. *The Companion to the Greek Lyric Poets.* Leiden, Netherlands: E. J. Brill, 1997.

Gigante, M. *Philodemus in Italy.* Ann Arbor: University of Michigan Press, 1995.

Golden, Mark. *Sport and Society in Ancient Greece.* New York: Cambridge University Press, 1998.

Gorman, Peter. *Pythagoras: A Life.* London: Routledge and Kegan Paul, 1979.

Gould, John. *Herodotus.* New York: St. Martin's Press, 1989.

Grainger, John D. *Seleukos Nikator: Constructing a Hellenistic Kingdom.* New York: Routledge, 1990.

Grant, Michael. *Hellenistic Greeks from Alexander to*

Cleopatra. London: Weidenfeld & Nicolson, 1990.

Grant, R. *Greek Apologists of the Second Century*. Philadelphia, Pa.: Westminster, 1988.

Graves, Robert. *The Greek Myths*. 2 vols. Rev. ed. Baltimore: Penguin, 1960.

Green, Peter. *Alexander to Actium: The Historical Evolution of the Hellenistic Age*. Berkeley: University of California Press, 1993.

_____. *The Greco-Persian Wars*. Berkeley: University of California Press, 1996.

Greer, Rowan A. *Origen*. Mahwah, N.J.: Paulist Press, 1988.

Gribble, D. *Alcibiades and Athens: A Study in Literary Presentation*. Oxford, England: Clarendon Press, 1999.

Griffin, Aubrey. *Sikyon*. Oxford, England: Clarendon Press, 1982.

Gruen, Erich S. *The Hellenistic World and the Coming of Rome*. Berkeley: University of California Press, 1984.

_____. *Heritage and Hellenism*. Berkeley: University of California Press, 1998.

Grundy, G. B. *The Great Persian War*. London: John Murray, 1901.

Guthrie, W. K. C. *A History of Greek Philosophy*. New York: Cambridge University Press, 1978-1990.

_____. *Orpheus and Greek Religion*. Reprint. Princeton, N.J.: Princeton University Press, 1993.

Gutzwiller, Kathryn J. *Theocritus' Pastoral Analogies: The Formation of a Genre*. Madison: University of Wisconsin Press, 1991.

Habicht, Christian. *Athens from Alexander to Antony*. Translated by Deborah Lucas Schneider. Cambridge, Mass.: Harvard University Press, 1999.

Hamilton, Charles D. *Agesilaus and the Failure of Spartan Hegemony*. Ithaca, N.Y.: Cornell University Press, 1991.

_____. *Sparta's Bitter Victories*. Ithaca, N.Y.: Cornell University Press, 1979.

Hammond, Nicholas G. L. *The Genius of Alexander the Great*. Chapel Hill: The University of North Carolina Press, 1997.

_____. *A History of Greece to 322 B.C.* 3d ed. Oxford, England: Oxford University Press, 1986.

_____. *The Miracle That Was Macedonia*. New York: St. Martin's Press, 1991.

_____. *Philip of Macedon*. Baltimore: Johns Hopkins University Press, 1994.

Hammond, Nicholas G. L., and G. T. Griffith. *A History of Macedonia*. Vols. 1-3. Oxford, England: Clarendon Press, 1979.

Hardy, D. A., ed. *Thera and the Agean World III*. London: The Thera Foundation, 1990.

Harris, E. *Aeschines and Athenian Politics*. New York: Oxford University Press, 1995.

Havelock, C. M. *The Aphrodite of Knidos and Her Successors*. Ann Arbor: University of Michigan Press, 1995.

Heath, Thomas L. *Aristarchus of Samos: The Ancient Copernicus*. New York: Clarendon Press, 1913.

Heckel, W. *The Marshals of Alexander's Empire*. London: Routledge, 1992.

Henle, Jane. *Greek Myths: A Vase Painter's Notebook*. Bloomington: Indiana University Press, 1973.

Henry, Madeleine M. *Prisoner of History: Aspasia of Miletus and Her Biographical Tradition*. Oxford, England: Oxford University Press, 1995.

Herington, John. *Aeschylus*. New Haven, Conn.: Yale University Press, 1986.

Higgins, Reynold. *Minoan and Mycenaean Art*. Rev. ed. London: Thames and Hudson, 1997.

Higgins, W. E. *Xenophon the Athenian*. Albany: State University of New York Press, 1977.

Hignett, C. *A History of the Athenian Constitution*. Oxford, England: Oxford University Press, 1952.

Hill, George Francis. *A History of Cyprus*. 4 vols. Cambridge, England: Cambridge University Press, 1940-1952.

Hodkinson, Stephen, and Anton Powell, eds. *Sparta: New Perspectives*. London: Duckworth, 1999.

Hooker, J. T. *The Ancient Spartans*. London: J. M. Dent, 1980.

Hopkinson, Neil, ed. *Studies in the Dionysiaca of Nonnus*. Cambridge, England: Cambridge Philological Society, 1994.

Hornblower, Simon. *Mausolus*. Oxford, England: Oxford University Press, 1982.

_____. *Thucydides*. Baltimore: Johns Hopkins University Press, 1987.

Hunter, R. L. *The Argonautica of Apollonius: Literary Studies*. New York: Cambridge University Press, 1993.

_____. *A Study of Daphnis and Chloe*. New York: Cambridge University Press, 1983.

Hunter, Richard, ed. *Studies in Heliodorus*. Cambridge, England: The Cambridge Philological Society, 1998.

_____. *Theocritus and the Archaeology of Greek Poetry*. Cambridge, England: Cambridge University Press, 1996.

Hurwit, Jeffrey M. *The Athenian Acropolis: History,*

Mythology, and Archaeology from the Neolithic Era to the Present. Cambridge, England: Cambridge University Press, 1999.

Hutchinson, G. O. *Hellenistic Poetry*. Oxford, England: Clarendon Press, 1988.

Huxley, G. L. *The Early Ionians*. London: Faber and Faber, 1966.

————. *Early Sparta*. London: Faber and Faber, 1962.

Inwood, Brad. *Ethics and Human Action in Early Stoicism*. Oxford, England: Clarendon Press, 1985.

Isager, Signe, and Jens Erik Skydsgaard. *Ancient Greek Agriculture: An Introduction*. New York: Routledge, 1995.

Jarratt, Susan. *Rereading the Sophists: Classical Rhetoric Refigured*. Carbondale: Southern Illinois University Press, 1991.

Jeffery, Lillian H. *Archaic Greece: The City-States c. 700-500 B.C.* New York: St. Martin's Press, 1976.

Jeffreys, Elizabeth, Michael Jeffreys, and Roger Scott. *The Chronicle of John Malalas*. Melbourne: Australian Association for Byzantine Studies, 1986.

Jenkins, Ian. *The Parthenon Frieze*. London: British Museum Press, 1994.

Jeppesen, K. *The Maussolleion at Halikarnassos*. Aarhus, Denmark: Aarhus University Press, 1986.

Johnson, F. P. *Lysippos*. Durham, N.C.: Duke University Press, 1927.

Kaegi, W. E., Jr. *Byzantium and the Decline of Rome*. Princeton, N.J.: Princeton University Press, 1968.

Kagan, Donald. *The Archidamian War*. Ithaca, N.Y.: Cornell University Press, 1974.

————. *The Fall of the Athenian Empire*. Ithaca, N.Y.: Cornell University Press, 1987.

Karageorghis, Vassos. *Ancient Cyprus: 7,000 Years of Art and Archaeology*. Baton Rouge: Louisiana State University Press, 1981.

————. *Cyprus: From the Stone Age to the Romans*. New York: Thames and Hudson, 1982.

Karavites, P. *Evil, Freedom, and the Road to Perfection in Clement of Alexandria*. Leiden, Netherlands: E. J. Brill, 1999.

Kelly, J. N. D. *Golden Mouth: The Story of John Chrysostom—Ascetic, Preacher, Bishop*. London: Duckworth, 1995.

Kennedy, G. *The Art of Persuasion in Greece*. Princeton, N.J.: Princeton University Press, 1963.

Kennell, Nigel M. *The Gymnasium of Virtue: Education and Culture in Ancient Sparta*. Chapel Hill: University of North Carolina Press, 1995.

Kincaid, C. A. *Successors of Alexander the Great*. Chicago: Argonaut, 1969.

King, Katherine Callen, ed. *Homer*. New York: Garland, 1994.

Kirk, G. S., J. E. Raven, and M. Schofield. *The Presocratic Philosophers*. 2d ed. Cambridge, England: Cambridge University Press, 1995.

Knoefel, Peter K., and Madeline C. Covi. *A Hellenistic Treatise on Poisonous Animals: The "Theriaca" of Nicander of Colophon, a Contribution to the History of Toxicology*. Lewiston, N.Y.: Edwin Mellen, 1991.

Knorr, Wilbur. *The Evolution of the Euclidean Elements*. Dordrecht, Netherlands: Reidel, 1975.

Kraut, R., ed. *The Cambridge Companion to Plato*. Cambridge, England: Cambridge University Press, 1993.

Krentz, Peter. *The Thirty at Athens*. Ithaca, N.Y.: Cornell University Press, 1982.

Kuhrt, Amélie, and Susan M. Sherwin-White, eds. *Hellenism in the East*. Berkeley: University of California Press, 1987.

Kurtz, Donna Carol. *Athenian White Lekythoi: Patterns and Painters*. Oxford, England: Clarendon Press, 1975.

Larsen, J. A. O. *Greek Federal States: Their Institutions and History*. Oxford, England: Clarendon Press, 1968.

Lazenby, John Francis. *The Defence of Greece, 490-479 B.C.* Warminster, England: Aris & Phillips, 1993.

————. *The Spartan Army*. Warminster, England: Aris & Phillips, 1985.

Lefkowitz, Mary. *The Lives of the Greek Poets*. Baltimore: Johns Hopkins University Press, 1981.

————. *Women in Greek Myth*. Baltimore: The Johns Hopkins University Press, 1986.

Lesher, J. H. *Xenophanes of Colophon*. Toronto: University of Toronto Press, 1992.

Lesky, Albin. *History of Greek Literature*. New York: Crowell, 1966.

Levin, Flora Rose. *The Harmonics of Nicomachus and the Pythagorean Tradition*. University Park, Pa.: American Philological Association, 1975.

Long, A. A. *The Cambridge Companion to Early Greek Philosophy*. Cambridge, England: Cambridge University Press, 1999.

————. *Hellenistic Philosophy, Stoics, Epicureans, Sceptics*. 2d ed. Berkeley: University of California Press, 1986.

————. *Stoic Studies*. Cambridge, England: Cambridge University Press, 1996.

Longrigg, James. *Greek Medicine from the Heroic to the Hellenistic Age*. New York: Routledge, 1998.

————. *Greek Rational Medicine: Philosophy from Alcmaeon to the Alexandrians*. New York: Routledge, 1993.

Lund, H. S. *Lysimachus*. New York: Routledge, 1992.

McCall, Marsh, Jr., ed. *Aeschylus: A Collection of Critical Essays*. Englewood Cliffs, N.J.: Prentice-Hall, 1972.

Macdonald, William L. *The Pantheon: Design, Meaning and Progeny*. Reprint. Cambridge, Mass.: Harvard University Press, 1998.

MacDowell, Douglass M. *Aristophanes and Athens: An Introduction to the Plays*. New York: Oxford University Press, 1995.

McGlew, J. *Tyranny and Political Culture in Ancient Greece*. Ithaca, N.Y.: Cornell University Press, 1993.

MacKendrick, Paul. *The Greek Stones Speak: The Story of Archaeology in Greek Lands*. Toronto: W. W. Norton, 1983.

McKirahan, Richard D., Jr. *Philosophy Before Socrates*. Indianapolis: Hackett, 1994.

MacQueen, B. D. *Myth, Rhetoric, and Fiction: A Reading of Longus's Daphnis and Chloe*. Lincoln: University of Nebraska Press, 1990.

Mango, Cyril. *The Art of the Byzantine Empire, 312-1453: Sources and Documents*. Toronto: University of Toronto Press, 1997.

Marazov, Ivan, ed. *Ancient Gold: The Wealth of the Thracians: Treasures from the Republic of Bulgaria*. New York: Abrams/Trust for Museum Exhibitions, 1998.

Martin, H. *Alcaeus*. New York: Twayne, 1972.

Mastromarco, Giuseppe. *The Public of Herondas*. Amsterdam, Netherlands: J. C. Gieben, 1984.

Mathews, Thomas F. *Byzantium: From Antiquity to the Renaissance*. Upper Saddle River, N.J.: Prentice Hall, 1998.

Mead, G. R. S. *Apollonious of Tyana*. Chicago: Ares, 1980.

Meier, Christian. *Athens: A Portrait of the City in Its Golden Age*. Translated by Robert Kimber and Rita Kimber. New York: Metropolitan Books, 1998.

Metcalf, D. M. *The Origins of the Anastasian Currency Reform*. Amsterdam, Netherlands: Hakkert, 1969.

Metropolitan Museum of Art. *Greek Art of the Aegean Islands*. New York: The Metropolitan Museum of Art, 1979.

Michelini, Ann Norris. *Euripides and the Tragic Tradition*. Madison: University of Wisconsin Press, 1987.

Missiou, Anna. *The Subversive Oratory of Andocides*. Cambridge, England: Cambridge University Press, 1992.

Mitsis, P. *Epicurus' Ethical Theory*. Ithaca, N.Y.: Cornell University Press, 1988.

Moon, Warren G., ed. *Polykleitos, the Doryphoros, and Tradition*. Madison: University of Wisconsin Press, 1995.

Moorhead, John. *Justinian*. New York: Longman, 1994.

Mosshammer, Alden A. *The Chronicle of Eusebius and the Greek Chronographic Tradition*. Lewisburg, Pa.: Bucknell University Press, 1979.

Mourelatos, Alexander P. D., ed. *The Pre-Socratics: A Collection of Critical Essays*. Garden City, N.Y.: Doubleday, 1993.

Mulroy, David. *Early Greek Lyric Poetry*. Ann Arbor: University of Michigan Press, 2000.

Munn, Mark. *The School of History: Athens in the Age of Socrates*. Berkeley: University of California Press, 2000.

Murray, Oswyn. *Early Greece*. London: Fontana Press, 1980.

Mussies, G. *Dio Chrysostom and the New Testament*. Leiden, Netherlands: E. J. Brill, 1972.

Myers, John L. *Herodotus: Father of History*. Chicago: H. Regency, 1971.

Mylonas, George E. *Eleusis and the Eleusinian Mysteries*. Princeton, N.J.: Princeton University Press, 1961.

Nagy, Gregory. *Homeric Questions*. Austin: University of Texas Press, 1996.

Nardo, Don, ed. *Readings on Sophocles*. San Diego: Greenhaven Press, 1997.

Nichols, Marianne. *Man, Myth, and Monument*. New York: William Morrow, 1975.

Nilsson, Martin P. *History of Greek Religion*. 2d ed. New York: W. W. Norton, 1964.

————. *The Mycenaean Origin of Greek Mythology*. Berkeley: University of California Press, 1932.

Norris, F. W. *Faith Gives Fullness to Reasoning: The Five Theological Orations of Gregory Nazianzen*. Leiden, Netherlands: E. J. Brill, 1997.

Norwich, John Julius. *Byzantium: The Early Centuries*. New York: Alfred A. Knopf, 1989.

Norwood, Gilbert. *Greek Comedy*. London: Methuen, 1931.

O'Brien, J. M. *Alexander the Great: The Invisible Enemy*. London: Routledge, 1994.

Oliva, P. *Sparta and Her Social Problems*. Amsterdam, Netherlands: Hakkert, 1971.

O'Meara, Dominic J. *Pythagoras Revived: Mathematics and Philosophy in Late Antiquity*. Oxford, England: Clarendon Press, 1989.

Osborne, Robin. *Archaic and Classical Greek Art*. New York: Oxford University Press, 1998.

Otto, Walter Friedrich. *Dionysus: Myth and Cult*. Translated by Robert B. Palmer. Bloomington: University of Indiana Press, 1965.

Owen, Clifford. *The Humanity of Thucydides*. Princeton, N.J.: Princeton University Press, 1994.

Page, D. *Sappho and Alcaeus*. London: Oxford University Press, 1955.

Palagia, Olga, and J. J. Pollitt, eds. *Personal Styles in Greek Sculpture*. Cambridge, England: Cambridge University Press, 1996.

Panteli, Stavros. *A New History of Cyprus, from the Earliest Times to the Present Day*. London: East-West Publications, 1984.

Pearson, L. *Early Ionian Historians*. Oxford, England: Clarendon Press, 1939.

Podlecki, Anthony J. *The Early Greek Poets and Their Times*. Vancouver: University of British Columbia Press, 1984.

_____. *The Political Background of Aeschylean Tragedy*. Ann Arbor: University of Michigan Press, 1966.

Pollitt, J. J. *Art in the Hellenistic Age*. Cambridge, England: Cambridge University Press, 1986.

_____. *The Art of Greece, 1400-31 B.C.: Sources and Documents*. Rev. ed. New York: Cambridge University Press, 1990.

Polter, Paul. *Hippocrates*. Cambridge, Mass.: Harvard University Press, 1995.

Pomeroy, Sarah B., Stanley M. Burstein, Walter Donlan, and Jennifer Tolbert Roberts. *Ancient Greece: A Political, Social, and Cultural History*. New York: Oxford University Press, 1999.

Powell, Anton. *Athens and Sparta*. New York: Routledge, 1996.

_____. *The Greek World*. London: Routledge, 1995.

Pressfield, S. *Gates of Fire: An Epic Novel of the Battle of Thermopylae*. New York: Bantam Books, 1999.

Price, Simon. *Religions of the Ancient Greeks*. Cambridge, England: Cambridge University Press, 1999.

Pritchett, W. K. *Studies in Ancient Greek Topography*. Vol. 2. Berkeley: University of California Press, 1969.

Rankin, H. D. *Archilochus of Paros*. Park Ridge, N.J.: Noyes, 1977.

Rayor, Diane. *Sappho's Lyre: Archaic Lyric Women Poets of Ancient Greece*. Berkeley: University of California Press, 1991.

Reesor, Margaret E. *The Nature of Man in Early Stoic Philosophy*. New York: St. Martin's Press, 1989.

Reger, Gary. *Regionalism and Change in the Economy of Independent Delos*. Berkeley: University of California Press, 1994.

Renfrew, C., and M. Wagstaff, eds. *An Island Polity: The Archaeology of Exploitation on Melos*. Cambridge, England: Cambridge University Press, 1982.

Richardson, N. J. *The Homeric Hymn to Demeter*. Oxford, England: Oxford University Press, 1974.

Ridgway, Brunilde Sismondo. *Fourth-Century Styles in Greek Sculpture*. Madison: The University of Wisconsin Press, 1997.

Rist, John M. *Epicurus: An Introduction*. Cambridge, England: Cambridge University Press, 1972.

_____. *Plotinus: The Road to Reality*. Cambridge, England: Cambridge University Press, 1967.

Roberts, J. W. *The City of Sokrates: An Introduction to Classical Athens*. London: Routledge and Kegan Paul, 1998.

Robertson, Martin. *A History of Greek Art*. 2 vols. New York: Cambridge University Press, 1975.

Robins, R. H. *The Byzantine Grammarians: Their Place in History*. New York: Mouton de Gruyter, 1993.

Romm, James. *Herodotus*. New Haven, Conn.: Yale University Press, 1998.

Rostovzeff, M. *The Social and Economic History of the Hellenistic World*. 3 vols. Oxford, England: Clarendon Press, 1941.

Russo, C. F. *Aristophanes: An Author for the Stage*. New York: Routledge, 1997.

Rutherford, R. B. *Homer*. Oxford, England: Oxford University Press, 1996.

Sacks, David. *Encyclopedia of the Ancient Greek World*. New York: Facts on File, 1995.

Sage, M. M. *Cyprian*. Cambridge, Mass.: Philadelphia Patristic Foundation, 1975.

Salmon, J. B. *Wealthy Corinth*. New York: Oxford University Press, 1984.

Sanders, L. J. *Dionysius I of Syracuse and Greek Tyranny*. New York: Croom Helm, 1987.

Schiappa, Edward. *Protagoras and Logos: A Study in Greek Philosophy and Rhetoric*. Columbia: University of South Carolina Press, 1991.

Scholten, Joseph B. *The Politics of Plunder: Aitolians and their Koinon in the Early Hellenistic Era, 279-217* B.C. Berkeley: University of California Press, 2000.

Sealey, Raphael. *Demosthenes and His Time*. Oxford, England: Oxford University Press, 1982.

———. *A History of the Greek City States*. Berkeley: University of California Press, 1976.

Shanks, Michael. *Art and the Greek City State: An Interpretive Archaeology*. New York: Cambridge University Press, 1999.

Sharples, R. W. *Stoics, Epicureans, and Sceptics*. New York: Routledge, 1996.

Shipley, D. R. *A Commentary on Plutarch's Life of Agesilaos*. Oxford, England: Clarendon Press, 1997.

Shipley, G. *A History of Samos, 800-188* B.C. Oxford, England: Oxford University Press, 1987.

Smith, John Clark. *The Ancient Wisdom of Origen*. Cranberry, N.J.: Bucknell University Press, 1992.

Spatz, Lois. *Aeschylus*. Boston: Twayne, 1982.

Sprague, Rosamond Kent, ed. *The Older Sophists*. Columbia: University of South Carolina Press, 1972.

Stadter, Philip. *Arrian of Nicomedia*. Chapel Hill: University of North Carolina Press, 1980.

Stein, Sherman. *Archimedes: What Did He Do Besides Cry Eureka?* Washington, D.C.: Mathematical Association of America, 1999.

Stewart, Andrew F. *Greek Sculpture*. New Haven, Conn.: Yale University Press, 1990.

———. *Skopas of Paros*. Park Ridge, N.J.: Noyes Press, 1977.

Stierling, Henry. *The Pantheon*. Vol. I in *The Roman Empire*. Cologne, Germany: Taschen, 1996.

Stockton, D. *The Classical Athenian Democracy*. New York: Oxford University Press, 1990.

Strauss, Barry S. *Athens After the Peloponnesian War*. Ithaca, N.Y.: Cornell University Press, 1986.

Stroud, Ronald S. *Drakon's Law on Homicide*. Berkeley: University of California Press, 1968.

Swain, Simon. *Hellenism and Empire*. New York: Clarendon Press, 1996.

Talbert, R. J. A. *Timoleon and the Revival of Greek Sicily, 344-317* B.C. New York: Cambridge University Press, 1974.

Taran, Leonardo. *Speusippus of Athens: A Critical Study with a Collection of the Related Texts and Commentary*. Leiden, Netherlands: E. J. Brill, 1981.

Tate, Allen. *Longinus and the New Criticism: Essays of Four Decades*. Chicago: Swallow Press, 1968.

Taylor, C. C. W. *Socrates*. Oxford, England: Oxford University Press, 1998.

Tejera, V. *Rewriting the History of Ancient Greek Philosophy*. Westport, Conn.: Greenwood Press, 1997.

Thomson, George. *Aeschylus and Athens: A Study in the Social Origins of Drama*. London: Lawrence and Wishart, 1973.

Treadgold, Warren. *A History of Byzantine State and Society*. Stanford, Calif.: Stanford University Press, 1997.

Tritle, Lawrence, ed. *The Greek World in the Fourth Century: From the Fall of the Athenian Empire to the Successors of Alexander*. New York: Routledge, 1997.

Turner, Jane Shoar, ed. *The Dictionary of Art*. New York: Grove, 1996.

Usher, Mark David. *Homeric Stitchings: The Homeric Centos of the Empress Eudocia*. Lanham, Md.: Rowman and Littlefield, 1998.

Van Ophuijsen, Johannes M., and Marlein von Raalte. *Theophrastus: Reappraising the Sources*. New Brunswick, N.J.: Transaction Publishers, 1998.

Von Bothmer, Dietrich. *The Amasis Painter and His Word: Vase Painting in Sixth-Century* B.C. *Athens*. New York: Thames and Hudson, 1985.

Von Staden, Heinrich. *Herophilus: The Art of Medicine in Early Alexandria*. New York: Cambridge University Press, 1989.

Wacholder, Ben Zion. *Nicolaus of Damascus*. Berkeley: University of California Press, 1962. Reprint. Millwood, N.Y.: Kraus, 1980.

Walbank, F. W. *The Hellenistic World*. Rev. ed. Cambridge, Mass.: Harvard University Press, 1993.

———. *A Historical Commentary on Polybius*. 3 vols. Oxford, England: Clarendon Press, 1957-1979.

———. *Philip V of Macedon*. Cambridge, England: Cambridge University Press, 1940.

Wallace, R. W. *The Areopagus Council to 307* B.C. Baltimore: Johns Hopkins Press, 1989.

Walton, J. M., and P. D. Arnott. *Menander and the Making of Comedy*. Westport, Conn.: Greenwood, 1996.

Waywell, G. B. *The Freestanding Sculpture of the Mausoleum at Halicarnassus*. New York: Farrar, Straus, and Giroux, 1979.

Webster, T. B. L. *Hellenistic Poetry and Art*. New York: Barnes & Noble, 1964.

———. *Introduction to Menander*. Manchester, England: University of Manchester Press, 1974.

West, M. L. *Ancient Greek Music*. Oxford, England: Oxford University Press, 1993.

West, Thomas G., and Grace Starry West. *Four Texts on Socrates*. Ithaca, N.Y.: Cornell University Press, 1984.

White, Heather. *Studies in Late Greek Epic Poetry*. Amsterdam, Netherlands: Gieben, 1987.

_____. *Studies in the Poetry of Nicander*. Amsterdam, Netherlands: Hakkert, 1987.

Wiles, David. *Tragedy in Athens: Performance Space and Theatrical Meaning*. Cambridge, England: Cambridge University Press, 1997.

Will, Frederic. *Archilochus*. New York: Twayne, 1969.

Williams, Rowan. *Arius: Heresy and Tradition*. London: Darton, Longman & Todd, 1987.

Williams, Stephen, and Gerard Friell. *Theodosius: The Empire at Bay*. New Haven, Conn.: Yale University Press, 1994.

Williamson, Margaret. *Sappho's Immortal Daughters*. Cambridge, Mass.: Harvard University Press, 1995.

Winnington-Ingram, R. P. *Sophocles: An Interpretation*. Cambridge, England: Cambridge University Press, 1980.

Wood, Michael. *In Search of the Trojan War*. Berkeley: University of California Press, 1998.

Xenakis, Iason. *Epictetus: Philosopher-Therapist*. The Hague, Netherlands: Nijhoff, 1969.

Zimmermann, Bernhard. *Greek Tragedy: An Introduction*. Baltimore: Johns Hopkins University Press, 1991.

ISRAEL

Focuses on the history and culture of the ancient Israelites through the fall of Jerusalem in 70 C.E. Also some material subsequent on Jewish history. For Judaism see the Religion category.

Ahlström, Gösta. *The History of Ancient Palestine from the Paleolithic to Alexander's Conquest*. Minneapolis: Fortress Press, 1993.

_____. *Who Were the Israelites?* Winona Lake, Ind.: Eisenbrauns, 1986.

Bahat, Dan, with Chaim T. Rubinstein. *The Illustrated Atlas of Jerusalem*. New York: Simon and Schuster, 1990.

Barclay, J. M. G. *Jews in the Mediterranean Diaspora: From Alexander the Great to Trajan, 323 B.C.E.-117 C.E.* Berkeley: University of California Press, 1996.

Beegle, Dewey. *Moses, the Servant of Yahweh*. Grand Rapids, Mich.: Wm. B. Eerdmans, 1972.

Bergeaud, Jean. *Saint John the Baptist*. New York: Macmillan, 1963.

Berrigan, Daniel. *Isaiah*. Minneapolis: Fortress Press, 1996.

Bickerman, Elias. *The Maccabees: An Account of Their History from the Beginnings to the Fall of the House of the Hasmoneans*. New York: Shocken Books, 1947.

Birch, Bruce C., ed. *A Theological Introduction to the Old Testament*. Nashville: Abingdon, 1999.

Block, Daniel I. *The Book of Ezekiel*. Grand Rapids, Mich.: Wm. B. Eerdmans, 1998.

Brettler, Marc Zvi. *The Creation of History in Ancient Israel*. New York: Routledge, 1995.

Bright, John. *A History of Israel*. 3d ed. Philadelphia: Westminster Press, 1993.

Clements, Ronald E. *Ezekiel*. Louisville, Ky.: Westminster John Knox Press, 1996.

Coats, George. *Moses: Heroic Man, Man of God*. Sheffield, England: Sheffield Academic Press, 1988.

Cohen, Shaye. *From the Maccabees to the Mishnah*. Philadelphia: Westminster John Knox Press, 1995.

Crenshaw, James L. *Education in Ancient Israel: Across the Deadening Silence*. New York: Doubleday, 1998.

_____. *Samson: A Secret Betrayed, a Vow Ignored*. Atlanta: John Knox Press, 1978.

Cross, Frank Moore. *Canaanite Myth and Hebrew Epic*. Cambridge, Mass.: Harvard University Press, 1973.

Crossan, John. *Jesus: A Revolutionary Biography*. San Francisco: HarperCollins, 1995.

Culpepper, H. Alan. *John, the Son of Zebedee*. Minneapolis: Fortress, 2000.

DeVaux, Roland. *The Early History of Israel*. Philadelphia: Westminster Press, 1978.

Ehrlich, Carl S. *The Philistines in Transition: A History from c. 1000-730 B.C.E.* Vol. 10. In *Studies in the History and Culture of the Ancient Near East*. Leiden, Netherlands: E. J. Brill, 1996.

Eisenman, Robert H. *James, the Brother of Jesus: The Key to Unlocking the Secrets of Early Christianity and the Dead Sea Scrolls*. New York: Viking, 1997.

Finegan, Jack. *Let My People Go: A Journey Through Exodus*. New York: Harper and Row, 1963.

Finkelstein, Louis. *Akiba: Scholar, Saint, and Martyr*.

2d ed. New York: Schocken Books, 1962.

Fox, E. *Give Us a King: Samuel, Saul, and David*. New York: Schocken Books, 1999.

Golb, Norman. *Who Wrote the Dead Sea Scrolls? The Search for the Secret of Qumran*. New York: Charles Scribner's Sons, 1995.

Goodenough, E. R. *An Introduction to Philo Judaeus*. 2d ed. Lanham, Md.: University Press of America, 1986.

Gordon, Robert D. *I and II Samuel: A Commentary*. Grand Rapids, Mich.: Zondervan, 1986.

Gottwald, Norman K. *The Tribes of Yahweh*. Sheffield, England: Sheffield Academic Press, 1999.

Grabbe, Lester L. *Ezra-Nehemiah*. New York: Routledge, 1998.

Grant, Michael. *The History of Ancient Israel*. New York: Charles Scribner's Sons, 1984.

Graves, Robert, and Raphael Patai. *Hebrew Myths*. Garden City, N.Y.: Doubleday & Co., 1964.

Gray, J. *The Legacy of Canaan*. Leiden, Netherlands: E. J. Brill, 1965.

Hasel, Gerhard F. *Understanding the Book of Amos: Basic Issues in Current Interpretations*. Grand Rapids, Mich.: Baker, 1991.

Hayes, John H. *Amos, the Eighth-Century Prophet: His Times and His Preaching*. Nashville: Abingdon Press, 1988.

Holladay, William L. *Jeremiah*. 2 vols. Philadelphia: Fortress Press, 1989.

Jagersma, Henk. *A History of Israel from Alexander the Great to Bar Kochba*. Philadelphia: Fortress Press, 1986.

James, Fleming. *Personalities of the Old Testament*. New York: Charles Scribner's Sons, 1938.

Johnson, Paul. *A History of the Jews*. New York: Harper & Row, 1987.

Jones, A. H. M. *The Herods of Judaea*. Oxford, England: Clarendon Press, 1967.

Kennedy, Hugh. *The Prophet and the Age of the Caliphates*. New York: Longman, 1999.

Klein, Ralph W. *I Samuel*. Waco, Tex.: Word, 1983.

Kraeling, Carl H. *John the Baptist*. New York: Charles Scribner's Sons, 1951.

Levenson, Jon D. *Sinai and Zion: An Entry into the Jewish Bible*. Minneapolis: Winston, 1985.

Levy, Thomas E., ed. *The Archaeology of Society in the Holy Land*. New York: Facts on File, 1995.

Mays, James Luther. *Hosea*. Philadelphia: Westminster Press, 1969.

Miller, J. Maxwell, and John H. Hayes. *A History of Ancient Israel and Judah*. Philadelphia: Westminster Press, 1986.

Neusner, Jacob. *A History of the Jews in Babylonia*. Vol. 4. Leiden, Netherlands: E. J. Brill, 1969.

Orlinsky, Harry M. *Ancient Israel*. 2d ed. Ithaca, N.Y.: Cornell University Press, 1960.

Painter, John. *Just James: The Brother of Jesus in History and Tradition*. Columbia: University of South Carolina Press, 1997.

Pardes, Ilana. *The Biography of Ancient Israel: National Narratives in the Bible*. Berkeley: University of California Press, 2000.

Perdue, Leo G., Joseph Blenkinsopp, John J. Collins, and Carol Meyers. *Families in Ancient Israel*. Louisville, Ky.: Westminster John Knox Press, 1997.

Perdue, Leo G., and Brian W. Kovacs, eds. *A Prophet to the Nations: Essays in Jeremiah Studies*. Winona Lake, Ind.: Eisenbrauns, 1984.

Perkins, P. *Peter: Apostle for the Whole Church*. Minneapolis: Fortress Press, 2000.

Provan, Iain. *Hezekiah and the Book of Kings*. New York: Walter de Gruyter, 1988.

Richardson, Peter. *Herod: King of the Jews and Friend of the Romans*. Columbia: University of South Carolina Press, 1996.

Rogerson, John. *Chronicle of the Old Testament Kings: The Reign-by-Reign Record of the Rulers of Ancient Israel*. London: Thames and Hudson, 1999.

Schiffman, Lawrence. *Reclaiming the Dead Sea Scrolls*. New York: Doubleday, 1994.

Shanks, Hershel. *Jerusalem: An Archaeological Biography*. New York: Random House, 1995.

————. *The Mystery and Meaning of the Dead Sea Scrolls*. New York: Random House, 1998.

————, ed. *Ancient Israel*. Rev. and enlarged ed. Upper Saddle River, N.J.: Prentice Hall and the Biblical Archaeology Society, 1999.

Smith, Morton. *Palestinian Parties and Politics That Shaped the Old Testament*. 2d ed. London: Student Christian Movement Press, 1987.

Stemberger, Gunter. *Jewish Contemporaries of Jesus: Pharisees, Sadducees, Essenes*. Translated by Allan Mahnke. Minneapolis: Fortress Press, 1995.

Thieberger, Frederic. *King Solomon*. 1978. Reprint. New York: Hebrew Publishing, 1998.

Toews, W. *Monarchy and Religious Institutions in Israel Under Jeroboam I*. Atlanta: Scholars Press, 1993.

Uffenheimer, Benjamin. *Early Prophecy in Israel*. Jerusalem: Magnes, 1999.

VanderKam, James. *The Dead Sea Scrolls Today.* Grand Rapids, Mich.: Wm. B. Eerdmans, 1994.

Wilson, Robert R. *Prophecy and Society in Ancient Israel.* Philadelphia: Fortress, 1980.

Yadin, Yigael. *Bar-Kokhba.* London: Weidenfeld & Nicholson, 1971.

_____. *Masada.* New York: Welcom Rain, 1998.

Yadin, Yigael, and Jonas Greenfield, eds. *The Documents from the Bar Kokhba Period in the Cave of Letters.* Jerusalem: Israel Exploration Society, 1989.

MESOPOTAMIA

The cultures in this group are often referred to as the Near or Middle East. These include the cultures of ancient Iraq and Iran (Persia, Babylonia) as well as peoples who lived closer to the Mediterranean such as the Canaanites.

Aitken, Kenneth T. *The Aqhat Narrative: A Study in the Narrative Structure and Composition of an Ugaritic Tale.* Manchester, England: University of Manchester Press, 1990.

Bienkowski, and Alan Millard, eds. *Dictionary of the Ancient Near East.* Philadelphia: University of Pennsylvania Press, 2000.

Boyce, Mary. *A History of Zoroastrianism: The Early Period.* Leiden, Netherlands: E. J. Brill, 1975.

_____. *A History of Zoroastrianism: Under the Achaemenians.* Leiden, Netherlands: E. J. Brill, 1982.

_____. *Zoroastrians: Their Religious Beliefs and Practices.* London: Routledge and Kegan Paul, 1986.

Briant, Pierre. *From Cyrus to Alexander: A History of the Persian Empire.* Winona Lake, Ind.: Eisenbrauns, 1998.

Clark, Peter. *Zoroastrianism: An Introduction to an Ancient Faith.* Brighton: Sussex Academic Press, 1998.

Colledge, Malcolm A. R. *Parthian Art.* London: Thames and Hudson, 1977.

_____, ed. *The Parthian Period.* Leiden, Netherlands: E. J. Brill, 1986.

Cook, J. M. *The Persian Empire.* New York: Schocken Books, 1983.

Crawford, Harriet. *Sumer and the Sumerians.* New York: Cambridge University Press, 1991.

Culican, W. *The Medes and Persians.* New York: Praeger, 1965.

Curtis, J. E., and J. E. Reade. *Art and Empire: Treasures from Assyria in the British Museum.* London: British Museum Press, 1995.

Curtis, Vesta Sarkhosh. *Persian Myths.* Austin: University of Texas Press, 1993.

Dalley, Stephanie, trans. *Myths from Mesopotamia.* New York: Oxford University Press, 1989.

Dandamaev, M. A. *A Political History of the Achaemenid Empire.* Leiden, Netherlands: E. J. Brill, 1989.

Debevoise, N. C. *A Political History of Parthia.* Chicago: University of Chicago Press, 1938.

Driver, G. R., and J. Miles. *The Assyrian Laws.* 1935. Reprint. Darmstadt, Germany: Scientia Verlag Aalen, 1975.

Duchesne-Guillemin, Jacques. *Symbols and Values in Zoroastrianism.* New York: Harper and Row, 1966.

Frye, Richard. N. *History of Ancient Iran.* Munich: C. H. Beck, 1984.

Gelb, I. J. *Hurrians and Subarians.* Chicago: Oriental Institute Publications, 1944.

Gershevitch, Ilya, ed. *The Cambridge History of Iran.* Vol. 1. *The Median and Archaemenian Periods.* Cambridge, England: Cambridge University Press, 1985.

Gibson, J. C. L. *Canaanite Myths and Legends.* Edinburgh: T. and T. Clark, 1978.

Gnoli, Gherardo. *Zoroaster's Time and Homeland.* Naples, Italy: Instituto Universitario Orientale, 1980.

Göbl, Robert. *Sasanian Numismatics.* Brunswick, Germany: Klinkardt & Biermann, 1971.

Gray, John. *The Canaanites.* New York: Frederick A. Praeger, 1964.

_____. *The Legacy of Canaan.* 2d ed. Leiden, Netherlands: E. J. Brill, 1965.

_____. *Near Eastern Mythology.* 2d ed. New York: Peter Bedrick Books, 1982.

Grayson, A. K. *The Royal Inscriptions of Mesopotamia: The Assyrian Periods.* Vols. 1-2. Toronto: University of Toronto Press, 1987-1990.

Hallo, W. W., and W. K. Simpson. *The Ancient Near East: A History.* 2d ed. Fort Worth, Tex.: Harcourt Brace Jovanovich, 1998.

Harris, Rivkah. *Gender and Aging in Mesopotamia: The Gilgamesh Epic and Other Ancient Literature.* Norman: University of Oklahoma Press, 2000.

Hartz, Paula R. *Zoroastrianism*. New York: Facts on File, 1999.

Hassig, Ross. *Aztec Warfare: Imperial Expansion and Political Control*. Norman: University of Oklahoma Press, 1988.

————. *War and Society in Ancient Mesoamerica*. Berkeley: University of California Press, 1992.

Healy, Mark. *The Ancient Assyrians*. London: Osprey, 1992.

Henderson, John S. *The World of the Ancient Maya*. 2d ed. Ithaca, N.Y.: Cornell University Press, 1997.

Henning, Walter Bruno. *Zoroaster: Politician or Witch-Doctor?* London: Oxford University Press, 1951.

Henry, Donald O. *From Foraging to Agriculture: The Levant at the End of the Ice Age*. Philadelphia: University of Pennsylvania Press, 1989.

Hinnells, John R. *Persian Mythology*. 2d ed. New York: Peter Bedrick Books, 1985.

Hoerth, Alfred J., et al., eds. *Peoples of the Old Testament World*. Grand Rapids, Mich.: Baker, 1994.

Hooke, Samuel Henry. *Babylonian and Assyrian Religion*. New York: Hutchinson's University Library, 1953.

————. *Middle Eastern Mythology*. Baltimore: Penguin Books, 1963.

Insler, Stanley. *The Gathas of Zarathustra*. Leiden, Netherlands: E. J. Brill, 1978.

Jackson, A. V. William. *Zoroaster: The Prophet of Ancient Iran*. New York: Columbia University Press, 1926. Reprint. New York: AMS Press, 1965.

————. *Zoroastrian Studies*. New York: Columbia University Press, 1928. Reprint. New York: AMS Press, 1965.

Jacobsen, Thorkild. *The Treasures of Darkness: A History of Mesopotamian Religion*. New Haven, Conn.: Yale University Press, 1976.

Kramer, Samuel Noah. *Sumerian Mythology*. 2d ed. New York: Harper and Brothers, 1961.

————. *The Sumerians: Their History, Culture, and Character*. Chicago: University of Chicago Press, 1963.

Kramer, Samuel Noah, and the editors of Time-Life Books. *Cradle of Civilization*. New York: Time, 1967.

Kuhrt, Amelie. *The Ancient Near East, c. 3000-330 B.C.* 2 vols. London: Routledge, 1995.

Larsen, M. T. *The Old Assyrian City-State and Its Colonies*. Copenhagen: Akademisk Forlag, 1976.

Leick, Gwendolyn. *Who's Who in the Ancient Near East*. London: Routledge, 1999.

Lerner, J. D. *The Impact of Seleucid Decline on the Eastern Iranian Plateau*. Stuttgart, Germany: F. Steiner, 1999.

Lewis, Brian. *The Sargon Legend*. Cambridge, Mass.: American Schools of Oriental Research, 1980.

Lloyd, Seton. *The Archaeology of Mesopotamia: From the Old Stone Age to the Persian Conquest*. Rev. ed. New York: Thames and Hudson, 1984.

McCall, Henrietta. *Mesopotamian Myths*. Austin: University of Texas Press, 1990.

Mellaart, James. *The Neolithic of the Near East*. London: Thames and Hudson, 1975.

Meyers, Eric M., ed. *The Oxford Encyclopedia of Archaeology in the Near East*. Oxford, England: Oxford University Press, 1997.

Moscati, S., ed. *The Phoenicians*. New York: Rizzoli, 1999.

Nemet-Nejat, Karen. *Daily Life in Ancient Mesopotamia*. Westport, Conn.: Greenwood Press, 1998.

Nigosian, Solomon A. *The Zoroastrian Faith: Tradition and Modern Research*. Toronto: McGill-Queens University Press, 1993.

Nissen, Hans. *The Early History of the Ancient Near East, 9000-2000 B.C.* Chicago: University of Chicago Press, 1988.

Oates, D. *Studies in the Ancient History of Northern Iraq*. London: Oxford University Press, 1968.

Oates, Joan. *Babylon*. Rev. ed. New York: Thames and Hudson, 1986.

Obermann, Julian. *Ugaritic Mythology*. New Haven: Yale University Press, 1948.

Oppenheim, A. Leo. *Ancient Mesopotamia: Portrait of a Dead Civilization*. Compiled by Erica Reiner. Rev. ed. Chicago: University of Chicago Press, 1977.

Parker, Simon B., ed. *Ugaritic Narrative Poetry*. Atlanta: Scholars Press, 1997.

Pavry, Jal Dastur Cursetji. *The Zoroastrian Doctrine of a Future Life*. 2d ed. New York: Columbia University Press, 1965. Reprint. New York: AMS Press, 1965.

Pitard, Wayne T. *Ancient Damascus*. Winona Lake, Ind.: Eisenbrauns, 1987.

Pollock, Susan. *Ancient Mesopotamia: The Eden That Never Was*. Cambridge, England: Cambridge University Press, 1999.

Postgate, J. N. *Early Mesopotamia: Society and Economy at the Dawn of History*. New York: Routledge, 1994.

Pritchard, James B., ed. *The Ancient Near East*. Princeton, N.J.: Princeton University Press, 1958.

_____. *The Ancient Near East: An Anthology in Texts and Pictures*. Translated by William F. Albright. 2 vols. Princeton, N.J.: Princeton University Press, 1973.

_____. *The Ancient Near East in Pictures*. Princeton, N.J.: Princeton University Press, 1954.

_____. *Ancient Near Eastern Texts Relating to the Old Testament*. 3d ed. Princeton, N.J.: Princeton University Press, 1969.

Roaf, Michael. *Cultural Atlas of Mesopotamia and the Ancient Near East*. Oxford, England: Equinox, 1990.

Robson, Eleanor. *Mesopotamian Mathematics, 2100-1600 B.C.: Technical Constraints in Bureaucracy and Education*. New York: Clarendon Press, 1998.

Roux, Georges. *Ancient Iraq*. 2d ed. London: Penguin Books, 1992.

Saggs, H. W. F. *Everyday Life in Babylonia and Assyria*. New York: Dorset, 1987.

_____. *The Greatness That Was Babylon*. New York: New American Library, 1968.

_____. *The Might That Was Assyria*. London: Sidgwick & Jackson, 1984.

Sason, Jack M. et al., eds. *Civilizations of the Ancient Near East*. New York: Charles Scribner's Sons, 1995.

Seibert, Ilse. *Women in the Ancient Near East*. New York: Schram, 1974.

Snell, Daniel C. *Life in the Ancient Near East 3100-332 B.C.E.* New Haven, Conn.: Yale University Press, 1997.

Stoneman, Richard. *Palmyra and Its Empire: Zenobia's Revolt Against Rome*. Ann Arbor: University of Michigan Press, 1992.

Trude Dothan, and Moshe Dothan. *People of the Sea: The Search for the Philistines*. New York: Macmillan, 1992.

Tubb, J. *Canaanites*. Norman: University of Oklahoma Press, 1998.

Turton, Godfrey. *The Syrian Princesses*. London: Cassel, 1974.

Van de Mieroop, Marc. *The Ancient Mesopotamian City*. Oxford, England: Oxford University Press, 1998.

Van Driel, G. *The Cult of Assur*. Assen, Netherlands: Van Gorcum, 1969.

Vermuseren, M. J. *Mithras, the Secret God*. New York: Barnes & Noble, 1963.

Von Soden, Wolfram. *The Ancient Orient: An Introduction to the Study of the Ancient Near East*. Translated by Donald G. Schley. Grand Rapids, Mich.: Wm. B. Eerdmans, 1994.

Walker, C. B. F. *Cuneiform*. Berkeley: University of California Press, 1987.

Weiss, H., ed. *The Origins of Cities in Dry-Farming Syria and Mesopotamia in the Third Millennium B.C.* Guilford, Conn.: Four Quarters, 1986.

Wiesehöfer, Josef. *Ancient Persia, from 550 B.C. to 650 A.D.* London: I. B. Tauris, 1996.

Wilcox, Peter. *Rome's Enemies 3: Parthians and Sasanids*. Vol. 175. Oxford, England: Osprey, 1988.

Wiseman, D. *The Alalakh Tablets*. London: The British School of Archaeology in Iraq, 1953. Reprint. New York: AMS Press, 1983.

Yaar-Shater, Ehsan. *The Cambridge History of Iran*. Vol. 2. in *The Seleucid, Parthian and Sainian Periods*. Cambridge, England: Cambridge University Press, 1983.

Yarshater, Ehsan, ed. *Encyclopaedia Iranica*. London: Routledge and Kegan Paul, 1989.

Zaehner, R. C. *The Dawn and Twilight of Zoroastrianism*. New York: G. P. Putnam's Sons, 1961.

_____. *Zurvan: A Zoroastrian Dilemma*. Oxford, England: Oxford University Press, 1955.

OCEANIA

Australia, New Zealand, and the Pacific Islands.

Allen, Louis, A. *Time Before Morning: Art and Myth of the Australian Aborigines*. New York: Thomas Y. Crowell, 1975.

Bellwood, Peter S. *Man's Conquest of the Pacific*. New York: Oxford University Press, 1979.

Craig, Robert D. *Historical Dictionary of Polynesia*. Lanham, Md.: Scarecrow, 1993.

Docherty, James C. *Historical Dictionary of Australia*. 2d ed. Lanham, Md.: Scarecrow, 1999.

Flood, Josephine. *Rock Art of the Dreamtime: Images of Ancient Australia*. Melbourne, Victoria: Angus & Robertson, 1998.

Irwin, G. *The Prehistoric Exploration and Colonization of the Pacific*. Cambridge, England: Cambridge University Press, 1992.

Osborne, D. *The Archaeology of Palau Islands*. Honolulu: Bernice P. Bishop Museum, 1966.

Spoehr, Alexander. *Marianas Prehistory*. Chicago:

Chicago Natural History Museum, 1957.

Terrell, J. *Prehistory in the Pacific Islands*. Cambridge, England: Cambridge University Press, 1989.

Wuerch, William L., and Dirk Anthony Ballendorf. *Historical Dictionary of Guam and Micronesia*. Lanham, Md.: Scarecrow, 1994.

ROME

These books deal not only with the city of Rome but also with Italy and the Roman Empire. However, users should also consult Europe, Egypt, Greece, and Africa for some materials on the peoples of the Roman Empire.

Adam, Jean-Pierre. *Roman Construction: Material and Techniques*. 3d ed. Paris: Picard, 1995.

Adkins, Lesley, and Roy A. Adkins. *Handbook to Life in Ancient Rome*. New York: Facts on File, 1994.

Ahl, F. M. *Lucan: An Introduction*. Ithaca, N.Y.: Cornell University Press, 1976.

Aicher, P. *A Guide to the Aqueducts of Ancient Rome*. Wauconda, Ill.: Bolchazy-Carducci, 1995.

Alföldi, Andreas. *The Conversion of Constantine and Pagan Rome*. New York: Oxford University Press, 1998.

Anderson, J. C., Jr. *Roman Architecture and Society*. Baltimore: Johns Hopkins University Press, 1997.

Anderson, W. S. *Essays on Roman Satire*. Princeton, N.J.: Princeton University Press, 1982.

Armstrong, D. *Horace*. New Haven, Conn.: Yale University Press, 1989.

Astin, A. E. *Cato the Censor*. Oxford, England: Clarendon Press, 1978.

_____. *Scipio Aemilianus*. Oxford, England: Clarendon Press, 1967.

Augenti, Andrea, ed. *Art and Archaeology of Rome: From Ancient Times to the Baroque*. New York: Scala/Riverside Book Company, 2000.

Auguet, Roland. *Cruelty and Civilization: The Roman Games*. London: Routledge, 1994.

Ball, Robert J. *Tibullus the Elegist: A Critical Survey*. Göttingen, Germany: Vandenhoeck and Ruprecht, 1983.

Balsdon, John Percy Vyvian Dacre. *Roman Women: Their History and Habits*. Reprint. New York: Barnes & Noble, 1998.

Banti, Luisa. *Etruscan Cities and Their Culture*. Berkeley: University of California Press, 1973.

Barker, Graeme, and Tom Rasmussen. *The Etruscans*. Oxford, England: Blackwell, 1998.

Barnes, Timothy David. *Ammianus Marcellinus and the Representation of Historical Reality*. Ithaca, N.Y.: Cornell University Press, 1998.

_____. *Constantine and Eusebius*. Cambridge, Mass.: Harvard University Press, 1981.

Barrett, Anthony A. *Agrippina: Sex, Power, and Politics in the Early Empire*. New Haven, Conn.: Yale University Press, 1996.

_____. *Caligula: The Corruption of Power*. New Haven, Conn.: Yale University Press, 1990.

Barrow, R. H. *Prefect and Emperor: The Relationes of Symmachus, A.D. 384*. Oxford, England: Clarendon Press, 1973.

Bartman, Elizabeth. *Portraits of Livia: Imaging the Imperial Woman in Augustan Rome*. Cambridge, England: Cambridge University Press, 1999.

Barton, Carlin. *The Sorrows of the Ancient Romans*. Princeton, N.J.: Princeton University Press, 1993.

Bartsch, Shadi. *Ideology in Cold Blood: A Reading of Lucan's Civil War*. Cambridge, Mass.: Harvard University Press, 1997.

Baumann, Richard A. *Women and Politics in Ancient Rome*. London: Routledge, 1994.

Baylis, H. J. *Minucius Felix and His Place Among the Early Fathers of the Latin Church*. New York: Macmillan, 1928.

Beacham, Richard. *The Roman Theatre and Its Audience*. Cambridge, Mass.: Harvard University Press, 1991.

Benario, Herbert. *Introduction to Tacitus*. Athens: University of Georgia Press, 1975.

Bennett, Julian. *Trajan, Optimus Princeps: A Life and Times*. Bloomington: Indiana University Press, 1997.

Bernstein, Alvin H. *Tiberius Sempronius Gracchus: Tradition and Apostasy*. Ithaca, N.Y.: Cornell University Press, 1978.

Birley, Anthony R. *Hadrian: The Restless Emperor*. New York: Routledge, 1997.

_____. *Marcus Aurelius: A Biography*. New Haven, Conn.: Yale University Press, 1987.

_____. *Septimius Severus: The African Emperor*. New York: Routledge, 1999.

Blockley, R. C. *The Fragmentary Classicising Historians of the Later Roman Empire*. Liverpool, England: Francis Cairns, 1981.

Bonfante, Larissa. *Etruscan Life and Afterlife*. Detroit: Wayne State University Press, 1986.

Bonner, Stanley F. *Education in Ancient Rome from the Elder Cato to the Younger Pliny*. Berkeley: University of California Press, 1977.

Boren, Henry. *Roman Society: A Social, Economic, and Cultural History*. Boston: Houghton Mifflin, 1992.

Bowersock, G. *Julian the Apostate*. Cambridge, Mass.: Harvard University Press, 1978.

Boyle, A. J., ed. *The Imperial Muse: Ramus Essays on Roman Literature of the Empire, Flavian Epicist to Claudian*. Berwick, Australia: Aureal, 1990.

Bradley, Keith R. *Slavery and Rebellion in the Roman World*. Bloomington: Indiana University Press, 1989.

_____. *Slavery and Society in Rome*. New York: Cambridge University Press, 1994.

Braund, David. *Rome and the Friendly King: The Character of the Client Kingship*. New York: St. Martin's Press, 1984.

Braund, S. H. *Roman Satirists and Their Masks*. Bristol, England: Bristol Classical Press, 1996.

_____. *Roman Verse Satire*. Oxford, England: Oxford University Press, 1992.

Briggs, Ward W. *Ancient Roman Writers*. Farmington Heights, Mich.: Gale Group, 1999.

Bright, David F. *Haec mihi fingebam: Tibullus in His World*. Leiden, Netherlands: E. J. Brill, 1978.

Brown, Peter. *Augustine of Hippo*. Berkeley: University of California Press, 1967.

Bunson, Matthew. *A Dictionary of the Roman Empire*. New York: Oxford University Press, 1995.

Burckhardt, W. *The Age of Constantine the Great*. New York: Dorset Press, 1989.

Burke, Vernon J. *Wisdom from St. Augustine*. South Bend, Ind.: University of Notre Dame Press, 1984.

Burns, Thomas S. *Barbarians Within the Gates of Rome: A Study of Roman Military Policy and the Barbarians, c. 375-425* A.D. Bloomington: Indiana University Press, 1994.

Bury, J. B. *History of the Later Roman Empire: From the Death of Theodosius I to the Death of Justinian*. New York: Dover, 1978.

Cairns, Francis. *Tibullus: A Hellenistic Poet at Rome*. Cambridge, England: Cambridge University Press, 1979.

Cameron, Alan. *Claudian: Poetry and Propaganda at the Court of Honorius*. Oxford, England: Clarendon Press, 1970.

Cameron, Averil. *The Later Roman Empire:* A.D. *284-430*. Cambridge, Mass.: Harvard University Press, 1993.

Campbell, B. *The Emperor and the Roman Army*. Oxford, England: Oxford University Press, 1984.

Carter, J. M. *The Battle of Actium: The Rise and Triumph of Augustus Caesar*. London: Hamish Hamilton, 1970.

Cary, M., and H. H. Scullard. *A History of Rome: Down to the Reign of Constantine*. 3d. ed. New York: St. Martin's Press, 1976.

Castriota, David. *The Ara Pacis Augustae*. Princeton, N.J.: Princeton University Press, 1995.

Chadwick, Henry. *Augustine*. New York: Oxford University Press, 1986.

Champlin, Edward. *Fronto and Antonine Rome*. Cambridge, Mass.: Harvard University Press, 1980.

Charlesworth, M. P. *Trade Routes and Commerce of the Roman Empire*. 2d ed. Cambridge, England: Cambridge University Press, 1926.

Claridge, Amanda. *Rome*. Oxford, England: Oxford University Press, 1998.

Clarke, M. L. *The Noblest Rome*. London: Thames and Hudson, 1981.

Clausen, Wendell Vernon. *A Commentary on Virgil, Eclogues*. New York: Oxford University Press, 1994.

Clausen, Wendell Vernon, and E. J. Kenney. *Cambridge History of Classical Literature. Vol. 2, Latin Literature. Part 1, The Early Republic*. Cambridge, England: Cambridge University Press, 1983.

Clay, D. *Lucretius and Epicurus*. Ithaca, N.Y.: Cornell University Press, 1983.

Clover, Frank. *The Late Roman West and the Vandals*. Brookfield, Vt.: Variorum, 1993.

Coffey, M. *Roman Satire*. Bristol: Bristol Classical Press, 1989.

Conlin, Diane Atnally. *The Artists of the Ara Pacis*. Chapel Hill: University of North Carolina Press, 1997.

Conte, Gian Biagio. *Latin Literature: A History*. Baltimore: Johns Hopkins University Press, 1994.

Cornell, T. J. *The Beginnings of Rome: Italy and Rome from the Bronze Age to the Punic Wars, c. 1000-264* B.C. New York: Routledge, 1995.

Cornell, Tim, Boris Rankov, and Philip Sabin. *The Second Punic War: A Reappraisal*. London: University of London, 1996.

Cottrell, Leonard. *Hannibal, Enemy of Rome*. New York: Holt, Rinehart and Winston, 1992.

Crawford, M. H. *The Roman Republic*. 2d ed. Cambridge, Mass.: Harvard University Press, 1993.

Curchin, Leonard A. *Roman Spain: Conquest and Assimilation.* New York: Barnes & Noble, 1995.

Den Blois, L. *The Policy of the Emperor Gallienus.* Leiden, Netherlands: E. J. Brill, 1976.

Digeser, Elizabeth DePalma. *The Making of a Christian Empire: Lactantius and Rome.* Ithaca, N.Y.: Cornell University Press, 2000.

Dixon, Suzanne. *The Roman Mother.* London: Routledge, 1990.

Dodge, Theodore A. *Caesar.* Mechanicsburg, Pa.: Stackpole Books, 1995.

Dominik, William J. *The Mythic Voice of Statius: Power and Politics in the Thebaid.* Leiden, Netherlands: E. J. Brill, 1994.

―――, ed. *Roman Eloquence.* New York: Routledge, 1997.

Donaldson, I. *The Rapes of Lucretia.* Oxford, England: Oxford University Press, 1978.

Drake, H. A. *Constantine and the Bishops.* Baltimore: Johns Hopkins University Press, 2000.

Duckworth, G. *The Nature of Roman Comedy: A Study in Popular Entertainment.* Norman: University of Oklahoma Press, 1994.

Dudden, F. Holmes. *The Life and Times of St. Ambrose.* 2 vols. Oxford, England: Clarendon Press, 1935.

Dupont, Florence. *Daily Life in Ancient Rome.* New York: Oxford University Press, 1992.

Evans, G. R. *The Thought of Gregory the Great.* Cambridge, England: Cambridge University Press, 1986.

Evans, Harry B. *Water Distribution in Ancient Rome: The Evidence of Frontinus.* Ann Arbor: University of Michigan Press, 1994.

Favro, Diane. *The Urban Image of Augustan Rome.* Cambridge, England: Cambridge University Press, 1996.

Ferrero, Guglielmo. *The Women of the Caesars.* New York: Century, 1911.

Forehand, Walter. *Terence.* Boston: Twayne, 1985.

Frier, Bruce W. *The Rise of the Roman Jurists: Studies in Cicero's Pro Caecina.* Princeton, N.J.: Princeton University Press, 1985.

Galinsky, Karl. *Augustan Culture.* Princeton, N.J.: Princeton University Press, 1996.

Gardner, Jane F. *Roman Myths.* Austin: University of Texas Press, 1993.

―――. *Women in Roman Law and Society.* Bloomington: Indiana University Press, 1991.

Garzetti, Albino. *From Tiberius to the Antonines.* London: Methuen, 1974.

Gelzer, Matthias. *Caesar: Politician and Statesman.* Translated by Peter Needham. Cambridge, Mass.: Harvard University Press, 1968.

George, Judith. *Venantius Fortunatus: A Latin Poet in Merovingian Gaul.* Oxford, England: Clarendon Press, 1992.

Gibbon, Edward. *Decline and Fall of the Roman Empire.* New York: Modern Library, 1995.

Gold, Barbara, ed. *Literary and Artistic Patronage in Ancient Rome.* Austin: University of Texas Press, 1982.

Gowing, Alain M. *The Triumviral Narratives of Appian and Cassius Dio.* Ann Arbor: University of Michigan Press, 1992.

Grant, Micheal. *The Antonines: The Roman Empire in Transition.* London: Routledge, 1994.

―――. *Caesar.* New York: Barnes & Noble, 1997.

―――. *The Etruscans.* New York: Charles Scribner's Sons, 1980.

―――. *History of Rome.* Englewood Cliffs, N.J.: Prentice Hall, 1978.

―――. *The Roman Emperors: A Biographical Guide to the Rulers of Imperial Rome, 31* B.C.-A.D. *476.* New York: Charles Scribner's Sons, 1985.

―――. *Roman Myths.* New York: Dorset Press, 1984.

Graves, Robert. *I, Claudius.* New York: Random House, 1934.

Griffin, Miriam T. *Nero: The End of a Dynasty.* London: B. T. Batsford, 1996.

―――. *Seneca: A Philosopher in Politics.* Oxford, England: Clarendon Press, 1982.

Gruen, Erich S. *The Last Generation of the Roman Republic.* Berkeley: University of California Press, 1974.

Gurval, R. A. *Actium and Augustus: The Politics and Emotions of the Civil War.* Ann Arbor: University of Michigan Press, 1995.

Hadas, M. *A History of Latin Literature.* New York: Columbia University Press, 1952.

Hadzits, G. *Lucretius and His Influence.* New York: Cooper Square, 1963.

Haight, Elizabeth Hazelton. *Apuleius and His Influence.* New York: Cooper Square, 1963.

Hall, Jennifer. *Lucian's Satire.* New York: Arno Press, 1981.

Hall, John B. *Prolegomena to Claudian.* London: University of London, 1986.

Hallett, J., and M. B. Skinner, eds. *Roman Sexualities.* Princeton, N.J.: Princeton University Press, 1997.

Hammond, M. *The Antonine Monarchy*. Rome: The American Academy, 1959.

Hardie, Alex. *Statius and the Silvae: Poets, Patrons, and Epideixis in the Greco-Roman World*. Liverpool, England: Francis Cairns, 1983.

Harries, J. *Sidonius Apollinaris and the Fall of Rome*. Oxford, England: Clarendon Press, 1994.

Healy, John F. *Pliny the Elder on Science and Technology*. Oxford, England: Oxford University Press, 1999.

Healy, Mark. *Cannae, 216 B.C.* Osprey Military Campaign Series 36. Peterborough, England: Osprey, 1997.

Hemelrijk, Emily A. *Matrona Docta: Educated Women in the Roman Elite from Cornelia to Julia Domna*. New York: Routledge, 1999.

Hencken, Hugh. *Tarquinia and Etruscan Origins*. New York: Frederick A. Praeger, 1968.

Hershkowitz, Debra. *Valerius Flaccus' Argonautica: Abbreviated Voyages in Silver Latin Epic*. Oxford, England: Oxford University Press, 1998.

Hoffman, R. *Celsus: On the True Doctrine*. Oxford, England: Oxford University Press, 1987.

Hofmann, H. A., ed. *Latin Fiction: The Latin Novel in Context*. London: Routledge, 1999.

Holford-Strevens, L. A. *Aulus Gellius*. London: Duckworth, 1988.

Honore, Tony. *Ulpian*. Oxford, England: Clarendon Press, 1982.

Hus, Alain. *The Etruscans*. New York: Grove Press, 1963.

Hüttl, W. *Antoninus Pius*. New York: Arno Press, 1975.

Huzar, E. G. *Mark Antony: A Biography*. Minneapolis: University of Minnesota Press, 1978.

Johnson, William Roger. *Darkness Visible: A Study of Virgil's Aeneid*. Berkeley: University of California Press, 1976.

————. *Momentary Monsters: Lucan and His Heroes*. Ithaca, N.Y.: Cornell University Press, 1987.

Jones, A. H. M. *The Later Roman Empire, 284-602*. Norman: University of Oklahoma Press, 1964. Reprint. Baltimore: Johns Hopkins University Press, 1986.

Jones, C. P. *Culture and Society in Lucian*. Cambridge, Mass.: Harvard University Press, 1986.

Keaveney, Arthur. *Rome and the Unification of Italy*. London: Croom Helm, 1987.

————. *Sulla: The Last Republican*. London: Croom Helm, 1982.

Keller, Werner. *The Etruscans*. New York: Alfred A. Knopf, 1974.

Kelly, J. N. D. *Jerome: His Life, Writings, and Controversies*. London: Gerald Duckworth, 1975. Reprint. Peabody, Mass.: Hendrickson, 1998.

Kennedy, George. *Quintilian*. New York: Twayne, 1969.

Keppie, Lawrence. *The Making of the Roman Army*. New York: Barnes & Noble, 1994.

Kildahl, Phillip A. *Caius Marius*. New York: Twayne, 1968.

Kirwan, C. *Augustine*. London: Routledge, 1989.

Kleiner, Diana E. *Roman Sculpture*. New Haven, Conn.: Yale University Press, 1992.

Kleiner, Diana E., and Susan B. Matheson, eds. *I, Claudia: Women in Ancient Rome*. New Haven, Conn.: Yale University Art Gallery, 1996.

Konstan, David. *Roman Comedy*. Ithaca, N.Y.: Cornell University Press, 1983.

Lacey, W. K. *Augustus and the Principate: The Evolution of the System*. Leeds, England: Cairns, 1996.

Launsbury, R. C. *The Arts of Suetonius*. New York: Peter Lang, 1987.

Lazenby, J. F. *The First Punic War*. Stanford, Calif.: Stanford University Press, 1996.

————. *Hannibal's War: A Military History of the Second Punic War*. Warminster, England: Aris & Phillips, 1978.

Le Glay, Marcel. *History of Rome*. London: Blackwell, 1998.

Lee-Stecum, Parshia. *Powerplay in Tibullus*. Cambridge, England: Cambridge University Press, 1998.

Lepper, Frank. *Trajan's Parthian War*. Chicago: Ares, 1994.

Lepper, Frank, and Sheppard Frere. *Trajan's Column*. Gloucester, England: Alan Sutton, 1988.

Levick, B. M. *Claudius*. London: B. T. Batsford, 1990.

————. *Vespasian*. New York: Routledge, 1999.

Luce, T. J. *Livy: The Composition of His History*. Princeton, N.J.: Princeton University Press, 1977.

Luciani, Roberto. *The Colosseum*. Novara, Italy: Instituto Geografico De Agostini, 1990.

Luttwak, E. N. *The Grand Strategy of the Roman Empire from the First Century A.D. to the Third*. Baltimore: Johns Hopkins University Press, 1976.

Lyne, R. O. A. M. *The Latin Love Poets from Catullus to Horace*. Oxford, England: Oxford University Press, 1980.

MacDonald, William L. *The Architecture of the Roman Empire*. New Haven, Conn.: Yale University Press, 1982.

McGuire, Donald T. *Acts of Silence: Civil War, Tyranny, and Suicide in the Flavian Epics*. New York: Olms-Weidmann, 1997.

Mack, Sara. *Ovid*. New Haven, Conn.: Yale University Press, 1988.

MacKendrick, Paul. *Romans On The Rhine: Archaeology in Germany*. New York: Funk and Wagnalls, 1970.

Magie, David. *Roman Rule in Asia Minor*. Princeton, N.J.: Princeton University Press, 1950.

Malamud, Martha A. *A Poetics of Transformation: Prudentius and Classical Mythology*. Ithaca, N.Y.: Cornell University Press, 1989.

Marcellinus, Ammianus. *The Later Roman Empire*. Translated by Walter Hamilton. New York: Penguin Classics, 1986.

Marsh, D. *Lucian and the Latins*. Ann Arbor: University of Michigan Press, 1998.

Marsh, Frank Burr. *The Reign of Tiberius*. New York: Barnes and Noble, 1931.

Marshall, B. A. *Crassus: A Political Biography*. Amsterdam, Netherlands: Adolf M. Hakkert, 1976.

Martin, C. *Catullus*. New Haven, Conn.: Yale University Press, 1992.

Masson, Georgina. *A Concise History of Republican Rome*. London: Thames and Hudson, 1973.

Masters, J. *Poetry and Civil War in Lucan's "Bellum Civile."* Cambridge, England: Cambridge University Press, 1992.

Matthews, John. *The Roman Empire of Ammianus*. London: Duckworth, 1989.

———. *Western Aristocracies and Imperial Court* A.D. *364-425*. Oxford, England: Clarendon Press, 1990.

Meier, Christian. *Caesar: A Biography*. Translated by David McClintock. New York: HarperCollins, 1995.

Mellor, Ronald. *Tacitus*. New York: Routledge, 1994.

Mendell, Clarence W. *Tacitus: The Man and His Work*. Hamden, Conn.: Archon Books, 1970.

Millar, Fergus. *The Emperor in the Roman World*. London: Duckworth, 1977.

———. *A Study of Cassius Dio*. Oxford, England: Clarendon Press, 1964.

Milner, N. P. *Vegetius: Epitome of Military Science*. Liverpool, England: Liverpool University Press, 1993.

Minyard, D. *Lucretius and the Late Republic*. Leiden, Netherlands: E. J. Brill, 1985.

Mitchell, R. E. *Patricians and Plebeians: The Origins of the Roman State*. Ithaca, N.Y.: Cornell University Press, 1990.

Mitchell, Thomas N. *Cicero: The Ascending Years*. New Haven, Conn.: Yale University Press, 1979.

———. *Cicero: The Senior Statesman*. New Haven, Conn.: Yale University Press, 1991.

Moorhead, John. *Ambrose: Church and Society in the Late Roman World*. London: Longman, 1999.

Morford, M. P. O. *The Poet Lucan: Studies in Rhetorical Epic*. Oxford, England: Oxford University Press, 1967.

Motto, A. L., and J. R. Clark. *Senecan Tragedy*. Amsterdam, Netherlands: A. M. Hakkert, 1988.

Munzer, F. *Roman Aristocratic Parties and Families*. Translated by T. Ridley. Baltimore: Johns Hopkins University Press, 1999.

Nardo, Don. *The Roman Colosseum*. San Diego: Lucent Books, 1998.

Nardo, Richard, ed. *The Fall of the Roman Empire*. San Diego: Greenhaven Press, 1998.

Odahl, Charles M. *Constantine and the Christian Empire*. London: Routledge, 2001.

O'Day, Gerard. *The Poetry of Boethius*. London: Duckworth, 1991.

O'Donnell, J. J. *Cassiodorus*. Berkeley: University of California Press, 1979.

Ogilvie, R. M. *The Library of Lactantius*. Oxford, England: Clarendon Press, 1978.

O'Meara, Dominic J. *Plotinus: An Introduction to the Enneads*. Oxford, England: Oxford University Press, 1995.

Oost, Stewart Irvin. *Galla Placidia Augusta*. Chicago: University of Chicago Press, 1968.

Osborn, E. F. *Justin Martyr*. Tubingen, Germany: Mohr, 1973.

———. *Tertullian: First Theologian of the West*. New York: Cambridge University Press, 1997.

Otis, Brooks. *Virgil: A Study in Civilized Poetry*. Oxford, England: Clarendon Press, 1964.

Packer, J. E. *The Forum of Trajan at Rome*. Berkeley: University of California Press, 1996.

Pallottino, Massimo. *A History of Earliest Italy*. Translated by M. Ryle and K. Soper. Ann Arbor: University of Michigan Press, 1991.

Pearce, James B. *The Eclogues of Calpurnius Siculus, with an Introduction, Commentary, and Vocabulary*. San Antonio, Tex.: Scylax Press, 1990.

Peddie, John. *The Roman War Machine*. Conshohocken, Pa.: Combined Books, 1997.

Peebles, Bernard Mann. *The Poet Prudentius*. New York: McMullen Books, 1951.

Perowne, Stewart. *Roman Mythology*. 2d ed. New

York: Peter Bedrick Books, 1984.

Pollitt, J. J. *The Art of Rome c. 753* B.C.-A.D. *337: Sources and Documents*. Cambridge, England: Cambridge University Press, 1995.

Pöschl. *The Art of Vergil: Image and Symbol in the Aeneid*. Translated by Gerda Seligson. Ann Arbor: University of Michigan Press, 1962.

Potter, D. *Prophecy and History in the Crisis of the Roman Empire*. Oxford, England: Oxford University Press, 1990.

Potter, D. S., and D. J. Mattingly. *Life, Death, and Entertainment in the Roman Empire*. Ann Arbor: University of Michigan Press, 1997.

Quinn, Stephanie. *Why Vergil? A Collection of Interpretations*. Wauconda, Ill.: Bolchazy-Carducci, 2000.

Raaflaub, K., and M. Toher. *Between Republic and Empire: Interpretations of Augustus and His Principate*. Berkeley: University of California Press, 1990.

Rajak, Tessa. *Josephus: The Historian and His Society*. Philadelphia: Fortress Press, 1984.

Ramsey, Boniface. *Ambrose*. London: Routledge, 1997.

Rankin, D. *Tertullian and the Church*. New York: Cambridge University Press, 1995.

Rawson, Elizabeth. *Cicero: A Portrait*. Ithaca, N.Y.: Cornell University Press, 1983.

_____. *Intellectual Life in the Late Roman Republic*. Baltimore: Johns Hopkins University Press, 1985.

Reece, Richard. *Later Roman Empire*. Charleston, S.C.: Tempus, 1999.

Reinhold, M. *Marcus Agrippa*. Geneva, N.Y.: The W. F. Humphrey Press, 1933.

Richardson, Lawrence, Jr. *A New Topographical Dictionary of Ancient Rome*. Baltimore: Johns Hopkins University Press, 1992.

Roberts, Michael John. *Poetry and the Cult of the Martyrs: The Liber Peristephanon of Prudentius*. Ann Arbor: University of Michigan Press, 1993.

Robinson, Olivia F. *The Sources of Roman Law: Problems and Methods for Ancient Historians*. New York: Routledge, 1997.

Roetzel, Calvin J. *Paul: The Man and the Myth*. Columbia: University of South Carolina Press, 1998.

Rose, H. J. *Ancient Roman Religion*. New York: Harper & Row, 1959.

Rudd, Niall, ed. *Horace 2000, a Celebration: Essays for the Bimillennium*. Ann Arbor: University of Michigan Press, 1993.

_____, trans. *The Satires of Horace and Persius*. London: Penguin, 1974.

_____. *Themes in Roman Satire*. Norman: Univer-

sity of Oklahoma Press, 1986.

Ruebel, James S., ed. *Caesar and the Crisis of the Roman Aristocracy*. Tulsa: University of Oklahoma Press, 1994.

Russell, D. *Antonine Literature*. Oxford, England: Clarendon Press, 1990.

Salmon, E. T. *The Making of Roman Italy*. Ithaca, N.Y.: Cornell University Press, 1982.

Sandy, Gerald. *The Greek World of Apuleius*. New York: Brill, 1997.

Scarborough, John. *Roman Medicine*. London: Thames and Hudson, 1969.

Scarre, Christopher. *Chronicle of the Roman Emperors*. London: Thames and Hudson, 1995.

_____. *The Penguin Historical Atlas of Ancient Rome*. Hammondsworth, England: Penguin Books, 1995.

Scullard, Howard H. *A History of the Roman World 753 to 146* B.C. 4th ed. New York: Routledge, 1992.

_____. *Roman Politics, 220-150* B.C. 2d ed. Oxford, England: Clarendon Press, 1973.

_____. *Scipio Africanus in the Second Punic War*. Cambridge, England: Cambridge University Press, 1930.

_____. *Scipio Africanus: Soldier and Politician*. Ithaca, N.Y.: Cornell University Press, 1970.

Seager, Robin. *Tiberius*. Berkeley: University of California Press, 1972.

Sear, Frank. *Roman Architecture*. Ithaca, N.Y.: Cornell University Press, 1982.

Sedley, D. *Lucretius and the Transformation of Greek Wisdom*. New York: Cambridge, 1998.

Sherwin-White, A. N. *The Letters of Pliny: A Historical and Social Commentary*. Oxford, England: Oxford University Press, 1985.

_____. *Roman Foreign Policy in the East, 168* B.C. *to* A.D. *1*. Norman: University of Oklahoma Press, 1984.

Silverio, Francesco. *Trajan's Column*. Rome: Quasar, 1989.

Slater, N. W. *Reading Petronius*. Baltimore: Johns Hopkins University Press, 1990.

Smith, C. J. *Early Rome and Latium*. Oxford, England: Oxford University Press, 1996.

Smith, R. *Julian's Gods*. New York: Routledge, 1995.

Southern, Pat. *Augustus*. New York: Routledge, 1998.

_____. *Domitian: Tragic Tyrant*. Bloomington: Indiana University Press, 1997.

Spivey, Nigel J., and S. Stoddart. *Etruscan Italy*. London: B. T. Batsford, 1990.

Stahl, W. H. *Commentary on the Dream of Scipio*. New

York: Columbia University Press, 1952.

Stahl, W. H., and R. W. Johnson. *Martianus Capella and the Seven Liberal Arts*. 2 vols. New York: Columbia University Press, 1971-1977.

Stockton, D. *The Gracchi*. Oxford, England: Clarendon Press, 1979.

Sullivan, J. *Martial: The Unexpected Classic*. Cambridge, England: Cambridge University Press, 1991.

Syme, R. *The Augustan Aristocracy*. Oxford, England: Oxford University Press, 1986.

_____. *The Roman Revolution*. Oxford, England: Clarendon Press, 1939. Reprint. New York: Oxford University Press, 1987.

_____. *Sallust*. Berkeley: University of California Press, 1964.

Tatum, James. *Apuleius and The Golden Ass*. Ithaca, N.Y.: Cornell University Press, 1979.

Tatum, W. J. *The Patrician Tribune: Publius Clodius Pulcher*. Chapel Hill: University of North Carolina Press, 1999.

Tellegen-Couperus, Olga. *A Short History of Roman Law*. London: Routledge, 1993.

Turcan, Robert. *The Cults of the Roman Empire*. Translated by Antonia Nevill. Cambridge, Mass.: Blackwell, 1996.

Van Andel, G. K. *The Christian Concept of History in the Chronicle of Sulpicius Severus*. Amsterdam: Hakkert, 1976.

Varro. *On the Latin Language*. 2 vols. Cambridge, Mass.: Harvard University Press, 1938.

Veyne, Paul. *The Roman Empire*. Cambridge, Mass.: Harvard University Press, 1997.

Vogt, John. *The Decline of Rome*. New York: The New American Library, 1965.

Wallace-Hadrill, A. *Suetonius: The Scholar and His Caesars*. New Haven, Conn.: Yale University Press, 1984.

Walsh, P. G. *Livy: His Historical Aims and Methods*. Cambridge, England: Cambridge University Press, 1961.

_____. *The Roman Novel*. Cambridge, England: Cambridge University Press, 1970.

Ward, A. M. *Marcus Crassus and the Late Roman Republic*. Columbia: University of Missouri Press, 1977.

Ward, A. M., F. M. Heichelheim, and C. Yeo. *A History of the Roman People*. 3d ed. Upper Saddle River, N.J.: Prentice Hall, 1999.

Watson, Alaric. *Aurelian and the Third Century*. London: Routledge, 1999.

Wellesley, K. *The Long Year:* A.D. *69*. 2d ed. Bristol, England: Bristol Classical Press, 1989.

Wells, Colin, M. *The Roman Empire*. Cambridge, Mass.: Harvard University Press, 1995.

West, D. *The Imagery and Poetry of Lucretius*. Norman: University of Oklahoma Press, 1994.

Wilken, R. *The Christians as the Romans Saw Them*. New Haven, Conn.: Yale University Press, 1984.

Wilkinson, L. P. *Ovid Surveyed*. Cambridge, England: Cambridge University Press, 1962.

Williams, Daniel H. *Ambrose of Milan and the End of the Nicene-Arian Conflicts*. Oxford, England: Clarendon Press, 1995.

Williamson, G. A. *The World of Josephus*. Boston: Little, Brown, 1964.

Wills, Gary. *Saint Augustine*. New York: Viking Penguin, 1999.

Wiseman, T. P. *Catullus and His World: A Reappraisal*. Cambridge, England: Cambridge University Press, 1985.

_____. *Remus, a Roman Myth*. Cambridge, England: Cambridge University Press, 1995.

Wolfram, Herwig. *The Roman Empire and Its Germanic Peoples*. Translated by Thomas Dunlap. Berkeley: University of California Press, 1997.

Woodman, Tony, and David West, eds. *Poetry and Politics in the Age of Augustus*. New York: Cambridge University Press, 1984.

Zanker, P. *The Power of Images in the Age of Augustus*. Ann Arbor: University of Michigan Press, 1988.

SOUTH AND SOUTHEAST ASIA
Includes India, Pakistan, Bangladesh, the Indochinese peninsula, and Indonesia.

Arasaratnam, S. *Ceylon*. Englewood Cliffs, N.J.: Prentice-Hall, 1964.

Aurobindo, Ghose. *Essays on the Gita: Second Series*. Calcutta: Arya Publishing House, 1945.

Basham, A. L. *The Wonder That Was India*. New York: Grove Press, 1959.

Behl, Benoy K. *The Ajanta Caves: Artistic Wonder of Ancient Buddhist India*. New York: Abrams, 1998.

Boisselier, Jean. *Ceylon-Sri Lanka*. Geneva: Nagel, 1979.

Briggs, Lawrence Palmer. *The Ancient Khmer Empire*. Philadelphia: American Philosophical Society, 1951.

Cardona, George. *Recent Research in Paninian Studies*. Delhi: Motilal Banarsidass, 1999.

Caswell, James O. *Written and Unwritten: A New History of the Buddhist Caves at Yungang*. Vancouver: University of British Columbia Press, 1988.

Chapuis, Oscar M. *A History of Vietnam*. Westport, Conn.: Greenwood, 1995.

Chaube, S. P. *Education in Ancient and Medieval India: A Survey of the Main Features and a Critical Evaluation of Major Trends*. New Delhi: Vikas Publishing House, 1999.

Coedès, Georges. *The Indianized States of Southeast Asia*. Honolulu: East-West Center Press, 1968.

Cort, John, ed. *Open Boundaries: Jain Communities and Culture in Indian History*. Albany: State University of New York Press, 1998.

Coward, H. G. *Bhartrhari*. Boston: Twayne, 1976.

Czuma, Stanislaw J., and Rekha Morris. *Kushan Sculpture: Images from Early India*. Cleveland: The Cleveland Museum, 1985.

De Bary, William. *Sources of Indian Tradition*. New York: Columbia University Press, 1966.

Dundas, Paul. *The Jains*. New York: Routledge, 1992.

Embree, Ainslie T. *Sources of Indian Tradition*. 2d ed. New York: Columbia University Press, 1988.

Feuerstein, Georg, et al. *In Search of the Cradle of Civilization: New Light on Ancient India*. Wheaton, Ill.: Quest Books, 1995.

Frawley, David. *From the River of Heaven: Hindu and Vedic Knowledge for the Modern Age*. Salt Lake City, Utah: Morson Publishing, 1990.

Geertz, Clifford. *Agricultural Involution: The Processes of Ecological Change in Indonesia*. Berkeley: University of California Press, 1971.

Gupta, Sanjukta, Dirk Jan Hoens, and Teun Goudraan. *Hindu Tantrism*. Leiden, Netherlands: E. J. Brill, 1979.

Hall, D. G. E. *A History of South-East Asia*. 3d ed. London: Macmillan, 1968.

Hammond, Norman, ed. *South Asian Archaeology*. Ridge Park, N.J.: Noyes Press, 1973.

Hazra, R. C. *Studies in the Puranic Records on Hindu Rites and Customs*. Calcutta: University of Dacca, 1940.

Hiltebeitel, Alf. *Rethinking India's Oral and Classical Epics*. Chicago: University of Chicago Press, 1999.

Jain, Surender K., ed. *Glimpses of Jainism*. Delhi: Motilal Banarsidass, 1997.

Jaini, Padmanabh S., and Robert Goldman. *Gender and Salvation: Jaina Debates on the Spiritual Liberation of Women*. Berkeley: University of California Press, 1991.

Jouveau, Dubreuil, G. *Ancient History of the Deccan*. Pondicherry, India: Modern Press, 1920.

Keay, John. *India: A History*. New York: Atlantic Monthly Press, 2000.

Keightley, David. *The Ancestral Landscape: Time, Space, and Community in Late Shang China, c. 1200-1045 B.C.* Berkeley: Institute of Asian Studies, 2000.

Kenoyer, Jonathan Mark. *Ancient Cities of the Indus Valley Civilization*. Karachi: Oxford University Press and the American Institute of Pakistan Studies, 1998.

King, Richard. *An Introduction to Hindu and Buddhist Thought*. Washington, D.C.: Georgetown University Press, 2000.

Kinsley, David R. *Hinduism: A Cultural Perspective*. 2d ed. Englewood Cliffs, N.J.: Prentice Hall, 1993.

Knapp, Stephen. *The Secret Teachings of the Vedas: The Eastern Answers to the Mysteries of Life*. Detroit: World Relief Network, 1990.

Knox, Robert. *Amaravati: Buddhist Sculpture from the Great Stupa*. London: British Museum Press, 1992.

Krech, Shepard, III. *The Ecological Indian Myth and History*. New York: W. W. Norton, 1999.

Laidlaw, James. *Riches and Renunciation: Religion, Economy, and Society Among the Jain*. Oxford, England: Oxford Studies in Social and Cultural Anthropology, 1996.

LeBar, Frank M., Gerald C. Hickey, and John K. Musgrave. *Ethnic Groups of Mainland Southeast Asia*. New Haven, Conn.: Yale University Press, 1964.

Legge, J. D. *Indonesia*. Englewood Cliffs, N.J.: Prentice Hall, 1964.

Lipner, Julius. *Hindus: Their Religious Beliefs and Practices*. New York: Routledge, 1994.

Mackerras, Colin, ed. *East and Southeast Asia: A Multidisciplinary Survey*. Boulder, Colo.: Lynne Rienner, 1995.

Mahulkar, D. D., ed. *Essays on Panini*. Simla, India: Indian Institute of Advanced Study, 1998.

Majumdar, R. C., ed. *The History and Culture of the Indian People: The Age of Imperial Unity*. Vol. 2. Mumbai: Bharatiya Vidya Bhavan, 1968.

Marshall, John. *The Buddhist Art of Gandhara: The Story of the Early School, Its Birth, Growth, and Decline.* Cambridge, England: The Syndics of the Cambridge University Press, 1960.

Monanty, J. N. *Classical Indian Philosophy.* New York: Rowman & Littlefield, 2000.

Mookerji, Radhakumud. *Chandragupta Maurya and His Times.* 4th ed. Delhi: Motilal Banarsidass, 1966.

Nehru, Lolita. *Origins of the Gandhara Style: A Study of Contributory Influences.* New York: Oxford University Press, 1989.

Norman, K. R. *Pali Literature.* Wiesbaden, Germany: Otto Harrassowitz, 1983.

Osborne, Milton E. *Southeast Asia: An Illustrated Introductory History.* Sydney: Allen & Unwin, 1990.

Ramamurty, A. *The Central Philosophy of the Rig-Veda.* Columbia, Mo.: South Asia Books, 1992.

Raychaudhuri, Hemachandra. *Political History of Ancient India: From the Accession of Parikshit to the Extinction of the Gupta Dynasty.* Delhi: Oxford University Press, 1996.

Richman, Paula, ed. *Many Ramayanas: The Diversity of a Narrative Tradition in South Asia.* Berkeley: University of California Press, 1991.

Sahoo, Ananda Chandra. *Jaina Religion and Art.* Delhi: Agam Kala Prakashan, 1994.

Satri, Nilakanta, ed. *Age of the Nandas and Mauryas.* Delhi: Motilal Banarsidass, 1988.

Schwartzberg, Joseph E., ed. *A Historical Atlas of South Asia.* Chicago: University of Chicago Press, 1975.

Seckel, Dietrich. *Buddhist Art of East Asia.* Translated by Ulrich Mammitzsch. Bellington: Western Washington University, 1989.

Shah, Natubhai. *Jainism: The World of Conquerors.* Portland, Oreg.: Sussex Academic Press, 1998.

Sharma, Arvind. *The Philosophy of Religion and Advaita Vedanta: A Comparative Study in Religion and Reason.* University Park: Pennsylvania State University Press, 1995.

————, ed. *Essays on the Mahabharata.* Leiden, Netherlands: E. J. Brill, 1991.

Shastri, Ajay Mitra, ed. *The Age of the Satavahanas.* New Delhi: Aryan Books International, 1999.

Smith, Vincent A. *The Oxford History of India.* Edited by Percival Spear. 3d ed. Oxford, England: Clarendon Press, 1958.

Stevenson, Margaret. *The Heart of Jainism.* London: Oxford University Press, 1915.

Stone, Elizabeth Rosen. *The Buddhist Art of Nagarjunakonda.* Delhi: Motilal Banarsidass, 1994.

Stuart-Fox, Martin. *A History of Laos.* Cambridge, England: Cambridge University Press, 1997.

Sundararajam, K. R., and Bithika Mukerji, eds. *Hindu Spirituality I: Vedas Through Vedanta.* New York: The Crossroad Publishing Company, 1997.

Swami Prabhavananda. *Vedic Religion and Philosophy.* Los Angeles: Vedanta Press, 1983.

Tarn, W. W. *The Greeks in Bactria and India.* 2d ed. Cambridge, England: Cambridge University Press, 1952.

Taylor, Keith W. *The Birth of Vietnam.* Berkeley: University of California Press, 1991.

Thapar, Romila. *A History of India.* Vol. 1. London: Penguin, 1990.

Thomas, P. *Epics, Myths and Legends of India.* Singapore: Graham Brash, 1913. Reprint. London: Gresham, 1989.

Tinker, Hugh. *South Asia: A Short History.* New York: Praeger, 1966.

Vraiaprana, Pravrajika. *Vedanta: A Simple Introduction.* Los Angeles: Vedanta Press, 1999.

Walker, Benjamin. *Hindu World: An Encyclopedic Survey of Hinduism.* Vols. 1-2. London: Allen & Unwin, 1968.

Williams, Joanna Gottfried. *The Art of Gupta India: Empire and Province.* Princeton, N.J.: Princeton University Press, 1982.

Winternitz, M. *A History of Indian Literature.* 2 vols. Reprint. New York: Russell and Russell, 1971.

Wolpert, Stanley. *A New History of India.* New York: Oxford University Press, 2000.

Zaehner, R. C. *Hinduism.* Oxford, England: Oxford University Press, 1962.

Zimmer, Heinrich. *Myths and Symbols of Indian Art and Civilization.* New York: Harper and Row, 1962.

Zimmer, Heinrich, and Joseph Campbell, eds. *Philosophies of India.* Princeton, N.J.: Princeton University Press, 1969.

—*Thomas J. Sienkewicz*

ENCYCLOPEDIA OF

THE ANCIENT

WORLD

CATEGORIZED LIST OF ENTRIES

LIST OF CATEGORIES

AFRICA
Africa, East and South
Africa, North
Africa, West
Axum
Carthage
Ethiopia
Ghana
Madagascar
Makouria
Napata and Meroe
Nubia
Rift Valley system
Wawat
Yam

ANATOLIA AND ARMENIA
Anatolia
Armenia
Attalid Dynasty
Byzantine Empire

Constantinople
Cyprus
Lycia
Lydia
Phrygia
Urartu

ARCHITECTS
Anthemius of Tralles
Apollodorus the Architect
Callicrates
Ictinus
Imhotep
Paeonius
Vitruvius Pollio, Marcus

ART, ARCHITECTURE, AND MONUMENTS
African rock art, southern and eastern
Akapana pyramid

Alexandrian library
Amaravātī school
ʿAmr ibn al-ʿĀṣ Mosque
Andhradesha school
Appian Way
Ara Pacis
Art and architecture: The Americas
Art and architecture: East Asia
Art and architecture: Europe and the Mediterranean region
Art and architecture: India
Art and architecture: Southeast Asia
Art and architecture: West and South Africa
Artemis, temple of, at Ephesus
Buddhist cave temples
Cajamarca pottery
Colossus of Rome
Delphi
Flavian Amphitheater

Nilotes
Nobatae
Nubia
Olmecs
Omotic peoples
Philistines
Phoenicia
Phrygia
Picts
Pyu
Recuay
Sarmatians
Scythia
Sea Peoples
Slavs
Spain
Suebi
Sumerians
Ta-Seti
Tai
Thera
Tibu
Troy
Urartu
Vandals
Vendae
Wawat
Xiongnu
Yam
Zapotecs
Zealots
Znaga

CULTURES
Adena culture
Afanasievo culture
Afrasans
Aleutian tradition
American Paleo-Arctic tradition
Andronovo culture
Archaic North American culture
Archaic South American culture
Archaic tradition, northern
Arctic Small Tool tradition
Banpocun culture
Beaker people
Black Pottery culture
Boylston Street weir
California peoples
Chifumbaze culture

Clovis technological complex
Cochise culture
Copper Belt
Dalton tradition
Deptford culture
Dorset phase
Eastern African Microlithic/
    Khoisan peoples
Eastern peoples
Folsom technological complex
Fremont culture
Great Basin peoples
Halafian culture
Hallstatt culture
Helton phase
Hohokam culture
Indus Valley civilization
Ipiutak
Jōmon
Kachemak tradition
Karasuk culture
Kelteminar culture
Kitoi culture
La Tène culture
Laurel culture
Liangzhu culture
Lima culture
Locarno Beach
Longshan culture
Maritime Archaic
Marpole phase
Microblade tradition,
    Northwest
Middle Woodland tradition
Moche culture
Mogollon culture
Nasca culture
Natufian culture
Neolithic Age Europe
Nok culture
Norton tradition
Old Copper complex
Paleo-Indians in North America
Paleo-Indians in South America
Plains peoples
Plateau peoples
Poverty Point
Qijia culture
Rift Valley system
Saint Mungo phase

Samarran culture
Sonota culture
Southwest peoples
Subarctic peoples
Sutton Hoo
Ta-Seti
Thom's Creek
Ubaid culture
Villanovan culture
Yangshao culture
Yayoi culture
Yue
Yuezhi culture

DOCUMENTS
Aiñkururnūru
Akanāṉūṟu
Aqhat epic
Āraṇyakas
Atrahasis epic
Avesta
Bhagavadgītā
Bible: Jewish
Bible: New Testament
Book of the Dead
Brāhmaṇas
Caṅkam
Chunqiu
Damascus document
Dead Sea Scrolls
Dhammapada
Djanggawul cycle
Dreaming
Gilgamesh epic
Hammurabi's code
Han Feizi
Harivaṃśa
Huainanzi
Jātakas
Kalittokai
Kuruntokai
Mahābhārata
Milinda-pañha
Muʿallaqāt, Al-
Mulanshi
Naṟṟiṇai
Nāṭya-śāstra
Nihon shoki
Palermo stone
Paripāṭal

v

Procopius
Pytheas
Sallust
Salvianus
Severus, Sulpicius
Sima Qian
Strabo
Tacitus
Theodoret of Cyrrhus
Thucydides
Vegetius Renatus, Flavius
Velleius Paterculus, Marcus
Xenophon

LAWGIVERS, LAWS, AND EDICTS
Draco
Gortyn, law code of
Government and law
Justinian I
Justinian's codes
Milan, Edict of
Solon
Twelve Tables, The
Ulpian

LEAGUES
Achaean League
Aetolian League
Latin League and War

MEDICINE AND MEDICAL PRACTITIONERS
Aretaeus of Cappadocia
Diocles of Carystus
Erasistratus
Galen
Ge Hong
Herophilus
Hippocrates
Imhotep
Medicine and health
Oribasius
Soranus of Ephesus
Vātsyāyana

MESOAMERICA
Altar de Sacrificios
Atlatl
Ball game, Mesoamerican
Caribbean

Chichén Itzá
Cholula
Cobá
Dzibilchaltún
El Tajín
Monte Albán
Palenque
TeotihuacánTIkal
Uxmal

MIDDLE EAST
Achaemenian Dynasty
Arabia
Arsacid Dynasty
Assyria
Babylonia
Fertile Crescent
Islam
Parthia
Persia
Sāsānian Empire
Umayyad Dynasty

NEAR EAST
Herodian Dynasty
Israel
Phoenicia
Seleucid Dynasty

OCEANIA
Australia, Tasmania, New Zealand
Hawaii
Melanesia
Micronesia
Polynesia
Sea Peoples

ORATORS
Aeschines
Andocides
Antiphone
Apuleius, Lucius
Cato the Censor
Cicero
Demosthenes
Fronto, Marcus Cornelius
Isaeus
Scaevola, Quintus Mucius (Auger)
Second Sophistic
Symmachus, Quintus Aurelius

OVERVIEWS
Agriculture and animal husbandry
Art and architecture: The Americas
Art and architecture: East Asia
Art and architecture: Europe and the Mediterranean region
Art and architecture: India
Art and architecture: Southeast Asia
Art and architecture: West and South Africa
Calendars and chronology
Daily life and customs
Death and burial
Education and training
Government and law
Languages and literature
Medicine and health
Navigation and transportation
Performing arts
Philosophy
Religion and ritual
Science
Settlements and social structure
Sports and entertainment
Technology
Trade and commerce
War and weapons
Women's life
Writing systems

PAINTERS
Achilles Painter
Amasis Painter
Gu Kaizhi
Wang Xizhi
Xie He
Yan Liben

PHILOSOPHERS AND PHILOSOPHY
Apollonius of Tyana
Archytas of Tarentum
Aristides
Aristotle
Asaṅga
Augustine, Saint
Bhartṛhari
Boethius

Celsus
Cicero
Daoism
Demetrius Phalereus
Democritus
Dio Chrysostom
Diogenes of Sinope
Dong Zhongshu
Epictetus
Epicurus
Gaudapāda
Gorgias
Hui Shi
Hypatia
Isocrates
Legalists
Leucippus
Lucretius
Meleager of Gadara
Mencius
Mozi
Neoplatonism
Nicomachus of Gerasa
Panaetius of Rhodes
Parmenides
Philo of Alexandria
Philodemus
Philosophy
Plato
Plotinus
Plutarch
Porphyry
Posidonius
Pre-Socratic philosophers
Prtagoras
Pyrrhon of Elis
Pythagoras
Second Sophistic
Seneca the Elder
Seneca the Younger
Socrates
Speusippus
Themistius
Theophrastus
Vasubandhu
Wang Bi
Wang Chong
Xenophanes
Xunzi
Yang Xiong

Zeno of Citium
Zeno of Elea

POETS, PLAYWRIGHTS, AND PERFORMERS

Accius, Lucius
Aeschylus
Agathias
Agathon
Alcaeus of Lesbos
Alcman
Amaru
Anacreon
Aneirin
Apollonius Rhodius
Appar
Aratus
Archilochus of Paros
Aristophanes
Ashvaghosa
Ausonius, Decimus Magnus
Bacchylides
Bāṇa
Bhartṛhari
Bhāsa
Bhavabhūti
Callimachus of Cyrene
Calpurnius Siculus, Titus
Campantar
Cao Zhi
Cātanār
Catullus
Claudian
Crates of Athens
Cratinus
Dallán Forgaill
Ennius, Quintus
Erinna
Eudocia
Eupolis
Euripides
Fortunatus, Venantius
Herodas
Hesiod
Homer
Horace
Ibycus
Iḷaṅkō Aṭikaḷ
Ion of Chios
Juvenal

Kālidāsa
Lucan
Lucilius, Gaius (poet)
Lucilius, Gaius (satirist)
Lucretius
Mahendravarman I
Manilius, Marcus
Meleager of Gadara
Menander (playwright)
Menippus of Gadara
Mimaji
Mimnermus
Moschus of Syracuse
Naevius, Gnaeus
Nemesianus
Nicander of Colophon
Nonnus of Panopolis
Ovid
Pacuvius, Marcus
Paulinus of Nola, Saint
Persius Flaccus, Aulus
Petronius Arbiter
Philodemus
Phineas
Pindar
Plautus
Propertius
Publius Syrus
Qu Yuan
Quintus Smyrnaeus
Rutilius Claudius Namatianus
Sappho
Semonides
Seneca the Younger
Sima Xiangru
Simon Magus
Simonides
Solomon
Solon
Sophocles
Statius, Publius Papinius
Stesichorus
Śūdraka
Sulpicia
Taliesin
Tao Qian
Terence
Terpander of Lesbos
Theocritus of Syracuse
Theognis

Thespis
Tibullus, Albius
Tiruttakkatevar
Tiruvaḷḷuvar
Tyrtaeus
Valerius Flaccus, Gaius
Vālmīki
Vergil
Viśākhadatta
Xenophanes
Xie Lingyun
Yannai
Yose ben Yose

RELIGION

Advaita
Ājīvikas
Apedemak
Āraṇyakas
Arianism
Avesta
Bhagavadgītā
Bible: Jewish
Brāhmaṇas
Brahmanism
Buddhism
Buddhist cave temples
Chalcedon, Council of
Christianity
Confucianism
Damascus document
Daoism
Dead Sea Scrolls
Dhammapada
Divinity
Donatism
Essenes
Exodus
Gnosticism
Harivaṃśa
Henotheism
Hinduism
Huainanzi
Isis, cult of
Islam
Jainism
Jātakas
Jewish diaspora
Judaism
Mahābhārata

Mahābodhi temple
Manichaeanism
Mao Shan revelations
Milinda-pañha
Mithrism
Monophysitism
Montanism
Nārāyaṇa
Nicaea, Council of
Orphism
Pārvatī Devī temple
Pelagianism
Peruṅkatai
Purāṇas
Qurʾān
Religion and ritual
Septuagint
Shintō
Sūtras
Suttanipāta
Talmud
Tantras
Tipiṭaka
Upaniṣads
Vedas
Vedism
Wujing
Zealots
Zhuangzi
Zoroastrianism
Zurvanism

RELIGIOUS FIGURES

Agapetus, Saint
Aidan, Saint
ʿĀʾishah bint Abī Bakr
Akiba beb Joseph
Alexandria patriarchs
Ambrose
Amos
Ānanda
Aneirin
Anthony of Egypt, Saint
Apollonius of Tyana
Appar
Arkamani
Asaṅga
Athanasius of Alexandria, Saint
Augustine, Saint
Augustine of Canterbury, Saint

Bar Kokhba
Basil of Cappadocia, Saint
Benedict Biscop, Saint
Benedict of Nursia, Saint
Bodhidharma
Buddha
Cassian
Clement I
Columba, Saint
Confucius
Cyprian of Carthage, Saint
Cyril of Alexandria, Saint
Dallán Forgaill
Denis, Saint
Elijah
Eudocia
Eusebius of Caesarea
Ezekiel
Faxian
Fortunatus, Venantius
Frumentius, Saint
Gośāla Maskarīputra
Gregory of Nazianzus
Gregory the Great
He Yan
Helena, Saint
Hilary of Poitiers, Saint
Hosea
Huiyuan
Ḥusayn
Ignatius of Antioch
Irenaeus, Saint
Isaiah
Isidore of Seville, Saint
James the Apostle
Jeremiah
Jerome, Saint
Jesus Christ
Johanan ben Zakkai
John Chrysostom, Saint
John the Baptist, Saint
John the Evangelist, Saint
Jordanes
Justin Martyr, Saint
Karaikkal Ammaiyar
Lactantius, Lucius Caelius
    Firmianus
Laozi
Leo I, Saint
Liu Xie

Maccabees
Mary
Mencius
Minucius Felix, Marcus
Moses
Muḥammad
Nestorius
Nine Saints
Origen
Pachomius, Saint
Patrick, Saint
Paul, Saint
Paulinus, Saint
Paulinus of Nola, Saint
Peter, Saint
Peyar
Philo of Alexandria
Phineas
Poykai
Priscillian
Prudentius, Aurelius Clemens
Pūtān
Radegunda, Saint
Salvianus
Samuel
Saul
Sidonius Apollinaris
Simon Magus
Solomon
Sylvester I, Saint
Tertullian
Theodoret of Cyrrhus
Theodosius of Alexandria
Vardhamāna
Vasubandhu
Xuanzang
Xunzi
Xushen
Yannai
Yose ben Yose
Zengzi
Zhiyi
Zi Si
Zoroaster

**RULERS AND MILITARY/
POLITICAL LEADERS**
ʿAbd al-Malik
ʿAbd Allāh ibn al-ʿAbbās
ʿAbd Allāh ibn az-Zubayr

ʿAbd Allāh ibn Saʿd ibn Abī Sarḥ
Abraha
Abū Bakr
Ælle
Aemilius Paullus, Lucius
Aeneas
Æthelbert
Agesilaus II of Sparta
Agricola, Gnaeus Julius
Agrippa, Marcus Vispanius
Ahab
Akhenaton
Akiba beb Joseph
Alaric I
Alaric II
Alboin
Alcibiades of Athens
Alexander the Great
ʿAlī ibn Abī Ṭālib
Anastasius I
Andocides
Ankhesenamen
Antiochus the Great
Antipater
Antiphon
Antoninus Pius
Antony, Marc
Archidamus II of Sparta
Archidamus III of Sparta
Ardashīr I
Argishti I
Aristides of Athens
Arminius
Artabanus I-V
Artavasdes II of Armenia
Artemisia I
Artemisia II
Arthur
Ashurbanipal
Aśoka
Astyages
Atossa
Attila
Augustus
Aurelianus, Lucius Domitius
Avitus, Eparchius
Bar Kokhba
Bathsheba
Belisarius
Ben-Hadad I

Boudicca
Brasidas of Sparta
Brutus
Caesar, Julius
Caligula
Camillus, Marcus Furius
Cao Cao
Caracalla
Caratacus
Cartimandua
Cassander
Cassius
Cassivellaunus
Catiline
Cato the Censor
Cato the Younger
Chandragupta Maurya
Chlotar I
Cicero
Cimon
Claudius
Claudius Caecus, Appius
Cleisthenes of Athens
Cleisthenes of Sicyon
Cleon of Athens
Cleopatra VII
Clodia
Clodius Pulcher, Publius
Clovis
Commius
Constans I
Constantine the Great
Constantius I-III
Corbulo, Gnaeus Domitius
Coriolanus, Gnaeus Marcius
Crassus, Marcus Licinius
Critias of Athens
Croesus
Cunobelinus
Cyaxares
Cypselus of Corinth
Cyrus the Great
Darius the Great
Darius III
Demetrius Phalereus
Demetrius Poliorcetes
Demosthenes
Diadochi
Dido
Diocletian

Teutoburg Forest, Battle of
Thapsus, Battle of
Thermopylae, Battle of
War and weapons
Zama, Battle of

WOMEN
Acte, Claudia
Agariste
Agrippina the Elder
Agrippina the Younger
ʿĀʾishah bint Abī Bakr
Ankhesenamen
Antonia the Elder
Antonia the Younger
Anyte of Tegea
Arria the Elder
Artemisia I
Artemisia II
Atossa
Bathsheba
Boudicca
Cartimandua
Cleopatra VII
Cornelia
Dido
Erinna
Eudocia
Eudoxia, Aelia
Faustina I
Faustina II
Fulvia
Hatshepsut
Hortensia
Hypatia
Jingū
Julia (daughter of Augustus)
Julia (daughter of Julius Caesar)
Julia Domna

Julia Mamaea
Livia Drusilla
Lucretia
Messallina, Valeria
Nefertiti
Octavia
Olympias
Poppaea Sabina
Sabina, Vibia
Sammu-ramat
Scribonia
Sempronia
Sophonisba of Numidia
Theodora
Verginia
Women's life
Wu Hou
Zenobia

WRITERS AND SCRIBES
Achilles Tatius
Aesop
Alexander Polyhistor, Lucius
    Cornelius
Anyte of Tegea
Apuleius, Lucius
Aristarchus of Samothrace
Aristides of Miletus
Aspasia of Miletus
Āśvalāyana
Atticus, Titus Pomponius
Bharata Muni
Bhāravi
Budhasvāmin
Capella, Martianus
Cassiodorus
Celsus, Aulus Cornelius
Clement of Alexandria
Columella

Daṇḍin
Ezra
Gellius, Aulus
Guṇāḍhya
Heliodorus of Emesa
Hyginus (land surveyor)
Hyginus, Gaius Julius
Iamblichus of Syria
Ling Lun
Liu Xie
Liu Yiqing
Livius Andronicus, Lucius
Longinus
Longus
Lu Ji
Lucian
Lysias
Macrobius, Aurelius Theodosius
Maecenas, Gaius
Martial
Palladius, Rutilius Taurus
    Aemilianus
Phaedrus
Philochorus
Philostratus, Flavius
Pliny the Elder
Pliny the Younger
Protagoras
Quintilian
Seneca the Elder
Shang Yang
Śyāmilaka
Tao Hongjing
Tōlāmoḷittēvar
Tullius Tiro, Marcus
Valerius Probus, Marcus
Varro, Marcus Terentius
Vegetius Renatus, Flavius
Wang Xizhi

PERSONAGES INDEX

SUBJECT INDEX

Apuleius, Lucius, 266-267, 287, 836
Apuleius, Philosophus Platonicus. *See* Apuleius, Lucius
Aqhat epic, 267
Aqiba ben Joseph. *See* Akiba ben Joseph
Aquatic tradition, 839-840
Aqueducts; Imperial Rome, 539, 961; Olmecs, 852; Republican Rome, 419
Aquitani, 552
Ara Pacis, 257-258, 268
Arab invasion; North Africa, 202
Arabia, 268-270, 659, 1095; literature, 68; science, 120; trade, 147; writing, 171
Arabic script, 171
Arakanese, 270-271
Aramaeans. *See* Arameans
Aramaic script, 171
Arameans, 243, 271-272, 304, 624
Āraṇyakas, 66, 272-273, 1120
Aratus (poet), 273
Aratus of Sicyon, 182
Arausio, Battle of, 273-274
Arawak, 274-275, 381
Arbela, 303
Arbogast, 1072
Arcadius, 222, 514, 519, 1073
Arch, discovery of, 142
Archagatus, 80
Archaic North American culture, 275, 353, 486, 609
Archaic South American culture, 275-276
Archaic tradition, northern, 276-277, 851
Archelaus (Macedonian king), 283, 517, 746
Archelaus (philosopher), 651
Archidamian War, 277-278, 355, 835
Archidamus II of Sparta, 210, 277-278
Archidamus III of Sparta, 278-279
Archilochus of Paros, 279
Archimedes, 279-280, 285, 505, 617
Architecture; the Americas, 6-9; Athens, 641; Babylonia, 327; Byzantine Empire, 253, 367-368, 594; Chavín de Huántar, 245, 402; Chichén Itzá, 403; China, 1135; Classical Greece, 374, 596; Cobá, 427; Crete, 444; Dzibilchaltún, 484; East Asia, 9-13; El Tajín, 499; Ethiopia, 510; Etruscans, 512;

Europe, 13-20; Hellenistic Greece, 891, 1163; Imperial Rome, 262, 268, 317, 530, 593, 764, 868, 961, 1097, 1131; India, 20-25, 755; Israel, 665; Japan, 671; Jeroboam I, 676; Kerma, 705; Koguryo, 710; La Florida pyramid, 715; Lima culture, 727; Maya, 771-772; Mediterranean, 13-20; Mixtecs, 799; Moche culture, 629; Mogollon culture, 802; Monte Albán, 808; Muslim, 239; Mycenaean Greece, 815; Niger-Congo, 837; Olmecs, 853; Palenque, 862; Pallava Dynasty, 866; Pharaonic Egypt, 493, 1020; Phoenicia, 900; Polynesia, 919; religious, 648; Republican Rome, 956, 969; South Africa, 28-31; Southeast Asia, 25-28; Teotihuacán, 1063; Uxmal, 1109; West Africa, 28-31; Zapotecs, 1158. *See also* Indian temple architecture
Archytas of Tarentum, 280-281, 515
Arctic cultures, 697
Arctic Small Tool tradition, 281, 482, 845
Ardashīr I, 281-282, 295, 872, 884, 986, 1007
Aretaeus of Cappadocia, 282
Aretaiou Kappadokou ta Sozomena (Aretaeus of Cappadocia), 282
Argead Dynasty, 283
Argentina, 180
Argishti I, 283-284, 983, 1108
Argishti II, 416
Argonautica (Apollonius Rhodius), 264
Argonautica (Valerius Flaccus), 1114
Arianism, 207, 223, 284, 307, 336, 384, 399, 413, 426, 536, 541, 617, 717, 833-834, 1043, 1051, 1070, 1072
Ariovistus, 546
Aristagoras, 622, 652
Aristarchus of Samos, 285, 582
Aristarchus of Samothrace, 230, 261, 286, 581, 809
Aristides (sophist), 286-287, 995
Aristides of Athens, 287
Aristides of Miletus, 287-288
Aristides Quintilianus, 99
Aristides the Just. *See* Aristides of Athens

Aristides Theodorus, Publius Aelius. *See* Aristides (Sophist)
Aristocles. *See* Plato
Aristogiton, 603
Aristophanes (comic poet), 70, 94, 134, 193, 288-289, 310, 422, 443, 517, 651, 1021; on Agathon, 209; on Crates of Athens, 443
Aristophanes of Byzantium, 230, 286
Aristotle, 69, 102, 119, 134, 193, 289-290, 310, 443, 467, 469, 910, 917, 941, 1034, 1074, 1139, 1164; on Agathon, 209; on Draco, 483; on Leucippus, 724; on Pittacus of Mytilene, 905; on Pre-Socratic philosophers, 926; on Zeno, 1162
Arithmētikē eisagōgē (Nicomachus), 836
Arius, 284, 413, 834
Ark of the Covenant, 323
Arkamani, 290
Arkhidamos son of Zeuxidamos. *See* Archidamus II of Sparta
Arles, Council of, 1051
Armenia, 291-292, 296, 464, 823, 884, 1007, 1087
Armenian church, 292
Armies; Byzantine Empire, 367; Etruscan, 511; Imperial Rome, 959; Republican Rome, 765, 967
Armin. *See* Arminius
Arminius, 292, 766, 1067
Arnuwandas III, 623
Arpad, 1086
Arqamani. *See* Arkamani
Arria Major. *See* Arria the Elder
Arria the Elder, 293-294
Arria the Younger, 293
Arrian, 294, 503; on Lycia, 739
Ars amatoria (Ovid), 858
Ars major (Donatus), 481
Ars minor (Donatus), 481
Ars poetica (Horace), 628
Arsaces, 871, 884
Arsaces II. *See* Artabanus I
Arsaces IV. *See* Mithradates I
Arsacid Dynasty, 294-295
Arshtivaiga. *See* Astyages
Arsinoë, 743, 932
Art; Amarna style, 219, 1101; the Americas, 6-9; Archaic Greece, 235, 570; Australia, 320; Berbers, 342; Buddhist, 248, 364; California peoples, 372; Celts, 397; Chadic

Urartu, 243, 283, 291, 304, 983-985,
1086, 1108-1109
Urewe ware, 334
Urhi-Teshub, 815
Uriah the Hittite, 336
Urien, 1057
Urnfield culture, 394, 597, 1129
Uruthirasanman, 218
Usermare Ramses. *See* Rameses II
Utayana Kumara Kaviyam (Durvinta),
887
'Uthmān ibn 'Affān, 178-179, 217,
270, 661, 1109
Uttararāmacarita (Bhavabhūti), 346
Utu-Hegal, 221, 1107
Uvakhshtra. *See* Cyaxares
Uxmal, 1109-1110

Vāgīsha. *See* Appar
Vairāgyaśatakai (Bhartṛhari), 345
Vaiśeśika philosophy, 1049
Vaiṣṇavism, 936
Vākāṭaka Dynasty, 589, 649, 1111
Vākyapadīya (Bhartṛhari), 345
Valagam Ba. *See* Vaṭṭagāmaṇi
Valens, 188, 238, 284, 561, 565, 1111-
1112
Valentinian I, 238, 565, 1052, 1111-
1112
Valentinian II, 514, 1052, 1072
Valentinian III, 400, 438, 515, 1112-
1113, 1116
Valerian, 454, 547, 884, 1007, 1113-
1114
Valerianus, Publius Licinius. *See*
Valerian
Valerius Flaccus, Gaius, 760, 1114
Valerius Flaccus, Lucius, 391
Valerius Maximus, 628, 1114-1115
Valerius Messalla Corvinus, Marcus,
1046, 1085
Valerius Probus, Marcus, 1115
Vallia. *See* Wallia
Vālmīki, 67, 301, 950, 1115-1116
Vandals, 221, 323, 339, 379, 384, 535,
542, 928, 1032, 1116, 1124, 1132;
Arianism, 284
Vardhamāna, 22, 113, 560, 647, 668,
1117-1118
Variae (Cassiodorus), 387
Varro, Marcus Terentius, 378, 500, 528,
781, 866, 962, 969, 1012, 1118
Varuṇa, 797
Varus. *See* Quinctilius Varus, Publius

Vasubandhu, 299, 1118-1119
Vātsyāyana, 1119
Vātsyāyana Mallanāga. *See*
Vātsyāyana
Vaṭṭagāmaṇi, 1036, 1120
Vaṭṭagāmaṇi Abhaya. *See* Vaṭṭagāmaṇi
Vedānta philosophy, 103, 1049
Vedas, 66, 112, 344, 645, 1048, 1106,
1120-1121
Veddas, 1035
Vedism, 618, 1121-1122
Vegeculture, 3, 5
Vegetius Renatus, Flavius, 1123
Velleius Paterculus, Marcus, 450,
1123-1124
Vendae, 1124
Venutius, 386
Veracruz civilization, 499
Vercingetorix, 226, 396, 431, 535,
547, 1124-1125
Vergil, 71, 134, 191, 257, 273, 317,
374, 383, 473, 481, 501, 504, 614,
637, 731, 750, 809, 859, 897, 961,
1069, 1114-1115, 1125-1126; on
sports, 130; on Troy, 1100
Vergilius Maro, Publius. *See* Vergil
Verginia, 1127
Verus, Lucius, 258, 525, 540, 763
Vesālī, Council of, 362, 673
Vespasian, 450, 475, 480, 497, 530,
533, 681, 685, 921, 946, 957, 1091,
1095, 1127-1128
Vestal Virgins, 109
Vesuvius, Mount, eruption of, 912-
913, 921, 1092
Via Appia. *See* Appian Way
Vietnam, 1128-1129, 1137, 1154; art,
25; Confucianism, 433
Vigilius, 684
Vijaya, Prince, 1035
Vijñanavāda. *See* Yogācara,
Mahāyānist
Vijñāptimatratasiddhi (Vasubandhu),
1119
Vikramāditya (king of Ujjain), 234
Vikramāditya I, 698
Vikramorvaśīya (Kālidāsa), 699
Villanovan culture, 1129
Vima Kadphises, 700, 714
Vinaya Piṭaka, 673, 1089
Vindhyaśakti, 1111
Vindolanda tablets, 1130
Vipsania Agrippina. *See* Agrippina the
Elder

Virgil. *See* Vergil
Virgin Mary. *See* Mary
Viśākhadatta, 703, 1130
Vishnu, 343, 355, 363, 602-603, 619,
821, 825, 890, 925, 936-937, 1122
Visigoths, 188, 222-223, 401, 425,
438, 535, 538, 561, 1032, 1043,
1072, 1111, 1132. *See also* Goths
Viṣṇu. *See* Vishnu
Viṣṇugupta. *See* Kauṭilya
Vita Constantini (Eusebius of
Caesarea), 519
Vita S. Antonii (Athanasius of
Alexander), 307
Vita S. Martini (Severus), 1004
Vitellius, Aulus, 533
Vitruvius Pollio, Marcus, 1131
Volcanic explosions; Thera, 1075
Vologases V, 295
Vonones, 295
Vortigern, 250
Vouillé, Battle of, 223, 536, 538, 562
Vulgate, 677
Vyāsa, 67

Wagadu. *See* Ghana
Wagadu Empire. *See* Ghana
Wales, 211
Wallia, 1132
Walya. *See* Wallia
Wang Bi, 607, 1132-1133
Wang Chong, 1133
Wang Ch'ung. *See* Wang Chong
Wang Chung-jen. *See* Wang Chong
Wang Hsi-chih. *See* Wang Xizhi
Wang Mang, 588
Wang Pi. *See* Wang Bi
Wang Xianzhi, 1134
Wang Xizhi, 1133-1134
Wang Zhongren. *See* Wang Chong
Warfare, 151-160; Archaic Greece,
572; Axum, 324; Babylonia, 327;
Carthage, 385; Celts, 397; Classical
Greece, 576; France, 537;
Germany, 555; Hellenistic and
Roman Greece, 579; Island Carib,
381; Koguryo, 710; Macedonia,
747; Maya, 233, 774; Melanesia,
776; Mixtecs, 798; Mongolia, 805;
Mycenaean Greece, 585; Nasca
culture, 824; Neolithic Age Europe,
830; Parthia, 795; Scythia, 994;
Slavs, 1019; Sumerians, 1046;
technology, 139; Zapotecs, 1159

Yishao. *See* Wang Xizhi
Yoga, 102, 217, 343, 1060
Yogācara, 550, 1118; Mahāyānist,
    299
Yogācara-bhūmi-shāstra, 300
Yohanan ben Zakkai. *See* Johanan ben
    Zakkai
Yose ben Yose, 1153
Yu, 1141
Yüan Hung. *See* Xiaowen Di
Yuanhong. *See* Xiaowen Di
Yue, 1153-1154
Yue ware, 1154
Yuefushi Ji, 813
Yüeh. *See* Yue
Yüeh ware. *See* Yue ware
Yüeh-chih. *See* Yuezhi
Yuezhi culture, 714, 1014, 1155
Yuga Purāna, 778
Yungang, 12, 364
Yupik culture, 845
Yūsuf Asʿar, 181

Zadokites, 461
Zak K'uk', 165
Zama, Battle of, 202, 384, 601, 935,
    990, 1156

Zapotecs, 798, 800, 807, 1156-1159
Zarathustra. *See* Zoroaster
Zawi Chemi Shanidar, 1
Zayd bin Thābit, 948
Zealots, 663, 685, 689, 768, 1160
Zenaga. *See* Znaga
Zengzi, 1160, 1168
Zeno (emperor), 242, 563, 722, 850,
    1070
Zeno of Citium, 102, 273, 1161-1162
Zeno of Elea, 724, 870, 1162
Zeno the Stoic. *See* Zeno of Citium
Zenobia, 270, 318, 1162-1163
Zenodotus, 230, 581
Zeus at Pergamum, Great Altar of,
    313, 516, 582, 1163
Zeuxis of Heraclea, 261, 578, 1163-
    1164
Zhang Daoling, 462
Zhang Hua, 122
Zhang Qian, 1014
Zhangdi, 1164
Zhangzhi, 1134
Zheng. *See* Shi Huangdi
Zheng Yin, 553
Zhengzhou, 1141
Zhiyi, 1164-1165

Zhongyao, 1134
Zhou Dynasty, 129, 155, 406, 433,
    780, 1153, 1165-1166; art, 10;
    medicine, 81
Zhou style, 1166
Zhouyi Zhu (Wang Bi), 1132
Zhuangzi, 105, 462, 607, 632, 1143,
    1166-1167
Zhuge Liang, 1167
Zi Si, 780, 1168
Zidantas I, 1063
Ziggurats, Mesopotamia, 14
Zixu Fu (Sima Xiangru), 1016
Znaga, 1168
Zoroaster, 113, 322, 1169-1170
Zoroastrianism, 50, 68, 113, 282, 291,
    322, 459, 884, 986, 1007, 1169-
    1171
Zosher. *See* Djoser
Zoskales, 1171
Zrvan. *See* Zurvan
Zu Chongzhi, 122
Zuhayr ibn Abī-Sulmā Rabīʿa, 811
Zuozhuan, 414
Zurvan, 1171
Zurvanism, 1171-1172
Zurwan. *See* Zurvan